THE END OF THE WORLD

WHAT THE BIBLE SAYS
ABOUT THE FUTURE

Andrew W. Wilson

BIBLICAL CHRISTIANITY VOLUME 9

The End of the World: What the Bible Says about the Future

Copyright © 2021 Andrew W. Wilson. All rights reserved. No part of this publication may be reproduced or transmitted in any form or by any means, electronic or mechanical, including photocopy, recording or otherwise, except for brief quotations in printed reviews, without the written permission of the publisher.

Believers Publications, P. O. Box 485, North Lakes, Qld, 4509, Australia.
www.believerspublications.com

Scripture quotations, unless otherwise noted, are taken from the New King James Version, copyright © 1979, 1980, 1982 by Thomas Nelson, Inc. Used by permission. All rights reserved. Scripture quotations marked (KJV) are taken from The Holy Bible, Authorized King James Version. Scripture quotations marked (ESV) are taken from The Holy Bible, English Standard Version® (ESV®), copyright © 2001 by Crossway Bibles, a publishing ministry of Good News Publishers. Used by permission. All rights reserved. Scripture quotations marked (NIV) are taken from the Holy Bible, New International Version®, NIV®, copyright © 1973, 1978, 1984, 2011 by Biblica, Inc.™ Used by permission of Zondervan. All rights reserved worldwide. www.zondervan.com The "NIV" and "New International Version" are registered in the United States Patent and Trademark Office by Biblica, Inc.™

Copyright © 2021 Andrew W. Wilson

All rights reserved.

ISBN: 978-0994397775

CONTENTS

	Introduction	5
	A Parable: The Case of Four Clues	8

Part One: How is it All Going to End?

1	Paradise Restored	37
2	Trouble in Paradise?	51
3	The Millennium	65

Theology: Three Views of the Future and the Kingdom

4	Amillennialism	95
5	Postmillennialism	116
6	Premillennialism	127
7	The Kingdom of God	146

Part Two: the Tribulation: Countdown to Armageddon

8	The Tribulation: Past, Present or Future?	171
9	Apocalypse: the End of the World as we Know it	188
10	Antichrist: Satan Come Down to Earth	205
11	Armageddon: How and When will it Happen?	227
12	The Timetable of the Tribulation: Daniel's 70 Weeks	254

Part Three: Does Israel Have a Special Destiny?

13	Israel's National Conversion: Romans 11	289
14	Israel at Armageddon: Zechariah 12-14	301
15	Israel's National Restoration: Jeremiah 30-33	310
16	Israel's Spiritual Rebirth: Ezekiel 36-37	321
17	Ezekiel's Temple: Ezekiel 40-48	329
18	Will there be a Third Temple?	340
19	Has the Church replaced Israel?	352

Part Four: Will the Church Go Through the Tribulation?

20	The Rapture: Which View is Right?	377
21	The Great Puzzle of Bible Prophecy: Matthew 24-25	409
22	The Lord's Coming: 1 Thessalonians	439
23	The Coming of Antichrist: 2 Thessalonians	450
24	The Church in Revelation	464
	Glossary	487

INTRODUCTION

The book of Revelation describes half of the world's population (or more) being wiped out. At current numbers, that means three or four billion people will die. Imagine most of the world's great cities destroyed, their shiny skyscrapers reduced to piles of smouldering rubble. And all this happens in the book of Revelation before we even get to the cataclysmic battle of Armageddon.

Before all that, Revelation says there is going to be a one-world government headed by Antichrist. No one will be able to buy or sell without having the 'mark of the beast' (666) on their right hand or forehead. Those who won't worship Antichrist will be put to death.

But are we meant to understand the book of Revelation literally? And if so, how and when are all these events going to happen? Are we about to see a one-world government and the rise of Antichrist? And is the church going to be taken out of this world before all these events happen?

Many Christians give very different answers to these questions today. Some say all these events will literally happen. Others say all these events happened in the first century under the Roman emperors – Revelation was just using code-language. Others say that Revelation is using symbolism to teach spiritual lessons about how Christians should live today. Many Christians are confused and not sure what to make of all this.

Whatever we think of the book of Revelation, we are certainly living in troubling times. I saw a newspaper headline a while ago, printed in bold capitals: 'The End of the World'. Quoting a famous scientist, it warned that unless action is taken on climate change, we are doomed to environmental devastation: increasing droughts, floods, fires, hurricanes and rising sea levels. At the same time, a deadly coronavirus is killing millions of people across the globe, with bodies burned in the streets or buried in mass graves as health systems are unable to cope with the numbers of sick and dying. Some of the world's most powerful nations are also becoming increasingly aggressive, leading to fears that a small spark could lead to war. Islamic terrorism has not disappeared either, threatening world peace. Meanwhile, Western society is crumbling, with tensions – racial, religious, political – nearing boiling point. With rising rates of drug use, crime, illegal immigration and family breakdown, Western civilization seems to be tearing itself apart. Technological developments that have shrunk the world to a global village now also mean that governments have the ability to assume the role of George Orwell's 'Big Brother'. They can spy on their own citizens, squash free speech, and control people's movements, activities and livelihoods. In the background, the world's economy teeters on the brink of another massive meltdown.

Things are not looking good. Where is our world heading? The only things missing from the picture described in the book of Revelation are that we have not yet seen the massive meteorite strikes, the invasion of demonic aliens (Rev. 9), or the totalitarian one-world government that it also adds to the picture.

It could be argued that some of the picture I have painted is mere overblown hysteria. But it hardly seems a stretch of the imagination to say that our world is like a train whose brakes have failed. With multiple doomsday scenarios converging, the locomotive is only increasing speed and about to crash.

This book is not an apocalyptic horror novel – although it will describe some of these scenarios in more detail. It is not an attempt to imagine the future by looking at trends in the political, scientific or economic spheres. Instead, this is a book that attempts to explain what the Bible says is going to happen at the end of the world.

Although I have been working on this book for a number of years, I am finishing it in the midst of a global pandemic. Many people in Western societies are worried about the state of the world, Christians included, and wondering where it is headed.

Just last month, I had a complete stranger knock at my door to try to prove to me (as I listened patiently for about an hour) that the world will end in 2024 because of the alignment of 12 stars in 2017, which fulfils Revelation 12:1, and which (he said) was the sign that the last seven years of earth's history have commenced. He told me that Donald Trump will become US President again, and launch a world war, Armageddon.

Some people have another theory: the global pandemic was planned and deliberately started by the world's elite, not only to depopulate the planet, but also to bring in a one-world socialist government, which is also needed to deal with the so-called 'climate catastrophe'. They are forcing Covid vaccines and passports on us, controlling who is able to buy and sell, just like the 'mark of the beast' (666) in the book of Revelation.

Many Christians wonder about Christ's words, where He said the world would be like the days of Noah just before His return (Matthew 24:37-39). In Noah's day, the world was so full of violence, immorality

Introduction

and corruption that God sent a flood and wiped out the human race. Are we in the last days before Christ's return?

There has never been a time when Christians have been more confused about what the Bible says about the future. Not only is the subject of Bible prophecy one of the most hotly debated issues in theology, but the internet makes the problem worse, with every possible opinion – from the traditional to the trendy – paraded before people who are unsure what to believe, concerned about current trends, and full of questions about what the Bible says about the end of the world:

- Is there going to be a one-world government?
- Will there be an Antichrist, and how can we recognize him?
- How (and when) does the battle of Armageddon happen?
- Is the church going to be 'raptured' before the tribulation?

This book is a comprehensive exploration of what the Bible says about future events. It provides in-depth coverage of all the main questions and all the main passages in the Bible about future events. But it is written, not just for those who have been students of Bible prophecy for many years, but also for the ordinary Christian who has no knowledge, and perhaps even no interest, in this subject. For this reason, I ask those who are serious students of Bible prophecy to be patient with the introduction that follows. In it, we are going to assume that the reader knows nothing, and to help open up the subject, we are going to use a parable.

A PARABLE: THE CASE OF FOUR CLUES

Hercule Holmes was in the sitting-room of his Baker Street flat reading the morning paper. It was late in July 1914 and the world was edging towards war. Not even Holmes himself was sure how things would turn out. It was going to be a hot day again, and he was just about to get up and open a window when the doorbell rang. Descending the stairs, he opened the door to find a young lady of beautiful appearance, with neither spot nor wrinkle on her complexion. She was evidently of some noble or wealthy family, and Holmes decided upon the former, for despite the temperature she wore silk gloves and an expensive hat, yet there was not about her the flashy show of jewels that announced commercial success.

"Mr. Hercule Holmes?", she asked, and upon Holmes' affirmative reply, she held out her card. Holmes saw to his satisfaction that he had been correct. He had not heard of Lady Amethyst Wingate before, but he knew of her father, Lord Wingate of Gresham Hall, Suffolk.

"How may I be of assistance, Lady Wingate?"

"I would like you to take my case, as they say", she replied. "I have received a letter and I would like some help in deciphering its meaning".

Thus began what Holmes later liked to call the Case of Four Clues. The first clue, of course, was the letter sent to Amethyst Wingate hinting at the existence, and the whereabouts, of a long-lost treasure. It only took Holmes a few days to unravel what the letter meant, but before Holmes could have the pleasure of a journey into the country to visit Gresham Hall for himself, Lady Wingate had disappeared, suddenly and without the slightest trace. She was eating and drinking with other guests at a wedding, when she literally disappeared. Other guests swore that one moment she was there, and then in the twinkling of an eye, she was gone. Her mysterious disappearance was all the news for a few days, but then the Great War broke out and Holmes' services were required in London by the government. Holmes was sure that the disappearance of Lady Wingate was related to the treasure letter, but did not think that there was any connection between the treasure (and the disappearance) and the Great War. What eventually cracked the case were the multiple reports of a mysterious, one-legged, homeless tramp in neighbouring Suffolk villages, and then the footprint he left in the garden outside one of the windows of

Gresham Hall. It was only then that it all started to make some sense.

The story is now so well-known, of course, that the four chief suspects, Professor Plum, Colonel Mustard, Mrs. Peacock and Hogarth the butler, are household names. But few people realize how personally taxing the investigations were that led to Hercule Holmes solving the mystery, working out what happened to the missing aristocrat, apprehending and identifying the one legged intruder and, once the war was over, finding the treasure.

Why Use a Detective Story as a Parable?

Here is where we must leave the Case of Four Clues. This little detective story is merely a parable to help us understand an even greater mystery: what the Bible says about future events. Before I show why the Case of Four Clues is similar to what the Bible says about the end of the world and explain what the four main clues of Bible prophecy are, let me give two reasons why our fictional parable might help some people with the subject of future events.

First, there are many Christians who struggle to understand the subject of Bible prophecy. This is hardly surprising, considering all the jargon used about the subject. In our detective story, we have avoided as much as possible words like Armageddon, apocalypse, eschatology, millennium, antichrist, tribulation, rapture, and the abomination of desolation. Mind you, every workplace on earth has its special jargon – from a surgical theatre to a building site. So to understand what the Bible says about the future, you will have to learn a few new words – but nowhere near as many as you do to become a nurse or car mechanic. You can use the glossary at the end of the book to help with this. Nevertheless, the entire subject of Bible prophecy is hard to understand. Prophetical books in the Bible (like Revelation) are puzzling – with their mysterious numbers (666), and their talk of beasts with seven heads and ten horns.

Sadly, there is no one place we can go in the Bible to see the future all mapped out chronologically. There are no divinely-inspired coloured charts showing what is going to happen and when. God has put together the Bible in such a way that only those who seek with all their heart shall find. We must connect different pieces of the puzzle together from all over the Bible, and this requires a detailed knowledge of both the Old Testament and the New. Putting all the events together in the right order is a difficult mystery to solve. The first main purpose of The Case of Four Clues is to help make the subject of Bible prophecy a little easier to understand. Some people might prefer a coloured chart, but I don't really think that coloured charts actually help people as much as 'using the little grey cells'.

Second, there are also some Christians who have a very negative attitude towards the subject of the end of the world. This again is not surprising, considering the embarrassing date-setters who have repeatedly predicted Christ's return – and without exception failed to get it right, just as Christ said they would. Some Christians are positively prophecy-phobic. They feel that future events is a divisive subject that breeds quarrels and fruitless speculative debate. One commenter on an internet page wrote, 'I wish Christ would come today to put an end to these discussions'.

Some Christians dismiss any interest in what the Bible says about the future as fanaticism – eschatomania. They see themselves as calm, level-headed types not given to sensational conspiracy theories. They trot out the tired old joke about being pan-millennial – it will all pan out in the end. But a dismissive attitude to what God's Word says about future events, as if it is beneath cultivated tastes, is not helpful. The second reason for using this parable, therefore, is to try to tempt those with dismissive and negative attitudes to read about future events in the Bible, even if just for a little, by approaching the subject from a different angle.

Christians should not have a negative attitude to Bible prophecy. The three principal Christian graces are faith, love and hope – yet in today's Christian world, there is very little preaching on the subject of our future hope in Christ. True, there is often talk of hope, but it is mostly about earthly hopes, not the future hope the Bible speaks of. We should be interested in what the Bible says about the future because about 27% of the Bible is devoted to prophecies of future events[1]. If we love the Bible, we should be interested in what its prophetic parts say, just as we love its other parts. Our God knows the end from the beginning, and in His Word He tells us about it: He is the God 'declaring the end from the beginning, and from ancient times things that are not yet done, saying, "My counsel shall stand, and I will do all My pleasure"' (Isa 46:10). History is His story, and in the Bible, God tells us where it is going. Finally, we should be interested in what the Bible says about the future because prophecy is ultimately about the Lord Jesus Christ. Revelation 19:10 says, 'the testimony of Jesus is the spirit of prophecy'. Jesus Christ is the central figure in what is going to happen in the future.

Forgive me if using this fictional detective story seems to trivialize what the Bible says about the future. Bible prophecy is important, and whether

---

[1] J. Barton Payne, *Encyclopedia of Bible Prophecy*, Grand Rapids: Baker, 1980, pp674-5

you are a beginner, or befuddled, or consider the subject beneath you, my encouragement is that you need to listen to what God's Word says. If this little parable helps in some small way to do that, it will have been worthwhile.

How to be a Good (or a Bad) Detective

We need to address one more issue before we dive back into our detective story and explain the parable. Many Christians believe that the key to understanding future events is to interpret the Bible the right way. Some say that this means interpreting the Bible literally rather than allegorically (or vice versa), others say that listening to how the New Testament interprets the Old Testament is the key (or vice versa), while others say a particular passage in the Bible is the secret to understanding all the rest.

Instead of adopting any of these approaches, I suggest an even more basic method for solving the mystery. We need to observe three universally-agreed rules of a good detective. Firstly, we need to try to be as personally detached in our investigation as possible. That is, we need to be as impartial as we can in evaluating the evidence and suspects. We need to try to be aware of our own prejudices and avoid indulging them. In fictional detective stories, the good detective is often contrasted with an easily-swayed police officer who rashly jumps to conclusions based on the flimsiest of suspicions, or superficial reactions to certain characters. Similarly, in the matter of Bible prophecy, most Christians come from a certain tradition and it is only natural for us to be inclined to support the traditional view we have been taught. Today also, many Christians are easily influenced by the internet, so that we tend to watch videos or read articles that support our preferred point of view. This 'echo chamber' effect means we only listen to arguments that confirm our prejudices. Instead of such an approach, we need to try to keep an impartial, open mind.

Secondly, being a good detective means that we also need to consider all possible explanations. Sadly, many Christians do not take this approach to Bible prophecy. When talking about the subject, they start off by assuming that their view is correct, and then proceed to fill in all the details, proof-texting the Bible by picking out odd verses to back up their view. Instead of mentioning any alternative viewpoints, they patronizingly dismiss them as silly or heretical. There are four main views held by Christians about what the Bible says is going to happen in the future, and we need to give all these four explanations a fair hearing. We cannot simply rule some Christian explanations of future events 'out of court' because of our personal preferences, or denominational prejudices. Instead, we must consider all possible explanations, or to use detective language, line up all the suspects, using a process of elimination to whittle down our options when we are confronted with Bible passages dealing with future events.

This method of evaluating all the options and then eliminating the unworkable is actually how the apostles approached Bible prophecy. For example, in perhaps the most famous case of fulfilled prophecy, Peter explained on the day of Pentecost that the prophecies in Psalm 16 and 110 about God's 'Holy One not seeing corruption' and instead sitting at God's right hand could not have referred to David (even though he was the author of these psalms), because David's grave was still occupied in Jerusalem. Peter said that these prophecies must instead refer to the resurrection of the Messiah, Jesus (Acts 2:25-36).

Sir Arthur Conan-Doyle's fictional character Sherlock Holmes famously said, 'Once you eliminate the impossible, whatever remains, no matter how improbable, must be the truth'. So here is the second rule for being a good detective: consider all the possible explanations, evaluate them fairly, and eliminate those that do not explain all the evidence.

Thirdly, and most important of all, we need to investigate all the evidence. In this case, this means studying all the Bible says about the future. As the godly R. C. Chapman said, 'Every error may be based upon some part of Scripture taken from its connection; but no error can stand the test of all Scripture'. Sherlock Holmes said, 'It is a capital mistake to theorize before you have all the evidence. Insensibly one begins to twist facts to suit theories, instead of theories to suit facts'.

Sadly, many Christians base their views on Bible prophecy on a very small selection of Bible passages. Here is how to be a really bad detective: pick one piece of evidence that supports your viewpoint and ignore all the rest of what the Bible says on the subject.

We live in an age of low levels of biblical literacy. In fact, there are many people who are positively disinclined to study certain books in the Bible that are largely focused on prophecy. It is not uncommon to find someone (particularly on the internet) who is vocally self-assured about their position on Bible prophecy, yet has never studied certain important books in the Bible. But unless we have thoroughly investigated all the evidence, we cannot claim to have mastered the subject.

In practical terms, investigating all the evidence means that, at the very least, you need to have studied the book of Isaiah ('the Prince of the Prophets'), Jeremiah's Book of Consolation (Jeremiah chapters 30-33), Ezekiel's Restoration prophecies (chapters 34-48), Daniel's visions of the future (chapters 7-12), Zechariah's Second Burden (Zechariah chapters

12-14), the Olivet Discourse (Matthew chapters 24-25), Paul's treatment of the subject of Israel (Romans chapters 9-11), Paul's two letters to the Thessalonians and finally, the book of Revelation. If we may compare solving the puzzle of Bible prophecy to climbing 8,850 metres to the top of Mt. Everest (because it really is the hardest puzzle in the Bible to solve), then if you have never studied all these parts of the Bible, you have not yet even got to Base Camp at 5,364 metres. If you have studied them all, you now have all the pieces of the puzzle, but you still have to connect them together in the right way. However, don't despair: in this book, we will carefully unpack these important parts of the Bible, opening them up and setting out what they say in simple terms.

These are some of the most difficult parts of the Bible to understand, but it is essential to know what the Bible is saying in these books to solve this mystery. The study of Bible prophecy takes long, hard work, and yet many Christians today who have hardly even read the entire Bible right through are nevertheless sure in their claim that they understand what it teaches about future events.

Dealing with all the evidence not only applies on the large scale – by looking at the whole Bible – it also applies at the level of detail, that is, in our examination of a particular verse or paragraph. It is possible to pick out one little part of a Bible prophecy that aligns with a preferred explanation, but ignore other features of the same prophecy, sometimes in the same verse, which cannot be explained by this same view. This selective approach cherry picks little pieces of evidence that side with a particular theory and ignores other elements. We are going to try to practice hermeneutical consistency, that is, look for the explanation that consistently interprets the most evidence.

So here are our three rules for budding Bible prophecy detectives: firstly, try to be as open-minded and impartial as possible, secondly, consider all possible explanations, and thirdly, thoroughly investigate all the evidence.

Back to the Detective Story Again

To return to our detective story, the four clues are the lost treasure, the missing aristocrat, the Great War, and the one-legged homeless tramp. In the same way, there are four important clues to understand what the Bible says will happen in the future. That is, there are four subjects which, if investigated fully and fairly, will help us work out what will happen in the future. The good news is that if we correctly solve all four clues we will arrive at a true understanding of what the Bible says about the end of the

THE END OF THE WORLD

world. These four clues (or Bible subjects) are:

a. the Millennium,
b. the Great Tribulation,
c. the Lord's coming, and
d. the Nation of Israel.

We are going to liken these four great subjects of Bible prophecy to the four clues in our detective story. Here is a table setting out the four clues alongside the four main puzzles of Bible prophecy (we will later explain how they correspond to each other):

Clues	Detective Story	Bible Prophecy
1	The Long Lost Treasure	The Millennium
2	The Great War	The Great Tribulation
3	The Missing Aristocrat	The Lord's Coming
4	One-Legged Homeless Man	The Nation of Israel

Next, remember that there are also four main suspects in our detective story (Professor Plum, Colonel Mustard, Mrs. Peacock and Hogarth the butler). These four characters correspond to the four main solutions, or schools of thought, about the puzzle of Bible prophecy:

1. amillennialism,
2. postmillennialism,
3. historic premillennialism, and
4. futuristic (or dispensational) premillennialism.

Sorry about all the long words! Again, please don't be put off by the jargon used to describe the four main views of the future – we don't need to worry about what they all mean yet. To help with the big words, here is a table setting out the four suspects in our detective story and the corresponding schools of thought about Bible prophecy:

Answers	Detective Story Suspects	Bible Prophecy Theories
1	Professor Plum	Amillennialism
2	Colonel Mustard	Postmillennialism
3	Mrs. Peacock	Historic Premillennialism
4	Hogarth the Butler	Futuristic Premillennialism

Let us now introduce our four suspects:
- Amillennialism is a bit like Professor Plum. With a prestigious position at an ancient university, he is a socially awkward and slightly absent-minded academic, who does not enjoy discussing complex matters with those he considers beneath his intellectual calibre.
- Postmillennialism is like Colonel Mustard, a retired military man, a relic of the colonial age who still harbours an imperialistic desire to conquer the world.
- Historic Premillennialism is like Mrs. Peacock, a grand old dame with pearls and musk perfume, who prides herself on holding views on 'good authority' and is careful to maintain the approval of high society.
- Finally, Futuristic Premillennialism is represented by Hogarth the butler, a busy little man with some annoying lower-class habits, including the use of overpowering mints to disguise his bad breath, lately come into the employment of the family of the missing aristocrat.

Amillennialism (the view of Professor Plum) was first set out formally by Augustine the fifth century church 'Father'. As a result, it is the view of future events held by the Roman Catholic church and the Eastern Orthodox churches, and afterwards, of the Anglican church, the Lutheran church, the Presbyterian church (mostly), and the Methodist church. Even though many of these 'mainline' churches are now liberal in their theology (i.e. they don't actually believe the Bible is the word of God), still many Bible-believers within these churches hold to amillennialism.

Postmillennialism (Colonel Mustard) was a view of future events first formally set out by Daniel Whitby (1638–1726), an English clergyman. It became quite popular over the next two centuries of rapid technological and social progress, as missionaries spread the Christian message throughout the world. Today it is a minority view.

Premillennialism is the view almost universally held by the earliest church 'Fathers' in the first three centuries after Christ. It made a comeback in the last few centuries and is the view held by most evangelicals (particularly Americans) and Pentecostals today. The main difference between the two forms of premillennialism is this: historic premillennialism (Mrs. Peacock) believes the church will go through the great tribulation, while futuristic premillennialism (Hogarth the Butler), believes in a pre-tribulation rapture that takes the church out of the world before the tribulation period (we will explain all these terms soon!).

Readers will notice that all four answers to the puzzle of Bible Prophecy contain the word 'millennial'. The first clue is also called the 'millennium'. This is a good place to start explaining the four clues to the future.

Clue No. 1: the Millennium

The word millennium comes from Latin and means '1000 years'. It refers to a 1000 year period in which Christ reigns with His saints in Revelation 20 (where it is mentioned six times).

The millennium presents us with the first clue in the mystery of Bible prophecy. This clue is not easy to solve – in fact, we will need other clues to help us do this. But here is the question: will there be a future paradise on earth, a prolonged golden age, a return to Eden's conditions?

In our detective story, remember that a letter hints at the whereabouts of a long-lost treasure. This treasure is so huge that whoever finds it will be able to live the rest of their life in luxury and splendour. But the question immediately arises: is this treasure real or just a legend? Some characters scoff at the idea of the long-lost treasure, but other people take the long-lost treasure very seriously. What about the Bible? Does it prophesy a future golden age of material and spiritual blessing on earth?

In the Old Testament there are many prophecies of a wonderful future age: world peace and prosperity – swords beaten into plowshares and spears into pruninghooks (Isaiah 2:4), the lion lying down with the calf (not the lamb, Isaiah 11:6), the deserts blossoming like the rose (Isaiah 35:1), and 'the earth full of the knowledge of the LORD as the waters cover the sea' (Isaiah 11:9) when the Messiah reigns (see Isaiah 11:10). It is an age of environmental, social, political and spiritual harmony. Is this literally going to happen?

Professor Plum, representing Amillennialism (meaning 'no millennium'), responds with an emphatic No: all this talk of a future golden age on earth is for the birds. There is no future utopia on earth, because Christ is reigning *now* spiritually – in the hearts of those who love Him. The present church age is the millennium, the period of Christ's spiritual reign. There is no future 'golden age' on this earth – there is only this church age, and then after the heavens and earth have been burned up and passed away, eternity in the new heavens and earth.

"Preposterous!" replies Colonel Mustard, representing Postmillennialism, his cheeks growing red with rage. Colonel Mustard takes the promises of a future golden age on earth literally, believing that the church will be so successful preaching the gospel that it will transform the world and bring about its Christianization, ushering in a 1000-year reign of peace, justice and joy on earth. After this, Christ will return.

Premillennialism (represented by Mrs. Peacock and Hogarth the butler) also takes the millennium literally. It says that Christ will return before (i.e. pre-) the millennium. After His return, Christ will reign for 1000 years with the saints in a period of unparalleled blessing for planet earth. After this 1000 year period, the dead will be raised and judged, and the eternal state will begin in the new heavens and earth.

View	Amillennialism	Postmillennialism	Historic Premillennialism	Futuristic Premillennialism
Belief	No literal millennium	Millennium before Christ returns	Millennium after Christ returns	Millennium after Christ returns

If this helps, here is a chart (the down arrow shows Christ's return):

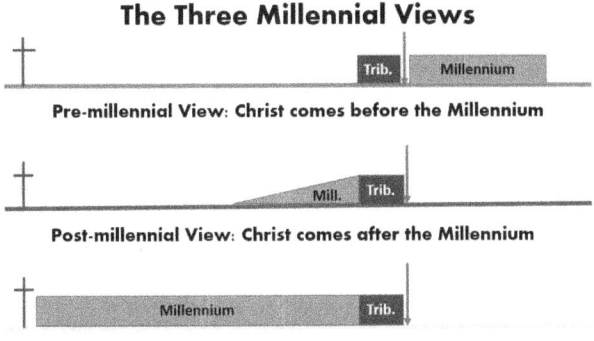

What shall we make of the millennium? One thing seems obvious: we are not living in earth's 'golden age' now. In the 20th century alone, 100 million people died at the hands of atheist regimes. It seems hard to believe that this is the paradise on earth the prophets longed for.

Postmillennialism, by contrast, says that things are getting better and better, and we are on the verge of earth's 'golden age' through the preaching of the gospel. But with all the mounting godlessness, we seem to be on the verge of the collapse of Western civilization, and a dystopian new dark age. The triumphant tone of postmillennialism (Colonel Mustard) seems a little out of place.

We will look at the evidence for and against the different millennial positions in Part One of the book. This is a complex matter, but thankfully the other three clues help us understand more about which view of the millennium is correct. Notice also, as we move on to the next clue, the box marked 'Trib.' in the chart before: this stands for the great tribulation.

Clue No. 2: the Great Tribulation

The second clue to understanding future events is the great tribulation. In Matthew's gospel, Jesus spoke about a period of unparalleled trouble on earth called the great tribulation in Matthew 24:21:

> for then there will be great tribulation, such as has not been since the beginning of the world until this time, no, nor ever shall be.

Similarly, in Revelation 7:14, we read about 'the great tribulation'. Is this 'great tribulation' something that happened in the past, or is it something happening in the present, or something that will happen in the future? Many Christians have different views on this matter, and this clue is crucial to understanding what the Bible says about the future.

In our imaginary detective story, we have compared the great tribulation to World War One. We will look at this question of the great tribulation in more detail in Part Two of the book. However, there are three main views about the great tribulation: the preterist, the historicist, and the futurist.

1. **Preterist** (from the Latin *praeter* meaning 'past'): The great tribulation occurred in the past, and Christ's words about it referred to the destruction of the Jewish temple in AD 70 by the Romans.
2. **Historicist**: The great tribulation is already happening in the present day. Historic premillennialists (like Mrs. Peacock) take this position: the church age right now is the great tribulation.
3. **Futurist**: Futuristic premillennialists (Hogarth the butler) hold that the great tribulation will occur in the future just before the return of Christ (as do most amillennialists and postmillennialists).

	Amill.	Postmill. Preterism	Historic Premill.	Futuristic Premill.
Tribulation?	Future	Past / Future	Present	Future

Thankfully, this clue is not so difficult to resolve. As mentioned, most historic premillennialists believe that we are already living in the great tribulation, which is, in fact, the entire church age. Theologian Wayne Grudem speaks for other historic premillennialists when he writes:

> Since the first century, there have been many periods of violent and intense persecution of Christians, and even in our century much of it

has occurred over large portions of the globe [in communist and Muslim lands].... It would be difficult to convince some Christians in this century who have undergone decades of persecution for their faith ... that such a great tribulation has certainly not yet occurred. They have longed and prayed for years for Christ to come and rescue them from the tribulation that they are enduring. ... [T]hough we may think that Jesus' words [about the great tribulation] indicate the likelihood of a yet greater persecution coming in the future, it is difficult to be certain of this. It seems appropriate to conclude that it is unlikely but possible that the prediction of a great tribulation has already been fulfilled[2].

However, there are certain characteristics of the great tribulation period that are difficult to see in our current day and age. Is the Antichrist ruling the whole world – so that his one-world government has authority over 'every tribe, tongue and nation' (Rev. 13:7)? Is the Antichrist doing amazing miracles by Satan's power (2 Thess. 2:9), or enforcing a law that says that people cannot buy or sell unless they take the 'mark of the Beast' – the number 666 (Rev. 13:16-18)? Has one half of the world's population been killed by the seal and trumpet judgments of Revelation chapters 6-9? Is God currently sending a 'strong delusion' upon the world so that unbelievers 'should believe the lie', so 'they all may be condemned who did not believe the truth' (2 Thess. 2:11-12)? No Christians believe that God is currently deliberately deceiving unbelievers so that they perish. It is more likely that all these things the Bible talks about are going to happen in the future tribulation period.

Further, the idea that we are currently living through the worst period of persecution for believers in the history of the world seems hard to believe. Christians in much of the world still attend church unmolested (and even fall off to sleep), go on luxury ocean cruises, live in pampered opulence undreamed of in centuries gone by, and even hold positions as heads of state in some nations. The fact that most Christians live in peace today hardly seems consistent with the idea that we are living through a worldwide reign of terror or the greatest time of tribulation in the history of the world. If we were now living in the great tribulation period, there would not be the slightest doubt about it. It would be like living in Europe during World War One – no one would deny it.

There are many clear descriptions given in the Bible about the characteristics of the 'great tribulation' and none of these signs are

---

[2] Wayne Grudem, *Systematic Theology*, IVP, 1994, p1102

currently happening. Christ Himself teaches in Matthew 24:22 that the great tribulation will be so cataclysmic that all life would be wiped off the face of the earth if it were allowed to continue too long. It seems pretty obvious that we are not living in earth's 'darkest hour'. Historic premillennialism (Mrs. Peacock) therefore seems a little confused.

Other Christians (preterists) believe that the great tribulation happened in the past, in the years AD 66 to AD 70. Undoubtedly, the Jewish War against Rome which led to the destruction of the Jewish temple in AD 70 was one of the most traumatic periods of time in ancient history. Most estimates put the deaths at about a million Jews. However, there is a fatal problem with the idea that the great tribulation occurred in AD 67-70. It is found in Christ's own words in Matthew 24:29-31 (notice particularly the very first word):

> Immediately after the tribulation of those days, the sun will be darkened, and the moon will not give its light, the stars will fall from heaven and the powers of the heavens will be shaken. Then the sign of the Son of Man will appear in heaven, and then all the tribes of the earth will mourn and they will see the Son of Man coming on the clouds of heaven with power and great glory. And He will send His angels with a great sound of a trumpet and they will gather together His elect from the four winds, from one end of heaven to the other.

Christ told us that His second coming would *immediately* follow the end of the great tribulation. That rules out AD 66-70 as a contender for the great tribulation for the simple reason that Jesus did not visibly return in AD 70. Further, the Bible teaches that the resurrection of the dead occurs at the time of Christ's return – the two events of Christ's return and the resurrection cannot be separated[3]. The fact that the resurrection did not occur in AD 70 further disproves any notion that Christ returned in AD 70. The suggestion that the resurrection and Jesus' visible return occurred in AD 70 is heresy and nonsense.

Seeing Christ's second coming has not yet occurred, but is still in the future, we can be confident that the great tribulation is also still in the future. This is what most Christians believe: amillennialists, postmillennialists and futuristic premillennialists.

But why do most historic premillennialists believe that we are already

---

[3] 'Partial Preterists' believe that Christ returned 'spiritually' in AD 70 but that the resurrection of the dead will not occur till Christ's return (again) at the end of the age. This divides Christ's return from the resurrection, two things which the Bible does not separate.

living in the great tribulation? They are driven to this idea because of the next of our four clues: the coming of the Lord.

Clue No. 3: the Lord's Coming

All Christians agree that the Lord is coming. But there is also a puzzle associated with the Lord's coming. In 1 Thessalonians 4:16-17, Paul writes about the 'rapture', a term used to describe Christians being 'caught up' into the air at the Lord's coming:

> For the Lord Himself will descend from heaven with a shout, with the voice of an archangel, and with the trumpet of God. And the dead in Christ will rise first. Then we who are alive and remain shall be caught up together with them in the clouds to meet the Lord in the air. And thus we shall always be with the Lord.

Paul also speaks of the change that will happen to believers who are still alive at the coming of the Lord in 1 Corinthians 15:51-52:

> Behold, I tell you a mystery: We shall not all sleep [i.e. die], but we shall all be changed in a moment, in the twinkling of an eye, at the last trumpet. For the trumpet will sound, and the dead will be raised incorruptible, and we shall be changed.

To return to our detective story, our third clue is the disappearance of Lady Wingate. We will liken this mysterious disappearance to the rapture: in a twinkling of an eye, millions of living and resurrected Christians are going to rise up into the air to be with Christ.

The great puzzle here is whether this rapture event happens before the great tribulation or after it. Christians hold different opinions on this question (futuristic premillennialists hold to a rapture before the tribulation, while others hold to a post-tribulation rapture), and this is one of the most difficult problems to solve in relation to future events.

To see why this clue is such a difficult puzzle, consider a question: could the Lord return at any moment? In some places in the Bible it seems that Christ's coming could happen at any time, as a sudden surprise, whereas on the other hand, if the Lord's return only happens after the 'great tribulation' period in the future, then Christ's coming will not be a sudden surprise – there will be obvious signs that Christ is about to return. Christians fall into two camps on this question.

Firstly, some Christians believe that Christ's coming could happen at any moment. They point to Bible verses like Matthew 24:36 which tell us that no man (or even angel) knows the day or hour of Christ's coming. In fact, Jesus' words in the following verses tell us of His coming being a surprise, just like in the days of Noah:

> as the days of Noah were, so also will the coming of the Son of Man be, for as in the days before the flood, they were eating and drinking, marrying and giving in marriage, until the day Noah entered the ark, and ***did not know*** until the flood came and took them all away; so also will the coming of the Son of Man be (Matt. 24:37-39).

Christ's point here is ***not*** that the sign of His coming is increased violence, immorality and corruption (although this was undoubtedly true of Noah's day). Christ is saying here that people were eating, drinking, and even getting married. Activities like getting married or eating are not sinful – nor signs of great tribulation. Christ's point is that just as people in Noah's day were getting on with their lives in conditions of perfect normality, unaware of coming judgment, and the flood came as a total surprise and destroyed them, so it will be in the day when He comes.

Christ proceeds to illustrate the exact same point that His coming will take people by complete surprise in the next few paragraphs. He says 'Watch therefore, for you do not know what hour your Lord is coming' (Matt. 24:42), 'Therefore you also be ready, for the Son of Man is coming at an hour you do not expect' (Matt. 24:44), and 'Watch therefore, for you know neither the day nor the hour in which the Son of Man is coming' (Matt. 25:13).

Other verses in the New Testament tell us that the coming of the Lord is 'near'[4], or that He will come like a thief in the night[5], or that believers should be looking for, and eagerly awaiting, Christ's coming[6]. All these Bible verses indicate that Christ's coming could happen at any time, on a day of which no one knows.

Martyn Lloyd-Jones wrote about Philippians 4:5, 'In all that we do we must always remember that the Lord may return at any time. His coming is always at hand, yes, but we do not know when, and so we must always live in the realization that he is coming'[7]. Gordon Fee writes about 1 Corinthians 1:7 ('waiting for the coming of our Lord Jesus Christ') that

---

[4] James 5:8, Rom. 13:11, 1 Pet. 4:7, Phil. 4:5, Heb. 10:37
[5] Matt. 12:43, 1 Thess. 5:2, 2 Pet. 3:10, Rev. 16:15
[6] Luke 12:36, 1 Cor. 1:7, Phil. 3:20, 1 Thess. 1:10, James 5:7
[7] D. M. Lloyd-Jones, *Life of Peace*, London: Hodder and Stoughton, 1990, p162

Paul had an 'ever present' concern about Christ's 'imminent return'[8]. R. C. H. Lenski wrote about 1 Corinthians 15:51-52: 'The simple fact is that Paul did not know when Christ would return ... All that he knew, and all that we know, is that Christ may come at any time'[9].

Secondly, on the other hand, other Christians believe that Christ's coming cannot be 'at hand', because a number of important events must take place before it comes. The theologian Louis Berkhof writes:

> According to Scripture several important events must occur before the return of the Lord, and therefore it cannot be called imminent[10].

The following events are described as signs that Christ is about to come:

- the 'abomination of desolation' (Matt. 24:15), marking the start of
- the great tribulation (Matt. 24:21),
- Antichrist's one-world government (2 Thess. 2:3-4, Rev. 13:7),
- Antichrist's miracles, worldwide worship (2 Thess. 2:9, Rev. 13:8)
- the signs in the sun, moon and stars (Matt. 24:29), and
- The Battle of Armageddon (Rev. 19:11ff.).

There are other signs too (we will look at a dozen of them later in the book), and these signs raise the question: How can Christ's coming be a surprise that could happen at any moment in conditions of perfect normality if all of these unmistakable signs must occur *before* He returns?

Certain places in the Bible tell us exactly how long the 'great tribulation' will last: 42 months, or 1260 days, or 'time, times and half a time' (Daniel 7:25, 12:7, Rev. 11:2, 3, 12:6, 14, 13:5). All of these different expressions equate to the same amount of time: three and a half years. Thus, once the three-and-a-half year 'great tribulation' has begun it will be as easy as looking at a calendar to tell when Christ is returning. How then can His return be a surprise? Robert Thomas puts the puzzle this way:

> All would agree that events of the tribulation period will be recognizable. Once that period has begun, His coming has to occur within a specified number of years. [However, if we believe that Christ

---

[8] Gordon Fee, *The First Epistle to the Corinthians*, Grand Rapids: Eerdmans, 1987, p42
[9] R. C. H. Lenski, *An Interpretation of Paul's First and Second Epistle to the Corinthians*, Columbus, OH: Wartburg Press, 1946, p737
[10] Louis Berkhof, *Systematic Theology*, Grand Rapids: Eerdmans, 1941, p696

comes after the 'great tribulation'] Christ's warnings to watch for His coming are meaningless until [the 'great tribulation'] arrives. The church need not watch as He commanded. And when that ['great tribulation'] arrives, imminence will no longer prevail because His coming will not be totally unexpected. It will have specified events to signal at least approximately, if not exactly, how far away it is[11].

Douglas Moo states that this is a real problem for all viewpoints:

All interpreters, whether they believe the discourse [i.e. Matthew 24-25] is addressed to the church or to Israel, face the difficulty of explaining how an event [i.e. Christ's return] heralded by specific signs can yet be one of which it is said 'no one knows the day and hour[12].

Postmillennialists have the biggest problem with statements of Scripture which tell us that the coming of the Lord is 'near' or 'at hand', because postmillennialists believe that the millennium (the 1000 year 'golden age'), must occur *before* Christ returns. That means that Christ's coming is at least 1000 years away in the future. Christ is not coming any time soon. Why should Christians be on the tip-toes of expectancy for Christ's return if He is not coming for such a long time? This is a big problem with postmillennialism (Col. Mustard).

Whichever way we look at this puzzle of Christ's coming, whether as a surprise in normal conditions or as preceded by unmistakable signs, it seems difficult to simultaneously believe in both a future great tribulation (Clue No. 2) and an any-moment Lord's coming (Clue No. 3), because the two clues stand in direct contradiction to each other. We either have the signs of the great tribulation period, or the surprise of the Lord's coming. Either Christ is 'at hand', coming 'at an hour we do not expect' (Matt. 24:44), or His coming is preceded by unmistakable events during the great tribulation which will form a countdown to Christ's return.

This dilemma is solved by different Christians as follows:

- Preterists believe that the Lord could come at any moment, because the signs of the great tribulation have already occurred – in AD 70.
- Historical premillennialists believe that the Lord could come very soon

---

[11] Robert Thomas, "Imminence in the New Testament, especially Paul's Thessalonian Epistles", *The Masters Seminary Journal* 13/2 (Fall 2002) 191-214, p206

[12] Douglas Moo, "A Case for the Posttribulation Rapture" in *Three Views on the Rapture*, ed. Alan Hultberg, Zondervan, 2010, p237

because the great tribulation is already underway at the moment.
- Amillennialists and Postmillennialists (who are not preterists) tend to ignore the verses about Christ's coming being 'at hand', and say that Christ cannot come at any moment because there are still many events that must occur before the Lord's coming, particularly the signs of the great tribulation period.
- Futuristic premillennialists have an unusual solution to this puzzle. They hold to the counter-intuitive idea that Christ's coming is *both* a surprise and also preceded by the signs of the great tribulation. This is because they believe that Christ's coming will occur in two stages. First, Christ is coming, as a surprise, before the great tribulation *for* His church, to take it out of the world. Then, at the end of the great tribulation Christ will return *with* His church at the battle of Armageddon to reign over the world during the millennium. A two-stage return of Christ neatly solves the puzzle of the Lord's coming; however, other Christians argue that this solution is altogether too neat and is, indeed, contrived.

The truth is that whichever way we approach this third clue, it is a tricky problem to solve. If we dismiss the large amount of biblical evidence that tells us that Christ's return will be a surprise, we are guilty of resorting to an unlikely solution to the problem, and likewise if we try to ignore all the biblical evidence of unmistakable signs preceding Christ's return. To hold both positions at the same time also seems strained. All the alternative solutions leave us with difficulties.

Here again we see the big difference between the two varieties of premillennialism. Historic premillennialists (Mrs. Peacock) hold to a post-tribulation rapture after the church has gone through the great tribulation, whereas futuristic premillennialists (Hogarth the butler) hold to a pre-tribulation rapture of the church before the great tribulation.

Our second and third clues clash to produce a problem for virtually every Bible prophecy position. We can either accept that Christ's coming will be preceded by signs and not be a surprise, or vice versa. The problem is that there are numerous Bible verses which teach both truths.

If futuristic premillennialism's solution (two comings of Christ) seems strained, historic premillennialism also seems confused, in that it teaches that we are already in the great tribulation period now, so that Christ's coming (a) could happen at any moment, and yet (b) only happens after the great tribulation.

Christ's Coming	Amillennial	Postmillennial	Historic Premillennial	Futuristic Premillennial
After *future* Tribulation	✓	✓	✗ ?	✓
At any moment	✗	✗	✓ ?	✓

The puzzle of the Lord's coming – is it preceded by the signs of the great tribulation, or is it a surprise in times of normality? – is the most difficult question to answer in relation to Bible prophecy. However, thankfully, there is another clue that provides amazing help in solving the mystery.

Clue No. 4: the Nation of Israel

If there were only three clues, we would be left confused. But there is one more important clue: the nation of Israel. Some Christians dismiss Israel as irrelevant to future events, but Israel is a subject we cannot ignore: it takes up the first three-quarters of the Bible. Israel is the easiest of our clues to solve, and it helps unlock some of the others. Horatius Bonar wrote, 'The prophecies concerning Israel are the key to all the rest'[13].

The nation of Israel is represented in our detective story by the homeless, one legged tramp who is not only seen multiple times in the villages near Gresham Hall, but has also left his footprint at the scene. Who is this very strange character, this 'odd man out', hobbled and handicapped by injury, who seems most interested in the treasure? What is his relationship to the other characters in the story? Does the homeless stranger have any claim on the legendary horde of treasure? And what is the homeless man's relationship to the missing aristocrat?

To return to the real world, why does the nation of Israel leave its footprints all over, not only Holy Scripture, but also history? Do God's plans for the future include the nation of Israel, or is the church the 'only game in town' now as far as God is concerned? H. N. Ridderbos wrote:

> The existence of Israel once again becomes a bone of contention, this time in a theoretical and theological sense. Do the misery and suffering of Israel in the past and in the present prove that God's doom has rested and will rest upon her, as has been alleged time and again in so-called Christian theology? Or is Israel's lasting existence and, in a way, her invincibility, God's finger in history, that Israel is the object of His

---

[13] Horatius Bonar, *Prophetic Landmarks*, J. Nisbet and Co., 1847, p228

special providence and proof of her glorious future, the future that has been beheld and foretold by Israel's own seers and prophets?[14]

Christians are divided over the question of Israel, and this is another significant issue we have to resolve if we are going to get a clear view of future events. Will the nation of Israel one day believe in Jesus as their Messiah? What is the relationship of the nation of Israel to the Church? And what happens to the nation of Israel at the return of Christ?

The question may be boiled down to this: does the Bible predict a future restoration of Israel, in national, territorial, political and spiritual terms? We have already seen, in the 20th century, the return of the Jewish nation to their own land. Is this the greatest modern fulfilment of Bible prophecy, happening literally right before our eyes? And what about the idea of a national spiritual revival, the turning of the Jewish nation to faith in Christ? At the moment, individual Jews are turning to Christ, but will the whole nation of Israel one day believe?

Amillennialism (Prof. Plum) answers 'no' to these questions. It insists that the Church has replaced national Israel; the Jewish nation has no further purpose in God's plans. From a human standpoint, the idea of a Jewish national conversion seems very unlikely. The Jews are the most anti-Christian nation in the world. For 2000 years, they have refused to adopt Christianity, even under severe persecution. But many Christians believe the Bible teaches that Israel will one day be converted. Romans 11:26 seems to say that Israel is going to turn to Christ: 'And so all Israel will be saved, as it is written: "The Deliverer will come out of Zion, and He will turn away ungodliness from Jacob"'.

This raises another question: if Israel is saved, what happens to the Jewish nation when they turn to Christ? Does Israel just merge into the church, like individual Jews do today when they believe in Christ? Or does Israel have a distinct future separate from the church?

The Old Testament prophets, particularly Isaiah, Jeremiah, Ezekiel, Daniel and Zechariah, are essential for understanding what will happen to Israel in the future. Sadly, today, many Christians have never studied (or even read) these books. One of the greatest problems with modern day attempts to unravel the mystery of Bible prophecy is the great ignorance of the Old Testament, and particularly the writings of the prophets. How is it possible to understand prophecy if we do not study the prophets?

---

[14] H. N. Ridderbos, "The Future of Israel", in *Prophecy in the Making: Messages Prepared for the Jerusalem Conference on Biblical Prophecy*, ed. C. F. H. Henry, Carol Stream, IL: Creation, 1971, p316

THE END OF THE WORLD

Many people think that, after listening to one or two sermons, or watching two or three Youtube videos, they have a good idea of how to piece together future events. But instead of consuming such spiritual 'fast food' off the internet, we must spend time doing in-depth study of the whole Bible. In Part Three of the book, we are going to look into the question of the role of the nation of Israel in future events, and to do this, we will be looking at some important passages in the Old Testament prophets.

But here, for a start, consider what Zechariah chapters 12-14 teach about the future of the nation of Israel. These chapters have been held, from the earliest Christian commentators (like Justin Martyr and Augustine) right up to modern day expositors, to refer to the conversion of the nation of Israel at the end of time. These three chapters in Zechariah show us that the conversion of Israel (Clue 4) is directly connected with the return of Christ (Clue 3). Notice what Zechariah says in chapters 12:9 to 13:3:

> It shall be in that day that I will seek to destroy all the nations that come against Jerusalem. [10] And I will pour on the house of David and on the inhabitants of Jerusalem the Spirit of grace and supplication; then they will look on Me whom they pierced. Yes, they will mourn for Him as one mourns for his only son, and grieve for Him as one grieves for a firstborn. [11] In that day there shall be a great mourning in Jerusalem, like the mourning at Hadad Rimmon in the plain of Megiddo. [12] And the land shall mourn, every family by itself: the family of the house of David by itself, and their wives by themselves; the family of the house of Nathan by itself, and their wives by themselves; [13] the family of the house of Levi by itself, and their wives by themselves; the family of Shimei by itself, and their wives by themselves; [14] all the families that remain, every family by itself, and their wives by themselves. 13:1 In that day a fountain shall be opened for the house of David and for the inhabitants of Jerusalem, for sin and for uncleanness. [2] It shall be in that day, says the LORD of hosts, that I will cut off the names of the idols from the land, and they shall no longer be remembered. I will also cause the prophets and the unclean spirit to depart from the land. [3] It shall come to pass that if anyone still prophesies, then his father and mother who begot him will say to him, 'You shall not live, because you have spoken lies in the name of the LORD'. And his father and mother who begot him shall thrust him through when he prophesies.

Zechariah 12 and 13 teach that Israel turns to their Messiah at the visible return of Christ. Israel's national spiritual conversion happens at the very climax of the battle of Armageddon, as Christ descends from heaven to rescue the nation of Israel from annihilation.

In the verses immediately prior, Zechariah 12:1-8, we have a description of a terrible siege of Jerusalem by all the nations, a siege which is relieved by divine intervention, by the coming of Christ himself, destroying all the surrounding armies. Such a siege has never yet happened – for example, the great siege of AD 70 was not relieved by God's intervention, (nor did Christ visibly return after it). This divinely-delivered siege must yet be in the future – it is Armageddon. Zechariah says that Israel will be converted to Christ as He returns to save their nation from annihilation. They will look on Him whom they pierced, and they will mourn for Him as one mourns for his only son (verse 10). This verse in Zechariah is quoted in Revelation 1:7 as part of its description of the return of Christ:

> Behold, He is coming with clouds, and every eye will see Him, even they who pierced Him. And all the tribes of the earth [or, land] will mourn because of Him. Even so, Amen.

Zechariah is also quoted in a verse we have referred to earlier – Matthew 24:30 and its description of Christ's return:

> then all the tribes of the earth will mourn and they will see the Son of Man coming on the clouds of heaven with power and great glory.

These two verses show that Zechariah is describing the return of Christ – the same event Jesus spoke about in Matthew 24 and John in Revelation 1. The return of Christ is also described in Zechariah 14:3-5:

> Then the LORD will go forth and fight against those nations, as He fights in the day of battle. ⁴ And in that day His feet will stand on the Mount of Olives … Thus the LORD my God will come, and all the saints with You.

This is again a description of the visible return of Christ to earth. As a result of visibly seeing Christ return to deliver them from Armageddon, Israel will believe in their Messiah, their sins will be forgiven, and they will go into mourning, just as Matthew 24:30 and Revelation 1:7 state.

Israel's national conversion is a crucial clue to the future, because it eliminates three of our four suspects. Amillennialists not only believe there is no national conversion or future for Israel, but they also believe that when Christ returns everything ends: time is no more, and the resurrection of the dead occurs. After being judged, all people go straight into the eternal state. In amillennialism, there is no glorious reign of Christ on earth after His return (the millennium). Yet, Zechariah 13 tells us that after the return of Christ, the new Jewish believers in Christ are not taken out of this world. Instead, the Jewish nation (and other nations too, see Zech. 14) continue to live on the earth, and the Jews spend the next month repenting and mourning for their long years of rejection of their Messiah. In fact, Zechariah 14:9 says, 'The LORD shall be King over all the earth'. So, Israel's continued earthly existence after their national conversion at the return of Christ appears to eliminate amillennialism as a valid explanation of future events. Life on this earth does not end at the return of Christ. Zechariah teaches that Christ is returning to earth to reign as King, and that there *is* a millennium.

Amillennialist commentators struggle so much with Zechariah's prophecy that some of them (like Calvin) even refuse to acknowledge that this prophecy is referring to Christ and His return. This is despite the fact that verses in Zechariah are repeatedly quoted in the New Testament and directly applied to Christ Himself and the events associated with His return[15]. Zechariah is indeed prophesying about Christ and His return, for the inspired New Testament authors tell us so.

This passage in Zechariah also poses problems for postmillennialism, for while postmillennialists believe that there will be a future national conversion of Israel, and that the saved nation of Israel experiences and enjoys the millennium, postmillennialists do not believe that the nation of Israel is saved *at the return of Christ*. They believe that the nation of Israel is saved by gospel preaching at least 1000 years before the return of Christ. They believe that Israel is saved before the millennium, 1000 years before the return of Christ. But Zechariah tells us the very opposite: the nation of Israel is saved at the very time of the return of Christ. Zechariah's prophecy is thus difficult to reconcile with postmillennialism.

Most historic premillennialists accept that Israel will experience a

---

[15] Compare Zech. 12:10 and John 19:37 ('they shall look on Him whom they pierced'), Zech. 13:7 and Matt. 26:31 ('strike the shepherd and the sheep will be scattered'), Zech. 14:5 and Jude 14 (the Lord coming with His saints), Zech. 14:6-7 and Matt. 24:29, 36 (the signs in the heavens of the dimmed lights), Zech. 14:8 with Ezek. 47:1-12, Joel 3:18 and Rev. 22:1-2 (living waters flowing from Jerusalem).

national spiritual conversion, but they believe that this will happen sometime during this church age, so that Israel becomes part of the church and, in effect, ceases to have a separate spiritual identity. In this scenario, when Christ returns, all believers – Jews and Gentiles – will be resurrected and raptured together as members of the one Church at the end of the great tribulation.

But Zechariah seems to teach the very opposite. Israel remains on earth during and after the return of Christ and mourns and repents of its sin of rejecting the Messiah. Zechariah makes no mention of Israel's 'rapture' as Christ descends from heaven. Rather, Israel remains on earth in the same unchanged, mortal bodies they had before Christ's return.

While the New Testament teaches that the Church experiences the change that occurs at the rapture and resurrection, Zechariah shows us that Israel does not. Some people in Israel will still sin after Christ's return, and get put to death (Zech. 13:2-3), neither of which are possible for people in resurrected, transformed, glorified, immortal bodies. Instead of being resurrected and raptured, Israel repents of its sin of rejecting God's Son and continues to live on earth as a nation of mortal saints, with their own national identity, enjoying the millennial reign of Christ.

Israel and the church are thus distinct. Zechariah shows that Israel does not merge into the church at the time of its national conversion. Israel is not saved during the church age – it is saved *after* the church age is finished, at the return of Christ. Israel has its own distinct spiritual identity, journey and destiny. So while historic premillennialism only allows a spiritual revival for Israel during the church age, Zechariah teaches that Israel has a future restoration, not only in spiritual, but also in national and territorial terms: Israel lives on into the millennium as a nation of mortal, unglorified believers.

Other OT prophecies, including Ezekiel 38-39 and Jeremiah 30, show that Israel is converted at the end of the great tribulation, after which Israel remains on earth as Christ reigns over them. Likewise, Matthew 23:39 proves that Israel is converted at the return of Christ. We will look at these passages in more detail later in the book, and see that they show that Israel has a different future pathway to that of the church.

This distinction between Israel and the Church is a key feature of futuristic premillennialism, or as it is sometimes called, *dispensational* premillennialism. 'Dispensational' is a dirty word in some Christian circles today, but it is actually a biblical term (see 1 Cor. 9:17, Col. 1:25, KJV, literally meaning 'economy, administration or stewardship'). It teaches that down through history God has done things in different ways (or under different economies, if you will). For example, before Christ, believers were under the law, and in the future, during the 'great tribulation', different conditions will exist when God will send a strong delusion on unbelievers (2 Thess. 2:11, something which is not happening today). After that, God will bring in the 'dispensation of the fullness of times' (Eph. 1:10, KJV) when Christ will head up all things in heaven and earth – the millennium. The fact that God administers things in different ways at different times explains why there is a difference between Israel and the church. Futuristic (or dispensational) premillennialism holds that there is a distinction between God's plans for the nation of Israel and the church. Israel and the church have distinct pathways in God's purposes. We will look at the future of Israel in more detail in Part Three of the book.

Conclusion

All four Christian views about Bible prophecy believe (in their own ways) in our four clues: the millennium, the great tribulation, the Lord's coming and the nation of Israel[16]. The main difference between the four views is a matter of timing: they put these events in a different order:

Amillennial	**Postmillennial**	**Hist. Premill.**	**Fut. Premill.**
Millennium	Israel Saved	Great Trib.	Lord's Coming
Israel saved(?)	Millennium	Israel Saved	Great Trib.
Great Trib.	Great Trib.	Lord's Coming	Israel Saved
Lord's Coming	Lord's Coming	Millennium	Millennium

Amillennialism believes we are in earth's golden age – the millennium – right now, while historic premillennialism says we are currently in earth's darkest hour – the great tribulation. Neither seems true. Postmillennialism says that we are on the verge of earth's golden age, but that Christ is not coming back for at least 1000 years, despite many verses teaching Christ could come at any time. Futuristic premillennialism teaches that the Lord's coming could happen at any moment, and the tribulation is still in the future. Perhaps the most decisive clue is the nation of Israel: futuristic premillennialism believes that the conversion of Israel happens at the battle of Armageddon at the end of the great tribulation, and that saved Israel goes into the millennium as a nation of mortal saints, so that Israel is distinct from the church. Amillennialism, postmillennialism and historic

---

[16] Amillennialism does not believe in a literal millennium, nor do some amillennialists accept that all Israel will be saved (amillennialists deny the national restoration of Israel).

premillennialism fail to correctly present God's future plans for Israel.

So there you have it. The butler did it. Futuristic (or dispensational) premillennialism, although not without problems, seems to explain more of the biblical evidence than any other view of Bible prophecy.

The true order of end-time events is this: we are in the church age (not the tribulation, or the millennium), next comes the rapture, then the tribulation period, and out of that crisis a one-world government rises under the tyrannical rule of the Antichrist. Eventually, a rebellion against Antichrist's rule leads to world war, Armageddon, when Christ returns, Israel is converted, and then there is Christ's millennial reign.

Futuristic Premillennialism is also the most widely-held view of future events by evangelical Christians today[17]. The Church 'Fathers' of the first few centuries after Christ also held to these four beliefs (as we shall see): a literal millennium, a future great tribulation, the conversion of Israel at the return of Christ, and the imminence of the Lord's coming (although they did not 'put it all together' or resolve all the apparent contradictions).

	Amillennial	Postmill. / Preterism	Historic Premill.	Futuristic Premill.
Literal Millennium?	✗	?	✓	✓
Future Tribulation?	✓	✗	✗ ?	✓
Lord's return Imminent?	✗	✓	✓ ?	✓
Israel restored?	✗	✗	✗ ?	✓

Notice that each of the four 'answers' to the puzzle of Bible prophecy are able to correctly explain some of the clues (they have ticks in some boxes). All four views have some valuable insights into what the Bible teaches about the future. But only futuristic premillennialism provides a solution that appears to correctly explain *all* the clues. The only unique feature of futuristic premillennialism is its teaching of a pre-tribulation rapture, but

---

[17] Lifeway Research (2016) surveyed 1000 Protestant senior pastors in the USA. 36% believe the Lord will come and rapture the church before the Great Tribulation, 18% believe He will come and rapture the church after the Great Tribulation, 8% believe the rapture occurs midway through the tribulation period, 25% say that there is no such thing as a literal rapture, 8% do not agree with any of these views, and 4% are not sure. Results for other countries are not available.

the idea of the rapture itself is not unique to futuristic premillennialism. Virtually all positions hold that there is a rapture at Christ's return; it is over the timing of the rapture that views differ.

Putting on our Lawyer's Hat

Thus far in the book, we have approached the subject of Bible prophecy as if it were a detective puzzle. From now on, however, we are going to stop pretending to be detectives and instead proceed more like lawyers. That is, think of this introductory chapter like a lawyer's 'opening statement', laying out the case. The rest of this book is going to call upon various (scriptural) witnesses which set out the evidence about the four main 'clues' in more detail. Feel free to turn to the section of the book that deals with the evidence you are most interested in.

In **Part One**, we will look at the evidence that shows there is going to be a literal millennium. Here we see the wonderful picture that the Bible paints of the future for our world when its true King returns.

After Part One, there is a digression, a **Theology section**, setting out the arguments for and against amillennialism, postmillennialism and premillennialism, respectively, and looking at the important subject of the kingdom of God.

In **Part Two**, we will look at the darkest hour of this world's history still to come, the great tribulation. Here we will see what the Bible teaches about Antichrist and the battle of Armageddon, among other approaching apocalyptic calamities.

In **Part Three**, we will look at what the Bible says about the future of the nation of Israel, its conversion and restoration.

Finally, in **Part Four**, we will look at what the Bible teaches about the coming of our Lord Jesus Christ and the hope of the Church.

Whether you agree or disagree with the solution to the puzzle of future events I have suggested, or maybe are still not sure what to believe, I encourage you to continue to explore what the Bible teaches about future events in the rest of the book. While I suggest futuristic premillennialism is the best explanation of the end of the world, I will nevertheless strive to fairly (and fully) present the best arguments for (and against) all the other viewpoints so that you can evaluate them.

May the Lord help and bless you as you read with an open Bible and an open heart, ready to believe what God's Word teaches about the end of the world.

PART ONE:

How is it all Going to End?

1 PARADISE RESTORED

When I was about ten years old, I had to pick out a book from the state school library to read. I chose *The Last Battle* by someone called C. S. Lewis. I had never heard of him before, but the book's title sounded exciting. So I read the book, and I still remember my reaction: I had never before read such a miserable book.

The Last Battle is Lewis' final *Narnia* story, and it explains how the world of Narnia ends. *The Last Battle* won the Carnegie Medal in 1956, the top British award for children's literature, so it must have been a great book, but I cannot believe they consulted many ten-year old boys before they awarded the prize. I have since read the other books in Lewis' *Narnia* series, and enjoyed most of them. I have re-read *The Last Battle* as an adult too, but I still feel the same way about it as I did when a child: it is a miserable book.

The Last Battle parallels in some ways how the Bible tells us our world will end, and its storyline is roughly as follows. Shift, the cleverest, ugliest and the most wrinkled of the apes, persuades his dim-witted friend Puzzle the Donkey to dress up in a lion's skin. He proclaims that Aslan (the Christ-figure of the *Narnia* stories) has returned. As news spreads that Aslan has come, all the creatures start to obey the dressed-up donkey. However, the Donkey (under the influence of Shift the Ape) starts issuing tyrannical orders that seem very unlike the real Aslan. Brave King Tirian, the last king of Narnia, with a few faithful followers, fights back against the ape and the false-Aslan. Up until this point, the book is full of good and exciting stuff.

However, here is the point which I found unsatisfying as a boy: King Tirian and his small band of followers do not win this final battle; instead they are all either killed or captured, one by one. It is all very sad.

In fact, the word 'battle' in the title almost amounts to false-advertising: King Tirian only has one unicorn, two children, a dwarf and half a dozen animals in his 'army'. Nor does the real Aslan come to their rescue. Instead, after his followers have lost the last battle, Aslan arrives and proceeds to destroy Narnia: time is no more, the stars fall, the sun is extinguished, the earth is stripped back to bare rock and the sea comes up over the land, leaving it in watery darkness. It is all very bleak and even some of the characters cry as they watch Narnia being destroyed. All Aslan's followers go through a door to live in a parallel universe, Aslan's country – heaven. Here is a line that sums up the book: 'all worlds draw to an end, except Aslan's own country'.

Certain elements of *The Last Battle* help us to understand what the Bible says will happen at the end of our world. Just like in Lewis' story, Satan will raise up a man who is the Antichrist – a counterfeit Christ. The rule of this Antichrist over the earth will be tyrannical – all will have to worship him or die. This period is sometimes called the great tribulation. Not only will the Antichrist persecute those who refuse to worship him, but God will also send terrible calamities upon the earth, particularly on those who follow the Antichrist. Finally, at the end of the great tribulation, Christ will come and defeat the Antichrist at the Battle of Armageddon.

As a boy, my biggest problem with *The Last Battle* was that the good guys didn't really win. As an adult, my issue is with another question the book raises: does our world end when Christ returns, in the same way Aslan destroyed Narnia, or does Christ return to defeat the Antichrist and reign here on earth? What happens to Christians when Christ returns: do we all get whisked off to heaven, like Aslan's loyal followers going to his own land? Is our Christian hope to sit on the clouds strumming harps in one big, never-ending church service in the sky? Or do we reign here on earth with Christ?

Christians hold two views on this subject. Some believe that our future is spiritual and heavenly. C. S. Lewis seems to have held this opinion. He wrote:

> God will invade ... When that happens, it is the end of the world. When the author walks on to the stage the play is over. God is going to invade, all right: but what is the good of saying you are on His side then, when you see the whole natural universe melting away like a dream and something else – something it never entered your head to conceive – comes crashing in; something so beautiful to some of us and so terrible to others that none of us will have any choice left?[1]

Other Christians believe that our future is physical and earthly. This second view teaches that Jesus doesn't return to wipe out Planet Earth and take His people off to heaven. Instead, Christ returns to restore this world to be the Paradise He originally created it to be. Which is true?

---

[1] C. S. Lewis, *Mere Christianity*, London: William Collins, 2016, p65.

Isaiah's Picture of the Future Paradise

In this chapter we are going to look at what Isaiah says about the future. What better place to start our study of end-time events than by turning to the prophets. Both the Lord Jesus and his apostles argued that their teachings were based on 'all things which are written in the Law and in the Prophets' (Acts 24:14).

Isaiah's name means 'Jehovah is salvation', and Isaiah has been called the Prince of the Prophets. His prophecy gives us one of the most glorious visions of the future. We will look at ten features of Isaiah's future paradise.

1. World Peace (Isaiah 2:1-4)

> The word that Isaiah the son of Amoz saw concerning Judah and Jerusalem. ² Now it shall come to pass in the latter days that the mountain of the LORD'S house shall be established on the top of the mountains, and shall be exalted above the hills; and all nations shall flow to it. ³ Many people shall come and say, "Come, and let us go up to the mountain of the LORD, to the house of the God of Jacob; He will teach us His ways, and we shall walk in His paths." For out of Zion shall go forth the law, and the word of the LORD from Jerusalem. ⁴ He shall judge between the nations, and rebuke many people; they shall beat their swords into plowshares, and their spears into pruning hooks; nation shall not lift up sword against nation, neither shall they learn war anymore.

The words of Isaiah 2:4 are engraved on the United Nations building in New York: 'they shall beat their swords into plowshares, and their spears into pruning hooks; nation shall not lift up sword against nation, neither shall they learn war any more'. Sadly, despite the best efforts of the United Nations, our world still has no peace. World military spending sits at nearly 2 trillion U.S. dollars p.a. in 2020. There are no signs of nations converting tanks into tractors, or other weapons into farm machinery. Nor has any nation stopped training soldiers in military academies. Yet Isaiah prophesies a coming day in which there will finally be peace on earth (verse 4).

M. R. DeHaan writes, 'The Bible is replete with prophecies of a coming age of peace and prosperity. It will be a time when war will be utterly unknown. Not a single armament plant will be operating, not a soldier or sailor will be in uniform, no military camps will exist, and not one cent will be spent for armaments of war, not a single penny will be used for defense, much less for offensive warfare. Can you imagine such an age, when all nations shall be at perfect peace, all the resources available for enjoyment, all industry engaged in the articles of a peaceful luxury[2].

2. National Blessing

Not only is all the world at peace, but all the nations have turned to the Lord and walk in God's ways. All the nations shall come up to God's house in Jerusalem to learn of God's ways (verse 2). In fact, Isaiah 11:9 says that the earth will be full of the knowledge of the Lord. Here we read that all nations will follow His ways (verses 2 and 3).

Imagine all the nations of the earth being truly God-fearing, following God's ways yet with their own distinctive cultural flavours: Italy without the Mafia, Arab lands without Islam, India without idolatry, Africa without corrupt dictators, and the West without godless political correctness.

Some Christians argue that Isaiah's prophecy is being fulfilled now in the church: all the nations are coming to the house of God (the Church) to learn 'His ways' (2:3). Theologian Robert Strimple writes, 'The ancient prophecies of Isaiah 2:2-4 and Micah 4:1-3 of "many peoples" from "all nations" streaming to Jerusalem will not be fulfilled [in the] future ... by terrestrial pilgrimages to an earthly city. Praise God, that blessed prophecy is being fulfilled *now* as men and women of every tribe on the face of the earth call upon the name of Zion's King and become citizens of "the Jerusalem that is above"'[3].

However, while the church is indeed a blessing to the nations through the gospel, the church has not brought an end to international wars, nor the manufacture of weapons (verse 4). If the church is not the fulfilment of the prophecy in verse 4, then it makes it difficult to see the church in verses 2 and 3 which speak about the nations learning God's ways. The two promises of world peace and walking in God's ways go together. The two activities are related, for world peace depends upon all nations being God-fearing, and both happen at the same time: 'in the latter days' (v2).

Another problem with seeing this prophecy as being fulfilled in the church is that, if we take the blessings promised to Israel in Isaiah 2 and apply them to the church, should we not apply the curses that follow Isaiah 2:5 and in Isaiah 3 to the church as well? If we try and read the church into 'Judah' and 'Jerusalem' (v1), or 'Jacob' and 'Zion' (v3), then what shall we

---

[2] M. R. DeHaan, *The Great Society*, Radio Bible Class, 1965, pp7-8
[3] Robert Strimple, "Amillennialism" in *Three Views on the Millennium and Beyond*, ed. D. L. Bock, Zondervan, 1999, p93, emphasis in original

do when we encounter the same terms in Isaiah chapter 3? Such a method of reading ourselves into scripture, picking out a few words from a passage but ignoring the context, might give us some comforting thoughts, but it does not really seem to be what the prophecy was originally intended to teach. Nor is it a consistent approach to interpreting the Bible, for while reading the church into one verse about Israel in Isaiah might seem plausible, it cannot be maintained beyond a few phrases. It is particularly significant that Strimple does not even mention verse 4 and its promise of world peace, nor the verses from 5 onwards, with their curses upon Israel for their idolatry. No one takes these to refer to the church.

It seems difficult to take Isaiah's prophecy as being fulfilled in our present day and age. Isaiah's prophecy does not picture a few people from many nations following the Lord, as presently, but many people (verse 3) from all nations (verse 2). Isaiah pictures the whole world following God's ways (see Isaiah 11:9). He is referring to something quite different to our present church age when there are 'few who are saved' (Luke 13:23).

3. The Reign of the Rightful King (Isaiah 9:6-7)

> 6 For unto us a Child is born, unto us a Son is given; and the government will be upon His shoulder. And His name will be called Wonderful, Counsellor, Mighty God, Everlasting Father, Prince of Peace. 7 Of the increase of His government and peace there will be no end, upon the throne of David and over His kingdom, to order it and establish it with judgment and justice from that time forward, even forever. The zeal of the LORD of hosts will perform this.

Isaiah's vision of world peace depends upon the coming of God's King to rule – the reign of the Messiah. Only when the 'Prince of Peace' sits upon the throne will He finally bring peace on earth. The restoration of the nations from the ruinous policies of their rulers likewise requires the arrival of God's appointed King. Isaiah speaks of the reign of this great King in other passages too: Isaiah chapters 11, 12, 32, 33 and 35.

Imagine a world without politicians or elections, without corruption in high places or the crushing of the masses under the heel of despots. With the perfect ruler sitting upon the throne, earthly Paradise follows.

Isaiah 9:6 shows us that the Messiah is both God and man – a child born, and yet the Mighty God, the Everlasting Father, the Son given. He is the King of Israel: 'of the increase of His government and peace there will be no end, upon the throne of David and over His Kingdom'. Only the Lord Jesus Christ matches the personal requirements of this job description.

Think of it – the One who was rejected, shamefully treated, hung upon a cross by His own creatures, and mocked with a crown of thorns – will instead sit upon the throne of His glory. He will be vindicated in the very place where He was despised and rejected – on earth.

Notice too that the Messiah will reign with 'judgment and justice' (9:7). This leads on to our next passage.

4. Social Justice (Isaiah 11:1-5)

> [1] There shall come forth a Rod from the stem of Jesse, and a Branch shall grow out of his roots. [2] The Spirit of the LORD shall rest upon Him, the Spirit of wisdom and understanding, the Spirit of counsel and might, the Spirit of knowledge and of the fear of the LORD. [3] His delight is in the fear of the LORD, and He shall not judge by the sight of His eyes, nor decide by the hearing of His ears; [4] But with righteousness He shall judge the poor, and decide with equity for the meek of the earth; he shall strike the earth with the rod of His mouth, and with the breath of His lips He shall slay the wicked. [5] Righteousness shall be the belt of His loins, and faithfulness the belt of His waist.

Because of the coming of the rightful King (11:1), filled with the Spirit of God (11:2), there will finally be righteousness and justice on the earth. He will bring the oppression of the poor to an end (11:4). He will come to the aid of the meek of the earth, and will also deal with the wicked, so that no longer will evil flourish: 'with the breath of His mouth He will slay the wicked' (11:5).

Imagine human society without crime, poverty, drugs, corruption, or injustice. With a King whose 'delight is in the fear of the LORD', characterised by righteousness and faithfulness (as opposed to human politicians with their self-promotion, corruption and broken promises), the world will finally be a paradise. Isaiah is prophesying the perfect society.

5. Natural Harmony (Isaiah 11:6-9)

> [6] The wolf also shall dwell with the lamb, the leopard shall lie down with the young goat, the calf and the young lion and the fatling

together; and a little child shall lead them. ⁷ The cow and the bear shall graze; their young ones shall lie down together; and the lion shall eat straw like the ox. ⁸ The nursing child shall play by the cobra's hole, and the weaned child shall put his hand in the viper's den. ⁹ They shall not hurt nor destroy in all My holy mountain.

Isaiah prophesies the removal of the curse from the natural realm: natural enemies in the animal kingdom, predators and prey, are at peace with each other: 'they shall not hurt nor destroy in all my holy mountain'.

Again, some Christians have argued that this prophecy applies to the spiritual blessings of the present church age. For example, some suggest that the lion and the lamb symbolise a man who was very violent in unconverted days sitting down in church alongside his meek, mild Christian brother.

John Calvin comments on the same prophecy in Isaiah 65:25 as follows: 'yet beyond all controversy the Prophet speaks allegorically of bloody and violent men, whose cruel and savage nature shall be subdued, when they submit to the yoke of Christ'.

This interpretation is indeed spiritually heart-warming, but the problem is the difficulty of accounting for all the animals in the picture. Who are the cows and goats among our congregations? Are these the less intelligent members of our churches? If we are to spiritualize the animals, surely the viper must refers to Satan, and if so, what does it mean that the little child is playing with the snake? Surely the prophet should be warning against any spiritually dangerous contact instead of encouraging such liaisons. And what about the straw that the lion eats, and the fact that the cow and the bear are grazing together (v7)? On the face of it, this seems to be teaching the end of carnivory and a return to a vegetarian diet among the animals, like in Eden (Gen. 1:29-30). Lions eating straw is a good thing. But if we spiritualize this vegetarian diet, what shall we say that the straw means?

If we try to read a secret, hidden, mystical meaning into the animals in this prophecy, we could perhaps view some of the animals in terms of certain character traits (lambs are meek and gentle), but we could alternatively take the animals to mean nations (the bear in v 7 is Russia?) or even sporting teams (various candidates suggest themselves).

What controls or limits are there to our spiritualizing of the passage, to help us know that our explanation is correct or not? Is there anything to stop someone choosing some other fanciful explanation for the animals? There seems to be no limit, other than imagination, to what we can make the Bible say if we choose to take it symbolically.

The problem is not simply taking the animals symbolically. All Christians accept that in certain books, there are various animals that are used as symbols. In the visions of Daniel 7 and 8 animals represent kingdoms – the lion represented Babylon, the bear Medo-Persia, the leopard Greece (Ch. 7), the ram Medo-Persia and the goat Greece (Dan. 8). The problem is not simply the attempt to interpret symbolically. Nor is the problem simply confined to interpretational inconsistency – the picking and choosing of one or two animals and ignoring others. The biggest problem is that there really is no limit to what we can make the Bible say if we read it like this.

The most natural way of understanding the prophecy is to take the animals simply to mean animals, and grass to mean grass. But there are other dangers in trying to read pleasant and edifying spiritual lessons into this prophecy rather than reading the words as they stand.

Take the story of a Jew who opened the New Testament and asked a Christian clergyman whether he believed the angel Gabriel's words to Mary in Luke 1:32 would be literally fulfilled: 'The Lord shall give to Him the throne of His father, David, and He shall reign over the house of Jacob forever'. The clergyman said, 'I do not; I take it to be figurative language describing Christ's reign over the church'. 'Well, then,' said the Jew, 'neither do I believe literally the words of Gabriel which say that this Son of David would be born of a virgin. I take them to be merely a figurative way of describing the remarkable purity of the person who is the subject of the prophecy'. The lesson here is this: if we start taking some things literally and some things allegorically or 'spiritually' in the same prophecy, picking and choosing what we like out of the Bible, we end up imposing our own preferences upon the Bible.

The normal control mechanism for interpreting Scripture is Scripture itself, but Calvin's interpretation suggested above (the animals represent various personality types) offers us no cross-references to confirm its validity. By contrast, Daniel's prophecies in chapters 7 and 8 about the animals are interpreted and explained by Daniel in the same chapters, so that we have scriptural warrant for taking Daniel's animals symbolically as empires. Calvin's interpretation, by contrast, is not substantiated by Scripture. As a result, the symbolic interpretation is limited only by the lengths our imagination is prepared to go.

The alternative method of interpretation (indeed, the default) is to let the words take their normal meaning. Instead of using imaginative licence, the most natural way of understanding the prophecy is to take the animals simply to mean animals. This verse is telling us that one day the animal creation will be at peace, with each other and with humans. Instead of eating each other, the animals will again be vegetarian: 'the lion shall eat straw like the ox'. This is the way things were at the beginning of Creation where the animals were vegetarian (Gen. 1:30). Here we have returned to Eden's paradise.

6. Spiritual Blessing (Isaiah 11:9b)

The prophecy in Isaiah 11 reaches its climax in verse 9b with the words, 'for the earth shall be full of the knowledge of the LORD as the waters cover the sea'.

No longer will the God-fearing people of the earth be a persecuted minority. Everybody will know God. Notice that the scene pictured here is not in heaven above: 'the *earth* shall be full of the knowledge of the LORD' (Isaiah 11:9).

7. Jewish Restoration (Isaiah 11:10-16)

Isaiah's prophecy continues:

> [10] And in that day there shall be a Root of Jesse, who shall stand as a banner to the people; for the Gentiles shall seek Him, and His resting place shall be glorious. [11] It shall come to pass in that day that the Lord shall set His hand again the second time to recover the remnant of His people who are left, from Assyria and Egypt, from Pathros and Cush, from Elam and Shinar, from Hamath and the islands of the sea. [12] He will set up a banner for the nations, and will assemble the outcasts of Israel, and gather together the dispersed of Judah from the four corners of the earth (Isa 11:11-12).

Isaiah's prophecy continues, foretelling the re-gathering of the Jewish people 'from the four corners of the earth' (v12). The dispersed of Israel shall return to their own land and enjoy Christ's reign. This is not a prediction of the return from the Babylonian captivity, for it happens when the true King (verse 1), the Messiah, finally reigns. By contrast, the Babylonian return occurred before Messiah's coming, and was not accompanied by any of the social, natural or spiritual blessings of this chapter.

We have already seen that Isaiah 2:1-4 describes Jewish restoration: the passage is 'concerning Judah and Jerusalem' (2:1); 'the mountain of the LORD'S house shall be established on top of the mountains and shall be exalted above the hills and all nations shall flow into it ... for out of Zion shall go forth the law, and the word of the LORD from Jerusalem'.

Micah 4 states this even more clearly. Micah's parallel prophecy reads virtually word for word the same as Isaiah 2, except that Micah goes further than Isaiah and concludes in verse 8 with these words: 'And you, O tower of the flock, the stronghold of the daughter of Zion, to you shall it come, even the former dominion shall come, the kingdom of the daughter of Jerusalem'.

Israel will be restored to its former glory and dominion, and be the centre of God's blessing on earth.

8. Environmental Beauty (Isaiah 35:1-2, 6b-7)

> The wilderness and the wasteland shall be glad for them, and the desert shall rejoice and blossom as the rose; ² It shall blossom abundantly and rejoice, Even with joy and singing. The glory of Lebanon shall be given to it, the excellence of Carmel and Sharon. They shall see the glory of the LORD, the excellency of our God. ... ⁶ᵇ For waters shall burst forth in the wilderness, and streams in the desert. ⁷ The parched ground shall become a pool, and the thirsty land springs of water; in the habitation of jackals, where each lay, there shall be grass with reeds and rushes.

Isaiah 35 speaks of the environmental blessings of that day: the desert will 'rejoice and blossom as the rose' (35:1). Imagine the great deserts of the world, like the Sahara, or central Australia, or the Arabian desert, nearly the size of India, being turned into fertile and productive places – with flower shows! Psalm 72:16 likewise speaks of the environmental blessing of Messiah's reign: 'there will be an abundance of grain in the earth, on the top of the mountains; its fruit shall wave like Lebanon'.

We are subjected to a constant bombardment of warnings about impending environmental catastrophes: global warming, deforestation, desertification, droughts, famines, and water shortages. Whether these doomsday warnings are fully justified or not, it is true that certain places in the world currently face serious environmental challenges. Here the Bible prophesies an age to come of environmental prosperity and plenty, not in heaven, but on the earth.

What a day it will be when we no longer have to endure the twin evils of corporate greed destroying the earth (Revelation 11:18) and environmental alarmists pushing their false-religion of nature-worship upon us.

9. Bodily Healing (Isaiah 35:3-6)

> ³ Strengthen the weak hands, and make firm the feeble knees. ⁴ Say to those who are fearful-hearted, "Be strong, do not fear! Behold, your God will come with vengeance, with the recompense of God; He will come and save you." ⁵ Then the eyes of the blind shall be opened, and the ears of the deaf shall be unstopped. ⁶ Then the lame shall leap like a deer, and the tongue of the dumb sing.

Isaiah prophesies that 'the eyes of the blind shall be opened, and the ears of the deaf shall be unstopped, then the lame shall leap like a deer, and the tongue of the dumb sing'. There will no longer be any more bodily disease or disability.

It is possible to understand these verses to refer to the way that Christ healed the sick during His public ministry. However, it is difficult to understand Isaiah 35 in its entirety as applying to Christ's earthly ministry. For example, Christ did not make the deserts 'blossom as the rose'. If we take the bodily healing literally, interpretational consistency demands that we also take the environmental blessings literally. The passage requires a yet future fulfilment. Seeing Christ did not fulfil the environmental prophecy at His first coming, it seems the passage requires a yet future fulfilment.

It is true, however, that Christ's ministry was a foretaste of this yet-future glorious period; Christ's miracles were signs of 'the powers of the age to come' (Hebrews 6:5). His miracles were not only a proof that He was the Messiah, but also a glimpse and foreshadowing of the glories of His future reign.

10. The Rejection of the Wicked (Isaiah 34)

In addition to paradise restored, we also have the punishment of those who do not know God. It is not until the world has been purged and the wicked punished that the earth will enjoy God's blessings. We will not quote Isaiah 34 in its entirety here, but verse 2 gives us a flavour of its contents:

> the indignation of the LORD is against all nations, and His fury against all their armies; He has utterly destroyed them, He has given them over to the slaughter.

Isaiah chapters 13 to 24 list all the nations that God is going to judge, starting with Babylon and its King, then moving on to all the other nations (Assyria, Philistia, Moab, Syria, Ethiopia, Egypt and Tyre), until in chapter 24, God's judgment falls upon the whole earth. 'Behold, the LORD makes the earth empty and makes it waste, distorts its surface and scatters abroad its inhabitants' (24:1). 'The earth is violently broken, the earth is split open, the earth is shaken exceedingly. The earth shall reel to and fro like a drunkard, and shall totter like a hut; its transgression shall be heavy upon it, and it will fall, and not rise again' (24:19-20).

Not only is the earth punished, but also God's heavenly enemies. We read in Isaiah 24:

> [21] It shall come to pass in that day that the LORD will punish on high the host of exalted ones, and on the earth the kings of the earth. [22] They will be gathered together, as prisoners are gathered in the pit, and will be shut up in the prison; after many days they will be punished. [23] Then the moon will be disgraced and the sun ashamed; for the LORD of hosts will reign on Mount Zion and in Jerusalem and before His elders, gloriously (Isaiah 24:21-23).

Only after God has judged a wicked world will paradise be re-established.

Paradise Restored in the Book of Revelation

It is not just Isaiah who talks about this future paradise. When we turn to the end of the Bible, in Revelation 21:9 – 22:5, we see Isaiah's future paradise presented to us again in the New Jerusalem descending from heaven. John describes a number of features that remind us of the original paradise in the Garden of Eden: there is a river (22:1), the tree of life (22:2), the healing of the nations (22:2), and no more curse (22:3). Here is the original paradise restored. The Earth is not destroyed at Christ's coming – it is instead liberated, rejuvenated and it finally becomes the paradise God created it to be in the beginning.

Other Bible passages that teach that Paradise will be Restored

The New Testament refers to 'Paradise Restored' in many places. Here are ten New Testament verses:

1. In Acts 3:21, Peter preaches that '… heaven must receive (Him, Christ) until the times of restoration of all things'. When Christ returns, everything is going to be restored like in the original paradise.

2. Christ spoke of the 'regeneration, when the Son of Man sits on the throne of His glory' (Matt. 19:28). 'Regeneration' here literally means 'new birth' – not of the individual, but of the whole creation.
3. Romans 8:19-22 tells how the whole 'creation itself also will be delivered from the bondage of corruption into the glorious liberty of the children of God' (v21).
4. Christ promised that 'the meek shall inherit the earth' (Matt. 5:5).
5. Christ said to the sheep in Matthew 25:34, 'inherit the kingdom prepared for you from the foundation of the world'.
6. Christ told us to pray for the coming paradise: 'Thy kingdom come, thy will be done on earth as it is in heaven' (Matt. 6:10).
7. Hebrews 2:5 speaks of 'the world to come', which is not going to be subject to angels, but ruled by men.
8. Abraham is the 'heir of the world' (Rom. 4:13).
9. 1 Corinthians 6:2 says that the 'saints will judge (i.e. administer, rule) the world'.
10. Rev. 5:10 says that the saved 'will reign on the earth'.

Summary

Isaiah foretells a future day of justice and joy, harmony and plenty. The earth itself will be restored to the paradise it was originally created to be. To borrow language from Milton's *Paradise Lost*:

> Earth be chang'd to Heav'n, and Heav'n to Earth,
> One Kingdom, Joy and Union without end.

Let us draw three conclusions from Isaiah's prophecies.

1. Isaiah is telling us of a kingdom to come: the Messiah, the Prince of Peace, will sit upon the throne as King.
2. Isaiah's kingdom is not the present church age. The nations are still at war with each other today, the earth is not full of the knowledge of the Lord as the waters cover the sea, the world still has many environmental problems, social problems and physical diseases, and the curse upon the animal creation has not been lifted. Isaiah's prophecy has not been fulfilled in the church. Isaiah's kingdom is still future.
3. This promised kingdom is earthly: there are nations, animals, and deserts blossoming.

THE END OF THE WORLD

In chapter 26 of his prophecy, Isaiah uses the beautiful imagery of a great feast to picture God's coming Kingdom (Isaiah 25:6-9):

> [6] And in this mountain the LORD of hosts will make for all people a feast of choice pieces, a feast of wines on the lees, of fat things full of marrow, of well-refined wines on the lees. [7] And He will destroy on this mountain the surface of the covering cast over all people, and the veil that is spread over all nations. [8] He will swallow up death forever, and the Lord GOD will wipe away tears from all faces; the rebuke of His people He will take away from all the earth; for the LORD has spoken. [9] And it will be said in that day: "Behold, this is our God; we have waited for Him, and He will save us. This is the LORD; we have waited for Him; we will be glad and rejoice in His salvation."

It will be a time of great joy and satisfaction. God will wipe away tears from all faces, and death will be swallowed up forever. God's people will be glad and rejoice in Him. Isaiah 35:10 says, 'the redeemed of the Lord shall return and come to Zion with singing, with everlasting joy on their heads. They shall obtain joy and gladness and sorrow and sighing shall flee away'.

2 TROUBLE IN PARADISE?

One of my favourite books is *Heaven* by Randy Alcorn. In fact, my wife and I like this book so much that we have given copies to a number of Christian friends. This is not to suggest that they might be going there soon and need to start getting ready, but just because the book is so encouraging and informative. Here's why I like the book.

Alcorn argues against the view of heaven that some Christians hold who think of heaven as a place of 'eternal tedium', where we 'float around in the clouds with nothing to do but strum a harp … it's all so terribly boring'[1]. Alcorn does this by showing that God's purpose is for us to ultimately enjoy a new Heaven and a new Earth (Rev. 21:1). He writes:

> If God's plan was merely to take mankind to the present Heaven, or to a Heaven that was the dwelling place of spirit beings, there would be no need for New Heavens and a New Earth. Why refashion the stars of the heavens and the continents of the earth? God could just destroy this original creation and put it all behind him. But he won't do that. … He isn't going to abandon his creation. He's going to restore it. We won't go to Heaven and leave Earth behind. Rather, God will bring Heaven and Earth together into the same dimension … God's perfect plan is "to bring all things in heaven and on earth together under one head, even Christ" (Ephesians 1:10)[2].

Many people today campaign against environmental pollution, or social injustice, or other problems our world is facing. The Bible's message is that this is what God Himself promises to do, as we have seen from the vision of the future in Isaiah. All the terrible things that blight our present earthly existence will be removed, and all our deepest longings will be satisfied. The believer's hope is not a ghostly, spiritual existence, but a resurrected life in the New Heavens and Earth.

---

[1] Randy Alcorn, *Heaven*, Carol Stream, IL: Tyndale House, 2004, p6
[2] Alcorn, *Heaven*, pp88, 90

THE END OF THE WORLD

Problems in Paradise?

In the last chapter, we looked at the wonderful future that Isaiah presents, the hope of Paradise restored. In this chapter, however, we are going to see that there are some problems with Isaiah's Paradise. Some observant readers may have already noticed some things that in Isaiah's Paradise that are not quite perfect.

Isaiah 65:17-25 gives us another description of Isaiah's future paradise, and some of these imperfect features become a little more obvious:

> [17] For behold, I create new heavens and a new earth; and the former shall not be remembered or come to mind. [18] But be glad and rejoice forever in what I create; for behold, I create Jerusalem as a rejoicing, and her people a joy. [19] I will rejoice in Jerusalem, and joy in My people; the voice of weeping shall no longer be heard in her, nor the voice of crying. [20] No more shall an infant from there live but a few days, nor an old man who has not fulfilled his days; for the child shall die one hundred years old, but the sinner being one hundred years old shall be accursed. [21] They shall build houses and inhabit them; they shall plant vineyards and eat their fruit. [22] They shall not build and another inhabit; they shall not plant and another eat; for as the days of a tree, so shall be the days of My people, and My elect shall long enjoy the work of their hands. [23] They shall not labour in vain, nor bring forth children for trouble; for they shall be the descendants of the blessed of the LORD, and their offspring with them. [24] It shall come to pass that before they call, I will answer; and while they are still speaking, I will hear. [25] The wolf and the lamb shall feed together, the lion shall eat straw like the ox, and dust shall be the serpent's food. They shall not hurt nor destroy in all My holy mountain, says the LORD.

Notice in the last verse 25 that we have the same description we saw in Isaiah 11: the curse is lifted from the animal creation, the wolf and the lamb feed together, the lion eats straw, and so on. Isaiah 65 seems to speak about the same paradise that we read about earlier in Isaiah 11 with the animals feeding together. Notice too that people are still labouring and working, planting vineyards and building houses (verses 22-23) – this is a picture of earthly life. Here we have another description of Isaiah's paradise, adding to what we learn from Isaiah chapters 2, 9, 11, 25 and 35.

Our first reaction to Isaiah's paradise is naturally to think that it occurs in the eternal state. However, there are a number of puzzling features of

Isaiah's paradise that are very difficult to understand in terms of the eternal state. Look at three problems in this passage:

Problem 1: Death
In this passage we read of people dying. Isaiah says that for a person to die at one hundred years will be considered to die young – 'the child shall die one hundred years old' (verse 20). Thus, there still seems to be death in Isaiah's paradise. Peoples' lifespans will be like the 'days of a tree' (verse 22) – they will live for many hundreds of years. But this is not quite the same thing as living forever. Trees do not live forever – only a few thousand years at the very most, and many trees only live for decades.

How can there be death in paradise? How can Isaiah be picturing the eternal state when 'there is no more death' (Rev. 21:4)? In the eternal state death, 'the last enemy' (1 Cor. 15:26), has been destroyed.

Problem 2: Birth
Notice too that there will be birth in Isaiah's Paradise, for we read of infants in verse 20. The word used in literally 'suckling', the breast-feeding child. Then again, in verse 23 we read, 'they shall not bring forth children for trouble, for they shall be the descendants of the blessed of the LORD, and their offspring with them'. This presents a problem because this suggests that the final resurrection has not yet occurred, for in the resurrection they neither marry nor are given in marriage (Luke 20:35). If people neither marry nor are given in marriage in the resurrected, eternal state, then neither are they going to be having children. So where do the infants come from?

Problem 3: Sin
Isaiah 65:20 also says that there will still be sinners who live (and die) on earth: 'the sinner being one hundred years old shall be accursed'. How can there still be sin in Paradise? This again argues against the eternal state, for there will be no more sin in the eternal state. The Great Judgment Day, when sin will finally be banished forever (Rev. 20:15-20), must not yet have occurred.

While the majority of English Bible translations have the word 'sinner' in Isaiah 65:20, some Bibles translate this verse differently. The NIV says, 'the one who *fails to reach* a hundred will be considered accursed'. The difference here involves translating 'sinning' to mean 'falling short', which is a possible rendering (other Bibles which have a similar translation are the NASB, the NRSV and the NLT). However, the fact that the word 'cursed' is found in the verse implies the presence of sin anyway, and even these Bibles do not remove the references to birth, death and being accursed in the context, so the removal of 'sin' does not get rid of the problems with this passage. In fact, the Hebrew root word for sin (*chatah*) is translated 'sin' about 200 times, and 'miss' only one time[3] (Judges 20:16 - stone slingers not 'missing' the target), while another possible case from Holladay's Hebrew lexicon is Job 5:24 ('finding nothing amiss'). So the evidence is 100 to 1 for 'sin' as the correct rendering in Isaiah 65:20. It is best to understand the verse talking about sinners being accursed.

Isaiah 65 presents us with a puzzle, in that it seems to refer to some features of paradise while containing conditions that will not be found in the eternal state. Before we try to resolve this conundrum, we need to think back briefly to the passages that we have already seen in Isaiah 2, 9, 11, where we find some of these same features present: birth, death, and sin.

Birth, Death, Sin, Cursing, Learning, Rebuking and Judging in Isaiah 2, 9 and 11

These problems are not confined to Isaiah 65. They are also found in the other passages that we have already looked at in Isaiah 2, 9, 11, where we find these same features present. There are also problems in other passages in Isaiah that we have not yet looked at, like Isaiah 66.

- In Isaiah 11 we have seen that the nursing (i.e. breast-feeding) child plays by the snake's hole, and the weaned (no longer breast-feeding) child puts his hand in the viper's den. There are newborn children and toddlers in Isaiah 11, at different stages of childhood development. But how can there be children born after the resurrection, when there is no more marriage (Luke 20:35)? There will be no new-born children in eternity.
- The King in Isaiah 9 is characterized by justice: 'upon the throne of David and over His kingdom to order it and establish it with judgment and justice'. Similarly, the King of Isaiah 11 is also characterized by justice: 'with righteousness He shall judge the poor, and decide with equity for the meek of the earth' (11:4). The same verse goes on to speak about how the King will judge criminals: 'with the breath of His lips He shall slay the wicked' (11:4). But there will be no sin, nor need for judgment, let alone executions, during the eternal state.
- In Isaiah 2, we read about how the nations will come to Jerusalem to

---

[3] using Strong's concordance's data for the KJV

learn, and how the King will rebuke nations. But it would seem strange for people to still learn God's ways in the eternal state, or for nations to need to be rebuked for their behavior in eternity. Believers will then 'know even as they are known' (1 Cor. 13:12), and we will be perfect. Will there even be nations in the eternal state? Hasn't Christ put an end to national distinctions among the people of God – so that there is no more Jew or Gentile?

- Isaiah 66:20-23 also describe the new heavens and new earth, but they do not seem to be describing the eternal state, for we read of the children of Israel being regathered and brought to Jerusalem by Gentiles, and being taken by God as priests and Levites (vs20-21), so that all flesh will worship God on the Sabbaths and New Moons (vs23)). It would seem strange that the eternal state would revert to Old Testament forms of worship involving the Levitical order and special priestly castes, Sabbath-keeping, and worship on special Jewish holy days. This all seems to be more consistent with life in the old creation than the new creation.

Thus, we see the same problems of sin, death and birth in Isaiah chapters 2, 9 and 11 as we have seen in Isaiah 65, as well as judging, rebuking and learning, and Isaiah 66 introduces other complications. How can there still be these problems in Paradise?

When does Isaiah's Paradise Occur?

Isaiah 65 (and all the other paradise passages in Isaiah) present us with a conundrum. On the one hand, these passages have features which seem to match the eternal state. Isaiah describes the new heavens and new earth (65:17, 66:22), which seems to refer to the eternal state. Furthermore, Isaiah 65:18 speaks about being glad and rejoicing 'forever', which again suggests the eternal state. Isaiah 9:7 uses 'forever' language too. It speaks of the King reigning forever: 'Of the increase of His government and peace there will be no end, upon the throne of David and over His kingdom, to order it and establish it with judgment and justice from that time forward, even forever'.

But on the other hand, it is hard to see how Isaiah's vision can describe the eternal state, with the references to birth, death, sin, judgment, rebuking and learning God's ways. These are not things that we would expect to find in the perfection of the eternal state.

There appear to be four possible answers to the puzzle of Isaiah's paradise with its combination of paradise yet imperfection.

Firstly, Isaiah could be speaking about the present day in which we live. As we have already seen, certain commentators (like Calvin) take Isaiah's vision to refer to the present church age, with the wolf and the lamb representing violent and timid men coming together in the church. These commentators say that the Old Testament prophecies of a glorious future are fulfilled in the church.

However, we have already established that Isaiah is not speaking about the present church age in which we live. The earth is not full of the knowledge of the LORD (Isaiah 11:9), nor are we enjoying conditions of paradise politically, socially, or environmentally. Isaiah is speaking about a future state of paradise that is like heaven on earth. Yet it also shares features of the present day in which we live, with birth, death and sin.

It is hard to take this first option seriously, for sadly, a quick glance at the world around us, or even at the state of the church, shows that we are a long way from heaven on earth. How would any Old Testament prophet look at the (quite frankly) pathetic condition of the world in our present day, spiritually and in every other way, and describe it as paradise? Isaiah is not prophesying about the present day church era in which we live.

Secondly, Isaiah could be speaking about the eternal state. Anthony Hoekema writes, 'In his redemptive activity, God does not destroy the works of his hands, but cleanses them from sin and perfects them, so that they may finally reach the goal for which he created them. Applied to the problem at hand, this principle means that the new earth to which we look forward will not be totally different from the present one, but will be a renewal and glorification of the earth on which we now live'[4].

This answer is an improvement over the previous one, in that eternity will certainly be paradise for those who belong to Christ. But as we look more closely at the details of Isaiah's prophecy, there are plenty of problems in paradise. How can there be sin, death, birth and all the other imperfections in the eternal state? Isaiah's paradise falls short of the perfect conditions of eternal bliss.

A third solution, building on this second one, is to suggest that Isaiah is speaking about the eternal state, but that he is presenting a 'spiritual vision' of eternity. Therefore he talks in earthly terms that we understand (animals, houses, trees, vineyards, fruit, labour and prayer) but only to give us a glimpse of things beyond our wildest imagination.

C. S. Lewis would probably agree with this third approach. He wrote, 'All the scriptural imagery (harps, crowns, gold, etc.) is, of course, a merely

---

[4] Anthony Hoekema, *The Bible and the Future*, Grand Rapids: Eerdmans, 1979, p73

symbolic attempt to express the inexpressible. Musical instruments are mentioned because for many people (not all) music is the thing known in the present life which most strongly suggests ecstasy and infinity. Crowns are mentioned to suggest the fact that those who are united with God in eternity share His splendour and power and joy. Gold is mentioned to suggest the timelessness of Heaven (gold does not rust) and the preciousness of it. People who take these symbols literally might as well think that when Christ told us to be like doves, He meant that we were to lay eggs'[5].

Some commentators who argue that Isaiah is describing the eternal state using concepts familiar to us today include Christopher Wright, who says that the prophets, when speaking of the future paradise, 'could only do so meaningfully by using terms and realities that existed in their past or present experience'[6]. Alex Motyer writes, 'throughout this passage, Isaiah uses aspects of present life to create impressions of the life that is yet to come. It will be a life totally provided for (13), totally happy (19cd), totally secure (22-23), and totally at peace (24-25). Things we have no real capacity to understand can be expressed only through things we know and experience. So it is that in the present order of things death cuts off life before it has begun or before it has fully matured. But it will not be so then'[7].

The problem with this argument is that Isaiah uses language that is the exact opposite of the eternal state. He speaks of people dying and being cursed for their sin. But in the eternal state, there will be 'no more death', nor sin. The argument that Isaiah is using metaphors to describe the indescribable does not work here, because Isaiah's 'picture-language' *contradicts* the central truths they are supposed to foretell. The idea that Isaiah is using present concepts to teach about the incomprehensible future is like someone using the metaphor of a wolf to describe Christ's love for His sheep, or of a loving mother to describe Satan.

Why couldn't Isaiah have just spoken about people living forever or never dying? Why couldn't Isaiah have simply omitted the parts about people sinning or new-born babies, while still keeping the bits about world peace and environmental paradise? The Hebrew language is not lacking in words to state the simple New Testament truths of 'no more sin or death'.

---

[5] C. S. Lewis, *Mere Christianity*, p137
[6] Christopher Wright, "A Christian Approach to Old Testament Prophecy Concerning Israel", in *Jerusalem Past and Present in the Purposes of God*, ed. P. W. L. Walker, Cambridge: Tyndale House, 1992, p3
[7] J. Alec Motyer, *The Prophecy of Isaiah*, IVP, 1996, p530

Because Isaiah's paradise falls short of the perfect conditions of the eternal state, this third explanation also fails. It ends up being another attempt to avoid the actual words of the text. If, in our attempt to understand future events, we wish to start with Scripture (not with a theological system) and base our understanding on God's Word rather than imposing a human framework upon it, we must take the actual words of Scripture seriously.

We have earlier seen some of the problems with this 'spiritualizing' approach when we looked at the way some commentators try to make Isaiah's prophecies fit the present church age. Here again, while it might be possible to select certain features of Isaiah's prophecy and spiritualize them, it remains very difficult to spiritualize sin, or death, or judgment, let alone explain how they can exist in the eternal state. Surely, if Isaiah was simply giving us a 'spiritual vision' of the glories of eternity, he would have said there is *no* sin, death or judgment. Nor are these elements (sin, death, and judgment) trivial or side-issues in Isaiah's prophecy – they are central features in certain passages.

Worse still, there is an inherent inconsistency in the 'spiritualizing' method. Randy Alcorn writes, 'It's worth restating that we should expect Isaiah's prophecies about the Messiah's second coming and the New Earth to be literally fulfilled because his detailed prophecies regarding the Messiah's first coming were literally fulfilled (e.g. Isaiah 52:13, 53:4-12)'[8].

The idea that the way to deal with inconvenient details in Isaiah is to spiritualize them, or to ignore them altogether, amounts to 'photoshopping the Bible'. We are transforming words to mean something else, 'airbrushing' out the parts we don't like. This is a dangerous approach to Bible interpretation – anybody can use this method to get rid of things in the Bible they don't like: miracles, genocides, Satan, even God Himself. Therefore, this third solution provides little real relief from the real problems that Isaiah's prophecy presents. If we believe that every word of Scripture is inspired, then the details matter. We cannot just change words' meanings, or pick certain elements we like in God's Word and ignore others that are inconvenient to our theological way of thinking.

The fourth and final option for explaining Isaiah's paradise is to simply take God's words at face value. It is a picture of a future (not a present) state, on earth (not in heaven) that contains conditions of paradise (but also features of our present fallen world, albeit greatly reduced), and so is not the eternal state in all its perfection. Yet it is very close to perfection.

---

[8] Alcorn, *Heaven*, p148

Isaiah's paradise contains certain elements of eternal conditions (like everlasting joy and Christ's unending reign), but also some features of our earthly existence in a sinful world. It is therefore an intermediate state, a half-way house, a transitional stage between now and eternity in which we enjoy paradise upon earth, but are not yet in the final, perfect eternal state.

This fourth interpretation has a number of advantages. First, it takes the words of the prophecy at their plain, face value meaning. It does not cherry-pick certain parts of the prophecy, or resort to 'airbrushing' inconvenient details out of the Bible, or spiritually 'photoshop' them to mean something different. Second, it explains and incorporates more of the scriptural evidence into its explanation than the other options. It thus remains the only viable option still standing once we have eliminated those options which do not fully or faithfully explain what Scripture says.

The Vestibule of Eternity

Isaiah's vision contains a mixture of paradise conditions and present problems (birth, death, sin – albeit much reduced) as well as eternal blessings (everlasting joy, Christ's unending reign). If we were to plot the features of Isaiah's Paradise on a line with 'Now' at one end and 'Eternity' at the other, Isaiah's Paradise would be very close to 'Eternity', while still falling short of it. Isaiah's paradise seems to be an almost-there stage, between now and eternity, in which there are conditions of paradise upon earth, but yet not the final, perfect eternal state.

Now   Isaiah's Paradise   Eternity

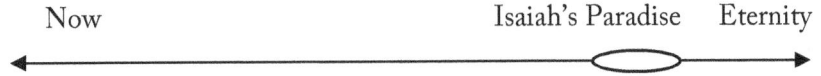

Some Bible scholars suggest that the best way to understand Isaiah's future paradise is to turn to Revelation 20, where after Christ's victorious return at Armageddon (Rev. 19), we read about a 1000-year period of glorious blessing on earth, yet before the eternal state (Rev. 21). Theologians call this period of Christ's reign on earth after His return the 'millennium' (meaning 1000 years).

This is a controversial idea that we will look at in the next chapter, but I suggest that if we consider the details of Isaiah's prophecy carefully we are forced to conclude that Isaiah's paradise is:

a.   an earthly (not heavenly) scene
b.   a paradise (which means that it is not the present church age, for the church age falls far short of paradise),

c. not perfect (which means that it is not the eternal state),
d. still in the future, because it has not yet come, which means that it must be before the eternal state, and
e. difficult to spiritualize as the present church era or the eternal state. I suggest that if we consider Isaiah's prophecy carefully, we are driven towards the idea of something like a period before the eternal state in which there are many features of paradise and yet there are still remnant traces of the present age.

The commentators Keil and Delitzsch write:

> But to what part of the history of salvation are we to look for a place for the fulfilment of such prophecies as these of the state of peace prevailing in nature around the church, except in the millennium? A prophet was certainly no fanatic, so that we could say, these are beautiful dreams.... The prophet here promises a new age, in which the patriarchal measure of human life will return, in which death will no more break off the life that is just beginning to bloom, and in which the war of man with the animal world will be exchanged for peace without danger. And when is all this to occur? Certainly not in the blessed life beyond the grave, to which it would be both absurd and impossible to refer these promises, since they presuppose a continued mixture of sinners with the righteous, and merely a limitation of the power of death, not its utter destruction[9].

Many theologians describe the kingdom of God using the expression 'already/not-yet', pointing out that while the future kingdom paradise is not yet come today in our church age, yet certain spiritual features of the future kingdom are already present, like the forgiveness of sins and the indwelling Holy Spirit. Isaiah's prophecy suggests that we may adapt this terminology by speaking of another stage of God's Kingdom after the church age but before the eternal state: the 'almost/not-fully' aspect of the kingdom of God.

The Perfection of the Kingdom of God			
OT Period	Church Period	Millennium	Eternity
Anticipated	Already/not yet	Almost/not fully	Achieved

---

[9] Keil and Delitzsch, *Commentary on the Old Testament*, Isaiah 65

Some preachers of a previous era used to refer to Isaiah's paradise as 'the vestibule of eternity'. Mark Hitchcock in his book, *The End*, compares the relationship between Isaiah's paradise (which he sees as the 1000-year reign of Christ spoken of in Revelation 20, the 'millennium') and Eternity to the front porch and a house. He writes:

> Christ will rule over His kingdom on this present earth for one thousand years, and He will reign forever. The future kingdom of God has two parts or phases. Phase one is the millennial reign of Christ on this earth (Revelation 20:1-6), and phase two is the eternal state (Revelation 22:5). As I once heard it described, the Millennium is the front porch of eternity[10].

Why is it Called the New Heavens and New Earth?

There is, however, one problem with this interpretation. If we take Isaiah's paradise as a transitional period before the eternal state, then what do we make of the fact that Isaiah describes it as 'new heavens and new earth' (Isaiah 65:17 and 66:22)? This suggests the eternal state, because Revelation 21:1 speaks of 'a new heaven and a new earth' after the Great White throne judgment of Revelation 20:11-15.

There are a number of answers to this question:

1. the word 'new' in Hebrew (*chodesh*) also means 'fresh', 'renewed', 'repaired' and 'restored'. Thus, in its verbal form, in 1 Samuel 11:14, Samuel said, 'Let us ... renew the kingdom', in 2 Chronicles 24:4 'Joash set his heart on repairing the house of the LORD', while in Psalm 104:30, God's Spirit 'renews the face of the ground'. Thus, Isaiah's vision presents to us the renovated earth and heavens.
2. as a result of God's judgments upon the earth preceding the return of Christ (as we read in 2 Peter 3:7-10, and in the book of Revelation), the whole world is going to be destroyed by fire, judgments, plagues, war and pestilence. The earth will need to be renewed and re-created.
3. for all those who are resurrected at the coming of Christ, this period of Messiah's reign will indeed be the eternal new beginning that will seamlessly progress into the eternal future in the new heavens and earth, and thus references to everlasting joy (v18) and Christ's eternal reign (Isaiah 9:7) are true for them. The eternal existence of the saints in their glorified bodies will commence at their resurrection, which

---

[10] Mark Hitchcock, *101 Answers to the Most Asked Questions About the End Times*, Sisters, OR: Multnomah, 2001, p212

occurs before Christ's millennial reign.
4. if, as we have suggested, this is a transitional phase of Christ's kingdom leading into the eternal state, then there is sense in which this is the beginning phase of the new heavens and earth.

Just as our resurrection bodies will not be entirely new creations but rather new-and-transformed versions of our current bodies, so too the new heavens and new earth are going to be redeemed, renovated and liberated versions of the current heavens and earth (see Romans 8:19-23).

It would therefore appear that the new heavens and new earth that Isaiah sees is not the eternal state, but the redeemed and restored creation that Christ reigns over in a period before the perfect conditions of the eternal state.

Appendix: Is the New Jerusalem in Revelation 21:9-22:5 the Eternal State or the Millennium?

Is the New Jerusalem, described in Revelation 21:9-22:5, the millennium, or the eternal state? It is clear that Revelation 21:9-22:5 describes Paradise, with features reminiscent of the original paradise in the Garden of Eden: the river (22:1), the tree of life (22:2), the healing of the nations (22:2), and no more curse (22:3).

On the one hand, we would most naturally expect that the New Jerusalem here is describing the Eternal State, because this passage comes after the description of the resurrection, the Great White Throne judgment, and the New Heavens and Earth (Revelation 20:1 – 21:8).

Yet there are certain features of the New Jerusalem in Revelation 21:9-22:5 that seem hard to understand as part of the Eternal State. For example, in Revelation 21:24 we read that 'the nations shall walk in its light'[11] and that 'the kings of the earth bring their glory and honour into it'. This seems to describe a scene on earth, not in heaven. Further, it would seem strange if we were separated by nationality in eternity. It would be even more strange if there were certain special people who were 'kings' of nations eternally. We also read that the 'tree of life bore twelve fruits, each tree yielding its fruit every month … [which] were for the healing of the nations' (22:2), yet it would seem strange if there were months in eternity, or if there were any need in eternity for 'the healing of the nations' (22:2), either.

These details suggest that this passage is talking about the millennial

---

[11] Virtually all Greek manuscripts omit the words, 'of those who are saved', found in the KJV in Rev. 21:24.

period, in which there are still all of these present-worldly features: nations, kings, healing, and months. If so, this section (21:9-22:4) would then be understood as giving more detailed information about an event that has just been briefly described (the millennium), in the same way as other sections of Revelation are flashbacks (particularly the description of the judgment of the Great Harlot, Rev. 17:1-19:10).

On the other hand, certain features of this section are hard to understand as millennial conditions, particularly the dimensions of the New Jerusalem (21:16), which are so large as to be difficult to imagine on the present earth. How do we solve this puzzle?

I suggest that the solution is found in Isaiah's prophecy; Isaiah helps us to answer the question of whether the New Jerusalem described in Revelation 21:9 – 22:5 is the Eternal State or the Millennium. If we look at the cross-references in our Bibles for this passage, we find that all of the details of the New Jerusalem in Revelation 21:9 – 22:5 come from Isaiah's prophecy of paradise restored. Notice the connections:

Revelation 21:9 – 22:5	Isaiah 54 and 60
Rev. 21:19-20 – 'the foundations of the wall of the city [New Jerusalem] were adorned with all kinds of precious stones'	Isaiah 54:11-12 – the foundations are made of beautiful gems
Rev. 21:11 – 'having the glory of God'	Isaiah 60:1-2 – the glory of the Lord is risen upon you
Rev. 21:24 – 'and the nations shall walk in its light, and the kings of the earth shall bring their glory and honour into it'	Isaiah 60:3-7 – the Gentiles and kings will come to your light
Rev. 21:25 – 'Its gates shall not be shut at all by day'	Isaiah 60:11 – the gates will be open continually
Rev. 21:23 – 'the city had no need of the sun or the moon to shine in it, for the glory of God illuminated it'	Isa. 60:19-20 – the sun will no longer be the light, but the Lord will be your light

The fact that the details of the New Jerusalem in Revelation 21:9-22:5 are drawn almost entirely from Isaiah's prophecy is very suggestive. Isaiah's prophecy presents us with a picture of paradise, as we have already seen in chapters 2, 11, 35 and 65, that is this-worldly – with sin, death, birth, judging, learning and rebuking still present. The picture we see in Isaiah

54 and 60 fits into this same frame, for in these chapters we have further evidence of a present-worldly scene. Consider Isaiah 60:6-7:

> The multitude of camels shall cover your land, the dromedaries of Midian and Ephah; all those from Sheba shall come; they shall bring gold and incense, and they shall proclaim the praises of the LORD. 7 All the flocks of Kedar shall be gathered together to you, the rams of Nebaioth shall minister to you; they shall ascend with acceptance on My altar, and I will glorify the house of My glory (Isa. 60:6-7).

Not only does Isaiah 65 speak of present surrounding nations, animals, Gentiles and their kings coming to Zion to worship God, but we read of animal sacrifices being offered on the altar of God. This surely cannot be a scene from the eternal state. Isaiah 54 and 60 therefore seem part of the millennial picture we have seen Isaiah presenting throughout his book. It would appear that Isaiah consistently presents – throughout his entire prophecy – the same picture of paradise, not in the eternal state, but in the 'millennial' period just before it.

If so, then it would appear that Revelation 21:9-22:5 is also giving us a picture of the New Jerusalem in the Millennial period too. The fact that Isaiah chapters 54 and 60 are sandwiched in between other descriptions of the same paradise we find at the beginning (in chapters 2, 9, 11), middle (chapters 25 and 35) and end of Isaiah (chapters 65 and 66), there seems no good reason to think that chapters 54 and 60 are speaking about something different. Thus, Revelation 21:9 – 22:5 is not describing the eternal state, but rather the millennial reign of Christ.

However, we have every reason to think that the celestial city itself, New Jerusalem, will continue into the eternal state, for the New Jerusalem will outlive the millennium. Thus, although the New Jerusalem will exist in the Eternal State, the section of Revelation in 21:9-22:5 is enlarging our understanding of the conditions during the millennial reign of Christ briefly described in Revelation 20:4-6.

3 THE MILLENNIUM

As the end of the 20th century approached, doomsayers warned that computers would be unable to handle the change from the year 1999 to 2000. Electronic devices which recorded the date using only the last two digits of the year would interpret the year as 00 and would crash, bringing down entire infrastructure networks, plunging Western civilization into chaos. Nothing happened, of course. The Y2K or Millennium Bug, as it was also known, was just another urban myth.

Another millennial myth sprung up in relation to the year 1000 AD. Medieval historians told of the panic that gripped Europe at that time. The world would end in the 1001, it was said, when the Antichrist would appear, and Armageddon and Judgment Day would soon follow. As the big M (the Roman numeral for 1000) approached, people flocked to monasteries, sold their worldly goods, and gave the proceeds to God. In *Extraordinary Popular Delusions and the Madness of Crowds*, Charles Mackay wrote:

> A strange idea had taken possession of the popular mind at the close of the tenth and the commencement of the eleventh century. It was universally believed that the end of the world was at hand: that the thousand years of the Apocalypse were near completion, and that Jesus Christ would descend upon Jerusalem to judge mankind. All Christendom was in commotion. A panic terror seized upon the weak, the credulous and the guilty, who in those days formed more than nineteen-twentieths of the population. Forsaking their homes, kindred, and occupation, they crowded to Jerusalem to await the coming of the Lord, lightened, as they imagined, of a load of sin by their weary pilgrimage[1].

Ironically enough, however, the entire story of millennial madness in the year 1000 is just a myth. No eleventh century European historians make any mention of it. The story was first promoted in the 1500s, then

---

[1] Charles Mackay, *Extraordinary Popular Delusions and the Madness of Crowds*, 1853, p.356-7.

embellished with lurid details over the following centuries until it was debunked by historical scholarship in the 1800s.

It was around the turn of the 20th century that the word millennium became part of ordinary peoples' vocabulary. *Millennium* was pronounced the German word of the year for 1999[2]. Apart from theologians, most Christians had never heard the word before, or knew that it meant 1000 years, despite the fact that the Bible mentions a 1000 year period in the book of Revelation that Bible scholars refer to as 'the millennium'.

The turn of the millennium brought an increased interest among Christians in what the Bible says about the end of the world. A lot of Christian writers published books about future events. It also brought increased controversy over what the Bible teaches about Christ's return: will He reign for a thousand years on earth, or is this yet another Christian myth – to be taken no more seriously than Y2K?

What Shall we Make of the Millennium?
In the previous chapter, we looked at one of the great puzzles of Old Testament prophecy: how can there be birth, sin and death (and other less than perfect conditions) in the future paradise that Isaiah and the other prophets foretold? We concluded that it is difficult to understand these prophecies as foretelling either the present church age or the eternal state. They appear to be describing conditions that have characteristics of both periods, without being either. We therefore described it as an intermediate, transitional stage in the future before the eternal state.

This raises the question for our present chapter: is the paradise that Isaiah describes the same thing as the millennium that John describes in Revelation 20? The answer to that question depends, of course, upon what we make of the millennium in Revelation 20. In this chapter we will look at Revelation 20 and try to navigate our way through the millennial maze.

The fact that the word 'millennium' never occurs in our English Bibles, and that this 1000-year period is only mentioned in one passage in our Bible, and that this passage is in Revelation, the most obscure and difficult book in the Bible to interpret, might at first seem to suggest that the millennium is just irrelevant theological jargon, and that any discussion about it is an academic debate unrelated to real-world Christian living.

However, the Lord's coming is not irrelevant to Christian living, and Revelation 20, coming straight after Revelation 19 with its description of the coming of the Lord, either tells us about what happens after the Lord

---

[2] by the GfdS, the official Association for the German Language

comes, or before He comes. Thus, the millennium is closely related to how we understand Christ's coming. Furthermore, while we as Christians have many questions about future events, there are only really four big questions when it comes to interpreting Bible prophecy, and what we make of the millennium is the first of them. With the millennium we come to our first major crossroads in the study of the Lord's coming. What we make of the millennium is such a significant decision-point in our understanding of future events that it will have far-reaching ramifications and lead to very different destinations. Our understanding of what happens at the coming of the Lord hinges on what we make of the millennium.

The main question we need to consider about the millennium is whether this 1000-year period in Revelation 20 is to be understood literally or symbolically. To do that, we are going to look at six major questions about Revelation 20 to which people give different answers.

The Millennium in Revelation 20

Before we try to answer these questions, we need to familiarize ourselves with Revelation 20. In this chapter, we read six times about 'a thousand years'. This passage describes the following seven main events:

1. Satan is bound for a thousand years in the bottomless pit, 20:1-3, so that he might not deceive the nations until the thousand years are finished,
2. during which period resurrected believers reign with Christ for a thousand years, 20:4-6,
3. but the rest of the dead do not live again until the thousand years are finished, 20:5,
4. Satan is released again from his prison at the end of the thousand years to deceive the nations, 20:7,
5. leading to a world-wide rebellion against God, which ends in defeat, 20:8-10,
6. after which, the rest of the dead are resurrected and judged, 20:11-13
7. resulting in all those not found written in the Lamb's Book of Life being cast into the lake of fire, 20:14-15.

There are essentially two ways of understanding Revelation 20: symbolically or literally. How we decide to interpret this chapter changes a great many things we believe about the coming of Christ.

The literal interpretation takes Revelation 20 as a continuation of the narrative following on from Revelation 19:11-21, where Christ returns at the battle of Armageddon. Satan is then imprisoned for 1000 years, while Christ reigns with His saints on the earth. This is the millennial reign of Christ. After this, Satan is released from his imprisonment for a short time, and he provokes one final rebellion against God. Fire from heaven destroys these rebels, Satan is cast into the lake of fire, and after this the dead are raised and judged. The wicked are cast into the Lake of Fire forever.

The symbolic interpretation, on the other hand, argues that Revelation 20 is not telling us about Christ reigning upon earth in a literal, future, earthly kingdom. Instead, it symbolizes the saints reigning spiritually now in the church age. In other words, Revelation 20 describes the entire church age, pictured as the 1000-year reign of Christ, in which (a) Satan's activities are bound – in that the nations are no longer in darkness, but the Gospel message is being preached in all the world, (b) the saints are reigning spiritually alongside Christ, and (c) at the end of this church age Christ returns to defeat one final rebellion of Satan: Armageddon.

Rather than pronouncing at the outset that the passage is literal or symbolic, it would seem wiser to first study the verses and see whether a symbolic or literal approach is able to be consistently applied to the text, whether it makes logical sense, and whether it is being interpreted in a way consistent with other Scriptures. Thus, we need to approach the passage with an open mind, being prepared to 'test all things' (1 Thess. 5:21).

To work out which interpretation is more helpful in understanding this chapter, we are going to ask six questions.

1. What does Satan being bound and cast into the bottomless pit refer to?
2. What does it mean that some people 'live again'? Is this a literal resurrection or spiritual new life?
3. What does it mean that the saints reign with Christ? Does this refer to the saints literally reigning on earth in the future or does it refer to a spiritual reign of the saints in the present?
4. What is the battle in Revelation 20:7-10? Is it Armageddon or some other battle?
5. Is Revelation 20 best interpreted literally or symbolically?
6. How did the earliest Christians interpret Revelation 20?

Question 1: What is the Binding of Satan in the Bottomless Pit?
Rev. 20:1-3 reads:

> Then I saw an angel coming down from heaven, having the key to the bottomless pit and a great chain in his hand. ² He laid hold of the dragon, that serpent of old, who is the Devil and Satan, and bound him for a thousand years; ³ and he cast him into the bottomless pit, and shut him up, and set a seal on him, so that he should deceive the nations no more till the thousand years were finished. But after these things he must be released for a little while.

Those who argue that this passage is to be understood symbolically suggest that the binding of Satan in Revelation 20:1-3 has already happened during Christ's ministry upon earth and particularly as a result of His work on the cross. The binding of Satan is best explained by Christ's words in Matthew 12:29, 'how can one enter a strong man's house and plunder his goods, unless he first binds the strong man? And then he will plunder his house?' By this 'strong man' being bound, Christ was referring to Satan. The spread of the gospel throughout the world since Pentecost is nothing short of the plundering of Satan's dominions. Therefore, the binding is symbolic, the millennium is now, and Christ's reign is spiritual.

However, there are two problems with this interpretation. Firstly, the idea that Satan is presently bound in the bottomless pit (Rev. 20:2) so that he should 'deceive the nations no more till the thousand years were finished' (Rev. 20:3) seems hard to accept in view of many New Testament verses which tell us about Satan's current deception of the world and opposition to the Gospel.

- Satan is the 'god of this age' who blinds the minds of those who do not believe (2 Cor. 4:4).
- Paul spoke of Satan as 'the Prince of the power of the air, the spirit who now works in the sons of disobedience' (Eph. 2:2).
- Paul writes about our warfare against Satan in Eph. 6:12: 'we do not wrestle against flesh and blood, but against principalities, against powers, against the rulers of the darkness of this age, against spiritual hosts of wickedness in the heavenly places'.
- Paul tells us we need to take up the whole armour of God so we can stand against all the cunning wiles of the Devil (6:11). He says we need to take the shield of faith so that we may quench all the fiery darts of the wicked one' (6:16).
- In 2 Cor. 11:13-15, Satan 'transforms himself into an angel of light' in order to deceive people through his false-apostles (v13).
- 1 Pet. 5:8 says that Satan 'walks about as a roaring lion, seeking whom

he may devour'.
- 1 John 5:19 says that 'the whole world lies under the sway of the wicked one'.
- 2 Tim. 2:26 speaks of Satan taking people captive to do his will.

Satan hardly seems 'bound' in these New Testament passages. Not only do these verses say Satan is still very active, but certain verses describe the ways he deceives people still today. This seems hard to square with the symbolic interpretation of Revelation 20:1-3.

Robert Mounce writes, 'The elaborate measures taken to insure [Satan's] custody are most easily understood as implying the complete cessation of his influence on earth (rather than a curbing of his activities)'[3].

Furthermore, the evidence from the many verses quoted above describing Satan's present deception seems far more weighty than the one reference from Christ's life in which He spoke in a parable about casting out demons. It would appear unwarranted for us to extend the parable to the entire church age and teach that it means that Satan is no longer active.

A second difficulty with the symbolic interpretation comes, not from Scripture, but from world history: the fact that many continents have been in spiritual darkness for nearly 2000 years. Thus, the gospel did not come to the continents of North or South America for nearly 1500 years after Christ, neither did the gospel come to Africa (apart from its northern parts) until 1800 years after Christ. The gospel did not penetrate China or Japan or Australasia until the same period. For the vast majority of the so-called Christian era, all of these vast areas have been under the power of darkness, that is, controlled by Satan. Still today, while a large majority of the world's population are aware of the basic facts of the gospel (the life of Christ, etc.), they remain in unbelief, unsaved, blinded by the god of this age. The idea that Satan stopped deceiving the nations 2000 years ago is contradicted by the plain facts of history and the current state of world affairs.

Those who say that Satan is presently bound seem to be strangely unaware of the terrible spiritual power that Satan has over billions of people. Who is behind the cults which deny the deity of Christ and teach salvation by works, or behind the atheists publishing best-selling books attempting to discredit God's existence, if not Satan? Who traps the minds of millions in powerful world-religions like Islam, Hinduism, or Buddhism? As someone once remarked, if Satan is bound, he must be on

---

[3] Robert H. Mounce, *The Book of Revelation*, NICNT, Eerdmans, 1977, p353

a very long chain.

A. J. Hough's poem asks:

> Won't somebody step to the front forthwith,
> And make his bow, and show
> How the frauds and crimes of a single day spring up,
> We want to know!
> The Devil is fairly voted out, and of course the Devil's gone;
> But simple folk would like to know who carries his business on.

These are the two main arguments against the symbolic interpretation of Satan's binding – one from Scripture and one from world history. Both strongly suggest that a present symbolic binding of Satan is false.

Question 2: What are the First and Second Resurrections (vs 4-6)?

Revelation 20 tells us about two resurrections: 'the first resurrection' (20:5-6) implies that there is a second which follows, and just a few verses later, in Revelation 20:11-12, we have another resurrection after the 1000 years, in which the rest of the dead are raised ('the rest of the dead did not live again until the thousand years were finished', 20:5). The most straightforward way of reading these words is that there are two resurrections separated by 1000 years.

Those who adopt a symbolic approach suggest that the first resurrection is a 'spiritual' resurrection (new birth) that occurs in the present day for the individual Christian, while the second resurrection is a literal, physical resurrection that occurs at the end of time. However, there are two difficulties with this symbolic interpretation.

The first problem is that it introduces a logical impossibility, for verse 4 speaks of these 'living' people having earlier been 'beheaded for their witness to Jesus'. The symbolic approach thus teaches that some people are beheaded for Christ's sake (v4a) but after this they are spiritually 'born again' (v4b), i.e. converted to Christianity. Alva McClain says that this view puts forward 'the absurdity of having souls being regenerated *after* they've been beheaded for their faithfulness to Christ!'[4].

A second problem is the interpretational inconsistency involved in taking the first resurrection symbolically and the second literally. Dr. Henry Alford, the 19th century Greek scholar, wrote:

---

[4] Alva McClain, *The Greatness of the Kingdom: An Inductive Study of the Kingdom of God*, 1959, (reprint Winona Lake, IN: BMH, 1992), p488, emphasis in original

On one point I have ventured to speak strongly, because my conviction on it is strong, founded on the rules of fair and consistent interpretation. I mean, the necessity of accepting literally the first resurrection, and the millennial reign. It seems to me that if in a sentence where two resurrections are spoken of with no mark of distinction between them ... – in a sentence where, one resurrection having been related, "the rest of the dead" are afterwards mentioned, – we are at liberty to understand the former one figuratively and spiritually, and the latter literally and materially, then there is an end of all definite meaning in plain words, and the Apocalypse, or any other book, may mean any thing we please[5].

The symbolic view thus seems illogical and inconsistent. The reason why the symbolic interpretation switches back to a literal second resurrection is that, if both resurrections are symbolic of new spiritual life in Christ, the passage would be teaching universalism – the idea that all will be saved. Notice how the last phrase of verse 4 flows into verse 5 as follows:

> they lived (Gk. *ezesan*, i.e. were born again, according to the figurative interpretation) and reigned with Christ for a thousand years, but the rest of the dead did not live (Gk. *ezesan*) until the thousand years were finished.

It is obvious that the two phrases are connected, and that they contrast two groups of people, those who 'lived' and 'the rest of the dead'. If we take the first word 'lived' to refer to new birth, then consistency suggests that we should take the second word 'lived' in the same way. This means that the rest of humanity, the 'rest of the dead', refers to the spiritually dead, who are also going to live, i.e. be born again and have eternal life. This would mean that all people will be saved.

Of course, most proponents of the symbolic approach deny universalism and argue that we must not take the word 'lived' to mean the same thing in the two parts of this one sentence. But this produces the strange result of interpreting the first 'lived' spiritually and the second 'lived' literally, which as Alford says, is making words mean anything we please.

An alternative figurative approach is to take the first resurrection to be the translation of the soul from earth to heaven – by death (Hendriksen[6]).

---

[5] Henry Alford, *Greek New Testament*, Vol. 4, Revelation, Prolegomena, V, para 33
[6] William Hendiksen, *More than Conquerors*, Grand Rapids: Baker, 1939, p192

But this approach is not followed by many others for one obvious reason: to call death (and the soul going to heaven) a resurrection is a very strange use of language. To call death a 'resurrection' is like calling the colour white 'black'. Nowhere in the Bible is the word 'resurrection' ever used for death, or for the soul going to heaven.

It would therefore make more sense that a physical resurrection is being described in Revelation 20:4-6. That, in turn, argues that there is an interval of a thousand years between two literal, physical resurrections, those of the saints and the unsaved.

In short, the symbolic approach is more confused, and seems more unnatural, imposed and inconsistent, while the straightforward approach makes perfectly natural sense in context.

Question 3: What is the Reign of the Saints (vs4-6)? Is it a spiritual reign in the present age, or is it in the future and literal?

Verse 4 reads: 'And I saw thrones, and they sat on them, and judgment was committed to them'. Is this referring to the future or the present day? Augustine, the early amillennialist commentator, argued as follows:

> they reign with Him who do what the apostle says, "If ye be risen with Christ, mind the things which are above, where Christ sitteth at the right hand of God. Seek those things which are above, not the things which are on the earth." Of such persons he also says that their conversation is in heaven. In fine, they reign with Him who are so in His kingdom that they themselves are His kingdom.

As to the saints judging, Augustine says:

> It is not to be supposed that this refers to the last judgment, but to the seats of the rulers and to the rulers themselves by whom the Church is now governed. And no better interpretation of judgment being given can be produced than that which we have in the words, "What ye bind on earth shall be bound in heaven; and what ye loose on earth shall be loosed in heaven." Whence the apostle says, "What have I to do with judging them that are without? do not ye judge them that are within?"

Thus, the saints reigning and judging refers, according to Augustine, to the present-day spiritual blessings of the believer and the government of the church. An alternative suggestion is that the saints 'judging' in verse 4 simply means that 'the ransomed souls in heaven praise Christ for His righteous judgments' (Hendriksen[7]). But this seems to play fast and loose with language: praising Christ is a quite different thing to judging.

One argument used to support the symbolic view is that the best cross-reference to the reign of the saints in Revelation 20:4-6 is the picture of the martyrs under the altar in Revelation 6:9 - 'When He opened the fifth seal, I saw under the altar the souls of those who had been slain for the word of God and for the testimony which they held'.

Thus, Sam Storms, who takes the symbolic view, argues: 'That John is talking about the intermediate state [i.e. in between death and resurrection] in Revelation 20:4-6 seems obvious once the parallel with Revelation 6:9-11 is noted'. He states, 'That John is describing the same scene, namely, that of the blessedness of the intermediate state, seems beyond reasonable doubt'[8].

However, while all agree that the same people are involved (for both groups are described as 'those slain/beheaded for their witness', 6:9, 20:4), this does not prove that they are in the same *state* in both passages. In Revelation 6:9, the souls under the altar are crying out for justice, but they are told to rest and wait for a little while because there are other martyrs still to join their number. By contrast, those described in Revelation 20:4 are not under the altar, but sitting on thrones reigning. They are not crying out for justice, but themselves administering justice and judgment. They are not waiting a little while, but reigning for a thousand years – a long time. The people are the same but the two states are the exact opposite. The cry of the martyrs for justice in Revelation 6:9 appears to be answered by the reign of the martyrs with Christ in Revelation 20:4.

Waymeyer states, 'the problem with this argument is that similarities listed by Storms merely prove that both visions refer to the same group of individuals, not that both visions describe the same experience of those individuals'[9].

Another argument for a spiritual reign of the saints is the use of the word 'souls' to describe those reigning in Revelation 20:4. This suggests that the passage is not talking about resurrected saints reigning in bodies on earth in the future, but rather the disembodied souls of the saints in heaven in the present age.

The word 'souls' can certainly mean disembodied spirits, as in Revelation 6:9 – 'When He opened the fifth seal, I saw under the altar the souls of those who had been slain for the word of God and for the

---

[7] Hendriksen, *More Than Conquerors*, p192
[8] Sam Storms, *Kingdom Come: The Amillennial Alternative*, Mentor, 2013, p457-58
[9] Matt Waymeyer, *Amillennialism and the Age to Come*, Kress, 2016, p241

testimony which they held'. However, the Bible often uses the word 'souls' to refer to ordinary people alive on earth. We read that three thousand souls were saved at the day of Pentecost, eight souls were saved on Noah's ark, and 286 souls were saved from shipwreck in Acts 27. The book of Revelation itself uses the word 'souls' to refer to creatures living on earth in bodies (8:9, 12:11, 16:3, 18:13 and 18:14). In none of these verses is the word 'soul' used for a disembodied spirit, for the word 'soul' often just means 'person', or 'self', and it is even used to refer sometimes to animal life (as in Rev. 16:3).

Seiss replies to the argument that the word 'souls' proves that Rev. 20:4-6 refers to a spiritual reign as follows:

> That the word souls, in John's vision of the martyrs beneath the altar [i.e. in Rev. 6:9], means persons dead as to their bodies, it is very evident, not, however, from the meaning of the word [souls], but from the accompanying statement that the souls he saw were people slain on account of their faith. He sees the same people, persons, souls, here [in Rev. 20:4]; but this time *ezesan* – 'they lived again'. As mere souls separate from the body, they never were dead. John saw them, and heard them speaking, and beheld them invested in white robes, and recognized them as still living and waiting, though dead as to their bodies. The living again in which he now sees them, must therefore be a living in that in which they were dead when he first saw them, that is, corporeally dead[10].

These arguments for a symbolic understanding of the saints reigning are therefore not convincing. Consider the following other verses within the book of Revelation providing contextual help to explain this reign of the saints:

- Christ (in Rev. 2:26-27) promises to the overcomer in the church in Thyatira: 'to him I will give power over the nations – he shall rule them with a rod of iron; they shall be dashed to pieces like the potter's vessels'.
- 'To him who overcomes I will grant to sit with Me on My throne, as I also overcame and sat down with My Father on His throne' (Rev. 3:21)
- 'And have made them kings and priests to our God; and they shall reign on the earth' (Rev. 5:10)

---

[10] Joseph Seiss, *The Apocalypse*, Zondervan, 1962, p459-60

These verses seem to correspond with the saints reigning and judging with Christ in Revelation 20:4-6. Notice, too, that these verses are promises (in the future tense) given to the Christians of the seven churches in the present church age, rather than blessings currently enjoyed. Further, the promise to reign and judge relates to nations (i.e. on earth, Rev. 3:21), and this promise of a future earthly reign is made explicit in the passage where we read, 'they shall reign on the earth' (Rev. 5:10).

It is interesting that Augustine quotes Paul in 1 Corinthians 5:12 about the church judging those within (i.e. believers), but not those outside (unbelievers). A few verses later, in 1 Corinthians 6:2, Paul asks, 'Do you not know that the saints will judge the world?' By judging here, Paul is probably referring to the administration of the realm to come, for Christ makes His servants rulers over many things in the parables of the talents and pounds (Matthew 25 and Luke 19). Notice that the judgment Paul speaks of is not in the present tense, but in the future tense ('the saints *will* judge the world', 1 Corinthians 6:2). When Revelation 20:4 speaks of the saints judging, this would seem to correspond more closely with what Paul says in 1 Corinthians 6:2 (about the future) than in 1 Corinthians 5:12 (the present).

Finally, as to the question of where the reigning and judging takes place – in heaven or on earth – four verses appear significant.

Firstly, at the start of the passage we read of 'an angel coming down from heaven' to bind Satan (20:1). The scene in Revelation 20 is not in heaven but on earth, for John sees the angel descending, which suggests John is on earth.

Secondly, we read that the angel bound Satan, 'so that he should deceive the nations no more till the thousand years were finished' (Rev. 20:3). But nations are earthly, and therefore this suggests again the scene is earthly. Satan is not deceiving anyone in heaven, nor are there nations there.

Thirdly, in Revelation 20:7-9, all agree that the battle after the 1000 years occurs on earth. In fact, the word 'earth' occurs twice in verses 7-9. Thus, after the reign of the saints in Revelation 20:4-6, we again have an earthly scene – a battle upon the earth (Rev. 7-9).

Fourthly, earlier in Rev. 19:15, Christ comes at the battle of Armageddon, and 'out of His mouth goes a sharp sword, that with it He should strike the nations, and He Himself will rule them with a rod of iron'. Thus, the passage immediately before Rev. 20 looks forward to Christ, not only coming on a white horse and defeating His enemies, but also reigning on the earth (ruling the nations with a rod of iron).

This would suggest that the passage in Rev. 20:4-6, in between Satan's binding in vs 1-3 and the battle of verses 7-9, is also set on earth, and that it is the fulfilment of the promise of Rev 5:10 that the saints will reign 'on the earth'.

In summary, the symbolic interpretation of the saints reigning and judging in vs 4-6 again seems more strained, and more contrary to Scripture and common sense, than the straightforward fulfilment of the promise of the saints' future 'reign on the earth' (Rev. 5:10).

Question 4: What is the Battle in Revelation 20:7-9? Is this the Battle of Armageddon, or are there two Battles in Revelation 19 and 20?

Those who interpret Revelation 20 literally take it that there are two different battles: firstly, in Revelation 19:11-21, Christ is described returning on a white horse at the battle of Armageddon, but then a second battle occurs at the end of the 1000 years after Satan is released from prison (Rev. 20:7-10), where all the armies of the earth come up to attack the saints, only to be destroyed by fire from God out of heaven. One battle occurs before Revelation 20 – the battle of Armageddon (Rev. 19:11ff.), and the second battle occurs after the 1000 years.

On the other hand, those who take Revelation 20 symbolically suggest that the two battles, first in Revelation 19:11-21 and then secondly in Revelation 20:7-10, are the one and the same battle – Armageddon. According to this view, Revelation chapters 19 and 20 present two visions of the one battle. They argue the similarities between the two battles described in Revelation 19:11-21 and Revelation 20:7-9 point to the one same event. And if the battle of Revelation 20:7-10 is Armageddon, this means that the millennium described in Revelation 20:1-6 occurs before Armageddon – it must be the church age now.

The symbolic view requires us to accept that Revelation 20 is a new section of the book of Revelation that does not follow on from Rev. 19, but instead recapitulates, or summarizes, the entire church era. The alternative, literal, view holds that Revelation 20 flows on naturally from Revelation 19 and that the millennium follows Christ's return at the battle of Armageddon, which is then followed by another, second battle.

However, the symbolic view has a fatal flaw. Notice that, after the first battle in Revelation 19, we read about the Beast and the False Prophet (Satan's two henchmen) being captured and cast alive into the lake of fire: 'Then the beast was captured, and with him the false prophet who worked signs in his presence, by which he deceived those who received the mark of the beast and those who worshiped his image. These two were cast alive into the lake of fire burning with brimstone' (Rev. 19:20). However, in Revelation 20:10, after the 1000 years of Satan's captivity and the second battle, we are told that 'the Devil was cast into the lake of fire and brimstone, where the Beast and the False Prophet are, and they will be tormented day and night forever and ever' (Rev. 20:10).

This strongly suggests that the Beast and the False Prophet were already present in the lake of fire, having been cast there after the first battle (in Rev. 19:20), while the Devil only joins them after the thousand year imprisonment and the second battle (in Rev. 20:10). This logically implies that the battle of Revelation 19:20 happened earlier than the battle of 20:7-10, that the two battles are different events, and that the 1000 year period intervenes between them.

It is true that the word 'are' is not present in the Greek text of Rev. 20:10 – 'The devil, who deceived them, was cast into the lake of fire and brimstone where the beast and the false prophet *are*'. Some argue that inserting 'are' into the verse is a false-translation, and that the verse is not saying that the beast and false prophet were in the lake of fire prior to the Devil. However, the verb 'to be' is the most commonly implied verb in Greek that translators have to supply to make sense in English[11].

Further, Greek usually only leaves out a verb (forcing translators to supply it) when the context makes it obvious what the meaning is without it. There is no other verb demanded by context, and therefore the word 'are' is the best translation. There is no English Bible that gives any other sense to the verse than the idea that the beast and false prophet had already been cast into the lake of fire previously. When did this happen? Revelation 19:20 tells us: one thousand years before.

We may therefore conclude that there is no compelling reason to view the two battles as the same event. Instead, taking the two chapters chronologically seems a more natural way to read them. There are two battles in two consecutive chapters of Revelation 19 and 20. The first is the battle of Armageddon, at which the Beast and False-prophet are thrown into the lake of fire, while the second battle occurs after Satan's 1000-year imprisonment in the bottomless pit, after which he too is thrown into the lake of fire.

While Revelation 19 and 20 naturally read as two consecutive narratives, the symbolic interpretation depends upon Revelation 20:1-10 being a recapitulation, or summary, of the entire book of Revelation and the entire church period. In this scheme, Revelation 20:1 is seen as the

---

[11] see A. T. Robertson's *Grammar of the Greek New Testament*, 1914, p1202

commencement of a new vision that does not follow on sequentially from Revelation 19.

A big problem with taking Revelation 20:1-10 as a recapitulation of the entire church period is that the main features of Revelation 20 are nowhere else mentioned in the earlier chapters.

Thus, those adopting a symbolic approach frequently point out that the 1000 years are mentioned nowhere else in Scripture. But if Revelation 20 is a recapitulation, why are the 1000 years only mentioned in this chapter, and not in earlier parts of the book? Elsewhere in Revelation we find other time markers, like 42 months or 1260 days or three and a half days or five months. But all of these are short periods of time, whereas the 1000 years is taken by all expositors to be a long period. There is no correspondence between the 1000 years and these other time periods. They are not equivalent in any mathematical or verbal sense.

Nor, in the earlier chapters do we ever read of Satan's binding and imprisonment. Instead, Satan is active earlier in the book. He is cast down to the earth in Revelation 12:9, having great wrath (12:12). Indeed, there are numerous mentions of Satan deceiving people and indeed, the whole world (see Rev. 12:9, 13:14 and 18:23). No other passage in Revelation mentions Satan being bound or restricted from deceiving the nations. Revelation 20:1-3 stands in complete contrast to these earlier references to Satan's deceiving activity in Revelation, for in the millennium Satan will be unable to deceive the nations.

Nor do we read elsewhere in the book of the saints reigning. Instead, earlier in the book, we find the Beast reigning. The only other verse in Revelation (besides 20:4-6) which mentions the saints reigning is Revelation 5:10 which says, 'they will reign on the earth'. Notice the future tense, indicating that this was not yet happening in Revelation 5.

The fact that there is only one passage that mentions the saints reigning, or Satan's binding, or the 1000 years – Revelation 20 – suggests that Revelation 20 is not a recapitulation of the same events as transpire earlier in the book. Instead, these events must occur after the return of Christ described in Revelation 19.

Robert Mounce writes, 'The interpretation that discovers recapitulation for the segment 20:1-6 must at least bear the burden of proof'[12]. George Ladd writes, 'There is absolutely no hint of any recapitulation in chapter 20'[13].

---

[12] Mounce, *Revelation*, p352
[13] G. E. Ladd, "An Historical Premillennial Response", in *The Meaning of the Millennium: Four Views*, ed. Robert Clouse, IVP: Downers Grove, 1977, p190

Some who argue that Revelation 20 is a recapitulation of the entire period of church history argue that the opening words of the chapter, 'then I saw', indicate a new vision, from which it flows that a new section of the book is being introduced. But these are exactly the same words (in Greek: και ειδον) that are found in Rev. 19:11, 17, and 19, as well as 20:4, 11, 12 and 21:1 describing a series of events unfolding at Christ's return and the resurrection of the martyrs thereafter. This means that the words 'And I saw' at the beginning of Revelation 20 are no evidence of a new vision.

Many commentators argue that the section in which Revelation 20:1-10 is found begins in Revelation 19:11 and ends at 21:8, not just because these are the most natural breaks in the flow of the story, but also because before this we have the vision of Babylon the great harlot, and then, beginning in 21:9 we have the vision of the New Jerusalem, the Lamb's wife. The contrasts are obvious. The section from 19:11 to 21:8 shows how we get from the rule of the Beast and the harlot in Babylon to Christ ruling accompanied by His bride in the New Jerusalem. These are not two systems ruling the world at the same time (as in the symbolic view). Instead, one opposes the other, and the whole point of Revelation 19:11 to 21:8 is to show how one is replaced by the other at the return of Christ.

This section is the climax of the book of Revelation, fulfilling its opening promise of the revelation of Jesus Christ on the clouds of heaven (1:7). Not only does it provide the dramatic high-point of the book; this section also shows the aftermath of this epoch-making event – Christ's reign.

The uninspired chapter division in Revelation 20:1 is therefore no evidence of the start of a new vision, distinct from what went before. David Pawson writes that the separation of Revelation 19 and 20 is 'totally unwarranted'[14].

Question 5: Is Revelation 20 better Understood Literally or Symbolically?

Those who hold to a symbolic or spiritualized interpretation of Revelation 20 argue that the idea of a 1000-year reign of the saints is only found in one chapter of the most symbolic book in the Bible (Revelation 20). Therefore, it is reasonable to understand the passage symbolically or figuratively. On the other hand, they say, to build a doctrine like a literal, future, earthly reign of Christ upon this one passage is precarious.

Virtually all Christians take certain parts of Revelation symbolically.

---

[14] David Pawson, *Unlocking the Bible*, London: Collins, 2003, p1255

Even here in Revelation 20, no one thinks that Satan is going to be bound with a literal, physical, iron chain. On the other hand, we cannot dismiss everything in the book of Revelation as symbolic. For example, the author John (Rev. 1:9) is not a symbol, neither is Christ (Rev. 20:4, 6). No one insists that everything in Revelation 20 is symbolic.

Not even commentators who take Revelation 20 figuratively take everything in the passage symbolically. They do not take, for example, the saints who reign with Christ figuratively, nor do they take Satan figuratively, or the battle at the end of the passage, which they believe to be a literal battle. We might ask why they take the battle at the end of the passage literally, if Satan's imprisonment and the 1000 year reign of the saints at the beginning of the passage are figurative?

On the other hand, even those who take Revelation 20 literally are open to many things in Revelation being symbolic. Take the beast with seven heads and ten horns just a few chapters before (Rev. 17:3) – no one believes this is a literal animal. So, the question becomes, which view is more consistent: is it possible to take most things (or everything) in the passage literally, or is it possible to take it all symbolically? If we chop and change between the two approaches with no good reason, this inconsistency would count against the view we take. Therefore, the question is not whether we take the passage symbolically or literally. Instead, it is a case of which interpretation is better able to handle the passage in three important respects:

1. which is the more consistent approach,
2. which is the more logical approach, and
3. which approach is more in tune with the biblical evidence elsewhere.

To understand what I mean by a 'consistent' and 'logical' approach, consider the first commentator (to our knowledge) who tried to take a consistently symbolic approach to virtually everything in Revelation 20:1-10. Augustine described a literal interpretation of the passage as 'ridiculous fancies'. But notice how he dealt with one feature of the passage.

As we have already seen, Augustine took Satan being 'bound' to refer to Christ's victory over Satan at the cross, as a result of which the gospel goes out to all the nations of the world today and people are delivered from Satan's deception. This sounds good and it is certainly true that Christ's death at the cross has resulted in the gospel going out into all the world. However, Revelation 20:1-3 not only speaks about Satan being bound, but these verses also tell us that Satan was cast into the bottomless pit.

Augustine felt that he also needed to explain what the 'bottomless pit' was referring to. A consistent approach means that we cannot cherry pick one little feature from a Bible passage that seems to be interpreted by a particular view without also seeing if we can explain the other features found alongside it. Here is Augustine on the bottomless pit:

> By the abyss [i.e. bottomless pit] is meant the countless multitude of the wicked whose hearts are unfathomably deep in malignity against the Church of God; not that the devil was not there before, but he is said to be cast in thither, because, when prevented from harming believers, he takes more complete possession of the ungodly. ... "And shut him up, and set a seal upon him, that he should deceive the nations no more till the thousand years should be fulfilled." "Shut him up,"-- i.e., prohibited him from going out, from doing what was forbidden. And the addition of "set a seal upon him" seems to me to mean that it was designed to keep it a secret who belonged to the devil's party and who did not. For in this world this is a secret, for we cannot tell whether even the man who seems to stand shall fall, or whether he who seems to lie shall rise again (*The City of God*, 20:7).

Notice some of the logical contradictions involved in Augustine's argument:

1. Augustine says that Satan being cast into the abyss (the bottomless pit) means being cast into the hearts of the ungodly. However, as Augustine himself admits, Satan was already there. It seems strange for Satan to be cast into something when he was already there.
2. Augustine later says (in Revelation 20:7) that Satan is released from this prison so he can seduce souls. But if the 'prison' is 'men's souls', then it is a quite illogical argument that speaks of Satan being released from men's souls so as to enable him to seduce them.
3. Augustine interprets the seal upon Satan to refer to the secret identity of unbelievers, but aren't the vast majority of unbelievers easy to spot?

This is just a little sample of what is meant by a lack of consistent 'logic' in an interpretation. In addition to being illogical, Augustine's interpretation ignores clear scriptural explanations of key terms. For example, Augustine suggests that the 'bottomless pit' or 'abyss' means men's hearts (in the depth of their sinfulness), but the 'abyss' is mentioned in other places where it has nothing to do with men's hearts, but instead seems to be a prison-house for demonic forces: see Luke 8:31, Romans 10:7, and most significantly, Revelation 9:1, 11:7, 17:8.

A symbolic approach contains obvious dangers: what is to stop other expositors – less distinguished than Augustine – reading whatever imaginative nonsense they wish into the symbolism? How do we tell whose symbolism is correct? What limits shall we put on the imagination?

At least Augustine attempted to be consistently symbolical. What about the alternative approach: is it possible to take everything in the passage literally? Many elements are taken literally by everybody, and there are only two or three things in the passage which, in themselves, suggest a possible symbolic meaning: the 1000 years, because numbers sometimes have symbolic significance, and the key and chain in verse 1, because it is hard to imagine that physical constraints would imprison Satan. However, 2 Peter 2:4 speaks of demons being imprisoned in 'chains of darkness', so even the chain and key could be taken literally to refer to real (though not physical) constraints. It is, of course, also possible to take the 1000 years to mean 1000 literal years. It is thus possible to consistently explain the whole passage literally.

Nor is it wise to argue that the millennium is only found here in the Bible. Yes, the period of time – 1000 years – is only stated here. But those who take this passage literally believe that it refers to the coming Kingdom foretold by all the prophets in which the saints reign on earth with the Messiah in conditions that, while not perfect, are nevertheless a return to paradise. Isaiah is not the only prophet to foretell this period – other prophets also gives similar predictions. J. D. Pentecost has written that 'a larger body of prophetic Scripture is devoted to the subject of the millennium, developing its character and conditions, than any other one subject'[15]. Even those who take this passage symbolically argue that it refers to the entire church age, and the church age is not found only here in the Bible – it is found all through the New Testament. So whichever way we take the millennium, symbolically or literally, it is found elsewhere in the Bible. It is not true to say that Revelation 20 is the only passage which describes this period.

Question 6. How did the Earliest Christians Interpret Revelation 20?

Although the writings of early Church 'fathers' are not equal in authority to inspired Scripture, nevertheless some of these writings come from men who not only lived soon after the apostle John, but also had a personal

---

[15] J. Dwight Pentecost, *Things to Come*, Grand Rapids: Zondervan, 1964, p476

connection with the writer of Revelation. Their opinion on what Revelation 20 means therefore carries some weight.

Papias (AD 60–130) was a contemporary of Polycarp, who was a disciple of the apostle John. Eusebius the church historian stated that Papias received "doctrines of the faith" that came from the "friends" of the twelve apostles (*Ecclesiastical History*, III.39.2.). Eusebius says, "And Papias, of whom we are now speaking, confesses that he received the words of the apostles from those that followed them" (ibid., 39.7). Eusebius records that Papias believed things that "came to him from unwritten tradition" and "teachings of the Saviour." Among these beliefs were "that there will be a millennium after the resurrection of the dead, when the kingdom of Christ will be set up in material form on this earth" (*Ecclesiastical History*, 39.11–12). So Papias was a Christian who had close ties to John the Apostle and stated that the kingdom of Christ was future and earthly.

Irenaeus (c. 130–c. 202) was the bishop of Lyon and as a youth listened to Polycarp who knew the Apostle John. Just like Papias, Irenaeus took the passage in Revelation 20 to refer to a literal period of 1000 years in which Christ would reign on earth. In his book *Adversus Haereses* [Against Heresies], Irenaeus argued against Gnosticism which taught that matter (and this physical world) is evil by asserting that in the millennium God is going to restore the world to a state of paradise. Irenaeus wrote:

> When this Anti-Christ shall have devastated all things in this world, he will reign for three years and six months, and sit in the temple at Jerusalem; and then the Lord will come from heaven in the clouds, in the glory of the Father, sending this man and those who follow him into the lake of fire; but bringing in for the righteous the times of the kingdom, that is, the rest, the hallowed seventh day; and restoring to Abraham the promised inheritance, in which kingdom the Lord declared, that 'many coming from the east and the west should sit down with Abraham, Isaac, and Jacob[16].

Both Papias and Irenaeus had historical connections with the apostle John and taught a literal millennium after Christ's return. Nor was it just Papias and Irenaeus who believed in a literal millennium – this was the position of most early Christian writers. The church historian Philip Schaff wrote:

---

[16] Irenaeus, *Against Heresies*, Book V, chap 30, para 4

The Millennium

> The most striking point in the eschatology [view of the end-times] of the ante-Nicene age is the prominent chiliasm, or millenarianism, that is the belief of a visible reign of Christ in glory on earth with the risen saints for a thousand years, before the general resurrection and judgment. It was indeed not the doctrine of the church embodied in any creed or form of devotion, but a widely current opinion of distinguished teachers, such as Barnabas, Papias, Justin Martyr, Irenaeus, Tertullian, Methodius, and Lactantius[17].

While the writings of these early post-apostolic Christians are not authoritative, it would seem more likely that they had received this view of Revelation 20 passed down from the apostle John himself.

Summary
In this chapter, we have looked at the arguments and the evidence involved in one of the most important debates over future events. We conclude that the arguments for a symbolic interpretation of Revelation 20 are inconsistent and illogical at many points. By contrast, the literal approach makes straightforward, natural sense.

The question of whether Christ's reign over the earth for 1000 years is to be taken literally or symbolically has far-reaching ramifications in many directions, as we will see as we continue to explore events relating to the coming of the Lord. For the moment, we may say that this issue is significant for a number of reasons.

1. It shows that the book of Revelation also teaches what we have learnt about the paradise to come prophesied in Isaiah – both are referring to the millennium.
2. It therefore reinforces what our future hope looks like: Christ is returning to reign over this earth for 1000 years in paradise conditions before the eternal state.
3. It teaches us important lessons about sound principles of interpretation, not only in what the Bible says about future events in Revelation and elsewhere, but how we interpret Scripture generally. It shows how the question of a literal or symbolic interpretation is only one of a number of important interpretational issues, included among which are hermeneutical, logical and scriptural consistency.
4. It teaches that we must go back to the Bible and carefully evaluate

---

[17] Philip Schaff, *History of the Christian Church*, Charles Scribner, 1884, 2:614.

what it says rather than clinging to doctrines received by church tradition about future events, like the Roman Catholic view of future events, which endorses Augustine's illogical writings on this subject, or the teachings of the Reformed Churches about future events, which in Luther and Calvin's days also largely continued to adhere to an Augustinian framework of future events.
5. It strongly suggests that the best framework by which to understand future events is a pre-millennial return of Christ – that is, Christ is returning before the millennium. We will look at the two alternative theories (amillennialism and postmillennialism) in the next section of the book.

John Walvoord writes, 'Revelation, while subject to all types of scholarly abuse and divergent interpretation, if taken in its plain intent yields a simple outline of premillennial truth – first a time of great tribulation, then the second advent, the binding of Satan, the deliverance and blessing of the saints, a righteous government on earth for 1000 years, followed by the final judgments, and the new heaven and new earth'[18].

J. C. Ryle warns about one of the great dangers that results from the symbolic interpretation of Revelation 20: 'The Apostles went into one extreme – they stumbled at Christ's sufferings. We have gone into the other extreme – we have stumbled at Christ's glory. We have got into the confused habit of speaking of the kingdom of Christ as already set up among us, and have shut our eyes to the fact that the devil is still prince of this world, and served by the vast majority, and the Lord, like David in Adullam, though anointed – is not yet set upon His throne'[19].

Why the Millennium?

Why does God plan to have this 1000 year period called the millennium before we get to the eternal state? Why can't everything be nice and simple? Why can't we all just go to heaven when we die – and that's all there is to it? Or why can't we go straight into the eternal state? Why does there have to be this transitional period? Here are seven reasons for the millennium:

---

[18] John Walvoord, *The Millennial Kingdom*, Zondervan, 1959, p118
[19] J. C. Ryle, *Coming Events and Present Duties*, Memphis: Bottom of the Hill, 2012, p20, emphasis in original

1. The Millennium will vindicate Christ

Christ, the rightful King of heaven and earth, was publicly crucified outside His capital city when He came to earth. But one day, in the very same place, He will ascend the throne He rightly deserves. The One who was mocked with a crown of thorns, spat upon and hung from a cross by His own people will receive the glory and the crown. He will reign in the very scene where He was despised and rejected, the earth.

Isaiah 32:1 says, 'Behold, a king will reign in righteousness'. Isaiah 33:17 says, 'Your eyes will see the King in his beauty; they will see the land that is very far off', and verse 22 says, 'for the Lord is our Judge, the Lord is our Lawgiver, the Lord is our King'. Isaiah 35:2 says, 'they shall see the glory of the Lord, the excellence of our God'.

Charles Ryrie writes, 'Why does there need to be an earthly kingdom? Because He must be triumphant in the same arena where he was seemingly defeated. His rejection by the rulers of this world was on earth (1 Cor. 2:8). His exaltation must also be on this earth. And so it shall be when He comes again to rule this world in righteousness. He has waited long for His inheritance; soon He will receive it'[20].

E. W. Bullinger wrote in *The Witness of the Stars*:

> Come, then, and added to Thy many crowns,
> Receive yet one, the crown of all the earth,
> Thou who alone art worthy! It was Thine
> By ancient covenant, ere nature's birth,
> And Thou hast made it Thine by purchase since,
> And overpaid its value with Thy blood,
> Thy saints proclaim Thee King; and in their hearts
> Thy title is engraven with a pen
> Dipp'd in the fountain of eternal love

The hymnwriter Frances Ridley Havergal sums up the believer's response:

> Thou art coming, O our Saviour, coming God's anointed King!
> Every tongue Thy name confessing, well may we rejoice and sing.
> Thou art coming, thou art coming, Jesus our beloved Lord;
> Oh the joy to see Thee reigning, worshipped, glorified, adored.

---

[20] Charles Ryrie, *Basic Theology*, Chicago: Moody Press, 1999, p596

2. The Millennium will demonstrate God's Glory on planet earth

God created this earth a paradise, but man's sin spoiled the entire creation. God is not going to 'write-off' this world which He made, but is instead going to have the last word, the victory even here in this earthly scene. God is going to reclaim the world He created and reign over all things. The last, and final epoch of this earth's history will demonstrate God's triumph. Earth's glorious golden age is still to come, and we will be there to see it.

Alcorn writes, 'What lies behind our notion that God is going to destroy the earth and be done with it? I believe it's a weak theology of God. Though we'd never say it this way, we see him as a thwarted inventor whose creation failed. Having realized his mistake, he'll end up trashing most of what he made. His consolation for a failed Earth is that he rescues a few of us from the fire. But this idea is emphatically denied by Scripture. God has a magnificent plan, and he will not surrender Earth to the trash heap'[21].

3. The Millennium will Reward Faithful Followers of Christ

In Rev. 11:18 we are told that the time had come for God to reward His servants the prophets and the saints, and those who fear His name, both small and great. In Christ's parable of the pounds, the nobleman who had gone into a far country to receive a kingdom, given his property to his servants to trade with in his absence and then returned, said to the faithful servant, 'Well done, good servant, because you were faithful in a very little, have authority over ten cities' (Luke 19:17). Those who have been persecuted for Christ (Matt. 5:10-12), those who have not lived for this world's material possessions but for the kingdom to come (Luke 12:31-32), those who have taken up their cross, denied themselves, left all and followed Christ (Matt. 19:27-30) will be fully rewarded in that day.

4. God will keep the Covenants with His Old Testament People

J. D. Pentecost writes about the various Old Testament covenants (or promises) that God made: with Abraham (Gen. 12:2-3, 13:14-17, 15:7-21), with Israel under Moses (Ex. 19-24, Deut. 28 – 30), with David (2 Sam. 7:8-16, 23:5, 2 Chron. 7:18, 21:7), and the New Covenant (Jer. 31:31-34). Pentecost says that the millennium is necessary

in order to fulfil all God's eternal covenants made with Israel. Apart

---

[21] Alcorn, *Heaven*, p90

from the earthly theocratic kingdom [i.e. the millennium] there would be no fulfilment of the Abrahamic covenant, which promised Israel possession of the land, perpetuity as a nation, and universal blessings through that nation. Apart from the kingdom the Davidic covenant could not be fulfilled, which had promised Israel a king in David's line, a throne or recognized seat of authority from which that king would rule, and a people or kingdom over which the king reigned. Apart from that kingdom the Palestinian covenant, which promised Israel possession of the land, and blessings in the possession of it, would not be fulfilled. Apart from that theocratic kingdom the new covenant, which promised Israel a conversion, a new heart, and the fullness of God's blessings, would not be fulfilled[22].

J. M. Davies writes:

God's dealings with Israel in grace are based on the unconditional promises and covenants He made to and with Abraham and David. They are not nullified either by the Law or by Israel's failure ... [Writing about the covenant with Abraham] No conditions were imposed. There is no *if* in the passage, no suggestion that its implementation would be contingent upon faithfulness on Abraham's part. It would depend on the faithfulness of God entirely. One of the clauses of this covenant states that the land of Canaan is to be Israel's in perpetuity, an everlasting possession... [Writing about the covenant with David] This covenant also is spoken of as an everlasting covenant (2 Sam. 23:5). Its immutability is emphasized very strongly by Jeremiah ... [in] (33:20,21). The immutability of these covenants is evident in connection with the three deliverances of Israel recorded in the Bible. Israel's deliverance from Egypt and entrance into Canaan was based on the covenant with Abraham ... not because of any righteousness or merit of Israel ... Israel's deliverance from Babylon was on the same basis ... Israel's future deliverance (Ezek. 36:22, 32; Deut. 4:30) is based on this covenant (Lev. 26:42; Ezek. 16:60-63). Israel is reminded in unmistakable terms that this will not be because of any claim on her part: "Not for your sakes do I this, saith the Lord God, be it known unto you: be ashamed and confounded for your own ways, O house

---

[22] Pentecost, *Things to Come*, p474

of Israel ... I do not this for your sakes ... but for mine holy name's sake" (Ezek. 36:32, 22)[23].

5. The Millennium will Show the Depths of Human Sinfulness

At the end of the millennium, after 1000 years of Christ's reign in righteousness, Satan will be released and again deceive the nations, provoking a final revolt by mankind against God. This shows that even after 1000 years of paradise on earth, mankind is still sinful in nature and practice. The millennium will provide the final demonstration of our true condition; the weakness of men's hearts will be seen in how easily the entire world is swayed by Satan. J. B. Watson writes,

> It has been a matter of wonder why Satan, once he has been safely shut up in the Abyss, should be set at liberty again to recommence his campaign against the Lord and His people. The explanation surely lies here: he is permitted to be the agent by means of whom a final test is applied to the inhabitants of the world, a test which reveals two things: first, who among them is suited to have part in the New Earth which is about to replace the Old; second, the utter badness of fallen human nature and the impossibility of improving it[24].

6. The Millennium helps us to understand the eternal state

There is very little specifically told us in the Bible about the eternal state. Most of the information about the future relates instead to the millennial rule of Christ. Maybe that is because it would be difficult for us to understand what it means to live in eternity. But the paradise conditions of the millennium give us a little glimpse of the even greater joy and glory of the eternal state.

7. Because the Bible tells us so!

Ultimately, the reason we should believe in the millennium is because the Bible teaches it. We might find the idea of interposing a 1000-year interval before eternity surprising, or we might be reluctant to add another long, theological word to our vocabulary, or we might prefer it that God's thoughts and plans were more simple, in line with our simple minds, and that all the saved just went to heaven forever. However, we need to let God

---

[23] J. M. Davies, *Israel in Prophecy*, Westchester, IL: Good News Publishers, 1967, p16-18, emphasis in original.
[24] J. B. Watson, "The Final Rebellion", in *The Lord's Return in Grace and Glory*, eds. R. McElheran and W. Hoste, Kilmarnock: Ritchie, n.d., p125

be God, and we need to be guided by God's Word, not by our feelings or preferences or traditional understandings.

How Long will the Millennium Last?

Those who take the millennium figuratively and spiritually suggest that it is simply a long period of time. They argue that the 1000 years mentioned six times in the passage is symbolic of completeness (10x10x10 – 'three dimensional completeness'[25]). Leaving aside the question of why ten should symbolize 'completeness' (doesn't seven suggest completeness?), there are four factors which suggest the 1000 years should be taken literally.

Firstly, the two different ways that Revelation 20 expresses the 1000 years are significant. The words '*for* a thousand years' are found three times (vs2, 4, 6 – see ESV, NASB, NIV), and employ the normal expression used to measure the length of time[26]. The expression '*the* thousand years' is also found three times (vs3, 5, 7) and uses the article to specify a particular and definite period of time[27]. Putting both expressions together, as the passage does three times, suggests a definite period of time of specific duration rather than a vague and symbolic age.

Secondly, verse 6 seems to take the form of an explanation, or interpretation, of the vision in verses 4-5 immediately before, which describe the resurrected saints reigning with Christ for 1000 years. Verse 6 says: 'Blessed and holy is he who has part in the first resurrection. Over such the second death has no power, but they shall be priests of God and of Christ, and shall reign with Him for a thousand years'. Notice, however, that the interpretation in v6 does not use a different description to explain the 1000 years – it just repeats the figure. If the interpretation had instead used some other description like, 'they shall be priests of God and of Christ, and shall reign with Him as long as the stars do shine, until moons shall wax and wane no more', then there might be more reason for taking the 1000 years as symbolic of a very long period of time.

Thirdly, Satan is bound and shut away for 1000 years, according to Rev. 20:1-3. The 1000 year duration is mentioned twice in these verses, and then again in verse 7. It is hard to imagine Satan quietly accepting a period of time any longer than 1000 years – some long age of indeterminate duration. We can be sure that Satan will protest at the end

---

[25] Michael Wilcock, *I Saw Heaven Opened*, BST, Leicester: IVP, 1991, p60
[26] The expression in Greek uses the accusative case which measures duration
[27] There are small number of manuscripts which read 'the' in verse 6, but there is much stronger manuscript support for omitting it, to read 'a thousand years'.

of 1000 years, and will insist that God must keep His six-times repeated word and release him from his prison when the 1000 years expire.

Lastly, the saints will also perhaps feel disappointed if the period in which they are said to 'long enjoy the work of their hands' (Isaiah 65:22) is shorter than 1000 years. Even patriarchs like Adam and Methuselah lived nearly 1000 years. Shall the long-promised reward of the righteous on earth be less? Therefore, it seems that the 1000 years probably means just what it says.

THEOLOGY:

Three Views on the Millennium and the Kingdom

The following four chapters of the book may be skipped by those wanting to continue exploring what the Bible says about the end of the world. These four chapters look in more detail at the three main theological frameworks for understanding future events.

4 AMILLENNIALISM

In the year 312 AD, as Constantine advanced at the head of his army towards Rome, he claimed that he saw a vision of a cross in the sky with the words, 'In this sign, conquer'. After defeating his enemies at the Battle of the Milvian Bridge, Constantine became Roman Emperor. In the next year, 313, Constantine issued the Edict of Milan, which legalized Christianity as a religion in the empire, and from then on, the new Emperor was to give increasing support to the Christian church. The emerging Christian kingdom in Rome seemed to many to be the final triumph of God over the powers of darkness. The kingdom of Christ upon earth had arrived.

For two hundred and fifty years before the Edict of Milan, the early church had endured sporadic but severe persecution at the hands of the Roman Empire. During this period, Christians lived in expectation of the soon return of Christ to reign in power on the earth. They did not think of their future hope in terms of religious freedom through political action or a Christianized Empire obtained through the preaching of the gospel. Instead, they believed that Antichrist would arise and Christ would return to crush him and establish a kingdom of justice and joy on earth.

Most of the Christian writers of this era tended to think of the millennium in Revelation 20 as a literal 1000 year reign of Christ with His saints upon the earth after His return.

However, in 410 AD the Goths sacked Rome, and the impending collapse of the Empire shattered hopes of a Christian political empire on earth. The great theologian of the era, Augustine (354-430 AD), adopted a spiritual view of the millennium, teaching that Christ's reign spanned the period from His resurrection until His return. He wrote the following about the 1000 years in Revelation 20:

> During the 'thousand years' when the devil is bound, the saints also reign for a 'thousand years' and, doubtless, the two periods are identical and mean the span between Christ's first and second coming[1].

---

[1] Augustine, *The City of God*, xx. 9

He suggested that the millennium referred to the emerging Christian spiritual kingdom, the worldwide Church, not an earthly Christianized political empire. Augustine's view dominated the Middle Ages, and the Roman Catholic Church considered itself the kingdom of God on earth.

Luther and Calvin reacted against this view at the time of the Reformation, holding the Roman Catholic Church to be anti-Christian. They saw the reign of Christ as otherworldly: the spiritual reign of Christ and His saints in heaven.

Amillennialism (meaning 'no millennium') teaches that references to the reign of Christ do not refer a future, earthly kingdom after His second coming, an intermediate state of blessedness before the general resurrection and judgment. Instead, Christ is reigning over His church from heaven in the present Church age. Here again, the millennium is not a literal 1000-year reign. Millard Erickson writes:

> Literally, amillennialism is the idea that there will be no millennium, no earthly reign of Christ. The great final judgement will immediately follow the second coming and issue directly in the final states of the righteous and the wicked[2].

Thus, amillennialism is more focused on the present than the future. Most of the events that other prophecy views take to be future, amillennialism takes to be happening here and now.

An amillennialist has described the difference between the three viewpoints as follows: 'Premillennialists are waiting for the millennium, postmillennialists are working for it, but amillennialists are enjoying it'. The humorous tone of the amillennialist epitomises the general attitude of many amillennialists towards future events: they consider the subject embarrassing, if not a joke. As we saw in the last chapter, Augustine described a literal interpretation of Revelation 20 as 'ridiculous fancies'. Here is what Augustine said about the subject of the millennium more generally:

> In fact I myself at one time accepted such an opinion [the idea of a millennium]. But when these interpreters say that the rising saints are to spend their time in limitless gormandizing with such heaps of food and drink as not only go beyond all sense of decent restraint, but go utterly beyond belief, then such an interpretation becomes wholly

---

[2] Millard J. Erickson, *Christian Theology*, Grand Rapids: Baker Academic, 2nd. Ed., 1998, p1218

unacceptable save to the carnal minded. But the spiritual minded term those who can swallow the literal interpretation of the thousand years, Chiliasts, from the Greek *chilias*, a thousand, or millenarians from the corresponding Latin word. To refute them point by point would take too long. My present obligation will be rather to show how the scriptural passage in question ought to be understood (*City of God*, 20.7).

Other amillennialists go further and label any Christians interested in the subject of what the Bible says about future events as dangerous eccentrics, or fanatics. Calvin is a good example of this:

Not long after arose the millenarians who limited the reign of Christ to a thousand years. Their fiction is too puerile to require or deserve refutation. Nor does the Revelation which they quote in favour of their error afford them any support, for the term of a thousand years there mentioned refers not to the eternal blessedness of the church, but to the various agitations which awaited the church in its militant state upon the earth. . . Those who assign the children of God a thousand years to enjoy the inheritance of future life little think what dishonour they cast on Christ and his kingdom (*Institutes*, 3.25.5).

The Second Helvetic Confession, (A.D. 1566), an early Reformation Creed, said, 'We further condemn Jewish dreams that there will be a golden age on earth before the Day of Judgment, and that the pious, having subdued all their godless enemies, will possess all the kingdoms of the earth'.

The Roman Catholic Church is strongly amillennial. Cardinal Ratzinger (later to become Pope Benedict XVI) wrote:

The Antichrist's deception already begins to take shape in the world every time the claim is made to realize within history that messianic hope which can only be realized beyond history through the eschatological judgment. The Church has rejected even modified forms of this falsification of the kingdom to come under the name of millenarianism, especially the "intrinsically perverse" political form of a secular messianism[3].

---

[3] Joseph Cardinal Ratzinger, *Catechism of the Catholic Church*, New York: Doubleday, 1995, p194

One currently popular form of amillennialism is Kingdom-Now theology or, as it has been called, hyper-realized eschatology. Many charismatics, in line with the prosperity gospel, believe that all the blessings of the Messianic age are available for us to enjoy now. Bill Johnson writes, 'One of the tragedies of a weakened identity is how it affects our approach to Scripture. Many, if not most, theologians make the mistake of taking all the good stuff contained in the prophets and sweeping it under that mysterious rug called the Millennium. It is not my desire to debate that subject right now. But I do want to challenge our thinking and deal with our propensity to put off those things that require courage, faith, and action to another period of time. The mistaken idea is this: if it is good, it can't be for now'[4].

Arguments for Amillennialism

Amillennialism (meaning 'no millennium') teaches that there will be no future 1000-year reign of Christ on this earth after His return. Instead, Christ is reigning over His church from heaven in the present Church age. Some have called amillennialism Realised Eschatology, in that we are already realising and experiencing the blessings of the millennium.

Here in this chapter we shall look at the best arguments for the amillennialist position. As we have already seen, the amillennial view of the future does not handle Revelation 20 or the Old Testament prophets very well. However, amillennialists tend to dismiss Revelation 20 as 'one passage in a very symbolic book', and they tend to avoid detailed exposition of the prophets as well. Amillennialists do not appeal first or foremost to these parts of Scripture for their view of future events. This is because the strongest arguments for amillennialism lie elsewhere. Amillennialists argue that the following three principles provide a more sure way of understanding the Bible's picture of future events.

1. Spiritual

Amillennialists interpret the prophecies of the Old Testament spiritually, not literally. Indeed, they argue that we should interpret Old Testament prophecies Christologically (that is, seeing them fulfilled in Christ), because this is what the New Testament itself teaches about Israel's Old Testament promises. Kim Riddlebarger writes:

> The New Testament writers claimed that Jesus was the true Israel of

---

[4] Bill Johnson, *God is Good*, Destiny Image, 2016, p55

God and the fulfilment of Old Testament prophecies. So what remains of the dispensationalists' case that these prophecies will yet be fulfilled in a future millennium? They vanish in Jesus Christ, who has fulfilled them[5].

Amillennialists reinterpret Old Testament prophecies spiritually because they argue that this is what the apostolic New Testament writers themselves do. Here are three examples:

- Peter quotes Joel's prophecy about the pouring out of the Spirit in Acts 2:16-21 and says 'this is what was spoken by the prophet Joel'. The speaking in tongues at Pentecost was the fulfilment of Joel's prophecy. Thus, it is argued, the Church is the fulfilment of Joel's prophecies, not Israel in some still-to-be-fulfilled apocalyptic future. Amillennialist author John Stott writes, 'It is the unanimous conviction of New Testament authors that Jesus inaugurated the last days or Messianic age, and that the final proof of this was the outpouring of the Spirit, since this was the Old Testament promise of promises for the end-time. This being so, we must be careful not to re-quote Joel's prophecy as if we are still awaiting its fulfilment, or even as if its fulfilment has been only partial, and we await some future and complete fulfilment. For this is not how Peter understood and applied the text'[6].
- In Acts 15:13-17 James says that the prophecy that God would 'rebuild the tabernacle of David which has fallen down so that the rest of mankind may seek the Lord' (Amos 9:11-12) has been fulfilled in the salvation of Gentiles through the preaching of the gospel in the church. This is not a literal fulfilment of an Old Testament prophecy, but a spiritual one: David's tabernacle here means the church which is spiritually David's house. Philip Edgcumbe Hughes, an amillennialist, writes, 'Here is another remarkable instance of a "kingdom" passage, relating to the "dwelling of David", being interpreted in the most authoritative manner as finding its fulfilment in the events of the church age. Plainly, this synod of apostles and elders (Acts 15:6), whose judgment was expressed by James, understood the rebuilding of David's house to be accomplished in God's building of his church'[7].

---

[5] Kim Riddlebarger, *A Case for Amillennialism: Understanding the End Times*, Grand Rapids: Baker, 2003, p70
[6] John R. W. Stott, *The Message of Acts*, BST, Leicester: IVP, 1990, p73
[7] P. E. Hughes, *Interpreting Prophecy*, Eerdmans, 1976, p107

- Similarly, while Jeremiah 31:31-34 promised a new covenant that would be made 'with the house of Israel and with the house of Judah', that promise is fulfilled in the present church age (see the institution of the Lord's Supper in Luke 22:20, and also Heb. 8:8-13) – not literally (with Israel and Judah), but with the church.

Amillennialism argues that the New Testament re-interprets the Old Testament promises and prophecies spiritually, not literally, and applies them to the church, not to Israel. This is the key argument for amillennialism, often presented by advocates for the position. They argue that we must follow the authoritative and inspired method for interpreting Old Testament passages provided for us by the apostles in the New Testament. To the credit of amillennialists, we must acknowledge that this key argument is a biblical argument – it is not an appeal to tradition, or to a psychological preference (optimism), or to a philosophical system of thought. This argument therefore deserves not only to be taken seriously by all Bible students, but also to be subjected to the closest scrutiny.

Jeremiah 31

Let us take the last-mentioned passage in Jeremiah 31 first. It is true that verses like Luke 22:20 ('this cup is the new covenant in my blood') and Hebrews 8:8-13 take Jeremiah's New Covenant prophecy and show that it is fulfilled in the church. However, what is less frequently observed is that Romans 11:27 also quotes Jeremiah's New Covenant prophecy and states that it will be fulfilled in the *future*, when Israel as a nation is converted. Romans 11:26-27 read:

> And so all Israel will be saved, as it is written, "The Deliverer will come out of Zion, and He will turn away ungodliness from Jacob; [27] For this is My covenant with them, when I take away their sins".

Paul quotes from Jeremiah 31:31-34 directly in verse 27. Ernst Käsemann writes, 'Christianity is already living in the new covenant' while 'Israel will begin to do so only at the parousia'[8]. While there is, at present, a fulfilment of Jeremiah's prophecy in the church's experience of forgiveness and salvation, there is also a future fulfilment that has not yet occurred.

Further, if we look at the extended passage in Jeremiah 31:35-40, God

---

[8] E. Käsemann, *Commentary on Romans*, trans. and ed. G. W. Bromiley, Grand Rapids: Eerdmans, 1980, p314

not only introduces a new covenant but also promises that:

- Israel will never cease to be a nation before Him,
- God will never cast off all the seed of Israel for all that they have done,
- the city of Jerusalem will be rebuilt, be 'holy to the LORD', and will never be destroyed anymore.

It is hard to avoid the conclusion that Jeremiah's new covenant includes a promised blessing for the Jewish people nationally that still awaits a future fulfilment. In fact, the prophecy almost pre-supposes Israel's failure and unbelief ('If heaven above can be measured, and the foundations of the earth searched out beneath, I will also cast off all the seed of Israel for all that they have done, says the LORD', v37). God assures them that He will not cast them off, and promises their eventual restoration.

What we, in the church, cannot do is adopt a selective approach to Jeremiah's inspired prophecy, by appropriating certain verses from his prophecy about forgiveness of sin while at the same time ignoring these other words about Israel's future national blessing in the same context.

But this raises the question: if the new covenant promises future national and spiritual blessing for the Jewish people, how can it be appropriated by the (overwhelmingly Gentile) Church today? Simply because, as James 1:18 says, we in the Church are the 'firstfruits' of a yet greater harvest still to come. 'The earth shall be full of the knowledge of the LORD as the waters cover the sea' (Isaiah 11:9), the nation of Israel will one day be saved (Romans 11:26) and come into the blessings of the new covenant, and even the creation itself will be re-born (see Rom. 8:18-23). We Gentiles, by God's grace, are currently partaking (i.e. sharing, Rom. 11:17) in the blessings promised to Israel, even though we were not the direct recipients of the original promise. There is nothing in the New Testament that says that the church has somehow replaced Israel as the recipients of Jeremiah's prophecy, for that is what God's new covenant in Jeremiah explicitly promises not to do.

Thus, while amillennialism rightly argues that the prophesied blessings of the messianic age are to be understood spiritually as applying in the present day church, the full truth is that these blessings are more accurately described as already present spiritually and yet also promised to come, literally and tangibly, when Christ returns to earth to reign.

Acts 2
We see the same sort of partial fulfilment in Acts 2:16-21. It is true that

Acts 2 is the fulfilment of Joel 3. However, it is hard to see that Joel's prophecy has been completely fulfilled, for there are parts of Joel's prophecy that cannot really be said to have happened at Pentecost.

Has the 'great and awesome day of the LORD' (Joel 2:31, Acts 2:20) already come at Pentecost? If so, why do New Testament authors say it is still in the future (1 Thess. 5:2, 2 Thess. 2:2, 2 Peter 3:10)? Where were the 'blood and fire and vapour of smoke, the sun becoming dark and the moon being turned to blood' at Pentecost, or even at the cross? Yes, the sun went dark at Calvary, and there were tongues of fire at Pentecost, but where does Scripture testify to the smoke, or the moon being turned to blood?

Some amillennialists, to avoid the problem of selective cherry-picking of fulfilments, spiritualise all the celestial 'wonders and signs' that Joel prophesies: the sun going dark and the moon being turned to blood tell of the downfall of demonic powers. But they take the prophecy about 'sons and daughters prophesying' literally, seeing it fulfilled in the speaking in tongues, and they take the pouring out of the Spirit literally too. But it is impossible to have it both ways. If the tongues-speaking and the Spirit-pouring are literal, should not all the celestial signs have been seen literally? If they were, why does Scripture not report it?

Worse yet, it seems very hard to understand the pouring out of the Spirit at Pentecost as the complete fulfilment of the Old Testament prophecy. Remember, John Stott said that 'we must be careful not to re-quote Joel's prophecy as if we are still awaiting its fulfilment, or even as if its fulfilment has been only partial, and we await some future and complete fulfilment'. But what the prophets like Isaiah tell us will result from the pouring out of the Spirit is the glorious wonder of 'the earth [being] full of the knowledge of the LORD as the waters cover the sea'. Joel is promising (to use Stott's words), the 'promise of promises', an all-pervading, world-transforming outpouring of the Holy Spirit upon earth. Joel prophesies a torrential downpour of the Holy Spirit upon the earth, but at present we only experience occasional showers. If our troubled church age is enjoying the Old Testament 'promise of promises' – the paradise on earth the prophets foretold – we might be forgiven for wondering if we haven't been sold short by false advertising of the greatness of Messiah's kingdom.

The amillennialist is guilty of hermeneutical inconsistency, by either selectively ignoring, or by selectively spiritualising a number of the signs mentioned in Joel. Interpretational inconsistency is simply another way of saying that the amillennialist is guilty of double-standards, and such inconsistency casts serious doubt on the claimed fulfilment.

It would seem that Pentecost only partially fulfilled Joel's prophecy. Stott warns us not to 'requote Joel', as if Christians must not read the Old Testament on its own terms or interpret it in its own context. Stott's advice sounds reminiscent of the 2nd century heretic Marcion's attempt to get rid of the Old Testament from the Christian Bible. Why can't Christians turn to the Old Testament and re-quote its prophecies? Is not 'all Scripture God-breathed'? This approach to interpreting the Old Testament is very troubling; it is the silencing of Scripture rather than letting Scripture speak for itself, imposition upon rather than the exposition of Scripture.

Acts 15

Acts 15 is the go-to reference, perhaps the lynchpin, for the amillennialist argument. It is mentioned in many treatments of amillennialism as the definitive proof that the New Testament radically reinterprets the Old Testament, taking the Church as the fulfilment of Israel's Old Testament prophecies.

For example, Stuart Olyott says about Amos and Acts 15:

> If I were preaching on Amos 9:11-15 I might be tempted to tell my hearers that the prophet is saying that the Jews will one day have David's descendants restored to them as a royal family, and that in those days the land of Israel will have renewed influence and prosperity. On first sight, that is what the words appear to mean. But we must not rely on first sight. And we must certainly not interpret any passage without asking our sixth question [What light do other parts of Scripture shed on this passage?] As it happens, Acts 15:15-17 shed marvellous light on what Amos says. It shows us that his prediction finds its fulfilment in the conversion of the Gentiles and their becoming part of the Christian church. In doing so, it also gives us a key by which we can unlock the meaning of dozens of similar prophecies found in the Old Testament[9].

Robert Strimple similarly says:

> it is the inspired interpretation of Old Testament prophecy by the New Testament apostles that is the authoritative guide for our interpretation. How instructive in this regard is the record of the

---

[9] Stuart Olyott, *Preaching Pure and Simple*, Bryntirion Press, 2005, pp46-7

Jerusalem Council in Acts 15. ... James sees Amos 9:11-12 being fulfilled right before his eyes, so to speak[10].

However, the amillennialist interpretation of Acts 15 has three problems. Firstly, to understand these two passages in Amos and Acts, it is important not only to look carefully at the biblical text, but also at the historical context of the Jerusalem Council in Acts 15. James in his speech was trying to placate the Jewish Pharisaical law-keeping party in the early church (of which he was the leading figure). These Jewish Christians insisted on keeping the Old Testament law in full. This is seen later in Acts 21 where James (and the elders of the Jerusalem church) suggest it would be a good thing for the apostle Paul to offer animal sacrifices in the temple to keep everyone happy. In other words, neither James nor the Jewish Christians had any intention of abandoning or 'reinterpreting' the Old Testament. The Jewish Pharisaical party had objected violently to the minimal suggestion that uncircumcised Gentiles be admitted into the church. They did so because Gentiles did not keep the law. The adherence of these Pharisees to the literal truth and application of the Old Testament, its laws as well as its prophecies, was absolute. Now try to imagine the uproar that would have ensued if James had said (as amillennialists argue) that Amos was prophesying that the Jewish nation had been abandoned by God and replaced by the (soon to be largely Gentile) church. The response would have been unprintable.

If James had really meant that Amos was not to be understood literally, and that Israel's prophesied national hopes of earthly blessing were now being realized spiritually in the church, he would have been tossed out of the Jerusalem Council on his ear. There would have been robe-ripping, dust throwing, and maybe even fist fights. The Jerusalem faction of the church would have instantly divided off from the Gentile churches, and James would have forever ruptured the unity of the early church. The fact that James' diplomatic speech did not prompt violent responses, but was instead greeted by an outbreak of smiles, amicable agreement and handshakes all round, would appear to suggest that the amillennialist argument is a misreading of the historical situation, and not really comprehending what James was saying in his speech that day.

Here are Amos' words (9:11-15), from which James quoted:

On that day I will raise up the tabernacle of David, which has fallen

---

[10] Strimple, "Amillennialism", in *Three Views on the Millennium and Beyond*, pp96-97

down, And repair its damages; I will raise up its ruins, And rebuild it as in the days of old; That they may possess the remnant of Edom, And all the Gentiles who are called by My name," Says the LORD who does this thing. Behold, the days are coming," says the LORD, "When the plowman shall overtake the reaper, And the treader of grapes him who sows seed; The mountains shall drip with sweet wine, And all the hills shall flow with it. I will bring back the captives of My people Israel; They shall build the waste cities and inhabit them; They shall plant vineyards and drink wine from them; They shall also make gardens and eat fruit from them. I will plant them in their land, And no longer shall they be pulled up From the land I have given them," Says the LORD your God.

Everybody agrees (including amillennialist interpreters) that in Amos' original context, the prophet is foretelling Israel's future, earthly, national blessings in Messiah's kingdom.

So, what is James saying in Acts 15? Is James saying, as the amillennialist argues, that Amos is not talking about the future blessing of the nation of Israel, but rather that the Church is instead the fulfilment of the ancient prophecies to Israel? The second problem with the amillennial interpretation of this passage is its misreporting of an important word in James' speech. The amillennialist argues that James says that Amos' prophecy is being *fulfilled* in the salvation of the Gentiles. This is precisely the word that Philip Edgcumbe Hughes, Stuart Olyott and Robert Strimple use in their comments on this passage. But this is not what James actually says in Acts 15:14. James says that God taking a people for His name from the Gentiles *agrees* with Amos' prophecy: 'with this the words of the prophet *agree*, just as it is written' (Acts 15:15). The actual Greek word used is *symphonousin*, which one doesn't need to know much Greek to understand. We get our word 'symphony' from it; it means to 'sound together, to be in harmony, to agree, to be in accord with'. 'Fulfilment' is not quite the word mentioned by James.

Rather than reading James as radically reinterpreting Amos' message – transferring the promised blessings from Israel to the Gentile church – James is instead making the much milder and more diplomatic point that Amos' glorious vision of the future paradise describes God blessing the Gentiles *alongside* the nation of Israel. After all (says James, quoting the Greek Septuagint version of Amos), 'I will rebuild [David's tabernacle's] ruins, so that the rest of the mankind may seek the Lord, even all the Gentiles who are called by My name'. In other words, in the future paradise (for that is what Amos in his original context is talking about), Gentiles also will come into blessing, for God is their Creator too. And if that is so, the salvation of Gentiles in the present day *agrees* with the future foreseen in Amos' prophecy: Gentiles being saved now is 'in harmony' with that glorious future paradise when David's house is re-established, and Messiah reigns in the millennial period.

The idea that James was ripping Amos' words out of their Old Testament context, spiritually reinterpreting them, dispossessing the Jews of their divinely-promised blessings, and saying these Old Testament words were 'fulfilled' in the present-day evangelism of Gentiles is not warranted by, and goes beyond, James' actual words in Acts 15. Amos' prophecy is referring to some as-yet-unfulfilled period of earthly material blessing ('the plowman overtaking the reaper, the mountains dripping with new wine', etc.) in which the Gentiles would also share alongside Israel. James is taking Amos at face value.

But is there any evidence that James is thinking of a yet-future paradise, instead of the church age? Yes there is, and here we come to the third amillennialist misreading of James's speech: it fails to notice the significant words 'after this' inserted by James (Acts 15:16) before his quote from Amos. These words are not found in Amos. What does 'after this' refer to? It means 'after this' period in which we live, the church age. The words 'after this' suggest that Amos' prophecy is not being fulfilled in the present day in the church, but it will be fulfilled 'after this', in the future.

The commentator E. H. Trenchard summarises:

> The point was that God had announced universal blessings for the Gentiles in the end times, so that the calling out of a people to His name in this age finds its place in the general perspective of prophecy. Fulfilment of the prophecy is partial and analogical rather than literal, as in the case of 2:16-21. Unless the promises given through the prophets to Israel are interpreted with reference to the same people and in the same sense in which they were originally given, the exegesis of prophecy becomes a guessing game controlled only by the predilections of the expositors[11].

Here we see a danger we have noticed before. The amillennialist asks, Why should we take the time or trouble looking at the Old Testament prophecies in their original context if we already possess the special key

---

[11] E. H. Trenchard, "Acts", *Zondervan Bible Commentary: One Volume Illustrated Edition*, (originally, Pickering and Inglis, 1979), Grand Rapids: Zondervan, 2008, p1273

that unlocks their meaning in the New Testament? All that needs to be known about the future is found in the New Testament, so why bother looking at the Old? According to the amillennialist, if the apostles have radically re-interpreted the Old Testament, it becomes a dangerous business for us to go back there and try to read the Old Testament for ourselves. Don't requote Amos, as Stott would say. Instead, all the amillennialist needs to do is to read the New Testament about Jesus' mission in the gospels and the explanation of His significance in the epistles. The Old Testament becomes unnecessary and even positively misleading. Such is the dangerous tendency of a spiritualizing exposition.

Thus, on the positive side of the ledger, the amillennialist interpretation helpfully points out that there is a sense in which the Old Testament prophecies are being fulfilled (spiritually) in the present-day church. But negatively, the amillennialist position robs us of the important truths in the Old Testament that God promises to one day literally fulfil.

There are other cases of Old Testament promises which are claimed to be spiritually fulfilled in the New Testament. However, why cannot both a spiritual fulfilment and a literal one be true? For example, the Old Testament promises a river of water flowing from a future end-time temple (Ezekiel 47, Joel 3:18, Zechariah 14:8). But the New Testament teaches that this is a spiritual reality in the present day (cf. Jesus' words in John 7:38 about rivers of living water flowing out of the inward parts of those who believe in Him) as well as a future feature of the New Jerusalem (Revelation 22:1-2). Both the present spiritual fulfilment and a future literal fulfilment are true, and therefore amillennialism is partially correct in pointing out the present fulfilment, but incorrect in limiting the fulfilment to this present age. Similarly with the New Testament truth that Christians are Abraham's seed (Galatians 3:28), who 'walk in the steps of the faith which our father Abraham had' (Romans 4:12). Why should the fact that we are spiritually Abraham's seed somehow disqualify Jews from being Abraham's literal (and, one day, spiritual) seed? It is not a case of either/or, but both/and.

Augustine the father of amillennialism used the spiritualising method of interpreting Scripture extensively in his manifesto, *The City of God*. Some examples will show its dangers. Augustine took the three storeys of Noah's Ark to mean:

> the three graces commended by the apostle – faith, hope, and charity; or even more suitably they may be supposed to represent those three harvests in the gospel, thirty-fold, sixty-fold, an hundred-fold, or

chaste marriage dwelling in the ground floor, chaste widowhood in the upper, and chaste virginity in the top storey; or any better interpretation may be given, so long as the reference to this city [i.e. the City of God, the Church] is maintained[12].

Augustine obviously had a bee in his bonnet about celibacy as the ideal Christian state, and his imposition of this agenda on Noah's ark seems rather laughable today. But there is nothing to stop anyone else with a crazy 'spiritual' interpretation foisting it upon the Old Testament. This approach to interpreting the Bible was all the rage in the amillennialist centuries after Augustine.

Pope Gregory the Great (AD 600) followed on in this tradition of trying to read mystical hidden meanings into God's Word by interpreting the story of Job as follows: Job's three friends are the heretics, Job's seven sons are the twelve apostles, his 7000 sheep are God's faithful people, and his 3000 camels with humped backs are the depraved Gentiles.

These examples show us that spiritualising the Bible means that we can make it say virtually anything at all. Dean Farrar declared:

When once the principle of allegory is admitted, when once we start with the rule that whole passages and books of Scripture say one thing when they mean another, the reader is delivered bound hand and foot to the caprice of the interpreter. . . . Unhappily for the Church, unhappily for any real apprehension of Scripture, the allegorists, in spite of protest, were completely victorious[13].

Richard Hooker, the Anglican theologian (1554-1600), wrote, 'I hold it for a most infallible rule in exposition of sacred Scripture that where a literal construction will stand, the farthest from the letter is commonly the worst. There is nothing more dangerous than this licentious and deluding art which changeth the meaning of words as alchemy doth or would do the substance of metals, making of anything what it listeth [i.e. wishes] and bringeth in the end all truth to nothing'[14].

J. C. Ryle wrote about the danger of spiritualizing OT prophecies:

We have got into a vicious habit of taking all the [Old Testament]

---

[12] Augustine, *City of God*, Book 15, ch. 26
[13] F. W. Farrar, *History of Interpretation*, p238 (cited in J. Dwight Pentecost, *Things to Come*, Zondervan, 1958, p23.
[14] Richard Hooker, *Laws of Ecclesiastical Polity*, V. lix. 2

promises spiritually, and all the denunciations and threats literally. The denunciations against Babylon and Nineveh, and Edom, and Tyre, and Egypt, and the rebellious Jews, we have been content to take literally and hand over to our neighbours. The blessings and promises of glory to Zion, Jerusalem, Jacob, and Israel, we have taken spiritually, and comfortably applied them to ourselves and the Church of Christ. Now I believe this to have been an unfair system of interpreting Scripture. I hold that the first and primary sense of every Old Testament promise as well as threat is the literal one, and that Jacob means Jacob, Jerusalem means Jerusalem, Zion means Zion and Israel means Israel, as much as Egypt means Egypt, and Babylon means Babylon. The primary sense, I believe, we have sadly lost sight of[15].

The issue is not ultimately whether we should interpret the Bible figuratively or literally, for everybody agrees that the Bible contains figurative, poetic and symbolic language in some places, and there are elements of a non-literal interpretation in all approaches. The more important issue is consistency of interpretation. Amillennialists employ a selective hermeneutic, cherry-picking certain words, phrases and verses from Old Testament passages and spiritualising them, but taking other words and phrases literally, or ignoring other verses in the same passages which cannot be so easily spiritualised.

The problems with the spiritualising or allegorising approach to interpretation are three-fold: first, it is selective, and thus inconsistent, secondly it is imaginative, that is, allowing the interpreter unlimited scope for fanciful speculation, and thirdly, it is subjective, robbing us of any biblical certainty, for 'its basis of authority ceases to be the Scriptures, but the mind of the interpreter' (J. D. Pentecost)[16].

2. Simple

Amillennialists believe in a simple view of future events – amillennialism has no complicated charts. They believe there is only one general resurrection and one future judgement of all people (John 5:21-30) at the second coming of Christ. Before this, there is the church age and after this, the eternal state. In amillennialism, the two resurrections mentioned in Revelation 20:5 and 12, one before the 'millennium' for believers and one after for unbelievers, cannot both be literal resurrections; the first must be spiritual (i.e. new birth) and the second literal. The thousand year period

---

[15] Ryle, *Coming Events and Present Duties*, pp20-1
[16] J. D. Pentecost, *Things to Come*, p5

in between is the present church age in which the saints reign spiritually with Christ.

Amillennialists appeal to John 5:28-29 for one general resurrection and judgment. There Christ says, 'the hour is coming in which all who are in the graves will hear His voice and come forth' – those who have done good, to the resurrection of life, and those who have done evil to the resurrection of condemnation'. Emphasis is placed upon the word 'hour', which suggests that the resurrection of those who have done good and those who have done evil must occur at the same time.

However, John's gospel sometimes uses the word 'hour' in a non-literal and very general way. For example, in John 4:21-23, Jesus spoke about the hour coming when worshippers will worship the Father in spirit and in truth. Christ is not referring here to an hour of 60 minutes – this period has lasted nearly 2000 years. Furthermore, a few verses before Christ's words about the resurrection in John 5, we read Him say, 'Most assuredly, I say to you, the hour is coming, and now is, when the dead will hear the voice of the Son of God; and those who hear will live' (John 5:25). Again, this refers to the entire church age.

It is unlikely that Christ was trying to give a precise timetable of future events at the resurrection and judgment in John 5. Christ is talking about how we can be saved, rather than giving a detailed explanation of eschatology. John 5 therefore gives us a general explanation of resurrection and judgment to come, while other passages provide more specific details about when and how the resurrection will happen.

Revelation 20 mentions two separate resurrections, separated by 1000 years. As we have already seen, the amillennial exposition of this passage is plagued with difficulties. Another passage which seems to clearly teach that not all are raised at the same time is 1 Corinthians 15:22-26:

> For as in Adam all die, even so in Christ all shall be made alive. But each one in his own order: Christ the firstfruits, afterward [or literally, *then*] those who are Christ's at His coming. Then comes the end, when He delivers the kingdom to God the Father, when He puts an end to all rule and all authority and power. For He must reign till He has put all enemies under His feet. The last enemy that will be destroyed is death.

Notice the important words about the resurrection: 'each one in his own order' (i.e. rank or group, Gr. *tagma*). This implies that there are different groups of people yet to be raised in their own appointed rank and time.

Notice also 'then': first Christ's resurrection, *then* (Gr. *epeita*) those who are Christ's at His coming, *then* (Gr. *epeita*) comes the end when the last enemy (death) is destroyed, presumably by yet another resurrection, as we read in Revelation 20:14 where 'Death and Hades are cast into the lake of fire'. The passage gives us an order of events, and separate resurrections in the future.

Craig Blaising writes:

> In verses 23-24, Paul lists three stages of resurrection: Christ, those who belong to Christ (raised) at his coming, and the end. The grammatical structure indicates that "the end" is the third stage of resurrection, differentiated not only from Christ's resurrection but also from a resurrection of those who believe in Christ. The end also correlates with the final subjugation of death, the last enemy, and the moment at which Christ presents the kingdom to the Father. Prior to this "he must reign until he has put all his enemies under his feet" (15:25). The grammar of the text allows the possibility of an interval of a reign of Christ between the resurrection of believers and the final resurrection[17].

There is nothing in the Bible that says that there must only be one resurrection or judgment. The amillennialist insistence on a single resurrection appeals to the idea that the simplest explanation is best. However, the amillennialist insistence on simplicity is a philosophical and aesthetic preference, not a biblical requirement, and – in and of itself – it is not even a very good philosophical principle. A preference for simplicity runs the risk of being simplistic.

William of Occam, the medieval English Christian philosopher and theologian (1287–1347AD) stated his principle (later called Occam's Razor) as *numquam ponenda est pluralitas sine necessitate* ("Plurality must never be posited without necessity"). In other words, the best solution to a problem is the one that provides the simplest explanation, yet covers all the facts. Occam's Razor does not state that the best answer is always the simplest one, but rather that the best answer must cover all the facts in the simplest way. The idea that there is only one resurrection does not appear to adequately explain all of the relevant biblical evidence.

---

[17] Craig Blaising, "Premillennialism", in *Three Views on the Millennium and Beyond*, Zondervan, 1999, p204

3. Supersessionist

Amillennialists also believe that the nation of Israel has been superseded by the church. This is sometimes called Replacement Theology by its critics (promoters prefer the language of fulfilment). We will not go into detail with the arguments here; Israel is the subject of a later section of the book. The arguments for supercessionism are largely based on (a) texts in the New Testament which appear to equate Israel with the church, (b) a spiritualising hermeneutic that reinterprets Old Testament promises to Israel as applying to the church, and (c) seeing Israel as a symbol or type of God's ultimate purpose and focus – Christ's coming and the establishment of the church.

Bavinck writes, 'The shadow, while not itself the body, does point to the body but vanishes when the body itself appears'[18]. Thus not only animal sacrifices and the temple, but Israel itself has been replaced. Similarly, the land promises made by God to the Old Testament patriarchs are not going to be literally fulfilled in a Jewish homeland, either now or during the millennium, but will be fulfilled when the church one day inherits the new heavens and new earth.

Robert Strimple uses an illustration to argue that New Testament 'reinterpretations' of Old Testament promises to Israel are not violations of those promises:

> Consider a young man looking forward to entering a local college in the fall. In appreciation of his good work in high school, his father promises that he will give him "wheels" for his upcoming birthday so that the boy will have transportation as a commuting student. The son is overjoyed, thinking that Dad is going to buy him a motorbike! Birthday morning arrives, and Dad asks him whether he has been out in the driveway yet. The son hurries outside, but there is no motorbike there! Now, there is a $200,000 Ferrari sports car parked in the driveway, but no motorbike. Does the son come back to his father crying: "You have robbed me of my hope?" Obviously not. This is a rather materialistic illustration; but surely with regard to the reality of our spiritual blessings in Christ, the fulfillment by God's grace (both now and in the day of the consummation and the eternal state) far transcends the terms in which the promise has been revealed[19].

---

[18] H. Bavinck, *Reformed Dogmatics*, One Volume Abridged version, ed. John Bolt, Grand Rapids: Baker Academic, 2011, p730

[19] Strimple, "Amillennialism", in *Three Views on the Millennium*, pp99-10

Michael Vlach, however, argues that this analogy is unsatisfactory:

> With Strimple's analogy, the son who receives the Ferrari is the same son to whom the wheels were promised. But this is not really the case with the supercessionist view. According to supercessionism, the nation Israel is promised certain blessings, but in reality, these blessings have been given to another group, the church, an entity that is not national Israel. To pick up on Strimple's analogy ... on the son's birthday, the father reveals the presence of a recently adopted son to whom a $200,000 Ferrari is given. The father then turns to the first son and declares, "I am sorry, but my true son is this adopted son who represents everything our family name stands for". The first son says, "But father, you made a promise to me. I don't mind if out of your wealth you give great gifts to this new adopted member of the family, but giving blessings to this new son does not mean you fulfilled what you promised me"[20].

Amillennialists argue that not only are the Old Testament prophecies completely fulfilled in this present age, but so are types like animal sacrifices, the tabernacle, the feasts, the Exodus, the land, and even Israel itself. All these Old Testament types have been fulfilled in Christ. Thus, it is claimed, everything we read about in the Old Testament is seen again in the New Testament, but on a higher, spiritual, plane. Amillennialists argue that the fulfilment of all these types renders the types themselves redundant.

However, to take one example, the fact that Christ is the true vine (John 15) might appear to suggest that Christ has replaced Israel (which is pictured as a vine in Psalm 80, Isaiah 5, and Ezekiel 17). However, consider other symbols that John's gospel uses to point to spiritual realities: birth (John 3, a picture of the new birth), water (John 4 and 7, a symbol of the Holy Spirit), bread (John 6, a picture of Christ the source of eternal life), and shepherds (John 10, a picture of Christ's care for His people). Does the fact that Christ is the 'true bread' (John 6:32) mean that physical bread has now vanished from the earth, or is 'false' bread because the true bread has come? With Christ's coming, do Christians no longer need to eat physical bread? No, what Christ meant, it would seem, is that bread is a picture or a 'type' of a heavenly, ultimate, divine, reality. Physical bread is not false bread, nor superseded bread, but symbolic bread – pointing to

---

[20] Michael Vlach, *Has the Church Replaced Israel*, Nashville: B&H, 2010, p99

something beyond our physical, earthly existence in the realm of ultimate 'truth' and reality. Therefore, coming back to the true vine in John 15, it would seem possible to describe Israel (God's people) as a picture of Christ (and His people, the church), for both are described using this metaphor of the vine. For Christ to be the 'true' Vine, however, does not necessarily mean that Israel's claim to be God's people is now somehow redundant, or fraudulent, or superseded. Rather, as a type, Israel is a picture pointing to an unseen, spiritual, heavenly, eternal reality.

While Israel's ceremonial types are explicitly said to be fulfilled in the New Testament, it would seem more difficult to treat Israel's promises the same way, for direct promises are quite different to shadowy types. Michael Vlach writes, 'the nature of the unconditional promises to Israel makes it highly unlikely that typology would override what God has declared concerning national Israel'[21].

Here are some comments by J. C. Ryle on these topics.

> For many centuries there has prevailed in the Churches of Christ a strange, and to my mind, an unwarrantable mode of dealing with this word "Israel." It has been interpreted in many passages of the Psalms and Prophets, as if it meant nothing more than *Christian believers*. Have promises been held out to Israel? Men have been told continually that they are addressed to *Gentile saints* ... Against that system I have long protested, and I hope I shall always protest as long as I live. I do not deny that Israel was a peculiar *typical* people, and that God's relations to Israel were meant to be a type of His relations to His believing people all over the world ... What I protest against is the habit of *allegorizing* plain sayings of the Word of God concerning the *future history of the nation Israel* and explaining away the fullness of their contents in order to accommodate them to the Gentile Church! I believe the habit to be unwarranted by anything in Scripture, and to draw after it a long train of evil consequences. Where, I would venture to ask, in the whole New Testament shall we find any plain authority for applying the word "Israel" to anyone but the nation of Israel? I can find none. On the contrary, I observe that when the Apostle Paul quotes Old Testament prophecies about the privileges of the Gentiles in Gospel times, he is careful to quote texts which specifically mention the "Gentiles" by name. The fifteenth chapter of the Epistle to the Romans is a striking illustration of what I mean. ... But that *believing*

---

[21] Michael Vlach, *Has the Church Replaced Israel*, p116

Gentiles may be called "Israelites", I cannot see anywhere at all[22].

Conclusion

There is a good measure of truth to the amillennial view that the church is presently enjoying the spiritual blessings promised in the Old Testament – pardon for sin and peace with God. This is because the kingdom of God is both a present, spiritual kingdom as well as a future, earthly kingdom. The millennium, whichever way it is interpreted, is a prolonged time of unparalleled blessing for man on earth. Amillennialists would argue that it refers to the saints reigning spiritually with Christ now. But these last 2000 years have hardly fulfilled the glorious Old Testament promises of blessing on planet earth. The Americas have been in darkness for three-quarters of the Christian era, most of Africa until the 1800s, as well as most of China and India. Even Europe went through centuries of Roman Catholic superstition which almost blotted out the light of the gospel. The period of unparalleled paradise in Revelation 20, with Satan imprisoned and Christ's saints reigning, has not yet been realised. It occurs after Christ returns.

The amillennial approach is attractive to some because of its minimalism: there is only one resurrection, only one judgement, only one future battle. However, the problem with the amillennial approach is that its minimalism does not fully account for what the Bible says. It is not the natural way that we would read different passages, both in the Old Testament prophets and also in the New. Instead, it involves a radical reinterpretation of the Old Testament prophets and an interpretation of Revelation 20 that not only contradicts what the rest of the New Testament tells us about Satan's present powerful opposition to the gospel, but also contradicts itself within this passage by suggesting that people who have been beheaded can be born again or that the passage speaks of two different sorts of resurrections. It imposes a simplistic theological straitjacket upon the scriptural texts which we find the Bible repeatedly bursting out of, leaving the straitjacket of amillennialism in tatters.

---

[22] J. C. Ryle, *Coming Events and Present Duties*, p117-8, emphasis original

5 POSTMILLENNIALISM

A second view of future events is post-millennialism, the most recent of the three major schemes of eschatology. While some postmillennialists claim that it can be found in the 3rd century AD, fully-fledged postmillennialism had its heyday in the 17th to 19th centuries. Prominent postmillennialists from this period include John Owen, Isaac Watts, John Wesley, Jonathan Edwards, Charles Hodge and B. B. Warfield. A significant promoter of post-millennialism was Rev. Daniel Whitby (1638-1725), an English Unitarian, who wrote *A Treatise of the True Millennium*. Whitby gave the first systematic exposition of a post-millennial position and taught that, 'by the preaching of the Gospel Mohammedanism would be overthrown, the Jews converted, the Papal Church with the Pope (Antichrist) would be destroyed, and there would follow a 1000 years of righteousness and peace known as the Millennium; at the close of which there would be a short period of Apostasy, ending in the return of Christ'[1]. In other words, the world will gradually be converted to Christianity, resulting in 1000 years of peace, justice and joy on earth (the millennium), after which Christ would return to raise the dead and judge the world.

Postmillennialism coincided with a period of great progress in Western society: the industrial and scientific revolution, technological developments, various revivals including the Great Awakening, and the modern missionary movement. Progress was the 'spirit of the age', and manifested itself not only in Christian post-millennialism, but also in the secular world, with its ideas of evolutionary development, the perfectibility of society by education, and humanistic social movements. Post-millennialists like A. A. Hodge argued that many factors, in addition to the gospel, would bring in the promised kingdom, including science, civilization, and political actions:

> The process by which this kingdom grows through its successive stages towards its ultimate completion can of course be very inadequately understood by us. It implies the ceaseless operation of the mighty

---

[1] Clarence Larkin, *Dispensational Truth*, 1920, chapter 2

power of God working through all the forces and laws of nature and culminating in the supernatural manifestations of grace and of miracle. The Holy Ghost is everywhere present, and he works directly alike in the ways we distinguish as natural and as supernatural ... in all the growing of the seeds and all the blowing of the winds; in every event, even the least significant, which has advanced the interests of the human family[2].

However, the French Revolution, and the attendant collapse of the traditional social order throughout Europe, dealt a serious blow to postmillennial hopes. Then the devastation of the twentieth century's two world wars, theological liberalism with its denial of the cardinal doctrines of the faith, the rise of communism and the increasingly secular post-war period dented progressive hopes. Postmillennialism went into steep decline and today post-millennialism is very much a minority position in eschatology.

In the 19th and 20th centuries, post-millennialism largely evolved into liberalism. John Walvoord writes that a 'significant fact is that postmillennialism lends itself to liberalism with only minor adjustments. If millennial prophecies could be spiritualized, why not the doctrine of inspiration, the deity of Christ, the substitutional atonement, the doctrine of resurrection, and the final judgment? The principle of spiritualizing Scripture and avoiding its literal exegesis if applied to prophecy could as well be applied to other fields. In any event, the old conservative, Biblical postmillennialism has long since passed from the contemporary scene'[3].

A modern variant of postmillennialism is called Dominionism or Theonomy (meaning 'God's law'). This argues that Christians are to subdue the whole world now (not in some future age), using political and legislative means as much as spiritual. Theonomists argue for the imposition of Old Testament law as the basis for an ideal theocratic society, and believe that Moses' law still applies in full to society today, including the death penalty for homosexuals and rebellious teenagers. Theonomists teach that 'God has not called us to forsake the earth, but to impress heaven's pattern on earth'[4]. David Chilton argues that 'our goal is

---

[2] A. A. Hodge, *Popular Lectures on Theological Themes*, Philadelphia: Presbyterian Board of Publication, 1887, pp295-97
[3] John Walvoord, "Postmillennialism", https://bible.org/seriespage/millennial-series-part-2-postmillennialism #G49B0326
[4] Gary DeMar, as quoted in H. Wayne House and Thomas Ice, *Dominion Theology: Blessing or Curse?* Portland, OR: Multnomah, 1988

world dominion under Christ's Lordship, a "world takeover" if you will; but our strategy begins with reformation, reconstruction of the church. From that will flow social and political reconstruction, indeed a flowering of Christian civilisation'[5]. R. J. Rushdoony states that 'the saints must prepare to take over the world's governments and its courts'[6].

Gary North writes, 'the goal of establishing Christ's international kingdom can be presented to citizens of any nation'. He also writes, 'if the Christian church fails to build the visible kingdom by means of biblical law and the power of the gospel, despite the resurrection of Christ and the presence of the Holy Spirit, then what kind of religion are we preaching?'[7]. Notice in these quotes the references to citizens and nations – dominionism is very much a political action plan, attempting to take over the government of countries politically. Pay attention also to the reference to 'biblical law'. Because dominionists believe that the Old Testament law still applies (and must be applied politically) in society today, it is arguable that they hold to the Galatian heresy.

The Postmillennial view holds that Christ will return to earth after the millennium, which is a long period (not necessarily exactly 1000 years) of earthly blessing. Postmillennialism involves a three-step process: (1) The church preaches the gospel throughout the world so that most of the world will be Christianised, although not completely saved, (2) this ushers in the golden age of the millennium with its promised blessing for this earth, after which, (3) Christ shall return, raise the dead, and judge the world.

Kenneth Gentry defines post-millennialism as follows:

> Postmillennialism expects the proclaiming of the Spirit-blessed gospel of Jesus Christ to win the vast majority of human beings to salvation in the present age. Increasing gospel success will gradually produce a time in history prior to Christ's return in which faith, righteousness, peace, and prosperity will prevail in the affairs of people and of nations. After an extensive era of such conditions the Lord will return visibly, bodily, and in great glory, ending history with the general resurrection and the great judgement of all humankind'[8].

---

[5] David Chilton, *Paradise Restored: an Eschatology of Dominion*, Tyler, TX: Reconstruction Press, 1985, p12

[6] R. J. Rushdoony, "Government and the Christian", *The Rutherford Institute*, July-August 1984, p7

[7] quoted from H. Wayne House and Thomas Ice, *Dominion Theology: Blessing or Curse?* Portland, OR: Multnomah, 1988, pp409-11

[8] Kenneth L. Gentry Jr., "Postmillennialism" in *Three Views on the Millennium and Beyond*, Grand Rapids: Zondervan, 1999, p13-14

Lorraine Boettner gives the following explanation of postmillennialism:

> We have defined Postmillennialism as that view of the last things which holds that the kingdom of God is now being extended in the world through the preaching of the Gospel and the saving work of the Holy Spirit in the hearts of individuals, that the world eventually is to be Christianized, and that the return of Christ is to occur at the close of a long period of righteousness and peace commonly called the 'Millennium.' ... The Millennium to which the Postmillennialist looks forward is thus a golden age of spiritual prosperity during this present dispensation, that is, during the Church age, and is to be brought about through forces now active in the world. It is an indefinitely long period of time, perhaps much longer than a literal one thousand years. The changed character of individuals will be reflected in an uplifted social, economic, political and cultural life of mankind. ... This does not mean that there ever will be a time on this earth when every person will be a Christian, or that all sin will be abolished. But it does mean that evil in all its many forms eventually will be reduced to negligible proportions, that Christian principles will be the rule, not the exception, and that Christ will return to a truly Christianized world[9].

Arguments for Postmillennialism

Postmillennialists have four main arguments that support their view:

1. The Power of the Gospel

In Matthew 28:18, Christ assured us that 'all authority in heaven and earth is given to me'. Seeing Christ empowers the gospel message, and Christ's presence is among His people who are preaching it, the gospel must ultimately prevail. Similarly, in Romans 1:16 we read, 'the gospel is the power of God'. Because of this, the Gospel message must triumph (rather than be a failure). Again, Matthew 24:14 says, 'this gospel of the kingdom will be preached in all the world as a witness to all the nations, and then the end will come'. This points again to the spread and triumph of the gospel message.

It is true that Christ's power and presence will enable His church to preach the gospel in all the world, and the power of the Gospel will result in conversions from 'every tribe and tongue and people and nation' (Revelation 5:9). But we are given no assurance in the New Testament

---

[9] Loraine Boettner, *The Millennium*, Philadelphia: Presbyterian and Reformed, 1966, p14

that all the world will be Christianised. In fact, some passages suggest that there are only few who will be saved (Matthew 7:13-14). Again, while it is true that 'this gospel of the kingdom will be preached in all the world as a witness to all the nations, and then the end will come' (Matthew 24:14), this does not assure us that all the world will believe it; rather, it will provide a witness to all nations.

George Müller wrote:

> the notion entertained by many godly, excellent persons, that the world will be converted during the present dispensation by the preaching of the gospel, and that the millennium will thus finally be introduced is not according to the Holy Scriptures. The Gospel, indeed, was to be preached 'as a *testimony* to all nations', but it was not to be the means of the *conversion* of the world (Matt. 24:14). Moreover, from Acts 15:14 we learn that the character of the present dispensation, which is, that God takes out from among the Gentiles a people for His name, but does not convert all nations. This is confirmed by the parable of the wheat and the tares; for if the whole world were to be converted before the return of the Lord Jesus, there would be no truth in the explanation given of it by our Lord Himself. He tells us that the tares (the children of the wicked one) were to grow together with the wheat (the children of the kingdom) until the end of the age, namely up to the time of His own return[10].

2. The Persuasiveness of the Gospel

Postmillennialists accept Old Testament passages that speak of a glorious future on earth, but argue that these conditions will come through gospel persuasion, not by Divine intervention at Christ's return. Regarding the nations streaming up to Zion in Isaiah 2, Gentry writes, 'political force does not compel them; rather the grace of God constrains them'; 'He will not accomplish this catastrophically by external political imposition, but gradually by internal personal transformation'[11].

However, in the book of Revelation, we see that the Millennium is not brought in by the preaching of the Gospel, but by the terrible judgments of the tribulation period where God pours out His wrath upon an unbelieving world. Isaiah 2 does not tell us whether the 'millennial' conditions described are imposed by Christ's return or by the persuasive power of the gospel, but other prophets describe the same millennial

---

[10] George Müller, *The Second Coming of Christ*, Bristol Bible and Tract Depot, 1881
[11] Gentry, "Postmillennialism", in *Three Views on the Millennium and Beyond*, p37, 42

conditions, and immediately prior to such conditions tell of God's great judgment falling upon the world. Thus, Joel, prior to his 'millennial' passage in 3:17-21 says in verses 14-16, 'Multitudes, multitudes in the valley of decision! For the day of the LORD is near in the valley of decision. The sun and moon will grow dark, and the stars will diminish their brightness. The LORD also will roar from Zion, and utter His voice from Jerusalem; the heavens and earth will shake' (3:14-21). Zephaniah also describes the terrible Day of the LORD before paradise on earth: 'My determination is to gather the nations to my assembly of nations, to pour on them My indignation, all My fierce anger (3:8). Amos, prior to his 'millennial' passage in 9:11-15, says, 'Surely I will command and will sift the house of Israel among all nations, as grain is sifted in a sieve ... all the sinners of My people shall die by the sword' (9:9-10).

3. The Parables of Christ
Christ's parable of the sower speaks of the good seed bearing fruit - some a hundred-fold, some sixty, some thirty (Matt. 13:8, 23). Postmillennialists argue that this teaches the growth and spread of God's kingdom.

Christ's parable of the mustard seed describes the kingdom of God as a very small seed that grows until it becomes 'greater than all herbs, and becomes a tree, so that the birds of the air come and nest in its branches' (Matt. 13:31-32). Postmillennialists argue that this teaches that God's kingdom will grow spectacularly till it dominates all other kingdoms on earth. Gentry writes, 'The imagery relates something magnificent beyond comprehension ... [teaching] the dominance of Christ's kingdom'[12].

Similarly, Christ's parable of the leaven also describes yeast that grows and infiltrates the three measures of meal 'until all is leavened' (Matt 13:33). This parable is again about the kingdom of heaven, and it is argued that this pictures the steady growth of the Christian church, infiltrating and spreading the gospel throughout the world. Postmillennialists therefore believe that Christ taught the increasing Christianisation of the world through the spread of the gospel message.

However, these are not the only parables Christ told. Christ's parable of the Wheat and the Tares teaches that false-disciples will co-exist alongside true followers of Christ, seemingly in similar proportions, till the end (Matt. 13:24-30). He also told the parable of the Dragnet, the wicked and the righteous both being gathered in abundance by the net, and

---

[12] Gentry, "Postmillennialism", in *Three Views on the Millennium*, p39-40

separated at the judgment at the end of the age (Matt. 13:47-50). Christ also told the parable of the Wise and Foolish Virgins, which shows that at Christ's coming the true believer and the false professor will be found in equal numbers (Matt. 25.1-13). J. C. Ryle preached from the parable of the Wise and Foolish Virgins the following truth:

> the visible Church of Christ will always be a mixed body, until Christ comes again ... I there see wise and foolish virgins mingled together in one company - virgins with oil, and virgins with no oil, side by side. And I see this state of things going on until the very moment the Bridegroom appears... I frankly say, that I can find no standing ground for the common opinion that the visible Church will gradually advance to a state of perfection - that it will become better and better, holier and holier, up to the very end - and that little by little the whole body shall become full of light. I see no warrant in Scripture for believing that sin will gradually dwindle away in the earth, consume, melt, and disappear by inches, like the last snow-drift in spring... I know that thousands think in this way. All I can say is, that I cannot see it in God's Word[13].

Furthermore, the parables that the postmillennialist points to for proof are far from conclusive. The parables of the mustard seed and the leaven are not directly explained by Christ in the gospels. For the postmillennialist to claim that the true interpretation of these parables is the spread of the gospel throughout the world is to merely offer a biblically unsubstantiated opinion. In fact, leaven is repeatedly used elsewhere in the Bible (without any exception, some would argue) as a picture of the spread of evil. One of the most prominent Jewish feasts, the Feast of Unleavened Bread, required the ritual removal of leaven from homes as a pollutant, and no sacrifice to God by fire was allowed to contain leaven. Thus, it is far from certain that the parable of the leaven speaks of the spread of the gospel.

Although the parables are not directly interpreted by the Lord, it is more than coincidence that nearly all of Matthew's kingdom parables are referred to in nearby passages, and here we find the key to their interpretation:

- the parable of the weeds, Matt. 13:24-30, tells the story of how an enemy planted tares (i.e. weeds) alongside the master's wheat, who

---

[13] J. C. Ryle, *Coming Events and Present Duties*, p15-16

tells his servants not to try to pluck up the tares until harvest time, lest the wheat also be damaged. This parable is illustrated two chapters later by Christ's words in Matthew 15:13, 'every plant which My heavenly Father has not planted will be uprooted'. Christ's reference in Matthew 15 to plants (representing those not belonging to the Father) being uprooted shows a clear link to the weeds (i.e. false-professors) being uprooted in the parable in Matthew 13. The reference in Matthew 15 therefore further explains the earlier parable. This passage also shows the way Matthew's gospel works, explaining parables by other nearby statements.

- the parable of the mustard seed (Matt. 13:31-32) is explained by Christ's words in Matthew 17:20, 'if you have faith as a mustard seed, you will say to this mountain, Be cast into the sea and it will move, and nothing will be impossible for you'. Again, there can be no doubt of the connection between this statement and Christ's earlier parable.
- the parable of the leaven (Matt. 13:33) is interpreted by Christ's words three chapters later: 'beware of the leaven of the Pharisees and Sadducees' (Matt. 16:6, 11 and 12). These are the only references to leaven in Matthew's gospel, and the connection between the references are as close and clear as between the references to plants and mustard seed.

The mustard seed therefore seems to positively picture the dynamic power of faith, while the leaven/yeast pictures the spread of corruption. These parables present a mixed picture of both growth and corruption during this church age. We see this in the amazing way that the gospel spread in the first few centuries, conquering the Roman Empire, but we also observe the depths of spiritual corruption in the Roman Catholic Church that replaced the Roman Empire. Even the parable of the spectacular growth of the mustard seed contains a cautionary note: while postmillennialists like Gentry say that 'the imagery relates something magnificent beyond comprehension', the mustard tree is only three metres tall and, by comparison with other trees the Bible uses to picture a magnificent empire (the massive cedars of Lebanon, Isa. 10:33-34, Ezek. 31:3, Dan. 4:10) it presents a rather pathetic image of grandeur, just like the Roman Catholic Church's attempt to be a political world-power. Thus, there is no certain evidence of post-millennialism in Christ's parables.

4. Progress in History
Postmillennialists have historically been optimistic and confident that the

church will bring in the millennium of peace and righteousness during times of successful missionary advances. They confidently look forward to an end-times revival, trusting in God's Spirit's work.

However, postmillennialism underplays the important New Testament emphasis upon apostasy in the church. The later New Testament epistles point to the fact that in the 'last days perilous times will come' (2 Tim. 3:1), 'in the latter times some will depart from the faith, giving heed to deceiving spirits and doctrines of demons' (1 Tim. 4:1), that there will be widespread and growing sinfulness in the world, and spiritual decline and heresy in the Church. The description of the corruption of Christianity in the letters of 2 Peter and Jude makes for particularly bleak and unpleasant reading.

Two Problems with Post-millennialism

The first major problem with postmillennialism is that it pushes the Lord's coming off into the remote future. In the postmillennial scheme, the church's mission of preaching the gospel will eventually produce millennial conditions upon earth. Whether this millennium lasts 1000 years or is symbolic of a long but unspecified period of time (as most post-millennialists hold), it is not until this millennium is over that Christ returns. Thus, there are at least a thousand years (or more) until Christ comes.

By contrast, the New Testament teaches that 'the coming of the Lord is at hand' (James 5:8). Thus, postmillennialism undermines the New Testament emphasis on the imminent return of Christ and His command to watchfulness. Other New Testament references to the nearness of Christ's coming include Romans 8:23, 25, 1 Corinthians 1:7, 13:11-12; 16:22, Galatians 5:5, Philippians 3:20, 4:5; 1 Thessalonians 1:10, 4:17, 1 Timothy 6:14, Titus 2:13, Hebrews 9:28, 1 Peter 4:7; 2 Peter 1:19, 1 John 2:18; Revelation 1:3 and 22:20. The result is that postmillennialism robs the church of the hope of the soon return of Christ, and denies the New Testament teaching of the necessity of Christian watchfulness.

The second problem with postmillennialism it that it uses an overly-spiritualising approach to interpret Scripture. Take, for example, the post-millennialist Bible scholar B. B. Warfield's explanation of Revelation 19:11ff. with its description of Christ's return as a symbolic vision of the victorious preaching of the gospel throughout the entire present age.

> The section opens with a vision of the victory of the Word of God, the King of Kings and Lord of Lords over all His enemies. We see Him

come forth from heaven girt for war, followed by the armies of heaven.
... The thing symbolized is obviously the complete victory of the Son
of God over all the hosts of wickedness. ... The conquest is wrought
by the spoken word---in short, by the preaching of the gospel. ...
What we have here, in effect, is a picture of the whole period between
the first and second advents, seen from the point of view of heaven. It
is the period of advancing victory of the Son of God over the world...
. As emphatically as Paul, John teaches that the earthly history of the
Church is not a history merely of conflict with evil, but of conquest
over evil: and even more richly than Paul, John teaches that this
conquest will be decisive and complete. The whole meaning of the
vision of Revelation 19:11-21 is that Jesus Christ comes forth not to
war merely but to victory; and every detail of the picture is laid in with
a view precisely to emphasizing the thoroughness of this victory. The
Gospel of Christ is, John being witness, completely to conquer the
world. ... A progressively advancing conquest of the earth by Christ's
gospel implies a coming age deserving at least the relative name of
'golden'[14].

To maintain this interpretation, Warfield must spiritualize certain details in the passage while selectively ignoring others that do not fit his narrative. Thus, Warfield does not explain what the birds feasting on the dead bodies of kings and soldiers after Armageddon means, nor does he explain what it means that Christ 'treads the winepress of the fierceness and wrath of Almighty God' (19:15), nor does he explain what it means for the Beast and the False prophet to be captured and cast alive into the lake of fire (19:20). This interpretation is astonishing for its brazen subversion of the obvious meaning of the text. It represents the imposition of an artificial and alien narrative upon a passage of Scripture unable to bear it, and we can only marvel that such a great scholar should hold such a bizarre interpretation. Warfield's own words about the book of Revelation apply: 'It cannot be denied that the unlettered Christians who have gone to the book for comfort and strength amid dark days have understood it better than the scholars'[15].

For another example, Gentry writes about Isaiah 2: "'Judah" and "Jerusalem" represent the whole of the people of God, just as "Israel" and

---

[14] B.B. Warfield, "The Millennium and the Apocalypse," in *Biblical Doctrines*, New York: Oxford University Press, 1929, pp. 647-648, 662

[15] B. B. Warfield, "The Apocalypse" in *Selected Shorter Writings*, Ed. John Meeter, Phillipsburg, NJ: Presbyterian and Reformed, 1973, Vol. 2, p653

"Judah" do in Jeremiah 31:31, where the new covenant specifically applies to the international church in the New Testament … The references to the "mountain", the "house of the God of Jacob", and "Zion" refer to the church'[16]. However, as we have seen, such an interpretation of Isaiah 2 is untenable: the church has not brought peace to the nations or the end of the manufacture of armaments (Isaiah 2:4), nor is it consistent to apply the blessings of Isaiah 2:1-4 to the church but leave the curses of Isaiah 3 for earthly Israel. There is no real reason why Isaiah would have meant us to take terms like Judah or Jacob to refer to the international church, nor is there any hint of a progressive spread of God's truth worldwide in Isaiah 2.

To quote John Macarthur, postmillennialism and amillennialism involve:

> interpretive negligence … in that they, without biblical warrant, read the New Testament into the Old Testament, resulting in an eschatology that fits a predetermined theology. In so doing, they reinterpret the Old Testament in such a way that no one before the time of Christ would have recognized their conclusions[17].

Conclusion

The optimistic outlook of post-millennialism has its attractions and certain psychological benefits, but there does not seem to be any strong biblical basis for the view. The history of the 20th Century, with its two world wars and increasing atheism, has dealt a heavy blow to the optimism of most post-millennialists. As author Graham Scroggie wrote, 'It were better to be an intelligent pessimist than a blind optimist'[18]. Indeed, most postmillennialists admit that, even on their theory, Revelation 20:7-9 speaks of an outbreak of overwhelming, worldwide, Satanically-inspired opposition to God before Christ's return.

---

[16] Gentry, "Postmillenialism", in *Three Views on the Millennium*, p36
[17] John Macarthur, "Does the New Testament Reject Dispensational Premillennialism", in *Christ's Prophetic Plans*, eds. John Macarthur and Richard Mayhue, Chicago, IL: Moody Publishers, 2012, p161
[18] W. Graham Scroggie, *The Lord's Return*, Pickering and Inglis, n.d., p164

6 PREMILLENNIALISM

The premillennial view holds that Christ returns to earth again (in Revelation 19:11-21) before the millennium, His 1000-year reign (Revelation 20:1-10). The saints will be resurrected to reign with Christ during this millennium over the earth, which will experience paradise conditions. Charles Ryrie defines the premillennial view as follows:

> The millennium is the period of a thousand years of the visible, earthly reign of the Lord Jesus Christ who, after His return from heaven, will fulfil during that period the promises contained in the Abrahamic, Davidic and new covenants to Israel, will bring the whole world to a knowledge of God, and will lift the curse from the whole creation[1].

The History of Premillennialism

The last few centuries have seen a return to the view taught by the Church of the first few centuries. There has been a resurgence of belief in a literal reign of Christ upon the earth for 1000 years after His return. The French Revolution, the Napoleonic Wars, and the social upheavals that followed in European society in the 1800s, along with widespread nominal Christianity in the state churches, prompted many Christians to wonder where the world was heading. Many Christians believe that things are only going to get worse before they get better, and that the Bible teaches that Antichrist and his terrible great tribulation period must come before the return of Christ, and his 1000 year reign.

George Peters, after listing fifteen premillennial advocates from the first century (including various apostles, as claimed by Papias and Irenaeus, as well as Clement of Rome and Polycarp) and another nine second-century premillennial advocates (including Justin Martyr, Irenaeus, and Tertullian), points out that on the other side of the argument, not a single writer or name can be presented who opposed the premillennial view in the first two centuries. Peters concludes:

(1) That the common faith of the Church was Chiliastic (i.e.

---

[1] Charles Ryrie, *The Basis of the Premillennial Faith*, Loizeaux Brothers, 1953, p145-6

premillennial), and (2) that such a generality and unity of belief could only have been introduced ... by the founders of the Christian Church and the Elders appointed by them[2].

Adolf Harnack wrote, 'This doctrine of Christ's second advent, and the kingdom, appears so early that it might be questioned whether it ought not to be regarded as an essential part of the Christian religion'[3].

Papias (c. 60–163 AD), a disciple of the apostle John wrote, 'there will be a millennium after the resurrection of the dead, when the kingdom of Christ will be set up in material form on this earth'[4].

Justin Martyr (100 - 165 AD) wrote, 'for Isaiah spoke thus concerning this period of a thousand years'[5].

Irenaeus (130-202 AD) wrote:

When this Anti-Christ shall have devastated all things in this world, he will reign for three years and six months, and sit in the temple at Jerusalem; and then the Lord will come from heaven in the clouds, in the glory of the Father, sending this man and those who follow him into the lake of fire; but bringing in for the righteous the times of the kingdom, that is, the rest, the hallowed seventh day; and restoring to Abraham the promised inheritance, in which kingdom the Lord declared, that 'many coming from the east and the west should sit down with Abraham, Isaac, and Jacob[6].

The significance of some of these early Christian teachers lies not only in how close in time they were to the apostles, but also in their direct relationships with them. Papias is believed to have been a disciple of the apostle John, while Irenaeus was a disciple of Polycarp, who was a disciple of the apostle John. In addition, another notable fact about these teachers was their biblicism – they appealed directly and primarily to Scripture in making their arguments for a premillennial view of future events.

Arthur Skevington Wood writes: 'In considering the eschatology of Irenaeus – as indeed his teaching in its entirety – we must begin by taking note of the indisputable fact that he was essentially a biblical theologian. He made no claim to originality. He was content to rely on the Word of

---

[2] G. N. H. Peters, *The Theocratic Kingdom*, Grand Rapids: Kregel, 1952, pp494-496
[3] quoted by L. S. Chafer, *Systematic Theology*, Dallas Seminary Press, 1947, IV, p277
[4] Eusebius, *Ecclesiastical History*, 39:11-12
[5] Justin Martyr, *Dialogue with Trypho*, Ante-Nicene Fathers, 80, 1:239
[6] Irenaeus, *Against Heresies*, Book V, chap 30, para 4

God'[7]. There are good grounds for believing, therefore, that Papias, Irenaeus and other early post-apostolic church teachers were transmitting the biblical truth that the apostles taught on this matter.

The earliest opponents of the premillennial view (like the gnostic heretic Gaius) did so by casting doubt on the divine inspiration of the book of Revelation and by teaching the inherent evil of all things material (so any future earthly kingdom must be 'carnal' and sinful). Later, others (like Clement of Alexandria and Origen in Egypt) argued against it under the influence of Greek (Platonic) philosophy which adopted a mystical and allegorical interpretation of Scripture, not only out of embarrassment at certain things in the Bible, but out of a desire to make Christianity more palatable and compatible with Greek philosophy. None of these reasons have about them the nobility of faith. Of amillennialism we may say, with Pentecost, 'It was not the child of orthodoxy, but of heterodoxy'[8].

Walvoord writes of how the premillennialism of the post-apostolic period was eclipsed by amillennialism:

> The importance of Augustine to the history of amillennialism is derived from two reasons. First, there were no acceptable exponents of amillennialism before Augustine ... Prior to Augustine, amillennialism was associated with the heresies produced by the allegorizing and spiritualising school of theology at Alexandria, which not only opposed premillennialism, but subverted any literal exegesis of Scripture whatever[9].

Augustine's work *The City of God* not only advocated a present-day millennium, but also identified this kingdom of God with the Catholic church. Thus amillennialism suited the rising power of the Roman church, and amillennialism became the official doctrine of Roman Catholicism, as it is to this day. The Roman Catholic church saw its riches, power, indulgence and luxury as a fulfilment of the promised golden age foretold by the prophets, and thus the amillennial view not only replaced premillennialism but became more entrenched as the church sunk further into the mire of the Roman Catholic 'dark ages'.

Farrar writes of this period:

---

[7] A. Skevington Wood, "The Eschatology of Irenaeus", *The Evangelical Quarterly* 41.1 (Jan.-Mar. 1969), pp30-41
[8] Pentecost, *Things to Come*, p24
[9] Walvoord, "The Millennial Issue in Modern Theology", *Bibliotheca Sacra*, 106: p420-1

during the Dark Ages, from the seventh to the twelfth century, and during the scholastic epoch, from the twelfth to the sixteenth, there are but few of the many who toiled in this field who add a single essential principle, or furnished a single original contribution to the explanation of the Word of God[10].

Furthermore, the Roman Catholic church's allegorical approach to interpretation meant that only those specially trained in its dogmatic mysticism were permitted to read God's Word; ordinary people were told they could not understand the oracles of God, and were discouraged from reading it. The return to more literal interpretation by the reformers laid the foundation for the resurgence of premillennialism in the centuries after the Reformation.

Dwight Pentecost writes:

While the Reformers did not adopt the premillennial interpretation of the Scriptures, without exception they did return to the literal method of interpreting the Scriptures, which is the essential basis on which premillennialism rests. The logical application of this method of interpretation soon led many of the post-reformation writers to this position .... There emerged a stream of exegetes and expositors that brought premillennialism back to a place of prominence in Biblical interpretation. Among them will be found the greatest exegetes and expositors that the church has known, such as Bengel, Steir, Alford, Lange, Meyer, Fausset, Keach, Bonar, Ryle, Lillie, MacIntosh, Newton, Tregelles, Ellicott, Lightfoot, Westcott, Darby, to mention only a few. The statement of Alford, in speaking of the interpreters of the Apocalypse since the French Revolution, is pertinent: "The majority, both in number, learning and research, adopt the Premillennial Advent, following the plain and undeniable sense of the sacred text"[11].

Arguments for Premillennialism

Premillennialism takes a straightforward view of many Old Testament prophecies of a future paradise on earth, and argues that these are neither fulfilled in the present church age, nor do they apply to the eternal state. Premillennialists argue that God is not going to write off His physical creation, but that this world will be delivered from the curse and enjoy

---

[10] Farrar, *History of Interpretation*, New York: E. P. Dutton and Co., 1886, p245
[11] Pentecost, *Things to Come*, p390-1

redemption too (Rom. 8:19-22).

Premillennialism also argues that Old Testament promises of a glorious future for the nation of Israel with be fulfilled during this millennial period; God will not abandon his promises to, and purposes for, Israel, which will be fulfilled. These will not only result in the blessing of Israel itself (Romans 11:1-2, 11-12, 26-29), but of all the nations.

The premillennial view is based on a straightforward, consecutive reading of Revelation, with the events of chapter 20 following chapter 19 – Christ's reign follows His return. The premillennial view holds that there are two battles, one in chapter 19, and one in chapter 20, separated by the 1000 years. The premillennial view is that there are also two resurrections, with the millennium intervening in between, not a spiritual resurrection followed by a literal resurrection.

We may summarise the arguments for premillennialism under three headings:

1. Interpretational Consistency
The difference between the three millennial views is often said to be one of interpretation – the premillennial view adopts a more literal view of Scripture than the amillennial or postmillennial views. However, this is not the real issue: all three views agree that some things in the Bible are not meant to be taken literally.

Instead, the real difference is that the premillennial view adopts a more consistent approach to interpreting the Bible. The key issue is consistency, whether symbolic or literal. If we are not able to carry through a policy of interpretation consistently, we are guilty of hermeneutical double-standards. Here we will look at two examples of hermeneutical inconsistency involved in amillennial and postmillennial attempts to apply Old Testament prophetic passages about Israel to the church.

Take the well-known prophecy in Zechariah:

Rejoice greatly, O daughter of Zion! Shout, O daughter of Jerusalem! Behold, your King is coming to you; He is just and having salvation, lowly and riding on a donkey, a colt, the foal of a donkey. I will cut off the chariot from Ephraim and the horse from Jerusalem; the battle bow shall be cut off. He shall speak peace to the nations; His dominion shall be from sea to sea, and from the River to the ends of the earth (Zech. 9:9-10).

The first verse here is interpreted literally by all Christian expositors because the event it foretells literally happened: Christ rode into Jerusalem on a donkey. But if we take verse 9 literally, should we not also take verse 10 literally with its promise that the coming King will bring peace to the whole earth ('from the River to the ends of the earth') so that there are no longer any weapons of warfare (chariots, battle bows, etc)? It is hard to see how else we can consistently interpret the passage.

Eric Sauer writes:

> The expectation of a visible kingdom of God on the theatre of this earth is evident in the Old and New Testaments. In a hundred places it is the subject. To "spiritualize" them all is contrary to accurate exegesis. The promises of the first coming of Christ were fulfilled literally. Christ came literally from Bethlehem (Mic 5:2), rode literally on a donkey into Jerusalem (Zech. 9:9), was literally betrayed for thirty pieces of silver (Zech. 11:12), and on the cross was literally pierced in hands and feet (Psa. 22:16). They literally cast lots for His garments (Psa. 22:18), literally His bones were not broken (Psa. 34:20) and literally His side was pierced by a spear (Zech. 12:10).
>
> Combined with these prophecies of the first coming, there often stand in the very same sentence prophecies of the second coming, and by the plain meaning of the words, and by their later fulfillment in the life of Jesus of Nazareth, it is evident that the first part of such sentences is to be taken literally. Who therefore can justify the taking merely "spiritually" of the second part of one and the same sentence (e.g. Luke 1:31-33)? Who gives us the right to take Jews to mean Christians, Jerusalem to mean now only the church, and Canaan heaven? No, the "spiritualizing" of these promises of the Messianic kingdom, and a transference of them to some other corporate system, were nothing else than a veiled breach of covenant by God as regards Israel. But this is impossible[12].

For a second example, consider Micah 4:1-2, where we have the famous prophecy (also found in his contemporary, Isaiah, in chapter 2):

> Now it shall come to pass in the latter days that the mountain of the LORD'S house shall be established on the top of the mountains, and shall be exalted above the hills; and peoples shall flow to it. Many nations shall come and say, "Come, and let us go up to the mountain

---

[12] Eric Sauer, *From Eternity to Eternity*, Paternoster, 1994

of the LORD, to the house of the God of Jacob; He will teach us His ways, and we shall walk in His paths." For out of Zion the law shall go forth, and the word of the LORD from Jerusalem (Micah 4:1-2).

Both postmillennialist and amillennialist expositors celebrate this prophecy as a reference to the gospel being preached to all the nations in the present church age. They argue that because the church is the fulfilment of Old Testament prophecies originally made to Israel, therefore the references to Zion, Jacob and Jerusalem in this prophecy must be taken spiritually to refer to the church.

However, if we look at the verse immediately before this prophecy (Micah 3:12), we read, 'Therefore because of you Zion shall be plowed like a field, Jerusalem shall become heaps of ruins, and the mountain of the temple like the bare hills of the forest'. Here, the prophet Micah confronts the Jews with their sins and foretells God's coming judgment. In Micah 3:1-11 (the verses before this) we read of the Jews 'who build up Zion with bloodshed and Jerusalem with iniquity: her heads judge for a bribe, her priests teach for pay, and her prophets divine for money. Yet they lean on the LORD, and say, "Is not the LORD among us? No harm can come upon us"'.

These verses in Micah 3 are taken literally, and applied to Israel by all expositors, and for good reasons: not only is it difficult to understand the idea of the true 'church' being built up by iniquity, bloodshed and bribery, but crucially this passage in Micah 3:12 is quoted in the book of Jeremiah as prophesying a literal destruction of Jerusalem (see Jer. 26:18). Bearing in mind that there were no chapter divisions in the Bible originally, the problem that confronts us is how we should interpret the words Jerusalem and Zion in two consecutive verses. In one verse, Micah 3:12 prophesies the destruction of Jerusalem, while in the next verses, Micah 4:1-2, he prophesies Jerusalem the centre of worldwide worship of God.

The amillennialist and postmillennialist interpreters take the first reference (3:12) to Jerusalem literally and then in the next verse (4:1) take them spiritually to refer to the church. However, we cannot just rip one verse about Israel out of its context, spiritualise it to refer to the church, and ignore how the words Jerusalem and Zion are used in the immediately preceding verses. Such a method of interpretation is illegitimate.

If we continue reading down the passage, not only do we come to the prophecy of worldwide peace (as in Isaiah 2:4), 'They shall beat their swords into plowshares, and their spears into pruning hooks' etc., (Micah 4:3), a prophecy that cannot be said to have been fulfilled in the church, but in Micah 4:7-8, we also read:

> So the LORD will reign over them in Mount Zion from now on, even forever. And you, O tower of the flock, the stronghold of the daughter of Zion, to you shall it come, even the former dominion shall come, the kingdom of the daughter of Jerusalem.

Here in 4:7-8 the prophet Micah foretells that the former dominion of Jerusalem over the nations will return in a future day. David's kingdom will be re-established and the Lord Himself will reign from Jerusalem over the earth. Attempts to interpret this dominion spiritually are difficult, because the expression 'the former dominion' refers quite clearly to the Jewish kingdom of Old Testament days being re-established. It is difficult to understand this prophecy as foretelling some sort of 'spiritualised' church dominion, for the church never enjoyed any 'former dominion' in Old Testament days.

It is the inconsistency of the selective method of spiritualisation that undermines any confidence in it as a legitimate approach to reading God's Word. We cannot take one verse literally, but then the next verse spiritually, when the same words are used in both. This is the problem of hermeneutical inconsistency that plagues the spiritualising approach.

William Tyndale, the great reformer and Bible translator wrote:

> Thou shalt understand, therefore, that the Scripture hath but one sense, which is the literal sense. And that literal sense is the root and ground of all, and the anchor that never faileth, whereunto if thou cleave, thou canst never err or go out of the way. And if thou leave the literal sense, thou canst not but go out of the way. Neverthelater, the Scripture useth proverbs, similitudes, riddles, or allegories, as all other speeches do; but that which the proverb, similitude, riddle or allegory signifieth, is over the literal sense, which thou must seek out diligently[13].

By contrast, a spiritualising approach is not only more difficult to maintain, but it also leads to nonsense. Dean Farrar wrote:

> The exegesis of St. Augustine is marked by the most glaring defects ... Snatching up the Old Philonian and Rabbinic rule which had been

---

[13] quoted by C. A. Briggs, *General Introduction to the Study of Holy Scripture*, C. Scribner's Sons, 1899, p456-7

repeated for so many generations, that everything in Scripture which appeared to be unorthodox or immoral must be interpreted mystically, he introduced confusion into his dogma of supernatural inspiration by admitting that there are many passages "written by the Holy Ghost", which are objectionable when taken in their obvious sense. He also opened the door to arbitrary fancy[14]

Here are some more examples of the nonsense generated by the spiritualizing method by Augustine. He interprets the Garden of Eden in an allegorical fashion, saying that no one may deny that the garden of Eden signifies the life of the blessed, the four rivers of paradise are the four virtues – prudence, fortitude, temperance and justice – and the trees and their fruit are useful knowledge and godly behaviour. Alternately, Augustine suggests that the garden of Eden means the Church, so that the four rivers are the four gospels, the fruit trees are the saints, the fruit their works, and the tree of life is the holy of holies – Christ Himself[15]. Augustine is just making it up as he goes along, and he shows that the spiritualising method makes the Bible say anything we please.

Although there are some figurative expressions in the Bible that we must beware of swallowing literally, yet there is far more danger of trying to avoid the plain meaning of Scripture by mystical allegorising and spiritualising of it.

The premillennial approach is a far more normal and straight-forward way to interpret both the Old Testament prophets and Revelation 20. By comparison with the plain and simple approach of the premillennial view, the spiritualising approach to reading Revelation 20 is at certain points absurd (e.g. people being spiritually born again after being beheaded for their testimony to Christ, Rev. 20:4), as well as counter-factual (the idea that Satan is bound in our present age is hard to reconcile with the multitudes in darkness today).

The burden of proof lies with those who take Revelation 20 to mean something other than it appears on a natural and straight-forward reading. To put it another way, those who adopt an abnormal understanding of the words of Revelation 20 need to not only provide strong reasons for their view, but to also eliminate as impossible (or unlikely) the ordinary plain meaning of the passage. The Christian who trembles at God's Word is advised to take the far safer, faithful and humble approach of accepting what God's Word states plainly and simply, without trying to re-interpret

---

[14] Farrar, *History of Interpretation*, p236-7
[15] Augustine, *City of God*, Book 13, chap. 21

it to fit in with some complex theological or eschatological theory.

2. Christ's Own Teaching is Premillennial

Here we shall look at five verses which show that the Lord Jesus Himself taught a premillennial view:

In Matthew 19:28, we read Christ saying to His disciples, 'Assuredly I say to you, that in the regeneration, when the Son of Man sits on the throne of His glory, you who have followed Me will also sit on twelve thrones, judging the twelve tribes of Israel'. Christ sitting on the throne of His glory has not yet happened, for (as we will shortly see) Matthew 25 tells us it happens at the time of Christ's return in glory. It is here said to be accompanied by the 'regeneration', which means the 'new birth', not of the individual, but of the whole world, the 'restoration of all things' as Peter says in Acts 3:21, or (as Paul says) the 'creation itself will be delivered from the bondage of corruption into the glorious liberty of the children of God' (Rom. 8:21). Furthermore, the disciples are told that when Christ comes and reigns, they will also reign with Him, for 'judging the twelve tribes of Israel' here refers to dispensing justice and administering Christ's kingdom, just as Paul mentions in 1 Cor. 6:2, 'the saints will judge the world', and as Rev. 20:4 says, 'I saw thrones and they sat on them and judgment was committed to them'. Notice that both of the events Paul refers to – the creation being reborn and the saints judging – are put in the future tense, indicating that they were still yet to come in Paul's day. It is very difficult to take the verses we are considering as having been fulfilled in the past or present, and so we conclude that the kingdom reign of our Lord Jesus with His apostles on the earth is still in the future, and occurs after He returns. Christ's return is premillennial.

In Matthew 25:31-32 we read, 'When the Son of Man comes in His glory, and all the holy angels with Him, then He will sit on the throne of His glory. All the nations will be gathered before Him, and He will separate them one from another, as a shepherd separates his sheep from the goats'. Christ here speaks of three things: His coming in glory, His judgment of the nations, and His sitting on the throne of His glory. Christ coming in His glory refers to His second coming, while sitting upon the throne of His glory is another way of speaking about His kingdom reign. From this passage therefore we may conclude that Christ's reign here spoken of has not yet happened, for Christ has not come in glory with His holy angels, nor has He judged the nations, and separated the sheep from the goats. We read in verse 41 that the goats are cast into the lake of fire, which has not yet happened. It is impossible to argue that this is presently happening or has happened in the past. Therefore, Christ's kingdom is yet future, and this passage says it will occur after His return. Christ's coming is again premillennial.

In Matthew 23:37-39, we read Christ saying:

> O Jerusalem, Jerusalem, the one who kills the prophets and stones those who are sent to her! How often I wanted to gather your children together, as a hen gathers her chicks under her wings, but you were not willing! [38] See! Your house is left to you desolate; [39] for I say to you, you shall see Me no more till you say, "Blessed is He who comes in the name of the LORD!'".

In this passage, Christ promised that the nation of Israel would not always reject its true Messiah. Instead, the time would come for Israel's restoration, spiritually and nationally, and Christ states that this will not happen until His coming again.

The key word 'till' in verse 39 shows that Israel's national restoration:

(a) will definitely happen,
(b) will not happen gradually, but instantly
(c) does not happen during this church age, but
(d) happens at the coming of the Lord.

This again argues against postmillennialism which says that Israel will repent '1000 years' before Christ returns. Instead, Israel's restoration happens at Christ's return, at the dawn of the next, millennial age. Amillennialism is also disproven by this verse, for amillennialism says that there is no national restoration of Israel, and that Israel's promises have been spiritually fulfilled and appropriated by the church. Seeing Israel is converted at Christ's return, this passage also disproves historic premillennialism. In short, it teaches dispensational premillennialism.

In Matthew 26:29, at His institution of the Lord's Supper, Christ told His disciples, 'I say to you, I will not drink of this fruit of the vine from now on until that day when I drink it new with you in My Father's Kingdom' (see also Mark 14:25). Not only does this verse prove that the wine used at the Lord's Supper had not turned into blood (but remained wine, denying the doctrine of transubstantiation); it also teaches that Jesus expected an earthly, physical and tangible kingdom in the future. He tells His disciples that He looks forward to drinking wine with them in His future kingdom reign. This would not be expected to occur in heaven; it more naturally occurs on earth. The Lord's Supper is therefore a foretaste of fellowship with Christ in His Kingdom. Similarly, Luke's Gospel in its account of the institution of the Supper specifies that this 'drinking of the wine' in the future occurs when the kingdom of God comes, for Christ says, 'I say to you, I will not drink of the fruit of the vine until the kingdom of God comes' (Luke 22:18). Paul, in his record of the institution of the Lord's Supper, tells us that this will happen at the Lord's coming: we 'proclaim the Lord's death until He comes' (1 Cor. 11:26), indicating that Christians are to continue observing the Lord's Supper as a foretaste of the Kingdom until the Lord Himself comes. Thus, by putting these three verses together, we see that the kingdom of God is still in the future, it will be earthly not heavenly, and it will happen at the Lord's coming (1 Cor. 11:26). Christ's coming is therefore premillennial.

In Luke 19:11-27 Christ told a parable about His return because people 'thought the kingdom of God would appear immediately'. In verse 12, Christ likened Himself to a nobleman who went into a far country to receive a kingdom and would return later. In the meantime, he called ten of his servants and gave them a sum of money each, telling them to "do business till I come". These verses teach that the kingdom of God has a future aspect that has not yet been fulfilled and will not be realised until Christ's return. An exact parallel of this situation occurred 30 years before Jesus in the case of Archelaus, Herod the Great's son, who went to Rome after his father Herod's death to claim his father's crown. The Jews sent a delegation after him saying they didn't want Archelaus to be their new king. The very same words are used in Christ's parable: 'his citizens hated him and sent a delegation after him, saying, "We will not have this man to reign over us" (v14). Nevertheless, Rome granted the kingdom to Archelaus. In the same way, Jesus has gone back to his Father to receive a Kingdom and one day He will return to reign over it. This teaches us that the kingdom is not some heavenly realm. The kingdom of God will be established here on earth where Jesus will reign when he returns as King. Furthermore, the servants who traded with their Lord's money and made a profit were rewarded at their master's return by being given positions of authority in the kingdom: "Well done, good servant; because you were faithful in a very little, have authority over ten cities" (Luke 19:17). The fact that the rewards at the Lord's coming involve earthly authority again strongly suggests that Christ's return is premillennial, and that His kingdom will be established on this same earth under conditions similar to those which now exist, i.e. cities needing governors and administrators. This suggests the very opposite of the idea that at Christ's return we are ushered into the eternal state in an altogether different type of existence. In addition, as we saw in Mt 19:28, what Christ says here aligns with His disciples ruling over the 12 tribes of Israel.

In Acts 1:6, the disciples asked, 'Lord, will You at this time restore the kingdom to Israel?' Calvin commented: 'There are as many errors in this question as words. They ask him as concerning a kingdom; but they dream of an earthly kingdom, which should flow with riches, with dainties, with external peace, and with such like good things'.

However, in His reply, Christ did not deny the possibility of the restoration of the kingdom to Israel. Instead, He said, 'It is not for you to know the times or seasons which the Father has put in His own power' (Acts 1:7).

Campbell Morgan writes:

Christ rebuked, not their conception that the kingdom is to be restored to Israel – for that he never rebuked – but their desire to know when it would take place ... A popular interpretation of this is that Christ said to them: There is to be no restoration of the kingdom to Israel. Christ did not say so. What he said was: It is not for you to know the times or seasons. You have other work to do[16].

German theologian Eric Sauer states:

He did not rebuke them on account of their "fleshly conceptions" or give a general denial of the coming of the kingdom in a visible sense which they meant, but said only: "It is not for you to know times or seasons, which the Father has retained in his own power" (Acts 1:7) ... Now this very prophetic expression "times or seasons" proves that the kingdom of God will some day be actually set up[17].

The decisive evidence that shows the disciples were not wrong in expecting a future kingdom reign is seen in Acts 3:21, where Peter said about Christ, that 'heaven must receive [Him] until the times of restoration of all things, which God has spoken by the mouth of all His holy prophets since the world began'. If we allow Scripture to interpret Scripture, we notice that Acts 3:21 answers the question of Acts 1:6 (notice the words 'time/times' and 'restore/restoration' are found in both). We are left with little alternative but to conclude that there is a future restoration of the kingdom

---

[16] G. Campbell Morgan, *The Acts of the Apostles*, Glasgow: Pickering and Inglis, 1946, p19
[17] Eric Sauer, *The Triumph of the Crucified*, Exeter: Paternoster, 1964, p147

promised to the nation of Israel. The 'times of the restoration of all things' presumably includes Israel (why should 'all things' exclude Israel?), particularly in view of the fact that Peter was preaching inside the Temple courts in Acts 3 to 'Men of Israel' (3:11).

Michael Vlach points out that Acts 1:3 tells us that after His resurrection Christ was 'speaking about the kingdom of God' with His disciples for 40 days; 'It seems unlikely that the disciples could be misguided in their perceptions of the kingdom after having received 40 days of instruction about it from the risen Lord'. Vlach also notes that the Lord did not correct the disciples in Acts 1:7. This would appear to validate their understanding of Israel's restoration: 'If the disciples had been wrong, Jesus probably would have corrected their misconception as He did on other occasions'[18].

Calvin's comments, 'there are as many errors in this question as words', criticises the apostles of Christ, despite the fact they had personally been taught by Him during the forty days after His resurrection and before His ascension. Calvin does not present any argument refuting the disciples' expectation of a restoration of the kingdom to Israel. Who is more likely to be in error, the apostles of the risen Christ or John Calvin? There are many reasons to think that we are on safer ground to follow the apostles of Christ.

In their preaching and writing, the apostles also spoke of the kingdom of God as still future, echoing Christ's similar teachings (note the future tense and the words 'enter' or 'inherit'):

- We must through many tribulations enter the kingdom of God (Acts 14:22)
- of which [sins] I tell you beforehand, just as I also told you in time past, that those who practice such things will not inherit the kingdom of God. (Gal. 5:21)
- For this you know, that no fornicator, unclean person, nor covetous man, who is an idolater, has any inheritance in the kingdom of Christ and God (Eph. 5:5)
- for so an entrance will be supplied to you abundantly into the everlasting kingdom of our Lord and Saviour Jesus Christ (2 Pet. 1:11)

John Macarthur writes:

---

[18] Michael J. Vlach, *Has the Church Replaced Israel*, B&H Academic, 2010, p191

When considering the New Testament's treatment of the millennial issue, it must be done against the backdrop of first-century Jewish eschatology [i.e. Jewish hopes for a glorious, literal, earthly, future kingdom]. If the New Testament writers rejected the Futuristic Premillennialism that was so prevalent in their day, we would expect them to denounce it clearly and explicitly (just as they did in response to other issues, like the legalism of the Judaizers). A strong, overt condemnation would be necessary in order to overturn the widespread eschatology of Jewish believers based on the common understanding of Old Testament Scripture that had been passed down to them. The fact that no such denunciation exists is highly significant, especially when paired with New Testament passages where the literal interpretation of Old Testament prophecy is upheld[19].

3. Premillennialists believe that Christ's Kingdom will arrive Cataclysmically, not Gradually

Postmillennialists accept Old Testament passages that speak of a glorious future on earth, but argue that these conditions will come gradually through gospel persuasion, not by Divine force at Christ's return. Regarding the nations streaming up to Zion in Isaiah 2 (and hence Micah 4), Gentry, a postmillennialist, writes, 'political force does not compel them; rather the grace of God constrains them'[20]; 'He will not accomplish this catastrophically by external political imposition, but gradually by internal personal transformation'[21]. In the post-millennial scheme, the gospel is going to transform the world.

However, Isaiah 2 does not tell us whether the 'millennial' conditions described are imposed by Christ's return or by the persuasive power of the gospel. Other prophets describe the same millennial conditions, and immediately prior to such conditions they tell of God's great judgment falling upon the world.

- Amos, prior to his 'millennial' passage in 9:11-15 ('the mountains will drip with sweet wine ... I will bring back the captives of My people Israel ... I will plant them in their land'), says, 'Surely I will command and will sift the house of Israel among all nations, as grain is sifted in a sieve ... all the sinners of My people shall die by the sword' (9:9-10).

---

[19] "Does the New Testament Reject Futuristic Premillennialism?", in *Christ's Prophetic Plans*, eds. John Macarthur and Richard Mayhue, Moody, 2012, p164
[20] Gentry, "Postmillennialism", in *Three Views on the Millennium*, p37
[21] Ibid, p42

- Before Obadiah's 'millennial' paradise where 'the captives of this host of the children of Israel shall possess the land of the Canaanites', and 'the kingdom shall be the Lord's' (vs17-21), we read of terrible events in vs 15-16: 'the Day of the Lord upon all nations is near; as you have done, it shall be done to you'.
- Zephaniah describes Armageddon ('My determination is to gather the nations to my assembly of nations, to pour on them My indignation, all My fierce anger', Zeph. 3:8) before he speaks of the coming paradise on earth ('I will leave in your midst a meek and humble people, and they shall trust in the name of the Lord, the remnant of Israel shall do no unrighteousness ... Sing O daughter of Zion ... the King of Israel, the Lord, is in your midst', etc. Zeph. 3:9-20).
- Joel, prior to his 'millennial' passage in 3:17-21' ('you shall know that I am the LORD your God, dwelling in Zion My holy mountain ... the mountains shall drip with new wine ... all the brooks of Judah shall be flooded with water ... for the LORD dwells in Zion') says in verses 14-16, 'Multitudes, multitudes in the valley of decision! For the day of the LORD is near in the valley of decision. The sun and moon will grow dark, and the stars will diminish their brightness. The LORD also will roar from Zion, and utter His voice from Jerusalem; the heavens and earth will shake' (3:14-21).
- Isaiah chapters 24-25 speak also of the terrible judgments of the tribulation period before the establishment of Messiah's kingdom (see Isa. 24:3-5 and 19-20 for tribulation and 25:6, etc. for millennial joy)

All of these Old Testament prophets end on a high note, with Israel enjoying the blessing of God. But all of them foretell terrible judgment coming before this glorious paradise. This teaches that the kingdom reign of God on earth comes after the return of Christ, not before it (as in the amillennial or the postmillennial schemes), because God's judgments upon this world, including Armageddon, come at the end. In other words, all of these prophets are premillennial. Even Allis, an ardent amillennialist writer, admits, 'Old Testament prophecies if literally interpreted cannot be regarded as having been yet fulfilled or as being capable of fulfilment in this present age'[22].

Peters puts it a different way:

---

[22] Oswald T. Allis, *Prophecy and the Church*, Philadelphia: Presbyterian and Reformed, 1945, p238

Premillennialism

If no restoration [of Israel] was intended; if all was to be understood typically, or spiritually, or conditionally, then surely the language was most eminently calculated to deceive the hearers[23].

Seeing we do not believe that God deceives people, we can therefore take His Word for it when we read His Old Testament promises of a future millennial kingdom.

Furthermore, the postmillennial hope of a 'golden age' that is still in the future (before the return of the Lord), and which comes in gradually through the advance of the gospel (as well as science, education, political activism, social justice, etc.) is false. This world is not going to end with a whimper, but with a bang! In the book of Revelation, we see that the millennium is not brought in by the preaching of the Gospel, but by the terrible judgments of the tribulation period where God pours out His wrath upon an unbelieving world. This world is not getting spiritually better, but worse, and is heading for judgment. However, Christ is coming to reign, He will restore all things and give the entire creation its 'rebirth' and liberation. Best of all, He will have the glory.

Problems with Premillennialism

It must not be thought that there are no difficulties with the premillennial view of future events. Here are three problems that we will have to deal with as we proceed further in the book.

1. **A Return to Features of the Old Covenant**. One particularly difficult problem with premillennialism is that it appears to teach that during the millennial period there will be the re-introduction of various features of the Old Testament economy, with the return of Jewish priestly service in a rebuilt earthly Temple, and the reintroduction of animal sacrifices. Various Old Testament passages foretelling the paradise to come speak of these features, notably the description of the temple in Ezekiel 40-47, but also Isaiah 60, Jeremiah 33 and Zechariah 14. Surely, with Christ's death and His fulfilment of the Old Testament's sacrificial system there can be no going back to what were only shadows and pictures? We will consider this problem in more detail later in the book.
2. **Inferences involved in Premillennialism**. Most premillennialists believe in a number of things for which there are no clear biblical

---

[23] G. N. H. Peters, *The Theocratic Kingdom*, Funk and Wagnalls, 1884, book 2, p51

statements. For example, most premillennialists believe that the prophecy of the Seventy Weeks in Daniel 9 has a 'parenthesis' between the 69th week and the 70th week – the church age. This parenthesis means that the 70th week of Daniel's prophecy (the 'tribulation period') is still in the future at the end of time. However, Daniel's prophecy itself nowhere explicitly states that there is a parenthesis in God's program of future events for the world. Similarly, many premillennialists believe that there will be a 'rapture' of the church (1 Thess. 4:16-17) before the 70th week of Daniel's prophecy – a pre-tribulation rapture. However, there is no verse that explicitly states that the rapture will occur before the tribulation. Again, we will look at these issues in more detail later in the book, but one thing to bear in mind at this point is that many things about the future are not perfectly clear. There is no passage of the Bible which lays out all the future events in God's program in a clear, systematic, sequential fashion. All viewpoints attempt to compare Scripture with Scripture, connect the dots, and make inferences. This is true of premillennialism as much as the alternative views. What this ultimately means is that we must not be overly dogmatic where we run up against certain difficult problems. Neither, on the other hand, should we adopt an overly agnostic approach that refuses to believe things that seem to be clearly stated in the Word of God.

3. **An Unbalanced Approach to the Kingdom**: one problem with some forms of premillennialism has been an under-appreciation (or outright denial) of the fact that the kingdom of God has a present spiritual aspect as well as a future, literal aspect. We will consider the Bible's teaching about the kingdom of God in the next chapter, but just as it is possible for amillennialists to hold an unbalanced view of future events (holding that Old Testament prophecies and promises have been fulfilled in the present, and denying a yet future fulfilment), so it is possible for premillennialists to fall into the opposite trap, that of denying any present fulfilment of Old Testament promises and pushing all fulfilments into the future. As we have seen, various verses (like the New Covenant promise in Jeremiah 31) have a partial, spiritual fulfilment in the present day in the church age, as well as a future, literal fulfilment at the end of the age to Israel. Both sides – the present spiritual fulfilment, and the future complete fulfilment – are true.

Conclusion

While it appears that premillennialism is a more biblically faithful position to adopt, being the truth taught by the Old Testament prophets, the words of Christ Himself, the plain and straightforward sense of the book of Revelation (particularly chapters 19-20), and a more consistent and logical approach to interpreting the entire Bible, there are also truths taught by the other approaches that need to be heard. Ultimately, all of God's people, saved by grace through faith on the basis of Christ's death, will be together for eternity, and the common points of our faith are more important than our differences.

	Postmillennial	Amillennial	Premillennial
Description	Christ rules over the earth after the gospel has Christianized it	Christ rules over the church and in human hearts presently	Christ rules over the earth for 1000 years after He returns
Time of Reign	Future, before Christ returns	Now, before Christ returns	Future, after Christ returns
Process	Gradually, via gospel preaching	Imperceptibly, in human hearts	Suddenly, after the tribulation
Interpretation	Figurative	Figurative	Literal
Highpoint	17th-19th centuries	4th century onwards	1st-3rd, 19th-20th centuries
Church/Israel	Israel = Church	Israel = Church	Israel = Israel
Summary	Optimistic	Simplistic	Literalistic

7 THE KINGDOM OF GOD

The kingdom of God is not only one of the most important topics in the Bible (it is mentioned over one hundred times in the gospels alone), and therefore worth understanding for its own sake, but it also helps us to be balanced in our approach to what the Bible teaches about the future. In particular, it enables us to see that there are truths in both a literal and spiritual interpretation of Scripture.

Different Views of the Kingdom

There are many different ideas Christians hold about the kingdom of God.

1. **Heaven.** Some Christians think the kingdom of God is another way of talking about heaven. John 3:3 says, 'Except a man be born again, he cannot see the kingdom of God' (KJV). Growing up hearing this verse, I thought it was saying we need to be born again to go to heaven. However, Christ told his disciples to pray 'Thy kingdom come' (Matt. 6:10), and taught us that, with the coming of His kingdom, 'the meek shall inherit the earth' (Matt. 5:5). The kingdom of God in this last verse is not heaven – it is heaven come down to earth.
2. **The Roman Catholic Church.** The Roman Catholic Church considers itself to be the kingdom of God.
3. **A Spiritual Kingdom.** Many Christians today, and throughout church history, have believed that the kingdom of God refers to God reigning in the hearts of those who love and obey Him: an invisible, spiritual rule. Beginning with Jesus' ministry, the sphere of God's sovereign, saving action has arrived – the kingdom has come.
4. **Kingdom Now.** Some Christian groups hold to a 'Kingdom Now' theology, whose 'hope is entirely and exclusively for present blessings that often include financial prosperity, total physical healing (sometimes including ability to skip death) and supernatural powers that may even enable them to control the social world and turn it into Christ's domain'[1]. After all, the promises of no more sickness and abundant earthly blessing are part of the kingdom described in the

---

[1] Roger Olsen, *The Mosaic of Christian Belief*, Downers Grove, IL: IVP, 2002, p347

OT, and Jesus' ministry was also characterized by healing and abundant blessing (e.g. feeding the 5000). Other Christians consider their mission as 'kingdom work' which goes beyond merely preaching the gospel to include social justice, environmental concern, political involvement, and cultural enrichment. Such an approach is required because the purpose of mission is that God's kingly rule should permeate every area of earthly endeavour and fulfil the 'cultural mandate' of Genesis 1:26-30 – filling and subduing the earth[2]. Theonomists (who believe that Christians are called to establish the OT law of God on earth) likewise argue that a Kingdom Now perspective means that 'God has not called us to forsake the earth, but to impress heaven's pattern on earth'[3].

5. **The Universal Kingdom.** Another view of the kingdom of God is that God eternally rules over all things. Psalm 145:13 says, 'Your kingdom is an everlasting kingdom, and Your dominion endures throughout all generations' (see also Daniel 4:3, 34, 1 Chron. 29:11, and Psa. 93:1-2). On this view, God's rules everywhere – He always has and always will. However, God's universal reign needs to be distinguished from the kingdom of God. W. Hoste asks, 'Why should the Kingdom [of God] need setting up? Is it not universal? Through the rebellion of angels and men, immense tracts of the moral universe lie today outside the kingdom of God ... When Satan fell, a new kingdom was set up, an "imperium in imperio" – the kingdom of darkness – a dark blot on the hitherto unsullied universe of God... This kingdom received a vast extension when man fell. We little realise the immense triumph that accrued to Satan when the whole human race was swept at one blow into his kingdom'[4]. The kingdom of God, foreshadowed in David's rule, foretold by the prophets, and announced in the NT, is therefore God's re-establishment of His rightful dominion here on earth.

6. **A Jewish Kingdom.** John the Baptist and the Lord Jesus Christ came preaching, 'Repent, for the kingdom of heaven/God is at hand' (Matt. 3:2, 4:17, Mark 1:14). There can be no doubt that what the ordinary Jews of the day thought John was saying was that the Messianic

---

[2] see, for example, Arthur Glasser, "Biblical Theology of Mission" in *Evangelical Dictionary of World Missions*, ed. A. S. Moreau, Baker, 2000, pp127-131
[3] Gary DeMar, *End Times Fiction: a Biblical Consideration of the Left Behind Theology*, Nashville: Nelson, 2001, p203
[4] W. Hoste, "The Kingdom of God", in *The Collected Writings of W. Hoste*, Vol. 2: Prophetic, Kilmarnock: Ritchie, 1998, p7

kingdom promised in the prophets was about to appear. In their view, based on the OT, the kingdom of God is a future earthly paradise.
7. **The Postponed Kingdom.** Another view of the kingdom of God is that Christ came offering the Jewish people an immediate kingdom, but they rejected Him, and so the kingdom of God had to be postponed.

When I was a young Christian, I was quite puzzled by all the talk of the kingdom of God in the gospels. Once, at a big Christian gathering, I remember seeing someone wearing a T-shirt with the words 'the kingdom' emblazoned on it. I was puzzled by this, unsure what message the T-shirt was trying to convey. So, one day, I decided to write out all the references in the New Testament to the word 'kingdom' (over 150), hoping for a better understanding of what it meant. This is an exercise I recommend for Bible students today! I suggest that when we look at the New Testament, we see primarily two ideas about the kingdom of God.

A Future Kingdom
The primary sense in which the kingdom of God is mentioned in the New Testament is as a future realm over which our Lord Jesus Christ will reign when He returns. Notice some verses showing this:

- Christ said, 'Not everyone who says to me, "Lord, Lord" shall enter the Kingdom of Heaven, but he who does the will of My Father in Heaven. Many will say to me in that day, "Lord, have we not prophesied in Your name", etc.' (Matt. 7:21-22). The Kingdom is plainly here described as something in a future day, after the Judgment.
- Matthew 8:11: 'Many will come from east and west and sit down with Abraham, Isaac and Jacob in the Kingdom of Heaven'. This verse again speaks of the Kingdom of Heaven in the future tense. Here it appears to be after the resurrection of the dead.
- The Beatitudes (i.e. blessings) with which the Sermon on the Mount commences (5:3-12) are all about the blessings of the future Kingdom which true disciples will enjoy. This is clearly seen by the fact that the first and the last of the beatitudes concern the Kingdom. The first is 'Blessed are the poor in spirit, for theirs is the Kingdom of Heaven' and the last is 'Blessed are those who are persecuted for righteousness' sake for theirs is the Kingdom of Heaven'. Notice, though, that all the blessings in between these first and last concern the future. For

example, 'Blessed are those who mourn for they shall be comforted' (5:4) or 'Blessed are the pure in heart for they shall see God' (5:8). All the blessings are in the future tense. If we were to just take the first and last blessings in isolation we could perhaps argue that there is no future tense implied in the words. However, the context closes this loophole. Christ is saying that the blessing or reward of those who are poor in spirit or those who are persecuted for righteousness' sake is that they are the sorts of people who will inherit in the future the Kingdom.

- Christ tells His disciples to pray in His model prayer 'Thy Kingdom come' (6:10). The word 'come' here forces the Kingdom into the future. Thus, in this verse, the Kingdom had not yet come in Christ's day. Furthermore, this prayer is the model for a Christian in this age. Therefore the Kingdom has not come yet – for we are supposed to be still praying for its coming. The Lord's words which follow, 'Thy will be done on earth, as in heaven' are taken by some to define what 'Thy Kingdom come' means – people living in submission to God and doing His will here and now. However, 'Thy Kingdom come' involves more than sporadic outbursts of obedience to God's will. Whilst it is true that there is a present sense in the prayer for God's will to be done on earth, the words 'as in Heaven' show that this prayer will never be fully answered until the Kingdom comes in the future. Only then will earth truly be like Heaven. In its world-wide scope this prayer remains unanswered in this present age of evil and injustice.
- In Matthew 26:29 Christ promised His disciples 'I will not drink of this fruit of the vine from now on until that day when I drink it new with you in My Father's Kingdom'. Notice the future tense of the Kingdom ('until that day').

There are a good few mentions of the Kingdom in the future tense in the rest of the New Testament. Notice the future tense and the words 'enter' and 'inherit' in the following verses:

- Acts 14:22: 'We must through many tribulations enter the kingdom of God'. Paul taught his new converts that persecution in this life was to be expected by a disciple before entrance into the Kingdom. The Kingdom here is not God 'reigning in me'. It is not 'being a Christian'.
- 1 Corinthians 6:9: 'Do you not know that the unrighteous will not inherit the kingdom of God? Do not be deceived. Neither fornicators, nor idolaters, nor adulterers, nor homosexuals, nor sodomites, not thieves, nor covetous, nor drunkards, nor revilers, nor extortioners will

inherit the kingdom of God'. Continuance in unrighteous living is evidence that a person is not saved and so shall never enter into the Kingdom in the future.
- Galatians 5:21: '… of which I tell you beforehand, just as I also told you in time past, that those who practice such things will not inherit the kingdom of God'.
- Ephesians 5:5: 'For this you know, that no fornicator, unclean person, nor covetous man, who is an idolater, has any inheritance in the Kingdom of Christ and God'.
- 2 Peter 1:11: 'for so an entrance will be supplied to you abundantly into the everlasting Kingdom of our Lord and Saviour Jesus Christ'.

An Earthly Kingdom
This future Kingdom is also earthly and visible:

- In the beatitudes again we read 'Blessed are the meek, for they shall inherit the earth'. This gives the lie to the idea that the Kingdom of heaven simply refers to Heaven itself or to a present spiritual Kingdom in which Christ reigns from Heaven over His Church. There will be a future earthly Kingdom.
- In Matthew 26:29 Christ promised His disciples 'I will not drink of this fruit of the vine from now on until that day when I drink it new with you in My Father's Kingdom'. We have already noticed the future tense of the Kingdom ('until that day'), but here we also see the earthly reality of the Kingdom: drinking from this fruit of the vine.

Consider some more New Testament verses that prove that the future Kingdom will be earthly:

- Revelation 5:9-10: 'And they sang a new song, saying: You are worthy to take the scroll and to open its seals; for You were slain, and have redeemed us to God by Your blood out of every tribe and tongue and people and nation, and have made us kings and priests to our God; and we shall reign on the earth'.
- Ephesians 1:9-10: 'Having made known to us the mystery of His will, according to His good pleasure which He purposed in Himself; that in the dispensation of the fullness of the times He might gather together in one [or, *head up*] all things in Christ, both which are in Heaven and which are on earth – in Him'. This is speaking about God's Grand Plan for all time – that at the end, the fullness of times, the Christ – the Messiah – might head up all things both in the

heavens and upon the earth. Christ is not only going to be the Head in Heaven but also upon the Earth.
- 2 Peter 3:13: 'Nevertheless we, according to His promise look for new heavens and a new earth in which righteousness dwells'. God's plans are not just to take us to heaven – there will be a new earth too.
- Romans 4:13: 'For the promise to Abraham or to his seed that he would be the heir of the world was not through the law but through the righteousness of faith'. Abraham is going to inherit the world.

Some have suggested that John the Baptist's announcement that the kingdom of God was near meant that the kingdom of God would arrive in the personal coming of Jesus Christ. But when Jesus came, He did not preach that the kingdom of God is *here*. Instead, He too only says that the kingdom of God is near. The kingdom is still impending – it has not arrived. Furthermore, John also preached that divine judgment is imminent:

- 'even now the axe is laid to the root of the trees. Therefore every tree which does not bear good fruit is cut down and thrown into the fire' (Luke 3:9),
- 'His winnowing fan is in His hand and He will thoroughly clean out His threshing floor, and gather the wheat into His barn, but the chaff He will burn with unquenchable fire' (Luke 3:17),
- 'flee from the wrath to come' (Luke 3:7).

The warnings of impending judgment (in hell: 'unquenchable fire') went hand in hand with the promise of the imminent kingdom. Yet, none of the judgments arrived with Christ's ministry, or death and resurrection. John's warning of people being sent to the unquenchable fire – Hell – is, in fact, still in the future, awaiting the great Day of Judgment. Therefore, it would appear that just as the judgment is still future and pending, so is the kingdom.

God promised many times in the Old Testament that one day He would send the Messiah, His King, who would establish a Kingdom for God on earth in the place of the kingdoms of men (Daniel 2:44). It would be a Kingdom after God's original intentions for our world. Matthew 25:34 expresses this idea of a future, earthly kingdom: 'Then the King will say to those on His right hand, Come, you blessed of My Father, inherit the Kingdom prepared for you from the foundation of the world'.

A Present Spiritual Kingdom

In addition to the idea of a future earthly kingdom, the New Testament also clearly teaches a second truth: a present spiritual Kingdom which those of us who are believers are already inside. Consider these verses:

- Matthew 12:28 (and Luke 11:20): 'But if I cast out demons by the Spirit of God, surely the kingdom of God has come upon you'. Here Christ assures the Jews that the Kingdom had arrived by virtue of the fact that the King was in their midst.
- Luke 17:20: 'Now when He was asked by the Pharisees when the kingdom of God would come, He answered them and said, "The kingdom of God does not come with observation"'. Christ here says that the kingdom of God comes invisibly and spiritually, rather than with open manifestation. This refers to the present spiritual aspect, the 'mystery' form of the Kingdom. The following verse makes this clear.
- Luke 17:21: 'nor will they say, "See here!" or "See there!", for indeed the kingdom of God is within (or in the midst of) you'. This verse cannot be understood to mean that the kingdom of God was residing inside the Pharisees with whom Christ was talking. Nevertheless, it shows that the kingdom of God is now within people's hearts spiritually as they repent and receive Christ.
- Matthew 11:12 (and Luke 16:16): 'And from the days of John the Baptist until now the kingdom of heaven suffers violence, and the violent take it by force'. Christ's similar words in Luke 16:16 give the sense: 'The law and the prophets were until John. Since that time the kingdom of God has been preached, and everyone is pressing into it'. Here Christ speaks of the Kingdom being besieged by people seeking to enter it. The kingdom is present, and people are entering it by responding to the gospel message in repentance and faith in Christ.
- Romans 14:17: 'For the kingdom of God is not eating and drinking, but righteousness, joy and peace in the Holy Spirit'. The immediate context shows that this chapter refers to the way believers in the present day behave toward each other. Paul is saying that believers are not to become embroiled in disputes and divisions over minor matters like food and drink, but to make it our business to pursue righteousness, joy and peace, 'the fruits of His Lordship obeyed in the heart'[5]. Some would argue that this verse does not teach that the

---

[5] W. Hoste, "Mysteries of the New Testament", *Collected Writings*, Vol. 2, Ritchie, 1999,

kingdom is a present spiritual reality, but simply that in the future kingdom, the emphasis will not be on food or drink[6]. However, the problem in the church at Corinth was Christians dividing in the present; what relevance does the future kingdom have to this issue? This verse makes much more sense if the kingdom is a present spiritual reality whose subjects are not to fight and argue over minor issues.

- 1 Corinthians 4:20: 'For the kingdom of God is not in word but in power'. Again the context here shows that Paul was writing about present conditions among believers. He was warning that when he came to Corinth all the idle boasting of the Corinthians about their spiritual accomplishments would not save them from the rod of Paul's chastening. Some would argue that the context argues for a future kingdom[7]. However, the verses in the context pointed to (vs 5 & 8) are so far removed from verse 20, both in distance and content, that they really have no connection with what Paul is talking about in the immediate context of verse 20 – his imminent visit.

- Colossians 1:13: 'He has delivered us from the power of darkness and translated us into the Kingdom of the Son of His love'. Some argue that this refers to God's universal Kingdom reign, but this cannot be so, because everyone and everything is already in the universal reign. Or, it has been argued that this verse expresses our legal position (*de jure*, as heirs of the future kingdom) rather than our actual position (*de facto*, the kingdom as our present possession[8]). However, Paul here speaks of our translation into the Kingdom in the past tense, at conversion. Furthermore, our 'legal position' is just another fancy way of saying that we are already *spiritually* in the kingdom. We might similarly say we are seated together with Christ in the heavenlies (Eph. 2:6) – this is our spiritual position (or legal position, if you will), but not our actual physical position. Our spiritual position is a present reality – we are in the kingdom of the Son of His love.

- Matthew 13: The final proof of the fact that the kingdom of God has a present spiritual aspect is seen in the parables of Matthew 13. These parables of the kingdom all relate to activities that are being fulfilled

---

p79
[6] For example, Andy Woods writes, 'the verse simply highlights or emphasizes the fact that the coming kingdom will emphasize a spiritual component as well'. In other words, "in that coming kingdom the emphasis will not be on food but on spiritual realities" (*The Coming Kingdom*, Grace Gospel Press, 2016, p297-8)
[7] Alva J. McClain, *The Greatness of the Kingdom*, Zondervan, 1959, p435
[8] McClain, *The Greatness of the Kingdom*, p435

in this day and age. For example, the parables about the sowing of the seed, the growth of the wheat and the tares and the fishing net being cast all refer to present activities. Here we have the kingdom in mystery form, that is, in a new and unexpected sense not foretold in the Old Testament – a spiritual kingdom. In this present age, the kingdom is present, but unrecognised by the world. It's progress is invisible – like the growth of a crop; its success is variable – much seed fails on poor ground and fails to produce fruit; its ranks have been infiltrated by the Devil's children – like in the parable of the wheat and the tares; its character has been corrupted by the spread of moral and doctrinal evils – like in the parable of the leaven; its true value is hidden – like the treasure in the field and the pearl on the sea bed; and its results await the day of judgment – like in the parable of the dragnet. But despite all this, God is using the spiritual activities of the present age to prepare for the arrival of the glorious future when 'the righteous will shine forth as the sun in the kingdom of their Father' (Matt. 13:43).

Thus, like many things in the Bible, the Kingdom has two sides to it and to understand the Kingdom properly we must hold both truths: the kingdom is both a future, earthly kingdom and a present, spiritual kingdom.

How Can There Be Two Sides to the Kingdom?

We have seen on the one hand that the Kingdom is a present-day reality for believers whilst, on the other hand, we are yet to enter the Kingdom in a future day. How can both sides of the Kingdom be true? I suggest that the present spiritual aspect of the Kingdom is a preparatory stage for the future Kingdom. In the Bible, the future Kingdom is pictured as a great feast (Matt. 8:11, Luke 14:15, cf. Isaiah 25:6-8). But a good deal of preparation is required before all the guests can enjoy the food, as any cook or farmer will remind us. There must be cooking done. Before that, there must be a crop harvested by the farmer so that there will be food to cook. In Matthew's Gospel, these preparations for the coming kingdom are pictured in Christ's parables in Ch.13 where we read of the sowing of seed, the harvesting of the crop, the baking of bread and other activities. These are the present preparations for the future Kingdom feast: the preaching of the Gospel and the salvation of men and women in view of the future Kingdom.

In fact, one of the verses sometimes used to argue for a present spiritual kingdom actually teaches there are two sides to it. Christ's reply to Pilate in John 18:36 is sometimes half-quoted to convey the one-sided impression that the kingdom of God is the present Christian age. Christ says:

> My Kingdom is not of this world. If my Kingdom were of this world, My servants would fight, so that I should not be delivered to the Jews.

But the verse does not finish there. Notice that Christ went on to say:

> but now My Kingdom is not from here.

The word 'now' in this phrase is significant: it implies that while Christ's kingdom is presently not earthly and external, there will come a day when it will be. What does He mean by 'not from here'? Some have argued this means that Christ's kingdom is not from earth – it is not an earthly kingdom. However, Christ uses a different Greek adverb at the end of the verse: *enteuthen* (from here) instead of *ek* (of, from) used twice earlier in the verse, and while the word *ek* (of, from) talks about what kind of kingdom Christ presently has ('not of this world'), the word *enteuthen* tells us where His Kingdom will radiate out from.

Several Old Testament verses tell us that the Messianic kingdom will be headquartered in Jerusalem. Thus, Psalm 110:2 says, 'The LORD shall send the rod of Your strength **out of** Zion. Rule in the midst of Your enemies!' Isaiah 2 says about the future Messianic kingdom, 'Many people shall come and say, "Come, and let us go up to the mountain of the LORD, to the house of the God of Jacob; He will teach us His ways, and we shall walk in His paths." For **out of** Zion shall go forth the law, and the word of the LORD from Jerusalem' (Isa 2:3, and also Micah 4:2). Similarly, several other verses speak of God helping His people out of Zion (Psalm 14:7, 20:2, 50:2, 53:6, 128:5), while Joel 3:16 and Amos 1:2 speak of the Lord roaring from Zion.

What Christ was implying to Pilate was that although now His Kingdom was not based at Jerusalem, one day it will be. While He is not presently reigning from Jerusalem, one day His kingly rule will centre and spread out from there.

This verse teaches both sides of the Kingdom. Christ's Kingdom at the present is a spiritual Kingdom, but there is a day coming when it will be a physical, literal Kingdom on Earth. A properly balanced view of the Kingdom shows there are two sides to it.

The Kingdom and the Church

What is the relationship between the kingdom of God and the church? We have already seen that there is a present spiritual aspect to the kingdom of God. The parables of the Kingdom show that present gospel activities are part of the preparations God is making for the coming Kingdom. Christ likens the kingdom to sowing seed, harvesting a crop, baking bread and catching fish, etc., encouraging us to consider gospel activities as 'kingdom' work.

However, while these activities are part of the Kingdom program, it is not true to say that Christ's Kingdom is simply this Church era. It is not true to say that the Old Testament prophecies of the Kingdom are all fulfilled in the Church. Nor is it the case that 'We Christians in the Church are the Kingdom'.

To understand the relationship of the church and the kingdom, we need to ask what a kingdom is. Many theologians define the kingdom of God as simply the reign or rule of God. However, this is inadequate, for a kingdom involves three elements: the rule of a rightful king, willing subjects, and a secure domain. A king's authority must be exercised over some sphere. Someone who reigns over nothing is not a king. A King must reign over subjects, but a kingdom involves more than people – it requires people who willingly accept the king's rule. Rebels will not do.

A kingdom also requires a land. If we may take earthly kingdoms as an example, a people without their own land are not a kingdom (for example, the Jewish diaspora of the last 2000 years), nor is a land without any people. Nor are land and people enough, for Israel in New Testament times had people and land but did not have the rightful king ruling over them – they had Herod a foreign imposter and then the Romans.

The present situation is that Christ is the King in exile, who is at present gathering a people, and one day will invade this earth to reclaim his rightful domain – the whole earth – and take the crown. The church is part of what will make up the subjects of the kingdom, the people of God. We might call the church an underground resistance movement, working in enemy territory towards the day when the rightful king returns and establishes His kingdom.

God's covenants in the Old Testament promised all these essential elements of the kingdom: to Abraham were promised a people and a land, to David was promised the rightful king, and the New Covenant promised the spiritual change that would turn the hearts of the people willingly toward their king.

Thus, the kingdom of God is not simply another way of talking about

Heaven. Christ made it quite clear in the Sermon on the Mount that those who inherit the Kingdom are going to inherit the Earth (Matt. 5:5) as well as Heaven (Matt. 5:12). Nor secondly, is the term 'the kingdom of God' another way of speaking about the Church. In some of Christ's parables, the kingdom includes within it many unbelievers (e.g. the parable of the Wheat and the Tares, Matt. 13:24-29, 36-43). Nowhere in the New Testament do we find any statement which says The Kingdom = The Church, nor do we even read of Christ being the King of the Church. God's Kingdom involves far more than God simply reigning over those who love Him. God plans to reign over everything, everywhere. As the poet put it, 'He shall reign from pole to pole, with illimitable sway. He shall reign, when, like a scroll, yonder heavens have passed away'.

'Big Picture' Theology and the Kingdom of God

One currently influential issue related to the kingdom of God is the novel idea that the kingdom of God is the master-theme of the entire Bible[9]. The kingdom of God helps us to understand the 'big picture' of the Bible's storyline. Here is how Big Picture theology proceeds:

1. We should not preach the OT allegorically. That would be like the Sunday School message where the speaker told the story of David and Goliath, and dressed up as Goliath in armour. He proceeded to peel off a number of cardboard strips from his breastplate, each having a childhood sin written on it. These are the Goliaths we face in our lives, he said. Then out came David on stage and produced a sling labelled 'faith' and five stones which were obedience, service, Bible reading, prayer and fellowship. These enable us to overcome giants in our lives, said the preacher. This allegorical approach to the Bible is not the way the original story of David and Goliath was intended to be applied.
2. Nor should we preach the OT moralistically, says Big Picture theology, preaching about Abraham, Moses or David, and urging us to imitate their faith, humility or courage. No, that is only using the OT illustratively, and indeed legalistically. This is only preaching

---

[9] This approach originates from Moore Theological College, Sydney, from seeds planted by liberal theologian Gabriel Hebert (*The Bible from Within*, 1950), developed by evangelical theologian Donald Robinson, and popularized by Graeme Goldsworthy in his books, *Gospel and Kingdom* (1981), *According to Plan* (1991), *Gospel-Centred Hermeneutics* (2006), and *Christ-Centred Biblical Theology* (2012). It is also found in books by other writers talking about the Bible's 'Big Picture'.

man, not God our Saviour. The Bible is not about us – it is about Christ.
3. Instead, because the OT is Christian scripture, we should preach the OT with Christ as our focus, for Christ Himself said that the Law, the Prophets and the Psalms were about Him (Luke 24:44).
4. The way to preach the OT Christologically is to find the master-theme of the whole Bible. The Bible is a unity, and therefore, it must have one theme that ties everything together.
5. This master-theme is the kingdom of God. In the OT, we see the theme of the kingdom, particularly in David's dynasty. Here is where we reach the highpoint of the OT story. Similarly, in the NT, Jesus came preaching the kingdom of God. The kingdom is therefore the master-theme of the entire Bible, for it ties the OT and NT together.
6. What is the kingdom of God? According to Big Picture theology, the kingdom of God means God's people in God's place under God's rule. We can see the kingdom in Eden where Adam and Eve were God's people in God's place living under His rule. We even see it in the OT prophets, where people long for a return of the kingdom.
7. Lastly, the NT gospel transforms the OT concept of the Kingdom; indeed the gospel fulfils the OT hope of the coming Kingdom. Instead of coming as a military Messiah to fight against the Romans, Jesus won a greater victory, defeating sin by dying on the cross. God's people in the NT are not Jews, but all who are in Christ. God's place in the NT is not the land of Israel, but again Jesus himself – He is the true temple; the true Jerusalem is in heaven above where Jesus is.

Many of these points are helpful. However, there are also subtle problems with reading the Bible this way.

1. The fundamental problem with reading the Bible like this is that there is no reason why the whole Bible must have only one theme. The Bible is a unity, but there are multiple themes which bind it all together. These include the faith of many OT heroes, a theme that is dismissed as false by Big Picture theologians despite the NT itself emphasizing it (Hebrews 11). Another theme is redemption (the so-called scarlet cord that runs through the entire Bible), with its sacrifices pointing to Christ's death. Another theme is God's love: the 19th century evangelist Henry Moorhouse famously preached all the way through the Bible showing that God is love. Or we could speak about the glory of God as another unifying theme for the entire Bible. The kingdom of God is one theme that runs through the Bible and it is helpful to notice it, but the idea that there must

be only one theme is not only slightly totalitarian (there is one theme, and you shall have no other!), but also a novel theological idea. The OT hardly ever uses the term 'the kingdom of God'[10], and the NT itself does not state that the kingdom of God is the master theme of the Bible. It speaks of Christ in all the Scriptures (Luke 24:27). But even so, this does not mean that we find Christ in every chapter or verse of the OT. For example, Exodus 8 is about a plague of frogs, Isaiah 15 is about God's judgement on Moab, Psalm 119 is about God's Word. Christ binds together all the other themes because all the other themes of sin, grace, salvation, faith and God's glory are related – He is the centre, or goal. Thus, the first problem is the idea that the kingdom of God is the one and only master-theme of the Bible.

2. The result of saying that the OT is all about the kingdom of God is that we have predetermined what every passage is about before we have even opened up the Bible and read what it says. There is a story about a professor called Rob Plummer who was reading to his young daughter through a book called *The Big Picture Story Bible*. This children's book traces the storyline of the Bible and shows children how the Bible is all about the Kingdom. After he had read what the *Big Picture Story Bible* said about Joshua and the battle of Jericho, his little girl was confused. 'Where is the lady? Why did they leave out the lady?' she asked. You see, the *Big Picture Story Bible* told the girl that the real meaning of Joshua and the battle of Jericho is that God was going to give His people Israel the land of Canaan because God wanted to set up a kingdom. But it did not tell the story about how the spies bravely went into Jericho and or how Rahab's faith hid them. It left out one of the most important parts of the story altogether. It pre-determined what the passage was about. There is another story about a Sunday School teacher who asked her little children a question, What is grey, furry and lives up a tree? The children sat silently, no one wanting to respond. Eventually after a long wait, one child replied, 'it sounds like a koala, but I know that the answer to every question in Sunday School is Jesus'. This is what the Big Picture approach does: once we have pre-determined that the meaning of every story in the Bible is the kingdom, or even Jesus, then why do we need to bother reading the details? The Big Picture approach is therefore reductionist – it skims over the details and boils down every story in the Bible to the same simplistic

---

[10] The only two references are in 1 Chronicles 28:5 and 2 Chronicles 13:8 – 'the kingdom of the LORD'

formula[11]. But the Bible is not simplistic – it is a complex, interconnected web of important ideas, and this is the way God has put it together. If we believe that all Scripture is God-breathed and profitable, then we must insist that every word, and all the details, are there for a reason and cannot be omitted.

3.   Thirdly, this Big Picture approach results in repetitive preaching. If you are preaching a series of messages on the life of David, and you believe that the key to understanding the life of David is not really anything David did, but the fact that God was setting up a kingdom, and you want to preach the gospel to non-Christians from David's life, what do you do? What the Big Picture approach suggests is that you briefly summarize the story of David in the allocated passage, and then assure everyone that the story of David is really about a kingdom God was setting up, and then jump over to the NT where Jesus is the fulfilment of the kingdom, and urge people to have faith in Jesus and become members of his kingdom. Now, that is all well and good, but if you are preaching a series of ten messages on ten different passages from the life of David, you are going to get very repetitive, week after week, jumping to the 'kingdom bit'. Or, if you are preaching four messages through the book of Ruth, and your lesson is that God was preparing the way for the kingdom, then why bother with four messages saying the same thing? Why not have just have one sermon, skip the details, and jump straight to the final paragraph of Ruth where we find out she was David's great grandmother. Then tack on the kingdom bit. Why bother trying to see what the individual passages in Ruth or David's life teach? You don't need to look at the details or differences between the passages – they are all teaching the same simple lesson: the kingdom.

4.   The last problem with this way of reading the OT, is that it argues that the NT gospel fulfils the OT promise of the kingdom. Now this is true, of course, but the 'Big Picture' approach explicitly teaches that God will not fulfil his OT promises to Israel. It says that the blessings God promised to OT Israel will not be honoured literally, nor will the original recipients of those promises (the Jews) receive them, for those promises have been transferred to the NT church. We are the kingdom, for the church has replaced Israel. Further, it reinterprets the OT by importing

---

[11] Here we see the influence of Gabriel Hebert; being a liberal theologian critical of the evangelical approach to the verbal inspiration of Scripture, he found truth in over-arching themes rather than individual texts.

and imposing NT themes upon it. Instead of interpreting OT passages by looking to see what the actual words say in their original context, this approach radically reinterprets OT messages with non-literal meanings. It argues for the interpretive priority of the NT, insisting that the proper starting point for understanding OT texts is the NT, and that the NT changes OT texts. This robs the OT of its true meaning, imposing on it a theological framework (based on amillennialism with its flaws and half-truths), rather than letting Scripture speak for itself. The OT is Christian Scripture, but it is also Jewish scripture – it contains promises made to the Jewish people that God will honour and fulfil. They too will come into the blessings that God promised them in the OT, when the Messiah returns. In Romans 11:26, Paul assures that all Israel will be saved, at the second coming of Christ. Micah 4:8 says this, 'the former dominion shall come, the kingdom of the daughter of Jerusalem'.

In summary, then, the problem with the Big Picture approach is that it imposes a straitjacket on the Bible and insists that we must read it this way. Its definition and understanding of the kingdom of God is also a problem, because it based on amillennialist and replacement theology, and therefore the theme that is being imposed on the OT is not fully biblical. Instead of allowing the Bible to be read in all its multifaceted magnificence, Big Picture theology reduces it to a caricature, a simplistic drawing. If we imagine the Bible to be like the beautiful tapestried curtain in the OT tabernacle, what Big Picture theology does is to pull the purple (kingdom) thread out of the stitching, announcing this one thread to be the key to the panoramic picture. But in addition to missing the significance of the other coloured threads, ripping one thread out from the tapestry ruins the whole. God has communicated to us in the full-orbed splendour of His Word, and we need to remember that all Scripture is inspired by God, not just 'kingdom bits'.

The Postponed Kingdom?
It is not only amillennialists who make mistakes about the kingdom of God; so do premillennialists. The verse in Matthew 4:17 ('the Kingdom of Heaven is at hand') is interpreted by some to mean that Christ came announcing the imminent arrival of the Kingdom but when Israel rejected Him (by Chapter 12 of Matthew), the Kingdom had to be put off to the future. Christ changed His mind and instead of setting up the Kingdom, opted for Plan B and decided to set up His Church. One day, when the Church is complete, Christ will return to establish His Kingdom.

Now of course, again, there is some truth in this view. Nevertheless, I have caricatured it to present its obvious absurdities. In fact, I suspect that even those who sometimes advocate this view of the Kingdom will agree that when it is pushed to its logical conclusion it has certain ridiculous features.

All would agree that there was never going to be a Kingdom without the Cross. The Cross and the Church were never Plan B. Christ was never offering Himself to be King without the Cross first. In fact, it was Israel – not Christ – which wanted an immediate Kingdom. Israel wanted to make Christ their King in John 6:15 after the feeding of the five thousand. Similarly, at the triumphal entry into Jerusalem the crowd acclaimed Christ as the Son of David (i.e. the rightful King), and they welcomed His kingdom, saying, 'Blessed is the kingdom of our father David that comes in the name of the Lord' (Mark 11:10). The crowds were ready to accept a miracle-working Messiah who would overthrow their enemies the Romans and usher in the golden era of Israel's glory. Their stumbling block was precisely that Christ was not offering an immediate Kingdom.

On the road to Emmaus, the two disciples said, 'But we were hoping that it was He who was going to redeem Israel' (Luke 24:21). Christ said to them in reply, 'O fools, and slow of heart to believe all that the prophets have spoken: 26 Ought not Christ to have suffered these things, and to enter into his glory?' (Luke 24:25-26). Everything in God's purposes, including the future kingdom, depended upon Christ's death.

The Old Testament prophets foretold both a suffering Saviour and a delay before His reign. Thus, Daniel 9 prophesied Messiah's death and an interval of time before His rule, during which (among other things), Jerusalem and its temple would be destroyed: 'And after the sixty-two weeks Messiah shall be cut off, but not for Himself; and the people of the prince who is to come shall destroy the city and the sanctuary' (Dan. 9:26).

Proponents of the view that the kingdom of God was postponed argue that Matthew 3:2 and 4:17 ('Repent, for the kingdom of heaven is at hand') constitute an offer – the offer of the millennial kingdom. J. D. Pentecost writes that 'the kingdom announced and offered by the Lord Jesus was the same theocratic kingdom foretold through the Old Testament prophets'[12]. Andy Woods writes, 'Yet, the kingdom never became a reality for the nation and the world. Why? The rest of the story as unfolded in the Gospels explains how the leadership of first-century Israel tragically rejected the *offer* of the kingdom. Despite their unique opportunity to accept both the King and the Kingdom, the nation turned

---

[12] Pentecost, *Things to Come*, p447

down the *offer*'[13].

I suggest it is better to speak of the kingdom being announced rather than offered. Of, if we wish to speak of the kingdom being offered, we must reject the idea that there was ever any *immediate* kingdom offered. God's plan always involved the death of Christ.

Proponents of the postponed kingdom also argue that the kingdom's 'coming was contingent upon one thing: Israel receiving it by genuine repentance'[14]. But this is exactly what the nation of Israel did in response to John's preaching of the kingdom: 'Then all the land of Judea, and those from Jerusalem, went out to him and were all baptized by him in the Jordan river, confessing their sins' (Mark 1:5). If the kingdom was an offer contingent upon repentance, Israel fulfilled the condition.

The reason the kingdom did not immediately appear was not because Israel rejected the offer of the glorious kingdom foretold by the prophets, nor because they did not repent. Instead, the reason the kingdom did not immediately appear was because it was never going to immediately appear.

Israel was always destined to reject Christ, not just because the prophets foretold it, but also because Jews steeped in monotheism were never going to accept the God-man, nor would their conceptions of the future kingdom allow any room for a crucified Messiah. How could it be that their glorious King would be their sacrifice for sin, hung from a tree by the Gentiles?

Christ was rejected long before Matthew chapter 12. He was rejected in his hometown synagogue at the beginning of His ministry (Luke 4), He was rejected in Jerusalem in John 2, and He was rejected by the religious elite for forgiving sins (Mark 2:6), mixing with sinners (Mark 2:16), feasting instead of fasting (Mark 2: 18), and doing various things on the Sabbath (Mark 2:23 – 3:6). Even at this early stage of His ministry, He told how 'the days will come when the bridegroom will be taken away from them, and then they will fast in those days' (Mark 2:21).

The idea that Christ changed course, withdrew the offer of the immediate kingdom and instead set up the church is not true. Christ always envisaged a future Kingdom coming after a time of rejection and His absence. Christ spoke plainly of His rejection long before Matthew Chapter 12. Here are some examples:

---

[13] Andy Woods, *The Coming Kingdom*, Duluth: Grace Gospel Press, 2016, p221, emphasis added

[14] Stanley D. Toussaint, *Behold the King*, Kregel, 2005, p36

- In the Beatitudes, Christ insisted that those who would be persecuted and reviled for His name's sake would be possessors of the Kingdom of Heaven (5:10-12). This implies both His absence during this period which we now live in as well as the rejection of Him and His message as delivered by His disciples.
- Christ refers to His disciples as the light of the world in the Sermon on the Mount (5:14). Later on in John's Gospel He says that as long as He is in the world He is the Light of the World. He is therefore implying in Matthew 5 that His disciples are to represent Him in His absence as light in a world that is dark – dark because it has rejected Him and He is absent.

In these verses, Christ spoke of the period of His absence and rejection in which we now live. One other simple proof of the fact that Christ did not change plans midway through Matthew's Gospel and postpone the Kingdom is that 20 of the 50 references to the Kingdom of Heaven/God in Matthew occur after Chapter 13. In other words, Christ kept on talking about the Kingdom of Heaven after He was rejected by the nation of Israel[15].

In fact, Christ spent the forty days between His resurrection and the ascension 'speaking of the things pertaining to the kingdom of God' (Acts 1:4), and this would include more than teaching about a future paradise. Christ was talking with the disciples about how God's purposes for the spread of the gospel and the salvation of men and women had been accomplished through His death. The *Macarthur's Study Bible* rightly says, 'Here this expression refers to the sphere of salvation, the gracious domain of divine rule over believers' hearts ... This was the dominant theme during Christ's earthly ministry'.

This leads on to another closely related misunderstanding. Some teach that the Sermon on the Mount does not apply to Christians today. In fact, they teach that whole sections of Matthew's Gospel – notably chapters 5-7, 10 and 24-25 – have nothing to do with the present Church age. Rather, they say, in the Sermon on the Mount Christ was advertising to the nation of Israel the principles upon which His future Kingdom would be based, or that He was outlining the lifestyle required for 'Tribulation Saints' to

---

[15] In Matthew alone the Kingdom is mentioned approximately 52 times. Luke's Gospel has nearly as many references (about 45) and Mark's Gospel does not dodge the issue either – it has about 15. Only John's Gospel is quieter on the issue, referring to the Kingdom only about 5 times. (There are 8 references to the Kingdom in Acts and 20 in the Epistles and Revelation).

be saved – by works. The *Scofield Bible* largely is responsible for spreading this idea that the Sermon on the Mount is not for the Church. It says that 'the Sermon on the Mount in its primary application gives neither the privilege nor the duties of the Church'. It teaches that the Sermon on the Mount is the Constitution for the Government of the Kingdom in a future day. In other words, our Lord's words here were not spoken for those of us in the Church to live by – we have to go to the Epistles. The Sermon on the Mount, rather, was spoken for Israel's sake, however, they unfortunately did not really want the Kingdom and so Christ opted instead for Plan B - the Cross and the Church.

However, the idea that the Sermon on the Mount is for Israel in the future and not for Christians today is wrong. Here are three reasons:

1. Notice that the difficult conditions that a disciple is expected to cope with in the Sermon on the Mount apply to the days in which we live – not the perfect, peaceful days of the Kingdom to come. Christ's followers are persecuted (Matt. 5:10), but this will not happen when Christ returns to reign. His disciples, are mourning (5:4), but we will not be mourning when Christ reigns. We are to be peacemakers (5:9) and that implies conflict and war, of which there will be none when Christ reigns. We are smote on the cheek (5:39), giving to charity (6:1-4), praying (6:5-14), fasting (6:16-18) and needy (6:25-34).
2. Some teach that we as Christians are to go to the Epistles rather than the teachings of our Master. This is disproved by the fact that the teachings of our Lord form the basis of all the teachings in the Epistles. For example, we are taught in the Sermon on the Mount to be like our Father in Heaven (Matthew 5:48; cf. Ephesians 5:1, 1 Peter 1:14-17), we are to return blessing for cursing (5:44; cf. Romans 12:14), we are to forgive others even as we have been forgiven (6:14-15; cf. Ephesians 4:32), we are to trust God for our needs rather than be full of care and anxiety (6:25-34; cf. Philippians 4:6, 1 Peter 5:7) and we are not to judge our brethren (7:1-5; cf. James 4:11-12).
3. Finally, one of the most beautiful signs that the Sermon on the Mount is for disciples today is that it teaches us to enjoy a relationship with God as our Heavenly Father (mentioned 17 times). At the very centre and heart of the Sermon is the 'Lord's Prayer', which teaches us to address God as 'Our Father in Heaven'.

What is the Gospel of the Kingdom?

Finally, there is one further little associated misconception that needs clearing up. Some teach that Christ's message to Israel about the offer of an immediate kingdom (which we have mischievously called Plan A) is called 'the gospel of the Kingdom' and is a different gospel to the present gospel Christ has sent us into all the world to preach – 'the gospel of the grace of God'.

However, no less an authority than the Apostle Paul plainly disagrees with this notion. That the 'gospel of the Kingdom' is exactly the same gospel as the 'gospel of the grace of God' is seen in Acts 20:24-25, the only place the expression 'the gospel of the grace of God' is mentioned. There we read about Paul 'preaching the kingdom of God' in the very same breath as speaking about the 'gospel of the grace of God': 'But none of these things move me; nor do I count my life dear to myself, so that I may finish my race with joy, and the ministry which I received from the Lord Jesus, to testify to the gospel of the grace of God. And indeed, now I know that you all, among whom I have gone preaching the kingdom of God, will see my face no more'.

Furthermore, Paul described his message as 'repentance toward God and faith toward our Lord Jesus Christ' just three verses before in 20:21. Thus, Paul described the preaching of the kingdom of God, the gospel of the grace of God and the message of repentance and faith as the one and the same message. These terms are synonymous descriptions of the One Gospel.

These two terms indeed advertise two different aspects of the gospel; the gospel of the kingdom tells us of the glorious hope of the gospel, while the gospel of the grace of God explains the basis of the salvation it offers. But at their heart, they are the same message.

The fact that we find the apostles preaching many times about the kingdom of God in the book of Acts shows that the gospel of the kingdom was not just confined to the ministry of the Lord Jesus, or to some future tribulation period proclamation. See Acts 8:12, 14:22, 19:8, 20:25, 28:23. Notice two examples:

- In Acts 8:12 we read, 'But when they believed Philip as he preached the things concerning the kingdom of God and the name of Jesus Christ, both men and women were baptized'.
- The very last verse of the book of Acts reads: 'Paul dwelt two whole years in his own rented house and received all who came to him, preaching the kingdom of God and teaching the things which concern the Lord Jesus Christ with all confidence, no one forbidding him'.

The idea that there are a number of different gospels such as the gospel of the Kingdom, the gospel of the grace of God, the gospel of God, the gospel of Christ, etc., is erroneous. The Bible teaches that there is one 'everlasting gospel' (Revelation 14:6). Please observe that in Revelation 14:6 this 'everlasting gospel' is being preached by an angel during the very period of time, the 'great tribulation', when – according to some – the 'gospel of the Kingdom' is to be preached. This further proves that all men are saved by grace through faith in Christ in response to the one and only everlasting gospel. There is no other way to be saved, nor are there any other gospels – except false-gospels.

Admittedly, these different descriptions of the one true gospel advertise different aspects of that message, but it is still the same gospel. Christ preached the kingdom of God, His apostles preached it, and we should likewise preach that one day the King will return and reign. The message of a bright future on Planet Earth for those who repent and believe is indeed 'good news' and is still an important part of the message that God commissions us to preach to the world today. His Kingdom will soon be upon us. The final events that will climax in the establishment of that Kingdom could happen at any moment! Men must therefore repent and believe in Christ. Let us not be worried, either, that Christ's announcement that the Kingdom was at hand has remained unfulfilled for 2000 years. God counts a thousand years as a watch in the night.

PART TWO:

The Tribulation: Countdown to Armageddon

8 THE TRIBULATION: PAST, PRESENT OR FUTURE?

Christians from all three main eschatological positions believe that there will be a period of intense persecution and suffering on earth before Christ returns: the great tribulation.

Berkhof, an amillennialist, writes, 'The words of Jesus undoubtedly found a partial fulfilment in the days preceding the destruction of Jerusalem, but will evidently have a further fulfilment in the future in a tribulation far surpassing anything that has ever been experienced, Matt. 24:21, Mark 13:19'[1]. Augustine in the 5th century, the first to propose the idea of amillennialism, wrote about the 'judgment' of the tribulation:

> And at or in connection with that judgment the following events shall come to pass, as we have learned: Elias the Tishbite shall come, the Jews shall believe; Antichrist shall persecute; Christ shall judge; the dead shall rise; the good and the wicked shall be separated; the world shall be burned and renewed. All these things, we believe, shall come to pass; but how, or in what order, human understanding cannot perfectly teach us, but only the experience of the events themselves[2].

From a postmillennialist perspective, Charles Hodge writes, 'those days of tribulation which the Bible seems to teach are to immediately precede the coming of the Lord'[3].

Charles Ryrie (a premillennialist) writes:

> In describing the period of the great tribulation, the Lord said it will be a time 'such as has not occurred since the beginning of the world until not, nor ever shall' (Matt. 24:21). It will be a time of trouble unique in the history of the world ... The uniqueness of the Tribulation lies in its being worldwide and in its terror, which will cause men to

---

[1] Louis Berkhof, *Systematic Theology*, p700
[2] Augustine, *City of God*, book 20, ch. 30
[3] Charles Hodge, *Systematic Theology*, 1871-3, reprinted Eerdmans, 1977, 3:812

want to die rather than live[4].

Irenaeus, a premillennialist from the 2nd century, wrote:

> When this Anti-Christ shall have devastated all things in this world, he will reign for three years and six months, and sit in the temple at Jerusalem; and then the Lord will come from heaven in the clouds, in the glory of the Father, sending this man and those who follow him into the lake of fire; but bringing in for the righteous the times of the kingdom, that is, the rest, the hallowed seventh day; and restoring to Abraham the promised inheritance, in which kingdom the Lord declared, that 'many coming from the east and the west should sit down with Abraham, Isaac, and Jacob[5].

However, there are others who take a different view, and argue that the 'great tribulation' will not happen immediately before the return of Christ.

Two Alternative Viewpoints

Preterists (meaning 'past', from the Latin *praeter*) hold that the great tribulation period already happened in the past – it was actually the Roman destruction of Jerusalem in AD 70. Preterists also believe that Jesus 'returned' in AD 70 to watch over the destruction of the Temple, that Nero the Caesar of the mid AD 60s was the Antichrist, that the book of Revelation was written before, and foretold, the destruction of Jerusalem, and that this siege of Jerusalem was also the battle of Armageddon.

Therefore, there is no future 'great tribulation' period, nor future Antichrist, nor future battle of Armageddon. Some 'Partial Preterists' still believe there is a future coming of Christ and resurrection, but full preterists deny a future return of Christ and even argue that the resurrection of the dead happened in AD 70, going beyond the bounds of Christian orthodoxy.

Secondly, many of those who believe Christ will rapture the Church after the great tribulation (post-tribulation rapturists) also deny a future tribulation period. They argue that the tribulation period is already happening now. The great tribulation is the entire church age, or even the entirety of human history.

To help us get our bearings, and try to work out what we should believe about the tribulation, we are going to look at the seven verses that are

---

[4] Charles Ryrie, *Basic Theology*, Victor Books, 1986, p464
[5] Irenaeus, *Against Heresies*, Book V, chap 30, para 4

usually taken as clear references to the great tribulation period.

Biblical References
This time of intense suffering is referred to in a number of New Testament passages:

- In Matthew 24:21-22, Christ said, 'For then there will be great tribulation, such as has not been since the beginning of the world until this time, no, nor ever shall be. And unless those days were shortened, no flesh would be saved; but for the elect's sake those days will be shortened'.
- Mark 13:19 likewise describes this period: 'For in those days there will be tribulation, such as has not been since the beginning of the creation which God created until this time, nor ever shall be'.
- In Rev. 2:22, the Lord warns the church in Thyatira about the prophetess Jezebel, 'Indeed I will cast her into a sickbed, and those commit adultery with her into great tribulation, unless they repent of their deeds'.
- In Rev. 3:10, 'Because you have kept My command to persevere, I also will keep you from the hour of trial which shall come upon the whole world, to test those who dwell on the earth'.
- Similarly, in Rev. 7:14, we read that 'These are the ones who come out of the great tribulation, and washed their robes and made them white in the blood of the Lamb'.

The Bible also speaks about the 'great tribulation' in a number of passages in the OT:

- In Jeremiah 30:7 we read, 'Alas! For that day is great, so that none is like it; and it is the time of Jacob's trouble, but he shall be saved out of it'. Following on from their salvation out of this time of trouble, Jeremiah speaks of how Israel will 'serve the LORD their God, and David their king, whom I will raise up for them'. This refers to the future time when Christ reigns; this verse links the great tribulation with end-of-time events.
- Daniel 12:1 says, 'there shall be a time of trouble such as never was since there was a nation even to that time'. In the next verse (v2), Daniel speaks about the resurrection following on from this time of trouble: 'and many of those who sleep in the dust of the earth shall awake, some to everlasting life, some to shame and everlasting

contempt'.

Notice that neither of these Old Testament passages are referring to a period of tribulation experienced in Old Testament times, but a period of great trouble that will occur at the end of the world – at roughly the same time as the resurrection, and the kingdom of the Messiah.

Notice also that both of these Old Testament verses speak of a time of tribulation unparalleled in human history. E. W. Rogers writes:

> It is not possible to have more than one period of which unparalleled severity (either in the past or future) is predicated. It follows, therefore, that Jeremiah 30:5-7, Daniel 12:1, Matthew 24:21 and Joel 2:2 refer to the same time. "The great tribulation" is identical with "the time of Jacob's trouble"[6].

We see from these verses that the great tribulation is characterized by three things: firstly, unparalleled intensity, secondly, worldwide scope, and thirdly, a Jewish epicentre.

When does the Great Tribulation Occur?

There are three possible answers to the question of when the 'great tribulation' occurs. Some hold that it occurred in the past (in the period leading up to the destruction of Jerusalem in AD 70, or during the early Roman persecutions), some hold that it is occurring in the present church age – right now – but most agree that the great tribulation will occur in the future.

View One: The Great Tribulation has Already Happened

Not all Christians believe that the great tribulation will occur at the end of time. Preterists believe that the great tribulation occurred in the past, during the three-year Jewish War that led to Jerusalem's destruction in AD 70. However, despite the increasing popularity of this view, there are nine problems with the idea that the great tribulation happened in AD 70:

1. **AD 70 was not the greatest trouble the world has ever seen.** AD 70 wasn't the greatest period of suffering the world has ever seen, even for the Jewish people. Just over one million Jews died in the war with Rome (AD 67-70), but the Jews have had periods of even greater

---

[6] E. W. Rogers, *Concerning the Future*, Pickering and Inglis, 1962, p44, ft 10

suffering, like the Holocaust when six million died.

2. **Christ comes immediately after the Great Tribulation.** Christ said that 'immediately after the tribulation of those days' (Matt. 24:29), He would return: 'then the sign of the Son of Man will appear in heaven, and then all the tribes of the earth will , mourn, and they will see the Son of Man coming on the clouds of heaven with power and great glory' (Matt. 24:29-30). But Christ did not return immediately after AD 70. Preterists say that Jesus had a 'secret' coming in AD 70, but apart from struggling to think of how such an 'invisible' coming could ever be proved, the other significant problem with this idea is that Matthew 24:30 says that all people will see Jesus coming, resulting in 'all the tribes of the earth' mourning. This fulfills the prophecy of Zechariah 12:10 - 13:1, in which Israel recognises Jesus as the true Messiah, receives the Holy Spirit, mourns over their 'piercing' – crucifixion – of the Son of God, and has their sins washed away. None of this happened in AD 70 – there has been no Jewish repentance or conversion or salvation from sins, because they have not yet seen Christ's visible return to earth and believed in Him. Therefore, the great tribulation did not happen in AD 70 but must instead occur immediately before Christ returns.

3. **The Resurrection happens at Christ's Return.** Daniel 12:1-3 tells us that the resurrection happens straight after the great tribulation: 'At that time Michael shall stand up, the great prince who stands watch over the sons of your people; and there shall be a time of trouble, such as never was since there was a nation, even to that time. And at that time your people shall be delivered, every one who is found written in the book. And many of those who sleep in the dust of the earth shall awake, some to everlasting life, some to shame and everlasting contempt. Those who are wise shall shine like the brightness of the firmament, and those who turn many to righteousness like the stars forever and ever'. Since the resurrection has not yet happened, neither has the great tribulation. Partial preterists try to separate Christ's coming in AC 70 from the future resurrection, but 1 Thessalonians 4 shows that it is impossible to separate these two events.

4. **The Abomination of Desolation.** Matthew 24:15 says that the sign that the great tribulation has begun is the 'abomination of desolation'. Christ further says that to understand this great sign, we must read

Daniel's prophecy. Daniel mentions the 'abomination of desolation' three times in his prophecy, and the reference in Daniel 11:31 is very important, because it tells how Antiochus Epiphanes, a Syrian king, set up an 'abomination of desolation' in the Jewish temple. The intertestamental book of Maccabees tells us how Antiochus Epiphanes fulfilled this prophecy of Daniel's when he desecrated the Jewish temple from 167-164 BC by stopping the Jewish sacrifices, setting up 'an abomination of desolation' (a statue of Zeus), and sacrificed swine on the altar. Maccabees even uses the term 'abomination of desolation' (1 Macc. 1:54). The 'abomination of desolation' is therefore an idol statue set up in the Jewish temple. Other OT passages refer to idols as 'abominations' (see Deut. 7:25, 26, 27:15). But Jesus in Matt. 24:15 says that there is an 'abomination of desolation' yet to come in the future. Preterists argue that the Roman army's standards were worshipped as images of the Roman gods, and that these images were the 'abomination' that resulted in desolation in AD 70. However, there is a problem here: the Roman standards were only set up in the Jewish temple in AD 70 *after* the Jewish war was won, while Jesus says that the 'abomination of desolation' stands in the Holy Place (i.e. the temple, see Acts 6:13, 21:28) as the sign that the great tribulation is about to ***begin***. Therefore, the abomination of desolation cannot be the Roman Army's standards. In any case, it seems unlikely that the Roman army standards are an 'abomination' when we remember that Christ seemed far from outraged by Caesar's image on Roman coins brought to Him in the gospels. The abomination of desolation is instead an idolatrous statue that all the world will be forced to worship in the future. Again, therefore, the great tribulation did not happen in AD 67-70.

5. **When was Revelation written?** Preterists argue that the book of Revelation was written in the AD 60s and foretold the destruction of Jerusalem. The book of Revelation describes events which 'must take place after this' (Rev. 4:1, see also 1:1) – events which include the great tribulation (Rev. 7:14). Preterists therefore argue that the predictions in the book of Revelation, including the great tribulation, have all been fulfilled in the first century AD. But there is good evidence that the book of Revelation was written in the AD 90s, during the reign of the emperor Domitian, long after the events of AD 70. Irenaeus (AD 120-202), who was a close associate of Polycarp, the disciple of the apostle John, wrote, 'We will not, however, incur the risk of pronouncing

positively as to the name of the Antichrist, for if it were necessary that his name should be distinctively revealed in the present time, it would have been announced by him who beheld the apocalyptic vision. For that was seen not very long time since, but almost in our day, towards the end of Domitian's reign'[7]. Irenaeus thus confirms that Revelation was written in the AD 90s. Again, Irenaeus writes about the number 666, 'this number being found in all the most approved and ancient copies [of Revelation], and those men who saw John face to face bearing their testimony'[8], confirming again that Irenaeus had close links with John's immediate disciples, and that his information about the date of Revelation is correct. If so, the great tribulation could not have been the suffering associated with the fall of Jerusalem in AD 70 or the persecution by Nero in the 60s, for Revelation (written in the 90s) tells us that is was still to come in the future.

6. **Revelation 1:7 says that every eye will see Christ when He returns.** Revelation 1:7 is perhaps the key verse of the entire book of Revelation, and speaks about Christ's 'revelation' at His return: 'Behold, He is coming with clouds, and every eye will see Him, even they who pierced Him. And all the tribes of the earth will mourn because of Him. Even so, Amen'. Christ's return will be visible and unmistakable, however no one at the time of AD 70 – Christian or non-Christian – mentioned this event. Preterists argue for a secret, invisible, 'spiritual' return of Christ in AD 70 – contradicting what Scripture plainly says.

7. **Nero is the Antichrist?** Preterists argue that Nero was the Antichrist (so that the Antichrist reigned before their 'great tribulation' of AD67-70). They argue that this is proved by the letters of his name adding up to 666. However, to obtain this result involves mathematical trickery. Nero's name in Latin does not add up to 666, because Roman numerals (MCMLXVIII, etc.) do not work in the same alpha-numeric way that Greek or Hebrew letters do (i.e. every letter corresponding to a number). Nero only adds up to 666 if you add the word 'Caesar' to 'Nero', and then write his name out in Greek (Caesar Neron - notice the added 'n') and then transliterate this name into Hebrew. But this three-step approach is too tortured – why not just transliterate the Latin straight into Hebrew (and skip the Greek)

---

[7] Irenaeus, *Against Heresies*, Chapter 30
[8] *Against Heresies*, Ch. 30

if Hebrew is the language to count it in? Because it wouldn't work, of course! Why not just give the numerical value of the Greek version of Nero? Because neither Nero nor Caesar Nero adds up to 666 in Greek either. It is obvious that the name Nero is being 'fixed' (with letters and other names added) to meet the target number 666. Irenaeus the 2nd century writer does not even mention Nero as a possible contender for Antichrist. He mentions some possible names: Evanthas, Lateinos and Teitan as adding up to 666, but dismisses all such number games, writing 'We will not, however, incur the risk of pronouncing positively as to the name of Antichrist; for if it were necessary that his name should be distinctly revealed in this present time, it would have been announced by him who beheld the apocalyptic vision. For that was seen not very long time since, but almost in our day, towards the end of Domitian's reign'[9]. In short, seeing the book of Revelation was written after Nero, it cannot be him. Other problems with Nero as Antichrist include the fact that he did not have a resurrection 'experience' (as the real Antichrist does, Rev. 13:14), nor did Nero rule the entire world, so that he was given authority over 'every tribe, tongue, and nation' (Rev. 13:7), nor did all the world worship him (Rev. 13:8).

8. **Who was Nero's False Prophet?** If Nero was the first 'Beast' of Revelation 13, as preterists maintain, who was his 'Minister of Propaganda', the second 'Beast' of Revelation 13, who did supernatural miracles in his presence, making fire come down from heaven (Rev. 13:13), and who set up an image of Nero that breathed and spoke (Rev. 13:14-15)? Preterists do not say[10].

9. **The Temple in Revelation 11.** Preterists argue that the temple mentioned in Revelation 11 proves that the book must have been written before the destruction of the temple in AD 70, however what Revelation 11:1-2 tell us is that the *'city* is trampled by the Gentiles' while the *temple* is not destroyed. John was told 'Rise and measure the temple of God, the altar, and those who worship there. But leave out the court which is outside the temple, and do not measure it, for it has been given to the Gentiles. And they will tread the holy city underfoot for forty-two months' (Rev. 11:1-2). This is very different to what

---

[9] Irenaeus, *Against Heresies*, Ch. 30
[10] Preterist Kenneth Gentry entirely omits any reference to the second beast of Revelation 13 in *Four Views on the Book of Revelation*, Zondervan, 1998, pp37-92

happened in AD 67-70 – the temple was destroyed (not spared), and the siege of Jerusalem only lasted 7 months in AD 70, not 42 months. We will later show that Rev. 11 is not speaking of the Jewish temple in AD 70, but is instead speaking of a future (rebuilt) temple.

Preterists teach that the New Testament's prophecies were all fulfilled in AD 70, however Christ did not visibly return in AD 70. Therefore Preterism is a false-teaching.

Preterist Arguments
Having looked at the arguments against Preterism, and the reasons why the Preterist position is not true, we need (in fairness) to turn and look at the verses which Preterists argue show that the great tribulation occurred in AD 67-70. For those who are interested in studying the Preterist view further (those who are not interested may skip this section), there are three main verses that Preterists point to.

First, **Matthew 10:23** says, 'When they persecute you in this city, flee to another. For assuredly, I say to you, you will not have gone through the cities of Israel before the Son of Man comes'. The preterist position argues that Christ is here speaking about His second coming. Therefore, Jesus' Second Coming must have occurred in the first century AD.

However, Jesus' second coming is not the context of Jesus' remarks here. In fact, in Matthew 10, Jesus has not even openly told His disciples about His death, let alone His return. The context of this verse is persecution the disciples would endure on their missionary journey during the Lord's ministry. Christ says that 'a disciple is not above his teacher, nor a servant above his master ... If they have called the master of the house Beelzebub, how much more will they call those of his household' (Matt. 10:24-25). Christ is saying that the disciples would suffer persecution in the same way Christ Himself is suffering persecution. He is teaching that whatever persecution the disciples suffer on their missionary journey is in keeping with what Christ Himself is already experiencing.

Christ's coming in Matthew 10:23 is therefore not a reference to the Second Coming of Christ but to the First Coming of Christ, to suffer and die at Jerusalem. We see Jesus speaking of his 'coming' in the same way – to refer to His first coming – later in the same chapter. In Matthew 10:34-35, Jesus said that He did not come to bring peace on the earth, but a sword. Then in Matthew 10:35, he says, 'I have come to set a man against his father, a daughter against her mother', etc.

Christ's coming in Matthew 10:23 is not referring to His Second

Coming. The idea of Jesus' second coming is something which the disciples would have had no idea about. Jesus' Second Coming only starts to be mentioned much later in Matthew's Gospel, after He has told the disciples about His death in chapter 16. This text in Matthew 10:23, therefore, lends no weight to the Preterist view.

A second verse that Preterists use is **Matthew 16:28**, 'Assuredly, I say to you, there are some standing here who shall not taste death till they see the Son of Man coming in His kingdom'. Kenneth Gentry writes:

> In Mark 9:1 Jesus promises that some of his hearers will not 'taste death' before witnessing 'the kingdom of God come with power.' This almost certainly refers to the destruction of the temple at the behest of Christ[11].

However, no one saw Jesus 'coming' in AD 70 – even Preterists say it was a 'secret' coming. A better understanding of Matthew 16:28 is that it refers to the Transfiguration, when Jesus was transformed and seen in all His glory. Just look at the verse immediately before, 'For the Son of Man will come in the glory of His Father, with His angels, and then He will reward each according to his works' (Matt. 16:27). Notice the word 'glory' in this verse, because this gives us a clue as to what Jesus is talking about. In each of the three synoptic Gospels, we have the story of the transfiguration immediately after Jesus makes his statement about certain people not tasting death till they see the Son of Man coming in His kingdom. Matthew and Mark say that the Transfiguration happened six days afterwards, while Luke's gospel says 'about eight days after these sayings'.

Furthermore, Luke's gospel makes much of the word 'glory' when Christ was on the mount of Transfiguration. We read that Moses and Elijah appeared in glory (Luke 9:31), while the next verse says that the disciples awoke and 'saw His glory' (Luke 9:32). Peter also speaks about the Transfiguration in his second epistle: 'for He received from God the Father honour and glory when such a voice came to Him from the excellent glory' (2 Pet. 1:17). Peter, James and John saw a vision of Christ in His glory on the mountain, a glimpse of what He will look like when He returns in His Father's glory to reign in His millennial kingdom. This is what Matthew 16:28 is referring to – not AD 70.

Perhaps the best verse for the Preterist viewpoint is **Matthew 24:34**, 'Assuredly, I say to you, this generation will by no means pass away till all

---

[11] Kenneth Gentry, "A Preterist View of Revelation" in S. N. Gundry & C. M. Pate (Eds.), *Four Views on the Book of Revelation*, Zondervan, 1998, p43

these things take place'. In fact, this is the only verse in the Bible that presents a good case for the preterist position. It is saying that all the events of Matthew 24 – the abomination of desolation (v15), the great tribulation (v21) and the coming of Christ (v30) must all occur before 'this generation' (i.e. Jesus' generation) dies out. The only candidate for the fulfilment of Matthew 24 in 'this generation', according to the Preterist, is the events of AD 67-70.

However, there are again many problems with taking the events of Matthew 24 as fulfilled in AD 67-70, including those already mentioned: there was no 'abomination of desolation' in this period meeting the biblical description, and no one saw 'the Son of man coming on the clouds of heaven with power and great glory' (Matt. 24:30).

An alternative interpretation of Matthew 24:34 is that 'this generation' refers to the generation in which the great tribulation happens. That is, the generation that sees all the signs, from the abomination of desolation and the great tribulation through to the signs of the sun, moon and stars (Matt. 24:29-31), will also see Christ's visible return.

Preterists argue that if that were the case, the Bible would have said 'that generation', instead of 'this generation'. However, the word 'this' in the Hebrew and Greek languages is more flexible than the word in English and is sometimes used in the sense of 'that'. Thus, in the Hebrew Old Testament, in Exodus 12:8, God says to Moses about the Passover, 'Then they shall eat the flesh on *that* night; roasted in fire'. But literally in the Hebrew text, the word is 'this' night. This would not make sense to us in English – it would mean on that very same night in which God was speaking to Moses in Ex. 12:8 (a number of days before the Passover) the Israelites were to eat the Passover – which clearly is not the case. Consider also the following cases where the Greek word 'this' is translated as 'that' in our English Bibles (some using the plural form: 'those' for 'these'):

- in Luke 1:39, we read 'Mary arose in *those* days and went into the hill country'. However, in the Greek, it is literally 'these days'.
- In Luke 23:7, Herod was in Jerusalem 'in those days', according to our English Bibles, but the Greek literally reads in 'these days'.
- In John 4:18, our English Bibles read, 'in that you spoke truly', but the Greek says 'in this you spoke truly'
- In Acts 1:15 and 6:1 the Greek reads, 'and/now in these days', but our English bibles have 'in those days'
- In Acts 7:7 the Greek reads, 'and after this', but our English Bibles have 'and after that'.

These are some examples that show the way that Hebrew and Greek use the word 'this' while our English idiom demands 'that'.

The key to understanding the word 'this' is to look at the context and see what 'this' is referring to. In Matthew 24, Jesus had just said (in the verse before) that when 'you see all these things you know that He (or it) is near' (Matt. 24:33). 'All these things' refers to the events of Matt. 24 – the 'abomination of desolation' and the 'great tribulation'. Jesus is saying that these events will immediately precede His coming and that 'this generation' will visibly see Him coming.

Darrell Bock, writing about this saying in Luke 21:32, says that 'the generation that sees all these things refers to the generation present in verse 25. In other words, those who see the beginning of the end in the cosmic signs will see the arrival of the decisive era in the Son of Man's return. Once the events of the final act commence, they will take place rather quickly'[12]. In other words, those who see the beginning of the end (in the abomination of desolation and the 'great tribulation'), will also see the end, at the coming of Christ. The same people who see the signs will see the Son of God.

View Two: The Tribulation is Happening Now

A second alternative view to the idea that the great tribulation is in the future is that the great tribulation is occurring right now – in the present: the entire church age is great tribulation.

It might seem strange that some people believe that the entire church age is the great tribulation. But there is a very interesting reason why they believe this idea: it is because they have no other way to solve a major puzzle related to the coming of the Lord. The Bible teaches that Jesus could come at any time, but the Bible also says His coming will be preceded by another event – the great tribulation period that lasts three and a half years. If there is a specific great tribulation time period that comes before Christ's return, then Christ's coming cannot be imminent – at any moment – for no Christians would ever be surprised at Christ's coming (as the Bible tells us) if it is to be preceded by a clearly signposted and set period of time, like the great tribulation. Once the great tribulation period has started, Christians would be able to mark on their fridge calendars the very day of Christ's return – if they know their Bible – because the Bible tells us how long the great tribulation lasts. To escape the horns of this dilemma, therefore, some people deny that the great

---

[12] Darrell Bock, *Luke*, NIVAC, Zondervan, 1996, p538-9

tribulation is in the future, and argue that it is already happening.

Wayne Grudem writes, 'since the first century, there have been many periods of violent and intense persecution of Christians, and even in our century much of it has occurred over large portions of the globe, with Christians being horribly persecuted in the former Soviet Union, in communist China, and in Muslim countries. It would be difficult to convince some Christians in this century who have undergone decades of persecution for their faith, and have known that persecution to affect thousands of other Christians throughout large segments of the world, that such a great tribulation has certainly not yet occurred. ... Once again, though we may think that Jesus' words indicate the likelihood of a yet greater persecution coming in the future, it is difficult to be certain of this. It seems appropriate to conclude that it is unlikely but possible that the prediction of a great tribulation has already been fulfilled'[13].

Grudem tries to sit on the fence by saying that it is 'unlikely but possible' that the great tribulation is presently being fulfilled. But the idea that we are currently going through the great tribulation is hard to accept when we observe Christians falling off to sleep in church services on Sunday, living in luxury and indulgence, and even running for the highest political offices in many lands. It is not very hard to imagine a time of persecution far more severe than what we are presently going through. To suggest that what we currently experience is the worst tribulation that could possibly ever happen in the history of the world – which is how the Bible describes the great tribulation – is far from convincing.

Douglas Moo argues along similar lines. He queries whether 'the tribulations of the final tribulation are qualitatively different from the tribulation experienced by God's people throughout history'. Moo answers in the negative, and says that:

> the New Testament consistently predicts that believers will suffer tribulation. Nothing in these texts suggests that the suffering of the final tribulation will be any greater in degree than what many believers throughout the age must suffer[14].

This is like saying that the Jewish Holocaust was not really any different to any other suffering in the world's history because, on an individual level, we all die, and death is unpleasant.

---

[13] Wayne Grudem, *Systematic Theology*, p1102
[14] Douglas J. Moo, "A Case for the Posttribulation Rapture", *Three Views on the Rapture*, Grand Rapids: Zondervan, 1996, p191-2

Despite the strained idea that the great tribulation is currently occurring, the fact that some Christians suggest this alerts us to a major puzzle of Bible prophecy they are trying to solve: how can Christ's coming be preceded by unmistakable signs (including the great tribulation), but also be a surprise that no one will be able to predict? Thus Erickson, explaining the view of J. Barton Payne, writes, 'while the return of Christ will not take place until after the Tribulation, it can be expected at any moment, for the tribulation may already be occurring'[15].

Others hold that the entire church period is the great tribulation (e.g. we read that 'a great persecution arose' in Acts 8:1), and thus the church is already in the tribulation. Hendriksen, an amillennialist, commentating on Revelation 11, writes: the 'twelve hundred and sixty days ... is the period that extends from the moment of Christ's ascension almost until the judgment day ... It is the period of affliction; the present gospel age'[16].

Others argue that the great tribulation covers the entire period of the world's history, so that the great tribulation started with the Fall and finishes at Christ's coming. Fromow writes:

> The Church is *already* passing through the great tribulation' ... The term Great embraces the whole period of the Church's course on earth, and should not be confined to the final 3½ years of the second half of Daniel's seventieth week of intensive tribulation. It began with the first saints after the Fall, and includes all who have washed their robes and made them white in the blood of the Lamb until the Second Advent of Christ[17].

The major problem with the theory that the great tribulation is happening now, in the present, is that the great tribulation is described as a time unlike any other. Matthew 24:21 calls it 'great tribulation, such as has not been since the beginning of the world until this time, no, nor ever shall be'. Mark 13:19 says the same thing. Daniel 12:1 calls it a 'time of trouble such as never was since there was a nation even to that same time'. Jeremiah 30:7 says 'alas, for that day is great, so that none is like it'.

This prompts the question: if the great tribulation is a period of time unlike any other, then how can it also be a period of time just like every other? Walvoord writes, 'a period of trouble cannot be unprecedented and

---

[15] Millard Erickson, *Christian Theology*, Baker, 2nd ed., 1998, p1230

[16] Hendriksen, *More than Conquerors*, p129

[17] George Fromow, *Will the Church Pass Through the Tribulation?* London: Sovereign Grace Advent Testimony, n.d., p2

at the same time general throughout the age'[18].

The definite article, '*the* great tribulation' (lit. 'the tribulation, the great one', Rev. 7:14), shows us that this is not simply a period of relatively greater tribulation (such as the church occasionally suffers in some places), but instead a specific and definite time of tribulation that will make all other periods of persecution pale by comparison.

View Three: A Future Tribulation Period

The third option is that the tribulation period is in the future. Evidences for this include the fact that it is followed immediately by Christ's visible coming (Matt. 24:21-31), and that it occurs at the time of the resurrection (Dan. 12:1-2). Both of these events are still in the future – therefore so is the great tribulation. Further confirmation that it is in the future is found in the book of Revelation. If we compare what Revelation says about the normal tribulation that Christians presently experience with what it says about the great tribulation, we notice significant differences. Firstly, notice what it says about normal Christian tribulation experienced presently:

- John was experiencing tribulation and persecution (Rev. 1:9),
- The church in Smyrna was told that it was about to suffer persecution (Rev. 2:10): 'Do not fear any of those things which you are about to suffer. Indeed, the devil is about to throw some of you into prison, that you may be tested, and you will have tribulation ten days. Be faithful until death, and I will give you the crown of life'.
- The church in Pergamos had already experienced persecution: Antipas was called 'My faithful martyr, who was killed among you' (Rev. 2:13).

However, the book of Revelation points to something that goes beyond simply localised and sporadic persecution in the present, as in Smyrna or Pergamos, to a future time of worldwide, 'great tribulation':

- In Rev. 2:22, we read about Jezebel in the church of Thyatira, 'Indeed I will cast her into a sickbed, and those who commit adultery with her into ***great tribulation***, unless they repent of their deeds'.
- In Rev. 3:10, in the letter to the church in Philadelphia, we read of 'the ***hour of trial which shall come upon the whole world***, to test those who dwell on the earth'. Here we read of a trial which will come upon the whole world – it is not a localized case of persecution. Notice that

---

[18] John Walvoord, *The Rapture Question*, Zondervan, 1979, p158

this worldwide tribulation is spoken of as being still in the future.
- In Rev. 7:14, we read about a great multitude of people dressed in white robes who stand before God's throne in heaven. John asks who they are and the angel replies: 'These are the ones who come out of ***the great tribulation***, and washed their robes and made them white in the blood of the Lamb' (Rev. 7:14). Bear in mind that from Revelation 4:1 onwards, we are being shown future events ('things which must take place after this'). Therefore, the 'great tribulation' here in Revelation 7:14 is in the future from John's perspective. Notice also that literally, the verse should read 'these are the ones ***who are coming out*** of the great tribulation'. In other words, while the great tribulation was spoken of in the future tense in Revelation 2:22 and 3:10, here it is described in the present tense in Revelation 7:14. Notice that it is literally 'the tribulation, the great one'. It is not only great tribulation, but *the* great tribulation, a specific and definite period of unparalleled tribulation.

Thus, the book of Revelation sets apart the great tribulation as different in three ways from normal Christian hardship and persecution:

1. The great tribulation is worldwide: it is described as a test that will come on the whole world (Rev. 3:10). This is something that has never happened in Christian history – it is still in the future.
2. The great tribulation is intense: while many Christians have experienced nothing more than minimal to moderate persecution, there is a period here described as 'great tribulation' (2:22, 7:14). In some parts of the world there have been periods of intense persecution, but there has never been worldwide 'great tribulation' yet.
3. The great tribulation is future: John does not use the term 'great tribulation' to describe the sufferings of Christians in his day. Rather, it is described as a future event in Rev. 2:22 and 3:10, and described as presently happening in Rev. 7:14, a passage which (as we will prove) shows us future events.

'The great tribulation' in Revelation is the same as 'the great tribulation' spoken of by Christ. There is no reason why we should see them as different. In fact, there can only be one period of 'great tribulation' that can be described by the words 'such as has not been since the beginning of the world until this time, no, nor ever shall be' (Matt. 24:21), a 'time of trouble such as never was since there was a nation even to that same time'

(Daniel 12:1), and 'none is like it' (Jer. 30:7). It will occur at the end of this age, be worldwide in its scope and be unparalleled in its intensity.

In the following chapters, we will look at what happens during this period of time.

9 APOCALYPSE: THE END OF THE WORLD AS WE KNOW IT

The word 'apocalypse', in modern novels and films, refers to a terrible cataclysm in which the world is destroyed, either as a result of a nuclear war, or by a deadly virus, or by climate change, or by a volcanic eruption, or by famine, or an alien invasion, or an asteroid impact, or by the rise of technologically-advanced robots or artificial intelligence, or by the tyrannical rule of an evil political dictator. The Bible describes (virtually) all of these apocalyptic disasters happening one after another in the book of Revelation. In this chapter we will look at the apocalypse to come.

The word 'Revelation' comes from the Greek word 'apocalypse', which means an 'unveiling', a pulling back of the curtain that allows us to peer into the future. In the next few chapters we are going to answer some questions people have about the end of the world:

- Will there be a One-World government?
- How will we know who the Antichrist is?
- When (and how) does the Battle of Armageddon happen?

Before we look at these subjects in more detail, we need to answer an even more basic question.

Is the Book of Revelation Literally Going to Happen in the Future?
Many people turn to read the last book of the Bible, Revelation, first – either because they are worried about the state of the world and want to see how everything ends, or maybe they hope that rather than reading the entire Bible, they can skip to the last part. But most people only end up confused when they read Revelation. There is a good reason Revelation is the last book in the Bible: we need to read all the rest of the Bible to understand it.

Revelation is one of the most difficult books in the Bible to understand. To see whether Revelation is literally going to happen in the future or not, we need to look at the four main ways that Christians interpret it.

1. **Preterists** (meaning, 'past') take the book as a description of events that happened in the past, that is, in the first century, and particularly the persecutions in the time of John who wrote it. As a result, most of the book of Revelation concerns events that are now past history.
2. **Historicists** take the book of Revelation as a prophecy of the unfolding history of the church age now. They take many details allegorically.
3. **Idealists** take the book as a depiction of the struggles between God and Satan, of good and evil, in every age; this approach leans heavily on spiritualising and allegorising.
4. **Futurists** see the book as a prophecy of events that will occur at the end of the world just before Christ returns. This school adopts a very literal approach, and sees Revelation as still in the future.

To see how these different approaches work, let us take one passage, Revelation 9:1-11, where we read about the sounding of the fifth trumpet:

> Then the fifth angel sounded: And I saw a star fallen from heaven to the earth. To him was given the key to the bottomless pit. ² And he opened the bottomless pit, and smoke arose out of the pit like the smoke of a great furnace. So the sun and the air were darkened because of the smoke of the pit. ³ Then out of the smoke locusts came upon the earth. And to them was given power, as the scorpions of the earth have power. ⁴ They were commanded not to harm the grass of the earth, or any green thing, or any tree, but only those men who do not have the seal of God on their foreheads. ⁵ And they were not given authority to kill them, but to torment them for five months. Their torment was like the torment of a scorpion when it strikes a man. ⁶ In those days men will seek death and will not find it; they will desire to die, and death will flee from them. ⁷ The shape of the locusts was like horses prepared for battle. On their heads were crowns of something like gold, and their faces were like the faces of men. ⁸ They had hair like women's hair, and their teeth were like lions' teeth. ⁹ And they had breastplates like breastplates of iron, and the sound of their wings was like the sound of chariots with many horses running into battle. ¹⁰ They had tails like scorpions, and there were stings in their tails. Their power was to hurt men five months. ¹¹ And they had as king over them the angel of the bottomless pit, whose name in Hebrew is Abaddon, but in Greek he has the name Apollyon.

In this scene, smoke billows out of the bottomless pit, darkening the sun.

Out of this smoke come a plague of locusts with scorpions' tails, looking like battle-horses, with crowns of gold, men's faces, women's hair and the teeth of lions. They wear breastplates of iron, their wings sound like chariots rushing into war and in their tails they have a sting. What does this all mean?

Preterist interpreters refer the book of Revelation to first century events, particularly the Jewish War of AD 67-70 which led to the destruction of the temple in Jerusalem. The key to understanding the vision, they argue, is that the events of the book of Revelation were to 'soon take place' (Rev. 1:1). Revelation must have had something to say to John's readers and thus must have been fulfilled soon after it was written. They suggest that the woman's hair in the vision would have immediately suggested to first century Christians the long-haired barbarians who eventually brought down the Roman Empire. One problem with this view is that Christ did not visibly return in the first (or subsequent) centuries. As the return of Christ is the main focus of the entire book (see 1:7, 19:11ff.), this seems to be a major problem for the idea that the book has already been fulfilled.

Historicists argue that the book of Revelation was meant to foretell the entire panoramic sweep of church history, from the apostles to Christ's return. These interpreters take the seven seals (Revelation chapters 6-7) to refer to the times of the Roman Empire, with its wars, famines (seal three) and Christian martyrs (seal five), while the seven trumpets (Revelation chapters 8-10) refer to the Vandals, Goths and finally Islamic invaders who overthrew the Roman Empire. The vision of the fifth trumpet in Revelation 9 relates to the swarming hordes of Muslim invaders in the AD 600s, for just as locusts are an Eastern plague, and the words Arab and locust in Hebrew were almost the same, so the 'man's face' pictures the Arab's moustache and beard, the iron breastplates their coats of mail, the lion-like teeth their ferocity and the fact that they resembled horses is a pointer to Arab horsemanship. The king, of course, must refer to Mohammed.

The historicist view was particularly popular in the 19th century because the seven bowls (Revelation chapters 15-16) were seen as the fulfilment of Napoleon and his wars (he was the Antichrist, the Beast of Revelation chapters 13-19). They took the first bowl (a foul and loathsome sore coming upon men) to be the spreading plague of the French revolution, while the ensuing bowls depicted the wars in Europe that followed. For example, the third bowl's rivers turning to blood pictured the wars in Germany and Italy, and the sun's scorching heat in the fourth bowl showed the intense suffering inflicted by Napoleon upon Europe.

The problem with the historicist view is the fact that, in the light of the twentieth century's vastly greater upheavals, it is clear that Napoleon was not the Antichrist. These Napoleonic explanations 'were too near the period of the French Revolution to be able to gauge its importance correctly, or to see its correct position in history, and they laid far too much stress upon details which, in the light of later happenings, are seen to have been of relatively little importance'(Tatford)[1].

Futurists see in the vision of Revelation 9 a yet-future judgement that God is going to bring upon the world at the end of time. Some would even argue that nothing fits the description in Revelation 9 more precisely than a modern Apache attack helicopter with its whirring wings sounding like chariots rushing into battle – it has armour-plating, and it has guns in the front and the rear. This sadly illustrates the fact that many prophecy enthusiasts are engaged in newspaper exposition: reading current affairs into the Bible.

Fourthly, Idealists argue that Revelation 9 simply refers to the spiritual conditions that exist throughout the entire age in which we live. Therefore, the smoke that billows out of the opened pit at the beginning of the vision refers to the way Satan is blinding the eyes of people who do not believe the gospel today. The locusts represent the Devil's agents, spreading delusion and deception, superstition, idolatry and error. The commentator Matthew Henry argues that when the passage says that the locusts were not to harm the grass or any green thing or any tree (verse 4), this means that true believers are not to be led astray, whether young Christians or more mature believers.

The problem with some of these interpretations is that they skim over the surface of the Bible's page, selectively cherry-picking one or two elements from the vision which match up with their preferences, while ignoring (or stretching) other features that do not. Or, interpreters take one feature of the locusts literally (women's hair), but then take the others allegorically (gold crowns=victory).

Thus, William Hendriksen, who suggests that the smoke in the vision allegorically represents Satanic blinding and deception in this present day, says 'we do not think it at all necessary to allegorize the sun and the air'[2]. The reason he doesn't allegorize the sun and air quickly becomes obvious.

---

[1] Frederick Tatford, *Prophecy's Last Word: an Exposition of the Revelation*, London: Pickering and Inglis, 1947, 1969, p180

[2] William Hendriksen, *More than Conquerors*, London: The Tyndale Press, 1940, p120, footnote 1

If we take the second item in the vision, the sun, to represent the light of God's truth that is blocked out by the smoke of Satanic deception, then we must proceed down through the rest of the twenty different elements, interpreting each one. How much easier just to pick out one element and interpret it! While the smoke interpretation sounds believable, what shall we make of the locusts' hair, teeth, breastplates, scorpion-stings and so on. This becomes increasingly difficult, if not ridiculous. So Hendriksen contents himself with allegorizing one element, pronounces himself satisfied, and declares no need for further interpretation.

This is the arbitrary, selective and whimsical approach of idealism. Why must the one dominant element we allegorize be the smoke instead of, say, the women's hair? The allegorizing game that Hendriksen plays lacks any consistent rules or controls. It is simply licensing our imagination to make the Bible mean whatever we want.

I suggest there are four reasons that suggest that the best way to understand the book of Revelation is using the futurist approach:

1. Christ's coming is the main event of Revelation. Notice the way that Revelation 1:7 introduces Christ's return as the goal and highpoint of the story, right at the beginning of the book: 'Behold, He is coming with clouds, and every eye will see Him'. The climax of the book is found in Revelation 19:11-21 where Christ returns, riding on a white horse. Seeing Christ's coming is still future, so the events leading up to it in Revelation are also still future.

2. After Christ's return in Revelation 19, we have the millennium (Rev. 20:1-10), the judgment of the Great White Throne (Rev. 20:11-15) and the new heavens and earth (Rev. 21:1-8). These events are also still in the future.

3. The main body of Revelation occurs in the future, as we can see by looking at Revelation chapters 4-6. In 4:1, John is told to come up into heaven where Christ says, 'I will show you things which must take place after this'. In other words, these are events still in the future for John. But what is the scene John sees in Revelation chapters 4 and 5 – when the Lamb takes the scroll out of the hand of the throne-sitter (Rev. 5)? Is it showing us the Ascension of Christ? No, because after the Lamb takes the scroll and begins to open its seals, He unleashes terrible disasters on the earth. One quarter of the world's population dies after the first four seals (Rev. 6:1-8). Then, at the opening of the sixth seal, we have signs that are elsewhere described as accompanying Christ's return: there is a great earthquake, the sun goes black, the moon turns

blood-red, the stars fall, and all the people on earth hide, calling upon the mountains and rocks to fall upon them and hide them from the wrath of God' (Rev. 6:12-17). These appear to be the same signs that we find described in Matthew 24:29-30 occurring immediately before Christ's return: 'Immediately after the tribulation of those days the sun will be darkened, and the moon will not give its light; the stars will fall from heaven, and the powers of the heavens will be shaken. Then the sign of the Son of Man will appear in heaven, and then all the tribes of the earth will mourn, and they will see the Son of Man coming on the clouds of heaven with power and great glory'. There are other Bible verses about the sign of the sun, moon and stars being darkened (see Isa. 2:10-22, 13:9-13, 24:1-23, Joel 2:10, 31, 3:15, Amos 5:20, Zeph. 1:15, Acts 2:20). This is the great sign of the end-times. These are not events that are happening in the present, nor did these events happen in the past. Therefore, it would seem that the dreadful events described in Revelation chapters 4-6 occur just before the Lord's return, and are therefore still in the future. And if Revelation chapters 4-6 are still in the future, and Revelation chapters 19-22 are still in the future, it makes sense to believe that the chapters in between – the main body of the book, chapters 7-18 – are also still in the future.

4. Rev. 1:19 says that John was told to 'Write the things which you have seen, and the things which are, and the things which will take place after this'. This verse speaks about: (a) 'the things which you have seen' – that is, the vision of Christ John saw in Revelation chapter One, (b) 'the things which are' – that is, things in the present (from John's perspective): chapters Two and Three, which tell us about the seven churches, and (c) 'the things which will take place after this' – that is, chapters Four to Twenty-two, future events.

Thus, while there may be some parts of the book of Revelation that are flashbacks to the past (e.g. Rev. 12:1ff.), and while there are benefits in viewing parts of the book of Revelation as having lessons for us in the present, it seems abundantly obvious that Revelation chapters 4 to 22 are referring to future events connected with the return of Christ

As to whether we should take Revelation literally or not, all commentators agree that some things in the book are symbolic. But it is also important to note that the symbols actually refer to real things; the details are not merely decorative. We will see that the best way to proceed is not by prejudging the question, but by looking at the individual prophecies in their context.

Because Revelation is all about the return of Christ and the events that lead up to this, we are going to take the main body of the book, from chapters 4 to 18 as dealing with the period that culminates in the return of Christ.

What will this period, the 'apocalypse', be like? It will be World Wars 3 and 4 one after another, plus the Black Death, the plagues of Egypt, wave after wave of terrible natural disasters, meteorite strikes, extreme global warming, the French Revolution's Reign of Terror, the Jewish Holocaust, and an alien invasion, all rolled into one. About 50 million people died in World War 2, but in the apocalypse, over half of the world's population will die – and that is before we even get to the final world war, Armageddon. This means that, on current population figures, more than 4 billion people will die during just the first part of the apocalypse. The devastation that is going to happen in this 'tribulation' period will be unparalleled.

In the rest of this chapter, we are going to describe the main events of the Apocalypse, the book of Revelation.

1. World War X (chapters 6-7)
2. Hell on Earth (chapters 8-11)
3. A One-World Government (chapters 12-14)
4. The Downfall of the Evil Empire (chapters 15-18)

In the following two chapters, we will look at what the Bible says about the Antichrist and the battle of Armageddon.

World War X (Revelation 6-7)

The future apocalypse starts in Revelation 6 with what I am going to call World War X. We could call it World War 3, except for the fact that it is theoretically possible that there will be future world wars before we get to the 'tribulation period'. World War X, described in Revelation 6, will be the third last World War of all time: after it will be World War Y – the Battle of Armageddon at the end of the tribulation period, and then, at the end of Christ's one thousand year reign (Revelation 20:7-9), World War Z.

The Four Horsemen of the Apocalypse

In Revelation 6, we see Christ opening four seals, and as these seals are opened, four horseman ride out.

1. **The rider on the White Horse**: *'And I looked, and behold, a white horse. He who sat on it had a bow; and a crown was given to him, and he went out conquering and to conquer'* (Rev. 6:2). Some commentators suggest that the rider on the white horse is Antichrist conquering the world. However, no one takes the next three riders (vs3-8) to be literal individuals. Instead, the riders on the red, black and pale horses are taken as symbols of bloodshed, famine and death. It would seem unreasonable to take the first rider as a literal, historical person, while the following three riders are mere symbols. Consistency requires that we take them all as actual people, or all as symbolic personifications. To put it another way: if the first rider is the Antichrist, what are the names of the second, third and fourth riders? Seeing the second, third and fourth riders are not historical personages, it seems more consistent that the rider on the white horse is also a symbolic personification, like the other three. What then does the rider on the white horse symbolize? Some commentators argue that because we only read of a bow, but no arrows, therefore this must mean conquest by shrewd diplomacy, peacemaking skills and victory without actual war or bloodshed. However, the Bible normally mentions bows without arrows (see Gen. 49:24, Josh. 24:12, 1 Sam. 18:4, etc.), just as we talk of guns (without needing to mention bullets). The description of a white horse, a bow, a crown, and particularly the words, he 'went out conquering and to conquer' all combine to describe wars of victory. It is perfectly possible that the actual, literal Antichrist will be involved in these wars, and maybe it is during these wars that he rises to prominence. Perhaps this is when he, as the 'little horn', uproots three other horns (Dan. 7:8, 24), conquering three powerful states, for it is true, as John Macarthur writes that 'the little horn (Antichrist) blasts his way to the zenith of world rule'[3]. William Kelly writes that the rider on the white horse symbolises 'victory after victory by the prestige of his name and reputation'[4].
2. **The rider on the Red Horse**: *'Another horse, fiery red, went out. And it was granted to the one who sat on it to take peace from the earth, and that people should kill one another; and there was given to him a great sword'.* (Rev. 6:4). Many commentators take the red horse to refer to war, but we have already seen that the white horse best represents glorious wars of conquest. The following three horses follow after the white horse –

---

[3] *Macarthur Study Bible*, note on Daniel 7:24.
[4] William Kelly, *Lectures on the Book of Revelation*, W. H. Broom, 1871, p136

that is, they are the results of world conquest. Famine and disease (horses 3 and 4) are obvious consequences of war. But what does the red horse represent? Notice the words 'kill one another'; these words signify people turning upon each other, that is, their neighbours and fellow-citizens. Following on from international conflict, symbolized by the rider on the white horse, the result is seen in the rider on the red horse: the breakdown of government and law and order, leading to internal rioting, looting, burning, violence, and anarchy. Peace is taken from the earth, and many ordinary civilians are killed.

3. **The rider on the Black Horse**: *'When He opened the third seal, I heard the third living creature say, "Come and see." So I looked, and behold, a black horse, and he who sat on it had a pair of scales in his hand. ⁶ And I heard a voice in the midst of the four living creatures saying, "A quart of wheat for a denarius, and three quarts of barley for a denarius; and do not harm the oil and the wine."* (Rev. 6:5-6). With the breakdown of government, and law and order, the normal infrastructure of society collapses; here we have the outbreak of food shortages.

4. **The rider on the Pale Horse**: *'So I looked, and behold, a pale horse. And the name of him who sat on it was Death, and Hades followed with him. And power was given to them over a fourth of the earth, to kill with sword, with hunger, with death, and by the beasts of the earth'* (Rev. 6:8). The word 'pale' here is literally 'sickly green' (Gr. *chloros*). It speaks of sickness and disease. The result is that one quarter of the world's population dies from these first four seals being opened.

The seal judgments set off a chain reaction of cause and effect: starting with international war, anarchy and unrest follows, which leads to famine, and finally disease and death. Their effect is to cause chaos and instability on earth. By contrast, God is seen in heaven at the beginning of the vision securely seated upon His throne, as the rightful ruler of all things. On earth, where God's rightful rule is denied, chaos and instability are unleashed. In the seal judgments, therefore, God starts to take action to bring man's government of earth crashing down.

A One-World Government?

Please notice that there does not appear to be a One-world government in place when the seal judgments fall upon the earth. How could there be a one-world government if the nations of the world are engaged in wars of conquest against each other? Wars of conquest are precisely what a one-world government is designed to prevent; a world government would not allow such wars of conquest to happen. Furthermore, the second red horse-rider symbolizes anarchy and the breakdown of civil order – the very opposite of government.

Therefore, it is highly unlikely that there is any one-world government in place at the start of the tribulation period. It is more likely that the one-world government is set up later in the tribulation period to bring order out of the chaos that is unleashed upon the world by the opening of the seals and the four horse-riders of the apocalypse. In other words, the one-world government comes *out* of the events that commence with World War X.

In our present day and age, it would seem difficult to envisage a one-world government being set up. How would the wealthiest nations on earth be persuaded to give up their independence and allow others to rule over them? What would make the most powerful nations hand over their military weapons to a world government? A crisis of gigantic proportions would be required to make the nations of earth cede their sovereignty to a central one-world government.

What causes World War X? From heaven's vantage point, Christ looses the seals that cause the first white horse-rider to bring war to the world. But from an earthly perspective, we are not told what prompts nations to try to conquer each other here. However, (as this present writer believes, and as we will see in the final section of the book), it is the rapture of the church which commences the cascade of end-time events. Paul teaches in 1 Thessalonians 4 and 5 that it is the rapture of the church which initiates the Day of the Lord, the end-time tribulation period. The disappearance of millions of Christians from our world could easily explain something like World War X. The chaos that would ensue would lead to a breakdown of order, such instability would lead to international tensions, and provide the perfect opportunity for some nations to invade others. In short, it is not till after the rapture of the church that World War X occurs, and eventually, out of the chaos, a one-world government comes to power. While we have determined attempts today to set up a one-world government, these efforts will be unlikely to succeed until the coming of a crisis of much greater magnitude than any we currently experience.

Hell on Earth (Revelation 8-11)

In Revelation chapters 8-10 we have a second series of divine judgements: the seven trumpets. Trumpets are associated in Scripture with battle, warnings, and prayer. Israel's silver trumpets in Numbers 10 were used to call upon God for help as Israel went into battle, and Joshua used trumpets in the battle of Jericho (Joshua 6). In Revelation 8:1-5, the seven trumpets are blown in response to the prayers of the saints, calling for God to take vengeance against a godless world and to take up His power and reign. The seven trumpets show us God declaring war on the world and warning of calamities to come. Two of the trumpet judgments (the fifth and sixth) involve the imagery of horses going into battle. The imagery of war is also seen in the angel standing at the altar who took the censer full of fire from the altar and threw it to the earth. In the trumpets, it is almost as if heaven is bombarding the earth with fiery missiles. The first three trumpets involve things being thrown to the earth from heaven. Yet the trumpets not only announce war, but also send warning, telling of the need to repent, because still worse things are yet to come.

1. **The First Trumpet** (Rev. 8:7): hail and fire mingled with blood were thrown upon the earth; a third of vegetation is burned up
2. **The Second Trumpet** (Rev. 8:8-9): a great mountain burning with fire was thrown into the sea; a third of the sea became blood, a third of sea creatures died, and a third of ships was destroyed.
3. **The Third Trumpet** (Rev. 8:10-11): a great fiery star fell from heaven, and fell on the rivers and springs of water; a third of the waters became bitter, and many people died therefrom.
4. **The Fourth Trumpet** (Rev. 8:12-): a third of the sun, moon and stars were struck (note the violence of the word); a third were darkened.
5. **The Fifth Trumpet** (Rev. 9:1-12): a horde of demonic locust-like beings are released to sting like scorpions, and thus torment but not kill men, for five months.
6. **The Sixth Trumpet** (Rev. 9:13-21): an army of 200 million horsemen were released to kill one third of mankind.
7. **The Seventh Trumpet** (Rev. 11:15-19): after another parenthesis (in Chapters 10 and 11), the seventh trumpet sounds. Just like the case of the seventh seal, very little is described as happening, except that heaven rejoices and gives thanks for God taking His great power and reigning (11:17).

Four features of the trumpet judgments have strong overtones of hell: fire, torment, brimstone and demons. Five of the trumpet judgments involve fire (trumpets 1, 2, 3, 5 and 6). The fifth trumpet involves torment: the locust hordes 'were not given authority to kill them, but to torment them for five months. Their torment was like the torment of a scorpion when it strikes a man. In those days men will seek death and will not find it; they will desire to die and death will fell from them' (Rev. 9:5-6). The brimstone (or sulphur) is seen in the horsemen of the sixth trumpet who kill one third of mankind:

> And thus I saw the horses in the vision: those who sat on them had breastplates of fiery red, hyacinth blue and sulphur yellow; and the heads of the horses were like the heads of lions, and out of their mouths came fire, smoke and brimstone. By these three plagues a third of mankind was killed – by the fire and the smoke and the brimstone which came out of their mouths (Rev. 9:17-18).

The fifth and sixth trumpets seem to involve demons:

> And I saw a star fallen from heaven to the earth. To him was given the key to the bottomless pit. And he opened the bottomless pit and smoke arose out of the pit like the smoke of a great furnace. Then out of the smoke locusts came upon the earth. And to them was given power, as the scorpions of the earth have power (Rev. 9:1-3).

The locusts of the fifth trumpet, with their king, Abaddon or Apollyon, the angel of the bottomless pit (Rev. 9:11) are not normal locusts, but seem to be demons let loose upon the earth. In the sixth trumpet, the army of 200 million horsemen are possibly demonic forces too, who have lion's heads breathing deadly fire and smoke, and serpents for tails which harm and kill. As a result, one third of mankind dies (Rev. 9:15, 18).

John Walvoord writes: 'Never since Noah has such a substantial proportion of earth's population come under God's righteous judgment. It may be that the army here described continues to fight until the time of the second coming of Christ, and the number slain is the total number involved in the conflict'[5].

If the four horsemen in the seal judgments give us a picture of chaos unleashed on earth as a result of men rejecting the rightful rule of God, here in the seven trumpet we have a little taste of hell on earth. But even in these judgments, God in mercy is also calling the people of earth to repentance. However, we read:

> But the rest of mankind, who were not killed by these plagues, did not repent of the works of their hands, that they should not worship

---

[5] John Walvoord, *The Revelation of Jesus Christ*, Chicago: Moody, 1989, p167

demons, and idols of gold, silver, brass, stone, and wood, which can neither see nor hear nor walk. ^{21} And they did not repent of their murders or their sorceries or their sexual immorality or their thefts (Rev. 9:20-21).

One of the reasons for the tribulation period, therefore, is to punish and discipline the world so that it turns back to God. The vast majority of people do not repent.

A One-World Government (Revelation 12-14)

In Revelation chapters 12 to 14, we read about a one-world government. This one-world government is described coming up out of the sea, and resembles a leopard, a bear and lion (Rev. 13:2). This picture takes us back to Daniel 7 where the four world empires of Babylon, Medo-Persia, Greece and Rome are pictured as these animals. Significantly, we are told there that the 'four winds of heaven were stirring up the Great Sea' (i.e. the Mediterranean) and that the four beasts came up out of the sea (Dan. 7:2). The sea is sometimes used in the Bible as a picture of the Gentile nations (Isa. 60:5, 57:20, Rev. 17:15). So here we have the rise of a Gentile world-empire. This one-world government has seven characteristics:

1. **It is Satanic.** After Satan has been cast out of heaven and down 'to the earth' (Rev. 12:9, 12, 13), he reappears again in the form of two 'beasts', or wild animals (ruthless, evil men) in Revelation 13: Antichrist and his False-Prophet. Satan is described in 12:3 as a 'dragon having seven heads and ten horns', and this is how the first 'beast' of 13:1 is also described. The second beast of 13:11 is described as follows: 'he had two horns like a lamb and spoke like a dragon'. The final one-world empire will be Satanic.
2. **It is Supernatural.** Revelation 13:3 tells us about Antichrist's apparent death and resurrection; 'I saw one of his heads as if it had been mortally wounded, and his deadly wound was healed. And all the world marvelled and followed the beast'. Verse 13 tells us about the False Prophets: 'He performs great signs, so that he even makes fire come down from heaven on the earth in the sight of men'.
3. **It has Worldwide Worship.** This leads to worldwide worship of the beast: 'So they worshiped the dragon who gave authority to the beast; and they worshiped the beast, saying, "Who is like the beast? Who is able to make war with him?" (Rev. 13:4). Verse 8 says, 'all who dwell on the earth will worship him'.

4. **It is Blasphemous.** 'And he was given a mouth speaking great things and blasphemies, and he was given authority to continue1 for forty-two months. [6] Then he opened his mouth in blasphemy against God, to blaspheme His name, His tabernacle, and those who dwell in heaven. [7] It was granted to him to make war with the saints and to overcome them. (Rev. 13:5-7)
5. **It has Worldwide Power.** 'And authority was given him over every tribe1, tongue, and nation' (Rev. 13:7)
6. **It Controls the Worldwide Economy.** 'He causes all, both small and great, rich and poor, free and slave, to receive a mark on their right hand or on their foreheads, [17] and that no one may buy or sell except one who has the mark or1 the name of the beast, or the number of his name' (Rev. 13:16-17).
7. **It is a 10-part Empire.** Revelation 17:12 explains what the 10 horns on the beast are: 'The ten horns which you saw are ten kings who have received no kingdom as yet, but they receive authority for one hour as kings with the beast'. This reminds us of Daniel's vision of the great statue which had 10 toes made of iron and clay.

This empire is obviously not in existence today. Although there are behind-the-scenes attempts to move towards a world government today, there is no established worldwide government that controls the world's worship or economy, and the blasphemy of world leaders today is not as brazen and open as that of the Beast will be. We will look at the leader of this world empire, Antichrist, in more detail in the next chapter.

The Downfall of the Evil Empire (Rev. 15-18)

In Revelation 15 and 16, we have the third major series of judgments in Revelation: the bowls. These describe God's judgments falling upon the empire of Antichrist:

1. **Bowl 1**: poured upon the earth, a loathsome sore afflicts those with the mark of the Beast (Rev. 16:2).
2. **Bowl 2**: poured upon the sea, which became blood like that of a dead man, and every living creature in the sea died (Rev. 16:3).
3. **Bowl 3**: poured upon the rivers and springs of water, which became blood, in retribution for all the blood of God's saints and prophets shed on earth(Rev. 16:4-7).
4. **Bowl 4**: poured out on the sun, which scorches men with fire and great heat, so that they blaspheme God (Rev. 16:8-9).

5. **Bowl 5**: poured upon the throne of the Beast, so that his kingdom became full of darkness, and men gnawed their tongues because of the pain, and they blasphemed God (Rev. 16:10-11).
6. **Bowl 6**: poured out on the river Euphrates, which dried up, preparing the way for the kings of the east to come to the battle of Armageddon (Rev. 16:12-16).
7. **Bowl 7**: poured out into the air, resulting in a great earthquake and great hail (Rev. 16:17-21).

Notice the setting of these judgments in Revelation 15: a sea of glass, with those victorious over the Beast standing upon it, having harps and singing the song of Moses and the Lamb. This is imagery drawn from Israel's crossing the Red Sea. Furthermore, the seven bowl judgments are called seven plagues (Rev. 15:1, 6), and some of them resemble the plagues of Egypt (sores, sea turned to blood, darkness, frogs).

The bowl judgments are particularly focused on the Beast and his kingdom. Thus, the first bowl afflicts those with the mark of the Beast, the fifth is poured on the throne of the Beast, and the sixth results in the Beast sending out demonic spirits to gather the armies of the world to fight at the battle of Armageddon.

Notice the reaction to these judgments. Just as Pharaoh hardened his heart during the plagues of Egypt, twice we are told that men still did not repent of their deeds and give God glory (Rev. 16:9, 11). Three times we are told that men blasphemed God for these plagues (Rev. 16:9, 11 and 21). Just as the plagues of Egypt culminated in Pharaoh calling out his army to pursue the Israelites, so the Beast calls together the armies of the world for the battle of Armageddon.

The parallels between the plagues of Egypt and the bowls of Revelation teach that just as God brought down Pharaoh in the book of Exodus, God will bring down the evil empire of Satan's world ruler, the Beast.

Babylon the Great Destroyed

In Revelation chapters 17 and 18, we are shown the downfall of Babylon the Great. Babylon is the world-system opposed to God, and is symbolized in these two chapters by two different images. Firstly, it is pictured as a harlot (Rev. 17), and then secondly as a city (Rev. 18). The chief characteristic of the harlot is her adultery, teaching us of the world's spiritual unfaithfulness to God, its creator and true owner. The city is seen in chapter 18 as the centre of commercial activity: the trading and transporting of goods. These are but two sides of the work of the harlot:

sexual immorality for commercial gain. They speak of the way in which men have traded the worship of the true and living God for the temporary riches and pleasures of this world.

Many commentators argue that the harlot represents a future world-religion during the tribulation period. Nothing is more likely than a vast unified religion in the first half of the tribulation period after the rapture when all the world tries to pull together to overcome the devastation of the great judgments which fall upon it. A world government will emerge, the seven-headed, ten-horned beast (Rev. 17:3), having authority over all the world (Rev. 17:12-13), and the harlot world-religion will piggy-back upon it.

In Revelation 17:16-18 the ten-horned beast turns upon the harlot and devours her. The beast wishes to have all the power and glory, and not share it with another. In addition, the great riches the harlot has amassed arouse the beast's jealousy. It might seem strange that Babylon should be destroyed by the very beast upon which she rides – we might have expected God to destroy the harlot Himself. But history gives plenty of examples where the supreme political power refuses to tolerate a rival object of loyalty. Think of Henry VIII making himself the head of the Church of England, and pillaging its wealth, or the various communist powers of the 20th century proscribing and plundering the church.

Thus, at the mid-point of the tribulation, after devouring the one-world religion, Antichrist sets up his own system of worship in Jerusalem, forcing all the world to worship himself. By this means, all the world's many false-religions will be gathered into one body and bound together like the sheaves in Christ's parable (Matt. 13:30), ready for destruction at the end of time.

This section leads into Revelation 19 with the return of Christ and the descent of the New Jerusalem, the bride of the Lamb. The two cities, Babylon and Jerusalem, and the two women, the harlot and the bride, are obvious opposites. This section shows us how God removes the harlot in order that he might give the bride her rightful place.

Conclusion

If the seven seals show us God unleashing chaos on earth, and the seven trumpets show us God sending hell on earth, the seven bowls show us God moving towards victory on earth, which is achieved at the return of Christ. God repetitively demonstrates His control over earth, sea, and sky. The repetition of sevens takes us back to the first chapter of the Bible where God created the heavens and the earth in seven days. Here, God takes back control of His creation and rules over it. The seventh judgment in each series also carries the idea of rest or completion. Here in Christ's return, at last, creation finds its perfect rest.

10 ANTICHRIST: SATAN COME DOWN TO EARTH

The 1976 film *The Omen* is probably the most famous screen depiction of the Antichrist. Damien Thorn is adopted at birth by an American diplomat and his wife. As he grows, so do the number of gruesome events associated with him. His nanny hangs herself at his fifth birthday party, a priest who tells the adopted father that Damien is not human dies by being impaled by a spire thrown from a church roof, Damien knocks his pregnant adopted mother over a balcony causing serious injury (she is later murdered), a photographer investigating the mystery surrounding the child is decapitated and finally the father, who discovers the number 666 in the form of a birthmark on the child's head, is shot by the police as he tries to kill him on a church altar. The film ends with Damien grinning callously at the funeral of his adopted father and mother.

Various Christian expositors have attempted to describe the Antichrist. John Phillips painted the following picture of him:

> The world will go delirious with delight at his manifestation. He will be the seeming answer to all its needs. He will be filled with all the fullness of Satan. Handsome, with a charming, rakish, devil-may-care personality; a genius, superbly at home in all the scientific disciplines, brave as a lion, and with an air of mystery about him to tease the imagination or to chill the blood as occasion may serve, a brilliant conversationalist in a score of tongues, a soul-captivating orator, he will be the idol of all mankind[1].

Think of the most outstanding men in every field down through time and combine them into one person and you will have a little glimpse of the Antichrist. With the military ability of Napoleon Bonaparte, the evil genius of Adolf Hitler, the oratory of Martin Luther King, the intellect of Albert Einstein, the political skills of Franklin D. Roosevelt, the dazzling personality (and probably good looks) of a Hollywood actor, and the ruthless brutality of Joseph Stalin or Mao Tse-tung, the Antichrist will be

---

[1] John Phillips, *Exploring Revelation: an Expository Commentary*, Kregel, 2001, p166

a man of amazing abilities. He will be a man unlike any other. Besides the Lord Jesus Christ, he will be the greatest man in human history.

In this chapter, we will first clear away some controversies related to the Antichrist before proceeding to describe his career and analyze his character.

Controversy over the Antichrist

There are two minor controversies over the Antichrist. Those who are more interested in the story of the Antichrist's life and career may safely skip this little section about two obscure biblical debates.

1. Is the Antichrist to be Understood Literally or Figuratively?

Some commentators (particularly those who take the Bible allegorically) argue that the Antichrist is not a literal individual, but rather a spiritual force opposing Christianity. This idea is taken from 1 John 2:22 – 'Who is a liar but he who denies that Jesus is the Christ? He is antichrist who denies the Father and the Son'. B. B. Warfield argues that the Antichrist is not in the future, but the present, is not an individual but a multitude, and is not a person but a heresy[2]. However, there are two other verses about the Antichrist that show that He is a literal person in the future as well as a spiritual force in the present. 1 John 2:18 says, 'Little children, it is the last hour; and as you have heard that the Antichrist is coming, even now many antichrists have come, by which we know that it is the last hour'.

John does not dismiss the teaching that the Antichrist is coming as false. Instead, he adds an extra dimension to this teaching by saying that there are also now many antichrists in the present. F. F. Bruce comments, 'That Antichrist would come he [John] and his readers knew, and in the false teachers he discerned the agents, or at least the forerunners, of Antichrist, sharing his nature so completely that they could be called 'many antichrists'"[3].

1 John 4:3 is also significant: 'every spirit that does not confess that Jesus Christ has come in the flesh is not of God. And this is the spirit of the Antichrist, which you have heard was coming, and is now already in the world'. Notice in this verse (as in the previous), that he is called 'the Antichrist'. It does not say 'a spirit of Antichrist', but 'the spirit of *the* Antichrist', indicating he is a definite, real person. Thus, the Antichrist is both a spiritual influence in the present, spreading false-teaching, and a

---

[2] B. B. Warfield, "Antichrist" in *Selected Shorter Writings*, Vol. 1, Phillipsburg, NJ: Presbyterian and Reformed Publishing Company, 1970, pp356-362
[3] F. F. Bruce, *The Epistles of John*, Grand Rapids: Eerdmans, 1970, p65

real person in the future.

How can Antichrist be both a literal person and a spiritual influence? Because behind Antichrist is Satan himself, who both influences the world in the present spiritually, and will one day indwell a man, the Antichrist, and rule the world through him.

In Revelation 13:18, we read about the Antichrist by his name the Beast: 'here is wisdom: let him who has understanding calculate the number of the beast, for it is the number of a man: his number is 666'. This verse tells us that the Beast, or the Antichrist, is a man.

The identity of the Antichrist has been the subject of many suggestions down through history, from Nero to Napoleon. Many theologians (particularly at the time of the Reformation) have said that the Roman Catholic Pope is the antichrist. However, no Popes have ever died and risen again (Rev. 13:3). Revelation 13:8 tells us that 'all those who dwell on the earth will worship him'. We also read of the Antichrist as an object of worship in 2 Thessalonians 2:4 ('he sits as God in the temple of God') and of the Satanically-inspired, supernatural miracles he performs. Such a supernatural, world-wide worship of one man has not yet appeared.

Others suggest that the Beast and the False Prophet are not human individuals, but rather symbols of systems. John Stott argued that the Beast and the False-prophet are merely symbols of opposition to God, like the Great Harlot. He argued that the Beast is really Rome and any other violent state that oppresses the church[4]. However, we read that the Beast and the False-prophet are thrown 'alive' into the Lake of Fire (Rev. 19:20), where they are later joined by Satan himself and we read that 'they will be tormented day and night forever and ever' (20:10). These verses make it hard to imagine the Beast and the False-prophet as anything other than literal human beings. Unless we are prepared to dismiss the personality of the Devil, then the Beast must be a real person too.

2. Which Beast of Revelation 13 is the Antichrist?

The second controversy is over which person deserves to be called the Antichrist. The vast majority of Bible commentators use the term Antichrist for the first Beast of Revelation 13, Satan's future world-ruler. However, some Bible teachers argue that the name Antichrist should be reserved for the second 'beast' of Revelation 13, the False Prophet.

The False Prophet is the Beast's lieutenant, his 'Minister of Propaganda' who will cause the world to worship the Beast (Rev. 13:12).

---

[4] John Stott, *The Cross of Christ*, Leicester: IVP, 1986, p248-9

He will perform miracles (Rev. 13:13) and make an idol/image of the Beast (Rev. 13:14), which is called the abomination of desolation (Matt. 24:15). He will kill any people who do not worship it (Rev. 13:15), and force all people to take the mark of the Beast (Rev. 13:16), the number 666 (Rev. 13:18), without which people will not be able to buy or sell (Rev. 13:17).

Arguments for reserving the name 'Antichrist' for the False Prophet include the fact that the False Prophet is pictured as a lamb (Rev. 13:11), which makes him the counterfeit Messiah, thus the Antichrist. The False Prophet also appears to be Jewish, in that he arises out of the earth (Rev. 13:11). This stands in contrast to the first Beast of Revelation 13 which arises out of the sea. The sea seems to picture the Gentile nations; see Revelation 17:1, 15 – 'the waters which you saw, where the harlot sits, are people, multitudes, nations and tongues'. Other Old Testament references in Isaiah 57:20, 49:1 and Ezekiel 26:3 also picture the Gentiles being like the restless sea and equate the 'isles' of the sea with the Gentiles. Therefore the False Prophet, arising out of the land, would appear to be a Jew, and makes a more appropriate Antichrist, i.e. false-Messiah.

However, the majority of commentators consider it more appropriate to call the first Beast of Revelation 13 the Antichrist because:

- The first Beast of Revelation 13 rules the world, and is therefore the more appropriate counterpart to Christ, who reigns over the world after His return.
- The first Beast has a death and resurrection experience (Rev. 13:3), which makes him the more appropriate counterpart of Christ than the False Prophet.
- Just as Christ has His bride, the New Jerusalem, so too the first Beast has his consort, Babylon the Great, the mother of harlots (see Rev. 17:3, 7). Seeing New Jerusalem and Babylon are opposites and counterparts, so must also the first Beast and Christ be.
- The word antichrist is only found in John's writings in the New Testament. Here the word does not refer to Jewish upstarts claiming to be the Messiah (like the False-Prophet), but rather to false-teachers denying the deity of Christ. John's usage of the word antichrist therefore stresses 'opposition' to Christ rather than 'imitation' or 'substitution' of Christ. Pentecost writes, 'The word antichrist appears only in the Epistles of John. It is used in 1 John 2:18, 22, 4:3 and 2 John 7. A study of these references will reveal that John is principally concerned with an immediate doctrinal error – the denial of the person

of Christ... It would seem that John has the idea of opposition in mind rather than the idea of exchange. This idea of direct opposition to Christ seems to be the particular characterization of the first Beast [of Revelation 13], for he sets his kingdom against the kingdom of the Son of God. If antichrist must be identified with one of the two Beasts it would seem to be identified with the first'[5]. This would argue against the idea of the word Antichrist being used to identify a Jewish substitute Messiah, and instead point to the great opponent of Christ, Satan's future world-ruler.

- If the first Beast of Revelation 13 is the Antichrist, we have a parallel between the true Trinity of Father, Son and Holy Spirit and the evil trinity of the Devil, the Beast and the False Prophet. John Walvoord writes, 'Satan's program is always one of substitution. As Christians in their faith have a triune God – the Father, the Son, and the Holy Spirit – so the forces of evil will represent themselves as triune, with the Dragon, or Satan, corresponding to God the Father, the Beast corresponding to Christ as King of Kings and Lord of Lords, and the False Prophet corresponding to the Holy Spirit. Just as the task of the Holy Spirit is to cause all men to worship Christ and the Father, so the False Prophet will cause men to worship the Beast and the Dragon'[6]. F. F. Bruce writes, 'As the true Christ received His authority from the Father ..., so Antichrist receives authority from the dragon (verse 4); as the Holy Spirit glorifies the true Christ (John 16:14), so the false prophet glorifies the Antichrist'[7].
- The False Prophet is only a minor character in the Bible, playing a secondary role to the Beast. It is hard to link him with the major status given to the Antichrist.
- Following on from this, there is another very practical reason for calling the first Beast of Revelation 13 the Antichrist. Because the Bible talks about the first Beast of Revelation 13 far more than it does about the second Beast, we need a simple and easy way to refer to the first Beast of Revelation which is not a long-winded mouthful or an obscure title. If we are not going to use the term Antichrist to describe the first Beast of Revelation 13 (but are to reserve this for the False Prophet), we are left with a number of unfamiliar, secondary titles

---

[5] Pentecost, *Things to Come*, pp337-8
[6] John F. Walvoord, *Armageddon, Oil and the Middle East Crisis*, Zondervan, 1974, 1990, p181
[7] F. F. Bruce, "Revelation", (New International Bible Commentary, Pickering and Inglis, 1979) *Zondervan One Volume Illustrated Bible Commentary*, 2008, p1669

which are less than helpful in clearly distinguishing who we mean without lengthy explanations. The second Beast of Revelation already has a simple moniker, the False Prophet, and the simplest way to refer to the first Beast is as the Antichrist.
- Another practical reason for calling the first Beast of Revelation 13 the Antichrist is that this is the way virtually everyone in both the Christian and non-Christian world refer to him. Usage determines meaning, and on this basis alone, the name Antichrist belongs to the first Beast.

There is a sense in which both 'beasts' of Revelation 13 imitate Christ, the first Beast as the Ruler of the entire world, and the second Beast as the Jewish False-Messiah. While it is therefore possible to refer to either of the Beasts of Revelation 13 as the Antichrist without violating any biblical truth or text, for simplicity's sake we will refer to the first beast of Revelation 13 as the Antichrist, and the second beast as the False-prophet.

The list of names the Bible uses for the Antichrist include:

- The Little horn (Daniel 7:8)
- The Prince to come (Daniel 9:26)
- The Man of Sin (2 Thess. 2:3-4), the very personification of evil.
- The Son of Perdition (i.e. Destruction, 2 Thess. 2:3)
- The Lawless One (2 Thess. 2:9)
- The Antichrist (1 John 2:18).
- The Beast (Revelation 13:1)

The Career of Antichrist
His birth
Arnold Fruchtenbaum argues that the Antichrist will have a supernatural origin, a counterfeit virgin-birth. He takes this from Genesis 3:15, which says, *I will put enmity between you and the woman, and between your seed and her seed; he shall bruise your head and you shall bruise his heel*:

> If the Seed of the Woman is Messiah, the seed of Satan can only be the Antichrist. From this passage [Gen. 3:15], then, it can be deduced that Satan will counterfeit the virgin conception and will some day impregnate a Roman woman who will give birth to Satan's seed who is going to be the Antichrist. The woman herself may not be a virgin, but the conception of Antichrist will be through the supernatural power of Satan. By this means, the Antichrist will have a supernatural origin.

Another passage dealing with this is 2 Thessalonians 2:9: 'even he, whose coming is according to the working of Satan with all power and signs and lying wonders'. The Greek word translated working is the word *energeo*, which means "to energize." His coming, then, will be brought about by the energizing of Satan. In other words, the Antichrist comes into being by some supernatural means, and that supernatural means is a counterfeit virgin conception'.... The end-product will be a counterfeit god-man[8].

However, these passages offer no real support to the idea of a supernatural birth. The passage in 2 Thessalonians is talking about the miracles of the Antichrist, not his birth, when it describes Antichrist being empowered by Satan. Neither are we required to take the verse in Genesis to mean that the Antichrist is Satan's literal physical child, any more than we should take the verse to literally mean that Satan would personally bruise (only) Christ's heel, or that Christ would literally bruise Satan's physical head. The Bible mentions Satan's children in a spiritual sense in various places, including John 8:41-44 ('You are of your father the devil') and 1 John 3:10 ('the children of the devil are manifest'). Few Christians have ever taken Genesis 3:15 to mean a virgin birth for the Antichrist. There would need to be more explicit scriptural evidence for Christians to believe that Antichrist must have a virgin birth so he can counterfeit Christ's birth. It is better to understand the Antichrist as a man who is indwelled by Satan, just as Satan entered Judas (Luke 22:3), rather than a man who is Satan incarnate.

What Nationality is the Antichrist?
While there is no evidence that Antichrist must be virgin-born, it would seem correct that he is of Roman origin. There are three good reasons for believing this.

Firstly, Daniel 9:26 calls him the 'prince to come' and identifies 'his people' as those who destroyed the Jewish temple in AD 70, that is, the Romans. Secondly, the Antichrist is also described in Daniel's dream in Daniel 7 as arising out of the fourth world-empire, which is the Roman Empire. Thirdly, in Revelation 17 the Beast again arises out of a resurrected Roman empire.

Daniel 11:37 speaks of the Antichrist that 'he shall regard neither the God of his fathers nor the desire of women'. From this expression in

---

[8] Arnold Fruchtenbaum, *Footsteps of the Messiah*, Ariel, 2003, 2004, pp213,4

Daniel 11:37, some have argued that Antichrist is Jewish. However, it is doubtful that the expression in Daniel 11:37 ('he shall regard neither the God of his fathers') refers to the God of Israel, for three reasons. Firstly, the expression should be translated 'he shall regard neither the gods of his fathers'. Arnold Fruchtenbaum writes:

> In the whole context, Daniel 11:36-39, the term god is used a total of eight times. In the Hebrew text, six of these times it is in the singular and twice in the plural, one of which is the phrase in verse 37. The very fact that the plural form of 'god' is used in a context where the singular is found in the majority of cases makes this a reference to heathen deities and not a reference to the God of Israel[9].

Even if we translate the verse with the 'god' of his fathers, this description could apply to any god, not necessarily the God of Israel.

Secondly, in the context, Daniel is referring to Antiochus Epiphanes as a type of the Antichrist, and Antiochus was a Syrian king. It is only if we take this expression out of its context that we can argue that this verse is referring to a Jew. The king who does not regard the gods of his fathers is a Gentile, not a Jew.

Another third problem with Daniel 11:37 referring to a Jew is that he exalts and magnifies himself above every god (v36, cf. v37, 'he shall exalt himself above them all'). This is not true of the Jewish False-prophet of Revelation 13, who promotes the worship of the first Beast rather than himself. In 2 Thessalonians 2:4, we read about the Man of Sin 'who opposes and exalts himself above all that is called God or that is worshipped, so that he sits as God in the temple of God, showing himself that he is God'. This king in Daniel 11:36-39 is the same person as the Man of Sin in 2 Thessalonians. He is therefore the first Beast of Revelation 13.

His Kingdom and Rise to Power

Antichrist rules an end-time kingdom pictured as a beast with ten horns (Dan. 7:7, 20, 24, Rev. 13:1, 17:3, 7, 12). What is this kingdom? Most commentators argue that this kingdom is a revived Roman Empire. This agrees with the fact that Daniel 9:26 speaks of the 'prince to come' being a Roman. This also makes sense when we look at Daniel who gives us two visions of the four major world empires of history, the fourth (Roman)

---

[9] Fruchtenbaum, *The Footsteps of the Messiah*, Ariel, 2004, p209

empire merging into the fifth (end-time) kingdom.

Daniel 2	Daniel 7	Empires
head of gold	lion with eagle's wings	Babylon
chest of silver	bear with three ribs in mouth	Medo-Persia
belly and thighs of bronze	leopard with four wings	Greece
legs of iron	beast with iron teeth	Rome
feet of iron and clay with ten toes	little horn among ten horns	Antichrist's

On this basis, most commentators argue that the Antichrist will rule over a revived Roman Empire. Many also point to the European Union as a forerunner of this end-time kingdom.

However, there are problems with the idea that the Antichrist rules over a revived Roman empire. Firstly, in both Daniel 2 and 7, the end-time kingdom of Antichrist is pictured with ten toes and ten horns, indicating that the kingdom will be made up of ten parts. But neither the Roman Empire of history nor the modern European Union have ever been divided into ten parts. Further, it is important to notice that the 'revived Roman empire' is not composed of iron (in Daniel's vision), but rather of iron and clay, indicating that it is slightly different to the original Roman empire.

Twice we are told that Antichrist's end-time kingdom rules over the whole world, not just Europe. Thus, Daniel 7:23 says, 'it will devour the whole earth', and Revelation 13:7-8 says, 'authority was given him over every tribe, tongue and nation. All who dwell on the earth will worship him'. Antichrist also controls the economy of the whole world, for Revelation 13:16-17 says that no one may buy or sell without the mark of the beast. Antichrist's kingdom will therefore be a one-world government, with a one-world economy, not just a Roman Empire.

What the iron and clay represent is not immediately obvious. Some commentators from the middle of the twentieth century, living through the great clash of Western democracies with totalitarian Nazism and Communism, argued that the iron represents totalitarianism while the clay represents democracy. However, there seems little direct scriptural evidence that Antichrist's future Kingdom will be characterized by democratic freedoms, let alone elections in which people decide who governs them.

One possible solution to the question of what the iron and clay represents is that Antichrist's kingdom is a revived Roman Empire which also controls the entire world. It is not just a European or Mediterranean empire, as was Rome of old. This perhaps explains the mixture of the iron and clay: the iron speaks of parts of the kingdom which still demonstrate the characteristics of ancient Roman law, order, discipline and power. These parts of the kingdom include Europe and North America, which still display in their character and systems of government the disciplined strength of ancient Rome. The clay, on the other hand, speaks of the more wild, lawless, undisciplined and weak character of other parts of the world (Africa, South America, etc.).

Italy itself resembles a giant leg with a foot extending out into the Mediterranean Sea, a geographical embodiment of the Roman legs and feet in Daniel's vision. But consider modern Italy: it is a nation of two parts. Its northern part, extending as far south as Rome, is characterized by European industry and elegance, whereas the southern part of the country, under the influence of the mafia, is described (even by Italians) as more a part of Africa than it is of Europe. In the same way, Antichrist's future kingdom will be partly strong and partly fragile.

The significance of the iron and clay is that they do not truly mix and bond with each other. Antichrist's kingdom is going to fragment at its end, with the kings of the south and of the east attacking him (see Daniel 11: 40, 44 and Rev. 16:12). Antichrist's kingdom will fracture and fall apart.

Mark Hitchcock writes, 'It is best to interpret the mixture [of iron and clay feet] as representing the diverse racial, religious, or political factions that ultimately contribute to the downfall of this revived Roman Empire. Strong nations will intermingle with weak nations'[10].

This maybe explains why it is a ten-part kingdom – maybe it will encompass the ten main regions of the world: Europe, N. America, S. America, Russia, the Muslim world, Africa, China, India, Asia, and Oceania. Antichrist's kingdom will be partly strong, and partly weak. This kingdom will be centred in the old Roman Empire, but extend out to the ends of the earth.

Antichrist's kingdom is also described as a beast with seven heads. Revelation 13:1 says, 'I saw a beast rising up out of the sea, having seven heads and ten horns, and on his horns ten crowns', and Revelation 17:3 says 'I saw … a scarlet beast which was full of names of blasphemy, having seven heads and ten horns'.

---

[10] Mark Hitchcock, *The End*, Tyndale House, 2012, pp250-1

What are the seven heads and ten horns? Revelation 17:12 explains the ten horns: 'The ten horns which you saw are ten kings who have received no kingdom as yet, but they receive authority for one hour as kings with the beast'. The ten horns are ten rulers over his ten-part kingdom, who rule under the beast, that is, Antichrist.

What about the seven heads? There have been many suggestions for the seven heads. Some (wishing to make Nero or Domitian the Antichrist, and holding that Revelation was fulfilled in first century events) have suggested that this refers to seven Roman Emperors from Julius Caesar (or Augustus) onwards down to the apostle John's time. But the numbers don't add up. Others have argued that it refers to seven forms of Roman government: kings, consuls, dictators, decimvirs, triumvirs, emperors. However, these distinctions are trivial. Others, fastening upon the fact that 'the seven heads are seven mountains' (Rev. 17:9), suggest that this refers to the 'seven hills of Rome'. However, the next verse tells us that five of the mountains have fallen. As Arnold Fruchtenbaum points out, 'if this refers to Rome the city, then five hills should no longer be in existence ... contextually then, this is an impossible interpretation'[11]. The mountains are symbolic, not geographical.

To make things even more complicated, in addition to the seven heads and the seven mountains, Revelation 17:9-11 also speaks of seven kings: 'The seven heads are seven mountains on which the woman sits, and there are seven kings. Five have fallen, one is, and the other has not yet come, and when he comes, he must continue a short time. The beast that was, and is not, is himself also the eighth, and is of the seven, and is going to perdition'.

This actually helps to explain the situation. The seven heads = the seven mountains = the seven kings. It is obvious from verse 11 that the last head-mountain-king is the Antichrist himself. But how can the heads mean the same as mountains and kings? Because in the Bible, mountains often picture kingdoms or empires (e.g. Jer. 51:25, Dan 2:35), and because kings are the embodiment of their empires (e.g. Nebuchadnezzar, Alexander), therefore we can say that the seven heads represent seven kingdoms who have been embodied in their rulers.

The best explanation of the seven heads is that they are seven successive superpowers, world-empires that have ruled over the earth. Just as the great statue of Daniel 2 pictured the different empires merging into each other, the gold head becoming the silver chest, and then the bronze belly,

---

[11] Fruchtenbaum, *Footsteps of Messiah*, p41

etc., so each of these empires swallowed up the other before it. Rome replaced Greece which conquered Persia which took over Babylon. There was really only ever one Gentile empire – all the different forms were really the continuation of the others, oppressing the people of Israel.

Daniel only gives us these four empires, but there were two others before them. Just like the Medes and Persians defeated the Babylonians, so too before that, Babylon defeated the great Assyrian empire. Before Assyria, it was Egypt who ruled the region. Isaiah 52:4 tells us, 'For thus says the Lord GOD: "My people went down at first Into Egypt to dwell there; then the Assyrian oppressed them without cause"'.

J. A. Seiss writes:

> But what five imperial mountains like Rome had been and gone, up to that time? Is history so obscure as not to tell us with unmistakable certainty? Preceding Rome the world had but five great names or nationalities answering to imperial Rome, and those scarce a schoolboy ought to miss. They are Greece, Persia, Babylon, Assyria and Egypt; no more, and no less. And these were all imperial powers like Rome. Here, then, are six of these regal mountains; the seventh is not yet come. ... Daniel makes the number less; but he started with his own times, and looked only to the end of it. Here the account looks backward as well as forward[12].

Thus, while the ten horns are ten simultaneous rulers under the beast, the seven heads are seven successive empires upon the earth, each a manifestation of Satanic desire to rule the world and Satanic oppression of God's people.

Antichrist is pictured as a 'little horn' (Dan. 7:8), different to the other ten horns (Dan. 7:24), yet rising up among them. The Antichrist rises from humble origins, and he is an outsider. Perhaps he is racially different, or not from the ruling classes. Yet he will overthrow three horns, which are plucked out by the roots (Dan. 7:8), and subdued (Dan. 7:24). This suggests a decisive military defeat by Antichrist over these three major world powers. This military victory elevates him to the pinnacle of world power – all ten horns now fear and follow him. We read, 'The ten horns which you saw are ten kings who have received no kingdom as yet, but they receive authority for one hour as kings with the beast. [13] These are of one mind, and they will give their power and authority to the beast' (Rev.

---

[12] J. A. Seiss, *The Apocalypse*, Zondervan, 1962, p393

17:12-13).

His Seven-Year Treaty with the Jewish people.
Because Antichrist is politically and militarily all-powerful, he is able to enforce upon the Jewish people a treaty. Daniel 9:27 says, 'Then he shall confirm a covenant with many for one week'. The word 'confirm' here is a word derived from a root meaning 'strength, power', and suggests that he is going to impose his treaty upon Israel. The 'many' refers to the majority of the Jewish people, who will agree with this development. The word 'week' here literally means a period of seven, and refers to the seventieth 'week', the final seven-year period of Daniel's prophecy in Daniel 9.

Presumably, in view of current tensions in the Middle East, this verse is saying that Antichrist is going to solve the Jewish/Arab problem. In exchange for something that will satisfy the Palestinians (probably land), Antichrist is going to guarantee peace and safety to the Jewish state, as well as allowing them to worship God in a rebuilt Temple in Jerusalem, for Daniel 9:27 tells us that Antichrist is later to cause the daily sacrifices to stop: 'he shall bring an end to sacrifice and offering'. Antichrist is thus temporarily going to bring peace to the world, or at least to the troubled Middle-East. This will only give further reason for the world to worship and follow him. Antichrist will be proclaimed as the Prince of Peace.

His Death and Resurrection.
Antichrist will be mortally wounded and yet live, thus undergoing a Satanically-empowered resurrection. Revelation 13:3 says, 'And I saw one of his heads as if it had been mortally wounded, and his deadly wound was healed. And all the world marvelled and followed the beast'. In Revelation 13:14 we read that the false-prophet makes an image to 'the beast who was wounded by the sword and lived'. We also read about this event in Revelation 11:7 and 17:8, where we are told that he 'rises out of the bottomless pit'.

Commentators are divided over whether this is a genuine resurrection or not. The words 'I saw one of his heads *as if* it had been mortally wounded, and his deadly wound was healed' have been taken to suggest that his 'resurrection' is counterfeit and that he does not really die, or his experience is not a true resurrection. Other commentators, however, point out that the same words are used to describe Christ in Revelation 5:6: 'I looked and behold ... [there] stood a Lamb *as though* it had been slain'. These are exactly the same Greek words as in Revelation 13:3.

However, the point of Revelation 5:6 is that Christ, although bearing in his body the evidences of death, is not actually dead – He is alive. His wounds make it look as if he should be dead, but He stands nevertheless. By contrast, in Revelation 13:3 we have the exact reverse: it is as if the Antichrist has suffered a mortal wound and then was raised to life again, however the wound was not truly mortal. The word 'healed' in Revelation 13:3 also suggests restoration rather than resurrection. Thus, the fact that the words 'as if' are used to describe the resurrection of both Christ and the Antichrist does not prove that both died and rose again. On closer inspection, the opposite is true: Christ's resurrection makes it look as if he did not really die (but he did), while the Antichrist's wound makes it look as if he really did die (but he did not).

Satan has always been in the business of counterfeiting God's work, from the days of Pharaoh's magicians. It will be the same until the end of time. But maybe we should not rule out the possibility of a real resurrection; after all, Satan causes many other miracles to happen at this time (2 Thess. 2:9, Rev. 13:13). Whatever happens to the Antichrist, it is so close to a real resurrection that we read that he comes back from death, the bottomless pit (Rev. 11:7, 17:8). Whatever happens, this miracle will sway the entire world, producing amazement and then worship (Rev. 13:14). While the world did not believe in the death and resurrection of Christ, they will gladly welcome the death and resurrection of the Antichrist.

The Antichrist is Indwelt by Satan.
Revelation 12:7-12 shows Satan being cast down to earth (v9), 'having great wrath because he knows that he has a short time' (v12), and Revelation 13:1 shows Satan reappearing in the form of the Antichrist. Just as Judas Iscariot was indwelt, not just by any ordinary demon, but by Satan himself (John 13:27), so too will the Antichrist. Presumably this indwelling occurs at the time of his restoration to life, for we read that the Antichrist 'ascends out of the bottomless pit' (Rev. 11:7, 17:8). 2 Thessalonians 2:9 says that the 'coming of the lawless One is according to the working of Satan, with all power, signs and lying wonders'. It is from this time onwards that the Antichrist and his false-prophet perform their miracles by Satan's power.

John Phillips writes:

> With this master stroke of miracle, the devil brings the world to the feet of his messiah … It is this miracle of his resurrection that is given as the reason for the popularity of the Beast. No doubt the whole thing

will be stage-managed by Satan and the false prophet to make the greatest possible impact upon men. Their propaganda machine will see to it that the miracle is magnified and elaborated to the fullest extent[13].

The Abomination of Desolation.
Daniel 9:27 says that Antichrist will cause the sacrifice and offering in the rebuilt Jewish temple to cease, and instead he will set up the abomination of desolation (Matt. 24:15, Mark 13:14), an idol statue of himself that all the world must worship. Daniel 12:11 similarly says, 'And from the time that the daily sacrifice is taken away, and the abomination of desolation is set up, there shall be one thousand two hundred and ninety days'.

The word 'abomination' is used in various Old Testament passages to speak of idols. Deuteronomy 27:15 says, 'Cursed is the one who makes a carved or molded image, an ***abomination*** to the LORD, the work of the hands of the craftsman, and sets it up in secret. And all the people shall answer and say, Amen!' See other references in Deuteronomy 7:25-26, 2 Kings 23:13, Isaiah 44:19 and Ezekiel 16:36.

Revelation 13:14-15 says that the false prophet will 'make an image to the beast who was wounded by the sword and lived. He was granted power to give breath to the image of the beast, that the image should both speak and cause as many as would not worship the image of the beast to be killed'. Perhaps it is on the occasion that, as 2 Thessalonians 2:4 says, he will sit 'as God in the temple of God, showing himself that he is God'. In Mark 13:14, the Greek participle (*'standing'* where it ought not') is masculine[14] although it should be neuter (matching the neuter 'abomination'), indicating that the abomination of desolation is a person. This confirms the dual nature of the idol – both a person and a thing. The abomination of desolation will be the first instance of artificial life, a scientific marvel (or Satanically-engineered miracle).

No wonder Antichrist will be worshipped by the whole world (Revelation 13:4) – not only because of his personal recovery from death, or because he has rescued the world from the economic chaos described in the book of Revelation, or brought peace to the warring nations of the Middle East, or united the world under a One-world government, but also because of the abomination of desolation itself – a living replica of himself.

The abomination of desolation will usher in the great tribulation, a period of unparalleled persecution for all those not worshipping the

---

[13] John Phillips, *Exploring Revelation*, Kregel, 2001, p166-7
[14] *'hestekota'* is the perfect participle, masculine accusative singular, used in the Nestle-Aland text; in the TR and the Majority text it is *'hestos'* (neuter).

Antichrist. Christ warned of the abomination of desolation and said:

> Then let those who are in Judea flee to the mountains. [17] "Let him who is on the housetop not go down to take anything out of his house. [18] "And let him who is in the field not go back to get his clothes. [19] "But woe to those who are pregnant and to those who are nursing babies in those days! [20] "And pray that your flight may not be in winter or on the Sabbath. [21] "For then there will be great tribulation, such as has not been since the beginning of the world until this time, no, nor ever shall be. [22] "And unless those days were shortened, no flesh would be saved; but for the elect's sake those days will be shortened (Matt. 24:16-22).

Revelation 13:7 says, 'It was granted to him to make war with the saints and to overcome them' (see also Dan. 7:21).

The Mark of the Beast.
Antichrist will cement his political and religious power by his economic policy. He will force all people to take the mark of the beast. 'No one may buy or sell except one who has the mark or the name of the beast, or the number of his name' (Rev 13:17).

The Bible does not exactly tell us what the mark of the beast is – it could be a symbol that people are branded or tattooed with. Or it could be a computer code, or a silicon chip implanted under the skin – we are not sure. We are also told that people will be able to take the name of the beast, or the number of his name, 666. Revelation 13:18 tells us about the number 666: 'Here is wisdom. Let him who has understanding calculate the number of the beast, for it is the number of a man: His number is 666'.

Many people have wondered at what 666 refers to. Some who hold that the book of Revelation was fulfilled in first century events have argued that 666 refers to Nero, because the letters of 'Caesar Neron' (in Greek) add up to 666 when transliterated into Hebrew (in Greek and Hebrew, letters also functioned as numbers, so we can assign a numerical value to the letters). However, Nero is clearly not the Antichrist: he was never worshipped by the entire world, nor did he force all people to take the mark of the beast, nor did he set up an idol to be worshipped, nor rise from the dead.

Other Christians have been taught that the Roman Catholic Pope is the Antichrist. Most Popes have met one pre-requisite for the Antichrist, which is being Roman. However, no Popes have ever died and risen again, or controlled the world economy, or demanded worship, or used the number 666.

Many other candidates have been suggested for the Antichrist:

- Napoleon (his name totals 666 if translated into Arabic and two letters are omitted),
- Adolf Hitler (Hitler adds up to 666 if A=100, B=101, etc.),
- Ronald Wilson Reagan (six letters in each name, and the fact he survived a gunshot to the head),
- Mikhail Gorbachev (he had a birthmark on his forehead),
- Bill Clinton (William J. Clinton adds up to 666 in both Hebrew and Greek),
- Barack Obama (apparently the winning number in a lottery was 666 the day after he became president)
- Prince Charles (the name Prince Charles of Wales adds up to 666 in English, and the symbol on his coat of arms is the Welsh Dragon).

The problem is that many different combinations of letters add up to 666. It will only be after the Antichrist commences his career, and declares that his number is 666, that anyone will know for sure who it is. Perhaps the true Antichrist will openly take the number 666 as part of his brazen blasphemy and mockery of God.

John Walvoord writes,

> Though there may be more light cast on it at the time this prophecy is fulfilled, the passage itself declares that this number is man's number. In the Book of Revelation, the number 7 is one of the most significant numbers indicating perfection. Accordingly, there are seven seals, seven trumpets, seven bowls of the wrath of God, seven thunders, etc. This beast claims to be God, and if that were the case, he should be 777. This passage, in effect, says, "No, you are only 666. You are short of deity even though you were originally created in the image and likeness of God". Most of the speculation on the meaning of this number is without profit or theological significance[15].

He Kills the Two Witnesses.

The Antichrist is going to kill the two witnesses who have prophesied outside the temple in Jerusalem for three and a half years (Rev. 11:1-3). The two witnesses have brought terrible punishments upon the earth: no

---

[15] John. F. Walvoord, *The Prophecy Knowledge Handbook: All the Prophecies of Scripture Explained in One Volume*, Wheaton: SP Publications, 1990, p587

rainfall, turning waters to blood, and 'striking the earth with all plagues as often as they desire' (Rev. 11:6). Others will have tried to harm them, but 'fire proceeds from their mouth and devours their enemies' (Rev. 11:5).

Only Antichrist is able to overcome them. Revelation 11:7 says, 'when they finish their testimony, the beast that ascends out of the bottomless pit will make war against them, overcome them and kill them'. This further feeds the cult of the Antichrist and causes the whole world to worship him. They will say, '"Who is like the beast? Who is able to make war with him?"' (Rev. 13:4).

The End of the Antichrist.
Antichrist will be defeated at the Battle of Armageddon when Christ returns. In 2 Thessalonians 2:8 we read, 'whom the Lord will consume with the breath of His mouth and destroy with the brightness of His coming' (2 Thess. 2:8). In Revelation 19:20 we read that he will be cast alive into the Lake of Fire with the false Prophet where they will be tormented forever and ever (Rev. 20:10).

Arthur Pink writes:

> Scripture has solemnly recorded the end of various august evil personages. Some were overwhelmed by waters; some devoured by flames; some engulfed in the jaws of the earth; some stricken by a loathsome disease; some ignominiously slaughtered; some hanged; some eaten up of dogs; some consumed by worms. But to no sinful dweller on earth, save the Man of Sin, "the wicked One", has been appointed the terrible distinction of being consumed by the brightness of the personal appearing of the Lord Jesus Himself. Such shall be his unprecedented doom, an end that shall fittingly climax his ignoble origin, his amazing career, and his unparalleled wickedness[16].

The Character of Antichrist

Antiochus Epiphanes as a Type of Antichrist
In the book of Daniel, we are given a lot of information about a King of Syria called Antiochus Epiphanes (215-164 BC). The reason why so much attention is given to this king is that he did something remarkably similar to what the future Antichrist will do: he set up an idol in the Jewish Temple. This idol was called the abomination of desolation. Daniel 11:31,

---

[16] A. W. Pink, *The Antichrist*, Bible Truth Depot, 1923, pp119-120

says that 'forces shall be mustered by him and they shall defile the sanctuary fortress, then they shall take away the daily sacrifices, and place there the abomination of desolation'.

When we come over to the NT, the Lord Jesus Christ also speaks about a yet-future abomination of desolation. In Matthew 24:15 he says, 'Therefore, when you see the abomination of desolation spoken of by Daniel the prophet, standing in the holy place (whoever reads, let him understand) ... then there will be great tribulation (v21)'. Paul over in 2 Thess. 2:3-4 speaks of 'the man of sin being revealed, the son of perdition, who opposes and exalts himself above all that is called God or that is worshipped, so that he sits as god in the temple of God, showing himself that he is God'. The Book of Revelation 13:14 also speaks about how 'those who dwell on the earth are told to make an image to the beast'.

Antiochus Epiphanes is a prophetic picture, a type, of an even worse tyrant who is going to come into the world at the end: the Antichrist. Just like Antiochus Epiphanes, the Antichrist will set himself up as god, erect an idol and compel all to worship him.

Antiochus Epiphanes shares the following points of resemblance with the Antichrist:

- Antiochus Epiphanes said that he was god. He surnamed himself 'epiphanes', which means '(God) manifest, or appearing' (on earth). He minted coins saying 'God manifest'. This is just what Antichrist will do, too, as 2 Thess. 2:3-4 tell us: he 'sits as God in the temple of God showing himself as God'. (By the way, while Antiochus called himself 'epiphanes', his subjects called him 'epimanes', which means 'madman).
- Antiochus persecuted the Jews who wished to continue worshipping the God of Israel, just as Antichrist will persecute the saints in the great tribulation.
- Antiochus forcibly stopped the Jewish temple worship, sacrificing pigs on the altar, prohibiting the Jews to circumcise their sons, or read the Scriptures or observe the Sabbath.
- Antiochus set up an idol of the Greek god Zeus, just as the Antichrist is going to set up an image of himself to be worshipped, the abomination of desolation

What sort of Person will He Be?

We learn more about the character of Antichrist from Antiochus Epiphanes. From Daniel 11:21-35 we read about Antiochus' ten year reign and some of the terrible things he did. Again, there are strong resemblances between him and the Antichrist:

1. **He is vile and contemptible**. 'And in his place shall arise a vile person, to whom they will not give the honor of royalty; but he shall come in peaceably, and seize the kingdom by intrigue' (Dan 11:21). Antiochus Epiphanes was not the rightful heir to the throne, but when his brother the king was assassinated, he took his place, and then later murdered his infant nephew, one of the legitimate heirs.
2. **He is cunning and deceitful** (v21, 23); he pretends to be a man of peace. Verse 21 says 'he shall come in peaceably' (and v24 repeats this: 'he shall enter peaceably'). He not only seized the kingdom by intrigue (v21), but v23 says, 'he shall act deceitfully, for he shall come up and become strong with a small number of people'. In verse 26, he destroys his enemy by planting traitors within their ranks.
3. **He uses violence and force**; verse 22 says, 'with the force of a flood they shall be swept away from before him and be broken'. He is powerful and angry: verse 23 says 'he shall come up and become strong', and verse 28 speaks of his anger ('his heart shall be moved against the holy covenant'). Antiochus Epiphanes thus combined all sorts of contradictions within his personality. He pretends peace, but motivated by hatred he turns to war. He is contemptible and yet also a smooth operator. He is versatile and resourceful, cunning and ruthless, completely unscrupulous and unstoppable. He has no moral qualms or constraints and will do whatever it takes to get what he wants, until he is in a position of absolute power.

In Daniel 11:36-39, the narrative jumps from Antiochus Epiphanes to an end-time king. We can see that these verses are no longer talking about Antiochus Epiphanes because (a) none of the events from verse 36 onwards happened to Antiochus Epiphanes, and (b) the events described will occur at the very end of time, at the time of the resurrection (Dan. 12:2). From Daniel 11:36 onwards, the narrative shift from Antiochus Epiphanes to the anti-type: Antichrist himself. Note three things more we learn about Antichrist:

4. **Antichrist is self-willed**. We read, 'then the king will do according to his own will'. The same thing was said about Alexander the Great in Daniel 11:3 – he did whatever he wanted, conquering the entire world. Willfulness is the essence of sinfulness; instead of following God's

ways, we choose to go our own way. The Antichrist is 'the Man of Sin' (2 Thess. 2:3), the ultimate expression of human sinfulness.

5. **Antichrist exalts himself.** Daniel 11:36 says, 'he shall exalt and magnify himself above every god'. Just as Satan exalted himself, aspiring to be like God, so will Satan's seed, the Antichrist (Gen. 3:15). Just as Antiochus Epiphanes proclaimed himself 'God manifest', so will his antitype, Antichrist. This is what Satan promised Eve in the garden: you will be like God.

6. **Antichrist speaks blasphemies against God.** Daniel 11:36 says, 'he shall speak blasphemies against the God of gods'. Like many atheists, Antichrist will be an angry man, full of hatred towards God. Antichrist is described on numerous occasions venting this hatred and preaching against God. Daniel 7:8, 11, and 20 tell us that he 'speaks pompous (lit. great) things', while Daniel 7:25 elaborates that 'he shall speak pompous words against the Most High'. Revelation 13:5 says, 'he was given a mouth speaking great things and blasphemies'. Not only will the Antichrist speak against God – he will also take action, persecuting the saints of God. Revelation 13:7 says, 'it was granted to him to make war with the saints and to overcome them'.

What explains the character of Antiochus Epiphanes, and the Antichrist to come? In Daniel 8:24, we are told the secret of Antiochus Epiphanes: 'His power shall be mighty, but not by his own power' (Dan. 8:24). In other words, behind Antiochus, there was another Power. The book of Daniel teaches that behind earthly empires there are demonic powers. In Daniel 10:20, the angel who speaks to Daniel says that he was withstood by 'the prince of the kingdom of Persia' (10:13), and 'must return to fight the prince of Persia' (10:20). It would seem, therefore, that behind the King of Syria is another powerful demonic power.

In the same way, the Antichrist is going to be indwelt and energized, not simply by a powerful demon, but by the Prince of demons, Satan himself. Revelation 13:2 tells us that the Antichrist is a man who opposes God because he is indwelt by Satan. This explains his evil, cunning character.

A Contrast: Antichrist is the Opposite of Christ

The Antichrist is the exact opposite of our Lord Jesus, the true Messiah. This is what the word Antichrist means; 'anti' means 'the opposite' and it also means a 'substitute'. Antichrist opposes and substitutes himself for the true Christ. Mark Hitchcock writes: 'Satan never originated anything except sin. For six thousand years he has counterfeited the works of God. With the Antichrist, this pattern continues. He is Satan's ultimate masterpiece – the crowning counterfeit – and a false Christ and forgery of Jesus, the true Christ and Son of God'[17].

1. Antichrist is a King – for a short time, he reigns over the whole world. Our Lord Jesus is going to reign as king over this earth as the 'Christ' – the Messiah, God's anointed king – when He returns.
2. Antichrist has a counterfeit resurrection.
3. Antichrist exalts himself, whilst our Lord Jesus humbled himself.
4. Antichrist is self-willed, but the true Christ was totally selfless. He said, 'I have come down from heaven, not to do My own will, but the will of Him who sent Me' (John 6:38).
5. Antichrist makes himself greater than any god – Christ, on the other hand, as Philippians 2 says, 'being in the form of God, humbled himself, taking the form of a servant, and being made in the likeness of men'. He stooped from the heights of heaven to a manger, a cross and a tomb.
6. Antichrist prospers – 'and he shall prosper till the wrath has been accomplished' (Daniel 11:36). Everything goes well for Antichrist at first – everything seems to go his way. By contrast, at His first coming, Christ was rejected, despised and put to death. Nevertheless, the tables will be turned. As God's judgments in the tribulation period rain down upon the world and his empire crumbles, even his allies and subordinates will turn against him, bringing in Armageddon. Antichrist will be cast alive into the Lake of Fire, and ultimately Christ will prosper: Isaiah 52:13 says, 'Behold, My Servant shall deal prudently (or prosper), He shall be exalted and extolled and be very high'.

---

[17] Mark Hitchcock, *The End*, p255

11 ARMAGEDDON: HOW AND WHEN WILL IT HAPPEN?

In 1970, the American evangelical writer Hal Lindsey published his book, *The Late Great Planet Earth*. By 1973 (the year of my second-hand paperback copy), it had gone through 27 print runs, and by 1990 it had sold 28 million copies. The *New York Times* declared it to be the best-selling non-fiction book of the 1970s. In 1976, it was turned into a film that made 20 million dollars in United States movie theatres. *The Late Great Planet Earth* was the book that made the end of the world a popular subject.

In *The Late Great Planet Earth*, Lindsey looked out at the state of the world in the light of Bible prophecy and pointed to a number of signs that the end of the world was very near:

- Israel's rebirth as a nation in 1948, its capture of the city of Jerusalem in 1967, and the desire of the Jewish people to rebuild their ancient temple on the same site where a sacred Muslim mosque sits,
- The emergence of a powerful European Common Market as the precursor of a revived Roman Empire over which the Antichrist will rule
- The animosity of the Arab nations towards Israel, and the inevitability of another war with Israel (which happened, yet again, in 1973, three years after Lindsey's book was published).
- The brooding malevolent power of Russia, with important strategic interests in the Middle East guaranteeing Russian interference in any future Middle East conflict.
- The rise of China as a powerful force to fight at the battle of Armageddon, as predicted in the book of Revelation

Lindsey also peered into the future and predicted two other events:

- The decline and demise of the United States as the world's leading power and Israel's chief supporter and defender, leaving the door open to the attack of other nations against Israel. (Lindsey based America's

future decline upon the fact the USA is not mentioned in Bible prophecy).
- Christ would come again in 1988. Lindsey based this prediction on the passage in Matthew 24 in which Christ speaks of 'all these events' occurring in 'this generation'. Taking a generation to last 40 years, and starting with the re-establishment of the state of Israel in 1948, Lindsey suggested the prophecy meant that all the events of the great tribulation and return of Christ spoken of in Matthew 24 must happen within 40 years of 1948.

Whatever we think of Lindsey's signs and predictions, the Bible does indeed teach that there is going to be a future world war fought in the Middle East, a cataclysmic conflict at the end of human history: Armageddon.

Armageddon sums up in one word the worst fears of the world for its future. The word Armageddon itself is only found in one passage in the Bible: 'For they are spirits of demons, performing signs, which go out to the kings of the earth and of the whole world, to gather them to the battle of that great day of God Almighty. ... [16] And they gathered them together to the place called in Hebrew, Armageddon' (Rev. 16:14,16).

Armageddon literally means 'Mount Megiddo'. Megiddo was a strategic town in the north of Israel overlooking the great plain of Jezreel or Esdraelon, the site of many important battles in the Old Testament. The main action of the battle of Armageddon is not going to occur in the north of the land of Israel, but around Jerusalem itself, so perhaps the 'Mount' being referred to is Jerusalem itself, here being likened to the most notable battlefield of ancient Israel, Megiddo.

It is better to describe Armageddon as a war rather than a battle. It is a series of military campaigns rather than one single conflict. Indeed, the Greek word *polemos* used in Rev. 16:14 and translated 'battle' in many Bible versions really means a war rather than a battle.

It is difficult to trace the different movements that take place in this war with total certainty, and many commentators offer different scenarios of events. Another difficulty is in deciding which passages of Scripture apply to Armageddon. This is the most important question to consider.

Which Bible Passages describe the Battle of Armageddon?

Most commentators agree that Revelation 19:11-21 refers to Armageddon, as do Joel 3, Zechariah 12-14, and Revelation 14 and 16. Revelation 19 describes Christ riding out of heaven on a white horse, destroying the armies of the Beast and false-prophet, while Joel 3 and the last few chapters of Zechariah describe the great battles that are involved. Other more controversial passages that need to be evaluated include Daniel 11 and Ezekiel 38-39.

Zechariah 12-14: Jerusalem Besieged and Israel Converted

The last three chapters of Zechariah describe events that take place before, during and after the battle of Armageddon. We will explore these chapters in greater detail in the section of the book dealing with Israel's future conversion. However, here we need to give a brief overview of the ten main events described in these chapters because of their connection with the battle of Armageddon:

1. **The Lord is coming**, as Zechariah 14:5 describes: 'Thus, the LORD my God will come and all the saints with You'.
2. **The Lord is coming to fight a battle:** 'the LORD will go forth and fight against those nations, as He fights in the day of battle, ⁴ and in that day His feet will stand on the Mount of Olives' (Zech. 14:3-4).
3. **The Lord destroys His enemies with a plague**: 'this shall be the plague with which the LORD will strike all the people who fought against Jerusalem: their flesh shall dissolve while they stand on their feet, their eyes shall dissolve in their sockets, and their tongues shall dissolve in their mouths' (Zech. 14:12).
4. **The Lord's deliverance happens during a siege of Jerusalem** by all nations: 'I will gather all the nations to battle against Jerusalem' (Zech. 14:2).
5. **Two-thirds of the Jewish people will be killed**, and half of the city of Jerusalem will be captured in this siege: 'It shall come to pass in all the land', says the LORD, 'that two-thirds in it shall be cut off and die, but one-third shall be left in it' (Zech. 13:8), 'the city shall be taken, the houses rifled, and the women ravished; half the city shall go into captivity but the remnant of the people shall not be cut off from the city' (Zech. 14:2).
6. **The surviving Jewish people will turn to God** for help in their distress: 'I will bring the one-third through the fire, will refine them as silver is refined, and test them as gold is tested; they will call on My name and I will answer them. I will say, 'This is My people', and each one will say, 'The LORD is My God' (Zech. 13:9).
7. **The Jewish people will see Jesus Christ at His return** and believe:

'I will pour on the house of David and on the inhabitants of Jerusalem the Spirit of grace and supplication; then they will look on Me whom they pierced' (Zech. 12:10)

8. **The Jewish people will mourn over their rejection of Christ** and repent of their sinful ways: 'Yes, they will mourn for Him as one mourns for His only son and grieve for Him as one grieves for a firstborn' (Zech. 12:10).
9. **The Jewish people will be forgiven of their sins**: 'In that day a fountain will be opened for the house of David and for the inhabitants of Jerusalem, for sin and for uncleanness' (Zech. 13:1).
10. **The Lord will reign as King** over the whole earth after His coming and His victory over His enemies: 'And the LORD shall be King over all the earth' (Zechariah 14:9).

Here we clearly see the main contours of future events surrounding the Lord's return at the battle of Armageddon. Zechariah teaches a premillennial return of Christ.

Some spiritualizing commentators try to understand these chapters figuratively and apply them to the church in this gospel age, but (as we shall see in a later chapter) the attempt is not even close to convincing. When has there ever been a siege of Jerusalem since Zechariah's day in which the Lord defeated all the enemies of the Jews by making their flesh melt as they stood on their feet? Seventeen times in Zechariah's three chapters he uses the expression 'in that day', and we are told that these events occur in 'the day of the LORD' (Zech. 14:1), which the New Testament writers place in the future, at the end of time, and at the return of Christ (1 Thess. 5:2, 2 Thess. 2:3). This prophecy obviously awaits a future fulfillment.

Please notice the points 7, 8 and 9 in the outline of events above, and the conclusion that we must draw from them: the conversion of the Jewish nation occurs at the Lord's coming at the battle of Armageddon – not before. It is only at the physical, visible return of Christ that the Jewish nation experiences the pouring out of God's Spirit, supplication, mourning, repentance and cleansing from sin.

These points are extremely significant because they help us to understand how some other passages about the battle of Armageddon fit into the timeline of future events. It is to these other passages that we shall now turn.

Ezekiel 38-39: The Invasion by Gog

In Ezekiel chapters 38-39, the prophet describes a great invasion of Israel by an alliance of nations from the north, headed by a mysterious character named Gog. This invasion is destroyed by divine intervention. Commentators are divided over when this takes place, but notice that Ezekiel 38:8 says it will occur 'after many days', and 'in the latter years' (see also v16). This is an event at the end of time. Some place this invasion: (a) before the tribulation period, (b) in the middle of the tribulation, (c) at the end of the great tribulation, i.e. at the same time as the battle of Armageddon, (d) at the beginning of the millennium, or (e) after the millennium, as described in Rev. 20:7-9.

The most important verses in determining what is being described here, and when it occurs, are the last nine verses of the vision, Ezekiel 39:21-29. After having defeated this invasion, God says,

> I will set My glory among the nations; all the nations shall see My judgment which I have executed, and My hand which I have laid on them. 22 So the house of Israel shall know that I am the LORD their God from that day forward. 23 The Gentiles shall know that the house of Israel went into captivity for their iniquity; because they were unfaithful to Me, therefore I hid My face from them. I gave them into the hand of their enemies, and they all fell by the sword. 24 According to their uncleanness and according to their transgressions I have dealt with them, and hidden My face from them." 25 Therefore thus says the Lord GOD: "Now I will bring back the captives of Jacob, and have mercy on the whole house of Israel; and I will be jealous for My holy name-- 26 after they have borne their shame, and all their unfaithfulness in which they were unfaithful to Me, when they dwelt safely in their own land and no one made them afraid. 27 When I have brought them back from the peoples and gathered them out of their enemies' lands, and I am hallowed in them in the sight of many nations, 28 then they shall know that I am the LORD their God, who sent them into captivity among the nations, but also brought them back to their land, and left none of them captive any longer. 29 And I will not hide My face from them anymore; for I shall have poured out My Spirit on the house of Israel," says the Lord GOD.

It is very important to read these verses carefully, for they give us the most significant evidence about when this invasion occurs. Notice five results of God's victory over this invading force:

1. God sets His glory among the nations – they will all know that God has done this (v21)
2. The house of Israel will know that the LORD is their God from that day forward (vs22, 28).
3. In verse 25 we read God saying, 'Now I will bring back the captives of Jacob and have mercy on the whole house of Israel'.
4. God will not hide His face from Israel anymore (v29).
5. God will pour out His Spirit on the house of Israel (v29). In verse 29, after He has destroyed the invading enemies of Israel, God says, 'I will not hide My face from them anymore; for I shall have poured out My Spirit on the house of Israel'.

Here is the key point to notice: the nation of Israel is converted as a result of this battle in Ezekiel 38-39:

- God refuses to hide His face from Israel anymore (v29). However, this is not true until the very end of the tribulation, at the battle of Armageddon. God continues to hide His face from Israel – refusing to deliver them – until the very end of the tribulation period, as Zechariah describes.
- God has mercy upon Israel (v25). Again, this does not happen at the beginning or mid-point of the tribulation, for Israel's greatest suffering occurs in the second half of the tribulation.
- Israel comes to know that the LORD is their God (v28). But this only happens at the end of the tribulation. As a nation, Israel remain estranged from God till Christ returns at the end of the tribulation period.
- God's Spirit is poured out on Israel. However, as we have seen from the book of Zechariah, this only happens at the return of Christ (Zech. 12:10ff., Rom. 11:25-27), at the end of the tribulation.

All of these factors indicate that the great battle Ezekiel writes about cannot occur at the beginning or mid-point of the tribulation. William Peterson writes, 'The Holy Spirit is poured out as the nation is born again (Isa. 32:15-17, 66:8, Zech. 12:10) . . . This will not take place in the middle of the Tribulation'[1]. Ezekiel 39:29 eliminates any pre-tribulation or mid-tribulation invasion, because it is not until the very end of the tribulation period – at the battle of Armageddon – that Israel is converted at the

---

[1] W. A. Peterson, *Watching for the Morning*, 1990, p236

coming of Christ, and God's Spirit is poured out upon them.

Ironside agrees with this, writing in his commentary on Ezekiel 38:

> In Zechariah 14:1-4 we are told of the gathering of all nations against Jerusalem, an event which certainly takes place just prior to the manifestation of Christ as King, when His feet shall stand upon the Mount of Olives. It would seem, therefore, that these northern and eastern hordes must be included among the armies that will then invade Palestine, and therefore the onslaught depicted in this chapter will take place toward the close of the great tribulation.[2]

Ezekiel chapters 38-39 appear to be describing the Battle of Armageddon. Four other factors also align to support this position:

1. the description of the vultures feasting on the dead bodies of the soldiers at Armageddon in Rev. 19:17-18, 21 is remarkably similar to the description found here in Ezekiel 38:17-20.
2. the destruction of the invading force is not the result of any human action, but instead by divine intervention, just like at the battle of Armageddon. If Revelation 16:17-21 describes the battle of Armageddon (as many commentators suggest), then the great earthquake and the great hail described in those verses is matched here in Ezekiel 38:19-22.
3. This event happens at the end of time, yet it also is the beginning of a new relationship between God and Israel. Israel enters into covenant relationship of peace with God and continue to live in the land (34:25, 37:26 and see following verses). God's deliverance leads on to the blessings of the millennium, not the eternal state.
4. The description of a temple in Ezekiel 40-48 follows this battle in Ezekiel 38-39. We will see (in a later chapter) that this is best understood as a millennial temple. This suggests, again, that this is the last battle, Armageddon, before the millennium.

Some commentators suggest that the clearest scriptural parallel with this battle in Ezekiel 38-39 is the invasion described in Revelation 20:7-8 at the end of the millennium, where we read about Gog and Magog. However, there are serious difficulties with this identification:

---

[2] H. A. Ironside, *Ezekiel the Prophet*, London: Pickering and Inglis, 1949, p265

1. In the battle in Ezekiel 38-39, Israel as a nation are saved: they have God's Spirit poured out upon them, are regathered, receive His mercy, and do not have His face turned away any more. But all these things happen at the end of the Tribulation – Israel is not saved at the end of the thousand-year millennial reign of Christ in Revelation 20:7.
2. Why spend seven months burying all the bodies and cleansing the land (Ezek. 39:11-16) if this battle occurred after the millennium? Doesn't the resurrection of the dead at the Great White throne judgment happen straight after the battle of Revelation 20:7-10?
3. It would seem strange for Ezekiel to place this battle before the millennial temple described in Ezekiel 40-48, if it was the battle after the millennium in Revelation 20.

But this raises another question: if Ezekiel 38-39 is not describing the post-millennial battle of Gog and Magog, why are these two battles both described using the exact same terms for the enemy, Gog and Magog? The reason is that both battles share the exact same characteristic: a worldwide invasion of the land of Israel, masterminded by Satan himself. Fred Cundick writes, 'There is a moral identity, but not a historical one'[3].

Many other commentators argue that the great invasion of Ezekiel chapters 38-39 occurs at some other point in time. The main reason why many commentators argue for a different occasion is because we read that Israel is dwelling safely, securely and in peace in its own land (Ezek. 38:7, 11, 14). On this basis, these commentators argue that the invasion must happen either before the tribulation, at the mid-point of the tribulation or at the beginning of the millennium.

However, Israel will not be at peace, nor dwelling securely, before the tribulation period – Israel is constantly on guard against its many neighbouring enemies still today. Nor is an invasion early in the millennium viable, for although there will be peace in the millennium, there will be no more weaponry, armies or even ungodly enemies then (Isa. 2:4), and Israel will already have been converted before the millennium begins (not after this battle).

The mid-tribulation invasion theory has no great advantages either. The idea that Israel only enjoys peace and safety up until the mid-point of the tribulation is not true – they enjoy peace after it too. The Antichrist enforces a seven-year covenant with Israel, presumably some sort of peace

---

[3] Fred Cundick, *The Book of Ezekiel*, Precious Seed, 1971, p44

treaty (Dan. 9:27), but at the mid-point of the 7-year treaty we read that he causes the sacrifice and offering in the temple to cease, and sets up the abomination of desolation. We nowhere read that the peace treaty is broken at its mid-point by either Antichrist, or an invading army. We would expect the Antichrist to continue to protect the abomination of desolation which he sets up in a Jewish temple as the centre of his worldwide worship system at the mid-point of the tribulation. There seems no good reason why Antichrist would want war to break out between Israel and its neighbours at this point by ripping up the peace treaty. Although Antichrist persecutes those who do not worship his image, we do not read that he invades Israel at this point, or that he annuls the peace treaty he has brokered. It is more than likely therefore that Antichrist will continue to enforce the peace and security conditions of the treaty until later in the great tribulation.

The other problem with all these commentators' attempts to date the battle of Gog and Magog at some time other than the end of the great tribulation is that they must ignore the last nine verses of the oracle which tell us that Israel as a nation is converted as a result of God's destruction of this invasion-force.

Therefore, we conclude that Ezekiel chapters 38-39 are describing the Battle of Armageddon, just like Zechariah chapters 12-14.

Daniel 11:36-45: the Invasion of the King of the North

Daniel chapters 10-12 form one single final vision. Our English Bibles obscure this important fact that we have one single vision by splitting the vision into three chapters. It is of great importance to see how this vision ends. While the vision starts in chapter 10 with Daniel's encounter with the angel, and then in chapter 11 we have an overview of history from the Persian emperors of Daniel's day right down to the end of time, Daniel 12 concludes this vision with the great tribulation in verse 1 and then the resurrection of the dead in verse 2. Just before this, at the end of Daniel 11, we have a description of a series of battles which include the invasion of Israel by a man called 'the King of the North'. Therefore, it is obvious that some of these battles in Daniel's concluding vision are connected with the great tribulation and resurrection, and therefore relate to the end-times.

Let us quickly overview Daniel 11. Here Daniel predicts the history of the Persian emperors (verse 2), the coming of Alexander the Great (described in verse 3 as 'a mighty king [who] shall arise, who shall rule with great dominion, and do according to his will'), and then the division of Alexander's empire into four parts (verse 4). Attention moves to the conflict between two divisions of Alexander's empire: the kings of the north (Syria) and the south (Egypt). Their ongoing wars over a number of centuries (in the second and third centuries BC) are described in verses 5-20, with the land of Israel caught in the cross-fire in between.

The main focus of attention in the chapter, however, is the career of Antiochus Epiphanes in about 165 BC. One third of the chapter is devoted to his reign, from verses 21-35. The reason for this focus is that Antiochus Epiphanes is the prototype of the end-time Antichrist. Antiochus persecuted the Jewish people and set up the abomination of desolation and his actions mirror what the future Antichrist will do in the great tribulation (Matt. 24:15-31).

However, something strange happens at Daniel 11:36. At first sight, the verses from Daniel 11:36 to the end of the chapter continue to talk about the career of Antiochus Epiphanes. However there are many features that do not fit the character or career of Antiochus Epiphanes. Instead, the verses from 11:36 onwards are not talking about Antiochus Epiphanes, but rather about a yet-future Antichrist.

Here are six indications that verses 36 onwards are about the Antichrist and his end at the battle of Armageddon:

1. The description of the great battle in Daniel 11:40-45 starts with these words: 'At the time of the end' (11:40). This expression, 'the time of the end' occurs elsewhere in Daniel 8:17, 11:35, 12:4 and 12:9, and the last two references show that it refers to the end of the world, because Daniel 12 (as we are about to see) deals with the end of the world. Therefore, the reference to the 'time of the end' in 11:40, at the beginning of the description of the great battle' points to Armageddon, at the end of time.
2. In Daniel 12:1, which follows the war of 11:40-45 and is part of the same vision, we find that the vision describes the great tribulation: 'there shall be a time of trouble such as never was since there was a nation, even to that time, and at that time your people shall be delivered, every one who is found written in the book'. The tribulation under Antiochus Epiphanes, while it was terrible (100,000 Jews died), was hardly the worst trouble the Jews have ever had. Christ uses very similar words in Matthew 24:21 to speak of a yet-future abomination of desolation and great tribulation, not something that happened in 165 BC.
3. In Daniel 12:2, we find that the events described end with the

resurrection: 'many of those who sleep in the dust of the earth shall awake, some to everlasting life, some to shame and everlasting contempt'. The resurrection of the dead did not happen soon after 165 BC and the terrible persecution of Antiochus Epiphanes. The resurrection happens at the same time as this 'great tribulation', straight after the battle of Daniel 11:40-45. So, the great tribulation can't be something that happened in Antiochus' time. Nor can the great tribulation be something that happened around 70 AD, because the resurrection of the dead didn't happen then. We haven't had the resurrection yet, so these events must still be future.

4. In Daniel 11:40-45 we read about a great battle, but while all the battles up to verse 35 are easy to fit into the history of Antiochus' life, there is no recorded battle like this one. In fact, as we see in 11:30, the Romans ('ships from Kittim') intervened the last time Antiochus invaded Egypt, and put a stop to any more invasions of Egypt by Antiochus' northern (i.e. Syrian) army. When Antiochus invaded Egypt in 168 BC, the Roman envoy Gaius Popillius Laenas brought him a message from the Roman Senate ordering him to stop the attack. Antiochus responded that he would think it over, but Popillius drew a circle in the sand around Antiochus and told him that if he did not give the Roman Senate an answer before crossing the line in the sand, Rome would declare war. Antiochus withdrew from Egypt as a result, and never invaded Egypt again. So the last great battle described in Daniel 11:40-45 never happened in Antiochus' day, and has not happened yet – it too is still in the future.

5. In 11:45, we read about the end of the 'King of the North'. We would initially take the 'King of the North' to refer to Antiochus Epiphanes (this is the title of the kings of Syria used in the earlier part of the chapter). However Antiochus' end was nothing like Daniel 11:45. Instead, we will see that the King of the North in Daniel 11:45 is Antichrist himself. Following an invasion of Egypt (11:40-45) the King of the North returns to the land of Israel, where he meets his end. But this is not the way Antiochus Epiphanes died. After being stopped from attacking Egypt by the Romans, he went off to Persia, where he died of a fever. The 'end' of the King of the North described in 11:45 does not match the way Antiochus Epiphanes died.

6. The description of this King of the North in 11:36-39 fails to match up with Antiochus Epiphanes. For example, we are told in 11:37 that he will not regard any god at all. But this was not true of Antiochus; he honoured the standard Greek gods like Apollo and Zeus.

All of this evidence seems to point to the fact that from verse 36 onwards we are looking, not at the days of Antiochus Epiphanes in 165 BC, but further off to a still future Antichrist at the end of time. The battle described in Daniel 11:40-45 happens at the time of the great tribulation, showing how Antichrist 'shall come to his end' (Dan. 11:45). Straight after this we read of the resurrection of the dead. The battle described in Daniel 11:40-45 is therefore the great end-time battle of Armageddon.

Some commentators[4] argue that the war in these verses is not part of the Battle of Armageddon, but instead is a war that occurs in the middle of the great tribulation. In fact, they suggest that Antichrist's 'end' (Dan. 11:45) is actually his (near) death and resurrection, which they suggest occurs in the middle of the tribulation period. However, while they are probably correct that Antichrist's death and resurrection experience occurs at the mid-point of the tribulation, Antichrist's 'end' does not happen in the middle of the tribulation period – he continues right to the very end, to the Battle of Armageddon. It is therefore very hard to take Antichrist's 'end' as any event happening before the Battle of Armageddon. We certainly cannot refer Antichrist's 'end' to an event in the middle of the tribulation period.

So, we may conclude that Daniel 11:40-45 gives us a description of the events leading up to the end of Antichrist, and seeing these verses describe a major war, it seems correct to view this war as Armageddon.

Getting the Main Players at Armageddon Straight

If Daniel 11:40-45 and Ezekiel 38-39 are both descriptions of the Battle of Armageddon, then what is the relationship of Gog, the leader of the invasion in Ezekiel, with Antichrist, the King of the North in Daniel 11? Are they the same person or are there two separate invasions by two different armies? And who else is involved in the battle of Armageddon?

Many commentators argue that the Antichrist is the leader of the Western European nations (the revived Roman Empire), while Gog is the King of the Northern nations. Thus they suggest that there are four main players at Armageddon: the Antichrist (from the West), Gog and Magog (from the North), the King of the South (Daniel 11:45) and then the kings of the East (Rev. 16:12, Dan. 11:44). These commentators argue that the northern, southern and eastern kings all attack the Antichrist with his Jewish false-prophet in the land of Israel.

---

[4] Fruchtenbaum, *Footsteps of the Messiah*, p240; Hitchcock, *The End*, p464-5

J. D. Pentecost writes, 'the invasion of Palestine by the northern confederacy will bring the Beast and his armies to the defense of Israel as her protector'[5]. John Walvoord writes,

> Daniel's prophecy also described a great army from Africa, including not only Egypt but other countries of that continent. This army, probably numbering in the millions, will attack the Middle East from the South. At the same time Russia and the other armies to the North will mobilize another powerful military force to descend on the Holy Land and challenge the world dictator.... Apparently the world ruler will be able to crush some of the first attempts at revolt and gain some preliminary victories, especially in the South, and he will be able to drive back the invasion from Egypt and Africa. But even as the world dictator appears to gain control of the situation, a report will come of the advancing army from the East (Dan. 11:44).[6]

To help us think about who is involved in the battle of Armageddon, we need to look at three passages that describe it: Ezekiel 38-39, Daniel 11, and Revelation.

Who's Who in Daniel 11:40-45?

To understand who is involved in the battle of Armageddon, we need to consider how many warring parties are involved in Daniel 11:40-45. Here is the first verse (v40):

> At the time of the end the king of the South shall attack him; and the king of the North shall come against him like a whirlwind, with chariots, horsemen, and with many ships; and he shall enter the countries, overwhelm them, and pass through.

From this verse, there seem to be two warring parties, the king of the South and the king of the North. The king of the South first attacks the king of the North, and then the king of the North fights back against the king of the South and overwhelms him.

However, many commentators insert a third party into the verse[7],

---

[5] Pentecost, *Things to Come*, p355
[6] Walvoord, *Armageddon, Oil and the Middle East Crisis*, Zondervan, 1990, p179
[7] See, for example, G. N. H. Peters, *Theocratic Kingdom*, II, p654: 'And he shall enter into the countries" – this is perhaps the clause which has caused the greatest difficulty to critics, owing to the sudden transition from one person to another. If we were to confine ourselves

arguing that the first 'him' in the verse is another third person, who is being attacked by both the king of the South and the king of the North. This 'him' is taken by some to mean the Jewish False Prophet, caught in between the two kings of the North and the South, and by others to mean the Beast, the head of the revived Roman empire.

But to insert a third character into this verse (in addition to the Kings of the North and the South), as many commentators do, is an exceedingly strange way to read this passage. To see who the first 'him' of v40 is, we look back to nearest antecedent in the preceding verses, and this is the king of the North, described as 'the king' (v36), 'he' (v36), 'himself' (v36), 'he' (twice, v37), 'he (twice, v38), 'his' (v38), and 'he' (three time in verse 39). This king of the North has been the main subject of Daniel 11 from verse 21 onwards. In verses 21 to 35, the King of the North is Antiochus Epiphanes, and from verse 36 onwards, it is the antitype of Antiochus Epiphanes, in other words, Satan's end-time world-ruler, the Antichrist. Thus, when Daniel 11:40 says that the King of the South shall attack 'him', the object of his attack is the King of the North. In response, we read 'and the King of the North shall come against him' (that is, the King of the South). There are only two characters in this verse, and to insert a third character is without any warrant.

Some commentators take the entire passage about the 'willful king' in verses 36-39 to be about the Jewish False Prophet, but this is emphatically not the case, for the False Prophet does not exalt himself (v36, he exalts the Beast), nor does the False Prophet exalt himself above every God (v36; it is the Man of Sin who does this, for virtually the exact same words are used of the Man of Sin in 2 Thess. 2:4). As we saw in the previous chapter, the king who 'does not regard the gods of his fathers' (Dan. 11:37) is not Jewish at all. Antiochus Epiphanes is the King of the North throughout Daniel chapter 11 (up to verse 35), and therefore the antitype of Antiochus Epiphanes (who is seen from verse 36 onwards as the King of the North) is Antichrist, himself the King of the North.

There is no hint of another third party in the verse, nor any reason to read one into it. The only reason commentators have difficulty with this passage is because they introduce the difficulty themselves! The passage

---

to this prophecy, it would be impossible from the language to decide what king this was that is to enter into the countries; whether the King of the North, or of the South, or of the Roman Empire, but we are not left to conjecture upon this point. The king who is thus victorious at the time of the end we find in Dan. 2 and 7 and Rev.17 to be identified with the fourth beast, the Roman power. Taking other prophecies as interpreters, it refers to the Roman power under its last head, who shall invade other countries, thus implying that the King of the South and the King of the North have been unsuccessful against him.

only mentions two parties: the King of the North (Antichrist, the antitype of Antiochus Epiphanes) and the King of the South who attacks him. Baldwin states the matter succinctly: 'the offensive is taken by the southern power, to which the northern king responds with overwhelming numbers of men and supporting military equipment'[8].

Who's Who in Ezekiel 38-39?

If the Antichrist is being pictured in Daniel 11 as the King of the North, entering the 'glorious land' (Israel, v41) after it has been attacked by the king of the South, is Antichrist's attack the same attack from the north as described in Ezekiel 38-39? To answer this question, we must turn to the description of the nations that come to fight in Ezekiel 38-39. In Ezekiel 38:2-6 we have a list of the nations involved:

> Son of man, set your face against Gog, of the land of Magog, the prince of Rosh, Meshech, and Tubal, and prophesy against him ... [5] Persia, Ethiopia, and Libya are with them, all of them with shield and helmet; [6] Gomer and all its troops; the house of Togarmah from the far north and all its troops-- many people are with you (Ezek. 38:2, 5, 6).

Gog is the leader of this invasion force. Is this a name or a title? In the ancient Greek translation of the Hebrew Bible (the Septuagint, LXX), Gog was used to translate the name 'Agag' in Numbers 24:7. The name thus came to be used to refer to an enemy of God's people. This is why Gog is used to describe the leader of the rebellion against God at the end of the millennium. Gog may be the actual name of this leader, but it may also be a general title for the great enemy of God's people.

Many commentators take Rosh in verse 2 to refer to Russia. However, the word 'Rosh' can mean two things. Rosh can either be the name of a place (perhaps Russia) or it can be part of Gog's title. Rosh is a very common word in Hebrew (occurring over 600 times), meaning 'head' or 'chief', and thus many Bibles translate the expression, 'the chief prince of Meshech and Tubal' (KJV, NRSV, NIV, ESV). This seems a more natural way to understand the verse, particularly in view of the fact that wherever else Meshech and Tubal are found together in the Bible (Gen. 10:2, 1 Chron. 1:5, Ezek. 27:13 and Ezek. 32:26), there is no mention of Rosh.

Many suggestions have been offered to explain the nations that accompany Gog. Some have tried to match the names up with similar-

---

[8] Joyce Baldwin, *Daniel*, TOTC, IVP, 2009, p224

sounding names of modern nations. Thus, for some, Meshech is Moscow, Tubal is the Siberian city of Tobolsk, and Gomer is Germany. Others have identified these places as obscure ancient towns based on Assyrian inscriptions: thus, Meshech=Moschoi and Tubal=Tibarenoi, ancient cities in modern-day Turkey.

However, two facts suggest these names do not refer to obscure cities, whether ancient or modern. Firstly, there are certain other names in the list that we are very familiar with: Persia, Ethiopia and Libya. These are not obscure cities; all these names belong to important nations.

Secondly, and even more significantly, all of the rest of the obscure names in Ezekiel 38 are listed in Genesis 10 in the 'table of nations' of Noah's descendants. Thus, Genesis 10:2-3 reads:

> The sons of Japheth were Gomer, Magog, Madai, Javan, Tubal, Meshech, and Tiras. ³ The sons of Gomer were Ashkenaz, Riphath, and Togarmah.

All five of the names listed in Ezekiel 38 are found in Genesis 10:2-3: Magog, Meshech, Tubal, Gomer and Togarmah. Moreover, some of the other names listed in Genesis 10:2-3 are well known: Javan refers to Greece (Dan. 8:21, Zech. 9:13) and Madai to the Medes (Jer. 25:25, Esther 10:2). Thus, here in Ezekiel 38-39, we find the names of four of the seven sons of Japheth. These names do not refer to obscure cities in Turkey or Siberia. These are the names of the sons of Japheth, which would eventually grow to be the foremost people groups of the Gentile nations. In Genesis 10:5 we read, 'From these the coastland peoples of the Gentiles were separated into their lands, everyone according to his language, according to their families, into their nations'.

Just like Javan and Madai (the Greeks and Medes), Japheth's other five sons settled the vast European continent to the north and west of the Middle East. Ezekiel 27:13 lists Javan (Greece), Tubal and Meshech as trading partners of Tyre, straight after Tarshish (Spain) in verse 12, while Ezekiel 32:26 pictures the multitudes of Meshech and Tubal in Hell, lying slain alongside Egypt, Assyria and Elam (i.e. Persia) in the grave. These are not obscure towns in ancient Turkey – these are the mightiest nations of earth, proverbial for their power. In short, these names Magog, Meshech, Tubal and Gomer refer to the main Western and Northern European people groups. The other nation listed, 'the house of Togarmah' is described as from the 'far north' and probably refers to Russia and its allies.

In summary, the invasion of Israel in Ezekiel 38-39 comes from the all the sons of Japheth, the major divisions of mankind seen in Genesis 10. Here is a coalition of the nations of Europe to the west, Russia to the north, along with other allies from the east and south: Persia, Ethiopia and Libya. Gog is not just the leader of a coalition of obscure Turkish tribesmen and Russian peasants. Gog is the ruler of the world; under his power are all the major nations of earth. Gog is the great enemy of God's people. Gog is Antichrist.

Here are eight more reasons why the invasion of Gog in Ezekiel 38-39 is the same as that of Antichrist in Daniel 11:

1. Gog is described as 'he of whom I have spoken in former days by My servants the prophets of Israel, who prophesied for years in those days that I would bring you against them' (Ezekiel 38:17). Gog is a major figure of prophecy, not some minor warlord, or an obscure peripheral politician. This suggests that he is the Antichrist, the long-promised seed of the serpent prophesied from Genesis 3:15.
2. Notice that the nations in Gog's coalition come from all four points of the compass: the house of Togarmah from the far north (Russia?), Persia (east), Ethiopia (south) and Europe (west). This raises the question: how could one person be leader over nations from all four compass points in the great tribulation? The head or chief (Rosh) of all these diverse areas would have to be none other than the world-ruler, Antichrist himself.
3. The fact that the rebellion at the end of the millennium (Rev. 20:7) is also called Gog and Magog, and involves all the armies of the world, suggests that the forces in Ezekiel 38-39 involve a coalition of armies from a large part of the world. Just as Gog in Revelation 20:7 refers to the supreme world leader opposing Christ, so too Gog in Ezekiel 38-39 is the world leader of his day, Antichrist.
4. The 'prince to come' of Daniel 9:26-27 (Antichrist) is also called 'the desolator' in Daniel 9:27. He is the one who comes to plunder and lay the land waste. Seeing Antichrist is the desolator (Dan. 9:27), there is no need for a separate northern king who comes to plunder in addition to Antichrist. There is only one desolator in Daniel 9:27. This desolator matches the description of Gog coming to plunder.
5. Another indication that Gog's army is the same as the army of Antichrist in Daniel 11 is that some of the armies who are allied with Gog are specifically named, and they are the same as those described in Daniel 11. Thus, it is very significant that in both Ezekiel 38 and Daniel 11 we read that Ethiopia and Libya are involved in the attack

of Gog, the King of the North. These nations are listed as part of Gog's coalition in Ezekiel 38:5, but the same two nations are mentioned as fighting on the side of the King of the North rather than with the King of the South in Daniel 11:43: 'also the Libyans and Ethiopians shall follow at his heels'. For these two African nations, Ethiopia and Libya, to be mentioned as coalition partners of the Gog as well as the King of the North, when their natural alliances and interests would align with the King of the South, is strange and best explained by the fact that the two invasions are the same, Armageddon.

6. Another point of connection between Gog's invasion in Ezekiel and Daniel 11 is the description of the battle of Armageddon. Gog is described as coming upon Israel 'like a storm' in Ezekiel 38:9, 16. The same language is used of the king of the North in Daniel 11:40, 'the king of the North shall come against him like a whirlwind ... and shall overflow (KJV, ESV)'. The similar language of storms and overflowing flood waters seems to point to the two invasions being the same.

7. Another point to notice is that nowhere in either Daniel's or Ezekiel's descriptions of these invasions is there any mention of a King of the West. Both Pentecost and Walvoord (in the earlier quotes) insert another figure into the account, a Western ruler of a revived Roman empire, who intervenes in the battle between the King of the North and the King of the South. However, in the absence of any reference to a king of the West in either Ezekiel or Daniel, it is better to understand that Gog is the head of the revived Roman Empire, and that his attack is from the North, because Europe sits to the north (as well as the west) of Israel. Also notice that Daniel says that the King of the North comes with 'many ships'. In other words, the King of the North's attack comes from the West, across the Mediterranean, as well as overland from the north.

8. Finally, a question to consider: if Gog and Antichrist are two different people and invasions, why would God tell us in such detail about the defeat of Gog's army in Ezekiel, giving us two whole chapters about an obscure battle that is not part of the campaign of Armageddon, yet not tell us about the defeat of the even more significant army of Antichrist at the battle of Armageddon?

It would appear, therefore, that the war in Daniel 11:40-45 is the same invasion as described in Ezekiel 38-39, led by Gog. Gog is the same person as Antichrist. He is the King of the North.

Who is 'the Assyrian'?
Some commentators also refer to another person involved in the great end-time battle: 'the Assyrian'. Gaebelein writes:

> Who is the desolator? The King of the North, the Assyrian of the endtime; he is the one of whom we read in a previous chapter and whose terrible work against the apostate nation is here once more touched upon as falling into the second half of the last prophetic week[9].

The title 'the Assyrian' comes from two passages. Isaiah 14:25 says, 'I will break the Assyrian in My land, and on My mountains tread him underfoot. Then his yoke shall be removed from them, and his burden removed from their shoulders'. Micah 5:5-6 says, 'And this One shall be peace. When the Assyrian comes into our land, and when he treads in our palaces, then we will raise against him seven shepherds and eight princely men. ⁶ They shall waste with the sword the land of Assyria, and the land of Nimrod at its entrances; thus He shall deliver us from the Assyrian, when he comes into our land and when he treads within our borders'.

Is 'the Assyrian' the same person as the Antichrist, or another actor in the great end-time drama? Isaiah's mention of 'the Assyrian' comes in the exact same chapter where he describes the downfall of Satan himself: 'How are you fallen from heaven, O Lucifer, son of the morning! ... For you have said in your heart: "I will ascend into heaven, I will exalt my throne above the stars of God"' (Isa. 14:12-13). The downfall of Satan is part of a 'proverb against the king of Babylon' (Isa. 14:4), a taunting poem describing the king of Babylon descending into Hell. It is this same king who is called 'the Assyrian' later in the chapter. Thus, the Assyrian seems to be none other than the embodiment of Satan himself, the king of Babylon, the future world-ruler, that is, Antichrist.

But why would the Antichrist be called the Assyrian, if Antichrist is a Roman? One reason is that the great crisis of Isaiah and Micah's day was the invasion by the Assyrian king Sennacherib. Not only did Assyria, the world superpower of the day, conquer the northern kingdom of Israel, they also nearly conquered Judah. Only Jerusalem was left, under siege, until God sent an angel and killed 185,000 men in the Assyrian army. Just like Antichrist in a day to come, the Assyrian army came into the land and

---

[9] A. C. Gaebelein, *The Prophet Daniel*, Pickering and Inglis, n.d., pp149-150

attacked Jerusalem from the north. The Assyrian invasion occupies a large part of the first half of Isaiah's prophecy (notably chapters 7-11, 30-31 and 36-38), a place that is out of all proportion to an ancient battle. The reason why Isaiah's prophecy focuses so much attention on this ancient invasion seems to be because it is a little picture of the future invasion of Israel at the time of the battle of Armageddon. Just like in Isaiah's day, Israel will be invaded and Jerusalem will be besieged (Zech. 12:2), but God will intervene, save Israel and destroy the invader.

The same imagery of overflowing floodwater used in relation to Armageddon ('overflow', Dan. 11:40, KJV) is also used of the Assyrian invasion in Isaiah 8:80. 'He will pass through Judah, he will overflow and pass over, he will reach up to the neck; and the stretching out of his wings will fill the breadth of Your land, O Immanuel' (Isa. 8:8, and see 30:28).

Micah's mention of the Assyrian comes in a Messianic passage that looks forward to the coming of Christ to reign over the world as King. Jerusalem is besieged (Micah 5:1), presumably in Hezekiah's (and Micah's) day, then we read of Christ's birth in Bethlehem (verse 2), in verse 3 we read that Christ will give up Israel until the time of the end, when (in verse 4): 'He shall stand and feed His flock in the strength of the LORD, in the majesty of the name of the LORD His God; and they shall abide, for now He shall be great to the ends of the earth'. This is the context in which, in the next verse, we find the Assyrian coming into the land and God raising up leaders ('shepherds and princes') against him. Zechariah 12:5-6 speaks of the same thing: God saves Jerusalem in its end-time siege by 'the governors of Judah'. The siege of Jerusalem by Sennacherib the Assyrian king is a picture of the end-time siege of Jerusalem by the Antichrist.

So, the Assyrian is the term used for the northern invader in Isaiah and Micah's day. But besides the similarity between the Old Testament Assyrian invasion and Antichrist's end-time one, there is another reason why the Antichrist is called the Assyrian. This is because the Antichrist's end-time empire is the continuation of the line of ancient superpowers Rome-Greece-Persia-Babylon-Assyria-Egypt. Antichrist's empire is the same beast as the ancient Assyrian – it just has a different head on it[10].

---

[10] Evidence that Assyria is just the continuation of other world-empires opposed to God's people (starting with Egypt and continuing through Babylon, Persia, Greece and Rome) is seen in passages like Jeremiah 50:17-18, Ezekiel 31 (where Assyria is a picture of a Satanic empire, just like Egypt, and with overtones of Satan's pride in Ezekiel 28), and in the prominence given to Assyria in Nahum.

The Seven Stages of the Campaign of Armageddon

What happens at the Battle of Armageddon? What is the order of events? Here are seven stages involved in the Battle of Armageddon:

The Background

The Antichrist, Satan's future World-ruler, makes a seven-year covenant, a peace-treaty, with Israel (Dan. 9:27). Why would the Jews want a peace-treaty? Because the threat of invasion from their enemies, the Muslim nations around them. No doubt Israel will have to make some concessions, perhaps in land, but what will make the peace-treaty all the more enticing and desirable to the Jews is that, under this treaty, the Jews will have protection to resume their temple worship in Jerusalem.

At the half-way point of this treaty (Dan. 9:27), the Antichrist stops the Jewish temple worship and instead sets up the image of himself, the abomination of desolation, and orders the whole world to worship him. This is the start of the period called the great tribulation (see Matt. 24:21). Christ says in Matthew 24:15, that when you see the abomination of desolation standing the holy place (which is the temple in Jerusalem, as we see from Acts 6:13, 21:28), then get out of the land of Judea. Jews living in the land of Israel who have been converted to Christ during the first part of the tribulation period will heed Christ's words and flee the land. It is likely that they will head for the territory east and south-east of Israel, for we read in Daniel 11:41 that the countries of Edom, Moab and Ammon will escape Antichrist's massive invasion as it sweeps south into Israel and Egypt.

Stage One: The King of the South Attacks

Daniel 11:40 says that at the time of the end the king of the South will attack northwards into the land of Israel. The King of the South attacks 'him', that is Antichrist, in that the King of the South attacks the place of Antichrist's idol-worship. The king of the South refers to more than just the land of Egypt, and may include not only other African nations but also Muslim nations from the Arabian Gulf which also lie to the south of Israel. We read that certain African countries (Ethiopia, Libya, Dan. 11:43) do not side with the king of the South, but perhaps other Muslim nations in Africa will perhaps join the attack.

Why would Egypt with other African or Muslim allies attack Israel? Firstly because of the ancient Muslim hatred of Israel, and the provocation of Jewish Temple worship on a Muslim holy site. But secondly, after the Antichrist has reneged on one of the terms of the covenant – allowing the

Jews to worship in their temple – the king of the South will perhaps feel free to break the covenant of peace with Israel. In addition, it is possible that the Muslim hatred of idolatry will cause some to rise against the worship-system of Antichrist in Jerusalem and against the protector of the Jews.

Stage Two: Antichrist's Invasion

The attack from the South provokes a massive retaliation by the king of the North, Antichrist, who comes down from the north like a whirlwind, like an overflowing flood Daniel (11:40). Antichrist attacks not only by land, but also with 'many ships', coming across the Mediterranean from the north and west. Antichrist enters the glorious land (11:41), Israel, and passes on down into Egypt (11:42), conquering it, and plundering its treasures (11:43). Antichrist's invasion is motivated not only by self-defence against the king of the South and a desire to protect his position in the Middle East, but by a desire to plunder Israel (Ezek. 38:13-14). It is probable that Antichrist uses the attack of the king of the South as an opportunity and pretext for occupying and looting the land of Israel.

Israel, on the other hand, will still be trusting in its peace treaty with the Antichrist. Isaiah 28:14-18 speaks of the attitude of the Jews:

> Therefore hear the word of the LORD, you scornful men, who rule this people who are in Jerusalem, ^{15} Because you have said, "We have made a covenant with death, and with Sheol we are in agreement. When the overflowing scourge passes through, it will not come to us, for we have made lies our refuge, and under falsehood we have hidden ourselves." ^{16} Therefore thus says the Lord GOD: "Behold, I lay in Zion a stone for a foundation, a tried stone, a precious cornerstone, a sure foundation; whoever believes will not act hastily. ^{17} Also I will make justice the measuring line, and righteousness the plummet; the hail will sweep away the refuge of lies, and the waters will overflow the hiding place. ^{18} Your covenant with death will be annulled, and your agreement with Sheol will not stand; when the overflowing scourge passes through, then you will be trampled down by it.

Stage Three: News from the East

In Daniel 11:44, Antichrist who is still plundering Egypt, hears news from the east and the north that troubles him. This is the news of a great army from the east coming to join battle. Revelation 16:12 says, 'Then the sixth angel poured out his bowl on the great river Euphrates, and its water was dried up, so that the way of the kings from the east might be prepared'. The fact that this news troubles him suggests that the kings of the East are taking sides against Antichrist, rising up in rebellion. In Ezekiel 38:21 God says, "'I will call for a sword against Gog throughout all My mountains", says the Lord God. "Every man's sword will be against his brother"'. The great end-time battle of Armageddon starts as a conflict among the armies of the world.

Perhaps in response to this threat, in Revelation 16:13-14, we read that Satan, Antichrist and the false-prophet send out demons 'to the kings of the earth and of the whole world, to gather them to the battle of that great day of God Almighty'. Then in Revelation 16:16, we read, 'and they gathered them together to the place called in Hebrew, Armageddon'. All the armies of the world are converging on the land of Israel to get involved in this battle. As a result of this news, Antichrist moves north again into Israel (Daniel 11:45).

In Joel 3:2, God says, 'I will also gather all nations and bring them down to the Valley of Jehoshaphat; and I will enter into judgment with them there on account of My people Israel, whom they have scattered among the nations'. Again, Joel 3:8 says, 'Proclaim this among the nations: Prepare for war! Wake up the mighty men, let all the men of war draw near, let them come up'. God gathers the nations of the world together for war by provoking some nations to revolt against Antichrist, while Satan gathers other nations together to defend Antichrist.

Stage Four: Trouble in the land of Israel

What is the news from the north (Dan. 11:44) that troubles Antichrist? This perhaps refers to news from Israel itself. Israel is rising up in revolt against Antichrist too. In Zechariah 12-14, we read that Jerusalem is laid siege by all nations (12:2) and puts up stiff resistance to the invading armies. God says, 'Behold, I will make Jerusalem a cup of drunkenness to all the surrounding peoples, when they lay siege against Judah and Jerusalem. [3] And it shall happen in that day that I will make Jerusalem a very heavy stone for all peoples; all who would heave it away will surely be cut in pieces, though all nations of the earth are gathered against it' (Zech. 12:2-3). This is possibly what Micah speaks about too: 'When the Assyrian comes into our land, and when he treads in our palaces, then we will raise against him seven shepherds and eight princely men. [6] They shall waste with the sword the land of Assyria, and the land of Nimrod at its entrances; thus He shall deliver us from the Assyrian, when he comes into our land and when he treads within our borders' (Micah 5:5-6).

The armies that have invaded and passed through Israel cut off two-thirds of the Jewish people (Zech. 13:8-9), and only one-third of the Jews are left in it. These Jews are purified through this terrible ordeal (13:8), leading to their conversion at the appearing of Christ (Zech. 12:10-13:1). Half of Jerusalem is captured, plundered and taken into captivity (Zech. 14:2).

Stage Five: Christ Returns
Antichrist comes back into the land of Israel and sets up camp before the city of Jerusalem. Daniel 11:45 says that Antichrist 'will plant the tents of his palace ... towards the glorious holy mountain, yet he shall come to his end, and no one will help him'.

In Zechariah 14:3, the Lord himself goes forth to battle. Christ descends and his feet stand on the Mount of Olives (Zech. 14:4), causing the mount of Olives to split in two, making an escape corridor for the remainder of the Jews, who flee from the terrible destruction that is about to occur (14:5).

> Then the LORD will go forth and fight against those nations, as He fights in the day of battle. ⁴ And in that day His feet will stand on the Mount of Olives, which faces Jerusalem on the east. And the Mount of Olives shall be split in two, from east to west, making a very large valley; half of the mountain shall move toward the north and half of it toward the south. ⁵ Then you shall flee through My mountain valley, for the mountain valley shall reach to Azal. Yes, you shall flee as you fled from the earthquake in the days of Uzziah king of Judah. Thus the LORD my God will come, and all the saints with You (Zech. 14:3-5).

Acts 1:11 also suggests that the Lord returns to the Mount of Olives: the angels said, "Men of Galilee, why do you stand gazing up into heaven? This same Jesus, who was taken up from you into heaven, will so come in like manner as you saw Him go into heaven". Christ's return will be literal, visible and public; it will not be in the desert or in an inner room (Matt. 24:26). What more public arrival could Christ have than to return in full view of all the armies of the world gathered at Jerusalem?

Psalm 110:6-7 also suggests that Christ will return to the Mount of Olives: 'He shall judge among the nations, He shall fill the places with dead bodies, He shall execute the heads of many countries. ⁷ He shall drink of the brook by the wayside; therefore He shall lift up the head'.

Here Christ is pictured defeating the armies of Antichrist and then drinking from the brook, which causes Him to lift up His head in triumph. When Christ went to the garden of Gethsemane, He crossed the brook Kidron (John 18:1), just as King David did in the day of his rejection and deep distress (2 Sam. 15:23). But Christ is going to retrace His steps, coming from the Mount of Olives back to Jerusalem; He will remember His deep sufferings, and have the satisfaction of vindication and victory.

Zechariah 14:12-15 describes the destruction of the armies of the world: they are struck with a plague in which their flesh dissolves while they stand on their feet (14:12), their eyes dissolve in their sockets, and their tongues dissolve in their mouths. 2 Thessalonians 2:8 says, 'then the lawless One (the Antichrist) will be revealed, whom the Lord will consume with the breath of His mouth and destroy with the brightness of his coming'.

No wonder the Lord splits the Mount of Olives to allow the Jews to escape out of harm's way. Revelation 14:20 says, 'the winepress was trampled outside the city, and blood came out of the winepress, up to the horses bridles, for one thousand six hundred furlongs (184 miles, about 300 km). This 300 km trail of blood stretches from Armageddon in the north of Israel all the way down to Egypt where some of Antichrist's armies remain. It is hard to say whether this describes an actual river of blood, or rather just the blood-spattering, like the trampling of a winepress, from the millions of soldiers who are killed at the appearing of the Lord.

Aftermath: Preparations for the Reign of the King

Zechariah 14:8-9 describes the aftermath of the battle of Armageddon: 'And in that day it shall be that living waters shall flow from Jerusalem, half of them toward the eastern sea and half of them toward the western sea; in both summer and winter it shall occur. ⁹ And the LORD shall be King over all the earth. In that day it shall be – The LORD is one, and His name one'.

Certain events will take place before the Lord commences to reign. Daniel 12:11-12 speaks of two time-periods of 30 days and a further 45 days after the end of the great tribulation (which lasts 1260 days): 'And from the time that the daily sacrifice is taken away, and the abomination of desolation is set up, there shall be one thousand two hundred and ninety days. ¹² Blessed is he who waits, and comes to the one thousand three hundred and thirty-five days'.

What will happen during these two periods? We are not sure but there are certain things that need to happen before Christ reigns:

- The casting of Antichrist and the false-prophet into the lake of fire (Rev. 19:20)
- The sending of Satan into the bottomless pit (Rev. 20:1-3)
- The resurrection of tribulation saints (Rev. 20:4, Dan. 12:2)
- The judgment of the living nations (Matt. 25:31-46)
- The mourning of the people of Israel over Christ (Zech 12:10-14)
- The commencement of cleansing the land of the dead and their weapons (Ezek. 39:11-16)
- The gathering of scattered Israel back to their land (Isa. 11:11-12).

There are also other things we are not told about that we may presume will happen:
- The removal of the abomination of desolation from the temple
- The demolition of the defiled temple in preparation for millennial worship, and building of a new temple?
- The organization of the administration of the millennial kingdom.

Armageddon: The Return of the King

At Armageddon, we reach the great crisis as well as the climax of human history: Jesus Christ Himself returns to earth. Here we have the fulfilment of the promise given in the key verse of the book of Revelation right at its beginning (Rev. 1:7): 'Behold, He is coming with clouds, and every eye will see Him, even they who pierced Him. And all the tribes of the earth will mourn because of Him. Even so, Amen'.

> Now I saw heaven opened, and behold, a white horse. And He who sat on him was called Faithful and True, and in righteousness He judges and makes war. [12] His eyes were like a flame of fire, and on His head were many crowns. He had a name written that no one knew except Himself. [13] He was clothed with a robe dipped in blood, and His name is called The Word of God. [14] And the armies in heaven, clothed in fine linen, white and clean, followed Him on white horses. [15] Now out of His mouth goes a sharp sword, that with it He should strike the nations. And He Himself will rule them with a rod of iron. He Himself treads the winepress of the fierceness and wrath of Almighty God. [16] And He has on His robe and on His thigh a name written: King of Kings and Lord of Lords. (Rev. 19:11-16)

Christ comes riding on a white horse – as a mighty warrior – in contrast to when He rode into Jerusalem on a humble donkey. He is called 'faithful and true', and 'in righteousness He judges and makes war'. What a contrast with the wars of earthly kings, driven by corruption, lies, and greed. His eyes are like a flame of fire – holy anger drives Him to destroy the Antichrist. He is the rightful King of the Earth – 'on His head were many crowns'. He wears a garment dipped in blood, a reminder of Calvary; His return as King is the rightful sequel to the suffering He experienced there. The armies of heaven follow Him on white horses, clothed in white – the same fine linen, bright and clean, clothing the Bride earlier in the same chapter (Rev. 19:8). This tells us that God's people shall return with Christ, as Jude also writes: 'Behold, the Lord comes with ten thousands of His saints, to execute judgment upon all' (Jude 14-15). A sharp sword goes out of His mouth to strike the nations – a mere word from His lips, 'the breath of His mouth' (2 Thess. 2:8), destroys His enemies, showing that He is truly God. He treads the winepress of God's wrath – in His crushing fury He is unstoppable.

He has three names in this passage. First, a name that none but He Himself knows, teaching His divine omniscience, second, the Word of God, reminding us of His first coming, humbly as a man with the good news of salvation, and third, King of Kings and Lord of Lords, revealing His ultimate destiny: to rule over an empire that will never end. Three times also we read the word 'Himself': He Himself alone knows His name, He Himself will tread the winepress of the wrath of God, and He Himself will rule the nations with a rod of iron. He 'Himself' is coming back. As the angel said on the day of the ascension: 'This same Jesus, who was taken up from you into heaven, will so come in like manner as you saw Him go into heaven' (Acts 1:11).

12 THE TIMETABLE OF THE TRIBULATION: DANIEL'S 70 WEEKS

My family lived in England for a number of years, and in England there is an annual event called a Royal Variety Performance. Different musicians, singers, dancers, comedians, magicians and other acts perform for the Queen, and all the money from the concert goes to charity. Now, just imagine if someone were to predict – a year in advance – not only the names of the entertainers who would perform before the Queen, but also the order in which the different acts would occur, and set out the timetable for the evening's entertainment.

If someone were to correctly predict the order of events at such a concert, we would not call it a lucky guess. Maybe we would call it proof of psychic powers. But more likely, we would conclude they were in 'the know', or had somehow obtained access to inside information – maybe a leaked copy of the program. This would be a feat of prediction beyond the realm of possibility.

In the prophecy in Daniel's chapter 9, we have something very similar to such powers of prediction. Daniel 9 is not just one prophecy, but a prophecy of seven events from the time of Daniel to the End of Time. In Daniel's prophecy of the Seventy Weeks (or, Seventy Sevens[1]), we have a prophecy that sets out seven events, putting these seven events in order, and also setting them to a timetable of Seventy Weeks, or Sevens.

Why is Daniel 9 so Important?
There are two reasons why Daniel's prophecy of the Seventy Weeks (Daniel 9:23-27) is one of the most important passages in the Bible about future events.

The first reason is that the Lord Jesus Christ described Daniel as the key to understanding future events. In His Olivet Discourse (Matthew 24-25), speaking about future events, Christ said these words:

---

[1] The Hebrew word 'shabua' means a group of seven, and is most commonly applied to the seven days which make up a week, but it is clear that the prophecy could not have been fulfilled within 70 normal weeks of days. Hence it is generally taken to refer to 70 weeks (or sevens) of years, i.e. 490 years.

> Therefore when you see the abomination of desolation, ***spoken of by Daniel the prophet***, standing in the holy place (whoever reads, let him understand) (Matthew 24:15).

Christ was speaking about future events, and He said that unless we correctly understand Daniel's prophecy, and particularly what Daniel said about the 'abomination of desolation', then we will not understand what He is teaching about future events. If we consider Christ's words about the future to be the most important words on the subject in the Bible, then our view of future events will be confused unless we understand what Daniel wrote about the 'abomination of desolation'. That is precisely what we see all around us today: Christian confusion about future events.

Most of the confusion we see about 'future events' today is a result of not following Christ's advice here: we need to understand Daniel, and particularly 'the abomination of desolation', which is found in Daniel chapters 9, 11 and 12. Daniel's prophecies in these chapters, and particularly chapter 9, are not understood very well today, firstly because they are very difficult and complex passages to understand correctly, and secondly, because instead of being serious Bible students, most Christians today are characterized by the typical sins of our age: we are self-centred, easily distracted, spiritually lukewarm and lazy. Rather than doing the hard work of studying Daniel's difficult prophecies, we shrug our shoulders and adopt a casual, clueless, agnostic attitude: 'who knows what these passages are teaching?' This is not the attitude that Jesus was encouraging in Matthew 24. He said we *must* read and understand Daniel if we want to have any clear idea about future events. Many Christians, sadly, think they can ignore this advice and still understand future events.

Daniel 9 is one of the places in the Bible where we read about the 'abomination of desolation'. Therefore, Daniel 9 is an important key to understanding future events. If our Lord Jesus Christ directed us here to understand what He was saying about future events, this makes it an important prophecy in the Bible. We need to understand it correctly.

Another reason why Daniel's prophecy of the Seventy Sevens in Daniel 9:23-27 is so important is that it sets out the timetable of future events. Daniel's prophecy not only tells us that certain events are going to happen, but crucially, it also tells us when they will happen.

Jerome, the 4th/5th century A.D. translator of the Bible into Latin, wrote about Daniel's prophecy as follows:

> None of the prophets has so clearly spoken concerning Christ as has

this prophet Daniel. For not only did he assert that He would come, a prediction common to the other prophets as well, but also he set forth the very time at which He would come. Moreover he went through the various kings in order, stated the actual number of years involved, and announced beforehand the clearest signs of events to come[2].

Daniel's prophecy of the Seventy Sevens has been described as 'perhaps the most important not only in the Book of Daniel, but in the whole Bible' (A.C. Gaebelein)[3], 'the "backbone" of all prophecies' (J.M. Boice)[4], and the 'indispensable chronological key to all New Testament prophecy' (Alva J. McClain)[5]. Harry Ironside called it 'the most remarkable time prophecy of the Holy Scriptures'[6].

To help us see why Daniel 9 is so important, and what is at stake here, I am going to state at the outset the results of our investigation in this chapter. There are five important conclusions:

1. Daniel chapters 9, 11 and 12 prove that 'The abomination of desolation' is an idol statue set up in the Jewish temple.
2. Daniel 9 proves that there is a seven-year period (often called Daniel's Seventieth Week) in which the Antichrist is going to come to power and rule the world
3. This seven year period is still in the future.
4. The 'great tribulation' is the second half of Daniel's Seventieth Week, and thus, the 'great tribulation' is also still in the future.
5. Daniel 9, 11, 12, and various passages in Revelation prove that the great tribulation lasts for three and a half years.

The Key to Understanding: the 'Abomination of Desolation'
What is the 'abomination of desolation' that Christ spoke about in Matthew 24:15 as the key to understanding future events?

The abomination of desolation is mentioned three times in Daniel, as well as in Matthew 24 by Christ. From these four passages, we can work out what Christ is talking about, and understand why the abomination of

---

[2] Jerome's *Commentary on Daniel*, Prologue
[3] A. C. Gaebelein, *A Key to the Visions and Prophecies of the Book of Daniel*, Pickering & Inglis, n.d., pp129-30
[4] J. M. Boice (following Sir Edward Denny) in *Daniel, An Expositional Commentary*, Baker Books, 1989, p96.
[5] Alva J. McClain, *Daniel's Prophecy of the 70 Weeks*, BMH Books, 2007, p10
[6] H. A. Ironside, "The Great Prophecy of the Seventy Weeks", in *A Brief Outline of Things to Come*, ed. T. Epp, Moody, 1952, p16

The Timetable of the Tribulation: Daniel's Seventy Weeks

desolation is so significant. Here are the verses:

- **Daniel 9:27** – Then he shall confirm a covenant with many for one week; but in the middle of the week he shall bring an end to sacrifice and offering. And on the wing of abominations shall be one who makes desolate, even until the consummation, which is determined, is poured out on the desolate.
- **Daniel 11:31** – And forces shall be mustered by him, and they shall defile the sanctuary fortress; then they shall take away the daily sacrifices, and place there the abomination of desolation.
- **Daniel 12:11** – And from the time that the daily sacrifice is taken away, and the abomination of desolation is set up, there shall be one thousand two hundred and ninety days.
- **Matthew 24:15-30** – Therefore when you see the abomination of desolation, spoken of by Daniel the prophet, standing in the holy place (whoever reads, let him understand), then let those who are in Judea flee to the mountains. ... For then there will be great tribulation, such as has not been since the beginning of the world until this time, no, nor ever shall be. ... Immediately after the tribulation of those days the sun will be darkened, and the moon will not give its light ... Then the sign of the Son of Man will appear in heaven, and then all the tribes of the earth will mourn, and they will see the Son of Man coming on the clouds of heaven with power and great glory.

The verse in Daniel 9:27 is hard to understand, but notice the reference to 'abominations' and 'desolation' – there seems to be a connection to the other two verses in Daniel 11:31 and 12:11 that also speak of the 'abomination of desolation'. The verse in Daniel 11:31 is easier to understand, and all Bible commentators agree that it is talking about a statue of the Greek god Zeus that a Syrian King called Antiochus Epiphanes set up in the Jewish temple when he invaded Judea and stopped the Jewish temple sacrifices in Jerusalem in 167-164 BC.

The reference to the 'abomination of desolation' in Daniel 12:11 is very significant. Most Bible commentators agree that while Daniel 11:21-35 is talking about the career of Antiochus Epiphanes, yet the verses from Daniel 11:36 onwards to the end of the book (i.e. into Daniel chapter 12) were not fulfilled in the life of Antiochus Epiphanes. Bible-believing Christians believe that these verses deal with events at the end of the world, because Daniel 12:1-2 and 13 go on to speak about the resurrection of the dead at the end of time. Verse 1 also speaks about the 'great tribulation' occurring at roughly the same time as the resurrection of the dead: 'at that time ... there shall be a time of trouble such as never was since there was a nation, even to that time'. The verses at the end of Daniel 11 (vs 40-45) also speak about a great battle which found no fulfilment in the career of Antiochus Epiphanes, but which also must occur at the end of time, and (as we saw in a previous chapter), these verses are talking about the battle of Armageddon. Therefore, many Bible-believing scholars take Daniel 11:35-39 to be a description, not of Antiochus Epiphanes, but of Antichrist.

The key point to understand here is that the third reference to the 'abomination of desolation' that we find in Daniel 12:11 is not the statue of Zeus that was set up in 167-164 BC, but rather an 'abomination of desolation' (idol statue) that is going to be set up at the end of the world – at the same time as the 'great tribulation', the reign of the Antichrist, the Battle of Armageddon and the resurrection of the dead.

This is confirmed by Christ's own words in Matthew 24:15-30 where He speaks of a yet-future 'abomination of desolation' that will mark the beginning of the great tribulation (Matt. 24:15), which will occur immediately before Christ Himself returns (Matt. 24:29-30).

Many modern theologians argue that the 'abomination of desolation' was something that happened in AD 70 when the Romans destroyed the Jewish temple, but (apart from the fact that there was no such idol set up inside the Jewish temple before the Roman army came), Jesus' own words disprove an AD 67-70 'abomination of desolation' because He said that the great tribulation would happen *immediately* before He visibly returns. As Jesus did not visibly return in AD 70, the 'abomination of desolation' did not happen in AD 67-70, but is still in the future, and so is the great tribulation.

This is an incredibly significant finding, (not only because it shows that an AD 70 fulfilment as false), but because it also means that what Daniel tells us about the 'abomination of desolation' in Daniel 9:27 (where he refers to abominations and desolation) also most likely refers to a future, end-time 'abomination of desolation'. As we are about to see, Daniel's prophecy of the Seventy Weeks in chapter 9 helps us to understand the timetable of the 'great tribulation' period, how long it will last and what comes before and after it. In this chapter, we shall firstly give a brief outline of the seven events prophesied in the passage, before we explore it in more detail.

The Seven Events

Here are the seven events prophesied in Daniel chapter 9, verses 25 to 27:

1. A Decree for the Rebuilding of Jerusalem

Daniel 9:25: 'Know therefore and understand, that from the going forth of the command to restore and build Jerusalem …'

The first event is the command to rebuild the city of Jerusalem. In Daniel's day, Jerusalem lay in ruins, destroyed by the Babylonians. However, Daniel prophesied the city would be rebuilt. After Cyrus the Persian allowed the Jewish exiles to return from Babylon, the book of Nehemiah shows how this first event was fulfilled in the rebuilding of the city walls of Jerusalem.

2. The Coming of Messiah the Prince

Daniel 9:25-26: '… until Messiah the Prince, there shall be seven sevens and sixty-two sevens; the street shall be built again, and the wall, even in troublesome times. And after the sixty-two sevens Messiah shall be cut off, but not for Himself'[4].

Messiah is prophesied to come after a certain period of time, but he is to be cut off, which means he is to die a violent death. This refers to the coming and death of Jesus Christ; as Isaiah 53:8 says, 'He was cut off from the land of the living, for the transgression of my people He was stricken'.

3. The city and temple destroyed

Daniel 9:26: 'And the people of the prince who is to come shall destroy the city and the sanctuary'.

This refers to the destruction of the Jewish temple ('the sanctuary') and city by the Romans in AD 70. This was the one and only time the Jewish temple was ever destroyed after the return of the Jews from their exile in Babylon.

4. War to be Fought over Jerusalem until the Time of the End

Daniel 9:26: "till the end there shall be war, desolations are determined' (see RV, Darby, NASB, NIV, ESV).

The last phrase in Daniel 9:26 traces the fourth stage of God's program. The verse is saying that following the destruction of Jerusalem in AD 70 there are to be continual wars fought over the city of Jerusalem. The 'end' here refers to the end of time, as we will show.

5. A Prince to Come will make a treaty with Israel

Daniel 9:27: 'Then he shall confirm a covenant with many for one seven'.

'He' in this verse refers back to the last-mentioned person in the prophecy, the 'prince to come'. This 'prince to come' cannot be 'Messiah the Prince' of verse 25, because (a) Messiah was cut off, and (b) Christ's people did not destroy the temple in AD 70 (see verse 26). Instead, this 'prince to come' is another, second prince, who is yet to come. He makes a seven-year covenant (i.e. treaty) with Israel, presumably offering them peace and the opportunity to worship God in a Jewish temple again.

6. The Deal is broken and there is a period of Great Tribulation

Daniel 9:27: 'But in the middle of the seven he shall bring an end to sacrifice and offering'.

At the half-way point of this seven year treaty period, the prince to come (Antichrist) will usher in a period the NT calls the great tribulation: Jewish worship will be forbidden in the temple, he will set up an idol to himself (the 'abomination of desolation') in the temple (we also read about this in 2 Thessalonians 2 and Revelation 13), people will not be able to buy or sell without his mark (666), and fierce persecution of any who don't worship him or take his mark will follow for three and a half years.

7. Antichrist will be destroyed at the Battle of Armageddon

Daniel 9:27: 'And on the wing of abominations shall be one who makes desolate, even until the consummation, which is determined, is poured out on the desolator'.

We read at the end of verse 26, 'His end shall be with a flood', that is, an overwhelming and sudden military defeat, a defeat that is 'poured out on the desolator' (v27). This is the battle of Armageddon; we can read about this in various places in the Bible, particularly Revelation chapter 19.

The Most Amazing Prophecy in the Bible

Daniel's prophecy is perhaps the most amazing prophecy in the Bible. Here are four reasons why.

1.   Panoramic Scope:

Daniel's prophecy foretells events from the time of Daniel to the Time of the End. Whereas other Bible prophecies focus on one event, e.g. Christ's death, this prophecy gives the divine view of world history from Daniel's time till the Time of the End, including the central event, Christ's death, and the downfall of the Antichrist. It is amazing for its panoramic sweep.

2. Precise Timing:
Daniel's prophecy is amazing because of its precision – correctly predicting seven events in the right order. The prophecy not only puts the seven events in order but also sets them to a chronological timetable: seventy sevens. There is nothing else like this in the Bible or in the history of human prediction. Plenty of people in history have made vague and cryptic prophecies, and even some biblical prophecies are somewhat mysterious. There is nothing else like the specificity of Daniel's prophecy.

3. Personalities Involved:
Here we have the two great figures of history: Christ and Antichrist – the two most important men to ever live on earth. Many people down through history have fancied themselves ruling the world. Here in this prophecy, God tells us about the true Messiah, what will happen to him and when it will happen. Daniel's prophecy tells anybody who wishes to know how to identify the true Messiah: he will be cut off.

After this, the prophecy moves forward to the end of days, and tells us about the career of the other great figure of world history. This is a man that the whole world is going to follow and worship, the Antichrist. Daniel's prophecy is a story of two Messiahs, one true and one false. Here we have in one prophecy the two greatest characters of human history.

4. Paradoxical Truth:
Daniel's prophecy tells us the Messiah will die, while the Antichrist will reign. Here is the great surprise prediction in the prophecy. What Daniel's prophecy says will happen to the Messiah is the exact opposite of what any Jew in Daniel's time, or in Jesus' day, would ever have predicted. The Messiah, instead of inheriting the throne, is going to be killed. A murdered Messiah, to any Jew, is a contradiction in terms. Nevertheless, this is what God foretold through His prophet Daniel.

On the other hand, the second Prince gains the acceptance and welcome of the Jewish people as their Saviour. The Lord Jesus Christ spoke about this in John 5:43, 'I have come in My Father's name, and you do not receive Me; if another comes in his own name, him you will receive'.

One final thought: Christ is called Messiah the Prince in this prophecy. Yet all we are told about him is that he is going to be cut off. How then can he rightly be called a Prince if he does not reign? I suggest that we have here a hint of His resurrection. Daniel 8:11 and 25 also mention 'the

Prince of the host' and the 'Prince of princes' – these are titles that rightly belong to Christ. Also in Daniel 7:13-14 we read about the Son of Man who is brought before the Ancient of Days and he was given dominion and glory and a kingdom which will last forever. This is Christ, and he will reign. So if Messiah the Prince is cut off in Dan. 9:25, and he must also reign, that requires a resurrection.

Why do we not Hear about Daniel's Prophecy Nowadays?
Daniel's prophecy of the Seventy Weeks is important for various reasons:

1. Christ tells us in Matthew 24:15 that Daniel is the key to understanding future events.
2. Daniel's prophecy is one of the most amazing prophecies in the Bible,
3. Daniel's prophecy is a striking proof that Jesus is the true Messiah,
4. It is an evidence of the divine inspiration of Scripture

Yet, despite the importance of Daniel's prophecy, many theologians writing today about future events ignore any mention, let alone explanation, of this passage. Even in evangelical Christian circles, this prophecy is hardly mentioned at all. For example, in Josh McDowell's book, *Evidence that Demands a Verdict* (ranked 13th in *Christianity Today's* list of most influential evangelical books published after World War II), the first edition in 1972 devoted over five pages to Daniel 9 as an evidence for Christian faith. But in the expanded 2017 edition of the book co-authored with his son Sean McDowell, Daniel's prophecy is entirely omitted. Many modern Bible commentaries on Daniel offer vague expositions of this prophecy, and even admit to feeling 'at sea'. Leading modern evangelical systematic theology books that explore eschatology (the doctrine of future events) like those by Wayne Grudem or Millard Ericksen, hardly mention this prophecy at all. The result is that we are hearing less and less from either pulpit or pen about Daniel 9.

What is going on here? Why is this prophecy largely ignored today? I suggest there are two reasons that Daniel's prophecy of the Seventy Weeks has fallen out of fashion.

The first reason is that Daniels' prophecy is one of the most controversial passages in the entire Bible. The scholarly literature on Daniel's prophecy of the Seventy Weeks is voluminous. J. A. Montgomery said 'the history of the exegesis of the seventy weeks is the dismal swamp of Old Testament criticism'[7]. Barnes in his commentary writes, 'Of this passage, Professor Stuart ("Hints on the Interpretation of Prophecy," p. 104) remarks, "It would require a volume of considerable magnitude even to give a history of the ever-varying and contradictory opinions of critics respecting this "locus vexatissimus"'[8]. Sir Robert Anderson writes, 'Well may Professor Driver and Dean Farrar comment upon the hopeless divergence which marks "the bewildering mass of explanations" offered by the numberless expositors of this passage' (however, Anderson continues, 'there is no reason why the intelligent reader should follow these eminent critics who, in their "bewilderment," have adopted the most preposterous interpretation of it ever proposed')[9]. As a result of this controversy, many theologians are unsure about, and even embarrassed by, this prophecy.

The second reason that Daniel's prophecy is largely ignored today, even by evangelicals, is because of the chronology of the prophecy. Sir Robert Anderson's book, *The Coming Prince*, claimed that this prophecy predicted – to the very day – when the Messiah would appear. This passage in Anderson's book has been quoted many times by evangelicals, in print and from the pulpit, as proof of the supernatural character of Bible prophecy. However, few preachers quoting Anderson have bothered to double-check his calculations, and few have the ability to prove them correct. It has become clear, however, that Anderson's dates are not valid. For example, Anderson claimed that Christ died at Passover AD 33 (at an age of about 37!), but the AD 33 date has many serious problems, and the majority of Bible scholars believe that Christ actually died in AD 30 (at an age of about 33). It would appear that Sir Robert Anderson fudged his figures to get them to fit his preferred answer.

So the second reason for the silence about Daniel's prophecy today is embarrassment at the extravagant claim made by Sir Robert Anderson, a claim which has made believing Christians look too eager to accept anything that 'proves' the Bible, without even doing any careful checking of the evidence.

We are not going to delve into the dispute over Anderson's chronology here, but we do need to look into the broader controversy over Daniels' prophecy. The reason is simple: Christ Himself warned that if we did not read and understand Daniel's prophecy, the result would be confusion about future events generally, which is what we see today. Christ said

---

[7] J.A. Montgomery, *The Book of Daniel*, The International Critical Commentary, T. & T. Clark, 1927, p400.
[8] Albert Barnes' *Notes on the Bible*, commenting upon Daniel 9:24.
[9] Sir R. Anderson, *Daniel in the Critics Den*, James Nisbet and Co, 1909, p114.

Daniel's prophecy is the key to understanding future events. Once we correctly understand Daniel's prophecy, we unlock all the other things the Bible teaches on the subject of future events.

For this reason, it is important for us to venture briefly into the 'dismal swamp' and explore the controversy over this passage. Jumping into an interpretative quagmire doesn't sound inviting, but readers need not despair; we are going to drain the swamp (to coin a phrase).

Three Different Ways to View a Controversial Prophecy

The reason why Daniel 9 is such a difficult chapter to understand is because there are three very different ways to understand it. We need to first of all familiarize ourselves with these three views and what they say.

1. The Liberal View: Daniel 9 refers to the Past, not the Future.

Liberal theologians deny the miraculous and dismiss the amazing prophecies in the book of Daniel (like the rise of the Persian empire, the coming of Alexander the Great, and then the Romans) by holding to the conspiracy theory that the book of Daniel was written, not before, but after the events it supposedly foretold: an example of *vaticinium ex eventu* (Latin for 'prophesying after the event'). Rather than having been written by Daniel in the 6th Century BC, liberal scholars argue that an anonymous author in the 2nd Century BC wrote the book, using Daniel's name. The prophecies of Daniel (particularly in Daniel 8 and 11) focus on a period of history in the 2nd Century BC when the Jewish people suffered severe persecution under the Syrian king Antiochus Epiphanes. Liberal critics argue the book was intended to encourage faithful believers in the God of Israel during this severe persecution around 167-164 BC. The entire book is viewed by liberal theologians as a masterly fraud, a pious forgery.

Jerome wrote his commentary on Daniel, in part, to refute this theory, which was first put forward by the early anti-Christian writer, Porphyry:

> And because Porphyry saw that all these things had been fulfilled and could not deny that they had taken place, he overcame this evidence of historical accuracy by taking refuge in this evasion, contending that whatever is foretold concerning Antichrist at the end of the world was actually fulfilled in the reign of Antiochus Epiphanes, because of certain similarities to things which took place at his time. But this very attack testifies to Daniel's accuracy. For so striking was the reliability of what the prophet foretold, that he could not appear to unbelievers as a predictor of the future, but rather a narrator of things already past.

There are many problems with this theory which we can't list now, but here, for a start, are a few:

- The Dead Sea scrolls make it very difficult to believe that the book of Daniel was written in the 2nd century BC, for copies of Daniel from the 2nd century BC are included as Scripture among the Dead Sea scrolls, which would be unlikely if it had just recently been forged.
- Liberal scholars used to argue that one evidence that Daniel was forged in the 2nd century BC was that it contained historical mistakes that no one living in the 6th century would make (like the idea that Belshazzar was the last king of Babylon). These mistakes proved it was a late forgery. However, archaeological findings have vindicated Daniel and proved that the book is true (and the critics were wrong).
- From a Christian perspective, the biggest problem with the theory of the liberal theologians is that our Lord Jesus Christ himself testified to Daniel's historicity. In addition, Christ also said that Daniel's 'abomination of desolation' (Matthew 24:15) was still in the future, so the whole idea of Daniel's prophecy referred to Antiochus Epiphanes in the past is wrong.

However, it is important to notice that while we must dismiss the unbelieving conclusions of liberal scholars, nevertheless their view contains an element of truth within it. It is true that Daniel's book focuses a lot of attention on the persecution of the Jews under Antiochus Epiphanes. In Daniel 8 and 11, particularly, we have a clear outline of the events in which Antiochus brutally suppressed the Jews. The temple sacrifices were stopped, an altar was erected to the Greek god Zeus, called the 'abomination of desolation', swine were sacrificed and Jewish practices like circumcision, the reading of the scriptures and the eating of ritually clean foods were prohibited. Thousands of Jews were put to death for refusing to cease practicing the worship of the God of their fathers.

In Daniel 9, the liberal view holds that its 'prophecies' pointed to Antiochus' persecution. In Daniel 9:26-27, a 'ruler to come' (Antiochus) brings 'an end to sacrifice and offering'. 'Messiah the Prince', it is said, refers not to our Lord Jesus Christ, but to the Jewish High Priest Onias III who was murdered at the time of Antiochus' persecution. The reference to 'abominations', too, is exactly the way the Jews of Antiochus' day referred to the altars erected to Zeus.

Here is the key point: the liberal view, despite its serious flaws and problems, helpfully alerts us to the fact that Daniel's prophecy concerns events that resemble in a remarkable way Antiochus Epiphanes stopping the Jewish temple worship in 167 BC and setting up the 'abomination of desolation' (Dan. 11:31).

2. The Amillennial View: Daniel 9 refers to the Present, not the Future

The amillennial view of Daniel's prophecy, in contrast to the liberal view, is marked by devotion to the scriptures and to the person and work of Christ. More generally, the amillennial approach to Scripture sees Christ's work as the fulfilment of virtually all Old Testament prophecies. It therefore regards Daniel 9 as relating, not to the people of Israel or to any events still in the future, but solely to the spiritual blessings for the present-day Church won through the work of Christ.

The amillennial position takes 'Messiah the Prince' spoken of in Daniel 9:26 to refer to the Lord Jesus Christ, whose death is foretold in the words, 'and after the sixty-two weeks Messiah shall be cut off'. The covenant enforced in Daniel 9:27 refers, not to any treaty imposed by Antiochus Epiphanes (as in the liberal view), but to the New Covenant established by Christ. The cessation of sacrifices in the same verse points, not to any attempt to halt the proceedings in an earthly Temple by Antiochus Epiphanes (or Antichrist in the future), but to the fact that Christ's one sacrifice for sin for ever puts an end to animal sacrifices.

The problem here is that, instead of starting with Daniel's prophecy in its own context, the amillennial view instead imposes familiar concepts borrowed from the New Testament upon the passage. Further, it ignores parallels within the book of Daniel that help to explain the prophecy. For example, the references in Daniel 11 to Antiochus Epiphanes' halting of the 'daily sacrifices' (11:31) and his establishment of an 'abomination of desolation' (11:31) would seem to provide far more obvious clues to what the same terms mean when used in Daniel 9:27 than Christian themes like a New Covenant and Christ's death forever doing away with animal sacrifices.

In the amillennial view, Christ is the entire focus of the prophecy: his death, his new covenant and the end of the old covenant's animal sacrifices. But the amillennial interpretation disappoints in the way it avoids the obvious sense of the actual text of, and contextual clues within Daniel's prophecy. Instead, by illegitimately reading New Testament concepts into the passage, the amillennial view is guilty of fancifully spiritualizing Daniel's prophecy. It is imposition rather than exposition.

Thus, surprisingly, the liberal view, for all its faults, actually performs a useful service. It shows how much more appropriate it is to understand

Daniel's prophecy by the parallels we see in Antiochus' actions than the amillennial attempt to jump straight to New Testament theological themes.

3. The Premillennial View: Daniel 9 takes us from Christ to the Future

The Premillennial view of this passage is essentially the view already outlined – a prophecy about a series of seven events from Daniel's time till the End-time.

Premillennialists see the fulfilment of God's purposes involving not simply salvation in spiritual terms but also the restoration of the entire creation during a future reign of Christ over the earth. In particular, they believe that Israel the nation is eventually to be restored to God and that the Old Testament promises made to Israel of a glorious future are to be literally fulfilled in this millennial reign.

Premillennialists, like amillennialists, view Christ and his death as the focus of Daniel's prophecy, as of the entire Bible. However, premillennialists, while viewing Christ's death as the central event of world history, observe that a considerable portion of Scripture is concerned with history's final climax: the tumultuous events that will happen at the 'Time of the End' (Dan. 11:35, 40; 12:4, 9), just before the resurrection of the dead.

On the other hand, premillennialists agree with critical scholars that there are very strong parallels between the persecution by Antiochus Epiphanes in the second century BC and some of the details of Daniel's prophecy of the Seventy Weeks. Premillennialists explain this similarity by pointing to the fact that history repeats itself. All through the Bible there have been times of fierce persecution against God's people, from Pharaoh in Egypt, to Nebuchadnezzar in Daniel's day, and beyond. In addition, history gives us many examples of world rulers who have demanded worship, like Nebuchadnezzar, and the Roman Emperors. In the case of Daniel's prophecy, we could even say that history tends to be prophetic. Antiochus' persecution of the Jews is a little picture of a far greater time of persecution at the end of time, right before Christ's return: the 'great tribulation'. Another striking parallel between Antiochus and the future Antichrist is that Antiochus called himself Epiphanes, meaning 'manifestation', because he claimed to be the manifestation of God on earth. So too, the future Antichrist will also claim to be God (2 Thess. 2:4, Rev. 13:8, 12) and demand to be worshipped.

The premillennial view does not see the prophecy as solely fulfilled in Antiochus Epiphanes (as in the liberal view), or in Christ's ministry (as the amillennialist does), but sees it as also going on to speak about another 'prince to come', Antichrist, of whom Antiochus Epiphanes was only a foreshadowing. Antiochus is a historical figure whose career becomes a prophetic picture of someone greater than him. This future Antichrist will make a covenant with Israel for seven years, only to break it at its midpoint, set up an idol in a future Jewish temple, 'the abomination of desolation' and bring upon the Jews the period called the great tribulation.

The premillennial view therefore takes Daniel's prophecy as a sequential overview of the entire Divine program from Daniel's time until the End.

	Liberal	**Amillennial**	**Premillennial**
Seventy 'Weeks'	Literal Years	Symbolic	Literal 'Sevens'
'Messiah the Prince'	Onias the High Priest	Jesus Christ	Jesus Christ
Prince to Come	Antiochus	Jesus Christ	Antichrist
City destroyed	167 BC	AD 70	AD 70
Covenant	?	New Covenant	Antichrist's Covenant
Sacrifices Stop	167 BC	AD 70	Future
Abomination of Desolation	167 BC	AD 70	Future
End of 'Prince to Come'	167 BC	?	Future

The Setting and Context of the Prophecy

To further help in correctly interpreting the prophecy, and decide which of the three interpretations is correct, it is important to look at its context. This will help us see which interpretation – the liberal, the amillennial or the premillennial – better explains what Daniels' prophecy means.

What prompted Daniel's prophecy? In chapter 9, Daniel had been praying for the restoration of Israel from their exile in Babylon. In his prayer, Daniel confesses his peoples' sin, pleads for God's forgiveness, and calls upon God to restore Israel's fortunes by allowing God's holy city and its Temple to be rebuilt.

It is important to notice the emphasis in Daniel's prayer upon two things: firstly, the city of Jerusalem with its temple and secondly, the people of Israel. Notice firstly the emphasis upon the city of Jerusalem:

- 'O Lord, according to all Your righteousness, I pray, let Your anger and Your fury be turned away from **Your city Jerusalem, Your holy mountain**' (9:16);
- 'for the Lord's sake cause Your face to shine on **Your sanctuary**, which is desolate' (9:17);
- 'open Your eyes and see our desolations, and **the city** which is called by Your name' (9:18);
- 'Do not delay for Your own sake, my God, for **Your city** and Your people are called by Your name' (9:19).

Then secondly, notice that the restoration concerns Daniel's people, the nation of Israel:

- 'O Lord, righteousness belongs to You, but to us shame of face, as it is this day – to **the men of Judah, to the inhabitants of Jerusalem and all Israel**, those near and those far off in all the countries to which you have driven them, because of the unfaithfulness which they have committed against You' (9:7)
- 'Yes, **all Israel** has transgressed Your law, and has departed so as not to obey Your voice' (9:11)
- 'And now, O Lord our God, who brought **Your people** out of the land of Egypt with a mighty hand, and made Yourself a name, as it is this day – we have sinned, we have done wickedly' (9:15).
- 'Do not delay for Your own sake, my God, for Your city and **Your people** are called by Your name' (9:19).

The words 'city', 'sanctuary', 'Jerusalem', 'Israel' and 'people' are mentioned fifteen times in Daniel's prayer in verses 4 to 19. Similarly, in the prophecy itself (vs 24-27), we find the words 'Your people' (v24), 'Your holy city' (v24), 'Jerusalem' (v25), 'the city' (v26) and 'the sanctuary' (v26).

The prophecy is primarily about the nation of Israel. It would hardly seem necessary to labour the point that Daniel's prayer (vs 4-19) and Daniel's prophecy (vs 24-27) refer to Israel nationally – except for the fact that amillennialist commentators seem determined to avoid this conclusion, arguing that the prophecy does not really have to do with Israel nationally and territorially, but rather to the church spiritually. In particular, amillennialist commentators argue that Daniel's prophecy is fulfilled in Christ's death and the spiritual blessing of justification which flows from it. This is not to say that there is no spiritual element to Daniel's prophecy, as we shall see. However, the context of Daniel 9 with its focus upon Israel's national life means that limiting the prophecy to the spiritual is to give us but a partial view of the prophecy's message. Edward Dennett writes:

> 'It must also be borne in mind that this revelation entirely concerns the Jewish people and Jerusalem. It is strange indeed that this should need to be insisted upon, considering the language employed; but the tendency is so persistent in some quarters to explain away, by spiritualizing, the scriptures which have in view the future restoration of the chosen nation, that it becomes necessary to affirm and to hold fast their manifest application. Gabriel says to Daniel, "Thy people," and "thy holy city." Even a child, if he know but the elements of the New Testament, understands that Christians have no holy city upon earth. And should it be contended that it is the heavenly city, new Jerusalem, which is here indicated, it might well be enquired, When were its walls thrown down, so as to need rebuilding? No, the city prayed for is the city of which Gabriel speaks, as is evident from verse 25; and consequently Daniel's people are the Jews, and his city is the earthly Jerusalem'[10].

To take one example of the spiritualizing tendency, amillennialist E. J. Young applies the prophecy to 'the true people of God' (i.e. the church) and accuses Gaebelein of trying to 'restrict the reference'[11] by taking the prophecy to refer exclusively to the Jews.

It is true that the prophecy not only deals with the nation of Israel and their national/political restoration, but also with the deeper issue of their spiritual restoration through the forgiveness of their sins. Thus, Daniel's prayer of confession makes reference to the words 'sin' (and cognates) eight times, as well as synonyms like 'done wickedly', 'committed iniquity', 'rebelled', 'unfaithfulness', 'transgressed' ten times and to the word 'confession' two times. The idea of spiritual restoration is seen in the further fact that the angel Gabriel comes, in reply to Daniel's prayer, 'about the time of the evening sacrifice' (verse 21), signifying God's means for making atonement and providing forgiveness.

Thus, the setting of the prophecy is the nation of Israel and its restoration, both nationally and spiritually. The prophecy is not about the church and its spiritual blessings (although our spiritual blessings are based on the work of Christ too). The prophecy is about the nation of Israel.

---

[10] Edward Dennett, *Daniel the Prophet and the Times of the Gentiles*, Central Bible Truth Depot, 1967, p145

[11] Edward J. Young, *The Prophecy of Daniel*, Wm. B. Eerdmans Publishing Co., 1949, p197

The Purpose of the Prophecy

In addition to the context of the prophecy, it is also very important that we consider the purpose of the prophecy. It, too, helps us as we continue to decide between the rival interpretations. The purpose of the prophecy is carefully spelled out for us in Daniel 9:24, and it functions almost like the 'mission statement' of a modern corporation:

> *Seventy weeks are determined for your people and for your holy city, to finish the transgression, to make an end of sins, to make reconciliation for iniquity, to bring in everlasting righteousness, to seal up vision and prophecy, and to anoint the Most Holy.*

There are six objectives to be fulfilled:
1. to finish the transgression,
2. to make an end of sins,
3. to make reconciliation for iniquity,
4. to bring in everlasting righteousness,
5. to seal up vision and prophecy,
6. and to anoint the Most Holy

The prophecy is all about God's program for Israel's restoration, both nationally and spiritually. We see this purpose expressed in six goals in v24, the first three negative (doing away with sin) and the last three positive (telling us about three new things that are going to happen).

Amillennialists like Philip Mauro argue that 'when our Lord ascended into heaven and the Holy Spirit descended, there remained not one of the six items of Dan. 9:24 that was not fully accomplished'[12]. However, Calvary did not put an end to human transgression, for the word transgression in verse 24 refers to mankind's defiant rebelliousness which still continues today. Baldwin says: 'If this is to be finished, we are being told about the final triumph of God's kingdom and the end of human history'[13].

'To finish the transgression' means that Israel's 'rebellion will effectively finish at the return of Messiah to earth' (Tatford)[14]. Pentecost writes, 'The nation Israel, to whom the prophecy was addressed, simply has not experienced a single one of the prophesied benefits of Messiah's coming

---

[12] Philip Mauro, *The Seventy Weeks and the Great Tribulation*, Hamilton, 1923, p53.
[13] Joyce G. Baldwin, *Daniel*, Tyndale Old Testament Commentaries, IVP, 1978, p187.
[14] Frederick A. Tatford, *God's Program of the Ages*, Kregel Publications, 1967, p45.

as yet'[15]. Although Christ made an end of sins and reconciliation for iniquity at the cross, Israel as a nation will not experience these blessings until Christ returns and they look upon the One whom they pierced and mourn repentantly for Him (Zechariah 12:10); 'in that day a fountain shall be opened for the house of David and for the inhabitants of Jerusalem, for sin and for uncleanness' (Zechariah 13:1).

Nor did Christ's work on the cross 'seal up vision and prophecy'. Alva McClain asks:

> Where in the period of the Acts can we find any "sealing up of vision and prophecy"? On the contrary, it is during this very period and beyond that we find the greatest loosing of "vision and prophecy" in all the history of revelation. But at the second coming of our Lord in glory, which will take place at the close of the Seventieth Week, vision and prophecy will no longer be needed. The Word of God Himself will be present in visible manifestation, and His law will go forth from Jerusalem[16].

William Kelly writes:

> I would call your attention to this ... all his thoughts are about Israel and about Jerusalem. The prophecy is not about Christianity, but about Israel ... Some are startled and ask, Have we, then, nothing to do with "reconciliation for iniquity" and "everlasting righteousness"? I ask, Of whom does the verse speak? You will find other scriptures, which reveal our interest in the blotting out of sin, and the righteousness which we are made in Christ. But we must adhere to this golden rule in reading the word of God – never to force Scripture in order to make it bear upon ourselves or others ...Thus, if we take the Bible as it is, without being too anxious to find ourselves here or there ... we shall not feel that we have been taking other people's property, and claiming goods upon a tenure that can be disputed, but that what we have is what God has freely and assuredly given us[17].

Forgiveness of sin rests upon the same basis whether for Jew or Gentile, but the prophecy is concerned with more than simply the basis of forgiveness. It concerns the city of Jerusalem, the Jewish people, the

---

[15] Dwight Pentecost, *Things to Come*, p247
[16] Alva J. McClain, *Daniel's Prophecy of the Seventy Weeks*, BMH Books, 2007, p36
[17] William Kelly, *The Great Prophecies of Daniel*, Pickering and Inglis, 1897, pp152-4

prophetic Scriptures, the Temple sanctuary, Israel's sins, their promised Messiah, their great enemy and their eventual triumph; it is the prophecy itself which restricts itself to Jewish concerns.

Thus, again, the prophecy is not really about the church's spiritual blessings. Instead, the prophecy deals with the nation of Israel's national and political restoration, and also with the deeper issue of their spiritual restoration through the forgiveness of their sins. As we are going to see, it deals with God's program for the completion of human history.

Why the Premillennial Interpretation of the Seven Events is True
Before we look at the timetable of the tribulation, we must now return to the seven events prophesied in Daniel 9 and consider which of the three interpretations best explains its meaning. Then we will then be able to put together a timetable of God's program for the future.

1. A Decree for the Rebuilding of Jerusalem
Daniel 9:25: 'Know therefore and understand, that from the going forth of the command to restore and build Jerusalem ...'

The prophecy firstly states that there will be a command to rebuild the city of Jerusalem. In Daniel's day, Jerusalem lay in ruins, destroyed by the Babylonians. The latter part of this verse gives more details: 'the street (or 'open square') shall be built again, and the wall, even in troubled times'.

When was this command to rebuild Jerusalem given? There are four main possibilities. Some commentators take it to refer to Jeremiah's prophecies (in Jeremiah 25 or 29, written either in 605 BC or in 597 BC) of a return from exile. However, nothing in Jeremiah's two prophecies mentions the rebuilding of the city, but simply a seventy year exile and then a return. Secondly, many commentators prefer the decree of Cyrus in 539 BC, quoting Isaiah 44:28 and 45:13, allowing the exiles to return and rebuild the temple. Thirdly, others suggest the permission given to Ezra to return to Jerusalem in Ezra 7 in 458 BC, however the decree in Ezra 7 (authorizing Ezra to 'beautify the house' and to teach the law) made no mention of the rebuilding of the city. Finally, there was the permission given by Artaxerxes to Nehemiah to return and rebuild Jerusalem in 454 BC[18].

If we look at the actual wording of Daniel 9:25, it becomes clear that only the work of Nehemiah fulfils the prophecy. Daniel 9:25 refers, not to an ongoing regeneration project, but to the reconstitution of the city as a

---

[18] For the reason why this date, as opposed to 445, see the author's book, *The Most Amazing Prophecy in the Bible*

civic entity by means of walls and the open public square, the 'essential part of the city' (Brown, Driver, Briggs), equivalent to a Roman forum. The very fact that Nehemiah's book and its story of the rebuilding of Jerusalem is included in our Bible means, for those who believe that Scripture interprets Scripture, that only Nehemiah fulfils the prophecy, for it shows that (a) in Nehemiah's day the city still lay largely in ruins and (b) Jerusalem was reconstituted as a city with walls and 'open square' (Neh. 8:1).

2. A Period of Sixty-Nine Sevens till the Coming of Messiah the Prince

Daniel 9:25-26: '… until Messiah the Prince, there shall be seven sevens and sixty-two sevens; the street shall be built again, and the wall, even in troublesome times. And after the sixty-two sevens Messiah shall be cut off, but not for Himself'.

Messiah the Prince is not only prophesied to come after a certain period of time, but he is to be cut off, which means to die a violent death. This refers to the coming and death of our Lord Jesus Christ. The next expression 'but not for himself' is not an accurate translation (although it is true that Christ did not die for Himself; He died for us). The Hebrew literally says, and he 'shall have nothing'. Christ had no possessions, no clothes, no children, no justice, not even a tomb to be buried in. Politically, it means that He had nothing: the long promised King was not given was what rightfully His – the kingdom. His own people rejected him and gave Him nothing.

Some commentators suggest other possible 'anointed princes': Cyrus (Isa.45:1), Onias III (the Jewish High Priest in the days of Antiochus Epiphanes, or Zerubbabel or Joshua (Haggai 1:1). But Sir Robert Anderson cuts through the confusion: it is a 'preposterous interpretation' to suggest 'that any Jew … could anticipate "the complete redemption of Israel" apart from the advent of Messiah. It is absolutely certain that the vision points to the coming of Christ, and any other view of it is indeed "a resort of desperation"'[19]. Also certain is the fact that the Messiah must have come and died before AD 70 when the temple was destroyed. This is because the destruction of the temple is the next event in the prophetic timetable.

3. The city and temple destroyed

Daniel 9:26: 'And the people of the prince who is to come shall destroy

---

[19] Sir R. Anderson, *Daniel in the Critic's Den*, Nisbet, 1909, p114-5

the city and the sanctuary, and his end will be with a flood'.

These words can only refer to the destruction of the Jewish temple ('the sanctuary') and city by the Romans in AD 70. This was the one and only time the Jewish temple was ever destroyed after the return of the Jews from their exile in Babylon. 'Commentators who argue that Antiochus Epiphanes fulfilled this prophecy are at a loss to account for the fact that he destroyed neither the temple nor the city of Jerusalem' (Baldwin[20]).

The Jewish people rejected their Messiah and gave him nothing, and for this great sin, after forty years of Divine longsuffering offering the opportunity for repentance, God's judgment overtook them; they lost their city and temple and ended up with nothing.

Edward Dennett writes:

> The most careful attention must be given to the exact words used in this scripture ... Remark then, first, that it does not say that a prince shall come and destroy the city and the sanctuary, but that the people of the prince that shall come shall do so[21].

Critical commentators take the Prince here to refer to Antiochus Epiphanes, while some amillennial commentators see Titus the Roman general. The one person it cannot refer to is Messiah the Prince of verses 25 and 26a, for neither His Jewish people nor His Christian people destroyed the city and the sanctuary. This means, crucially, that there are actually two princes in Daniel's prophecy. Amillennialist commentator Matthew Henry argued that Christ destroyed the city and sanctuary through His agents, the Romans, however these were not 'His people'. The title 'the Prince to come' is explained by Montgomery, who argues that the expression distinguishes this second prince from the 'Prince of verse 25 by the epithet 'to come', either as some new one or in the sense of an invader, as the verb often implies, e.g. 1:1, 11:13, etc.'[22].

Dennett continues:

> In other words "the prince that shall come" applies to the future, and is indeed, as will be seen in the next verse, the imperial head of the revived Roman empire in the last days. The "people" are identified with him because they are Romans of the same kingdom that is yet to reappear,

---

[20] J. G. Baldwin, *Daniel*, TOTC, IVP, 1978, p190
[21] E. Dennett, *Daniel the Prophet and the Times of the Gentiles*, Central Bible Truth Depot, 1967, p150
[22] J. A. Montgomery, *Daniel*, ICC, T&T Clark, 1927, p383

and of which this prince will be the leader and the chief[23].

We read that the end of this second 'prince to come' will be with a flood. 'Flood' here is a metaphor describing sudden destruction, particularly in an overwhelming military defeat. We see this figure of speech in various Bible verses, for example Daniel 11 verses 10 ('overflow') and 22 ('flood'). A literal translation of this phrase reads: 'his (not 'its') end will be with a flood'[24]. Thus, the end referred to is not that of the city of Jerusalem, nor the war of AD 70[25]. Further, although 'sanctuary' is masculine, the nearest antecedent in the Hebrew is 'the prince to come'. The prince's end is in view, standing in contrast with his coming.

Liberal scholars take 'the prince to come' to be Antiochus, but his end was obscure. Although he died while on a military campaign in 164 BC, it was not in a battle – Josephus says he died of a 'distemper'; others say of 'worms and ulcers'. Neither (as some amillennialists assert) does the description apply to Titus, who did not die in war, but of a fever after dedicating the Colosseum in Rome to victory in the Jewish war.

The 'prince to come' is the Antichrist of the future, and his end is going to come in an overwhelming military defeat in the greatest battle of world history: Armageddon.

By the way: we see here a gap in the prophetic timetable. After the first 69 weeks, bringing us to Christ's death in AD 30, we have a forty year gap to the destruction of Jerusalem in AD 70. This gap does not fit into the Seventy Weeks. McClain writes, 'a gap in time between the Sixty-ninth and Seventieth Weeks is demanded by the historical fulfilment of the two predicted events of verse 26 [i.e. Christ's death and Jerusalem's destruction]… Both of them were *after*, not within, the Sixty-nine Weeks … Yet in the record of the prophecy, the destruction of the city is placed before the last week'[26]. This is highly significant, as we shall see.

4. War to be Fought over Jerusalem until the Time of the End
Daniel 9:26: 'and till the end there shall be war, desolations are determined'.

The last phrase in Daniel 9:26 traces the fourth stage of God's program: 'till the end there shall be war, desolations are determined' (see RV,

---

[23] Dennett, *Daniel the Prophet*, pp150-1
[24] see the RV, and Keil and Delitzsch; the word 'end' has the masculine suffix
[25] Both 'city' and 'war' are feminine in Hebrew and so do not match the masculine word 'end' earlier.
[26] McClain, *Daniel's Prophecy of the Seventy Weeks*, pp34-35.

NASB, NIV, ESV). Keil and Delitzsch write:

> 'we agree with the majority of interpreters in regarding [*milchamah*, war] as the predicate of the passage: "and to the end is war;" but we cannot refer [*qetz*, end] ... to the end of the prince, or ... to the end of the city, because [*qetz*, end] has neither a suffix nor an article. ... [*qetz*] without any limitation is the end generally, the end of the period in progress, the seventy [sevens] and corresponds to ['unto the end'] in Daniel 7:26, to the end of all things, Daniel 12:13. To the end war shall be = war shall continue during the whole of the last [seven]'.

The verse is saying that following the destruction of Jerusalem in AD 70 there are to be continual wars fought over the city of Jerusalem.
The commentator Gaebelein writes:

> these words give us the history of the Jewish people, of their land and their city, up to the present time. It is identical with what our Lord said, "and they shall fall by the edge of the sword, and shall be led away captive into all nations; and Jerusalem shall be trodden down of the Gentiles until the times of the Gentiles are fulfilled" (Luke 21:24)[27].

The history of Jerusalem after AD 70 is the history of war. The city of Jerusalem has changed hands seventeen times and the walls have been destroyed and rebuilt eight times. These include the city being taken by the Romans during the Bar Kochba revolt in A.D. 135 (killing half a million Jews), by the Muslims in A.D. 638, Crusaders in A.D. 1099, Saladin in A.D. 1187, Tartars in A.D. 1244, Egyptians in 1247 A.D., Mamluks in the 13th Century, Ottomans in A.D. 1517, the British in A.D. 1917 (when the author's great-grandfather entered Jerusalem with the British Eighth Army under General Allenby), Jordan in A.D. 1948 and the modern state of Israel in A.D. 1967. Still today, Palestine is a war-zone and Jerusalem is the most troublesome place on earth.

There could hardly be a more striking proof of fulfilled Biblical prophecy. Why Jerusalem should be such a troublesome nuisance is a mystery to most of the world's politicians, but why Jerusalem should be so war-torn, from a Christian point of view, is surely obvious: the Jews rejected the Prince of Peace; they will have no peace until they finally say, 'Blessed is He who comes in the name of the Lord' (Matthew 23:39).

---

[27] A. C. Gaebelein, *Daniel the Prophet*, Pickering and Inglis, n.d., p143

5. The Prince to Come will make a treaty with Israel

Daniel 9:27: 'Then he shall confirm a covenant with many for one seven'.

The prediction in verse 26 of continual wars over Jerusalem provides us with the setting for this final verse of the prophecy. 'He' in this verse refers back to the last-mentioned person in the prophecy, the 'prince to come', the second prince, Antichrist. The 'prince to come' (verse 26) will enforce a treaty with the Jews. 'The unusual verb used in make a strong covenant (*gabar*) bears this out for it has the implication of forcing an agreement by means of superior strength' (Baldwin[28]). Presumably this will involve a peace deal, solving the 'Jewish problem' in the Middle East and giving the Jews protection from their enemies and the freedom to worship God in such a way that the sacrificial system is resumed in a Jewish temple. Just as the majority of Jews in Jesus' day rejected the Christ, so the 'many' (the majority) of them will welcome the Antichrist and his treaty.

Dennett writes,

> What is asserted here is, that the future head of the revived Roman Empire will make a covenant with "the many", that is, with the mass or majority of the Jews, who at that time will again be in their own land; for the mention of the sacrifice and the oblation puts it beyond doubt that Jerusalem is in question, and that the temple has been rebuilt. This prince will then enter into an alliance with the Jews, with all of them save the godly remnant, professedly as befriending their cause, and as protecting them from their adversaries[29].

6. The Deal is broken and there is a period of Great Tribulation

Daniel 9:27: 'But in the middle of the seven he shall bring an end to sacrifice and offering, and on the wing of abominations shall be one who makes desolate'.

In the middle of the seven-year deal, the 'prince to come' will renege on his treaty and forcibly intervene to halt the Jewish temple sacrifices.

The references to 'bring(ing) an end to sacrifice and offering', to 'abominations' and 'desolation' in this verse connects this passage with Daniel 11:31 where we read the following about the forces of Antiochus Epiphanes: [They will] 'defile the sanctuary fortress; then shall they take away the daily sacrifices, and place there the abomination of desolation'.

---

[28] J. G. Baldwin, *Daniel*, TOTC, IVP, 1978, p191

[29] Edward Dennett, *Daniel the Prophet and the Times of the Gentiles*, Central Bible Truth Depot, 1967, pp153-4

Similarly, Daniel 12:11 tells us about a time at the end of the world (for Dan. 12:3 talks about the resurrection at the end of time) when similar things will happen: 'and from the time that the daily sacrifice is taken away, and the abomination of desolation is set up, there shall be one thousand two hundred and ninety days'.

In the New Testament, Christ prophesied that the 'abomination of desolation' was still to happen in the future (Matt. 24:15). This means that the liberal view (that says that Daniel's prophecy was fulfilled in the past, centuries before Christ during Antiochus Epiphanes' atrocities) is wrong. Further, Christ said that His coming would occur 'immediately after the tribulation of those days' (Matthew 24:29), and seeing the tribulation commenced with the setting up of an 'abomination of desolation' (Matt. 24:15), this means that the amillennial view (which argues that Daniel's prophecy was completely fulfilled in Christ's first coming and the destruction of Jerusalem in AD 70) is also wrong, because there is clearly still a yet-future, end-times fulfilment of 'the abomination of desolation' just before Christ returns.

Approaching the prophecy from the standpoint of what Christ Himself said about it in the Olivet Discourse leaves us with no alternative but to view Daniel's seventieth 'seven' as yet-future. Our Lord Jesus Christ's own words about a future abomination of desolation require that Daniel 9:27 is telling of the career of the yet-future Antichrist, of whom Antiochus Epiphanes was but a foreshadowing. The New Testament elsewhere tells us that the Antichrist will indeed set up an idol in the Jewish Temple and will force the entire world to worship it (2 Thessalonians 2:4 and Revelation 13:14-15).

The Antichrist will usher in a period described in terrible terms: the 'great tribulation' (Revelation 7:14) also spoken of by Christ in Matthew 24:21, 'a time of trouble, such as never was since there was a nation, even to that time' (Daniel 12:1). Jewish worship will be forbidden in the temple, he will set up an idol to himself (the 'abomination of desolation', Matthew 24:15, Mark 13:14, 2 Thessalonians Ch. 2 and Revelation Ch. 13), people will not be able to buy or sell without his mark (666), and fierce persecution of any who don't worship him or take his mark will follow for three and a half years.

7. Antichrist will be destroyed at the Battle of Armageddon
Daniel 9:27: 'even until the consummation, which is determined, is poured out on the desolator'.

We read at the end of verse 26, 'His end shall be with a flood', that is, an overwhelming and sudden military defeat will be 'poured out on the desolator' (see the end of verse 27). This is the battle of Armageddon of Revelation chapter 19.

Thus, God's purposes will finally be accomplished: God will spiritually restore the nation of Israel to Himself, he will punish the world for its godlessness and He will usher in Christ's reign over the earth (Revelation 20) where everything is restored: earth will finally revert to the Paradise it was created to be. Those of us who are Christ's, forgiven through His death, belonging to His bride the Church, will reign with Him there.

The Timetable of Future Events

1. The true Messiah must have come and died before AD 70, when the temple was destroyed, for the simple reason that Messiah's death (event two in Daniel's program) occurs before the temple's destruction (event three). Christ died in AD 30 in fulfilment of the vision, thus completing the 69th 'seven' – 483 years from the command for the re-establishment of Jerusalem. For more details on the chronology, see the author's book, *The Most Amazing Prophecy in the Bible*.

2. There is a forty-year gap between event two (Messiah's death) and event three (the destruction of the Temple). Thus, the 69th 'seven' (when Christ died) does not appear to have been followed immediately by the 70th (and last) 'seven'. The timetable of the seventy sevens in Daniel 9 does not state in which 'seven' the temple's destruction was to occur. Neither is there anything else particularly noteworthy that happened seven years after Christ's death in AD 30. Rebellion and transgression against God certainly did not cease, nor was there the sealing up of prophecy (v24), for the rest of the New Testament was not written in the seven years after Christ's death. Some suggest that the end of the seventieth week refers to Stephen's death or Paul's conversion in AD 33, but this is pure speculation. There is no hint of the fulfilment of the seventy weeks in Acts 8-9.

3. We therefore have a gap, or a parenthesis, in the timetable. In fact, the prophecy has three gaps in its schedule of future events: firstly the period from Daniel's day till the rebuilding of Jerusalem (a period of nearly 150 years), secondly, the forty years from Christ's death till the destruction of the Jewish temple in AD 70, and then thirdly, the unspecified gap described as 'war until the end' (v26). At the moment, we are living in this long gap in the Divine Program, between Christ's death and The End. There is nothing stated in the prophecy about how long this gap will last before the last three events take place. This

is why it is impossible to put a date on Christ's return (Matthew 24:36).
4. Verse 26 tells of the temple being destroyed, but verse 27 tells that the 'prince to come' will halt Jewish sacrifices. The prophecy therefore implies that despite the Temple's destruction in AD 70, there must be the reinstitution of Jewish temple services and sacrifices. This also implies that the Jews would once again return to their own land after their scattering among the nations by the Romans. Seeing the re-establishment of Jewish temple worship has still not occurred, the events of Daniel 9:27 are still in the future.
5. In verse 27 the timetable resumes with the mention of 'one seven', presumably the last, missing seven. Verse 27 also speaks of 'the middle (lit. 'half') of the seven'. The Bible repeatedly refers to a period of three and a half years in relation to future events. This period of three and a half years is described in four different ways: as 'half of the seven', as 'time, and times and half a time' (where 'times' is dual in Hebrew, i.e., meaning two), as forty-two months, and as 1260 days (Daniel 7:25, 12:7, Rev. 11:2, 3, 12:6, 14, 13:5). All of these different expressions equate to the same amount: three and a half years. The last seven years of world history before Christ's return will be divided into two halves, the second of which is called 'the great tribulation'.

The Period of the 'Great Tribulation'

What shall we make of the three and a half year period referenced in Daniel and Revelation? Amillennialist commentators treat it as symbolic of the entire church age; as a result, it means everything and yet means nothing. Thus Hendriksen, commentating on Rev. 11, writes: the 'twelve hundred and sixty days ... is the period that extends from the moment of Christ's ascension almost until the judgment day ... It is the period of affliction; the present gospel age'[30]. Mounce, although not amillennialist, describes this period in a symbolic way as the period of the church's persecution; it is 'a conventional symbol for a limited period of time during which evil would be allowed free rein'[31], 'the traditional period for religious persecution' (p254).

This vague approach to explaining the three and a half year time-marker is rendered dubious by the fact that it is (a) is a specific time period of unequalled persecution ('such as never was since there was a nation', Daniel 12:1) – not a description of the entire age, (b) that occurs just before

---

[30] Hendriksen, *More than Conquerors*, p129
[31] Mounce, *Revelation*, p221

the resurrection (Daniel 12:2), (c) that occurs just before the reign of the returning Messiah upon the earth (Dan. 7:14, 27), (d) during which time the great enemy of God's people reigns.

Notice what the Bible tells us about this three and a half year period:

- Daniel 7:25 says, 'He shall speak pompous words against the Most High, shall persecute the saints of the Most High, and shall intend to change times and law. Then the saints shall be given into his hand *for a time and times and half a time*'. 'He' here is the 'little horn' (see 7:8) who shall rise from the fourth (Roman) world empire – i.e. this cannot be Antiochus Epiphanes (who rose from the third, Greek, empire); it is the future Antichrist. This verse tells us that the he will persecute God's people for three and a half years.
- Daniel 12:7 says, 'Then I heard the man clothed in linen, who was above the waters of the river, when he held up his right hand and his left hand to heaven, and swore by Him who lives forever, that it shall be for *a time, times, and half a time*; and when the power of the holy people has been completely shattered, all these things shall be finished'. This passage tells us that the 'great tribulation' period of three and a half years will lead to the 'holy people' (see Dan. 12:1) being completely humbled and shattered, so that they are finally ready to receive their Messiah, Jesus Christ (see Zechariah 12-14).
- Revelation 11:2 says, 'leave out the court which is outside the temple, and do not measure it, for it has been given to the Gentiles, and they will tread the holy city underfoot for *forty-two months*'. Treading underfoot is another way of speaking of persecution and tribulation.
- Revelation 11:3 says, 'And I will give power to my two witnesses, and they will prophesy *one thousand two hundred and sixty days*, clothed in sackcloth'. We will investigate who these two prophetic witnesses are in a later chapter, but here we read that they witness for God during this same three and a half year period of tribulation.
- Revelation 12:6 says, 'the woman fled into the wilderness, where she has a place prepared by God, that they should feed her there *one thousand two hundred and sixty days*'. Here the woman (which refers to God's people) will be provided for and preserved ('fed') during the 'great tribulation' period of Satanic persecution.
- Revelation 12:14 tells us that 'the woman was given two wings of a great eagle, that she might fly into the wilderness to her place, where she is nourished for *a time and times and half a time*, from the presence

of the serpent'. Here we see that the two time periods, described in different ways in 12:6 and 14, both refer to the exact same period.

- Revelation 13:5 says, 'to him was given a mouth speaking great things and blasphemies, and he was given authority to continue for *forty-two months*'. It will be noticed that this is almost a direct quotation from our first passage in Daniel 7:25, connecting the 'forty two months' of Revelation 13:5 with 'the forty two months' of Daniel 7:25, and thereby equating the 'little horn' of Daniel 7 with the 'beast' of Revelation 13.

We conclude that the different time descriptions are the same length, and refer to the same period: the 'great tribulation'. Once we connect this period with Daniel 9:27 and its 'half a seven', i.e. three and a half years, we see again that Daniel's final 'seven' must still in the future. The second half of this final 'seven' is the 'great tribulation' spoken of by Christ in Matthew 24:21 which occurs 'immediately' before Christ's return (Matt. 24:29-31).

Early Christians who Held Daniel's Seventieth Week to be Future
Some argue against Daniel's seventieth week being in the future (or a gap in the prophetic program) by saying that this is a recent invention. However, various early Christian writers held to the same truth.

Irenaeus (about AD 186) wrote:

And the angel Gabriel, when explaining this vision, states with regard to this to this person: 'And towards the end of their kingdom a king of a most fierce countenance shall arise, one understanding [dark] questions, and exceedingly powerful, full of wonders; and he shall corrupt, direct, influence, and put strong men down, the holy people likewise; and his yoke shall be directed as a wreath [round their neck]; deceit shall be in his hand, and he shall be lifted up in his heart; he shall also ruin many by deceit, and lead many to perdition, bruising them in his hand like eggs'. **And then he points out the time that his tyranny shall last, during which the saints shall be put to flight, they who offer a pure sacrifice unto God: 'And in the midst of the week'**, he says, **'the sacrifice and the libation shall be taken away, and the abomination of desolation [shall be brought] into the temple even unto the consummation of the time shall the desolation be complete'. Now three years and six months constitute the half-**

week[32].

Notice that Irenaeus saw Daniel's last half-week as still in the future, not in AD 67-70 or in 167-164 BC. He held the great tribulation to be in the time of the Antichrist, which implies a gap in Daniel's prophetic program.

Hippolytus, in his commentary on Daniel (written between AD 202 and 211) wrote:

> **For after sixty-two weeks was fulfilled and after Christ has come and the Gospel has been preached in every place, times having been spun out, the end remains one week away,** in which Elijah and Enoch shall be present and **in its half the abomination of desolation, the Antichrist, shall appear who threatens desolation of the world.** After he comes, sacrifice and drink offering, which now in every way is offered by the nations to God, shall be taken away[33].

> **Just as also he spoke to Daniel, "And he shall establish a covenant with many for one week and it will be that in the half of the week he shall take away my sacrifice and drink offering", so that the one week may be shown as divided into two,** after the two witnesses will have preached for three and a half years, **the Antichrist will wage war against the saints the remainder of the week and will desolate all the world so that what was spoken may be fulfilled, "And they will give the abomination of desolation one thousand two hundred ninety days.** Blessed is he who endures to Christ and reaches the one thousand three hundred thirty-five days!"[34]

Hippolytus, interestingly enough, sees Antichrist himself as the 'abomination of desolation', which has some truth to it, considering the fact that 2 Thessalonians 2 says that the Man of Sin will sit in the temple of God showing himself that he is god. Similarly, Revelation 13 describes a living image of the Beast (i.e. Antichrist) as the object of idolatrous worship.

Conclusion

Daniel's prophecy of the Seventy Sevens gives us a timetable of future

---

[32] Irenaeus, *Against Heresies*, Book 5, Ch. 25
[33] Hippolytus, *Commentary on Daniel*, Book 4, 35.3
[34] Ibid, Book 4, 50.2

events: the future Antichrist will (a) make a seven year treaty with Israel, (b) halt Jewish worship in the temple at the half-way mark of this treaty, (c) set up the 'abomination of desolation', (d) ushering in the 'great tribulation', and (e) after three and a half years he will be destroyed at Christ's return.

PART THREE:

Does Israel Have a Special Destiny?

13 ISRAEL'S NATIONAL CONVERSION: ROMANS 11

In this chapter we begin to consider the question of whether the nation of Israel has a special destiny or future. In particular, does Scripture foretell that Israel is one day going to turn to Christ?

In addition to any interest we might have in Israel itself, how we interpret what the Bible says about Israel will also help us to interpret all the rest of the Bible. Horatius Bonar wrote:

> The prophecies concerning Israel are the key to all the rest. True principles of interpretation, in regard to them, will aid us in disentangling and illustrating all prophecy together. False principles as to them will most thoroughly perplex and over cloud the whole Word of God[1].

Many Christians would say the nation of Israel does not have a future in God's plans. Amillennialists believe that Israel has been replaced (or superseded, or fulfilled), by the church, and that God has no future purposes for the nation of Israel, except as individual Jews become members of the church through faith in Christ.

Luther in *The Jews and their Lies* wrote, 'the Jews, surely rejected by God, are no longer his people, and neither is he any longer their God'[2].

Herman Bavinck writes, 'Not only did Jesus not expect anything from the Jews in the present; in the future also he expected nothing for them'[3].

Bruce Waltke has written, 'The Jewish nation no longer has a place as the special people of God; that place has been taken by the Christian community which fulfils God's purpose for Israel'[4].

John Stott has said, 'I have recently come to the conclusion that political Zionism and Christian Zionism [the belief that the return of the

---

[1] Horatius Bonar, *Prophetic Landmarks: Concerning Christ's Pre-millennial Advent*, p228
[2] Luther, *The Jews and their Lies*, 1543
[3] Herman Bavinck, *Reformed Dogmatics*, 1895, 1 Vol. abridged, Baker, 2011, p733
[4] Bruce Waltke, "Kingdom Promises as Spiritual", in *Continuity and Discontinuity*, Crossway, 1988, p275

Jews to the Holy Land is in accordance with Bible prophecy] are biblically anathema to Christian faith'[5]. That is another way of saying that it is heresy to believe that God has any prophetic plans for the Jewish nation. Stott (and these other writers) are using very strong language!

Some Christians' statements about the Jews have involved shameful anti-Semitism. Luther (in *The Jews and Their Lies*) wrote:

> What shall we Christians do with this rejected and condemned people, the Jews? Since they live among us, we dare not tolerate their conduct, now that we are aware of their lying and reviling and blaspheming ... I shall give you my sincere advice.
>
> First, to set fire to their synagogues or schools and to bury and cover with dirt whatever will not burn, so that no man will ever again see a stone or cinder of them. This is to be done in honour of our Lord and of Christendom, so that God might see that we are Christians ... Second, I advise that their houses also be razed and destroyed ... Third I advise that all their prayer books and Talmudic writings, in which such idolatry, lies, cursing and blasphemy are taught, be taken from them ... Fourth, I advise that their rabbis be forbidden to teach henceforth on pain of loss of life and limb.

John Calvin wrote, 'God so blinded the whole people that they were like restive dogs. I have had much conversation with many Jews: I have never seen either a drop of piety or a grain of truth or ingeniousness – nay, I have never found common sense in any Jew'[6].

On the other hand, many Christians have argued that Israel has an important place in Bible prophecy. These Christians believe that the Bible teaches there is going to be a national conversion of Israel, a restoration to their land, and a special part for them to play in end-times events.

John Owen, the 17th century English theologian (a puritan post-millennialist), wrote: 'Moreover, it is granted that there shall be a time and season, during the continuance of the kingdom of the Messiah in this world, wherein the generality of the nation of the Jews, all the world over, shall be called and effectually brought unto the knowledge of the Messiah, our Lord Jesus Christ; with which mercy they shall also receive deliverance from their captivity, restoration unto their own land, with a blessed,

---

[5] quoted by Donald W. Wagner in *Anxious for Armageddon: A Call to Partnership for Middle Eastern and Western Christians*, Scottdale, PA: Herald, 1995, p80, explanatory emphasised text added

[6] John Calvin, "Daniel" Lecture XI, *Calvin's Commentaries*.

flourishing, and happy condition therein'[7].

John Gill, the 17th century Baptist commentator, writing on Deuteronomy 30:5, says, 'That the Jews upon their conversion in the latter day will return to the land of Judea again, and possess it, is the sense of many passages of Scripture; among others, see Jer. 30:18'.

Charles Spurgeon, the great 19th century Baptist preacher said, 'We look forward, then, for these two things. I am not going to theorize upon which of them will come first — whether they shall be restored first, and converted afterwards — or converted first and then restored. They are to be restored and they are to be converted, too'[8].

The salvation of the nation of Israel at the end of the world was also the virtually universal belief of early Church writers in the first few centuries after Christ. Origen, even though addicted to a spiritualizing method of interpretation, could write:

> Now indeed, until all the Gentiles come to salvation the riches of God are concentrated in the multitude of believers, but as long as Israel remains in its unbelief it will not be possible to say that the fullness of the Lord's portion has been attained. The people of Israel are still missing from the complete picture. But when the fullness of the Gentiles has come in and Israel comes to salvation at the end of time, then it will be the people which, although it existed long ago, will come at the last and complete the fullness of the Lord's portion and inheritance.

Augustine, although an amillennialist, wrote:

> And at or in connection with that judgment the following events shall come to pass, as we have learned: Elias the Tishbite shall come, the Jews shall believe; Antichrist shall persecute; Christ shall judge; the dead shall rise; the good and the wicked shall be separated; the world shall be burned and renewed. All these things, we believe, shall come to pass; but how, or in what order, human understanding cannot perfectly teach us, but only the experience of the events themselves[9].

---

[7] John Owen, *Complete Works*, Vol. 17, p560
[8] Spurgeon, *The Restoration and Conversion of the Jews. Ezekiel 37.1-10*, June 16, 1864
[9] Augustine, *City of God*, book 20, ch. 30

Tertullian (155-220 AD) wrote:

> He [God] will favour with His acceptance and blessing the circumcision also, even the race of Abraham, which by and by is to acknowledge Him[10].

John Chrysostom (349-407) the great preacher wrote:

> To show therefore that [Elijah] the Tishbite comes before that other [second] advent ... He said this ... And what is this reason? That when He is come, He may persuade the Jews to believe in Christ, and that they may not all utterly perish at His coming. Wherefore He too, guiding them on to that remembrance, saith, "And he shall restore all things"; that is, shall correct the unbelief of the Jews that are then in being[11].

Jerome, the translator of the Latin Vulgate Bible, wrote:

> When the Jews receive the faith at the end of the world, they will find themselves in dazzling light, as if our Lord were returning to them from Egypt[12].

Were these early (and later) Christians under God's anathema in their understanding of God's purposes for Israel, as Stott says? Or is it rather the case that Stott and other writers like him are just confused and perplexed because they have not correctly understood what God says about Israel?

Romans 11: Will there be a National Conversion of Israel?

One of the most important chapters dealing with the subject of Israel is Romans 11, where Paul addresses this subject of God's plans and purposes for Israel: 'has God cast away His people?' (verse 1), and again in verse 11, 'have they stumbled that they should fall?'. Paul answers these questions with an emphatic negative: Certainly not! The King James Version memorably renders it, God forbid! Then, in verses 25 and 26, he reveals a

---

[10] Tertullian, *Against Marcion* 5.9, Ante-Nicene Fathers 3:448
[11] Chrysostom, *The Gospel of Matthew* 57, NPNF[1] 10:352
[12] Jerome, *Commentary on St. Matthew*, 2, quoted in Michael Vlach, *Has the Church Replaced Israel*, B&H, 2010, p47

mystery: 'blindness in part has happened to Israel until the fullness of the Gentiles has come in, and so, all Israel will be saved'.

> For I do not desire, brethren, that you should be ignorant of this mystery, lest you should be wise in your own opinion, that blindness in part has happened to Israel until the fullness of the Gentiles has come in. 26 And so all Israel will be saved, as it is written: "The Deliverer will come out of Zion, And He will turn away ungodliness from Jacob; 27 For this is My covenant with them, When I take away their sins." 28 Concerning the gospel they are enemies for your sake, but concerning the election they are beloved for the sake of the fathers. 29 For the gifts and the calling of God are irrevocable (Rom. 11:25-29).

The expression in verse 26, 'all Israel will be saved', has been interpreted in a variety of ways. Calvin argued that 'all Israel' here means the entire church: 'Many understand this of the Jewish people, as though Paul had said, that religion would again be restored among them as before: but I extend the word Israel to all the people of God . . . and thus shall be completed the salvation of the whole Israel of God, which must be gathered from both [Jews and Gentiles]'[13].

The problem with Calvin's argument is that in the verses immediately before and after, Israel clearly refers to ethnic Israel: 'blindness in part has happened to Israel' (verse 25) and 'concerning the gospel, they are enemies for your sake' (verse 28). These verses cannot refer to the church. How is the church the enemy of the gospel?

John Murray writes, 'It is exegetically impossible to give to "Israel" in this verse any other denotation than that which belongs to the terms throughout this chapter'[14].

S. Lewis Johnson writes, 'It is exegetically and theologically highly unlikely that the term 'Israel,' having been used 10 times for the nation in ... Romans 9-11, should now suddenly without any special explanation refer to 'spiritual Israel,' composed of elect Jews and Gentiles'[15].

Other commentators deny a future national conversion of Israel by arguing that 'all Israel' (verse 26) refers to the last few Jews who will be converted before the end of the church age, thus making up the full-quota of Jews who become part of the church. Philip Hughes writes, '"All Israel"

---

[13] John Calvin, *Commentary on Romans*
[14] John Murray, *The Epistle to the Romans*, Vol. 2, Grand Rapids: Eerdmans, 1965, p96
[15] S. Lewis Johnson, "Evidence from Romans 9-11", in *A Case for Premillennialism*, ed. D. K. Campbell and J. L Townsend, Grand Rapids: Kregel, 1997, p202

or "the fullness of Israel," then, is the full number of those Jews ... who by God's grace hear and by faith receive the message of the Gospel'[16]. However, there seems little reason why Paul should need to write such a commonplace thing as 'thus the last trickle of Jews will be saved'.

Leon Morris points out that this is hardly a mystery: 'Now it is no 'mystery' that all the elect, Jews as well as Gentiles, will be saved. Nor is the conversion of a few Jews in each generation such as has happened until now the kind of thing that needs to be the subject of a special revelation'[17].

Nanos says, 'This [view] too, is redundant and hardly motivates Gentiles to humility. They [Paul's readers] already recognize that Jews who believe in Jesus as the Christ are saved, don't they? What does this position tell us about the 'stumbling of Israel'?'[18].

If Paul had meant to say that the last few Jews will eventually be saved, it would have been better to have said something like 'the last few of Israel will be saved', or 'the final remnant will be saved', not 'all Israel will be saved'.

F. F. Bruce writes, '"All Israel" is a recurring expression in Jewish literature, where it need not mean "every Jew without a single exception", but "Israel as a whole"'[19]. Sanday and Headlam write that all Israel means 'Israel as a whole, Israel as a nation, and not as necessarily including every individual Israelite'[20]. See 'all Israel' in 1 Chr. 11:1, 4, 13:5, 14:8, 15:3, etc.

Now, of course, it hardly needs to be stated that when the Bible says that 'all Israel will be saved', it is not meaning that all Jews of all time are going to be saved. What Romans 11 means (and what other OT passages show, as we will see in subsequent chapters) is that those Jews who are left alive at the return of Christ, the nation as a whole, are going to believe in Christ and be saved. As we shall see in the next chapter, more than two-thirds of the Jewish nation are going to die in the great tribulation, but those who are left at its end will turn to Christ and be saved.

Other Evidence in Romans 11 that Ethnic Israel will be Saved

There are five other pieces of evidence in Romans 11 that suggest that there is going to be a future national conversion of Israel.

Firstly, in Romans 11:1 Paul asks whether God has cast away Israel. He says, 'certainly not!', and his first proof is to point to a remnant of

---

[16] Philip. E. Hughes, *Interpreting Prophecy*, Eerdmans, 1976, p96.
[17] Leon Morris, *The Epistle to the Romans*, Grand Rapids: Eerdmans, 1988, p421
[18] M. D. Nanos, *The Mystery of Romans*, Minneapolis: Fortress, 1996, p256
[19] F. F. Bruce, *Romans*, TNTC, 1985, p209
[20] Sanday and Headlam, *Romans*, ICC, T&T Clark, 1902, p335

Jewish believers like himself, an Israelite, of the seed of Abraham, of the tribe of Benjamin (verse 1). Then in verses 2-5 he talks about how Elijah thought he was the only faithful Israelite left, and God told him that he had left 7000 men who had not bowed the knee to Baal. Elijah thought that Israel was spiritually finished, and that God had given up on them, but it was not so. The fact that there is a remnant of Jewish believers in Christ today disproves the idea that God has finished with Israel. God is showing mercy on individual Jews today and they are coming to Christ. It is not the case that God has fully or finally washed His hands of Jewish people.

In fact, if God had cast away Israel for their great sin of rejecting and crucifying God's Son, then we might expect there to be no Israelites left at all in the world. Israel would have gone the way of the Philistines, and the Hittites – vanished from the face of the earth. Israel would be no more than a museum curiosity or an historical footnote.

There have been theologians who held that God has rejected and replaced Israel, and who confidently stated that the people of Israel would never come back to their land. Kim Riddlebarger, an amillennialist, (and someone who believes that the church has replaced Israel), has admitted, 'We cannot repeat the mistakes of prior generations of amillennarians (such as Bavinck and Berkhof) who both said one of the sure signs that dispensationalism was false was that the dispensationalists kept predicting that Israel will become a nation. As we all know, Israel became a sovereign nation in 1948 despite Berkhof's and Bavinck's views to the contrary'[21]. The re-founding of the state of Israel in 1948 dealt a heavy blow to the idea that God has forever finished with Israel.

So, here is Paul's first argument in Romans 11. He says that the fact that there is a continuing remnant in Israel, and particularly godly, Christian Jews, is proof that God has not given up on Israel.

Secondly, Romans 11:12 asks, 'If their fall (literally, 'offence', i.e. their rejection and crucifixion of Christ) is riches for the world, and their failure riches for the Gentiles, how much more their fullness'. The word 'fullness' stands in contrast to the two words 'fall' and 'failure' in verse 12; if the fall and failure of the Jewish nation (seen in the scattered, and persecuted position the Jews have occupied for the last 1900 years) is to be replaced with 'fullness', this suggests not only their spiritual blessing (reversing their great sin of rejecting Christ), but also their national restoration and blessing.

---

[21] Kim Riddlebarger, "Answers to Questions: Part 2", The Riddleblog, http://kimriddlebarger.squaresspace.com/answers-to-questions-2/

Thirdly, verse 15 says, 'If their being cast away is the reconciling of the world, what will their acceptance be but life from the dead' (v15). 'Acceptance' (by God) and 'life from the dead' again hint at a future spiritual restoration for Israel.

Fourthly, Paul's metaphor of the olive tree (vs 16-24) leads us to think that while Israel (the olive branch) is currently broken off (v17) and the Gentiles (the wild olive branch) has been grafted into the tree, how much more natural is the re-grafting in of Israel: 'For if you were cut out of the olive tree which is wild by nature, and were grafted contrary to nature into a cultivated olive tree, how much more will these, who are natural branches, be grafted into their own olive tree?' (Rom. 11:24). The suggestion of 'grafting in' again of olive branches (Israel) into the olive tree speaks of Israel's national, spiritual restoration.

Fifthly, verse 25 says that 'blindness in part has happened to Israel until the fullness of the Gentiles has come in'. In this verse we see that (a) 'until' suggests that Jewish restoration is not happening in the present, but will happen in the future, for the Jews will continue in partial blindness until a future day, (b) partial blindness is not going to continue forever, which suggests that it is going to give way to sight, i.e. future Jewish belief, and (c) 'fullness' is the same word as in verse 12, where it speaks of the fullness of Gentile blessing in salvation, in which case Israel's 'fullness' here would appear to refer to future Jewish blessing in salvation.

The Olive Tree Illustration

In Romans 11:16-24, Paul uses an illustration of an olive tree to show God's purposes for Israel. The natural olive branches (picturing Israel) have been broken off and replaced by wild olive branches (picturing Gentiles) grafted into the tree. This shows God's present replacement of Israel with the church. In fact, many theologians argue that there is only one 'people of God', the true Church which is comprised of Old Testament Jewish believers and New Testament Christian believers. Wayne Grudem writes, 'when Jewish people according to the flesh are saved in large numbers at some time in the future, they will not constitute a separate people of God or be like a separate olive tree, but they "will be grafted back into their own olive tree" (Rom. 11:24)[22].

This illustration of the olive tree is a favourite argument of those who believe that the church has replaced Israel. They point out that there is only one olive tree – not two trees (Israel, and the church, with separate

---

[22] Wayne Grudem, *Systematic Theology*, p861

destinies). Further, they point out that the natural branches (the Jewish people) have been broken off the tree and replaced by the wild olive branches (that is, the Gentiles). Thus, it is argued, Paul's illustration teaches replacement theology. However, it is dangerous to build doctrine on illustrations (or parables) in the Bible unless the doctrine is explicitly taught in the Bible itself. Having said this, there are four things that we should notice carefully in this illustration of the olive tree:

1. While the natural branches have been broken off the tree, Paul says that the natural olive branches (the Jewish people) are one day going to be re-grafted into the tree. See verses 23 and 24: if it is possible to graft in the wild olive branches, it is even easier to re-graft in the natural branches. Paul is again hinting that the replacement we see in the illustration is not final or permanent. He goes on in verses 25 and 26 to promise that all Israel are one day going to be saved.
2. As we read down through the illustration, both the natural branches (the Jews) and the wild olive branches (the Gentiles) remain distinct. They are called different names throughout the illustration. It is not as though the 'wild' olive branches become 'natural' olive branches after they are grafted in. Gardeners graft branches of certain trees into different trees, for example, a lemon branch may be grafted into an orange tree, but the grafted lemon branch does not start growing oranges. Instead, the new branch grafted in still grows lemons on an orange tree. The branches maintain their difference and distinction. So, there is still a distinction between Jewish and Gentile branches throughout the illustration.
3. While those who hold to replacement theology point to the fact that there is only one tree, it is important to notice that Paul takes us back to the very 'root' of the tree (in vs 16 and 18) that supports everything. Nowhere does he call the root of the tree 'Israel', as if we Gentile Christians are now part of Israel, nor does Paul call the root of the tree the 'church' as if the church refers to all people down through time who are saved. Paul says neither of these things. Most commentators suggest that by referring to the root, he means Abraham. But there were saints before Abraham even came into existence, like Noah and Abel and Melchizedek and Job. Nor is Abraham part of Israel, inasmuch as Israel – i.e. Jacob – was his grandson, not vice versa. It is true that Christians are the spiritual children of Abraham, as the NT teaches (Gal. 3:29). Indeed, all believers down through time are 'the people of God' (meaning that we belong to God, Heb. 4:9, 11:25, 1

Pet. 2:10). But that does not necessarily mean that the Church is 'Israel', nor that Israel was the church in the OT. After all, Abraham was told that he would be the father of many nations, not just Israel. So, it is true that NT and OT saints share in many blessings of a spiritual nature, but our shared spiritual blessings do not prove that there are no differences or distinctions between Israel and the church. Nor do our shared spiritual blessings mean that Israel is finished, forever rejected by God, or replaced and fulfilled by the church.
4. Instead, this parable teaches that similarity and differences, continuity and discontinuity, mark the relationship of Israel and the Church.

Paul in fact strongly warns us Gentile believers in Romans 11:18, 'Do not boast against the branches, but if you do boast, remember that you do not support the root, but the root supports you'. In other words, we Christians are piggybacking on a Jewish religion, we Gentiles are the Jonny-come-latelies to the party, and Paul says we should show some respect towards the Jewish people. In v20, he says, do not be haughty but fear.

When our family were in Israel about ten years ago, we went along to the Holocaust Memorial Museum, Yad Vashem. Right at the very beginning of the exhibition, to explain the historical causes of the Holocaust, there was a quote from Augustine, the famous 5th century Christian, about the Jews: "Slay them not ... scatter them abroad." I was somewhat upset to read this quote, trying to pin the blame for the Holocaust on early Christians. Augustine is not even saying to kill the Jews, and secondly, he is quoting the words of Psalm 59, from the Hebrew Bible. But the reality is that Church authorities down through time have sometimes authorized and encouraged the persecution of Jews. Christianity has not paid much attention to what Paul warns against here. Paul's point in the illustration of the olive tree is to discourage Christian anti-Semitism, to discourage the bad attitudes that have occasionally been shown by Christians towards the Jews.

When will the Future Jewish National Conversion Occur?

Romans 11 also tells us when Jewish restoration will occur. The words 'all Israel will be saved' (verse 26) are put it in the future tense ('will be'), pointing to a yet-future Jewish spiritual restoration. We read that it will happen after 'the fullness of the Gentiles' (v25).

Osborne writes, 'after the Gentile mission is complete (v. 25), Israel will experience a national revival and come to Christ'[23].

The end of verse 26 tells us that this national spiritual restoration will happen at the return of Christ: 'and so all Israel will be saved, as it is written, 'The Deliverer will come out of Zion and He will turn away ungodliness from Jacob, for this is My covenant with them, when I take away their sins' (Romans 9:26b-27).

The salvation of Israel depends upon the coming of Israel's Saviour, the Lord Jesus Christ, and verse 26 strongly suggests that Israel's national conversion will occur at the return of Christ.

Israel are not going to be saved as part of the church, because Israel is not saved until Christ's coming. Verse 26 speaks of 'all Israel' being saved when the Deliverer comes out of Zion. And if Israel is saved at Christ's coming, then it is saved *after* the church age is complete.

We cannot leave Romans 11 without looking at v27. I once had a conversation with a friend who said this: 'In Jeremiah 31:31-34, God promised a new covenant that would be made 'with the house of Israel and with the house of Judah', but when we come to the NT, that promise is now fulfilled in the church (see Luke 22:20, and also Heb. 8:8-13). The prophecy in Jeremiah is not fulfilled literally (with Israel and Judah), but instead spiritually – with us today. Doesn't the NT re-interpret the OT in a non-literal way? Doesn't this mean that the church has replaced Israel?

It is true that the church today enjoys the blessings of the New Covenant. But look at Romans 11:27 – it says that one day Israel is going to come into the New Covenant, too, when God takes away their sins. That hasn't happened yet – Israel are still in their sins, their Deliverer hasn't come yet. Walter Kaiser writes that Romans 11:27 'is nothing less than a reference to the New Covenant of Jer. 31:31-34'[24]. 'Ernst Käsemann writes, 'Christianity is already living in the new covenant' while 'Israel will begin to do so only at the parousia'[25] (that is, at Christ's coming). While there is, at present, a fulfilment of Jeremiah's prophecy in the church's experience of forgiveness, there is also a future fulfilment to ethnic Israel that has not yet occurred.

Other passages in the New Testament also promise a national

---

[23] Grant R. Osborne, *Romans*, IVP, 2010, p306

[24] Walter C. Kaiser Jr., "Kingdom Promises as Spiritual and National: Discontinuity Between the Testaments," in *Continuity and Discontinuity: Perspectives on the Relationship Between the Old and New Testaments: S. Lewis Johnson Festschrift*. Ed John S. Feinberg, Crossway, 1987, p302

[25] Ernst Käsemann, *Commentary on Romans*, trans. and ed. G. W. Bromiley, Grand Rapids: Eerdmans, 1980, p314

conversion of Israel. In Matthew 23:38, Christ curses the nation ('your house is left to you desolate'), but in verse 39 He goes on to say, 'you shall see Me no more till you say, "Blessed is He who comes in the name of the LORD"'. Christ promises that Israel will one day acknowledge Him as their Messiah. He says this will happen when they see Him coming again. In fact, Christ says that He will not return again until Israel acknowledges Him: 'you shall see Me no more until you say, "Blessed is He who comes in the name of the LORD"'.

One preacher used rather impolite language in commenting on the word 'until' in this verse by saying that the problem with those who do not believe in a future national conversion for Israel is not theological, it is educational: they cannot read, for the word 'until' in Matthew 23:39 guarantees Israel's future conversion.

Matthew 23:29 is one of six important occurrences of the word 'until' in Scripture. Luke 21:24 tells us how long it will be until Israel is restored to its own land: 'they will fall by the edge of the sword, and be led away captive into all nations. And Jerusalem will be trampled by Gentiles until the times of the Gentiles are fulfilled'. Romans 11:25 tells us about Israel's future national conversion: 'For I do not desire, brethren, that you should be ignorant of this mystery, lest you should be wise in your own opinion, that blindness in part has happened to Israel until the fullness of the Gentiles has come in'. Matthew 23:39 tells us how long it will be until Israel believes in Christ. All three occurrences of 'until' assure us that these things will eventually happen. Other references to 'until' include Psalm 110:1, Micah 5:3 and Zephaniah 3:8.

Geoffrey Bull comments on the meaning of 'until' in Scripture:

> The word 'until' in Scripture bespeaks a God-originated determination. It was up *until* the daybreak that the Angel wrestled with the man called Jacob. The shepherd went on searching *until* he found his wayward sheep. The woman swept her house *until* she grasped her precious piece. God is in earnest. He yearns to find us one by one, and bring us home[26].

The same is true of God's determination to restore Israel too. Her future salvation is therefore certain.

---

[26] Geoffrey T. Bull, *Love-Song in Harvest: an Interpretation of the Book of Ruth*, London: Pickering and Inglis, 1972, pp82-3, emphasis in original.

14 ISRAEL AT ARMAGEDDON: ZECHARIAH 12-14

A few years ago, I was due to preach at a meeting on Zechariah chapters 12-14. A lady was present that day named Patricia from Papua New Guinea and after the meeting Patricia spoke to one of the ladies who had attended. Patricia said, 'I love Zechariah. I read chapter 1, and the Lord showed something to me. I read chapter 2, and the Lord showed something to me. I read chapter 3, and the Lord showed something to me'. On Patricia went, through chapters 4 to 11. Day after day, it was the same result. But then she said, 'I read chapter 12 and I got nothing. Why Lord? I read chapter 13 and I got nothing. I read chapter 14 and I had the same result: nothing. What is the problem?'

Then Patricia said, "I came along to the meeting today, and I saw a book on the book table about Zechariah. Wonderful! Then I heard that the speaker was to speak about Zechariah chapters 12-14. I wanted to hear what he has to say. Now I know why I did not get anything from Zechariah chapters 12-14. They were not written about me!"

I believe that Patricia was correct. Zechariah chapters 12-14 were not written about Christians – they were written about the nation of Israel and its future conversion to Christ. This has been the view of Christians from the beginning of the church. Justin Martyr, from the 2nd Century, wrote:

> And what the people of the Jews shall say and do, when they see Him coming in glory, has thus been predicted by Zechariah the prophet: 'I will command the four winds to gather the scattered children; I will command the north wind to bring them, and the south wind, that it keep not back. And then in Jerusalem there shall be great lamentation, not the lamentation of mouths or of lips, but the lamentation of the heart; and they shall not rend their garments, but their hearts. Tribe by tribe they shall mourn, and then they shall look on Him whom they have pierced; and they shall say, Why, O Lord, hast Thou made us to err from Thy way? The glory which our fathers blessed, has for us been turned into shame[1].

---

[1] Justin Martyr, First Apology 52, *Ante-Nicene Fathers*, 1:180

Even Augustine the amillennialist, wrote:

> It is a familiar theme in the conversation and heart of the faithful, that in the last days before the judgment the Jews shall believe in the true Christ, that is, our Christ, by means of this great and admirable prophet Elias who shall expound the law to them[2].

In the next chapter of the same book, Augustine quoted Zechariah 12:

> In like manner the Lord, speaking by the same prophet, says, 'And it shall come to pass in that day, that I will seek to destroy all the nations that come against Jerusalem. And I will pour upon the house of David, and upon the inhabitants of Jerusalem, the spirit of grace and mercy, and they shall look upon me because they have insulted me, and they shall mourn for Him as for one very dear, and shall be in bitterness as for an only-begotten. To whom but to God does it belong to destroy all the nations that are hostile to the holy city Jerusalem, which 'come against it', that is, are opposed to it, or, as some translate, 'come upon it', as if putting it down under them, or to pour out upon the house of David and the inhabitants of Jerusalem the spirit of grace and mercy? This belongs doubtless to God, and it is to God the prophet ascribes the words, and yet Christ shows that He is the God who does these so great and divine things, when He goes on to say, 'And they shall look upon me because they have insulted me, and they shall mourn for Him as if for one very dear, or beloved, and shall be in bitterness for Him as for an only-begotten. *For in that day the Jews – those of them, at least, who shall receive the spirit of grace and mercy – when they see Him coming in His majesty, and recognize that it is he whom they, in the person of their parents, insulted when He came before them in His humiliation, shall repent of insulting Him in His passion*[3].

The Bible commentator Merrill Unger describes this last section of Zechariah's prophecy as 'one of the most magnificent eschatological [i.e. end-time] vistas to be found in the Word of God as well as *one of the most disbelieved portions of Holy Writ*'[4]. Notice what Unger says: the problem with Zechariah 12-14 is not that it is particularly hard to understand; the

---

[2] Augustine, *City of God*, Book XX, chapter 29
[3] Ibid., Book XX, chapter 30
[4] Merrill F. Unger, *Zechariah: Prophet of Messiah's Glory*, Zondervan, 1963, p208, emphasis in original.

problem is that some Christians refuse to believe what it says.

Zechariah chapters 12-14 have been understood from the very beginning of the church to refer to the future conversion of the nation of Israel. As we shall see, attempts to try to apply these chapters to present day Christian life result in confusion, so that some of the greatest commentators attempting to apply them to the Church today have given up in despair. Patricia was right: these chapters were not written about us.

If, as we saw in the previous chapter, Romans 11 teaches a future national conversion of Israel, it does so very briefly. Romans 11 does not shed great light upon the subject of how Israel's national conversion happens, nor does Paul tell us where he got his information about Israel's national conversion from. Thankfully, God has not left us in the dark about how Israel are going to be saved. The prophecy of Zechariah describes how it will occur in chapters 12 – 14. These three chapters answer the important questions of when Israel's national conversion will take place, and how will it take place.

Zechariah 12:1-9 – Jerusalem Besieged and Delivered

In chapter 12:1-9, Zechariah says that 'all the surrounding peoples . . . lay siege against Judah and Jerusalem' (v2), but that 'the LORD will save the tents of Judah (v7) . . . 'defend the inhabitants of Jerusalem' (v8) and . . . 'seek to destroy all the nations that come against Jerusalem' (v9).

This passage describes a military conflict between Israel and the surrounding nations: it mentions a siege, horses and riders; it tells of God's desire to defend the inhabitants of Jerusalem and destroy all the nations that come against it. As we saw in a previous chapter, Zechariah is here referring to the battle of Armageddon at the end of time.

Some commentators argue that this passage is not referring to Israel, but to the church. Calvin interprets this passage to mean that 'though the whole world conspired against the Church, there would yet be sufficient power in God to repel and check all their assaults . . . when the ungodly assail the Church of God, all things seem to threaten its ruin; but God declares that they shall be like chaff or wood'[5].

H. C. Leupold writes, 'The claims made for Jerusalem's future find their ultimate fulfilment in the true Zion of God – His church. . . . The whole passage speaks of God's sovereign care and protection of the church of the Old and New Testaments through the ages'[6].

Richard Phillips applies this passage to the church today. Verse 6 is

---

[5] John Calvin, *Commentary*, Zech. 12:4, 6
[6] Leupold, *Exposition of Zechariah*, Baker, 1981, p234

typical of his approach: 'In that day I will make the governors of Judah like a firepan in the woodpile, and like a fiery torch in the sheaves; they shall devour all the surrounding peoples'. Phillips writes, 'This is what the church needs, blazing pastors who stand firm against the world in reliance on God, spreading his Word like fire'[7]. This is indeed what the church needs today – fiery preaching of the Word of God. But is this really what Zechariah was prophesying?

Tim Chester in *Zechariah: God's Big Plan for Struggling Christians* writes, 'In [Zechariah] chapter 12, we see the world opposing God's people. But God helps us to stand firm and ultimately He will give us victory ... Zechariah 12 is being fulfilled today in the work of the church, as Christians proclaim the gospel of Jesus Christ to a hostile world, and in the church's experience of persecution'[8].

Chester advises readers to substitute the word 'church' every time we come across Israel, Judah, or Jerusalem. He says: 'Read the following quotes from Zechariah 12, where 'church' replaces 'Judah' or 'Jerusalem' (p40). Thus, according to Chester, we should change the words in verse 2 to read, 'I am going to make the church a cup that sends all the surrounding nations reeling', and verse 3 as, 'I will make the church an immovable rock for all the nations; all who try to move it will injure themselves', and verse 8 as 'On that day the Lord will shield those of the church, so that the feeblest among them will be like David'.

But have a look at verse 7: 'The LORD will save the tents of Judah first, so that the glory of the house of David and the glory of the inhabitants of Jerusalem shall not become greater than that of Judah'. Let us try to read verse 7 as Chester has suggested, replacing all references to Israel, Judah, Jerusalem and the house of David with the word 'church'. According to Chester, this means: "The LORD will save the church first, so that the glory of the church and the glory of the church shall not become greater than that of the church'. No wonder Chester makes no comment about this verse in his study guide – his interpretation of this verse renders it ridiculous.

Such an interpretation (spiritualizing selected verses and ignoring others which do not make sense when read the same way) might give us some comforting present-day Christian life-applications. But it is not a safe or sane way to interpret Scripture. Why not just stick with what the

---

[7] Richard Phillips, *Zechariah*, Reformed Expository Commentary, Philippsburg, NJ: P & R Publishing, 2007, p263
[8] Tim Chester, *Zechariah: God's Big Plan for Struggling Christians*, The Good Book Company, 2005, pp40-41, 62

Bible actually says? Why not let the Bible itself show us how to apply these verses – to Israel, Judah and Jerusalem? Here is the problem with the spiritualizing approach to Scripture: words never take their normal meaning, and passages are never allowed to make straightforward sense. Instead, they must be de-coded, allegorized and twisted to mean other things.

Another problem with spiritualizing Zechariah to refer to the church is that the prophecy tells us that God is going to destroy those nations that fight against Jerusalem: 'It shall be in that day that I will seek to destroy all the nations that come against Jerusalem [or, as some would have it, the Church]' (v9). If Zechariah is prophesying the destruction of all the church's persecutors, we have not yet seen it happen – for the church is still being persecuted.

Richard Phillips points to the Spanish Armada (1588) as an example of God's destruction of those persecuting the church[9], but the Armada was an exceptional event. No doubt it is true that God sometimes rescues His persecuted people today, but do the prophecies of God's Word only come true in rare and exceptional circumstances? There have been many thousands of Christians martyred down through history, and many still being persecuted today. God is not destroying the church's persecutors. If we believe that God's Word is true and faithful, then the fulfilment of this prophecy must be pointing to a yet-future day, when God will destroy all the nations persecuting His people. The commentators who apply this passage to the present day experience of the church are wrong on two counts: it does not refer to the church, and it does not refer to the present.

It seems more appropriate to take Zechariah 12 to refer to a future deliverance of Jerusalem and Judah. This passage does not, in its primary meaning, teach us about present day troubles of the church; it is about a future deliverance of Israel. Further confirmation of this is seen in the next section.

Zechariah 12:10-13:6 – the Conversion of Israel

Zechariah shows us that Israel's future national conversion occurs when they look upon Christ, 'whom they have pierced' (12:10).

Following on from God's destruction of the nations that fight against Israel, we read about Israel's national conversion in 12:10 through to 13:6. Zechariah 12:10 says:

---

[9] Phillips, *Zechariah*, p261

And I will pour on the house of David and on the inhabitants of Jerusalem the Spirit of grace and supplication; then they will look on Me whom they pierced. Yes, they will mourn for Him as one mourns for his only son, and grieve for Him as one grieves for a firstborn.

In verses 11-14, we read about all the families of Israel mourning, 'every family by itself' (Zech. 12:14). In Zechariah 13:1, we read: 'In that day a fountain shall be opened for the house of David and for the inhabitants of Jerusalem, for sin and for uncleanness'. In 13:2-6, we read about the idols and false-prophets being cut off from the land.

Some commentators who spiritualize the first part of Zechariah 12 to refer to the church admit that this passage is speaking about the national conversion of Israel, as described in Romans 11. Others, however, argue that the conversion spoken about here applies to God's people in the church generally (not to Israel) and occurs in the present (not the future).

Some commentators do not even take the piercing literally. Calvin takes the piercing metaphorically. He says: '"they will look upon Me whom they have pierced" does not refer to the piercing of Christ upon the cross, but to people provoking and offending God generally by their sins'. But this is clearly wrong, because John's gospel (19:37) says that this prophecy was fulfilled literally, not metaphorically, in Christ's crucifixion. Calvin admits this but argues that Christ's piercing was but a visible symbol of the many ways and times people have provoked God. Therefore, Calvin takes this prophecy to be fulfilled whenever people today turn to God and repent of all the times they have hurt Him.

Revelation 1:7 also shows us that the prophecy applies literally to Christ, not metaphorically to God: 'Behold, He is coming with clouds, and every eye will see Him, even they who pierced Him. And all the tribes of the earth (or, land) will mourn because of Him. Even so, Amen'. This verse shows us that the prophecy will be fulfilled in the future, at Christ's return.

Zechariah's prophecy has not yet been fulfilled. While Christ's piercing has been fulfilled at the cross, 'Every eye will see Him' refers to a yet-future event: at Christ's return. This is when Israel will be converted. The final passage in Zechariah tells us about Christ's return.

Zechariah 14 – the Return of Christ

Zechariah 14:1-4 tells us that God is going to gather all nations to battle against Jerusalem (v2), but 'the LORD will go forth and fight against those nations, as He fights in the day of battle. And in that day His feet will stand on the Mount of Olives' (v3-4). Verse 5 says, 'the LORD my God will come and all the saints with You' (v5). In that day, there will be no light (vs 6-7), living waters will flow out of Jerusalem (v8), and 'the LORD will be King over all the earth' (v9).

This seems to promise the return of Christ to reign on earth. But some commentators are not so sure. In fact, this is where the spiritualizers abandon their foolish interpretation in exasperation. Martin Luther said: 'Here, in this chapter, I give up, for I am not sure what the prophet is talking about'[10].

How is it possible for Luther to be left puzzled and unsure of the Bible's meaning when it says 'the LORD my God will come'? Has Luther never read the New Testament about the Lord's return? The spiritualizing principle of interpretation turns the simplest expressions into puzzles.

Calvin was not prepared to give up so quickly. He did not take the passage to refer to a literal return of Christ. Rather, he spiritualized it to teach God's deliverance of the Church from its troubles:

> God's power would be then conspicuous in putting enemies to flight. He indeed illustrates here his discourse by figurative expressions . . . The Prophet then, in order to aid our weakness, adds a vivid representation, as though God stood before their eyes. . . . The import of the whole is, —that God's power would be so remarkable in the deliverance of his Church, as though God manifested himself in a visible form and reviewed the battle from the top of the mountain, and gave orders how everything was to be done[11].

Despite the fact that the NT teaches that Christ is literally going to return, Calvin refuses to see Christ in this passage. He says it is about God metaphorically appearing and manifesting Himself in the deliverance of the church from its persecutors.

Some amillennial commentators accept that this passage is referring to Christ's return, but refuse to accept that it has any Jewish application. They take the return of Christ literally, but the parts about Christ coming to fight at Jerusalem spiritually.

Thus Thomas Moore, after surveying attempts to explain this passage in Maccabean times and in the destruction of Jerusalem in A.D. 70, writes, 'It is evident that no events have yet occurred in history to which these predictions are applicable without much forcing', but he then argues that

---

[10] Luther's Works, St Louis: Concordia, 1973, 20:337
[11] John Calvin, *Commentary*, Zechariah 14:4, emphasis added

the passage 'predicts glory to God and triumph to his Church, taking Jerusalem here as the symbol of the Theocracy, or the Church of the future'[12].

John Dickson and Greg Clarke in a chapter of their book called, "The Rapture, Israel, and other Christian Myths", write that some Christians believe that:

> Jesus the Judge will return to Jerusalem itself because Zechariah 14:4 prophesies, 'On that day his feet will stand on the Mount of Olives, east of Jerusalem'. An apocalyptic scene is . . . [simply] an imaginative way of saying 'he'll come home[13].

Dickson and Clarke accept that the passage is teaching about Christ's return, but cannot bring themselves to allow that His feet will stand on the Mount of Olives, because that would mean that Christ returns to the literal, earthly Jerusalem. It would also mean that Israel has a future in God's plans. These plainly taught truths are so unpalatable to amillennialist commentators that they twist the Scriptures to mean something else. The idea that Israel has a future in God's plans is a 'myth' that they must debunk.

Some time ago I had a conversation with a theological lecturer who was very antagonistic to what he termed 'Christian Zionism'. He argued that a certain 'framework' for understanding Scripture shows us that ethnic Israel has no future in God's plans. I suggested that if we impose our theological frameworks on the Bible, we not only stop the Bible speaking for itself, but we even end up reducing the Old Testament to fairytales. He asked what I meant, so I went through Zechariah 12-14, showing that Israel is going to be converted at the return of Christ. But at the suggestion that Christ is going to be visibly seen by people all over the world, he started to scoff: this idea is a scientific impossibility! I didn't say it directly to his face, but he had just proven my point: he had just treated what the Bible says about the visible return of Christ as a fairytale.

Summary

Zechariah presents us with one final vision in three chapters. It is a vision of 'the day of the LORD' (Zechariah 14:1), God's great end-time

---

[12] Thomas Moore, *Zechariah*, Geneva Series Commentary, Edinburgh: Banner of Truth Trust, 1958, p218-9

[13] John Dickson and Greg Clarke, *666 and All That, The Truth about the Future*, Aquila, 2007, p45

judgment of the world. The expression 'in that day' is woven through these three chapters 17 times, linking them together. Chapters 12 and 14 both speak of a great battle of 'all the nations' against Jerusalem, from which the Lord rescues the Jewish nation. This is the same battle, and therefore, all three chapters are referring to the Jewish people: we cannot take the first chapter and apply it to the persecuted church of our day, then take the second chapter and refer it to Jewish national conversion, or ignore the fact that Christ returns to Jerusalem in the third chapter. Nor can we take some of the passages to refer to the present day, for the expression 'in that day' refers to a period of trouble and salvation for the Jewish people, which is followed by the Lord returning and reigning as King over all the earth. None of this has happened yet; it is all still in the future.

We learn five lessons from this prophecy. Firstly, that Israel will be converted at the literal, physical, visible return of Christ. Secondly, that Israel will be converted through and after a period of great tribulation when all the nations of earth besiege and attack Jerusalem and Judah. Thirdly, that Israel must obviously be back in its own land, in unbelief, for all this to happen. Fourthly, Israel is not converted as part of the church, for it is converted after the visible return of Christ, which means it does not take part in the rapture and resurrection of the church (1 Thess. 4:13-18). Finally, after Christ's return, believing Israel lives on in mortal bodies on the earth enjoying the reign of the Lord over all the earth, in other words, during the millennium. As a result, we conclude that amillennialism, postmillennialism, and historic premillennialism are all false (for the reasons given in the introduction, The Case of Four Clues):

- Amillennialism is false because the Lord reigns over all the earth after His return at the battle of Armageddon,
- Postmillennialism is false because Israel's conversion does not happen 1000 years before Christ's return, but at His return, and
- Historic Premillennialism is false because Israel is not converted as part of the church, during the church age, but believing Israel lives on as unglorified, mortal saints into the millennium. Israel and the Church are distinct and different entities.

Despite the tortured exposition of Zechariah by some commentators, and their best attempts to mangle its meaning, we see here a vision of hope which clearly teaches a future for the nation of Israel, their time of great tribulation, their national conversion, and their millennial blessing.

15 ISRAEL'S NATIONAL RESTORATION: JEREMIAH 30-33

Having seen in previous chapters that Israel is going to experience a national conversion (Romans 11), and that this will occur at the time of the return of Christ at the battle of Armageddon (Zechariah 12-14), we turn in this chapter to consider the question of whether Israel's future restoration is merely spiritual, or will it also be national, territorial, and political?

To see why this question is important, consider the reaction of some Christians to the re-establishment of the nation of Israel in their ancient homeland. While many Christians believe the return of the Jews to the land of Israel in the 20th century is the fulfilment of biblical prophecy, many modern theologians argue that this event has no significance for Christians and has no connection with Bible prophecy. Colin Chapman writes,

> When the New Testament writers like John had seen the significance of the land and the nation in the context of the kingdom of God which had come into being in Jesus of Nazareth, they ceased to look forward to a literal fulfilment of Old Testament prophecies of a return to the land and a restoration of a Jewish state. The one and only fulfilment of all promises and prophecies was already there before their eyes in the person of Jesus. The way they interpreted the Old Testament should be the norm for the Christian interpretation of the Old Testament today[1].

When we turn to the Word of God, however, we find a different story. As we have just seen, Zechariah 12-14 teaches that Israel will be in their own land when Christ returns. In a previous chapter, we saw that Daniel 9 also teaches us that Israel will be in the land during the last 'seven' years.

J. C. Ryle, the famous evangelical Bishop of Liverpool (1816 – 1900), once preached a sermon on Jeremiah 31:10, which reads (in its printed

---

[1] Colin Chapman, *Whose Promised Land? The Continuing Conflict over Israel and Palestine*, Oxford: Lion, 2015, p262

form), 'Hear the word of the Lord, O nations, and declare it in the isles afar off, and say, He who scattered Israel will gather him, and keep him as a shepherd does his flock'. Ryle said this:

> Reader, however great the difficulties surrounding many parts of unfulfilled prophecy, two points appear to my own mind to stand out as plainly as if written by a sunbeam. One of these points is the second personal advent of our Lord Jesus Christ before the Millennium. The other of these points is the future literal gathering of the Jewish nation and their restoration to their own land. I tell no man that these two truths are essential to salvation and that he cannot be saved, unless he sees them with my eyes. But I tell any man that these truths appear to me distinctly set down in holy Scripture, and that the denial of them is as astonishing and incomprehensible to my own mind, as the denial of the divinity of Christ.
>
> Now what says our text about the future prospects of the Jews? It says, "He who scattered Israel – will gather him." That gathering is an event which plainly is yet to come.

Ryle, who lived in the 19th century, did not see the re-establishment of the state of Israel in 1948, or even the Balfour Declaration of 1917 promising British support for a Jewish homeland in Palestine. His view was based solely on Scripture. In his sermon he stated:

> Reader, I believe that the interpretation I have just given, is in entire harmony with many other plain prophecies of Scripture. Time would fail me, if I were to quote a tenth part of the texts which teach the same truth. Out of the sixteen prophets of the Old Testament, there are at least ten in which the gathering and restoration of the Jews in the latter days are expressly mentioned.

Ryle proceeds in his sermon to quote one passage from each of these ten prophets: Isaiah 11:11-12, Ezekiel 37:21, Hosea 1:11, 3:4-5, Joel 3:20, Amos 9:14-15, Obadiah 1:17, Micah 4:6-7, Zephaniah 3:14-20, Zechariah 10:6-10, and Jeremiah 30:3, 11.

Walter Kaiser Jr., President-Emeritus at Gordon-Conwell Theological Seminary, writes, 'It is impossible to read, teach, and preach on the prophets of the Old Testament without bumping into the promise of a return of Israel to her land again and again, something like one verse out of every eight verses in the prophets!!!'[2]

As Ryle says, time does not permit us to look at all the passages that teach of Israel's prophesied return to their land from exile. Furthermore, the almost total ignorance of the Old Testament prophets by most modern Christians means that the passages listed above are nothing more than meaningless Bible references, mere names and numbers. In this chapter, however, we will focus on one of the most important prophetical passages in the Bible: Jeremiah 30-33. As we shall see, the Bible plainly declares that the nation of Israel will be in their own homeland when Christ returns.

Jeremiah 30-33: The Restoration of Israel

Jeremiah has been called the weeping prophet; his book is a message of doom in view of Jerusalem's coming destruction by Nebuchadnezzar. However, in chapters 30-33, Jeremiah is given a glimpse of future hope. These chapters have been called the Book of Consolation. Here we find the comfort of Israel. In these chapters, he writes of Israel's restoration.

Is Jeremiah's promised Restoration merely the Return from Babylon?

Jeremiah 30:1-3 read as follows:

> The word that came to Jeremiah from the LORD, saying, "Thus speaks the LORD God of Israel, saying: 'Write in a book for yourself all the words that I have spoken to you. For behold, the days are coming,' says the LORD, 'that I will bring back from captivity My people Israel and Judah,' says the LORD. 'And I will cause them to return to the land that I gave to their fathers, and they shall possess it.'" (Jer. 30:1-3).

The first possible way to understand Jeremiah's promises of Israel's restoration is that they refer to Israel returning from Babylonian captivity after seventy years. It is true that Jeremiah writes of such a return, particularly in chapters 25 and 29. However in chapters 30-33, Jeremiah looks much further into the future. This can be seen from the following seven facts:

1. **It occurs at the Time of the Great Tribulation** (vs 4-7): the return from captivity and exile that Jeremiah prophecies in verses 1-3 is

---

[2] Walter c. Kaiser, Jr., "What's So Important about Pre-millennialism?", http://www.walterckaiserjr.com/Israel%20and%20pre-millennialism.html

described further in verses 4-7: *'Now these are the words that the LORD spoke concerning Israel and Judah. For thus says the LORD: 'We have heard a voice of trembling, Of fear, and not of peace. Ask now, and see, Whether a man is ever in labor with child? So why do I see every man with his hands on his loins like a woman in labor, And all faces turned pale?* **Alas! For that day is great, so that none is like it; And it is the time of Jacob's trouble'** (Jer. 30:5-7). The return of Israel happens in a day of unparalleled suffering. This is the exact opposite of what happened when Judah returned from Babylon. Seeing that all the Bible references to a day that is unlike any other in the severity of its suffering can only refer to the same one event (how can multiple different events all be greater than any other?), therefore Jeremiah must be speaking of the great tribulation period, which Jesus also describes as 'great tribulation, such as has not been since the beginning of the world, nor ever shall be' (Matt. 24:21). This is further confirmed by what follows:

2. **Israel will be Saved out of it** (vs 7-8). There have been many times of great trouble the Jews have gone through (including Jerusalem's siege and destruction by Nebuchadnezzar, and the siege and destruction of Jerusalem by the Romans in AD 70), but only one period fulfils the two qualifications given here: (1) it ends in divine deliverance, and (2) it results in Israel's return from captivity. This is the future great tribulation. *'But **he shall be saved out of it**. For it shall come to pass in that day,' Says the LORD of hosts, That I will break his yoke from your neck, and will burst your bonds; foreigners shall no more enslave them'* (Jer. 30:7-8). The fact that Israel is saved out of this terrible time of suffering means that it cannot refer to the Jewish War of AD 70 (for Israel were not delivered out of it), nor can it refer to the destruction of Jerusalem by Nebuchadnezzar, for they were not delivered by God from this catastrophe. Furthermore, this time of great tribulation must still be in the future because of ...

3. **The Reign of their King, the Messiah** (vs 9): *'But they shall serve the LORD their God, and **David their king**, whom I will raise up for them'* (Jer. 30:9). Jeremiah cannot be referring to the return from captivity after the exile in Babylon because Israel's King did not reign again after the return from the Babylonian captivity. Therefore this is referring to a restoration far beyond the Babylonian captivity. This ushers in ...

4. **The Restoration of Israel** (vs 10-11). *'Therefore do not fear, O My servant Jacob,' says the LORD, 'Nor be dismayed, O Israel; For behold, I will save you from afar, And your seed from the land of their captivity.*

Jacob shall return*, have rest and be quiet, And no one shall make him afraid. For I am with you,' says the LORD, 'to save you; Though I make a full end of all nations where I have scattered you, Yet I will not make a complete end of you. But I will correct you in justice, And will not let you go altogether unpunished.'* (Jer. 30:10-11). Here we have the promise of the return of the scattered people of the nation of Israel to their own homeland at the time of their deliverance from the great tribulation and the reign of the Messiah. In fact, these two verses are so important to Jeremiah that he repeats them again at the very end of his book, in Jeremiah 46:27-28 (there is only one other passage that is so significant that he repeats the same words again, Jeremiah 10:12-16, repeated in Jeremiah 51:15-19, a beautiful description of God). The promise of Israel's restoration is so important in Jeremiah's eyes that, along with description of the character of God in Jeremiah 10, it is also repeated at the end of the book.

5. **Israel's Sins will be Punished but God will also Restore them** (vs12-17). God assures Israel that they are going into captivity for their sins, but yet He says: *'I will restore health to you and heal you of your wounds,' says the LORD, 'Because they called you an outcast saying: "This is Zion; No one seeks her."'* (Jer. 30:17).

6. **Israel will Return to their Land and to their God** (vs 18-22). These verses are so beautiful and full of hope that we must quote them in full: *"Thus says the LORD: 'Behold, I will bring back the captivity of Jacob's tents, And have mercy on his dwelling places; The city shall be built upon its own mound, And the palace shall remain according to its own plan. Then out of them shall proceed thanksgiving and the voice of those who make merry; I will multiply them, and they shall not diminish; I will also glorify them, and they shall not be small. Their children also shall be as before, and their congregation shall be established before Me; and I will punish all who oppress them. Their nobles shall be from among them, and their governor shall come from their midst; then I will cause him to draw near, and he shall approach Me; for who is this who pledged his heart to approach Me?' says the LORD.* ***You shall be My people, And I will be your God.****"* (Jer. 30:18-22). Not only is the nation of Israel restored to their land, but they are restored to their God. God says, 'You shall be my people, and I will be your God'.

7. **This will occur in the End-time** (vs 23-24): *'Behold, the whirlwind of the LORD goes forth with fury, a continuing whirlwind; it will fall violently on the head of the wicked. The fierce anger of the LORD will not return until He has done it, and until He has performed the intents of His*

heart. *In the latter days you will consider it'* (Jer. 30:23-24). This concluding passage finishes with an important line: God says that we will consider these things in the 'latter days', or literally in Hebrew, 'the end of days'. This whole passage is therefore looking beyond the Babylonian captivity to the last days.

Jeremiah is therefore prophesying the final and complete restoration of Israel. Notice, too, that this promise relates to the nation of ethnic Israel and the return to their literal land of Israel. We cannot take this promise as a message to the Church, for the Church never had any land that 'God gave to our fathers' (Jer. 30:3), nor was the Church ever divided into two groups, Israel and Judah (Jer. 30:3), nor did the Church ever go into captivity (Jer. 30:2). This entire prophecy refers to ethnic Israel.

Notice: Jeremiah 30 teaches that Israel is converted to God after the great tribulation, and then Christ reigns over Israel in their own land. It is premillennial and teaches a post-tribulation conversion of Israel.

Jeremiah 31: the Prophecy of the New Covenant

In the next chapter, Jeremiah 31, we have a subject familiar to Christians, the establishment of the New Testament (or Covenant) in verses 31-40. However, before we come to these important verses, the earlier verses of this chapter also clearly teach the restoration of national Israel.

We will not look in great detail at the first 30 verses of this chapter. It is similar to the previous chapter in content, as it concerns Israel's **reunification** (vs1-2), **rebuilding** (vs3-6), **return** from captivity (vs7-17), **repentance** (vs18-22), and **restoration** (vs23-30). How do we know that this promise of return from captivity refers to the end-time rather than simply the return from Babylon? For five reasons:

1. Because of the context of the previous chapter which, as we have showed, must refer to something greater than the Babylonian captivity. We should assume that the return from captivity (in both of these adjoining chapters) refers to the same event.
2. Because in the very first verse of this chapter, we read, 'at the same time'. That is, at the same time as the 'great tribulation', and the reign of the Messiah mentioned in the previous chapter. This chapter's events refer to the same time as we read about in the last verse of the previous chapter: 'the end of days'. This chapter is thus also describing a great end-time return from captivity.
3. Certain features of this chapter cannot be said to have been fulfilled in

the return from the Babylonian captivity. For example, the reunification of 'all Israel' (v1), 'the house of Israel and the house of Judah' (v27), including even Ephraim (vs 5, 6, 9, 18-20, that is, the northern tribes which did not return from Babylonian captivity), cannot be said to have been accomplished in the return from Babylon.

4. The return from captivity in this chapter is specifically stated to be from far more than Babylon: 'Behold, I will bring them from the north country, and gather them from the ends of the earth' (vs 8). Indeed, there is no mention of Babylon or a return from Babylon at all in the chapter.

5. The perfect conditions of the returned people in verses 7-14 suggests God's ultimate blessing and redemption of Israel. By contrast, the conditions of Israel after the return from Babylon were very difficult. Thus, consider the beautiful picture found in verses 11-14, *'For the LORD has redeemed Jacob, and ransomed him from the hand of one stronger than he. Therefore they shall come and sing in the height of Zion, streaming to the goodness of the LORD-- for wheat and new wine and oil, for the young of the flock and the herd; their souls shall be like a well-watered garden, and they shall sorrow no more at all. "Then shall the virgin rejoice in the dance, and the young men and the old, together; for I will turn their mourning to joy, will comfort them, and make them rejoice rather than sorrow. I will satiate the soul of the priests with abundance, And My people shall be satisfied with My goodness, says the LORD."* (Jer. 31:7-14). Notice particularly the promise that 'they shall sorrow no more at all'. In addition to the perpetual nature of the promised joy, these words are reminiscent of Revelation 21:4 ('there shall be no more sorrow'), and the ultimate blessing of the end-times.

In the midst of these beautiful promises we have the verse quoted by J. C. Ryle: *Hear the word of the LORD, O nations, and declare it in the isles afar off, and say, 'He who scattered Israel will gather him, and keep him as a shepherd does his flock.'* (Jer. 31:10). As Ryle states, nothing could be clearer from the page of Scripture than the eventual restoration of the nation of Israel to their former homeland and glory under the Messiah.

The New Covenant (vs 31-40)
The highpoint of Jeremiah 31 is, of course, the promise of the New Covenant. This is a passage (and a concept) that Christians know from the various places it is quoted in the New Testament: Luke 22 (at the institution of the Lord's Supper), 2 Corinthians 3, and Hebrews 8.

> *Behold, the days are coming, says the LORD, when I will make a new covenant with the house of Israel and with the house of Judah-- not according to the covenant that I made with their fathers in the day that I took them by the hand to lead them out of the land of Egypt, My covenant which they broke, though I was a husband to them, says the LORD. But this is the covenant that I will make with the house of Israel after those days, says the LORD: I will put My law in their minds, and write it on their hearts; and I will be their God, and they shall be My people. No more shall every man teach his neighbor, and every man his brother, saying, 'Know the LORD,' for they all shall know Me, from the least of them to the greatest of them, says the LORD. For I will forgive their iniquity, and their sin I will remember no more. (Jer. 31:31-34).*

In this New Covenant, God promises three things:

1. **A New Relationship**: When God brought Israel out of Egypt, He was 'a husband' to them (v31), but they broke the covenant He made with them. In the New Covenant, God promises, 'I will be their God and they shall be My people', and further, 'they shall all know Me, from the least of them to the greatest of them'.
2. **God will Dwell Within**: God promises to 'put His law in their minds, and write it on their hearts'. Instead of being written on tablets of stone, like the Old Covenant, God will put the desire within His people to walk in His ways. Paul explains this in 2 Corinthians 3 as referring to the Holy Spirit dwelling within.
3. **Sins Forgiven**: 'For I will forgive their iniquity, and their sin I will remember no more'.

All these blessings are based on the death of Christ, as the New Testament teaches. This is why Christ said, on the night before His death, 'This cup is the new covenant in My blood, which is she for you' (Luke 22:20). It is only by Christ's death that our sins can be forgiven, our hearts made clean and fit places for the Holy Spirit to dwell in, and for us to be brought back into relationship with God as His people.

Is the New Covenant for the Church, or for Israel?

This raises the question (which we have already dealt with, but bears repetition), whether the New Covenant was made with the Church or with ethnic Israel. The answer the New Testament gives is, both. In Luke 22, 2 Corinthians 3 and Hebrews 8, we find that the blessings of the New

Covenant are applied to present day believers in Christ. However, significantly, Romans 11 also quotes these same words from Jeremiah and applies them to the nation of Israel in the day when 'all Israel will be saved' (Romans 11:26). Paul proceeds in the very next words to say, 'For this is My covenant with them when I take away their sins' (Romans 11:27, quoting from Jeremiah 31:33, 34). Thus, Jeremiah's New Covenant promise has a present-day (partial) fulfilment in the Church, and a future fulfilment – to Israel – that has not yet taken place.

Jeremiah 31:31-40 give us four reasons to believe that the promise originally made to ethnic Israel will also be fulfilled to ethnic Israel:

1. The covenant is made with 'the house of Israel and the house of Judah' (v31). This refers to ethnic Israel in its two-fold division in Jeremiah's day. How is the church divided into a northern and southern kingdom? God continues: it is not a 'covenant like the one that I made with *their fathers* in the day I took them by the hand to lead them out of the land of Egypt'. It is made with the same people whose fathers came out of Egypt and who received the Old Covenant – that is, with ethnic Israel.
2. God specifically assures ethnic Israel of their continued existence before Him in verses 35-36, linking Israel's existence with that of the created order: *'Thus says the LORD, who gives the sun for a light by day, the ordinances of the moon and the stars for a light by night, who disturbs the sea, and its waves roar (The LORD of hosts is His name): If those ordinances depart from before Me, says the LORD, then the seed of Israel shall also cease from being a nation before Me forever.'*
3. God explicitly promises not to reject Israel for all their sins in verse 37: *'Thus says the LORD: "If heaven above can be measured, and the foundations of the earth searched out beneath, I will also cast off all the seed of Israel for all that they have done, says the LORD'*. All their sins would have to include their greatest sin, that of rejection of God's Son. Therefore, Israel's rejection of Christ does not annul the promises made to Israel.
4. Finally, in verses 38-40, God promises the restoration of Jerusalem (naming various geographical places, like the Tower of Hananel, Gareb, Goath, the Brook Kidron, and the Horse Gate, which cannot apply to the church, but instead apply to the literal earthly Jerusalem), and this is undoubtedly an end-time restoration (not just the return from Babylon) because the promise concludes with these words: *'it shall not be rooted up nor overthrown for ever'* (v40). Jerusalem was

overthrown again after the Babylonian captivity, first in AD 70, and many times since.

Thus, the promise of the New Covenant is made to ethnic Israel, and entails their eventual restoration to God spiritually (by the forgiveness of sins), and this is linked indissolubly with their return to their own land geographically.

Jeremiah 32 and 33: Jeremiah's Purchase of the Land

In Jeremiah chapters 32 and 33, the Lord tells Jeremiah to buy a piece of ground. This is very surprising to Jeremiah because he is in prison, the Babylonians are besieging Jerusalem, and he knows the Babylonians will conquer the kingdom. But Jeremiah pays the price for the land, and signs and seals the purchase documents. Then the prophet turns to God in protest, asking why God wants him to buy the field.

In Jeremiah 32:36-41, God responds by saying that although the city will be captured by the Babylonians,

- God will regather Israel out of all the countries where He is going to drive them, and bring them back (v37),
- God will be their God, and they will be His people (v38),
- God will give them a heart to fear Him forever (v39),
- God will make an everlasting covenant with them, and will not turn away from doing them good, so that they will fear God and not depart from Him (v40), and
- God will do them good and plant them in their own land (v41).

Jeremiah's purchase of the title deeds for the field is therefore a prophetic picture of the fact that God is one day going to bring the nation of Israel back to their own land. It is quite clear, too, that this restoration (a) applies to national Israel – not the Church, and (b) is not the return from Babylon, but the eventual complete restoration of Israel. We see this from the twin facts that, firstly, the land is prominent here in this passage – the Church is nowhere promised the title deeds to 'this land' (v41), the geographical land of Israel – and secondly, the restoration is spiritual as well as physical, in that Israel will never more depart from God, nor will God ever turn away from doing them good – this was not true of the return from Babylon, for Israel turned away from God's Messiah, and God turned away from the nation and they suffered even worse punishment and exile in AD 70.

In Jeremiah 33, God's word comes again to Jeremiah in prison, reinforcing the message that Jerusalem will fall (vs4-5). Yet God comforts Jeremiah with the following beautiful promises:
- He will one day bring healing to the nation (v6)
- He will cause the captives of Judah and Israel to return and rebuild (v7)
- God will cleanse them from all their sins and pardon all iniquity (v8)
- God will do them good and bring prosperity (v9)
- God promises to bring joy and gladness, the happiness of weddings, and the praise of the Lord (vs10-13)
- God's promise is connected with the coming of the Branch of the LORD, the reign of our Lord Jesus Christ – and this does not refer to His first coming but His second, for we read that Judah and Jerusalem will be saved and dwell safely (vs14-16)
- David will never lack a man to sit on the throne of Israel, nor will the priests and Levites lack a man to offer burnt and grain offerings (vs17-18)

God finishes by assuring Jeremiah that His covenant with David is as unbreakable as His covenant with the day and night. Listen to the beautiful promise of Israel's restoration with which the prophecy finishes:

> Thus says the LORD: "If My covenant is not with day and night, and if I have not appointed the ordinances of heaven and earth, then I will cast away the descendants of Jacob and David My servant, so that I will not take any of his descendants to be rulers over the descendants of Abraham, Isaac, and Jacob. For I will cause their captives to return, and will have mercy on them" (Jer. 33:25-26).

Conclusion

Jeremiah teaches that Israel is to be restored to its land prior to the return of Christ, that it must go through the great tribulation in unbelief, at the end of which it will be converted to God, and after which Christ will reign over them in the land. Jeremiah therefore shows us that amillennialism is false (for Christ reigns over Israel in the land of their fathers after His return), that post-millennialism is false (Israel is converted at the return of Christ, not 1000 years before), and historic premillennialism is false (for Israel is not transformed and raptured at the return of Christ, but lives on in the land as mortal saints).

16 ISRAEL'S SPIRITUAL REBIRTH: EKEZIEL 36-37

To further prove that Israel's regathering to her own land is an explicit prophecy of Scripture, we must turn to Ezekiel.

The Valley of Dry Bones: National Restoration

In Ezekiel 37 the prophet is taken by the Spirit of God and set down in a valley that is full of dry bones, and told to prophesy to these bones, and lo and behold, the bones come together to form skeletons, and then flesh covers them to form bodies, and finally, he is told to prophesy again, and the dead bodies come alive, and form a great army.

Some Christians take this prophecy to mean that it is possible for spiritually dead people to come to life in Christ today. The Christian singer Lauren Daigle wrote a song in 2016 called, *Come Alive*, based on Ezekiel's prophecy about the valley of dry bones. She says she wrote it because a friend at church went away from the Lord and became a prodigal son. The song was written for this young man's mother, and Daigle believes that it is possible for us to "speak with authority" to those who are spiritually dead and they will come alive and return to God.

I once heard a testimony of a young woman. She had grown up in a broken home and her life was a mess. When she grew a bit older, she started seeking God, and went to church, where she heard a message on Ezekiel 37 and the Valley of Dry Bones – about how God can change peoples' lives. She responded to this message, turned to God, and turned her life around. She is now employed in a good profession, and helping to serve God in her church. It truly is wonderful that God can bring about new life today.

So, it is undoubtedly true that God's Word can do amazing things in peoples' lives and draw them back to Himself. But our question here is whether Ezekiel's prophecy primarily applies to us today or to Israel in the future? Let us look at the passage.

Verses 1-3 – A Seemingly Impossible Situation

In verses 1-3 we are presented with a seemingly impossible situation. Notice the way that in the first two verses we are told that the valley is full of bones (v1), that they were very many in number, and that they were very dry (v2). These bones were long dead – there did not appear to be any hope for them, and it seems impossible to believe that they can come to life. Even Ezekiel himself is reluctant to believe that they can come alive again in verse 3. When God asks, "Can these bones live?" Ezekiel just says, "O Lord God, You know". So here we have a seemingly impossible situation – a situation of death, in a very spiritually dry and desolate place.

Verses 4-6 – God's Promise
But verses 4-6 tell us about God's promise. In verse 4, Ezekiel is told to prophesy to the bones – this must have seemed a futile thing to do: bones can't hear. But Ezekiel prophesies in verse 5, and notice the expression he uses for God: Lord God, or in Hebrew, Adonai Yahweh. God is the sovereign master of everything; He is Adonai, the Lord. He can do whatever He pleases.

Then in verse 5, God says, "I will" (and the word I is emphatic here) – God promises that He himself will bring these bones to life by His power. In verse 6 He promises to put flesh on the bones, cover them with skin, put breath in them and they will live. God promises to do this and, of course, all God's promises are true. Finally, in v6, God attaches His own credibility to this promise: when God has done this, 'you will know that I am the Lord'. Here is a prophecy of something that God promises He will do.

Verses 7-10 – God's Power
In verses 7-10 we see God's power to fulfil His promise. As Ezekiel prophecies, the bones come together, flesh and skin covers them, breath enters them, and they stand up on their feet.

But notice carefully that the bones come to life in two stages. Firstly, in verses 7-8 the dead bones join together. There is a regathering of the bones. Then, the flesh and skin cover them, but they are still dead bodies lying in the dust. There is still no life. Then, in verses 9-10, Ezekiel is told to prophesy a second time, and breath enters the dead bodies, so that they live, and they stand up on their feet. God's power brings new life from death.

Verses 11-14 – the Explanation
In verses 11-14 God gives Ezekiel the explanation of this prophecy. In verse 11, God says that these dead bones represent Israel: 'these bones are the whole house of Israel' (v11). Israel has been complaining, as a nation,

that their hope has been destroyed. They have been taken captive to Babylon. Their nation is finished, so they think.

But in verse 12, God promises that He is going to bring the nation of Israel back to their homeland. Verse 12 says, 'I will open your graves ... and bring you into the land of Israel'. So there is going to be a regathering to the land of Israel.

Then in verse 14, God promises to put His Spirit in them, and they shall live. There is going to be spiritual new birth for the nation of Israel. Then, God repeats His earlier promise in verse 12 – He is going to place them in their own land again.

Please notice the two promises here, based on the two-stages of the miracle. Israel is promised that they will be regathered to their own land, the land of Israel, and then secondly, they are promised that they will experience spiritual new birth. God's Spirit will come into them.

But to prove that this prophecy primarily concerns the nation of Israel, we need to look at the context, the passages before and after this chapter in the book of Ezekiel. As we will see, this prophecy is not primarily about Christians today, but about the nation of Israel being restored to their homeland, and spiritually reborn. In other words, the primary lesson is that Israel has a future, nationally and spiritually.

Ezekiel 36: The Prophecy of New Birth

Ezekiel 36 is the great chapter in the Old Testament on spiritual new birth. This is the chapter that our Lord Jesus was referring to when He spoke to Nicodemus about being born again and said, 'Are you the teacher of Israel and do not know these things?' (John 3:10).

Ezekiel's prophecy has three stages: return from exile, spiritual rebirth, and living on in the millennium.

Firstly, **there is a return from exile**. Look at verse 17: 'Son of man, when the house of Israel dwelt in their own land, they defiled it by their own ways and deeds; to Me their way was like the uncleanness of a woman in her customary impurity'.

As a result, Israel was sent into exile – see verse 19: 'So I scattered them among the nations, and they were dispersed throughout the countries; I judged them according to their ways and their deeds'.

But God promises in verse 24 that He is going to bring them back from exile: 'For I will take you from among the nations, gather you out of all countries, and bring you into your own land'. So, God first of all promises a national regathering to the land of Israel.

Secondly, **there is a promise of spiritual new birth**. Look at Ezekiel

36:25: 'I will sprinkle clean water on you, and you shall be clean, I will cleanse you from all your filthiness, and from all your idols. I will give you a new heart and put a new spirit within you. I will take the heart of stone out of your flesh and give you a heart of flesh. I will put My Spirit within you and cause you to walk in My statutes, and you will keep my judgments and do them'.

Ezekiel is prophesying a national spiritual rebirth. This has not yet happened, for Israel is still in unbelief today. This promise of spiritual rebirth will only happen at the return of Christ, as we saw in Zechariah.

Thirdly, **there is a promise that Israel will live in the land**. Notice the next verse (28): 'Then you shall dwell in the land that I gave to your fathers, you shall be my people, and I will be your God.

Verse 33 also speaks of Israel continuing to live in the land: 'On the day that I cleanse you from all your iniquities, I will also enable you to dwell in the cities and the ruins shall be rebuilt. The desolate land shall be filled instead of lying desolate in the sight of all who pass by. So they will say, this land that was desolate has become like the garden of Eden'.

Notice that this promise is not talking about Israel living in the Eternal State in the new heavens and earth. It speaks about the ruins being rebuilt, and the desolate land being filled. It would seem unlikely that there would be any ruins in the eternal state, that need to be rebuilt.

The Prophecy of the Two Sticks: National Regathering

Finally, we turn to the passage that follows immediately after the vision of the valley of dry bones: Ezekiel 37:15-28. Here we have the prophecy about the two sticks. Ezekiel is told to take two sticks (one called Judah and the other called Joseph, or Ephraim – the two sticks thus refer to the southern and northern Kingdoms of Israel), and join the two sticks together in his hand to form one stick.

What does this mean? Look at Ezekiel 37 verse 21: 'Thus says the Lord God, "Surely I will take the children of Israel from among the nations, wherever they have gone, and will gather them from every side and bring them into their own land"'.

This is the message of regathering. In verse 22 God says, 'I will make them one nation in the land, on the mountains of Israel, and one king will be over them' (the Messiah) 'and they shall no longer be two nations, nor shall they ever be divided into two kingdoms again'. Verse 24 tells how they will have David as their king again (the Messiah). This is looking far beyond the return from the Babylonian exile to the eventual coming of the Messiah.

It is very hard to take this prophecy and refer it to the church. Is the church divided into two kingdoms? Some spiritualizing commentators argue that this prophecy simply means that there will one day be true unity among all God's people in the church.

However, if this is the case, what does it mean when verse 25 says, 'Then they shall dwell in *the land* that I have *given to Jacob my servant*, where *your fathers dwelt*; and they shall dwell there, they, their children, and their children's children, forever, and My servant David shall be their prince forever'.

Notice the emphasis on the land in these verses: it is called the land where their fathers dwelt, the land that God gave to Jacob His servant. Who are the 'fathers' of the church, and in what land did they dwell? What land did God give to His servant Jacob? The prophecy is plainly speaking about the land of Israel, and foretells a future restoration of the people of Israel, ethnically, nationally, territorially and politically.

Does this Apply to Christians Today, or to Israel in the Future?

Is it possible to apply Ezekiel's prophecies about the new birth, the valley of dry bones and the two sticks to Christians today? Perhaps we Christians are 'spiritual' Israel and have replaced national Israel in God's affections through the spiritual new birth we have experienced? But while we know from John's Gospel that we need to be born again (and so the prophecy about new birth may be applied to Christians today), yet it would seem difficult for us to dwell in the land God gave to Jacob, the land where Ezekiel's fathers dwelt (v25). Unless we physically live in the land of Israel, it is very difficult to apply those words to Christians today.

The passage most naturally and directly applies to the actual nation of Israel. Israel is spoken of here – not New Testament Gentile Christians. God is promising the nation of Israel that they are going to be regathered to their land, and then are going to experience spiritual rebirth as they are indwelt by God's Spirit, and they are going to live in the land of Israel again under their Messiah. Israel therefore has a future, involving national regathering, spiritual rebirth and dwelling in their own land under the reign of the Messiah.

The passage about the dry bones can be applied to our Christian spiritual new birth, because we experience the same thing. But in its primary application, it refers to the nation of Israel. These are God's promises for the future blessing of the people of Israel – the ethnic, national, territorial and political entity called Israel – which is going to experience spiritual rebirth when they believe in their Messiah, and then live in their ancient land, being ruled by Him.

Two Re-gatherings

As we look at these passages which teach an end-times regathering of the people of Israel, it becomes clear that there are actually two re-gatherings to the land. One regathering to the land is in unbelief, and the other is after the return of Christ, when Israel has believed in Him.

Once their Messiah has come and reigns on earth, Israel will be regathered. This regathering is found in a number of passages, including Isaiah 11:11-16. The famous prophecy in Isaiah 11 first describes Messiah's reign (vs1-5), in paradise conditions (the wolf shall dwell with the lamb, etc., vs6-9), the 'earth [being] full of the knowledge of the LORD as the waters cover the sea (v9b). Then, in verse 10 we read that the Root of Jesse shall stand as a banner to the people. In the verses following we read:

> It shall come to pass in that day that the Lord shall set His hand again the second time to recover the remnant of His people who are left, from Assyria and Egypt, from Pathros and Cush, from Elam and Shinar, from Hamath and the islands of the sea. [12] He will set up a banner for the nations, and will assemble the outcasts of Israel, and gather together the dispersed of Judah from the four corners of the earth. [13] Also the envy of Ephraim shall depart, and the adversaries of Judah shall be cut off; Ephraim shall not envy Judah, and Judah shall not harass Ephraim. [14] But they shall fly down upon the shoulder of the Philistines toward the west; together they shall plunder the people of the East; they shall lay their hand on Edom and Moab; and the people of Ammon shall obey them. [15] The LORD will utterly destroy the tongue of the Sea of Egypt; with His mighty wind He will shake His fist over the River, and strike it in the seven streams, and make men cross over dry-shod. [16] There will be a highway for the remnant of His people who will be left from Assyria, as it was for Israel in the day that he came up from the land of Egypt.

Notice particularly verses 11 and 12: 'It shall come to pass in that day that the Lord shall set His hand again *the second time* to recover the remnant of His people who are left … and will assemble the outcasts of Israel, and gather together the dispersed of Judah from the four corners of the earth'.

The words 'the second time' are particularly significant. The first regathering of Israel from all the surrounding nations occurred after the seventy year Babylonian exile. Isaiah cannot here be talking about the return from Babylon, for he calls it a second regathering. Instead, the prophet is looking to the great end-time regathering of Israel.

This is further proved by the fact that this end-time regathering happens after the establishment of Messiah's kingdom on earth. Christ's millennial kingdom is described in verses 1-9, then Isaiah describes the end-time regathering of the people of Israel.

Other similar passages which teach this regathering under Messiah are found in a number of places. Consider Amos 9:13-15, which are the last three verses of the prophecy of Amos, and speak of the blessings of the millennium:

> Behold, the days are coming, says the LORD, when the plowman shall overtake the reaper, and the treader of grapes him who sows seed; the mountains shall drip with sweet wine, and all the hills shall flow with it. [14] I will bring back the captives of My people Israel; they shall build the waste cities and inhabit them; they shall plant vineyards and drink wine from them; they shall also make gardens and eat fruit from them. [15] I will plant them in their land, and no longer shall they be pulled up from the land I have given them, says the LORD your God.

Other verses which teach a regathering after Messiah's return are Isaiah 27:12-13, Jeremiah 31:7-10, Zech. 10:8-12, and most importantly, as we shall see, Matthew 24:31.

However, there must also be a return to the land in unbelief, before the Messiah returns and reigns, for the simple reason that Israel does not turn to Christ as a nation until Christ's return at the end of the tribulation, and Israel is already in the land during this tribulation period.

Luke 21:24 seems to promise such a return: Christ said about the people of Israel, 'and they will fall by the edge of the sword, and be led away captive into all nations. And Jerusalem will be trampled by Gentiles until the times of the Gentiles are fulfilled'. The word 'until' implies that one day Israel's scattering among the nations and Jerusalem's occupation by the Gentiles would come to an end. But, in the following verses, Luke 21:25-27, Christ goes on to speak about the signs which precede Christ's coming, during the great tribulation ('on earth, distress of nations, with perplexity . . . men's hearts failing them from fear and the expectation of those things which are coming on the earth', v26), culminating in Christ's return (v27).

In other words, the Jews seem to be back in their land, and returned from their scattering among the nations (v24) before the great tribulation (v26), and return of Christ (v27).

We have already seen that another passage also teaches this return in unbelief: Ezekiel 36:22-24, which teaches a 'gathering' before their 'sprinkling' and new birth (vs25-27).

One final evidence that the Bible teaches a return to the land in unbelief is the fact that the Jewish temple will have been rebuilt and the sacrifices re-instituted during the first half of the tribulation period. We have already seen this from Daniel 9:27. The idea that the Jews are going to rebuild their Temple is a controversial topic, which we shall evaluate in our next chapter.

Conclusion

In this chapter we have seen, from multiple scriptures, that nothing could be plainer than the fact that God repeatedly promised, in both the Old and New Testaments, to regather His earthly people Israel at the time of Messiah's reign over an earth restored to paradise.

17 EZEKIEL'S TEMPLE

In Ezekiel chapters 40 to 48 God gives the prophet, in a vision, a tour of a temple in the land of Israel. It is obviously not a temple in existence in Ezekiel's time, for the temple had recently been destroyed by Nebuchadnezzar and the Babylonians. Not only are the exact dimensions of many parts of this temple listed, but the manner of its operation is described – including the various animal sacrifices that are to be offered. The glory of God re-enters and fills this temple in Ezekiel 43 – a fitting conclusion to the book of Ezekiel which commenced with the glory of God departing from the temple Solomon had originally built. In following chapters, there are rules decreed for how its priests – and a prince – are to live. Finally, in a scene reminiscent of the New Jerusalem in the book of Revelation, a river of living water flows out from this temple and heals the land.

These are some of the most difficult chapters in the Bible to interpret, whichever view of the future we hold. Calvin (writing from an amillennialist position) found these chapters so difficult that he solved the problem of Ezekiel's temple by not commenting on the second half of Ezekiel at all, despite commentating on every other chapter in the Old Testament Law, Psalms and Prophets. These chapters are also difficult for futuristic (or dispensational) premillennialists, who see in them a literal description of a millennial temple, because this would involve a return to animal sacrifices. To have literal sacrifices in a future earthly temple would be winding the clock of redemptive history backwards, to revert to the former shadows and pictures instead of holding the reality – Christ.

What, then, are we to make of Ezekiel's temple? In this chapter, we shall look at what Ezekiel's temple is all about.

Possible Interpretations

We shall start out by listing and evaluating the seven possible interpretations of Ezekiel's temple:
1. **The Past.** Ezekiel's vision was a flashback to Solomon's temple that had recently been destroyed.
2. **The Immediate Future.** Ezekiel's vision was of a post-exilic temple, given either to lay out the plans and measurements of such

a temple, or to encourage the rebuilding of another temple on the return of the exiles from Babylon.

3. **The Medium Future.** Ezekiel's vision was of Herod's temple. That is, Ezekiel's vision was fulfilled in the dimensions of Herod's temple.
4. **The Spiritual Ideal.** Ezekiel's vision was of an ideal temple. Rather than promoting or predicting a literal temple, Ezekiel was given the vision to teach Israel spiritual lessons.
5. **The Church.** The temple in Ezekiel's vision was a picture of the Church.
6. **The Millennium.** Ezekiel's vision was of a Millennial temple built during the reign of Christ on earth in a future day.
7. **The Eternal.** Ezekiel's vision refers to the Eternal State and teaches us about future conditions in Eternity.

Perhaps there are other interpretations or explanations of Ezekiel's temple, and some of the seven interpretations overlap somewhat, but seven is sufficient for present consideration.

Some of these interpretations are easily discounted. The first interpretation (Solomon's temple) is answered by the fact that Ezekiel is shown the glory of God re-entering the Temple. Such a process of re-entry would be impossible after Solomon's temple had been destroyed. Ezekiel is also told about the sacrifices necessary for the consecration – i.e. re-establishment – of the altar in 44:18-27, which again implies a future temple. Finally, if it was Solomon's temple Ezekiel saw, why are we nowhere told this fact directly?

The last interpretation, a temple (whether literal or spiritual) in the eternal state, is at first sight attractive because of the cross-references to the New Jerusalem in the book of Revelation – the river of life, and the trees on the bank growing fruit, and leaves for healing (Ezek. 47:1-12, cf. Rev. 22:1-2). But on closer inspection, this option becomes difficult to maintain. There will surely be no animal sacrifices in the eternal state, for the simple reason that there will no longer be any sin. Neither sin nor repeated sacrifices will feature in eternity.

The second and third interpretations (Zerubbabel's and Herod's temples) are likewise unsatisfactory explanations of Ezekiel's vision, for the simple reason that they do not match the details of the vision given to Ezekiel. Where was the river coming out of the temple (Ezekiel 47) in Zerubbabel's or Herod's day? It is obvious when we compare Ezekiel's vision with the similar pictures of a river of life in Joel 3:18, Zechariah 14:8

or Revelation 22:1 that the river in Ezekiel must either be river of life in the future or it is simply a 'spiritual' river and not a physical river at all.

Furthermore, the physical dimensions of Ezekiel's temple go far beyond anything Zerubbabel or Herod could have possibly built. The scale is too grand. Indeed, it would be impossible (according to some computations) to geographically fit the temple and associated tribal boundaries into the modern land of Israel – without some serious earth-movement. Ezekiel's temple court area (about 1 square mile) would itself have been larger than the size of ancient Jerusalem itself. The temple area would be ten miles north of the city (45:1-8), virtually up in Samaria. It is obvious that this temple complex cannot be located in Jerusalem, and the city is never described as Jerusalem anyway. So it is impossible for Ezekiel's temple to be the one rebuilt by Zerubbabel in Jerusalem, which was renovated by Herod.

Some argue for a post-exilic temple on the grounds that the promised blessings (like the river of life) were conditional upon the Jews actually building the temple. However, it is worth reminding ourselves at this point of the context of Ezekiel's prophecy, in which the return of the glory of God to the temple in chapters 40-48 happens after the fulfilment of the Messianic hope and the complete restoration of Israel in chapters 33-39. Ezekiel's temple is connected, in some way, with Messianic blessing – not simply the post-exilic situation. Furthermore, Ezekiel's temple counter-balances the first section of the prophecy (chapters 1-11) in which God's glory departs from the temple. The scene in chapters 40-48 is thus not a temporary restoration of the temple, such as happened under Zerubbabel or Herod, but the fulfilment of Israel's hope under the Messiah which finally brings closure to all its years of sin and failure. Ezekiel's temple is a symbol of the final redemption.

So, we must narrow our interpretation down to either some ideal temple, teaching spiritual lessons either to Israel or to the church today, or a literal millennial temple. This last option would include cataclysmic earth-movements, of the like predicted by the prophets accompanying Christ's return – for example, Isaiah (24:19-23), Zechariah (14:3-10) and Joel (3:16) – as a pre-requisite for a literal, physical temple foreseen by Ezekiel. We must choose between a spiritual, ideal temple or a literal, millennial temple.

The problem with the spiritualization of these chapters is the abundance of specific measurements and detailed architectural terms (26 of them, according to some commentators). What spiritual lesson do we learn from the fact that the temple's gateways had three chambers on either side, each six cubits wide? Is there is a moral here? Do the gateways symbolize judgment, as in ancient Israel? Are the six chambers, each six cubits wide, meant to teach us something about the true pattern of church government? What is the spiritual significance of the fact that a gateway is thirteen cubits long (Ezekiel 40:11)? Does thirteen stand for bad luck? What spiritual lesson do we draw from all the numbers and architectural elements?

The fact that so many specific details are given (just like in Moses' tabernacle and Solomon's temple), and that so few are explained in the inspired prophecy, argues against a spiritualized temple. Put simply, if the temple is meant to teach spiritual morals, why are there so few spiritual lessons taught in these chapters? As mentioned, even those commentators who are most keen to put their sanctified imagination to use by offering spiritualized interpretations struggle to find any here.

Furthermore, specific geographical locations argue against a spiritualized meaning. We are told that the fishermen shall stand by the river from En-gedi to En-eglaim (47:10). We are given specific geographical notes about the boundaries of the tribes in chapter 48 – reference is made to Damascus, Hamath, Meribah, Kadesh and the Great Sea. These geographical details do not encourage a spiritualized ideal but point to a real-world places.

Of course, there are some spiritual lessons to be taken from these chapters. The temple's cherubim no doubt teach about God's holiness, the palm trees about God's self-sufficiency. Furthermore, God specifically tells Ezekiel to point out to Israel several lessons from the temple, concerning their sinfulness (43:10ff) and true equity (45:9ff). These spiritual lessons do not stand in the way of us taking Ezekiel's temple as a literal temple, for spiritual lessons may be drawn from the Tabernacle and Solomon's temple (see Hebrews 9:5). All literal temples in the Bible taught spiritual lessons; the question here is whether a symbolic and imaginary temple can have so many detailed specifications without being a real temple. If we are to interpret and apply these chapters spiritually, there are too many intricate measurements and architectural details to moralize upon.

A final problem with identifying Ezekiel's temple with either some spiritual ideal state or with the Church is that the New Testament nowhere interprets these chapters in this way. The New Testament refers to the Tabernacle and Solomon's Temple and draws lessons from them, but nowhere do we read New Testament authors mentioning Ezekiel in the same breath. They ignore Ezekiel's temple when drawing typological lessons from Old Testament temples.

A variant on the spiritual interpretation is the apocalyptic interpretation. That is, Ezekiel's temple section is written in the apocalyptic genre which uses grotesque otherworldly symbols (like beasts with seven heads and ten horns) to teach spiritual lessons. This is an increasingly common ploy by Bible commentators: claim that a passage is apocalyptic and then discount any literal meaning or fulfilment. However, apart from the fact that this section lacks the standard features of apocalyptic works (e.g. grotesque symbolism, cosmic drama) and instead reads like the very down-to-earth instructions for Solomon's temple's construction (2 Chronicles 3 and 4), the end-result of this approach is unsatisfying. Consider the lessons that John Taylor suggests we take from this 'apocalyptic vision':

> This was Ezekiel's pattern for the Messianic age that was to come. It lay in the future, and yet it grew out of the present. It was expressed in tangible terms and yet these were merely the forms in which the general principles of God's activity were enshrined. The vision of the temple was in fact a kind of incarnation of all that God could do for His people in the age that was about to dawn[1].

The lessons from the precise details are mystical, that is, shrouded in the mists of theological mumbo-jumbo. Taylor continues ...

> On this view, which of all the interpretations seems to take the most realistic view of the literary character of the material with which we are dealing, the message of Ezekiel in these chapters may be summarized as follows:

(a) The perfection of God's plan for His restored people, symbolically expressed in the immaculate symmetry of the temple building;
(b) The centrality of worship in the new age, its importance being expressed in the scrupulous concern for detail in the observance of its rites;
(c) The abiding presence of the Lord in the midst of His people;
(d) The blessings that will flow from God's presence to the barren places of the earth (the river of life);
(e) The orderly allocation of duties and privileges to all God's people, as shown both in the temple duties and in the apportionment of

---

[1] John B. Taylor, *Ezekiel*, Tyndale OT Commentaries, IVP, 1969, p253

the land (a theme taken up in Rev. 7:4-8)[2].

These general lessons are followed by very little in the way of practical spiritual application or relevance to readers, ancient or modern, as Taylor makes a few brief, bland notes on each of Ezekiel's chapters. Rather than teaching divinely powerful practical spiritual lessons, the apocalyptic approach interprets precise measurements as vague nothings. By imposing a foreign 'apocalyptic genre' upon the temple vision, these nine chapters are rendered spiritually fruitless.

This brings us to the last option, a millennial temple. There are, as we have indicated, a number of features that point to this solution, chiefly the fact that this appears to be a temple which is placed in Ezekiel's prophecy after the battle of Armageddon (Ezekiel 38-39), following on from a Jewish ethnic, national, conversion, regathering to their land and political re-establishment under the Messiah (chapters 34-39). Further, this temple does not appear to be in the eternal state, for there are sacrifices offered for sins.

Further Evidence that Ezekiel's temple is in the Millennium:
We find references in Ezekiel chapters 40-48 to the same sorts of things we see in Isaiah 65-66 (and other millennial passages like Isaiah 2, 11, etc.): sin, death, birth, learning, judging:

- **Death**: Ezekiel 44:25 speaks about death occurring: [the priests] 'shall not defile themselves by coming near a dead person. Only for father or mother, for son or daughter, for brother or unmarried sister may they defile themselves ... he must offer his sin offering in the inner court, says the Lord God'.
- **Birth**: Ezekiel 47:22 speaks of 'strangers who dwell among you and who bear children among you'. Similarly, in Ezekiel 46:16 we read of the prince who 'gives a gift of some of his inheritance to any of his sons, it shall belong to his sons'. People will have children in the state described by Ezekiel chapters 40-48.
- **Sin**: we read of sin offerings in 42:13 and other verses (which presumes that there is sin committed). In addition, in 45:8, the princes are told to no more oppress God's people, and in 45:9 we read, 'Thus says the Lord God, Enough, O princes of Israel! Remove violence and plundering, execute justice and righteousness, and stop dispossessing

---

[2] Ibid, p253-4

my people ... you shall have honest scales, an honest ephah and an honest bath'.
- **Judging**: In 44:24, the priests are told 'in controversy they shall stand as judges, and judge it according to My judgments'. This again implies sin, so that right and wrong may be identified and blame apportioned.
- **Teaching**: In 44:23, the priests are also to teach the people, implying that there is not perfect knowledge of God, as in the eternal, glorified state: 'they shall teach My people the difference between the holy and the unholy, and cause them to discern between the clean and the unclean'.
- **Time**: there are Sabbath sacrifices and New Moon sacrifices, the latter more important than the former, maybe because the New Moon sacrifices are important for calendar calculation (and the dates for the yearly feasts). In the eternal state, there will no longer be time the way we think of it, and therefore, in the Millennium of 1000 years, the calculation of time will still be relevant and important.

All of these features of the millennium have been seen in Isaiah's vision of the paradise to come – the millennium. Ezekiel's temple, which contains these same features, is therefore a millennial one too.

However, there are two problems with the idea that the millennium is in view. Firstly, there is the problem of animal sacrifices, which seems anachronistic – a reverting to Old Testament shadows and types, and secondly, the mention of a prince in these chapters, which we would assume to be Christ Himself in a millennial interpretation, yet there are problems identifying the prince with our Lord Jesus.

Animal Sacrifices

Animal sacrifices are not just a problem for the view that Ezekiel is prophesying a future millennial temple. Animal sacrifices are also a problem for the idea that the church is in view here. For, if we start spiritualizing the sacrifices, we must face up to what the sacred text actually says about them. Who are the Zadokite priests (44:15) in the church who alone are able to offer these sacrifices? (Christ is not a Zadokite priest, he is from a different order of priest). What are we to make of all the mechanics of animal sacrifice: the chambers where they wash the burnt offerings, and stone tables where they slaughter the offerings, and stone tables where they lay the instruments of slaughter, as well as hooks, perhaps to hang the carcasses (Ezek. 40:38-43)? What do these stone tables mean for us in the church today, or the hooks, and why are all these procedural details given? Why are we given lists of all the different animals sacrificed (bulls, kids of the goats, lambs, rams, grain, oil) and different types of sacrifices (sin offerings, burnt offerings, grain offerings, peace offerings, drink offerings)? If these all simply refer to Christ's once-for-all death, why are we not given one simple sacrifice here? If we may simply generalize the whole matter by pointing to the sacrifice of Christ, why the need for the multiplied details?

Remember, too, that God told Ezekiel to 'make known to them the design of the temple and its arrangement, its exits and its entrances, its entire design and all its ordinances [i.e. rules to be obeyed], all its forms and all its laws. Write it down in their sight, so that they may *keep* its whole design and all its ordinances and *perform* them' (43:11). God said these instructions about animal sacrifices need to be obeyed. But all these rules and instructions do not apply to the church today, either literally or spiritually. Why are we given details of the chambers and stone tables where we must sacrifice, and the implements we must use to do so, if we do not need to obey any of these rules? Nor will it do to argue that all these implements point to Christ's sacrifice, for we do not need to repeat Christ's sacrifice. Yet Ezekiel says that the details are given so that the sacrifices may be *performed*. In what way, then, should we sacrifice Christ afresh on stone tables in special chambers?

It becomes clear that Ezekiel's temple does not directly apply to us in the Church at all. We seem to have got by for 2000 years by largely ignoring Ezekiel, so it hardly seems essential for the Church's continued existence to read and obey Ezekiel's instructions regarding the sacrifices and order of worship in the temple.

The second thing we need to observe about the animal sacrifices here in Ezekiel is that they are not the same sacrifices as we find in the Law of Moses. Thus, if we compare the sacrifices in Ezekiel 45:18-25 with Numbers 28-29, we see:

1. The day of atonement (which was on the 10th day of the 7th month in Lev. 16) is moved to the first day of the first month (Ezek. 45:18), and the offerings for the day of atonement are completely different in Ezekiel to those in Leviticus (there is no scapegoat offering, etc.)
2. Ezekiel has thus added a feast on the first day of the year, which is not found in the Law of Moses.
3. There are only two other feasts in Ezekiel - Passover/Unleavened bread (Ezek. 45:21-24) and Tabernacles (Ezek. 45:25), and again, the sacrifices are very different to Numbers 28:19-21 (Passover) and

Numbers 29:12-38 (Tabernacles).
4. There are no feasts of first-fruits, or Pentecost (i.e. weeks) or trumpets in Ezekiel.
5. The holy city in Ezekiel is geographically different to where Jerusalem is. In Ezekiel, the holy city is in the exact centre of the land of Israel geographically. Ezekiel is describing a transformed geopolitical reality.

If it is the case that the sacrifices here in Ezekiel are not those offered under the Mosaic Law, we do not have a reversion to Old Testament times. The sacrificial system in Ezekiel is not a 'going back' to the Law of Moses. These considerations, particularly the changes to the laws concerning offerings, apparently led to some Jews rejecting Ezekiel as inspired Scripture. Ezekiel is a great puzzle to Jews as well as to many Christians!

How can there be Animal Sacrifices in the Millennium?
Strange as it may sound, the animal sacrifices mentioned in Ezekiel's temple actually make a positive argument for the millennial option. As we have already argued, the mention of animal sacrifices in Ezekiel's temple rules out the 'eternal state' option, because this would mean sin in the eternal state. However, as Isaiah 2, 9, 11, and 65 teach (see chapters 1 and 2 of this book), there will still be sins committed in the millennium.

Consider the question of what to do with sin in the millennium: what action will be taken against sin in that near-perfect state? Certain options and possibilities suggest themselves: mortals committing sin in the millennium could all be executed. After all, the wages of sin is death. No doubt, some serious sins will meet this penalty (see Isaiah 11:4 and 65:20) But the death penalty for all sins would leave no mortal standing long before the end of the millennium. At the other end of the scale, sins could receive some mild 'slap on the wrist' – a penalty, a monetary fine, or public shaming, acting as a deterrent. Or, sins could be treated using a religious remedy, some form of prayer-apology – like Roman Catholic confession.

Options like these would achieve the objective of helping remind citizens of the millennium that sin cannot be ignored, but must be repented of and punished. In other words, there must be some 'teaching aid' about sin in the millennium. Furthermore, other Old Testament passages mention animal sacrifices in the millennium – Isaiah 56:6-7, Isaiah 60:7, Jeremiah 33:15-18 and Zechariah 14:21. Without some form of remedial action against sin in the millennium, civil government would break down, or on the other hand, if the penalty was too harsh, no flesh would survive.

Animal sacrifices would seem to present just such a 'teaching aid', combining elements of a penalty, public deterrent and religious penance, achieving the same objectives as seen above:

- To sacrifice animals for sin would require the public acknowledgement of sin. There would be no 'sweeping under the carpet' of sin in the millennium.
- As such, there would be much less of the careless attitude toward sin that we find today. The millennium's ideal, holy and just society would remain functional, placing limits and penalties on sin.
- Animal sacrifices would stand as lessons about the seriousness of sin, the holiness of God, the fact that only death can pay for sin, the fact that only a substitute can save the sinner and a pointer to the one sacrifice for sins for ever – Christ.

In short, the reason for animal sacrifices would be their teaching value. Animal sacrifices would not really wind back the clock because animal sacrifices never truly paid for sins. Animal sacrifices only teach lessons about sin and other eternal and important truths.

As we have just seen, the sacrifices in Ezekiel's temple are not really a retrogression. They underline the fact that sacrifices in the Old Testament were multifaceted in their purpose (as they will be in the Millennium), they did not take away sin, and a large part of their purpose was purely didactic: moral and spiritual education.

Neither is it true to think that God saving the Jewish nation in the future is 'going backwards', for the entire world (both Jews and the other nations) will then know God: 'the earth shall be full of the knowledge of the Lord as the waters cover the sea' (Isaiah 11:9). It is going forwards to the completion of God's purposes.

As a result, Christ's one sacrifice for sin forever is no more denied by animal sacrifices in the millennium than it was by animal sacrifices in the Old Testament. The Old Testament sacrifices were types whose value was in teaching about Christ's sacrifice. Any future animal sacrifices would likewise be pictures that deny nothing about Christ's sacrifice.

Who is the Prince?

The second problem with identifying Ezekiel's temple with a millennial age is the person of the Prince mentioned in these chapters. Is he the same Prince as mentioned in Ezekiel 34:24 and 37:24? These references would appear to point to Christ because the shepherd prince fulfils the same roles as both God and yet David in chapter 34. The reference to the prince in 37:24 would appear to refer to the same prince as found in Ezekiel's temple because in 37:27 God promises His tabernacle shall be among them, as fulfilled in Ezekiel 40-48.

But then, if the Prince in Ezekiel's temple is Christ, why does He offer sin offerings for Himself (45:22) and who are His sons to whom He may give an inheritance (46:16)? Does not the mention of a sin offering imply a sinning Prince, does not mention of the sons of the Prince imply an earthly Prince, and does not an inheritance imply a mortal Prince?

Perhaps there are ways of reconciling Ezekiel's temple prince with Christ, but the most natural answers to these questions would appear to cast serious doubt upon the identification. Some dispensationalists have therefore argued that the Prince is not Christ, but a mortal Jewish Prince under Christ. This seems the best answer.

The problem of the Prince is even more acute for amillennialist theologians. Because they see parallels in Ezekiel's prophecy with other prophetic books, and because they take these other prophecies to represent the Church, they are driven to read Christ into Ezekiel's Prince (by trying to see 'Christ in all the Scriptures'). However, the same problems apply. The amillennialist theologian does not even have the fallback option of a Jewish prince, because to him, the Jews are 'history'. We affirm with Paul, however, that the Jews are not 'history', 'for the gifts and calling of God are irrevocable' (Romans 11:29).

Conclusion

Ezekiel's temple is millennial, for despite some difficulties, the millennial view seems superior to any other. There is no satisfying alternative to the simple acceptance of what Ezekiel's prophecy pictures in the future after Israel's regathering and spiritual rebirth (chapters 36-37) after the battle of Armageddon (chapters 38-39). For those who are not premillennialists, the challenge is to provide a satisfying counter-exposition of Ezekiel. Professor Daniel Block, who wrote the New International Commentary on the Old Testament on Ezekiel put it this way in personal discussion with a friend of mine: people arguing against a premillennial view of Ezekiel are typically NT theologians – they rarely have to give expositions or write expository papers that grapple in detail with the relevant OT passages.

18: WILL THERE BE A THIRD TEMPLE?

In September 2000, Ariel Sharon, then Israel's opposition leader and later Prime Minister, walked up into the Temple Mount in Jerusalem. His visit prompted protests and riots by Palestinians all over the land of Israel. This was the cause of the Second Intifada, or Uprising, which lasted till 2005, during which time about 3000 Palestinians and 1000 Israelis died. It was called the Al-Aqsa Intifada, after the Al-Aqsa mosque which sits on Temple Mount.

Sharon walked onto the Temple Mount with his bodyguards to make a political statement: Israel (under a government he hoped to lead) would never relinquish control of the Temple Mount in peace negotiations with the Palestinians. His mere presence on the mount was enough to spark furious reactions.

More recently, in 2017, three Muslim gunmen shot two Israeli police officers in Jerusalem in the so-called Temple Mount Crisis, after which Jewish soldiers chased the gunmen into the Temple Mount complex where they were killed. The Jewish authorities closed off access to the Temple Mount and then imposed metal detectors and security cameras on the Mount, which led to riots. Eventually the Jewish government backed down, removed all the security measures and the situation settled down.

The Temple Mount is the holiest site in Judaism and third holiest site in Islam. Muslims do not acknowledge the presence of the two previous Jewish temples on Temple mount (first Solomon's, and then Zerubbabel's, which underwent renovations by Herod the Great).

I have in my study a large triangular piece of broken tile, coloured turquoise blue. It was given to me by my uncle, Dr. Victor Wilson, who visited the land of Israel on a number of occasions. This blue tile comes from the Al-Aqsa Mosque on the Temple Mount in Jerusalem, from rubbish recovered during one of the periodic renovations. The Al-Aqsa Mosque is the most famous building in the land of Israel; its golden dome sitting on top of Temple Mount dominates the Old City of Jerusalem.

From a political perspective, it seems unlikely that the Jews will rebuild the Temple. The Israeli government has been steadfastly opposed to any moves to rebuild the Temple or even to allow Jews freedom to pray on Temple Mount. Secular Jews are very wary of the prospect of a third temple. Not only do they think it would unleash violent protests from the Palestinians and possibly even war with the Muslim world, they worry that it would lead to Israel becoming more religious and that this might lead to the same sort of religious mania among the Jewish zealots that occurred at the time of the destruction of the Second Temple by the Romans.

The Jews have been back in control of the land since 1948, and regained control of Jerusalem in 1967. If they haven't started to rebuild the temple in the last 50 years, it seems unlikely they will any time soon. If such happened, we might soon be facing World War Three. What Jewish government would risk that?

On the other hand, there are a number of organizations in Israel whose goal is to rebuild the Temple. They are engaged in preparing vessels and architectural plans for the temple, and training priests.

Our interest here is not focused on the political maneuverings in the land of Israel, but on the scriptures. Does the Bible teach that the Jews are going to rebuild the Temple?

Revelation 11: a Future Temple in Jerusalem?

Revelation 11 is one of the most interesting chapters in the Bible relating to Israel and its future. This chapter enables us to draw a number of very important conclusions about future events. Before we look at it, we need to briefly mention three other passages that suggest that there is going to be another Jewish temple.

Matthew 24:15 speaks about an idol-statue called 'the abomination of desolation' 'standing in the holy place'. Some commentators take Matthew 24 to have been fulfilled in the events surrounding AD 70. However, there is one verse that conclusively refutes this idea, and shows us that the 'great tribulation' this passage speaks about is yet future. Verse 29 tells us that 'immediately after' the great tribulation (v21) of those days, Christ will return (v30-31). Seeing that Christ has not yet returned, the great tribulation immediately before that has not yet occurred. The expression 'the holy place' is only mentioned four more times in the New Testament: Acts 6:13, 21:28, Hebrews 9:12, 9:25. The references in Acts and in Hebrews 9:25 refer to the Jewish temple in Jerusalem, and the reference in Hebrews 9:12 refers to heaven itself. Seeing it is impossible to have an abomination in heaven, it would appear that the future abomination of desolation will be in a literal temple in Jerusalem.

2 Thessalonians 2:4 also speaks of the Man of Sin who will sit in the temple of God showing himself to be God. As the Antichrist has not yet appeared, he must yet sit in the temple of God. In fact, the two verses in

Matthew 24:15 and 2 Thessalonians 2:4, about the 'abomination of desolation' and the Man of Sin sitting in the temple of God, are really referring to the same thing. They suggest that there must yet be a future Jewish temple in Jerusalem, for the Man of Sin's appearance and the idol-statue he sets up both occur in the temple of God.

The third reference is found in the Old Testament in the book of Daniel where we read in Daniel 9:27 that the Antichrist, the 'prince to come', is going to put a stop to the animal sacrifices in the Jewish temple, and Daniel 12:11 tells us that he will set up the abomination of desolation, just like Daniel 11:31 tells us that Antiochus Epiphanes set up an idol-statue of the Greek god Zeus in the temple in Jerusalem in 167 BC. These are the passages in Daniel that Christ referred His hearers to in his teaching about future events.in the Olivet Discourse.

The Temple, City and Two Witnesses in Revelation 11

Revelation 11 gives us perhaps the most intriguing information on this question of whether there is going to be a future Jewish temple. The first three verses of Revelation 11 read:

> Then I was given a reed like a measuring rod. And the angel stood, saying, "Rise and measure the temple of God, the altar, and those who worship there. But leave out the court which is outside the temple, and do not measure it, for it has been given to the Gentiles. And they will tread the holy city underfoot for forty-two months". And I will give power to my two witnesses, and they will prophesy one thousand two hundred and sixty-days, clothed in sackcloth' (Revelation 11:1-3)

In these verses we read about two witnesses who prophesy outside this temple. We read more about these two witnesses in verses 4-6:

- if anyone wants to harm them, fire proceeds from their mouth and destroys them.
- they have power to shut heaven so no rain falls, they have power to turn water to blood, and to strike the earth with plagues as often as they desire.
- in verses 7-10, the two witnesses are killed, and their bodies lie in the street of the city for three and a half days,
- after this they are raised to life by God and taken up to heaven in a cloud (vs 11-12).
- Then an earthquake kills 7000 people and one tenth of the city is

destroyed (vs 13-14).

We need to ask three questions at this point: (1) what is the temple that John is told to measure in the first two verses, (2) what is the city that is mentioned in this passage, and (3) who are the two witnesses here?

What is this Temple in Revelation 11?
There are, logically speaking, four possible options for the temple. It could be heavenly, historical, spiritual or future.

1. Firstly, the temple here could be heavenly. After all, the book of Revelation refers to God's temple in heaven. For example, at the end of this same chapter, Revelation 11:19, we read, 'then the temple of God was opened in heaven'. However, verse 2 would seem to indicate that this temple is not in heaven, for John is told not to measure the outer court, for the Gentiles will tread the holy city underfoot for forty-two months. 'Trampling underfoot' is a way to describe the brutal occupation of a city by a conquering army, or at least the control by foreigners. This does not sound like something that would or could happen in heaven. If this were a heavenly temple, why would Gentiles only be allowed access to heaven's outer courts, not inside the temple itself? How would two of God's servants be killed in heaven by 'the Beast that ascends from the bottomless pit'? How would there be an earthquake in heaven? Reading the entire passage, heaven does not seem like a natural way to understand this temple.

2. Secondly, it could be historical: Herod's Temple. Sometimes, the book of Revelation looks backwards in history rather than forwards. For example, Revelation 12 gives us a flashback historically to the birth of Christ. So, this passage could be a retrospective view of the Second Temple that was destroyed by the Romans in AD 70. This would explain the Jewish temple being trampled by the Gentiles. However, the prophecy in Revelation 11 seems to exempt the actual temple from destruction, whereas the Romans not only trampled the city, but also destroyed the Temple itself. Furthermore, there were no fire-breathing prophetic witnesses who devoured their enemies in AD 70. The Jewish temple had been destroyed for about 20 years by the time John wrote the book of Revelation, and Revelation 4:1 tells us that John was shown 'things which must take place after this' – events that were yet future. Thus, the Jewish second temple does not seem to be what John's vision

is trying to depict.

3. Thirdly, many commentators take this temple symbolically, and say that it is a spiritual temple, the church. The New Testament pictures the church as a holy temple (e.g. Ephesians 2:21). Leon Morris writes, 'The altar … points to the sacrificial nature of Christian service'[1]. This spiritualizing interpretation is the preferred choice for many interpreters. The trampling of the temple's outer courts, they suggest, symbolizes the persecution of the church.

4. Fourthly, we could take the temple to be the opposite of these three views. That is, instead of being a heavenly temple, we could take it to be an earthly temple. Instead of seeing it as an historical temple, we could take it to be a future temple. Instead of a spiritual temple, we could take it to be a physical temple. Putting it all together, we could view this as an earthly, future, physical temple. Inside this temple there are worshippers, but the city outside is occupied by a foreign power during a period of three and a half years, during which period two prophets witness for God. There is no particular difficulty or internal contradiction in Revelation 11 to prevent us understanding the temple as a future, earthly physical temple. However, to see whether this is indeed what is being pictured here, we need ask a second question and enquire what the name of the city is outside the temple.

What is the City?

The spiritual interpretation (the temple is the Church) becomes difficult to maintain once we look at the context and realize that the temple is located in a city. This city is described in three verses in Revelation 11. Firstly, it is called 'the holy city' (verse 2), secondly, 'the great city which spiritually is called Sodom and Egypt, where also their Lord was crucified' (verse 8), then thirdly, a city which is hit by an earthquake in verse 13: 'in the same hour there was a great earthquake and a tenth of the city fell; in the earthquake seven thousand people were killed, and the rest were afraid and gave glory to the God of heaven'.

This city appears to be the one and the same city throughout the passage. For example, the 'holy city' is trampled underfoot by Gentiles for the same period of time, forty two months (v2), that the two witnesses prophecy, 1260 days (v3). The dead bodies of the two witnesses 'lie in the

---

[1] Leon Morris, *Revelation*, TNTC, IVP, 1987, p142

street of the great city' (v8). That is, the witnesses lie unburied where they died, which is the same place where they prophesied (i.e. in the city, v3), and no one seems to dispute that the city in verse 13 is the same as the city in verse 8. The city is one and the same throughout the story.

What is this city? The spiritualizers take the city to refer to the church. But here is where things start to get slightly difficult for this interpretation, if not downright comical. Those who argue that the temple is the church also say that the 'holy city' (v2) is the church. In addition, they also say that the altar and the worshippers are symbols of the church. So, the temple, the altar, the worshippers, and the city are all pictures of the church.

David Aune voices some disquiet with this interpretation: 'the over-allegorization of the passage has essentially removed the clear apocalyptic orientation that the passage exhibits. How, one asks, can the temple, the altar, and the worshippers all stand for the people of God?'[2].

These commentators actually go one step further and argue that the two witnesses who prophesy outside the temple (verses 3ff.) are also the church. So, here is the spiritualized interpretation: 'the two witnesses' who prophesy in the street of 'the holy city' outside 'the temple' which contains an 'altar' with 'worshippers' are really the church witnessing in the church outside the church which contains a church with a church. The spiritualizing is all getting a bit too silly.

But that is not the end of it. There is worse to come, for these commentators are also guilty of a glaring inconsistency. They say that the city in verse 2 is the church, but in verse 8 they change tune and say the city is the 'world'[3], because in v8 the city is described as 'spiritually Sodom and Egypt, where also their Lord was crucified'. It is possible, perhaps, to take the 'holy city' to refer to the church, but it seems difficult for the city just a few verses later, which is called Sodom and Egypt, to also be the church.

Revelation 11 refers to a city three times (in verses 2, 8, and 13), and it is clear the chapter is not talking about three different cities. The most natural interpretation is that verses 2, 8 and 13 are talking about the same city. To argue that the city in verse 2 is the church, but then in verses 8 and 13 it is the wicked world is a very clumsy backflip. These commentators doggedly allegorize everything they can in the passage to refer to the church (until it becomes ridiculous), but they refuse to interpret the one common element in the story, the city, to consistently mean the same thing. Such an interpretation shows the lengths some will go to fit

---

[2] David Aune, *Revelation 6-16*, WBC, Nashville: Thomas Nelson, 1998, p598
[3] E.g. Morris, *Revelation*, p141

Revelation 11 into their pre-determined theological framework, instead of just letting the words of Scripture speak for themselves.

What city is this referring to? There is only one sensible answer: the city described here in Revelation 11 is the actual city of Jerusalem, which is both 'the holy city' where 'the temple of God' is located, and also the place 'where the Lord was crucified' (verse 8). The fact that the city is hit by an earthquake in which one tenth of the city falls and seven thousand people die would also seem to suggest that it is a city full of buildings and inhabited by people, not an allegorical, spiritualized city. In other words, it a normal, real-life city: Jerusalem.

Back to the Temple (again)
If the city is literal, earthly Jerusalem, then the temple is a literal temple in Jerusalem. The temple is not a historic temple (AD 70) nor the heavenly temple where God dwells, nor a figurative temple (the church): it is the opposite of all these, a future, earthly, physical temple. Seeing John is prophesying things still to come (Rev. 4:1), and seeing the temple in Jerusalem was destroyed before the time John wrote the book of Revelation, it would appear that Revelation 11 is teaching us about a future, earthly temple in the city of Jerusalem. This means that there is a temple yet to be rebuilt by Jews in Jerusalem that exists during the 'great tribulation' period ('the forty-two months' or '1260 days').

A future Jewish temple in Jerusalem is a significant result of our study of Revelation 11, a result we see confirmed from a number of other passages (Matthew 24, 2 Thessalonians 2, Daniel 9) in which Christ and the apostles also speak of a future Jewish temple.

One reason this temple is significant is that it would appear that Israel as a nation would have to build this temple while still following the Jewish religion, rather than converted to Christianity. This future temple will be built by Jews still in unbelief in Christ – for why would Jews who believed in Jesus as the Messiah wish to rebuild a temple in Jerusalem? This suggests, too, that Israel's conversion to Christ in Romans 11 and Zechariah 12-14 does not happen until after this Temple has been built.

Furthermore, from a psychological point of view, considering how greatly the Jewish nation's religious zeal would be excited by a re-established temple, and how greatly such a temple would reinvigorate Judaism itself as a religion, it would seem that some event of seismic proportions would be required to later turn them away from Judaism to faith in Christ. Only Christ's visible return at the end of the great tribulation will be enough to bring about Israel's national conversion.

Sadly, a future Jewish temple in Jerusalem means, from a geopolitical perspective, that there are many more upheavals still to come in the Middle East. Some people might perhaps dismiss this interpretation of a future temple yet to be rebuilt in Jerusalem on the grounds that the author is 'anxious for Armageddon'. However, this is not true. The author has no apocalyptic death-wish. The author studied this passage long before he had clearly come to any certainty about eschatological answers or views of prophecy. The author was simply trying to understand, with an open and honest mind, what this passage in the Bible was saying.

The Two Witnesses (Revelation 11)
Following on from the description of the Jewish temple in the city of Jerusalem, we read about the Two Witnesses (Rev. 11:3-6):

> And I will give power to my two witnesses, and they will prophesy one thousand two hundred and sixty days, clothed in sackcloth. These are the two olive trees and the two lampstands standing before the God of the earth. And if anyone wants to harm them, fire proceeds from their mouth and devours their enemies. And if anyone wants to harm them, he must be killed in this manner. These have power to shut heaven, so that no rain falls in the days of their prophecy; and they have power over waters to turn them to blood, and to strike the earth with all plagues, as often as they desire.

Who are these Two Witnesses? Some commentators argue that these two witnesses are the church. Morris argues that because the two witnesses are described as lampstands in verse 4 (just like the seven churches of Revelation chapters 2 and 3), the two witnesses here collectively represent the faithful witnessing members of the church.

However, there are a number of reasons why it seems unlikely that these two witnesses are the church. Commentators who teach that the two witnesses are the church say that they are preaching the gospel. But notice that the two prophets also kill their enemies who try to harm them:

> if anyone wants to harm them, fire proceeds from their mouth and devours their enemies; and if anyone wants to harm them, he must be killed in this manner (v5).

How does the church kill its enemies? The flame-throwing, we are told, is the preaching of the gospel, because God's word is like fire (e.g. Mounce[4]). However, these commentators do not explain how calling down drought, turning water to blood and sending all manner of plagues upon the earth are descriptions of the 'good news' of the grace of God.

Morris argues that the rain-stopping, blood curdling and plagues-sending prophets express 'the truth that God's servants in the new dispensation [i.e. the church] have just as great resources as did Moses and Elijah in the old'[5]. But there seems to be far more emphasis upon the plagues themselves than the resources of the Christian. Hendriksen argues that 'Chapter 11 now gives us a description of the 'bitter' experiences which the true Church must endure when it preaches the 'sweet' gospel of salvation'[6]. But it is not immediately obvious how incinerating ones enemies with a flame-thrower illustrates the 'sweetness' of salvation. How does calling down all sorts of destructive plagues upon the earth symbolize 'good news'? Indeed, Hendriksen soon abandons the 'sweetness and light' and instead starts hectoring and threatening: 'Indeed, in a most real sense, the church still smites the earth with every plague! Be very, very careful, O wicked world. ... But even if anyone would like to harm the true ministers and missionaries, he will be destroyed similarly'[7]. Hendriksen here suggests we take the plagues 'in a most real sense', that is, literally. But he does not explain how the church smites the earth 'in a most real sense'.

Some commentators allegorize the plagues to mean 'troubling the conscience'. Thus, Beale writes that their witness 'unleashes torment toward those who remain ultimately unrepentant. The torments anticipate the final judgment and harden the reprobate in this sinful stance, making them ever more ripe for the punishment of the great day. These torments primarily affect the spiritual realm of a person, especially plaguing his or her conscience'[8]. But we are not told why there are four different varieties of spiritualized torment needed (fire, blood, drought and plagues); nor are we told what different effects these various spiritual torments have upon the consciences of sinful men.

In verses 7 to 10, these two witnesses are killed by the 'beast that ascends out of the bottomless pit', and their bodies lie unburied for three and a half days in the city where 'also their Lord was crucified'. Then in verses 11 and 12, they come back to life and ascend to heaven before the

---

[4] Mounce, *Revelation*, pp224-5
[5] Morris, *Revelation*, page 49
[6] Hendriksen, *More than Conquerors*, p126
[7] Ibid, p157
[8] G. K. Beale, *Book of Revelation*, NIGTC, Eerdmans, 1999, p584

eyes of their enemies. What does this all mean? These commentators take the dead bodies of the two witnesses lying unburied in the street for three and half days to mean that at the end of the age, Satan will overcome the church (for three and half days – i.e. 'a very brief time', Hendriksen[9]). Here is a 'brief period of apparent defeat for the church' (Wilcock[10]). They take this to symbolize the 'great tribulation'.

Surprisingly, the ascension mentioned here is taken literally: it is the 'rapture' of the church. 'This is no secret rapture!' says Hendriksen triumphantly[11]. Mounce enthusiastically agrees: 'the triumph of the witnesses is no secret rapture'[12]. All of a sudden, the spiritualizers turn biblical literalists, although almost everything else up to this point they have taken allegorically. They join in the mockery of a secret rapture with as much glee as the earth-dwellers rejoicing over the death of the two prophets.

Who are the two witnesses? Plainly, they are not the church. Contrary to what Morris suggests, the reference to the lampstands is not primarily pointing back to Revelation chapters 2 and 3; instead, the imagery of 'the two olive trees and two lampstands' (v4) seems to come from the book of Zechariah 4:2-3 where we have a lampstand standing beside two olive trees. These pictures are interpreted to mean 'the two anointed ones who stand beside the Lord of the whole earth' (Zech. 4:14), just like 'the two witnesses stand… before the God of the earth' (Rev. 11:4). In the context in Zechariah, they appear to refer to Zerubbabel and Joshua, the two men God raised up to rebuild the temple after the Babylonian exile.

This would seem to indicate that here in Revelation, as in Zechariah, the Bible is referring to two individuals. In addition, notice two ways that these witnesses bear more resemblance to Old Testament Jewish prophets than to the New Testament church. They are clothed in sackcloth, a common Old Testament form of mourning, and the plagues these prophets send upon the earth are reminiscent of the plagues Moses brought upon Egypt and Elijah brought upon Ahab's kingdom. Thus, these three points of reference (Zechariah, sackcloth, and plagues) take us back to Old Testament individuals, conditions and ministries. These two witnesses have more in common with the Old Testament than the New, and in them, we seem to have the reappearance of an Old Testament prophetic ministry. (Some would argue that we have the actual

---

[9] Hendriksen, *More than Conquerors*, p131
[10] Michael Wilcock, *The Message of Revelation*, BST, IVP, 1984, p106
[11] Hendriksen, p131
[12] Mounce, p228

reincarnation of Moses and Elijah, but this is neither stated in the passage, nor necessary).

It seems more reasonable to interpret this passage at its face value and understand these two witnesses who prophesy dressed in sackcloth for 1260 days as two actual people who witness for God during the great tribulation (outside a future, literal, earthly Jewish temple). Interpreting this passage at face value makes more sense than selectively spiritualizing it. The alternative, spiritualizing, scheme stands as a witness to the truth of the old adage: 'If the plain sense makes good sense, seek no other sense, lest it become nonsense'.

When do these two Prophets minister?
Do these two witnesses minister in the first half of the tribulation, or the second half – in the great tribulation? It is possible to argue that it is in the first half of the Tribulation period for the following reasons. (1) Verse 1 could suggest this, where we read about 'the altar, and those who worship there'. This might appear to indicate that the Jewish temple sacrifices are still being offered, and the Jewish people are worshipping in the temple. If the two witnesses minister during this time period, this would mean during the first half of the tribulation period. (2) The fact that 'the beast who ascends from the bottomless pit' kills the two witnesses. This is the way Revelation describes the resurrection of the Antichrist (Rev. 17:8, cf. 13:3). If Antichrist kills the two witnesses after he has been raised from the dead, his Satanically-empowered resurrection and killing of the two witnesses provide two reasons why the whole world will worship him. If the Antichrist is raised from the dead at the mid-point of the tribulation period to start his worldwide worship and the period of 'great tribulation', why would he wait until the end of the tribulation to kill the two witnesses if, being Satanically-indwelt, he has power to do so at any time?

Other commentators argue that the two prophets minister in the second half of the tribulation. Arguments for this position include the following: (1) that the 1260 days is always spoken of the second half of the tribulation period, the great tribulation, (2) that the trampling of Jerusalem occurs in the great tribulation during the worship of the Antichrist, and (3) that the seventh trumpet which follows the ministry of the two witnesses leads on to the millennium, for in the seventh trumpet (11:15) we have the announcement that the 'kingdoms of this world have become the kingdoms of our Lord and of His Christ'. (4) The Gentiles do not tread down the outer court of the Temple and the city of Jerusalem (Rev. 11:2) until the time of the great tribulation. Up until the abomination of desolation, the temple in Jerusalem is reinstated for Jewish worship, and Jews will be unmolested in worshipping the God of their fathers there. It would thus appear more likely that this is the second half of Daniel's seventieth week – the great tribulation.

Conclusion

Revelation 11 teaches that there will be a future temple in Jerusalem at whose altar Jewish worshippers will offer sacrifices in the future, and outside which two prophets will testify for God.

Many commentators tell us that Revelation 11 is 'extraordinarily difficult to interpret'[13]. The commentators' cries of "difficult" and "obscure" are a sign (to quote Bonar again) that 'false principles [of interpretation] most thoroughly perplex and over cloud the whole Word of God'. However, if we follow the simple procedure of considering all the alternative interpretations and eliminating those that are untenable, we find ourselves left with one remarkably simple and clear picture: there must yet be a temple built in Jerusalem by Jews who have still not turned to Christ.

---

[13] E.g. Morris, *Revelation*, p140

19 HAS THE CHURCH REPLACED ISRAEL?

Many theologians argue that the Church has replaced Israel. N. T. Wright says, 'Through the Messiah and the preaching which heralds him, Israel is transformed from being an ethnic people into a worldwide family . . . The Christians regarded themselves as a new family, directly descended from the family of Israel, but now transformed . . . they claimed to be the continuation of Israel in a new situation'[1]. Bruce Waltke writes, 'the kingdom promises are comprehensively fulfilled in the church, not in restored national Israel'[2].

In one sense, of course, all Christians would agree that the church has indeed replaced Israel, inasmuch as the church is the vehicle for God's activity in the world today, and Israel is not. The church has replaced Israel as the direct object of God's program of spiritual blessing in the world in our present age, which is why dispensationalists call this the 'church age'. After His parable of the wicked vinedressers, the Lord said to the Jews, 'Therefore I say to you, the kingdom of God will be taken from you and given to a nation bearing the fruits of it' (Matt. 22:43). The Lord appears to be talking about the church here, for the church is called a 'holy nation' in 1 Peter 2:9. Perhaps a better way to phrase the question, therefore, is to ask whether the church has *permanently* replaced Israel.

There are good biblical reasons to think that the church has not permanently replaced Israel. Instead, Israel has been shunted into a siding while the gospel express roars past, but Israel remains a distinct and important part of God's plans. Amillennialists, Postmillennialists and Historic Premillennialists all believe that the Church today is 'spiritual' Israel, and vice versa: Israel in the OT was the Church, and Israel and the Church are the one and the same thing.

In this chapter, we shall consider the question of whether this is true. Just at the level of word-usage, however, this seems doubtful, in that the Bible does not seem to use the words 'Israel' and 'the Church' interchangeably. Thus, it is significant that the word 'Israel' occurs 21

---

[1] N. T. Wright, *The New Testament and the People of God*, London: SPCK, 1992, pp447, 457
[2] Bruce Waltke, "Kingdom Promises as Spiritual", in *Continuity and Discontinuity: Perspectives on the Relationship between the Old and New Testaments*, ed. J. S. Feinberg, Wheaton, IL: Crossway, 1988, p264

times in the book of Acts and each occurrence refers to the ethnic people of Israel nationally. This is despite the fact that the book of Acts shows us the Church co-existing alongside national Israel during this period. Israel and the Church are two clearly distinguished and distinct groups of people. Charles Ryrie points to evidence from Romans 10, and says, 'In Paul's prayer for natural Israel (Rom. 10:1) there is a clear reference to Israel as a national people distinct from and outside the church'[3]. Arnold Fruchtenbaum points out that the word 'Israel' is used 73 times in the New Testament and is always used of ethnic Jews: 'Of these seventy-three citations, the vast majority refer to national, ethnic Israel. A few refer specifically to Jewish believers who still are ethnic Jews'[4].

Why do some theologians argue that the church is the true or new Israel, or spiritual Israel? A number of New Testament verses are sometimes claimed to equate Israel and the Church. Leon Morris gives a handy summary of this argument:

> The church can be referred to as the twelve tribes (James 1:1, cf. Matt. 19:28, Luke 22:30) and this is probably the thought when a letter is sent to 'the dispersion' (1 Pet. 1:1). The Christian appears to be the true Jew (Rom. 2:29) and the church the "Israel of God" (Gal. 6:16). Descriptions of the old Israel are piled up and applied to the church (1 Pet. 2:9, Eph. 1:11, 14). It is the church which is God's 'peculiar people' (Titus 2:4), and Christ's own who are 'Abraham's seed' (Gal. 3:29) and 'the circumcision' (Phil. 3:3)[5].

We shall look at eight verses with particular reference to this question: Acts 1:6, 7:36, Rom. 2:29, 9:6-8, 9:33, Gal. 6:16, James 1:1, 1 Peter 1:1.

Acts 1:6

In Acts 1:6, the disciples asked, 'Lord, will You at this time restore the kingdom to Israel?' Calvin commented: 'There are as many errors in this question as words. They ask him as concerning a kingdom; but they dream of an earthly kingdom, which should flow with riches, with dainties, with external peace, and with such like good things'.

However, in His reply, Christ did not deny the restoration of the kingdom to Israel. He did not say, 'O fools and slow of heart to understand

---

[3] Charles Ryrie, *Dispensationalism*, Chicago: Moody, 1995, p127
[4] Arnold Fruchtenbaum, "Israel and the Church", in *Issues in Dispensationalism*, ed. W. R. Willis and J. R. Master (Chicago: Moody, 1994, p120
[5] Leon Morris, *Revelation*, p114

all I have been teaching, do you not know that the Church is Israel and Israel is the Church?' Instead, the Lord said, 'It is not for you to know the times or seasons which the Father has put in His own power' (Acts 1:7). Campbell Morgan writes, 'Christ rebuked, not their conception that the kingdom is to be restored to Israel – for that he never rebuked – but their desire to know when it would take place . . . A popular interpretation of this is that Christ said to them: There is to be no restoration of the kingdom to Israel. Christ did not say so. What he said was: It is not for you to know the times or seasons. You have other work to do'[6].

Michael Vlach points out that Acts 1:3 tells us that after His resurrection Christ was 'speaking about the kingdom of God' with His disciples for 40 days; 'It seems unlikely that the disciples could be misguided in their perceptions of the kingdom after having received 40 days of instruction about it from the risen Lord'[7]. Vlach also argues that the fact that the Lord did not correct the disciples in Acts 1:7 would appear to validate their understanding of Israel's restoration: 'If the disciples had been wrong, Jesus probably would have corrected their misconception as He did on other occasions'[8].

Even more significantly, in Acts 3:21 Peter said about Christ, 'heaven must receive [Him] until the times of restoration of all things, which God has spoken by the mouth of all His holy prophets since the world began'. If we allow Scripture to interpret Scripture, and notice the way that Acts 3:21 answers the question of Acts 1:6 (the words 'restore/restoration' and 'time/times' are found in both verses), we are left with little alternative than to conclude that there is a future restoration of the kingdom promised to the nation of Israel. The 'times of the restoration of *all* things' presumably includes Israel, particularly in view of the fact that Peter was preaching inside the Temple courts in Acts 3 to 'Men of Israel' (3:11).

Calvin's comment, 'there are as many errors in this question as words', disparages the apostles of Christ who had been taught by Him during the forty days between His resurrection and ascension. To set oneself as an authority above the apostles of the risen Christ is a rather presumptuous claim to make. It is alarming to see Calvin doing so here.

Acts 7:38

In Acts 7:38, Stephen calls Israel the 'Church in the wilderness' (KJV). From this, some have argued that Israel was the Church in the Old

---

[6] G. Campbell Morgan, *The Acts of the Apostles*, Pickering and Inglis, 1946, p19
[7] Michael Vlach, *Has the Church Replaced Israel*, B&H, 2010, p191
[8] Ibid.

Testament. However, the Greek word for 'church', *ekklesia*, simply means a gathering or assembly of people. It was originally used to describe a Greek civic or political gathering, but by New Testament times it simply meant a 'gathering' in the most general of terms. Thus, it is also used in Acts 19:32 and 40 to refer to the mob of rioting Ephesian idolaters, people who were far from believers in the true God and certainly not members of any Christian church. The word cannot be restricted to simply the Christian Church. Rather, the context determines what sort of gathering is referred to. There were many types of gatherings of people in the Roman world and the mere designation of these gatherings as *ekklesiai* does not grant them Church or Christian status. Likewise, to call the congregation of Israel in the wilderness an *ekklesia* was not an attempt by Stephen to identify them as part of the Christian Church, but simply a descriptive term used for gatherings in general.

Another similar argument is based on the Hebrew word *qahal* translated by 'assembly' or 'congregation' many times in the Old Testament. The fact that Israel is often referred to as the 'congregation' (particularly in the wilderness) and the further fact that this word is equivalent to the Greek word *ekklesia* (it is so translated in the Septuagint, the Greek OT) is taken by some to prove the equivalence of Israel with the Church.

However, again, the Hebrew word *qahal* has no technical meaning – it refers to gatherings of all sorts in the Old Testament. Brown, Driver, Briggs define it as 'an assembly specially convoked ... for evil counsel (Gen. 49:6, etc.), for civil affairs (Prov. 5:14, etc.), for war or invasion, (Num. 22:4, etc.), a company of returning exiles, (Jer. 31:8, etc.), for religious purposes, (Deut. 5:19, etc.), for feasts, fasts and worship (2 Chron. 20:5, etc.)'. *Qahal* was not a technical term for Israel as the people of God.

The argument, therefore, that *ekklesia* means the church, and that *qahal* means Israel, and therefore that the church is the continuation of Israel, is based on nothing more than ignorance of the usage of these words.

James 1:1 and 1 Peter 1:1

To the twelve tribe scattered abroad', 'to the pilgrims of the Dispersion (James 1:1, 1 Peter 1:1)

James' reference to the Christian recipients of his letter being 'the twelve tribes which are scattered abroad' is often taken to show that the Christian church is now the true Israel. Thus, F. F. Bruce, writing in *New Testament History* calls the Church 'the true remnant of the people of God, the Israel of the new age'[9], for as he later goes on to say, 'that the Jewish Christians continued for decades to regard themselves as the true remnant of Israel, the 'twelve tribes', is implied by the superscription of the Epistle of James'[10]. Likewise, Peter addressed his first letter to the 'pilgrims of the Diaspora'. This word 'diaspora' refers to the 'dispersion' or 'scattering' of Jews throughout the Roman world – there were more Jews outside Israel in the days of Christ than living in Israel. Peter's use of the word 'diaspora' when addressing his Christian readers has also led to the conclusion that he regarded, and addressed, the church as Israel.

However, F. F. Bruce himself refers twelve times in his *New Testament History* to the word 'diaspora' and in every case it simply refers to the ethnic Jewish communities scattered throughout the Roman Empire, not to Christians. The term, in its ordinary and common usage, refers to Jews, not to Christians. Thus, the question becomes: should we take the terms 'the twelve tribes' and 'diaspora' at their face-value meaning – referring to ethnic Jews – or should we read into them a cryptic significance demonstrating that the Church is the 'true' Israel?

A problem with the idea that 'the twelve tribes' refers to the church is that Paul used this term in Acts 26:7 before King Agrippa to refer to the Jewish nation. Thus, the NT apostles seem to use it in its ordinary sense.

Galatians 2:7-9 tells us that the mission of both Peter and James was principally to preach the gospel to the 'circumcision', to Jews, whilst Paul's mission was to be to the 'uncircumcision', the Gentiles. Both James' and Peters' letters assume their readers lived a Jewish way of life:

- the believers met in a 'synagogue' (James 2:2)
- the believers lived 'among the Gentiles' (1 Peter 2:12)
- James writes about the Jewish Law, teaching his readers of a properly Christian understanding of the law as the law of freedom (James 1:25, 2:8, 2:12)
- God is referred to as 'the Lord of Sabaoth', a Hebrew title for God (James 5:4)
- Peter reminds his readers of the Christian significance of events of Jewish historical importance –the girding up of the loins (1:13), the Passover lamb (1:19) and the temple (2:5).

---

[9] F. F. Bruce, *New Testament History,* Pickering and Inglis, 1982, p196
[10] Ibid, p200

No doubt the commission God gave to Peter and James, to preach the good news of Christ to Jews, would also have involved shepherding such people after they became Christians. Thus, it is not impossible to take James' and Peter's words at their ordinary meaning: they were writing to Jewish people amongst the Jewish Dispersion who had become Christians. Seeing that James and Peter, as apostles to the Jews, can be understood in their plain and normal sense as writing to Jewish believers, why should we try to read a cryptic significance into the expressions they use to greet their Jewish readers? That is not to say that Gentile Christians cannot benefit from these letters – just as we benefit from Paul's letters to the Corinthians although we never lived in first century Corinth. Simply put, the terms 'the twelve tribes' and 'diaspora' used in the address line of James' and Peter's letters are to be taken as referring to the actual original recipients of these letters – Jewish Christians who lived outside Israel. There is no warrant for reading other deeper meanings into these words, much less basing a doctrine of replacement upon them.

Romans 2:29
'But he is a Jew who is one inwardly; and circumcision is that of the heart, in spirit, not in letter; whose praise is not from men but from God.

Wayne Grudem writes, 'Paul recognizes that though there is a literal or natural sense in which people who physically descended from Abraham are to be called Jews, there is also a deeper or spiritual sense in which a "true Jew" is one who is inwardly a believer and whose heart has been cleansed by God'[11].

However, if we read this verse in its context, and if we look at other Bible references to the circumcision of the heart, it becomes clear that Paul is not writing about Christians who have been forgiven of their sins.

In Romans 2, Paul is not (yet) showing us the way of salvation; he is teaching that all people are sinners (Romans 1), even Jews (Romans 2), and warning us of God's judgment. Paul clearly states that God is going to judge all people on the basis of their deeds, that is, their works (Rom. 2:6), whether Jews or Gentiles. In verse 13, Paul states that one way someone can escape God's judgment is to be perfectly sinless: 'the doers of the law will be justified'. That is, those who continually and perfectly keep the law of God will escape God's judgment. These verses puzzle some Christians because they seem to teach salvation by works. However, Paul is not teaching salvation by works, because he is not talking about salvation

---

[11] Wayne Grudem, *Systematic Theology*, p861

at all – yet. He is simply showing that the standard of works-righteousness is perfection, a standard all men fall short of, as he goes on to state in Romans 3:23. From there onwards he proceeds to show how we are saved through the redemption that is in Christ Jesus, and faith in Him.

But before Paul gets to Romans 3, he deals with the Jewish legalist who thinks he is going to inherit eternal life because of his Jewish birth and law-keeping (Romans 2:17-29). Here, Paul shows that the Jew fails to keep the law, and is as guilty as the Gentile. Paul says that circumcision is irrelevant to the question of who will inherit eternal life; all that counts is perfectly keeping the law of God, whether a person is a Jew or Gentile (2:26-29).

Paul thus concludes his argument in verse 29 – not by introducing Christian salvation – but by showing the futility of Jewish confidence in circumcision. He says that 'he is a Jew who is one inwardly; and circumcision is that of the heart, in spirit, not in letter; whose praise is not from men but from God' (Rom. 2:29). The same expression is used in Deuteronomy 10:16, 30:6 and Jeremiah 4:4, not to teach forgiveness of sin through faith in Christ, but to warn proud Jewish hearts that the external trappings of religion are not enough: 'therefore circumcise the foreskin of your heart, and be stiff-necked no longer' (Deuteronomy 10:16).

Nowhere in Romans 2 has Paul yet introduced the idea of salvation by grace through faith in Christ. Nor is there any reason to read the Holy Spirit (many Bible versions capitalize the word Spirit in verse 29), and therefore conversion, into the verse. Paul is contrasting outward externals like circumcision with the inner man of the spirit. 'Receiving praise from God' shows that this verse is not talking about salvation, for which God gets all the glory and praise (Eph. 1:6), but about someone perfectly keeping God's law, by which they would merit eternal life and God's praise by their own efforts. There has only been one Man who has ever lived up to the standard of perfect righteousness, circumcision of the heart, and rightly deserved eternal life and the praise of God by His own efforts – our Lord Jesus Christ.

Therefore, we conclude that Romans 2:29 is not speaking about Christian salvation, not is it saying that a Christian is a 'true Jew'. Nor is the verse referring to believing (i.e. Christian) Jews who have received spiritual circumcision of the heart – not by their own efforts but by God's grace (cf. Fruchtenbaum's argument that Paul is trying to make a distinction between believing and non-believing ethnic Jews[12]). No, the

---

[12] Arnold Fruchtenbaum, "Israel and the Church", in *Issues in Dispensationalism*, ed. W. R. Willis and J. R. Masters, Chicago: Moody, 1994, p128

passage says nothing about faith in Christ, whether by Jews or Gentiles. Paul leaves faith in Christ till Romans 3 and 4. Paul is trying to show Jews that they stand guilty before God, just like the Gentiles. Paul even writes about the theoretical case of a Gentile who perfectly keeps the law of God written on his heart (not that anyone has ever done so), but only to show Jews that externals like nationality and circumcision will not avail in the Day of Judgment.

William MacDonald writes, 'A real Jew is the one who is not only a descendant of Abraham but who also manifests a godly life. This passage does not teach that all believers are Jews, nor that the church is the Israel of God. Paul is talking about those who are born of Jewish parentage and is insisting that the mere fact of birth and the ordinance of circumcision are not enough... A real Jew is one whose character is such as to receive praise from God'[13].

The argument of Grudem here is based on a misunderstanding of the flow of Paul's argument in Romans; Grudem is jumping ahead to things that Paul has not yet introduced.

Galatians 6:16 – 'The Israel of God'

Perhaps the most common argument made to prove that Israel has replaced the Church is found in Galatians 6:15-16: 'For in Christ Jesus neither circumcision nor uncircumcision avails anything, but a new creation. And as many as walk according to this rule, peace and mercy be upon them, and upon the Israel of God'.

Because the word 'and' here (Gk: *kai*) can also be translated 'even', this verse is read by some as follows: 'mercy and peace upon those who are a new creation in Christ Jesus, even upon the Israel of God'. In other words, those in Christ are the Israel of God, the true Israel.

However, there are a number of problems with this interpretation of Galatians 6:16. Firstly, although the Greek word *kai* sometimes means 'even' (e.g. 1 Cor. 2:10), it is far more commonly used to simply mean 'and'. S. Lewis Johnson writes about this verse, 'We should avoid the rarer grammatical usages when the common ones make good sense'[14]. Therefore, it is doubtful that we should translate the verse with 'even' here, and the more natural way to understand it is 'and'. This means that Paul is referring to two different groups of people: 'mercy and peace upon those who are a new creation in Christ and upon [a second group of people] the

---

[13] William MacDonald, *Believers Bible Commentary*, Nelson, 1995, p 1685
[14] S. Lewis Johnson, "Paul and the Israel of God", in *Essays in Honor of J. Dwight Pentecost*, ed. Stanley D. Toussaint and Charles H. Dyer, Moody, 1986, p187

Israel of God'.

As we shall see when we look at our next reference in Romans 9:6-8, Paul is not equating the 'Israel of God' with the church. Instead, the 'Israel of God' refers to Jewish believers in Christ, a subset of all those who are 'in Christ'. The verse is pronouncing a special blessing on Jews in Christ who walk by faith, and by contrast calling down a curse (Gal. 1:8, 9, 5:10, 12) upon the false-brethren (Gal. 2:4), the Judaizers causing all the problems in the churches of Galatia.

The very ambiguity of the word 'and/even' here means that the verse does not explicitly state that the church is Israel. The argument, at best, falls short of proof.

A more serious problem with this argument is that there is another passage in Scripture which teaches us what the 'Israel of God' refers to, Romans 9:6 – and it is not the Church.

Romans 9:6-8

Romans 9:6 says, 'They are not all Israel which are of Israel'. Grudem writes, 'Paul here implies that the true children of Abraham, those who are in the most true sense "Israel," are not the nation of Israel by physical descent from Abraham but those who have believed in Christ'[15].

But what Paul means by 'they are not all Israel who are of Israel' becomes clear in the words that follow: 'nor are they all children because they are the seed of Abraham; but, In Isaac your seed shall be called. ⁸ That is, those who are the children of the flesh, these are not the children of God; but the children of the promise are counted as the seed' (Rom 9:7-8).

What Paul means here is not that believing Gentiles are the 'true Israel', but rather that Jews who believe in Christ are, in the most true sense, "Israel". In other words, the true Israel is the subset of national, ethnic Israel who are also children of God by faith in Jesus Christ. To quote even Douglas J. Moo in his commentary on Romans (who, by the way, believes the Israel of God in Galatians 6:16 refers to the Church): 'There is, Paul suggests, in keeping with the OT 'remnant' theology, a spiritual Israel within a larger ethnic Israel. Paul may elsewhere use 'Israel' to denote the entire people of God, both Jew and Gentile (Galatians 6:16). Here, however, as the sequel makes clear, he is thinking only of Jews'[16].

In modern parlance, the true Israel of Romans 9:6-8 are the so-called Messianic Jews or 'Jews for Jesus'. The 'true Israel' in these verses has

---

[15] Grudem, *Systematic Theology*, p861
[16] Douglas Moo, Romans, *New Bible Commentary*, IVP, 1994, p1143

nothing to do with any idea of anyone outside of ethnic Israel, or the incorporation of Gentiles who have become Christians, into Israel. These verses are not teaching that the Church is the 'true Israel'. Rather, the verses in Romans 9:6-8 are teaching an Israel within Israel. The true Israel is the Jewish section of the Church.

Galatians 6:16 (again)

Therefore, returning again to the verse in Galatians 6:16, the 'Israel of God' means Jewish believers in Christ, the true Israel within ethnic Israel, as opposed to those ethnic unbelieving Jews or Judaizing false-brethren persecuting the Galatian Christians.

One further problem with the view that 'the Israel of God' means the Christian Church is the fact that nowhere else in the NT is the identification of the Church with Israel made. We would expect Paul to have explicitly spelled out that the Church was now the true Israel in Romans chapters 9 to 11 if this were the case, for these chapters are dealing with the vexed question of what God's purposes for Israel involve. However, these chapters are completely devoid of any explicit identification of the church as the true Israel.

The verse in Galatians 6:16 is the best example of identification that can be produced, but it is at best ambiguous and at worst simply mistaken. This is significant, for we would expect the New Testament to repeatedly and explicitly affirm such an important point as the fact that the Church was now the new, true Israel. To first century Jews, whether Christian or not, the question of who was or was not an Israelite was of great importance.

If we are going to base our doctrinal position about the relationship of Israel and the Church on actual New Testament verses, we are going to need something more than a solitary, ambiguous expression in Galatians 6:16. We should be able to point to such an identification in repeated and explicit references. Instead, the New Testament provides nothing in the way of direct identification of Israel with the Church. The only help (by way of cross-references) about what the Israel of God in Galatians 6:16 might be is found in the verses in Romans 9:6-8 which speak not about the Israel of God encompassing both Jewish and Gentile Christians, but the very opposite, a restricted segment of Judaism, those believing in Christ.

Romans 9:23-26

> And that He might make known the riches of His glory on the vessels of mercy, which He had prepared beforehand for glory, 24 even us whom He called, not of the Jews only, but also of the Gentiles? 25 As He says also in Hosea: "I will call them My people, who were not My people, And her beloved, who was not beloved. 26 And it shall come to pass in the place where it was said to them, 'You are not My people,' there they shall be called sons of the living God'.

In Hosea, God calls Israel Lo-Ruhamah ('no mercy', Hos. 1:6) and Lo-Ammi ('not My people', Hos. 1:9) but then goes on to say in Hos. 1:10 that, 'in the place where it was said to them, 'You are not My people', there it shall be said to them, 'You are the sons of the living God', 'My people' and those shown 'mercy' (Hos. 2:1).

But here in Romans, Paul takes this quote from Hosea, which in its original context refers to ethnic Israel, and applies it to the church. He says it applies to 'the vessels of mercy', 'even us whom He called, not of the Jews only, but also of the Gentiles' (Rom. 9:24).

Those who suggest that the church has replaced Israel argue that Paul's inspired New Testament interpretation provides us with guidance for how we should understand Hosea's message. The inspired New Testament proves that the church has replaced Israel.

But there are two problems with this argument. Firstly, the story of Hosea presents a problem for this explanation. Hosea was told to marry a prostitute who would turn away from him and commit adultery (Hos. 1:2). But then Hosea was told to redeem and take her back to himself again (3:1-5). This was to be a picture of God's mercy on spiritually adulterous Israel. The story of Hosea is saying that God will eventually bring back faithless Israel to Himself. The story of Hosea suggests that God has not replaced Israel, and taken a different wife instead, the church.

Further, the actual wording of Hosea, interpreted in its original context, assures us that the same people Israel who were unfaithful to God were going to be taken again as His people, and 'in the same place' (Hos. 1:10-11). That is, God's restoration of unfaithful Israel will happen in the land of Israel. Hosea is saying that specific people (Israel) in a specific place (the land of Israel) will one day again be joined to God. It is not possible to retain any biblical integrity if we selectively ignore these statements, cherry-pick other parts of the prophecy, rip them out of their original context, and apply them to the church.

Unless we are willing to deny the inspiration of the words of the book of Hosea, and deny its storyline and meaning, we cannot accept the idea that God has replaced Israel. But how then can Paul take this Old Testament quote and apply it to a different group of people, the church?

There are two things that need to be observed about Paul's treatment of Hosea. The first is that that Paul is not denying the original context or meaning of Hosea's prophecy. Paul specifically says that this prophecy in Hosea applies 'not [to] the Jews only' (Rom. 9:24). In other words, it applies to its original recipients, the Jews. But Paul also extends and expands its application to the Gentiles also.

How can Paul take Hosea and apply his prophecy to the Gentiles, though, if it was originally spoken to the Jews? The answer is that while Hosea literally applies to Israel, Paul applies it ultra-literally here to also include the Gentiles. What do I mean by ultra-literally? Just that the words 'not God's people' (in and of themselves) normally refer to Gentiles, so that Paul can take the prophecy and apply it to Gentiles, in that Gentiles were once not God's people, nor had they been shown mercy by God. But now that Gentiles have become God's people, Hosea has become true for them, even though it was not directly spoken to them. We could put it this way: Hosea's words, in context, apply to Israel, but in an ultra-literal sense, they are also true of Gentiles.

Thus, Paul is not repudiating Hosea's original message, nor is he replacing Israel with the church. After all, Romans chapters 9-11 are the very chapters in which Paul insists that God has not cast off Israel (Rom. 11:1-2), but that eventually all Israel will be saved (Rom. 11:26). Instead, Paul expands the application of the prophecy to also include Gentiles as well as Israel. That might surprise us as an unusual way to handle Scripture, but it is not true to say that Paul denies the original meaning or application.

Other Verses
Appeals are sometimes made to other verses to identify the church with Israel, for example, the verses quoted by Morris: 1 Pet. 2:9, Eph. 1:11, 14, Titus 2:4, Gal. 3:29, and Phil. 3:3. However, while these verses show that the church and Israel have things in common (they are both God's people, Abraham's children, God's possession, the circumcision, etc.), yet none of these verses go the necessary step further and describe the church as the new Israel or the true Israel. These verses show us that the church shares in many of Israel's blessings, but not that the church supersedes or replaces Israel. The Church is the 'people of God' just as much as Israel were 'the

people of God', because we belong to God just as Israel did. There is a continuity between Israel and the Church – we belong to God – as well as discontinuity.

Summary
None of these oft-quoted proof-texts prove that the Christian Church is to be understood as the new or true Israel. The biblical case for the Church being the true Israel is as weak as the watered-down grape juice some churches put out at the Lord's Supper. There is not one verse that clearly states this idea. We conclude with the words of Michael Vlach: the idea that the church has replaced Israel is 'not a biblical doctrine. There are compelling scriptural reasons in both Testaments to believe in a future salvation and restoration of the nation Israel'[17].

New Testament Evidence of a Distinction between Israel and the Church

In addition to the failure of the arguments for identifying the Church as the New Israel, we shall here look at the two main arguments for a distinction between Israel and the Church: firstly, the church is a new thing, and secondly, the church is a different thing from Israel.

The Church is a New Thing

When did the church begin? Does the church include all the Israelites of the Old Testament or does it only include New Testament believers?

The first argument for a distinctly New Testament church is found in Christ's own references to the Church in the Gospels. These seem to provide good evidence that the church only started in the New Testament, for it is noticeable that His references to the church are in the future tense.

- And I also say to you that you are Peter, and on this rock I will build My church (Matthew 16:18)
- And other sheep I have which are not of this fold; them also I must bring, and they will hear My voice; and there will be one flock and one shepherd (John 10:16)

Both of these verses speak of Christ bringing His Church into existence in the future. Notice in passing that Christ refers to the Church in very personal terms here – He calls it 'My church' and says 'I have other sheep'.

---

[17] Michael Vlach, *Has the Church Replaced Israel*, p3

Christ uses the term 'My Church' in Mt 16, when he is making a clear distinction between people who believe in Him like Peter, who had just confessed Him as the Christ the Son of the Living God, and the crowds who do not believe in Him (but who are still members of Israel).

The fact that so little reference is made to the Church in the gospels (the word is only used twice in the gospels) is best explained on the ground that it did not yet exist. If it did already exist, why did Christ not make more reference to it, give more teaching or explanation about it, or make clear that his followers were already members of His church? Instead, Christ hardly mentioned the church in the gospels, instead majoring on the Kingdom.

A second argument for the church only starting in the New Testament involves the prominent metaphor of the Church, the building. The New Testament repeatedly stresses the fact that Christ is the Church's foundation or corner-stone. However, notice that in Ephesians 2:20, the New Testament apostles and prophets are the next layer of the foundation on top of Christ:

> having been built on the foundation of the apostles and prophets, Jesus Christ Himself being the chief cornerstone (Eph. 2:20).

If it were true that the Church is a continuation of Old Testament Israel, then surely it would have been more correct to state that the church is built on the foundation of patriarchs, prophets, priests and kings, on top of which rest the apostles. In what sense are apostles the foundation of the church if it started with Adam? Rather, everything starts with Christ and His apostles – the patriarchs and kings are not a part of the picture at all.

It is clear that Ephesians 2:20 is referring to New Testament prophets (rather than Old Testament prophets), and in proof of this we may notice what Paul says later in Ephesians:

- as it has now been revealed by the Spirit to His holy apostles and prophets that the Gentiles should be fellow heirs, of the same body, and partakers of His promise in Christ through the gospel (Ephesians 3:5-6)
- And He Himself gave some to be apostles, some prophets, some evangelists, and some pastors and teachers, for the equipping of the saints for the work of ministry, for the edifying of the body of Christ (Ephesians 4:11-12)

Quite obviously, Paul is referring to New Testament prophets when he links them with apostles (and other New Testament gifts) in these references in Ephesians. Therefore, the reference to the Church 'being built on the foundation of the apostles and prophets' is referring to New Testament prophets, not Old Testament prophets. The church is a New Testament entity, not an Old Testament carry-over.

A third argument which suggests that the church is something new comes from Ephesians 3, where Paul speaks of the mystery (v3):

> as it has now been revealed by the Spirit to His holy apostles and prophets that the Gentiles should be fellow heirs, of the same body, and partakers of His promise in Christ through the gospel (Ephesians 3:5-6)

Paul's great subject in Ephesians 3 is that the church, composed of Jews and Gentiles, is a mystery. In Ephesians 5:32, Paul again directly states that the church is a mystery:

> This is a great mystery, but I speak concerning Christ and the Church.

The New Testament speaks of the Church as a mystery. The word 'mystery' does not mean a riddle or an enigma when it is used in the New Testament. Instead, it means something once hidden and unknown, but now revealed and understood.

Notice two logical implications of the fact that the church is a mystery:

1. The idea that Gentiles were going to be blessed by God was not a mystery in the Old Testament. It was not hidden or unknown. It is mentioned in various places: Genesis 12:3 (the promise to Abraham that all nations would be blessed), Isaiah 2:2-4 (the promise that the Gentile nations would learn God's laws and ways), Isaiah 11:9 (the promise that the earth would be full of the knowledge of God as the waters cover the sea), Amos 9:12 (the promise quoted by James in Acts 15 that the Gentiles would be blessed), and Malachi 1:11 (the promise that 'from the rising of the sun to the going down of the same', God's name would be great among the Gentiles). Therefore, while future Gentile spiritual blessing is not a mystery that is hidden or unknown in the Old Testament, Paul here states that the church which is jointly composed of Jew and Gentile is a mystery. The church therefore must be something new which is not taught in the Old Testament.
2. On the other hand, the term mystery cannot be applied to Israel. Israel

was never a mystery, either in Old Testament days, or even today. Everybody in the geographical region of Israel in Old Testament days knew of the existence of Israel. There was no special revelation required for a Philistine to understand what Israel was. Neither does it require spiritual illumination today for a non-Christian to understand what the nation Israel is.

This leaves the argument that the church is the same thing as Israel with a problem. Maybe there are ways it could be solved, but it would appear from the fact that the mystery of the Church was not revealed until Christ and His apostles (Eph 3:5), that the Church is something that came into existence at this point, and did not exist before, as Israel did.

Fourthly, while we are still in Ephesians, the Church is spoken of as an entirely new concept in Ephesians 2:15: 'having abolished in His flesh the enmity, that is, the law of commandments contained in ordinances, so as to create in Himself *one new man* from the two [i.e. the Jew and the Gentile], thus making peace'.

Notice that Christ has created something new that did not exist before – a new man. Whereas before there were Jews and Gentiles, now in the Church an entirely novel creation is introduced – the Christian. Notice the many other 'new' things introduced by Christ:

- He gave us new wine and new garments (Mt. 9:16-17) – not a patched-up or filled-out version of Judaism, but a distinctly new religion.
- He brought a new doctrine (Mk 1:27)
- He gave us a new commandment, to love one another (John 13:34) – notice, not an additional commandment, but a new commandment.
- He instituted a new covenant (Mt. 26, 1 Cor1, 2 Cor 3, Heb 8, 9, 12).
- We are a new creation (2 Cor. 5:17, Gal. 6:15), something not in existence beforehand.
- He has made a new (and living) way into God's presence (Heb 10:20)

Someone might argue that 'new' can mean 'reinvigorated, restored, or reformed, superseding and more advanced than others of the same kind'. But Christ did not come to reinvigorate or reform (or patch up) Judaism. His coming brought about a new creation – something new that did not exist before. It would instead appear to be the case that the intention behind Christ's institution of all these new things was to introduce something which never existed before.

Of course, there are similarities, parallels and continuities between Israel and the Church, and we must not try to say that Israel and the Church are to be distinguished as light from darkness. But the new/old distinction means that these similarities cannot be taken to mean there is no difference at all nor any distinction between Israel and the Church. Rather, the introduction of so many new things indicates that there is a discontinuity of such magnitude between Israel and the Church that the two may not be considered to share the same identity.

A fifth argument for a distinctly New Testament church comes from Colossians 1:18 which seems to state that the Church started with Christ, and that it started with Christ in resurrection: 'And He is the head of the body, the church, who is the beginning, the firstborn from the dead, that in all things He may have the pre-eminence'.

The phrase 'who is the beginning' is ambiguous. Is it saying that Christ is the beginning of the Church or of the Resurrection? The answer would seem to be that Christ is the beginning of both the Church and the great resurrection harvest.

This much is clear: the main subject of the verse is the Church. The main focus is not upon the doctrine of resurrection, but on Christ's pre-eminence in the Church. Seeing then that the main subject of the verse is Christ's relationship to the Church it seems warranted to apply the statement that 'Christ is the beginning' to the Church as well as to the resurrection which follows on. We might summarize the teaching of the verse by saying that it defines Christ's relationship to the Church – in addition to being the head of the body, He is the beginning of the Church ... by his resurrection.

Here is the main point, then. The Church did not start with Abraham or Adam. Rather, the Church started with Christ. Furthermore, it started with Christ in resurrection, as Colossians 1:18 tells us, not Christ in creation, to which Paul had earlier referred.

One might object to this argument by saying that the verse is using the word 'beginning' here in the sense of 'source', as in Christ is the 'cause' behind the Church's existence, or the 'reason' that the Church exists. Although it is true that Christ is the one who brought the Church into existence, Paul's argument about Christ's pre-eminence in the Church seems to go beyond this to indicate a temporal factor. We see this from the parallels between Paul's argument about Christ's pre-eminence in Creation and in the Church:

- Christ is pre-eminent in Creation because (a) He created it (Col 1:16),

and also (b) because He was 'before' it (Colossians 1:17).
- Likewise, Christ is pre-eminent in the Church ('He is the head') because (a) it came into existence through His resurrection (Col 1:18) and (b) He was 'the beginning' of the Church (Col 1:18).

Just as Christ is pre-eminent in creation because He was before it and created it (verses 16 and 17), so too, Paul wants us to notice the parallel in relation to the Church. 'Christ ... who is the beginning' has pre-eminence in the Church because it *began* with His resurrection.

Paul's argument in Colossians is intended to cut off the claim of false-teachers that they know of a better way for the Colossians to live (whether under Jewish law or under pagan religious practices). Paul's argument is that the Church must stick to its founding principles – 'that which is from the beginning' to use the language of 1 John – and Christ is the One with whom the Church began. Christ has priority over any other human teachers in the Church or their doctrines – He was there at the beginning.

A sixth argument for the church commencing only in New Testament times is that membership in the Church involves spiritual union with Christ Himself through participation in Christ's death, burial, resurrection and new life in Christ. The confirmation that such a spiritual union with Christ had indeed taken place was seen by the indwelling of God's Spirit in different groups of people newly admitted to the Church (Samaritans – Acts 8:17, Gentiles Acts 10:44, see also Acts 1:4-5 and 1 Cor. 12:13). Thus, the coming of the Holy Spirit is linked in a special way with entrance into the Church, marking out the Church as a spiritual body. In this, the Church is distinct from Israel, a physical nation, none of whose members were indwelt by God's Spirit in the permanent way that all Christians in the Church are. The special links between the Church and the Spirit of God mark out Pentecost as the most plausible candidate for the inception point of the Church.

The Church is a Different Thing

There are many differences between Old Testament Israel and the New Testament church, but we will briefly consider three:

a. The work of the Holy Spirit is quite different in Israel to what we find in the Church. The Holy Spirit was not resident in people in the Old Testament. Instead, the Holy Spirit came upon certain people for certain tasks and for periods of time. Samson is a case in point. We read that 'the Spirit of the LORD began to move upon him' (Judges

13:25) and then 'the Spirit of the LORD came mightily upon him (14:6, 14:19, 15:14), but then we later read that 'the LORD had departed from him (16:20). Likewise, the Holy Spirit came upon Saul (1 Sam. 10:10) but later left him when David was anointed by Samuel (1 Sam 16). David himself, felt it necessary to pray that God would not remove His Spirit from him after his sin with Bathsheba (Psalm 51:11). The situation is completely different with believers in the Church who are promised that (a) all believers are indwelt by the Spirit (Romans 8:9) – not just certain Christian leaders and (b) that the Spirit will be with us forever (John 14:16).

b. Another difference is between the Sabbath day and the Lord's Day. Not a few Christians are guilty of confusing the two, but the differences are abundant and obvious. Keeping the Sabbath is commandment number four in the Decalogue, but whilst all the other nine commandments are repeated in the New Testament, the Sabbath law is not, despite the dread seriousness with which the Old Testament treated violations of it. Instead, the Christians in the New Testament meet together on the First Day of the Week (John 20:1, 19, 26, Acts 20:7, 1 Cor. 16:2), which is likely the same as the Lord's Day of Revelation 1:10. However, the First Day of the New Testament is not a Sabbath in which work is unable to be performed. Instead, it is the day of Christian gathering. The Sabbath was given as a reminder of Creation (Exodus 20:8-11), because it was on the seventh Day that God rested. On the other hand, the Christian observance of the First Day of the Week points to the day of Christ's resurrection. We may therefore say that the Sabbath is a reminder for an earthly people of the proper place they should give to their Creator, whereas the Christian First Day of the week is a reminder of the new creation inaugurated in Christ's resurrection, applying only to a spiritual institution, the church. The differences, on one level, are minor – just shifting the 'special' day by 24 hours. However, at a deeper level, they are symbolic of a ground-shift in God's purposes. Both 'special days' converge together in their future emphasis upon a Sabbath Rest when the New Creation is complete, but at the present their divergences flag a profound difference between Israel and the Church.

c. There are many other significant differences which arise from the fact that the New Testament Christian is not under the Old Testament law. We do not offer animal sacrifices, nor do we abstain from certain foods, nor is there any longer the keeping of certain feast days like Passover (failure to keep which resulted in excommunication from Israel, Numbers 9:13), nor can there be a separation between Jew and Gentile in the Church, as there was in Old Testament times. Many other examples could be given to show that the Church is different in many important practical ways from Israel.

Israel has a Distinct Future
Even in the future state when all God's people are together, there is a difference noted between Israel and the church. For example, in Revelation 21:10-14, the New Jerusalem is described with twelve gates named after the 'twelve tribes of the children of Israel' and twelve foundations upon which are the names of the apostles of the Lamb. We have already argued earlier in the book that this passage is describing the New Jerusalem in the millennium, as can be seen from all the parallels in Isaiah. The fact that Israel and the Church are both named as partakers in the New Jerusalem shows, on the one hand, the unity of Israel and the Church as 'people of God', jointly sharing in the blessings of that age, but it also maintains a distinction between the two. Michael Vlach comments:

> The 12 tribes of Israel are distinguished from the "Lamb's 12 apostles" of verse 14. Thus, this passage shows that the Israel-church distinction is still maintained to some degree even in the eternal state. This passage also rules out any idea that the 12 tribes of Israel were only a temporary type that has been superseded by the 12 apostles. The 12 tribes of Israel, who are the foundation of national Israel, are viewed as distinct from the 12 apostles (see Eph. 2:20). As [Robert] Thomas puts it, "It is significant that John brings together the 12 tribes of Israel and the 12 apostles here, and makes a distinction between them. Jesus did the same earlier (Matt. 19:28; Luke 22:30). This distinction shows the wrongness of identifying the 12 tribes in 7:4-8 with the church"[18].

Romans 11, as we have seen, teaches a future Jewish turning in faith to Christ at the time of His coming. Even commentators who do not consider Israel to have any future distinctive position or role in God's purposes consider this to be the unavoidable interpretation of the passage.

---

[18] Michael J. Vlach, *Has the Church Replaced Israel?* p198-9

For example, Grudem argues that:

> Even on the nondispensational view, a person may hold that there will be a future large-scale conversion of the Jewish people (Rom. 11:12, 15, 23-24, 25-26, 28-31)[19].

However, the idea of a national conversion for Israel is really only possible if there is something special about the nation of Israel. Of no other nation does Scripture offer a prophecy of wholesale conversion on an ethnic basis. Thus, to admit a future national conversion and yet say that the Jews are not a special nation is contradictory.

Theologians like Grudem argue that Israel will be converted and become part of the Church at Christ's coming, but there are major problems with this idea. Various Scriptures seem to indicate this national conversion event will happen at the time of Christ's coming – not before it (cf. Zechariah 12:10). Furthermore, these converted Israelites continue to live on earth after this event in the same state in which they lived before, mourning for Christ (see Zechariah 12:10-14), abolishing idolatry and false-prophets from the land (Zech. 13:2-3). In other words, Israel will not participate in the resurrection of believers in the Church. They are not part of the Church whose *terminus ad quem* is the rapture and resurrection. While the church will be transformed and resurrected, Israel will have been 'left behind' and persist as a nation after Christ's coming, living on during His millennial reign (Zech. 14:9-21).

Paul's argument for a future national conversion of Israel in Romans 11 is based on the fulfilment of Old Testament prophecy (Isaiah 59:20-21) and on Israel's ancient election as God's special people (Romans 11:2, 28). Such 'special nation status' is incompatible with the church-age principle that 'there is no distinction between Jew and Gentile, for the same Lord over all is rich to all who call upon Him' (Romans 10:12).

The real crux of the issue, in relation to Israel and the Church, is not when the Jews' special status kicks in again – whether at Christ's return or before. The real issue is whether the Jews have a special place in the future at all. This is the main reason why some amillennialist theologians are prepared to argue the absurd proposition that Romans 11 is not teaching a future Jewish national conversion (e.g. Robert Strimple[20]). If nearly everyone else agrees that sometime in the future this 'special status' becomes operative again, then the only issue is the minor technicality of

---

[19] Wayne Grudem, *Systematic Theology*, p861
[20] Robert Strimple, "Amillennialism", in *Three Views on the Millennium*, pp112-8

the timing.

The very idea of a future Jewish national revival can only be truly understood on the basis that to some degree the Jews are different to the church. Therefore we conclude that the Jewish nation has a special destiny, that Israel is different, and that Israel and the Church are not the same.

Are God's Promises and Covenants with Israel Unconditional?

God's covenants with the Jewish nation (promising to bless them with descendants, the land of Canaan, a son of David upon the throne, and the forgiveness of sins), are the subject of some debate. Some argue that these covenants are conditional – that is, because of Israel's disobedience, God is no longer bound to keep the promises He made. Or some instead argue that these covenants were fulfilled in the past, at the conquest of Canaan or David's reign, and thus are no longer valid. Instead, God has transferred His promises of blessing to the Church, which has replaced Israel. However, if we look at these covenants, with the exception of the Mosaic covenant (which had many conditions attached), we see that they were unconditional and eternal covenants. That is, the covenants were Divine promises made to the nation of Israel that did not depend upon Israel's obedience, nor did they expire. These promises therefore remain in place:

- In **Genesis 12:7**, God promised to give Abraham both descendants and the land of Canaan.
- In Genesis **15:18**, God ratified this promise by sacrifice, stating again that the land of Canaan had been given to Abraham's descendants. Significantly, this covenant was one-sided. That is, whereas in other similar cases of covenants ratified by sacrifice, both parties walked down the middle of the divided sacrifices (e.g. Jer. 34:18-19), signifying that both parties would keep the terms of the covenant (or be cut in pieces?), here only God passed between the divided animal sacrifices, as Abraham had been put into a deep sleep (Gen. 15:12ff).
- In **Genesis 17:7, 13 and 19**, this covenant with Abraham is re-affirmed and stated to be an 'everlasting covenant'.
- In **Genesis 48:3-4**, Jacob recounted the story of his encounter with God at Bethel (Genesis 28), and adds that God gave the land of Canaan to his descendants as an 'everlasting possession'.
- In **Jeremiah 31:35-37**, the New Covenant guarantees that God will never cast off the seed of Israel from being a nation, even despite all they have done.
- **Hebrews 6:13-18** tells us that God's promise to Abraham is certain

and immutable, confirmed by an oath.

C. F. Lincoln writes,

> All of Israel's covenants are called eternal except the Mosaic covenant which is declared to be temporal, i.e., it was to continue only until the coming of the Promised Seed. For this detail see as follows: (1) The Abrahamic Covenant is called "eternal" in Genesis 17:7, 13, 19; I Chronicles 16:17; Psalm 105:10; (2) The Palestinian Covenant is called "eternal" in Ezekiel 16:60; (3) The Davidic Covenant is called "eternal" in II Samuel 23:5; Isaiah 55:3; and Ezekiel 37:25; and (4) The New Covenant is called "eternal" in Isaiah 24:5; 61:8: Jeremiah 32:40; 50:5; and Hebrews 13:20[21].

The argument that the covenant promises made with Israel were fulfilled historically in the conquest of the land of Canaan (1 Kings 4:21-24) are disproved by the 'eternal' nature of these covenants. By contrast with the Mosaic Covenant, whose blessings were conditional upon Israel's obedience (e.g. Deut. 29:9), the promises made to the patriarchs were not conditional upon their obedience, but were instead unconditional, that is, dependent upon God's faithfulness. Some amillennialists argue that conditions may attach to promises without being specifically stated[22] (as in Jonah 3:4 where Jonah unconditionally threatened Nineveh's destruction in forty days), however this argument thereby admits that there are no conditions attached to any of the four unconditional covenants (Abrahamic, Palestinian, Davidic, New). It is an argument from silence.

Conclusion

We may now answer our original question: does Israel have a special role to play in future events, a distinctive destiny in Bible prophecy? The evidence we have looked at seems conclusive: Israel is going to experience a national conversion at the return of Christ, after having gone through the great tribulation, having returned to their own homeland, largely in unbelief, and having rebuilt a Jewish temple in Jerusalem. All of these prophecies provide good reasons for seeing a distinctive role and place for Israel during the great tribulation prior to Christ's return.

---

[21] Charles Fred Lincoln, *The Covenants*, unpublished doctoral dissertation, Dallas Theological Seminary, Dallas, Texas, 1942, p181
[22] Oswald Allis, *Prophecy and the Church*, Philadelphia: P&R, 1945, p32

PART FOUR:

Will the Church Go Through the Tribulation?

20 THE RAPTURE: WHICH VIEW IS RIGHT?

In 2009, Eternal Earth-Bound Pets USA, for the sum of $135, offered to look after the left-behind pets of Christians who had been 'raptured', that is, caught up to heaven at the return of Jesus Christ. Rather than leave the pets of true believers to starve to death after their owners had left the planet, an avowed atheist contractor would come within 24 hours of the rapture to the home of Christians, collect their pets, adopt them and care for them. The company's website had the following on its question and answer page:

Q: Is this a Joke?

A: No. This is a serious offer to our Christian friends who believe in the Second Coming and honestly care about the future of their pets after the Rapture occurs.

The company was interviewed by news reporters and claimed that it had 250 Christian clients signed up. But eventually it was revealed (when being investigated for insurance fraud), that the company was a hoax, and had neither clients nor contractors, nor had it received a cent of revenue in three years of existence.

The 'rapture', as a term used to describe Christians going to heaven at the return of Christ, was propelled into the wider public consciousness through the best-selling 1995 *Left Behind* novels (and movies) by Tim LaHaye and Jerry Jenkins. These novels described the disappearance of millions of Christians in an instant of time, leaving behind not only their cars with engines running and airplanes mid-flight, but also their clothes, dentures, and other personal effects still on the seats.

Before that, in 1988, Eric Whisenant published *88 Reasons Why the Rapture Will Be in 1988*. Three million copies were printed, and 200,000 sent to pastors in the United States for free. His main reason for the 1988 date was that it was 40 years from the founding of the modern state of Israel in 1948. After this date failed to eventuate, he amended his predictions to 1989, 1993 and 1994.

American Christian radio host Harold Camping predicted the rapture would occur in May 21, 2011, 7000 years after Noah's flood (which he dated at 4990 BC). After the date passed, Camping claimed that it had been a spiritual day of judgment and that the real date of the rapture was October 21, 2011, which was also the date of the end of the world. No surprise, this date also passed without event.

No wonder most people (many Christians included) dismiss the entire idea of the rapture as joke – a Christian attempt to sensationalize Christ's return and make it sound like some science fiction TV show with people being teleported into space. Some Christians call the rapture a myth, or a misinterpretation of the Bible.

But even the current Roman Catholic Pope Francis appears to believe in the rapture:

> This is the future that awaits us and this is the fact that brings us to pose so much resistance: resistance to the transformation of our bodies. Also – resistance to Christian identity. I'll say more: perhaps we are not so much afraid of the Apocalypse of the Evil One, of the Antichrist who must come first – perhaps we are not so afraid [of him]. Perhaps we are not so afraid of the voice of the Archangel or the sound of his trumpet – that shall sound the victory of the Lord. Fear of our resurrection, however, we have: we shall all be transformed. That transformation shall be the end of our Christian journey[1].

When the Pope here uses the word 'transformation' (or 'change'), he is quoting from 1 Corinthians 15:51-52 (which describes the rapture):

> Behold, I tell you a mystery: We shall not all sleep [i.e. die], but we shall all be changed – in a moment, in the twinkling of an eye, at the last trumpet. For the trumpet will sound, and the dead will be raised incorruptible, and we shall be changed.

The other main passage in the New Testament that talks about the rapture is 1 Thessalonians 4:16-17:

> For the Lord Himself will descend from heaven with a shout, with the voice of an archangel, and with the trumpet of God. And the dead in Christ will rise first. Then we who are alive and remain shall be caught up together with them in the clouds to meet the Lord in the

---

[1] Pope Francis, homily in St. Martha's House, Rome, on 14th September, 2014

air. And thus we shall always be with the Lord.

The word 'rapture' is not found in our English Bibles, but it comes from the Latin Bible in 1 Thessalonians 4:17. *Rapiemur* (from *rapio*) is the Latin word for 'caught up' in verse 17[2]. The 'rapture' therefore refers to resurrected and living believers being 'caught up' to meet the Lord in the air at His coming.

The subject of the rapture is highly controversial today. According to a 2016 survey of 1000 American Senior Protestant pastors[3], 36% said they believe the Lord will come and rapture the church before the tribulation, 18% believe He will come and rapture the church after the tribulation, 8% believe the rapture occurs midway through the tribulation period, 25% say that there is no such thing as a literal rapture of Christians being caught up into the air, 8% do not agree with any of these views, and 4% are not sure. Looking at these results, the only thing we can say for sure is that there is a lot of confusion about what is going to happen when Christ returns.

One thing can be stated right at the outset. The rapture is not a myth. The logic of the Lord's coming demands that believers who are still alive at the Lord's coming must also be changed and receive 'resurrection' bodies, without going through death, just like the dead who are to be raised.

There are some Christians who try to deny a literal rapture. For example, John Dickson and Greg Clarke write about 1 Thess. 4:17:

> this is clearly apocalyptic language. The expression "caught up together with them in the clouds" recalls Jesus' return on a cloud (Dan. 7:13, Mark 13:26 and elsewhere) – cloud riding is a symbol of authority in apocalyptic literature. Paul's point is that when Christ's judgment falls on the earth believers will not be dangerously underneath it; instead, they will be with the Judge on the 'cloud'. "In the air" just means at a safe distance from the judgment falling upon the world. There is no Rapture of the church in Paul's teaching. The idea is a Christian myth[4].

---

[2] The Greek word used is *harpazo*, and means to 'snatch away' or 'carry off'
[3] Telephone survey of 1000 Protestant Senior Pastors of all denominations, conducted Jan. 8-22, 2016, by LifeWay Research, sponsored by Charisma House Book Group.
[4] John Dickson and Greg Clarke, *666 and All That: The Truth about the Future*, Sydney: Aquila Press, 2007, p42. N. T. Wright also considers the rapture to be a myth; see *The Resurrection of the Son of God*, Minneapolis: Fortress, 2003, vol. 3, p215

But there is no reason to think that Paul's letter to the Thessalonians is 'apocalyptic literature'. It lacks all the standard features, particularly outlandish symbolism. One feature – clouds – is not sufficient to prove an apocalyptic genre, and there is nothing here to suggest that 1 Thessalonians 4:17 is talking about anything other than literal clouds. Furthermore, clouds in the Bible are primarily used to symbolize God's presence with His people, not judgment (see Exodus 13:21-22, 19:16, 40:34).

The main reason people object to the rapture, or describe it as a myth, seems to be embarrassment at the idea of Christians being caught up into the air. But if non-Christians are prepared to accept the possibility that one day science will allow people to be teleported in space, it seems strange that some modern evangelical Christians cannot believe God's Word when He says that He is going to catch us up into the air.

Further, the main miracle at the Lord's coming is the resurrection of dead believers. By comparison with this, any rapture of believers up into the air is a minor matter. Dickson and Clarke claim to be evangelicals, but they sound more like liberal theologians who do not believe in the supernatural. Why should God not be able to raise the dead or snatch believers up into the clouds if He says He will? And if Dickson and Clarke's 'clouds' are to be spiritualized, what shall we say about Jesus' own ascension, in which 'a cloud received Him out of their sight' (Acts 1:9)? Was Jesus' own rapture (the ascension) real, or just another myth?

The rapture is a real event that is going to happen at Christ's return. Most Christians believe in the rapture for the simple reason that 1 Thessalonians 4:16-17 tells us quite soberly that it will happen. The real disagreement among Christians is not whether there is going to be a rapture, but when the rapture occurs. Is it before the tribulation, in the middle of the tribulation or at the end of the tribulation? These are the three main views Christians hold about the rapture: the pre-tribulation rapture, the mid-tribulation rapture, and the post-tribulation rapture.

It is important to state at the outset that we cannot prove either a pre-tribulation rapture, a mid-tribulation rapture or a post-tribulation rapture. There is no verse in the New Testament that says that Christ will return before the Tribulation. Nor is there any verse in the New Testament that describes the rapture happening at the end of the Tribulation, or in the middle of the Tribulation. The future is not laid out anywhere in our Bible in a coloured chart depicting future events with arrows going everywhere. We are required to draw inferences from the biblical information by comparing scripture with scripture. We cannot 'prove' (in some mathematical sense) when the rapture happens.

But in this chapter we are going to evaluate the arguments for and against the three main views about when the rapture happens.

A Post-Tribulation Rapture

The first view we will examine is the post-tribulation rapture position. This view has three main arguments: it is scriptural, logical, and historical:

1. Scriptural: biblical cross references to the rapture show that it occurs at the end of the tribulation period,
2. Historical: the view of the church from the earliest ages was that the rapture would occur at the end of the tribulation period.
3. Logical: the simplest answer to when the rapture occurs is when Christ returns, and since we know that Christ returns at the end of the tribulation period, the rapture must be post-tribulational.

Scriptural Arguments for a Post-Tribulation Rapture

There are three common scriptural arguments for a post-tribulation rapture.

The Rapture in Matthew 24:29-31

Post-tribulation rapture ('post-trib') advocates argue that the description of Christ's return in Matthew 24:29-31 contains so many features in common with Paul's description of the rapture in 1 Thessalonians 4:15-17 that these passages must both refer to the same event. Seeing Christ's return in Matthew 24:29-31 occurs after the great tribulation, the rapture described in 1 Thessalonians 4:16-17 must likewise be post-tribulational. Notice the five common features in the table below: Christ's coming, clouds of heaven, angels, trumpets, and the gathering of God's people.

Matthew 24:29-31	1 Thessalonians 4:15-17
Immediately after the tribulation of those days the sun will be darkened, and the moon will not give its light; the stars will fall from heaven, and the powers of the heavens will be shaken. ³⁰ "Then the sign of the Son of Man will appear in heaven, and then all the tribes of the earth	¹⁵ For this we say to you by the word of the Lord, that we who are alive *and* remain until the **coming of the Lord** will by no means precede those who are asleep. ¹⁶ For the Lord Himself will descend from heaven with a shout, with the voice of an **archangel,** and with the **trumpet**

will mourn, and they will see the **Son of Man coming** on the **clouds** of heaven with power and great glory. [31] "And He will send His **angels** with a great sound of a **trumpet**, and they will **gather together** His elect from the four winds, from one end of heaven to the other.	**of God**. And the dead in Christ will rise first. [17] Then we who are alive *and* remain shall be **caught up together** with them in the **clouds** to meet the Lord in the air. And thus we shall always be with the Lord.

The argument that Matthew 24:29-31 parallels 1 Thessalonians 4:13-17 is powerful precisely because it is a biblical argument – one that lets Scripture interpret Scripture. However, it also has two major problems.

Problem 1: No Resurrection or Rapture in Matthew 24:29-31

The post-trib argument's biggest problem is that the verses in Matthew 24:29-31 do not make any reference to either a rapture or a resurrection of the dead. The actual words mention a gathering, but there is no resurrection of the dead, nor does the word 'gathering' necessarily entail people being caught up into the air. Thus, while there are some parallels between Matthew 24:29-31 and 1 Thessalonians 4:16-17, the main feature of 1 Thessalonians 4:16-17 – the resurrection of the dead – is missing in Matthew 24:29-31. Surely, if Matthew 24:29-31 was speaking of the resurrection, Christ would have mentioned this important event.

Problem 2: Christ is Referring to Something Else

The second major problem with seeing Matthew 24:29-31 as a post-tribulation rapture is that it overlooks other biblical cross-references. 1 Thessalonians 4:13-17 is not the only possible cross-reference to Matthew 24:29-31. There is, in fact, a much stronger Old Testament parallel to Matthew 24:29-31, and this cross-reference shows us that Matthew 24:29-31 is not referring to a resurrection or rapture, but something very different.

When Christ says that 'the angels will gather together His elect from the four winds, from one end of heaven to the other' (Matthew 24:31), Christ is quoting Nehemiah 1:9. Compare the two passages:

Matthew 24:31	Nehemiah 1:9
[31] "And He will send His angels with a great sound of a trumpet, and they will **gather** together His elect from the four winds, **from one end of heaven to the other.**	'but if you return to Me, and keep My commandments and do them, though some of you were cast out to **the farthest part of the heavens**, yet I will **gather** them from there, and bring them to the place which I have chosen as a dwelling for My name'.

Notice the way that Nehemiah refers, not only to a gathering, but to people being brought back 'from the farthest part of the heavens' – exactly the same words Christ used in Matthew 24:29-31. Nehemiah, in turn, was quoting Moses' words in Deuteronomy. In Deuteronomy 28:64, Moses had warned Israel that if they did not obey God's commandments but turned to other gods, God would 'scatter you among all peoples, from one end of the earth to the other, and there you will serve other gods'. Notice the promise that follows in Deuteronomy 30:3-4, as compared with Matthew 24:31:

Matthew 24:31	Deuteronomy 30:3-4
[31] "And He will send His angels with a great sound of a trumpet, and they will **gather** together His elect from the four winds, **from one end of heaven to the other.**	'the LORD your God will bring you back from captivity, and have compassion on you, and **gather** you again from all the nations where the Lord your God has scattered you. If any of you are driven out to **the farthest parts of heaven** (see ESV, KJV), from there the LORD your God will gather you, and from there He will bring you'.

When Moses (and Nehemiah) mention the 'farthest parts of heaven', they were talking about the re-gathering of scattered Israel from the far-flung corners of earth at the end of their exile. Other verses like Isaiah 13:5 and Deuteronomy 4:32 similarly show that 'the end of heaven' is simply a Hebraic way of talking about 'the ends of the earth'.

- They come from a far country, **from the end of heaven**-- the LORD and His weapons of indignation, to destroy the whole land. (Isa. 13:5)
- For ask now concerning the days that are past, which were before you, since the day that God created man on the earth, and ask **from one end of heaven to the other**, whether any great thing like this has happened, or anything like it has been heard. (Deut. 4:32)

When Christ speaks about gathering His elect from the 'four winds' in Matthew 24:31, it is best to understand the 'four winds' to refer to the four compass points. Consider what Jeremiah 49:36 says: 'Against Elam I will bring **the four winds** from the four quarters of heaven, and scatter them toward all those winds; there shall be no nations where the outcasts of Elam will not go'.

Another Old Testament parallel to the gathering in Matthew 24:31 is found in Zechariah 2:6, which in the Greek Septuagint (LXX) translation (in Zech. 2:10) reads: 'Up, up, flee from the land of the north, says the Lord, for I will gather you from **the four winds of the heavens,** says the Lord'. This passage is talking about the return of the Jews from the Babylonian captivity and their regathering to Israel in the days of Zechariah. Again, the same language ('gather from the four winds of the heavens') is used to speak – not of people being caught up into the clouds – but of Jews being regathered from their exile and scattering at the ends of the earth.

Being gathered from the 'four winds' in Matthew 24:31 and Zechariah 2 is also best understood as a reference to Israel's future regathering from the ends of the earth, as Isaiah 11:11-12 describes Israel's regathering:

> It shall come to pass in that day that the Lord shall set His hand again the second time to recover the remnant of His people who are left, from Assyria and Egypt, from Pathros and Cush, from Elam and Shinar, from Hamath and the islands of the sea. He will set up a banner for the nations, and will assemble the outcasts of Israel, and gather together the dispersed of Judah from *the four corners of the earth* (Isa. 11:11-12).

Israel's return from exile is also attended by another important feature: the sounding of a great trumpet, just as described in Matthew 24:31:

> And it shall come to pass in that day that the LORD will thresh, from the channel of the River to the Brook of Egypt; and you will be gathered one by one, O you children of Israel. So it shall be in that day:

the great trumpet will be blown; they will come, who are about to perish in the land of Assyria, and they who are outcasts in the land of Egypt, and shall worship the LORD in the holy mount at Jerusalem (Isa. 27:12-13)

Professor John Hart comments: 'Interestingly, the only places in the NT or the LXX where the Greek 'a great trumpet' is mentioned are in Matthew 24:31 and Isaiah 27:13. Neither 1 Corinthians 15 or 1 Thessalonians 4 (or Revelation) use this term. Both Matthew 24:29-31 and Isaiah 27:13 describe the gathering of Israel ... not the church'[5].

Notice also, while in Matthew 24 the elect are gathered *from* the winds and heavens (which we have seen refer to the ends of the earth), in 1 Thessalonians 4, the saints are caught up *into* the air. There is a significant difference between these two statements. Reading a rapture into Matthew 24:31 is eisegesis.

Thus, in evaluating the post-trib argument that Matthew 24:31 parallels 1 Thessalonians 4:16-17, the question is whether the similarities in both passages indicate direct parallels or incidental resemblances. It would appear that in Matthew 24:29-31, Christ is quoting Deuteronomy and Nehemiah. He is not talking about gathering His church up into the clouds to meet Himself in the air (as in 1 Thess. 4). He is instead talking about the re-gathering of the scattered nation of Israel from the ends of the earth to its ancient homeland when He returns to earth after the tribulation. The gathering in Matthew 24 is thus best understood as Jewish, rather than Christian, as the preceding context shows (e.g. 'let those in Judea flee to the mountains', 'on the sabbath').

The main pillar of the post-trib position, that Matthew 24:29-31 parallels 1 Thessalonians 4:13-17, and refers to the rapture of the church at the end of the tribulation, is thus a less convincing explanation than the alternative, viz. that Matthew 24:29-31 refers to the regathering of Israel. Even stronger parallels can be found between Matthew 24:29-31 and Deuteronomy, Nehemiah, Isaiah, Jeremiah and Zechariah, which tell us about a future Jewish regathering from all nations to Jerusalem. This all casts doubt on the idea that Matthew 24:29-31 is describing a post-tribulation rapture.

The Elect
Another post-trib argument is that Christ gathers His 'elect' (or, chosen

---
[5] John F. Hart, "Jesus and the Rapture", in *Evidence for the Rapture*, ed. J. F. Hart, Moody, 2015, p68

ones) in Matthew 24:31. Seeing the church is composed of the 'elect' in the New Testament (e.g. Rom. 8:37, 1 Thess. 1:4, 1 Pet. 1:2), this suggests that the church is gathered to Christ at the end of the tribulation period. However, Israel is also called God's elect in various places in the Old Testament:

- 'the LORD has chosen Jacob for Himself, Israel for His special treasure' (Ps. 135:4)
- 'you, Israel, are My servant, Jacob whom I have chosen, the descendants of Abraham My friend' (Isa. 41:8)
- 'Jacob my servant's sake, and Israel mine elect' (Isa. 45:4)
- 'I will bring forth descendants from Jacob, and from Judah an heir of My mountains; My elect shall inherit it, and My servants shall dwell there' (Isa. 65:9)

In reply, post-trib proponents argue that Israel and the church are one and the same people (i.e. Israel is the church in the Old Testament), chosen by God, so the fact that Israel is elect makes no difference – God's elect people, the church and Israel, will be gathered together by the rapture at the end of the tribulation. But this reasoning is faulty for four reasons:

1. It ignores the fact that when Israel is converted at the return of Christ (Zech. 12-14), they will not be raptured or resurrected, but remain on earth as mortal saints, which is very different to what happens to believers in the church at the rapture (1 Thess. 4:13-18).
2. It ignores the fact that in the immediate context of Matthew 24:1-31, Christ is speaking about Jewish people (e.g. 'those in Judea flee to the mountains', 'on the sabbath')
3. It ignores the biblical evidence we have seen in a previous chapter that Israel and the church are distinct entities,
4. It is guilty of circular reasoning, by assuming what needs to be proved – that the 'elect' in Matthew 24:31 is referring to the church.

Instead of proving that the 'elect' in Matthew 24:31 are the church, this post-trib argument falls short of what its proponents claim, for it is clear that there are other people in the Bible who are also elect, Israel. It therefore does not prove that the rapture of the church occurs at the end of the great tribulation.

The Meaning of 'Meet' (*apantesis*)

A third common argument made for a post-tribulation rapture is that the word 'meet' in 1 Thessalonians 4:17 (*apantesis* in Greek) has a technical meaning and refers to a welcoming party going out to greet a visiting dignitary and then escorting him back to the city. Thus, when Paul says that at the rapture we are going to 'meet' the Lord, this means that we will go to meet Christ and immediately return to earth with Him. If it is true that at the rapture, the church immediately returns with Christ to earth, then this means that the rapture occurs at the end of the tribulation period when Christ Himself comes to reign. Douglas Moo writes,

> The word used by Paul to describe the "meeting" between the living saints and their Lord in the air (*apantesis*) occurs in references to the visit of dignitaries and generally implies that the "delegation" accompanies the dignitary back to the delegation's point of origin… This would suggest that the saints, after meeting the Lord in the air, accompany him back to earth instead of going with him to heaven[6].

However, this argument is simply false – it is poor scholarship. *Thesaurus Linguae Graecae* (a database of Greek literature) produces 91 pages of citations of various forms of the word *apantesis* from several centuries before and after Paul, and only a minority of references describe such formal receptions[7]. The word *apantesis* rarely means 'to go out and escort a visitor back into town'; it usually just means 'meet' in the same way the word 'meet' is used in a non-technical way in English. Thus, even in the New Testament, we see the verb form of the word (*apantaw*) being used in Luke 17:12 where we read about Jesus entering a certain village, where 'there met Him ten men who were lepers, who stood afar off'. The ten lepers do not escort Jesus back into the town – they go off to the priests as Jesus told them. The argument that the meaning of *apantesis* proves a post-tribulation rapture is thus not correct.

Scriptural Problems with a Post-Tribulation Rapture

There are also four biblical problems with a post-tribulation rapture.

---

[6] Moo, in *Three Views on the Rapture*, 2010, pp200-1. Wayne Grudem also uses this argument in his *Systematic Theology*, IVP, 1994, p1134, footnote 41.
[7] See Michael R. Crosby, "Hellenistic Formal Receptions and Paul's use of APANTHSIS in 1 Thessalonians 4:17", *Bulletin for Biblical Research* 4 (1994), p19

The Denial of the Great Tribulation

One of the greatest problems with a post-tribulation rapture is the confusion displayed by post-tribulationists over the question of the 'great tribulation'. Most post-tribulationists insist that the great tribulation is already happening now, despite the fact that Christians are living in luxury, going to church every Sunday (some falling asleep) and even occupying positions as head of state in some countries. The (astonishing) idea that we are currently in the 'great tribulation' is what post-tribulationists actually teach, as can be seen in the following quotes:

- **George H. Fromow**: 'The church is already passing through the 'Great Tribulation' ... This term Great embraces the whole period of the Church's course on earth, and should not be confined to the final 3½ years or the second half of Daniel's seventieth week of intensive tribulation. It began with the first saints after the Fall, and includes all who have washed their robes and made them white in the blood of the Lamb until the Second Advent of Christ'[8].
- **George L. Rose**: 'The record left us in the book of The Acts of the Apostles leaves no room to doubt that, 'tribulation' began almost as soon as the Church was born ... At the time of Stephen's death 'there was a GREAT PERSECUTION against the church which was at Jerusalem ... Saul made havoc of the church, entering into every house, arresting men and women committed them to prison' (Acts 8:1-3). *This 'great persecution' mentioned in Acts 8:1 is called 'tribulation'* in Acts 11:19 therefore, 'great persecution' is 'great tribulation'[9].
- **J. Barton Payne** described the great tribulation as 'pasttribulation'. John Walvoord summarizes Payne's position as follows: 'Payne holds that the prophecies of the Tribulation have already been fulfilled or are in process of being fulfilled to such an extent that the coming of Christ could occur at any time'[10]. Payne therefore considered the post-tribulation return of Christ to be imminent: 'Each morning, as the Christian casts his glance into the blueness of the sky, he may thrill with the prayerful thought, "Perhaps today"'[11].
- **Douglas Moo**: 'Matthew 24:4-28//Mark 13:5-23 describes the entirety of the church age, which will be marked by great tribulation

---

[8] George H. Fromow, *Will the Church Pass through the Tribulation?* London: Sovereign Grace Advent Testimony, n.d., p2
[9] George L. Rose, *Tribulation Till Translation*, Glendale, California, 1942, pp68-9
[10] John Walvoord, *The Rapture Question*, Zondervan, 1979, p136
[11] J. Barton Payne, *The Imminent Appearing of Christ*, Eerdmans, 1962, p161

and by the important event of the Roman destruction of Jerusalem (= "the abomination that causes desolation") in AD 70. This must take place, Jesus suggests, before his parousia, and once it has taken place, his parousia is "near". Jesus may refer to the greatest distress of all time in this context (Matt. 24:21//Mark 13:29) as a hyperbolic way of emphasizing the suffering that the Roman destruction of the city would cause. But it is perhaps likelier that he refers to the sufferings of God's people throughout the "church age"[12].

- **Wayne Grudem**: 'since the first century, there have been many periods of violent and intense persecution of Christians, and even in our century much of it has occurred over large portions of the globe [in communist and Muslim lands].... It would be difficult to convince some Christians in this century who have undergone decades of persecution for their faith ... that such a great tribulation has certainly not yet occurred. They have longed and prayed for years for Christ to come and rescue them from the tribulation that they are enduring. ... [T]hough we may think that Jesus' words [about the great tribulation] indicate the likelihood of a yet greater persecution coming in the future, it is difficult to be certain of this. It seems appropriate to conclude that it is unlikely but possible that the prediction of a great tribulation has already been fulfilled'[13].
- **Don Carson** argues that the tribulation period is 'from the Ascension to the Second Advent'[14].
- **Craig Keener** holds the tribulation started in AD 66 and ends at Jesus' return[15].

But as John Hart asks, 'Can a time really be found in the church age about which it can be said, "unless those days were limited, no one would survive"?'[16].

Some post-tribulationists, like Moo, not only argue we are already in the great tribulation, but also deny a future abomination of desolation[17]. However, Daniel's references to an abomination of desolation[18] (to which

---

[12] Douglas J. Moo, *Three Views on the Rapture*, 2010, pp216-7
[13] Wayne Grudem, *Systematic Theology*, IVP, 1994, p1102
[14] D. A. Carson, *Matthew, Expositors Bible Commentary*, Zondervan, 1984, p495
[15] Craig Keener, *Matthew*, IVP, Downer's Grove, 1997, p349
[16] John Hart, *Evidence for the Rapture*, p67, footnote 19
[17] Moo, *Three Views*, p216.
[18] As we saw in a previous chapter, Daniel tells us that not only was there an 'abomination of desolation' in the times of Antiochus Epiphanes, Dan. 11:31, but there will also be an 'abomination of desolation' at the end of time, Dan. 12:11

the Lord specifically pointed in explanation of the abomination of desolation in Matthew 24:15), clearly point to a yet-future 'abomination of desolation' at the time of the resurrection (i.e. the end of the world, Daniel 12:11, and see references to the resurrection in verse 2 of that chapter). As far as Matthew's gospel is concerned, 'the abomination of desolation' (Matt. 24:15) is the signal for the start of the 'great tribulation' (Matt. 24:21), after which Christ 'immediately' (Matt. 24:29) comes (Matt. 24:30-31). Therefore the great tribulation cannot refer to AD 70. Nor did the abomination of desolation happen in AD 70. Nor is the great tribulation an age-long tribulation – it must occur immediately before Christ's return.

Why do post-tribulationists take such positions – denying a future 'great tribulation' and the signs (e.g. the abomination of desolation) associated with it, and instead argue that the entire age is 'the great tribulation'? The reason is because it is very difficult for post-tribulationists to reconcile two seemingly contradictory facts: (1) the many signs of the 'great tribulation' period leading up to Christ's coming, and (2) the many references describing Christ's coming as a surprise that could happen at any moment and which nobody will know is about to happen. This leads on to the second biblical problem with the post-trib position.

The Denial of Imminency

A second problem with a post-tribulation rapture is the Bible's teaching about the imminence of Christ's coming. The idea of imminence means that something is going to happen, but we do not know *when* it will occur. If a friend of mine who is an electrician offers to come over to my house to fix something, and he says he will come tomorrow but does not give me a time, then I have to be ready and dressed from early in the morning right through to the end of the day – he could come at any time. The same is true of Christ's coming. As we shall see in the next chapter, there are about fifty verses in the New Testament which teach that Christ could come at any time, so that Christians ought to be ready and watching, eagerly waiting for Him. This creates a problem for the post-trib position, for how is it possible that Christ can speak, on the one hand, of His return after the great tribulation, but on the other hand, at a time when nobody will know or expect it? J. Dwight Pentecost writes:

> A second major argument of the post-tribulation rapturists is the argument against imminency. It is evident that if belief in the imminent return of Christ is the Scriptural doctrine then the church

must be raptured before the signs of the tribulation period unfold. The adherent of that position discounts all the Scriptural admonitions to the church to watch for Christ and bids us watch for signs[19].

Some post-tribulationists, of course, simply deny imminence outright. Berkhof, as we earlier saw, wrote: 'According to Scripture several important events must occur before the return of the Lord, and therefore it cannot be called imminent'[20]. Berkhof's approach is simply to dismiss all the verses in the New Testament telling Christians to be ready, watching, and waiting, because we do not know when Christ is going to come.

But other post-tribulationists try other ways to explain away all these verses about the imminent return of Christ. Don Carson suggests 'imminent' could mean 'in any generation' rather than 'at any moment'[21]. But this is a definition of imminence which has not occurred to anyone else in the history of the English language, let alone in the history of theology. Worse, Carson's definition does not fairly represent the teaching of Christ in Matthew 24:36ff where He says that He could come at any day, and any hour – not in any generation.

The post-tribulationist G. E. Ladd in *The Blessed Hope* argues against the imminent return of Christ by suggesting that the repeated mention of the word 'watch' in Matthew 24 and 25 does not carry with it the idea that Christ could come at any moment[22]. Instead, Ladd argues it simply means that believers during the tribulation period should be 'watching' for signs of the return of Christ. Ladd here takes the word 'watch' to mean nothing more than 'spectate'. But the idea of watching in the context carries the thought of eagerly expecting something which might imminently happen. For example, in Matthew 24:44, we read, 'Therefore you also be *ready*, for the Son of Man is coming at an hour you do not expect'. The parable of the wise and foolish virgins in Matthew 25:1-13 likewise emphasizes the need for believers to be 'ready' (v10). That is what imminence really involves – not merely watching events unfold. As we will see, verses about imminence are found in many other passages besides Matthew 24 and 25

---

[19] J. Dwight Pentecost, *Things to Come*, Zondervan, 1964, p168
[20] Berkhof, *Systematic Theology*, 696
[21] '[T]he imminent return of Christ' then means Christ may return at any time. But the evangelical writers who use the word divide on whether 'imminent' in the sense of 'at any time' should be pressed to mean 'at any second' or something looser such as 'at any period' or 'in any generation. (D. A. Carson, "Matthew" 490)
[22] Ladd, *The Blessed Hope*, p112

and use many other words besides simply 'watch'. The problem with Ladd's argument is that we cannot simply focus on one word 'watch' to the exclusion of all the other different ways we are exhorted to be ready for Christ to come at any time. Aside from this, most believers during the tribulation are going to be martyred and so should be looking forward to their resurrection rather than the Lord's coming,

Robert Gundry, another post-tribulationist, gives the following definition of imminence:

> By common consent imminence means that so far as we know no predicted event will necessarily precede the coming of Christ. The concept incorporates three essential elements: suddenness, unexpectedness or incalculability, and a possibility of occurrence at any moment. But these elements would require only that Christ *might* come before the tribulation, not that He must. Imminence would only raise the possibility of pretribulationism on a sliding scale with mid- and post-tribulationism. It is singularly strange that the most popularly cherished argument for pretribulationism should suffer such an obvious and critical limitation[23].

Gundry is correct that his definition of imminence in the first two sentences enjoys common consent. However, it is obvious that once the seven-year tribulation period (Daniel's Seventieth Week) with all its predicted signs has commenced, it is no longer true to say that Christ could come at any hour, for certain carefully sequenced events must then take place before Christ comes, including the three-and-a-half-year great tribulation period with its cataclysmic signs culminating in the battle of Armageddon. Christ's coming is no longer imminent, for Christ cannot come for a set period of time. Any Bible reading believer during the tribulation would be able to calculate exactly when Christ will return: three and a half years after the setting up of the abomination of desolation. It is only in a pre-tribulation scene that Christ's coming can be called imminent according to Gundry's definition – with no predicted event preceding it. Gundry is right to say that imminence is more probable 'on a sliding scale with mid- and post-tribulationism'. But this is because imminence flatly contradicts post-tribulationism (and to a lesser extent, mid-tribulationism) which teach that certain unmistakable signs precede Christ's coming.

These are some of the post-trib attempts to explain the verses which

---

[23] Robert Gundry, *The Church and the Tribulation*, Zondervan, 1973, p29

teach imminence. It is no wonder they get themselves so tangled, for they are stuck in a difficult position. On the one hand, the Bible teaches that Christ's coming is imminent – it could happen at any time, with no predicted events preceding it – but on the other hand, the Bible also teaches that certain clearly-identifiable and unmistakable signs will precede Christ's coming. The verses about imminence present no problem for a pre-tribulation rapture, but it is a particularly difficult issue for the post-tribulation position. We will look at the imminence issue in more detail in the next chapter.

Who will populate the Millennial kingdom?
The third great problem with the post-trib position is the presence of birth, death and sin (Isaiah 11:4-8, 65:20ff.) during the millennium. This proves that there must be mortal saints, people in non-glorified, unresurrected and non-transformed bodies which have not been raptured, in the millennium. Also, the rebellion against Christ at the end of the millennium (described in Rev. 20:7-9) shows that there are many people by the end of the millennium who are not saved.

But if the rapture happens at the end of the tribulation, then all saved people alive are transformed and glorified, so that there are no non-glorified people left to enter the millennium. Under a post-trib scenario all Christians go through the tribulation and are transformed and raptured at the coming of Christ at its end. So, who are the people who live on into the millennium in unresurrected bodies? In the post-trib scheme, all saved people have received resurrection bodies at the rapture, and can neither sin nor die nor have children. So, who populates the millennium?

Charles Ryrie explains: 'When the millennium begins, some people have to be alive in unresurrected bodies, who can beget children and populate that kingdom . . . If there were only resurrected saints in the kingdom, then there would be no death, no increase in population, and no differences in the ages of millennial citizens (all of which are indicated as characterizing the kingdom – Isaiah 65:20; Zechariah 8:5; Revelation 20:8). Since resurrected people do not propagate, there would be no way to populate the kingdom unless some unresurrected people enter the Millennium. . . The initial group that will enter the Millennium will not only enter with natural bodies but will also be redeemed people who willingly submit to the rule of the King. . . By the end of the Millennium there will be innumerable rebels who will have given outward obedience to the King, but who, when given the opportunity by Satan after his release, will join his revolution against Christ'[24].

It would hardly seem possible that unsaved people from the tribulation period could enter the millennium, for they are not born again, (and John 3:3 says people must be born again to enter the Kingdom). Further, unsaved people will have taken the mark of the beast (Rev. 13:16), which results in eternal torment in the Lake of Fire:

> If anyone worships the beast and his image, and receives his mark on his forehead or on his hand, he himself shall also drink of the wine of the wrath of God, which is poured out full strength into the cup of His indignation. He shall be **tormented with fire and brimstone** in the presence of the holy angels and in the presence of the Lamb. And **the smoke of their torment ascends forever and ever; and they have no rest day or night, who worship the beast and his image, and whoever receives the mark of his name** (Rev. 14:9-11).

Those who repeatedly refused to repent during the judgments of the tribulation period (Rev. 9:20), but instead blasphemed God (Rev. 16:9, 11) will surely not be admitted to the kingdom. We also read that God will 'send them strong delusion that they should believe the lie, that they **all** may be condemned who did not believe the truth' (2 Thess. 2:11-12). There does not seem to be any hope for unbelievers during the tribulation to enter the millennial kingdom. How could Christ speak of entry to His kingdom in this present church age being so difficult, and so few finding it (Matt. 7:14), so that mere professors of Christ who call Him "Lord, Lord" but do not do the will of the Father (Matt. 7:21) are shut out from the kingdom, yet in the future the door is thrown wide open to all and sundry so that people who remained rank unbelievers during the great tribulation, or who sat on the fence, are let into the kingdom? This is surely impossible.

The post-trib view provides no satisfactory answer to this problem, and some post-tribulationists resort to desperate theories. Thus, Eckhard Schnabel suggests that the people who rebel against Christ at the end of the millennium are the unsaved at Christ's return, who were sent to Hades with Satan, and are brought back again when Satan is released![25]. Schnabel gets full marks for imagination, but his view does not have the slightest shred of scriptural support. Even though it solves the problem of the

---

[24] Charles Ryrie, *What You Should Know about the Rapture*, Moody Press, 1981, pp75-6
[25] Ekhard Schnabel, *Forty Questions about the End Times*, Kregel, 2011, pp226-8, 276

rebellion at the end of the millennium, it does not provide an explanation for birth, sin and death on earth throughout the millennium. Post-tribulationists must admit unsaved people into the millennium, which means that all those martyrs who laid down their lives during the great tribulation rather than worship the Beast died for nothing.

Israel and the Church

A fourth major problem with the post-tribulation position is that it fails to distinguish between Israel and the Church. As we saw in previous chapters dealing with Israel's conversion in Zechariah 12-14 and also Ezekiel 38-39, Israel is not converted as a nation before the return of Christ, or even during the great tribulation. God's plans for Israel take a different path to those for the Church. Israel as a nation is not converted as part of the church (although individual Jews are converted and become part of the church now). Instead, Israel is converted *after* Christ returns to rescue them at the battle of Armageddon, and they live on in non-glorified bodies into the millennium. This is in sharp contrast to what will happen to members of the church whose bodies are transformed and glorified at the rapture. Post-tribulation rapture advocates ignore the clear Old Testament prophecies about the conversion of Israel. Added to this, as we have seen in a previous chapter, the arguments for a distinction between Israel and the church are strong, with good evidence that the church is a new thing that only started at Pentecost (not being mentioned in the gospels except in prospect), with the word 'Israel' continuing to be used to mean ethnic Israel (as distinct to the church) in Acts and the epistles, except for one reference in Galatians 6:16 where 'the Israel of God' refers to ethnic Jewish believers in Christ in contrast to Judaizing false-brethren (and not referring to the church, or to Gentiles).

Logical Arguments for a Post-Tribulation Rapture

A second common argument for a post-tribulation rapture is that it is the most logical position to take because we would assume that Christ's return is a simple, straightforward affair, at the end of the tribulation period; a complex, multi-stage 'coming' is unwarranted. However, the fact that the saints are going to 'meet the Lord' at the rapture means that there must be some delay before Christ returns to fight the Battle of Armageddon. As John Hart argues, 'In *all* premillennial schemes, the Parousia [i.e. Christ's coming] includes a rapture that takes believers to meet Christ in the clouds, and afterward Christ returns with the saints to the earth. These two stages are separated by an interval of time. This interval is simply confined to a very small portion of the tribulation period in the posttribulational perspective.... [Midtribulation] theories have a more extended interval than posttribulationism. Pretribulationaism separates the rapture and the return of Christ by seven years'[26].

The idea that Christ's coming must be a simple, instantaneous event is an *a priori* assumption that some people bring to the discussion. Even Occam's Razor, which argues that we should prefer simpler explanations to those which are more complex is qualified: the simplest explanation *that adequately explains all the evidence* is to be preferred.

There is, by the same token, a logical riposte to the post-tribulation position: what is the point of a post-tribulation rapture? Why is there any need for believers to be caught up into the air if they are immediately going to come straight back to earth with Christ? Why not just experience the transformation of our bodies on earth and await Christ's coming there? Why the roller-coaster ride up into the air and then down again? Paige Patterson writes, 'The rationale for a posttribulation rapture of the church is hard to establish. ... what could be the purpose of this rapture when they return immediately to earth?'[27].

Another related argument that possibly falls under the 'logical' heading is this: Why would the Lord speak to His disciples on the Mount of Olives about future events if these events were to happen in the remote future to people other than the apostles or His followers? Why do we have the Olivet Discourse about the great tribulation recorded in our gospels if it is not for the church? Wayne Grudem asks, 'Is it likely that Jesus, in saying all these things [his Olivet Discourse in Matthew 24] *to his disciples*, intended his words to apply not to the church but only to a future earthly kingdom of Jewish people who would be converted during the tribulation?'[28]. On one point, Grudem is surely correct: the idea that Matthew 24-25 has nothing to say to the church seems unlikely and illogical.

We will look at Matthew 24 and 25 in more detail in the next chapter, and see that although there are also parts of these chapters concerning the great tribulation that are directly related to Jewish people ('those that are in Judea'), there is also material in these chapters that is best understood as addressed to Christ's followers in the church. As John Hart writes, 'Most pretribulationists have insisted that the group being addressed in the

---

[26] Hart, *Evidence for the Rapture*, p53, emphasis in original.
[27] Paige Patterson, *Revelation*, New American Commentary, Nashville: B&H Publishing, 2012, p41
[28] Wayne Grudem, *Systematic Theology*, 1994, p1135, emphasis in original

Discourse is Israel, not the church. It is true that the gospel of Matthew is addressed primarily to the Jews. However, it is also the only gospel to mention the "church" (*ekklesia*, Matt. 16:18; 18:17). The Great Commission in Matthew 28:19-20 is given to the church, not Israel. So it is not impossible that Matthew and Jesus address the church as well as Jews in different portions of the Discourse'[29].

In summary, while these logical arguments are common, they are not decisive, one way or other, in the debate over when the rapture happens. Logical arguments are not as powerful as scriptural ones.

Historical Arguments for a Post-Tribulation Rapture

The third key argument for a post-tribulation rapture is that this was the view of virtually all of the post-apostolic church 'fathers'. These early Christian writers believed in a literal millennium on earth after Christ's return, but they also held to a post-tribulation rapture. J. Barton Payne (a post-tribulation rapture advocate) writes,

> The ante-Nicene fathers [i.e. writers before the council of Nicaea in AD 325] ... held two basic convictions relative to the second coming of Christ: that it was imminent, and that it was post-tribulational[30].

The difficulty with holding these two views, as we have seen, is that they contradict each other. How can Christ's coming be imminent, so that it could happen today and we should be on the tip-toes of expectancy for it, if there is still to come a three and a half year period of 'great tribulation', easily identified by certain well-marked signs?

The reason the early church fathers held these two seemingly contradictory views is because their understanding of future events was not very well developed. The early Church 'Fathers' held to the four great 'clues' with which we started this book:

- A literal millennium
- A future great tribulation
- The conversion of Israel at the return of Christ
- The imminence of the Lord's coming at any moment

For example, Irenaeus (2nd century), speaks of the first two 'clues':

---

[29] Hart, *Evidence for the Rapture*, p66, footnote 5.
[30] J. Barton Payne, *The Imminent Appearing of Christ*, Eerdmans, 1962, pp15-16

> When this Anti-Christ shall have devastated all things in this world, he will reign for three years and six months, and sit in the temple at Jerusalem; and then the Lord will come from heaven in the clouds, in the glory of the Father, sending this man and those who follow him into the lake of fire; but bringing in for the righteous the times of the kingdom, that is, the rest, the hallowed seventh day; and restoring to Abraham the promised inheritance, in which kingdom the Lord declared, that 'many coming from the east and the west should sit down with Abraham, Isaac, and Jacob[31].

We have also quoted a number of Church Fathers who believed in the future conversion of the nation of Israel which is to occur at the return of Christ. But the early Church Fathers also believed in the imminence of the Lord's coming. Thus, Clement (writing about AD 96) said:

> Ye see how in a little while the fruit of the trees come to maturity. Of a truth, soon and suddenly shall His will be accomplished, as the Scriptures also bear witness, saying "Speedily will He come, and will not tarry"; and "The Lord shall suddenly come to His temple, even the Holy One, for whom ye look"[32].

The *Didache*, another early post-apostolic document (from the first or second centuries), says:

> Watch for your life's sake. Let not your lamps be quenched, nor your loins unloosed; but be ye ready, for ye know not the hour in which our Lord cometh[33].

But the early Christian writers also spoke about the Lord coming at the end of the great tribulation period to defeat Antichrist (as we have seen with Irenaeus). As to how it is possible to reconcile the two facts of imminency and the Lord's return at the end of the tribulation, as well as the conversion of Israel (after the Church), they were not very clear. It is probably best to say that they did not attempt to reconcile these doctrines. The reason for this was that their attention was on other issues, like the great doctrinal disputes over the nature of the Person of Christ. Walvoord writes:

---

[31] Irenaeus, *Against Heresies*, Book V, chap 30, para 4
[32] Clement, "Letter to the Corinthians", *The Ante-Nicene Fathers*, I, 11
[33] "Didache", *The Ante-Nicene Fathers*, VII, p382

How the coming of the Lord could be a daily expectation as is indicated by the early Fathers and at the same time have a lengthy series of events preceding the Second Advent was apparently not resolved in the early church. Some were undoubtedly post-tribulational, but others are not clear. If major doctrines like the Trinity and the procession of the Holy Spirit took centuries to find acceptable statement, it is hardly to be expected that the problems of eschatology would be all settled in the early centuries[34].

It is a curious fact that the normal order of subjects studied in theology (God, Christ, Holy Spirit, Man, Sin, Salvation, Sanctification, the Church, Future Events) follows the order in which doctrinal debates happened historically over the last 2000 years, so that while controversy over future events is now very common, it was largely ignored for the first 1800 years of the Church. Gerald Stanton wrote in 1956,

> During these past nineteen centuries, there has been a progressive refinement of the details of Christian theology, but not until the last one hundred years has Eschatology come to the front to receive the major attention and scrutiny of foremost Bible scholars. It is not that the doctrine of Christ's coming, or any of its special features, is new or novel, but that the doctrine has finally come into the place of prominence it rightfully deserves. With that prominence there has come a greater discernment of prophetic detail[35].

A Pre-Tribulation Rapture is a Late Invention

Another post-tribulation rapture argument, along similar lines, is that a pre-tribulation rapture is only a lately-invented doctrine, arising in the 1820s with John Nelson Darby. Professor Ben Witherington III, in a Youtube video entitled, *Where did Rapture Theology Come from*[36], states that:

> First thing to be said about a dispensational reading of the Bible is that it didn't exist before the 19th century. It really began in a little revival in Glasgow, Scotland, and there was a teenage girl named MacDonald, a good Scottish name, who claimed to have a vision of a pre-tribulation

---

[34] John Walvoord, *The Rapture Question*, Zondervan, 1979, p156
[35] Gerald B. Stanton, *Kept from the Hour*, Zondervan, 1956, pp.223-24.
[36] Ben Witherington III, *Where Did Rapture Theology Come From?* https://www.youtube.com/watch?v=d_cVXdr8mVs, Oct 8, 2014

rapture of the church out of this world into heaven. Now this event might have come and gone and not left much of a mark on the church except that there was a certain reverend named Darby there, who heard this, became convinced that this theology was correct, began preaching this, and Reverend Darby was one of the founders of the Plymouth Brethren denomination in the 19th century... Mr. Darby took his gospel of the rapture to the United States, and came in contact with the Billy Graham of his day, Dwight L. Moody ... who became the worldwide disseminator of this theology of dispensationalism and a pre-tribulation rapture on both sides of the Atlantic... This was a lay theological movement, not based on the study of the Greek New Testament or Hebrew Old Testament, that spread throughout the United States and the world.

However, if we read the words of Margaret MacDonald herself, we see that this story is not true. The claim that the pre-tribulation rapture had its origin in the utterances of a proto-Pentecostal Scottish teenage girl named Margaret MacDonald has been popularized by Dave MacPherson, a 'newsman turned rapture researcher', in his book, *The Great Rapture Hoax*. Here are Margaret MacDonald's words, which show clearly that she did not believe in a pre-tribulation rapture at all:

> now shall the awful sight of a false Christ be seen on this earth, and nothing but the living Christ in us can detect this awful attempt of the enemy to deceive. . . . The Spirit must and will be poured out on the church, that she may be purified and filled with God. . . . There will be outward trial too, but 'tis principally temptation. It is brought on by the outpouring of the Spirit, and will just increase in proportion as the Spirit is poured out. The trial of the Church is from the Antichrist. It is by being filled with the Spirit that we shall be kept. I frequently said, Oh be filled with the Spirit—have the light of God in you, that you may detect Satan—be full of eyes within—be clay in the hands of the potter— submit to be filled, filled with God. . . . This is what we are at present made to pray much for, that speedily we may all be made ready to meet our Lord in the air—and it will be. Jesus wants his bride. His desire is toward us[37].

One only has to read the above quote carefully to realize that Margaret

---

[37] Dave McPherson, *The Great Rapture Hoax*, New Puritan Library, 1983, pp127-8.

The Rapture: Which View is Right?

MacDonald was a post-tribulationist. Notice: 'the trial of the church is from the Antichrist'. She prophesied that the church would undergo a trial from the Antichrist, after which purging trial 'we may all be made ready to meet our Lord in the air'. There is no pre-tribulation rapture here, for the church (in her account) goes through the great tribulation, the trial of the Antichrist. She was a post-tribulation rapturist.

Another falsehood in Witherington's account is the suggestion that Darby was present when MacDonald made this prophecy. There is no evidence for this whatsoever. Darby was a Church of England clergyman from an aristocratic family, who came top of Classics (i.e. Greek and Latin) at Trinity College, Dublin (the main university in Ireland), who not only translated the Bible out of the original Greek and Hebrew into English, but also into French and German. All this means that Witherington is again wrong to describe the idea as a 'lay movement, not based on the study of the original languages of the Bible'. Contrary to Witherington, there is no evidence Darby ever had any contact with a Pentecostal girl in Glasgow. They did not meet, exchange letters or have any known connection.

Darby claimed to have come to his understanding of a dispensational view of Scripture (that the church and Israel are separate entities) while recovering from an accident in Ireland in 1827, three years before McDonald's utterance. This was a result of studying Isaiah 32 and 2 Thessalonians 2. Darby's dispensational distinction between Israel and the Church later led him to posit a pre-tribulation rapture as a logical corollary.

Others have argued that Darby got the pre-tribulation rapture from Edward Irving, another proto-Pentecostal. But apart from the fact that Darby was heavily critical of Irving's movement, Irving himself was also a post-tribulationist. Here is what Irving wrote:

> That the seventh seal had been opened, the seventh trumpet sounded, the seventh vial commended: but it is only to this last-mentioned portion of prophecy that we shall at present direct our attention. We have, blessed be God, lived to see the outpouring of the seventh vial, during the outpouring of which the Lord will come![38]

Irving here says that the Lord will come during the outpouring of the

---

[38] Edward Irving, *The Morning Watch*, December 1831, quoted by R. A. Huebner, *The Truth of the Pre-Tribulation Rapture Recovered*, Millington, NJ: Present Truth, 1973, pp22-23

seventh vial, which occurs at the end of the tribulation period. This means that Irving was a post-tribulationist.

F. F. Bruce (not a pre-tribulation rapture advocate) responded to the idea that Darby got his pre-tribulation rapture from Margaret MacDonald: 'Where did he [Darby] get it? [My] answer would be that it was in the air in the 1820s and 1830s among eager students of unfulfilled prophecy. . . . direct dependence by Darby on Margaret Macdonald is unlikely'[39].

As to the claim that dispensationalism didn't exist before Darby in the 19th century, Professor William Watson in his book *Dispensationalism before Darby* gives lengthy quotes from writers of the 17th and 18th centuries who believed in either a pre-tribulation rapture or a rapture some time before the return of Christ to earth, among them Robert Maton (1607-53), John Archer (1598-1682), Nathaniel Homes (1599-1692), Captain John Browne (1627-1677), William Sherwin (1674), M. Marsin (1696), Oliver Heywood (1630-1702), Increase Mather (1701), Cotton Mather (1727), John Asgill (1727), Sayer Rudd (1734), Morgan Edwards (ca. 1743), and Grantham Killingworth (1761). Also, in 1590 Francisco Ribera, a Jesuit, taught that a rapture (a gathering-of-the-elect) would happen 45 days before the end of a three and a half year great tribulation[40].

James Morris, in his book *Ancient Dispensational Truth*, quotes a sermon by Pseudo-Ephraim (c. 4th century), *On the Last Times, the Antichrist, and the End of the World*:

> Why therefore do we not reject every care of earthly actions and prepare ourselves for the meeting of the Lord Christ, so that he may draw us from the confusion, which overwhelms all the world? Believe you me, dearest brother, because the coming of the Lord is nigh, believe you me, because the end of the world is at hand, believe me, because it is the very last time. Or do you not believe unless you see with your eyes? See to it that this sentence be not fulfilled among you of the prophet who declares: 'Woe to those who desire to see the day of the Lord!' ***For all the saints and elect of God are gathered, prior to the tribulation that is to come, and are taken to the Lord lest they see the confusion that is to overwhelm the world because of our sins***[41].

---

[39] F. F. Bruce, "Review of The Unbelievable Pre-Trib Origin", in *Evangelical Quarterly*, 47 (January-March 1975), p58.
[40] See the Wikipedia article on the Rapture: https://en.wikipedia.org/wiki/Rapture
[41] Pseudo-Ephraim, 'On the Last Times, the Antichrist, and the End of the World', translated by Cameron Rhoades from C. P. Caspari, *Briefe, Abhandlungen und Predigten*

Lee Brainerd in *Recent Pre-Trib Findings in the Early Church Fathers*, quotes Eusebius (*Fragments in Luke, Luke 17:26*, Migne 24.584-585):

> Indeed, as all perished then except those gathered with Noah in the ark, so also at his coming, the ungodly in the season of apostasy ... shall perish ... At the time of the deluge, it (judgment) did not come and destroy all the inhabitants of the earth before (until) Noah entered into the ark. Therefore, in the same way, at the consummation of the age, it (this pattern) says (demands) that the cataclysm of the destruction of the ungodly shall not happen before those men who are found of God at that time are gathered into the ark and saved according to the pattern of Noah ... all the righteous and godly are to be separated from the ungodly and gathered into the heavenly ark of God. For in this way [comes the time] when not even one righteous man will be found any more among mankind. And when all the ungodly have been made atheists by the antichrist, and the whole world is overcome by apostasy, the wrath of God shall come upon the ungodly.

Post-tribulation rapture advocates place a great deal of emphasis upon history. But the lesson that history teaches is that down though time many people have struggled to piece together the puzzle of future events in different ways. The truth is that all historical arguments are of limited authority. All that ultimately matters is what God has told us in His word.

Summary

A post-tribulation rapture attracts many people because of its appearance of historical authority and its appeal to simplicity, but it does not correctly interpret the key passage in Matthew 24:15-31 about the great tribulation, reading the church and the rapture into these verses. Worse still, it is weighed down with difficult problems regarding who will people the millennium, Israel's distinct future, confusion about the 'great tribulation', and a denial of the imminence of the Lord's coming. This means that the post-tribulation rapture position does not offer a satisfactory explanation for all the major scriptural questions regarding future events.

The Mid-Tribulation Rapture Position

A second view on the future of the church is the mid-tribulation rapture position. This is very much a minority viewpoint. It holds that the rapture

---

aus den letzten zwei Jarhhunderten des kirchliche Alterthums und dem Anfang des Mittelaters (Christiania, 1890), pp208-20

and Christ's return to reign are separate events (as in the pre-tribulation rapture view). It thus avoids the problem of how it is possible for mortal saints, saved but not glorified, to enter the millennium (which the post-tribulation rapture position cannot solve). The mid-tribulation rapture position suggests that the church goes through part of the last seven year period before Christ's return, the 'Seventieth Week' of Daniel. However, crucially, mid-tribulation rapturists believe that the church will not be present to experience any of the time in which God's wrath is being poured out on the earth; they argue that God's wrath is only poured out on earth during later parts of this seven-year period, and that the rapture occurs before this happens. Here we will look at the arguments for, and issues relating, to this position.

The Last Trumpet
One of the arguments for a mid-tribulation rapture is that because the rapture occurs at the 'last trumpet' (1 Corinthians 15:52, cf. 1 Thess. 4:16), therefore, the rapture must occur at the same time as the seventh trumpet of Revelation 11:15 – which mid-tribulationists take to be the middle of the Seventieth Week. However, a trumpet also sounds at Christ's return at the very end of the great tribulation (see Matt. 24:31), so this argument is not very helpful to mid-tribulationists.

Paul's reference to the 'last trumpet' (1 Cor. 15:51) is probably not referring to something in the book of Revelation, for Revelation was not yet written when Paul wrote 1 Corinthians. Some have suggested Paul is referring to the last trumpet sounded in a Roman military camp, in which a series of trumpets were sounded for packing up and moving camp, the last of which signified 'march away'[42]. More likely, Paul was referring back to the trumpets in the book of Numbers, which were sounded for moving camp in the desert and gathering together in an assembly (Numbers 10:1-8), in which case the 'last trump' would mean the last journey we make on our Christian pilgrimage, and the great gathering call of God's people. Paul's point in referring to the last trumpet in 1 Corinthians 15:51 was to assure the Corinthians of the triumphant reality of our resurrection hope rather than trying to precisely settle the timing of the rapture.

The Wrath of God
Mid-tribulationists also argue that the seventh trumpet of Revelation 11:18 introduces the time of God's wrath upon earth: *'The nations were*

---

[42] H. A. Ironside, *Addresses on the First Epistle to the Corinthians*, Loizeaux, 1938, p529

*angry, and **Your wrath has come**, and the time of the dead, that they should be judged, and that You should reward Your servants the prophets and the saints, and those who fear Your name, small and great, and should destroy those who destroy the earth*' (Rev. 11:18). Mid-tribulationists take the second half of Revelation (starting at the end of chapter 11) as the time during which God's wrath is to be poured out on the earth, and indeed, the word 'wrath' occurs frequently in the chapters describing the bowls of God's wrath (Rev. 15:1, 7, 16:1). Accordingly, they hold that the rapture must happen somewhere before this point. However, the problem with this argument is that God's wrath is also found in passages in Revelation 6 and 7. Revelation 6:16-17 says:

'[Men] said to the mountains and rocks, "Fall on us and hide us from the face of Him who sits on the throne and from the wrath of the Lamb! For the great day of His wrath has come, and who is able to stand?" (Rev. 6:16-17).

This verse is not saying that God's wrath is *about to come*. Rather, the aorist tense ('the wrath *has come*') means it has already come. The Greek scholar Henry Alford writes, 'the virtually perfect tense of the aor. *elthen* here can hardly be questioned'. What Alford means is that the Greek aorist tense of the word 'come' here is effectively being used in a perfect tense, which grammatically refers to a past event that has continuing consequences in the present. In other words, God's wrath came before this point in Revelation 6:17 and continues on. This can be seen just by looking at the events of Revelation 6 in which the seals are opened and God's judgments fall upon the earth, resulting in one quarter of the world's population dying (see Rev. 6:8). If one quarter of the world's population dying is not God's wrath, then what is? The idea that God's wrath only commences at the end of the trumpet judgments (Rev. 11:15) is also impossible to accept for another similar reason, for it requires us to believe that all the terrible events entailed during the first six trumpets of Revelation 8 and 9 – resulting in the death of a further one-third of the world's population (Rev. 9:15) – are not somehow connected with God's wrath.

The mid-trib position also struggles to explain the reference to the 'great tribulation' in Revelation 7:14, which speaks of the great multitude who 'come out of *the great tribulation*, and washed their robes and made them white in the blood of the Lamb. (Rev. 7:14). According to the mid-trib position, the church does not go through the 'great tribulation' (the second half of Daniel's 'Seventieth Week') because this is the time of God's wrath. However, the reference to the 'great tribulation' in Revelation 7 shows that the 'great tribulation' is not just confined to the chapters in Revelation following the seventh trumpet in Revelation 11:15.

A Mid-Tribulation Rapture Denies Imminency

Mid-tribulation rapture proponents are forced to deny the doctrine of the imminence of Christ's return, which we will look at in more detail in the next chapter. This is because the Bible's teaching of the establishment of a seven-year treaty with Israel by the Antichrist, which starts Daniel's 'Seventieth Week', would mean that Christ cannot come at any point before this treaty was established, nor could Christ come for another three and a half years after this point – till the middle of the last seven years.

No Rapture in Revelation

A final problem with the mid-tribulation rapture position is that there is no clear description of a rapture occurring anywhere in the middle of the book of Revelation (just as there is no rapture at its end). Suggestions that identify the rapture midway through the book of Revelation are exegetically unconvincing. Consider some of the places some people have argued for a rapture in the middle of the book of Revelation:

- Revelation 11:11-12 ('Now after the three-and-a-half days the breath of life from God entered them, and they stood on their feet, and great fear fell on those who saw them. And they heard a loud voice from heaven saying to them, "Come up here". And they ascended to heaven in a cloud, and their enemies saw them'). But, as we have seen in a previous chapter about the rebuilt Jewish temple in Revelation 11, this is not the rapture of the church, but of two prophetic witnesses who are resurrected during the tribulation.
- Rev. 11:15 ('at the sounding of the seventh trumpet'). But there is no rapture or resurrection mentioned or described.
- Rev. 12:5 ('she bore a male child who was to rule all nations with a rod of iron. And her child was caught up (Gk: *harpazo*: 'raptured') to God and His throne'). However, this is Christ's 'rapture', His ascension, not the rapture of the church.
- Rev. 14:14-16 ('Then I looked, and behold, a white cloud, and on the cloud sat One like the Son of Man, having on His head a golden crown, and in His hand a sharp sickle. And another angel came out of the temple, crying with a loud voice to Him who sat on the cloud, "Thrust in Your sickle and reap, for the time has come for You to reap, for the harvest of the earth is ripe." So He who sat on the cloud thrust

in His sickle on the earth, and the earth was reaped'). However, apart from the fact that there is no description of people being caught up into the air (or even raised from the dead), this seems to be a harvest for judgment, not salvation, as the parallel in Joel 3:13 shows.

The Pre-Wrath Rapture Position

A recent variant of the mid-tribulation rapture position is the 'pre-wrath' rapture. This view holds that the church is raptured sometime after the 'great tribulation' has begun (i.e. after the abomination of desolation), but yet before the time that God's wrath is poured out on the earth. The obvious problem with this view, just as we have seen with the mid-trib view, is that God's wrath is poured out throughout the entire period of the Daniel's 'Seventieth Week', the final seven years, as can be seen in the reference to 'God's wrath' in Revelation 6:16-17 during the opening 'seal' judgments. If the seal and trumpet judgments in Revelation 6-11, instigated by heaven, leave one quarter and then one third of the world's population dead, how is this not part of God's wrath? A mid-tribulation rapture, and its more recent variant a pre-wrath rapture position, therefore seem unlikely.

A Partial Rapture?

Some have taught the partial rapture theory, that only those Christians who are living in a way that is worthy or ready for the Lord at His coming to rapture His church will go with Him, while those who are not worthy are left for the tribulation. This view has been based on the following verses:

- Watch therefore, and pray always that you may be counted worthy to escape all these things that will come to pass, and to stand before the Son of Man (Luke 21:36).
- So Christ was offered once to bear the sins of many. To those who eagerly wait for Him He will appear a second time, apart from sin, for salvation. (Heb. 9:28).
- Because you have kept My command to persevere, I also will keep you from the hour of trial which shall come upon the whole world, to test those who dwell on the earth (Rev. 3:10).
- The Parable of the Wise and Foolish Virgins in Matthew 25:1-13.

However, 1 Corinthians 15:51 says that all believers will taken at the rapture: 'we shall all be changed'. 1 Thessalonians 4:16-17 speaks of 'the dead in Christ' being raised again as well as 'we who are alive and remain' being raptured, not just a subset of the Church.

G. H. Lang argued that Luke 21:36 taught a number of things: '(1) that escape is possible from all those things of which Christ had been speaking, that is, from the whole End Times, (2) that that day of testing will be universal and inevitable… (3) that those who are to escape will be taken to where He, the Son of Man, will then be, that is, at the throne of the Father in the heavens, (4) that there is a fearful peril of disciples becoming worldly in heart and so being enmeshed in that last period (5) that hence it is needful to watch, and to pray ceaselessly, that so we may prevail over all obstacles and dangers and thus escape that era'[43].

However, the pre-tribulation rapture advocate would agree with virtually all of this, particularly the idea that God promises an escape from the entire period of future divine judgment on earth (i.e. Daniel's Seventieth Week), except the pre-tribulation rapture advocate would object to the idea that some special test of works-holiness is being applied to the rapture, for it is by grace we are saved through faith. A pre-tribulation rapture would indeed separate those who are truly saved from mere professors. The parable of the wise and foolish virgins illustrates this: those who are not truly saved, who do not possess the oil of the indwelling Holy Spirit, are left behind.

Conclusion

None of the rapture options we have looked at provide a satisfying solution to the question of when the rapture occurs. In the next chapter we will look at the central puzzle of the Lord's coming in the most important chapters related to future events in the Bible, Matthew 24 and 25. It is this great puzzle that suggests that the rapture happens before the tribulation period.

---

[43] G. H. Lang, *The Revelation of Jesus Christ*, Scribner, Armstrong and Co., 1874, pp88-89

21 THE GREAT PUZZLE OF BIBLE PROPHECY

The most important passage in the Bible about Christ's coming is found in the gospels, in Matthew chapters 24 and 25 (and parallel passages in Mark and Luke), commonly called the Olivet Discourse. Here we find Christ's own words on the subject of His return at the end of this age. However, Christ's words leave us with five puzzles.

Puzzle One: Is Christ's coming Preceded by Signs or is it a Surprise?
In Matthew 24:1-36, we have a number of signs that form a countdown to the coming of the Lord:

- the abomination of desolation (Matt. 24:15),
- the great tribulation (Matt. 24:21),
- signs in the heavens: the sun being darkened and the moon not giving its light (Matt. 24:29).

Following these signs, we read in verse 30: 'the sign of the Son of Man will appear in heaven, and then all the tribes of the earth will mourn, and they will see the Son of Man coming on the clouds of heaven with power and great glory'. This is a description of Christ's return.

The Lord is giving us a sequence of unmistakable signs that show us, in the words of Matthew 24:33, 'when you see all these things, know that it is near – at the doors'.

These signs provide a countdown to Christ's coming. Someone who saw the abomination of desolation set up, and understood what the Bible says about it (particularly the books of Daniel and Revelation, which tell us how long it is from the abomination of desolation till the end of the great tribulation), would be able to calculate how long it is till Christ returns. They would know that it is only three and a half years or 42 months, or 1260 days until Christ returns. They could immediately sit down and work out the date when Christ comes, and maybe even mark the date on their calendar. Christ's coming at the end of the great tribulation will not be a surprise, but will be preceded by unmistakable signs.

However, when we look at the second half of the Olivet Discourse, from Matthew 24:36 through to 25:13, Christ's coming is spoken of as a surprise, without any preceding signs at all.

- It is like Noah's flood: the people of his day 'did not know until the flood came and took them all away' (24:39). Many Christians have taken Christ's words about His coming being like the days of Noah to mean that the world will be especially wicked before Christ comes, and although this is doubtless true, it is not actually the lesson that Christ Himself draws from this comparison. The point the Lord makes is that the people of Noah's day were taken by complete surprise when the flood suddenly came, so that they had no time to be saved.
- Directly after this, Christ talks about the two in the field and the two at the mill, one of whom was taken and one of whom was left. What is the lesson we are supposed to take from this mysterious little paragraph? Christ tells us: '*Watch therefore, for you do not know what hour your Lord is coming*' (24:42). Christ's point is that His coming will be so sudden and such a surprise that two people standing right next to each other will be separated, one taken and the other left.
- Then Christ tells of His coming being like a thief in the night. The point is the same: 'know this, that if the master of the house had known what hour the thief would come, he would have watched and not allowed his house to be broken into. *Therefore you also be ready, for the Son of Man is coming at an hour you do not expect*' (24:43-44).
- In the parable of the Faithful and Wise servant, the lesson is exactly the same. We read, 'the master of that servant will come on a day when he is not looking for Him and at an hour that he is not aware of' (24:50).
- in the parable of the Ten Virgins, the Bridegroom comes in such a way that both the wise and foolish virgins are taken by surprise. Christ comments again, 'Watch therefore, for you know neither the day nor the hour in which the Son of Man is coming' (25:13).

There is a pattern in each of these five paragraphs: the time of the Master's coming is unknown and people are taken by surprise when it suddenly happens.

Nor is it just unbelievers who are taken unawares by Christ's coming (like the godless in Noah's day). Even true believers like the Faithful and Wise Servant and the five Wise Virgins do not know when He is coming. Christ says three times in these verses, 'Watch therefore, for you do not know what hour *your Lord* is coming' – in 24:42, 44 and 25:13.

This is puzzling because if Christ is coming after the abomination of desolation, after the great tribulation, and after the signs in the heavens (the sun being darkened, the moon turning to blood), there would be no excuse for believers to be unaware of Christ's coming. How would believers be taken by surprise at Christ's coming when Christ had just given such a list of tell-tale signs in Matthew 24:1-35? All believers would be on the tip-toes of excitement, knowing that Christ is about to come.

Even the unbelievers will know that the Lord is coming at the end of the great tribulation, for in the book of Revelation 6:15-17, we read:

> the kings of the earth, the great men, the rich men, the commanders, the mighty men, every slave and every free man, hid themselves in the caves and in the rocks of the mountains, and said to the mountains and rocks, "Fall on us and hide us from the face of Him who sits on the throne and from the wrath of the Lamb! For the great day of His wrath has come, and who is able to stand?

The events of the great tribulation will be so terrible that everyone – even the most ungodly – will be aware that something is up. There will be no blissful ignorance during the great tribulation – all will be forced to take sides. The ungodly will blaspheme God's name because of the terrible pains they endure, refusing to repent (Rev. 9:20-21, 13:5-6, 16:11).

So here we have a puzzling difference between the first half of the Olivet Discourse and the second half: the first half tells us of unmistakable signs that provide a countdown to Christ's return, but the second half of the Olivet Discourse tells us that Christ's coming will be a sudden event and a complete surprise. How do we reconcile this difference?

Puzzle Two: Is Christ's Coming preceded by Nightmare Conditions or Perfect Normality?

A second puzzle involves the way Christ describes completely different conditions in the first and second halves of the Olivet Discourse.

In the first part of the Olivet Discourse we have nightmare conditions:

- people fleeing homes and land (Matt. 24:16-20)
- the 'great tribulation, such as has not been since the beginning of the world' (Matt. 24:21),
- huge numbers of people dying: 'unless those days were shortened, no flesh would be saved' (Matt. 24:22)

- great spiritual deception: 'false christs and false-prophets will rise and show great signs and wonders to deceive, if possible, even the elect' (Matt. 24:24)
- apocalyptic calamities: 'the sun will be darkened, and the moon will not give its light, the stars will fall from heaven, and the powers of the heavens will be shaken' (Matt. 24:29).

But when we look at the second part of the Olivet Discourse, from Matthew 24:36 to 25:13, we have an entirely different picture. There we read of conditions of peace and safety in six consecutive paragraphs.

First, Christ tells us that in Noah's day they were eating and drinking, marrying and giving in marriage (Matt. 24:37-39). Some preachers read divorce statistics, homosexuality, and hedonistic pleasure-seeking into these verses. However the verses themselves say that the characteristics of the times when Christ comes will involve marrying and giving in marriage – not sexual immorality and rising divorce statistics. Christ says people will be eating and drinking. These are not sinful activities – these are just part of normal life. Most of us ate and drank today – it is perfectly normal. And that is precisely Christ's point: His coming in these verses is preceded by perfect normality. In fact, we would hardly expect marriage to be an outstanding characteristic of the tribulation period – half the world's population (or more) is wiped out, and we read that the rest of the people in the world did not repent of their idolatry, or 'their murders, or their sorceries, or their ***sexual immorality*** or their thefts' (Rev. 9:20-21). So, the situation Christ describes seems quite different to tribulation conditions. These seem to be normal domestic conditions.

Second, Christ speaks of people working, of two in the field (one taken and one left) and two grinding at the mill (one taken and one left, Matt. 24:40-42). These people do not seem to be suffering any tribulation, but rather seem to be getting on with normal, everyday life. These are people doing normal jobs. Here we have 'business as usual'. These seem to be different people to those Christ told to flee for their lives and leave their houses and fields in the great tribulation section in Matthew 24:17-18.

Third, Christ's coming is compared to the thief in Matthew 24:43-44. Seven times in the New Testament we are told that the Lord's Coming will be as a Thief in the Night (Matt 24:43, Luke 12:39, 1Thess 5:2, 4, 2 Peter 3:10, Rev. 3:3, Rev. 16:15). This is the ultimate metaphor of surprise, but not a pleasant one.

Fourth, in Matthew 24:45-51, Christ tells the parable of his coming being like a Master returning unexpectedly to find some servants working and another servant, suspecting the master is delaying his coming, getting himself drunk, and beating his fellow servants. The faithful and wise servant, appointed 'to give them food in due season', seems to picture the shepherd in the church feeding the flock. This parable seems to picture normal church life. There is no indication of persecution, or tribulation conditions.

Fifth, in the parable of the ten virgins (25:1-13), all of the virgins (not just the foolish) are asleep, unaware of the imminent arrival of the Bridegroom. But how could believers be spiritually asleep during the great tribulation and final countdown to the Lord's coming?

Then, finally, in the parable of the talents (25:14-30), we have three servants who are told to go out and trade with the Master's goods in his absence. The three servants seem to be getting on with 'business as usual'. But in the tribulation period, it will not be 'business as usual', for no one will be able to buy or sell unless they take the mark of the beast. The three servants in the parable are not in hiding or barricading the door against the agents of the Antichrist. Here is a picture of normal Christian service.

Nowhere in these six paragraphs in the second half of the Olivet Discourse do we read about divine judgments, or features of the great tribulation: catastrophes, persecution, war, famine, earthquakes, calamities or distress. There are no burning stars raining down from the sky, or people being beheaded because they refuse to take the Mark of the Beast. Instead, these paragraphs give the impression of normal life before Christ's coming - eating and drinking, marrying and giving in marriage, even careless Christians (24:48-50). These verses do not seem to be describing conditions of tribulation at all – there is not one feature of the tribulation period described in these verses from Matthew 24:36 onwards.

We might describe the contrast between the conditions in the two sections of the Olivet Discourse as Nightmare for people living through the great tribulation (Matt. 24:15-31) and Normality in the second part of the Discourse (Matt. 24:36 – 25:30), for believer as well as unbeliever.

So, here is a second puzzle. How is it possible that conditions of both nightmare and normality apply to the coming of Christ at the end of the great tribulation?

Puzzle Three: Is Christ's coming for the Jews or for Christians?
A third puzzling difference between the first and second half of the Olivet Discourse is that the first half of the Olivet Discourse (Matthew 24:15-31) is very Jewish, while the second half is more Christian.

Some Christians argue that Matthew chapters 24-25 are all Jewish, and have no application to the church, because the church is not going to go through the great tribulation. Other Christians argue that these chapters are all Christian, and that the church will go through the great tribulation, for (they ask), why would these chapters have been placed in our New Testament if they were not written for our benefit?

However, it is better to understand the Olivet Discourse as having a Jewish section and a Christian section. Notice the following five Jewish elements involved in the first half of the Olivet discourse:

1. The Olivet Discourse was spoken by Christ sitting on the Mount of Olives, overlooking the city of Jerusalem and its temple. It was prompted by the disciples' excitement at the grand buildings of the Temple in 24:1. In response, Christ prophesies the Temple's destruction (24:2-3). The disciples are filled with horror and they privately ask Christ about what the future holds. The background to the Olivet Discourse is the Temple in Jerusalem and the disciples' Jewish national pride.
2. In 24:15, Christ gives the sign of the onset of the great tribulation: 'when you see the abomination of desolation spoken of by Daniel the prophet standing in the holy place'. The 'holy place' is a reference to the Temple in Jerusalem – every time this expression 'the holy place' is used elsewhere in the New Testament, it refers to the Jewish temple in Jerusalem (Acts 6:13, 21:28, Hebrews 9:25) or heaven itself (Hebrews 9:12). Here we have a reference back to the prophet Daniel and the desecration of the Jewish temple by the setting up of an idol to Zeus in it in 167 BC by the Syrian king Antiochus Epiphanes. This idol was called the Abomination of Desolation (Dan. 11:31). This historical idolatrous abomination now becomes a prophetic prototype of a future end-time desecration of a Jewish temple (Dan. 12:11, cf. 9:27). To understanding the abomination of desolation, we need to understand the Jewish historical connection. Again, then, we have a Jewish historical setting for the great tribulation passage.
3. In 24:16, Christ says, 'let those in Judea flee to the mountains'. The great tribulation particularly affects those in the land of Israel; they are told to flee for their lives. Here we have a Jewish geographical focus.
4. In 24:17, Christ refers to Jewish conditions when he warns 'him who is on the housetop' not to go down to take anything from the house. Most Westerners don't live in flat-roofed houses, but most people in Israel and Jerusalem do. Here we have a piece of Jewish cultural colour.

5. In 24:20, Christ refers to Jewish religious practices when he says, 'pray that your flight may not be in winter or on the Sabbath'. For observant orthodox Jews, travelling a long distance would be a violation of the Sabbath. Even for a non-religious Jew today, there is very little transport or travel on the Sabbath. Here we have a Jewish religious and cultural context: the Sabbath.

These warnings were not given to Christians, because Christians are not under the Jewish Sabbath law, and would not be stopped from fleeing by concern for Sabbath regulations. Nor were these words spoken to Christians of all ages – but only to that future generation that will live through the great tribulation. Nor do these words apply to Christians living in different locations around the world – they apply to those living in Judea.

Christ's prophecy concerning the great tribulation contains multiple references to Jewish national, geographical, historical, religious and cultural life, but it does not have any direct connection or immediate reference to Christians. Other Old Testament Bible passages refer to the Jewish focus of the great tribulation (e.g. Jer. 31, Dan. 12), and while we know from other Bible passages that the great tribulation is a time of worldwide distress, yet here in the first half of the Olivet Discourse, the focus and spotlight falls on the Jewish nation.

The second half of the Olivet discourse, however, is very different. It contains a number of parables that have always been most naturally understood as Christian parables.

The parable of the Talents (Matt. 25:14-30) tells of three servants who are given their Master's goods and, while their Master was away, they traded with them. Notice, in verse 19, we are told that the Master came back 'after a long time'. There are some commentators who argue that Matthew 24-25 has nothing to do with the church, and that these are three tribulation saints. However, the great tribulation is a very short period – only three and a half years. This parable instead speaks about a 'long time', and most naturally applies to the entire Christian era. In our Master's absence, Christians are to be busy using our spiritual gifts. It is a Christian parable, and to try to read tribulation saints or conditions into it is a forced and unnatural interpretation.

Similarly, the parable of the faithful and wise servant in the Master's house (24:45-51) is a Christian parable stressing the importance of the need for shepherds to feed God's people in the church. This same parable is found in Luke's Gospel, almost word for word, but not in relation to any

Jewish tribulation conditions. Instead, it is found in Luke 12:42-46, amongst a number of chapters which are all about how a Christian disciple should live. Notice that one of the servants says 'My master is delaying His coming' (Matt. 24:48). This more naturally applies to the long wait we are in the midst of now – nearly 2000 years long – since Christ went back to heaven, rather than the short and specified period of the tribulation.

Again, in the parable of the Wise and Foolish Virgins we read in Matthew 25:5 that 'while the bridegroom was delayed they all slumbered and slept'. The word 'delay' again points to the waiting period of the Christian era. This parable, in addition, is all about a wedding, and this suggests Christ and the church, His Bride.

So, here we have a third difference between the two sections of the Olivet Discourse. The first part of it has a Jewish focus during the great tribulation period. In it we read of a future Jewish temple (where the abomination of desolation is set up), and its warnings are directed to Sabbath-keeping Jews.

The second part of the Olivet Discourse, however, not only contains no references to tribulation, or to specifically Jewish conditions, but also contains parables that most naturally apply to Christians in the church age. Christ's coming in these two sections seems to again be quite different.

Puzzle Four: Why is Matthew's Olivet Discourse Twice as Long as Mark and Luke?

Mark and Luke finish their accounts of the Olivet Discourse in different places to Matthew. If we compare the Olivet Discourse in Matthew, Mark and Luke's Gospels, the idea of two different sections to the Discourse makes sense.

If you study the table on the next page closely you will notice two particular features. Firstly, Matthew's account of Christ's Olivet Discourse is more than twice as long as Mark's and Luke's. Both Mark 13 and Luke 21 conclude Christ's Olivet Discourse before Matthew has even finished Ch. 24. Mark's column has dashes in the last seven boxes, showing that Mark does not include any of the material from Matthew 24:36 onwards. Secondly, notice that Luke's column only has dashes and references from Luke 12 and Luke 17 next to these blanks in Mark's column – but no references whatsoever in Luke 21. Thus, Mark's and Luke's accounts of Christ's Olivet prophecy both stop two-thirds of the way down the material in Matthew 24 (about 24:36).

Prophecies	Matt.	Mark	Luke
1. Christ's prophecy & Disciples' question about Temple's Destruction	24:1-3	13:1-4	21:5-7
2. Warning about false-signs of the end	24:4-14	13:5-13	21:8-19
3. Abominat'n of Des. & Gt. Tribulation	24:15-22	13:14-20	--[AD70]--
False-Christs	24:23-26	13:21-23	(17:23?)
(Coming like lightning, Eagles)	24:27, 28	-----	17:24, 37
4. The Coming of Christ	24:29-31	13:24-27	21:25-27
5. Parable of the Fig Tree	24:32-35	13:28-31	21:29-33
(No man knows the day)	24:36	13:32	-----
6. As in the days of Noah	24:37-39	-----	17:26, 27
7. Two in field, at the mill	24:40-42	-----	17:36, 35
8. The Thief in the night	24:43-44	-----	12:39, 40
9. The Faithful and Wise Servant	24:45-51	-----	12:42-46
10. The Ten Virgins	25:1-13	-----	-----
11. The Talents	25:14-30	-----	(19:11-27?)
12. The Sheep & the Goats	25:31-46	-----	-----

All three accounts of the Olivet Discourse part and go their separate ways at Matthew 24:36 – the verse where Christ says that no man knows the day of hour of His coming. After this point, Mark's gospel contains no more of the Olivet Discourse, nor does Luke's gospel, which instead places the same parables in very different contexts – not in Luke 21, but in chapters 12, 17 and 19.

What Matthew appears to have done is slotted in other sayings of Christ about future events at appropriate points in the Olivet Discourse, but mostly after Matthew 24:36. Evidence of this is seen in that in every case where Mark has blanks, Luke either has blanks too or has references in Chapters 12, 17 and 19 – not 21. Luke's Gospel shows us that the sayings that Mark omits were not spoken on the Mount of Olives at all – they were spoken elsewhere, in chapters 12, 17, and 19, and in quite different settings.

Matthew writes his gospel, not chronologically, but logically, that is thematically or topically. He groups Christ's teachings on various subjects into topical sections or blocks of material instead of separating them according to the original setting in which they were spoken. Matthew does the same thing in other parts of his gospel, too. For example, Christ's teachings in the Sermon on the Mount (Matthew 5-7) were recorded by Luke in different places in his gospel (Luke 6, 11 and 12, in very different settings) and similarly with the evangelistic instructions (Matthew 10)[1].

So, here we have another difference between the first and second parts of the Olivet Discourse. The first part was spoken on the Mount of Olives, but Mark and Luke's gospels show us that Christ spoke the other parables about future events after Matthew 24:36 on other occasions[2].

Puzzle Five: Is Christ coming to take us to Heaven or to Earth?
Leaving the Olivet Discourse, the fifth puzzling feature about Christ's coming is found in John 14:2-3, where Christ gave us a beautiful promise:

> In My Father's house are many mansions; if it were not so, I would have told you. I go to prepare a place for you. And if I go and prepare a place for you, I will come again and receive you to Myself, that where I am, there you may be also.

This verse appears to say that when Christ comes again, He will receive us

---

[1] See the author's book, *Matthew's Messiah: A Guide to Matthew's Gospel*

[2] The idea that there are different sections in the Olivet Discourse is not a novel idea at all. J. N. Darby in his *Synopsis*, and C. H. Mackintosh in his *Miscellaneous Writings*, both argue that the Olivet Discourse has different sections that apply (1) to the Jewish people, (2) to the church and (3) to the Gentile nations (in the last parable about the separation of the sheep from the goats, which Christ says refers to the Gentile nations being judged at His coming). More recently, Professor John F. Hart at Moody Bible Institute has argued the same: he suggests 'that Matthew 24:29-31 refers to the second coming – the return of Christ to the earth. But Matthew 24:36-44 speaks of a pretribulation rapture, and coincides with the sudden onset of the day of the Lord (the future tribulation of seven years)' (John. F. Hart, "Jesus and the Rapture: Matthew 24" in *Evidence for the Rapture: a Biblical Case for Pretribulationism*, Chicago: Moody Publishers, 2015, p46). Some dispensationalists reject this idea and say that Matthew 24-25 do not have anything to say to the church, however, you can't get much more dispensational than Darby, and yet Darby argues for different sections in the Olivet Discourse.

to Himself and take us to His Father's house. This seems to refer to heaven, for this is where Christ went after He finished His earthly ministry and left His disciples.

This verse presents us with another puzzle, because it seems to teach that the Christian is going to heaven when Christ comes again. This is strange, because the very idea of Christ's coming suggests a return to earth.

There are a number of possible interpretations of this verse. First, some have suggested that it is speaking about a Christian going to heaven at their death. Marcus Dods wrote, 'The promise is fulfilled in the death of the Christian'[3]. This is the way this verse is sometimes applied at funerals. However, while the Christian goes to heaven at death, this verse is talking about Christ's return, and nowhere does the Bible teach that Christ 'comes again' each time a believer dies to receive him or her to heaven.

Secondly, some have suggested that this verse refers to the promised descent of the Holy Spirit[4]. Thus, in John 14:18, Christ says, 'I will come to you' – a reference to the coming of the Holy Spirit. But this interpretation fails to do justice to what Christ says in 14:2, 'I will come again and receive you to myself, that where I am there you may be also'. At the Holy Spirit's descent, Christ did not receive the disciples to Himself. The words are not talking about the Holy Spirit. They are about Christ's second coming when we will be taken to heaven.

Thirdly, post-tribulationist Robert Gundry offers this interpretation:

> In order to console the disciples concerning His going away, Jesus tells them that His leaving will work to their advantage. He is going to prepare for them spiritual abodes within His own Person. Dwelling in these abiding places, they will belong to God's household ... Thus the rapture will not have the purpose of taking them to heaven. It rather follows from their being in Christ, in whom each believer already has an abode[5].

But this is theological gobble-gook and mystical mumbo-jumbo. It just muddies the waters. It is hard to see how such a bizarre explanation would have been understood by the disciples, let alone be of any comfort.

Fourthly, Douglas Moo argues that Christ did not promise the disciples He will take them to heaven when He comes, but simply that He will receive them to Himself, and that they will be with Him. He writes:

---

[3] Marcus Dods, *The Expositor's Greek Testament*, Hodder and Stoughton, 1:822
[4] Craig Keener, *Bible Background Commentary: New Testament*, IVP, 1993, p299
[5] Robert Gundry, *The Church and the Tribulation*, Zondervan, p154

'the text does not state that believers will go directly to heaven, but only that they will always be with the Lord'[6]. However, this explanation ignores the immediate context, in which Christ talks about many 'mansions' in the Father's house, and how He is going away to prepare a place for the disciples (v2). Christ repeats this promise again at the beginning of verse 3: 'And if I go and prepare a place for you, I will come again'. Why does Christ repeatedly talk about preparing abiding places for us in the Father's house, if we are not going there? Moo rips one phrase out of the context and ignores Christ's words which say that we are going to the Father's house – heaven.

Lastly, we could read the verse and take it at face value, and accept that it says that when Christ returns, He is going to take believers to heaven. Don Carson writes, 'The simplest explanation is best: *my Father's house* refers to heaven'[7]. But this is very puzzling: how is it possible that we are taken to heaven at Christ's coming, as John 14:3 seems to say, when other passages speak about Christ coming again to earth?

Three Possible Solutions to these Puzzling Features

How can these different descriptions about the Lord's coming be true at the same time? Some of them are diametrically opposed to each other: signs and surprise, nightmare and normality, heaven and earth. Post-tribulationist Douglas Moo writes, 'All interpreters, whether they believe the [Olivet] discourse is addressed to the Church or to Israel, face the difficulty of explaining how an advent heralded by specific signs can yet be one of which it is said, 'No one knows the day and hour'[8].

We cannot account for these differences by saying that perhaps unbelievers will not know the day or hour of Christ's coming, while believers will see the signs and be ready for Christ's coming. This solution will not work because in the second half of the Olivet discourse even the believers are told that '*you* do not know what hour *your Lord* is coming' (Matt. 24:42). Christ says that even the angels do not know the day or hour of Christ's coming (Matt. 24:36). Nor is it convincing to suggest that the different descriptions are due to different conditions in different parts of the world – great tribulation in certain places, but relative normality in other parts – for the Bible teaches that the tribulation period 'shall come upon the whole world to test those who dwell on the earth' (Rev. 3:10).

There are, historically speaking, only three solutions to these puzzles

---

[6] Moo, *Three Views on the Rapture*, Zondervan, 2010, p197
[7] D. A. Carson, *The Gospel according to John*, PNTC, Eerdmans, 1990, p489
[8] Douglas Moo, *Three Views on the Rapture*, Zondervan, 2010, p237

that have been offered with any seriousness. Firstly, some have denied that Christ's coming will be a surprise: it will be preceded by clear and unmistakable signs. Secondly, some have denied the signs and insisted that Christ's coming could occur at any moment. Thirdly, some accept that Christ's coming will be both a surprise and yet preceded by signs because there are actually two different comings. Christ comes first for His church before the tribulation period, and then secondly, Christ returns to reign after the tribulation.

Solution One: Christ's Coming Cannot Occur at any Time
Firstly, some deny that Christ's coming is near, or that it will be a surprise. Thus, Berkhof (an amillennialist) writes, 'According to Scripture several important events must occur before the return of the Lord, and therefore it cannot be called imminent'[9]. These events include the great tribulation, the coming of the Antichrist, the battle of Armageddon, and other tumultuous signs in the heavens.

Similarly, post-millennialists deny the imminence of Christ's coming because they believe that these signs (as well as all the millennium itself) must occur before Christ returns. For the post-millennialist, Christ's coming is still thousands of years away. As a result of denying the doctrine of imminence, the great event of Christ's coming is pushed over the horizon beyond any pressing concern.

However, numerous verses through the New Testament teach that Christ's coming is a surprise that could happen at any moment. In addition to the five verses we have seen in Matthew 24 and 25 that teach that Christ will come as a surprise, there are many other verses that teach that Christians should be ready at any moment for Christ's coming, for it is at hand:

- Luke 12:40 – 'Therefore you also be **ready**, for the Son of Man is coming at an hour you do not expect' (and see also verse 36).
- Luke 21:36 – '**Watch** therefore, and pray always that you may be counted worthy to escape all these things that will come to pass, and to stand before the Son of Man'.
- Romans 13:11-12 – 'The night is far spent, the day is at hand [lit. **drawn near**]. Therefore let us cast off the works of darkness, and let us put on the armour of light'

---

[9] Louis Berkhof, *Systematic Theology*, p696

- The early Christians used the watch-word 'Maranatha', meaning 'O Lord come!' (1 Cor. 16:22).
- Philippians 4:5 says 'The Lord is *at hand*'.
- 1 Thessalonians 5:2 says 'the day of the Lord will come like a thief in the night'.
- James 5:8 says 'the coming of the Lord is *at hand*'.
- 1 Peter 1:5 – '[we] are kept by the power of God through faith for salvation *ready* to be revealed in the last time' (and see 4:5).
- 1 Peter 4:7 says 'the end of all things is *at hand*'.
- 2 Peter 3:10 says the day of the Lord will come as a thief in the night
- 1 John 2:18 says 'it is the last hour'.
- Rev. 22:20 reads 'Surely I am coming quickly. Amen, even so, Come, Lord Jesus'.
- Other verses teach that the Christian is to live in constant expectation of the Lord's coming: Romans 8:23, 1 Corinthians 1:7, 15:51-52, Galatians 5:5, Philippians 3:20, 1 Thessalonians 1:10, 4:13-17, Titus 2:13, 1 Timothy 6:14, Hebrews 9:28, 1 John 2:28, 3:3.

Gordon Fee writes about 1 Corinthians 1:7 ('waiting for the coming of our Lord Jesus Christ') that Paul had an 'ever present' concern about Christ's 'imminent return'[10]. R. C. H. Lenski wrote about 1 Cor. 15:51-52: 'The simple fact is that Paul did not know when Christ would return ... All that he knew, and all that we know, is that Christ may come at any time'[11]. Martyn Lloyd-Jones wrote about Phil. 4:5, 'In all that we do we must always remember that the Lord may return at any time. His coming is always at hand, yes, but we do not know when, and so we must always live in the realization that he is coming'[12].

The word we use to say that Christ could return at any time is 'imminent', which comes from a Latin word 'overhanging'. Imminence does not mean that the Lord *must* come within my lifetime, but that He *may* come (E. W. Rogers). It does not mean that He *will* come today, but that He *could*. Imminence does not mean that Christ must be coming soon, or that nothing else can happen before it, but just that there is nothing to stop it happening at any moment.

Some argue against the doctrine of imminence by pointing to events

---

[10] Gordon Fee, *The First Epistle to the Corinthians*, Eerdmans, 1987, p42

[11] R. C. H. Lenski, *An Interpretation of Paul's First and Second Epistle to the Corinthians*, Columbus, OH: Wartburg Press, 1946, p737

[12] D. M. Lloyd-Jones, *Life of Peace*, London: Hodder and Stoughton, 1990, p162

predicted to occur before the Lord's coming, like Peter's death (John 21:18-19) or Paul's death (2 Tim. 4:8) or the destruction of the temple in Jerusalem (Matthew 24:1-2). But Paul's death no more denies imminence than any other Christian's death, for while Paul was ready to depart and be with Christ (Phil. 1:23) or remain on earth serving Him (Phil. 1:25), he also anticipated the Lord's coming in his own lifetime (see his use of 'we' in 1 Thess. 4:15, 17). The predictions of Peter's death and the temple's destruction were private and cryptic; it is probable that they were only fully understood after the event (see similar cases in John 2:22 and 12:16). For all the early disciples knew, Jesus could still have come beforehand.

Renald Showers writes, 'When an event is truly imminent, we never know exactly when it will happen. ... we should always be prepared for it to happen at any moment ... we cannot legitimately say that an imminent event will happen soon... an imminent event may take place within a short time, but it does not have to do so in order to be imminent'[13].

Algernon Pollock offers an illustration:

> Suppose a husband left England for Canada. He informs his wife that his business may take a lengthy period, or he may be able to settle it at once; and return by the next available steamer. True, at the first, she cannot expect her husband to return at ANY moment. The first two or three weeks she could safely say, "I am not expecting my husband for some time," but given time for the steamer to reach Canada, a day or two in which to settle his business, and a few days for the homeward journey, she could then say, "I expect my husband's return at ANY moment." She would be a foolish woman did she not expect him daily as the time wore on, and as week succeeded week her expectation would deepen[14].

Don Carson argues that the solution to the puzzle is that Christ's coming could happen 'in any generation'[15], and therefore it is not true to say that it will be a surprise that could happen at any moment. However, the verses we have seen from Matthew 24:36 onwards state that Christ's coming will be a surprise without forewarning, like a thief in the night, or like the flood of Noah, so that the Lord could say, 'Therefore, you also be ready, for the

---

[13] Renald Showers, *Maranatha, Our Lord, Come!* Friends of Israel, 1995, p127
[14] Algernon Pollock, *May Christ Come at Any Moment?* (see online at stempublishing.com/authors/pollock)
[15] D. A. Carson, "Matthew", in *The Expositors Bible Commentary*, Vol. 8, Grand Rapids: Zondervan, 1984, p490

Son of Man is coming at an hour which you do not expect' (Matt. 24:44), and 'Watch therefore, for you do not know what hour your Lord is coming' (Matt. 24:42). Carson's suggestion that Christ could come in any generation is a platitude that ends up telling us nothing.

Douglas Moo suggests a similar solution, arguing that 'Jesus' words about the unknown day ... apply to every generation except the last – that generation who, when it "sees these things happening," knows that Christ is at the very gates (Matt. 24:33-34). Or it may be that while the exact time cannot be known, one will be able to know the general time of the advent after the tribulation has begun'[16]. However, this again denies the verses from Matthew 24:36 onwards which speak of Christ coming upon unsuspecting believers and unbelievers alike as a sudden surprise. Moo highlights the signs and ignores the element of surprise.

The attempt to solve the puzzle by denying that Christ's coming will be a surprise that could happen at any moment does not satisfy. It simply dodges the chief difficulty: the mention of the doctrine of the imminence of the Lord's return in many New Testament verses.

Solution Two: There are No Signs before Christ comes
Secondly, some deny that any signs will precede the Lord's coming. However, the Bible speaks of at least twelve signs that will precede Christ's coming:

- The abomination of desolation (Matt. 24:15, Dan. 9:27).
- A rebuilt temple in Jerusalem (Matt. 24:15, Rev. 11, 2 Thess. 2:4)
- The great apostasy (2 Thess. 2:3)
- The great tribulation (Matt. 24:21, Dan. 12:1)
- The gospel preached to all nations (Matt. 24:14)
- Antichrist's appearance, one-world government and the mark of the beast - 666 (Rev. 13, 2 Thess. 2)
- Signs and wonders done by Antichrist (Matt. 24:24, 2 Thess. 2:9-10)
- Strong delusion sent by God on unbelievers (2 Thess. 2:11-12)
- Restraint on lawlessness withdrawn (2 Thess. 2:6-8)
- The battle of Armageddon (Zech. 12-14).
- Signs in the sun, moon and stars (Matt. 24:29-31)
- Israel's national conversion (Rom. 11:26, Zech. 12-13)

Preterists believe that all the signs mentioned in Matthew 24-25 happened

---

[16] Douglas Moo, *Three Views on the Rapture*, p237

in the first century AD in the siege of Jerusalem. But this runs up against the difficulty that Christ said that His coming occurs 'immediately after the tribulation' period (Matt. 24:29-31). Preterists try to get around this by arguing that Christ's coming occurred 'spiritually' in AD 70. Thus, R. T. France suggests that Christ's coming in the Olivet Discourse refers to the 'coming of God to receive vindication and authority' by the Temple's destruction and the punishment of 'the Jewish establishment which has rejected him'[17]. However, Christ insists that His coming will be visible and unmistakable: 'for as the lightning comes from the east and flashes to the west, so also will the coming of the Son of Man be' (Matt. 24:27) … 'they shall see the Son of Man coming on the clouds with power and great glory' (Matt. 24:30). Preterists step outside the boundaries of Christian orthodoxy when they state that Christ's coming is not bodily or visible.

Others deny the signs by arguing that we are already in the great tribulation, and therefore Christ's coming could occur at any moment. Grudem takes this approach, arguing that all the signs of Christ's coming (except the sun being darkened, the moon not giving light, and stars falling) may have already occurred. He therefore writes, 'all the signs have been fulfilled, and therefore Christ in fact could return at any moment'[18].

However, if the great tribulation is already upon us, then who is the Antichrist, and where are all the people wearing the mark of the beast – 666 – on their hand or forehead? Where are all the miraculous signs and lying wonders being done by the Antichrist and the False Prophet by the power of Satan (2 Thess. 2:9, Rev. 13:13)? Is God presently sending a strong delusion upon unbelievers so that they do not receive the truth (2 Thess. 2:11)? Are the armies of the world already mobilizing for the battle of Armageddon?

Grudem argues that because some people in the past thought that Napoleon or Hitler might be the Antichrist, then the Antichrist might have already come. But this is nonsense. If Napoleon or Hitler were the Antichrist, then Christ would have come in 1815 or 1945. Because He didn't, Napoleon and Hitler obviously weren't Antichrist. Grudem says that because some false predictions have been made about Antichrist, we should accept that it has already happened. This is as ridiculous as saying that because some people have (foolishly) suggested dates for the return of Christ, then we should accept that Christ has in fact already come. The logic of Grudem's argument here is so absurd it is right up there as a contender for the stupidest idea ever suggested by any theologian in

---

[17] R. T. France, *The Gospel according to Matthew*, Leicester: IVP, 1985, p344
[18] Grudem, *Systematic Theology*, p1100

history. The fact that the Antichrist has not yet come means that this sign has not yet been fulfilled, so we are not in the great tribulation.

Again, if we are already in the great tribulation, which is a time of persecution unlike any other, why are the vast majority of Christians enjoying comfortable conditions on earth and going unmolested to church every Sunday? How is it possible that there are Christian heads of state in the world today, if we live during the great tribulation? In what way is the present day far worse than any other period in Christian history? Where are all the people being 'beheaded for their witness to Jesus' because they had not 'worshipped the beast or his image, and had not received his mark on their foreheads or on their hands' (Rev. 20:4)? Where is the great apostasy, the general abandonment of the faith (2 Thess. 2:3)? If the great tribulation was already present when Grudem wrote his book in 1994, then why didn't Christ come three years later, in 1997 or thereabouts?

Grudem's solution is, in effect, a denial of all the biblical signs that must occur before the coming of Christ: the reality of the Antichrist, the great tribulation as a time of worldwide persecution unlike any other in history, and God's wrath being poured out upon the world. This does not represent a serious solution to the puzzle of how Christ's coming can be both a surprise and yet preceded by signs, nor how Christ's coming can be preceded by non-tribulation normality and yet at the same by nightmare.

Grudem appears to believe that the great tribulation will actually happen, but his is a watered-down great tribulation that is evacuated of any trouble or difficulty, and therefore unfaithful to the biblical witness. The strangest thing about Grudem's argument is that he himself is not convinced by it, for he repeatedly admits that his suggested 'fulfilments' of these signs are 'unlikely'[19]. The reason why Grudem is not convinced by his own argument is simple: it is so illogical that it ranks amongst the worst eschatological arguments ever suggested by a professional theologian.

Solution Three: A Coming in Two Stages

A third solution to the puzzle is that both the signs and the surprise are true, but do not occur at the same time. This third view accepts what the Bible teaches about the two very different descriptions of Christ's coming, without denying or diluting them, and without confusing or compromising them. It holds to both what the Bible says about the imminence of Christ's return and the fact that it will be preceded by unmistakable signs.

---

[19] Grudem, *Systematic Theology*, pp1101, 1102, 1103, 1104

It suggests that the differences between these descriptions of Christ's coming are real and significant. In the absence of any better attempts at harmonization, it holds that both sides of these paradoxical puzzles are true, because there are two different stages of Christ's coming, which will not occur at the same time, but as separate events.

These two different stages of Christ's coming occur at different times (one before the tribulation period, and one at the end of the tribulation period), in different manners (one as a sudden surprise, one publicly after signs), with the result that the church is taken to different places (firstly to heaven, and then secondly after the tribulation back to earth), and with different objects (firstly to take the church out of the tribulation period, and then to reign, after rescuing the Jewish nation at Armageddon).

The main objection to this solution is that the Bible never speaks of two separate comings of Christ at the end of the age. But the possibility that there are two stages to Christ's coming is similar to other biblical and theological paradoxes: Old Testament prophecies spoke of a suffering Messiah and a glorified Messiah, and yet nowhere was it explicitly stated in the Old Testament that there would be two separate comings of Christ, the first as a suffering servant, and the second, thousands of years later, to reign as King of Kings. Christ is fully God and truly human, yet the Bible never explains the mystery of how it is possible for one person to be both of these very different things. The kingdom of God is likewise both a present spiritual sphere and yet also a future earthly reign, although the Bible nowhere explicitly harmonizes the two sides of the Kingdom or sets out a timeline of their temporal relationship in any doctrinal statement. In the same way, we cannot simply dismiss this solution because the Bible never explicitly states that Christ's second coming will happen in two stages.

One reason why many theologians are reluctant to accept this solution, at a social and psychological level, is that with the success of works of fiction, like the *Left Behind* novels, it is considered a populist view, looked upon with disdain by professional theologians. There are, however, two very important theological reasons for considering this solution:

1. This solution maintains a distinction between Israel and the Church instead of denying a national future for Israel in spiritual, ethnic, national and territorial terms.
2. This solution is based on better hermeneutics. It avoids the absurdities of the allegorizing approach and instead attempts to read the Bible in a more natural and normal way. It holds to the plenary

inspiration of Scripture - by not prioritizing the New Testament over the Old Testament, by not interpreting certain New Testament verses in a way that overrides the original meaning of Old Testament verses, and by not misinterpreting Old Testament verses by ripping them out of context.

This third solution is what is called in science 'an inference to the best explanation'. It is an inference because it is not based on an explicit statement of Scripture. But this is because we do not have exhaustive information in the Bible about future events, and whatever view of future events a person holds must be pieced together from different passages.

But an 'inference to the best explanation' means three other things:

a. as a hypothesis, this solution provides an explanation for the evidence we have seen,
b. no other hypothesis provides a true solution,
c. therefore, this is the best available explanation and is probably true.

This third solution is based on a pre-tribulation rapture: the idea that Christ is going to come to take His church to heaven before the great tribulation then, after the great tribulation, He will come again with the church to reign on earth. He must come for His saints before He comes with His saints. It is to the subject of the rapture that we must now turn.

What is the Strange Event Described in Matthew 24:40-42?

Matthew 24:40-42 describes a strange event associated with Christ's coming:

> Then two men will be in the field: one will be taken and the other left. [41] Two women will be grinding at the mill: one will be taken and the other left. [42] Watch therefore, for you do not know what hour your Lord is coming.

There are seven pieces of evidence that point to this being a rapture:

A. Christ does not seem to be telling a parable here: the event is too vivid and mysterious. The description is not an everyday event like those normally employed in parables. Christ is describing in detail an actual event as it takes place in the future.
B. Neither does this event seem to refer to death, either by natural causes,

catastrophes, diseases or wars. Death by natural causes would not suddenly strike down healthy people like these workers. A catastrophic death would normally kill both of the two people standing next to each other, rather than just one. Here is something more discriminating than death.

C. It is an event that accompanies Christ's coming. Christ's words which follow show this: 'you do not know what hour your Lord is coming'.

D. This event occurs suddenly and instantaneously, without any warning. Christ's words which follow reinforce this lesson: 'you do not know what hour your Lord is coming'. No one can predict when it will occur, and the separation catches people unaware, as they go about their ordinary work. This matches the description of the rapture given in 1 Cor. 15:51-52: 'in a moment, in the twinkling of an eye'.

E. This is not a localized event, but one which happens to different people in different situations all over the world. Luke tells us that, in addition to the two in the field and at the mill, there will be two in one bed, one of whom will be taken, and the other left (Luke 17:34). This suggests that this same event will simultaneously affect some people during the night, while for others it will happen during the day. Nor is this event restricted to people of certain races, genders or social classes. Its impact is generalized – anybody who sleeps in a bed could be affected. It is universal in its effect.

F. Christ's description stresses separation rather than destruction. Two very similar people will be together, but one will be taken and the other left. Men and women will literally disappear right in front of the person they are standing beside.

G. Theologians from all camps accept that this is a rapture event. Post-tribulation rapture advocates like Reese, Moo and Gundry hold that this is the post-tribulation rapture[20], occurring at the end of the Tribulation period, at Christ's return. Pre-tribulation rapturists like John Walvoord also hold that this is a rapture, but suggest it a rapture of unbelievers[21], a rapture of the ungodly who are taken away to stand before Christ in judgment at the end of the Tribulation. Others suggest that it is a rapture of godly Jews at the end of the Tribulation.

Thus, it would seem that these verses describe a rapture. Who is 'raptured' and when this rapture happens are matters of debate, but most are agreed

---

[20] Reese, *The Approaching Advent of Christ*, p208, Gundry, *The Church and the Tribulation*, p137-8, Moo, *Three Views on the Rapture*, pp222-3
[21] John Walvoord, *The Rapture Question*, p189

that this is a rapture. In fact, it is hard to imagine a better description of the effects of the rapture. Some commentators argue that this is a post-tribulation rapture, and that when Christ returns at the end of the great tribulation, the church will be raptured, leaving the ungodly for judgment. However, there are five reasons for doubting that this is a post-tribulation rapture of believers.

1. **Context**: The main reason that post-tribulation rapture advocates hold that this scene happens at the end of the great tribulation is the general context: Christ's return (Matt. 24:30) in the Olivet Discourse. However, as we have seen, there are good reasons for doubting that the immediate context in the second half of the Olivet Discourse, from Matthew 24:36 onwards (where the two in the field, two at the mill paragraph is found) is the tribulation period. There is no suggestion anywhere in verses 40-42 of tribulation conditions. The two in the field and the two at the mill are getting on with normal life; they are not disturbed by any tribulation. Nor is there any hint of tribulation conditions anywhere in the surrounding paragraphs in the second half of the Olivet Discourse.
2. **Normality**: The verses immediately before the 'two in the field/mill' are about Noah and the Flood. The lesson is that the godless were completely unsuspecting of the judgment that was about to overtake them; they were 'eating and drinking, marrying and giving in marriage … and did not know until the flood came and took them all away' (Matt. 24:38-39). In the parallel passage, Luke adds that it will be like in the days of Lot: people were 'buying and selling, planting and building' (Luke 17:27-28). As John Hart writes, 'Matthew's and Luke's description seem too casual to take place during the second half of the tribulation. During the second half of the tribulation, no buying or selling will be done without the mark of the Beast (Rev. 13:17). The lifestyles depicted in the days of Noah and Lot are those that have existed in every generation since the earliest days of human history. This implies an emphasis on the normalcy and indifference that take place prior to the day of the Lord. The illustrations that follow verses 37-39 about two men working in the field and two women grinding at the mill (vv.41-42) also argue for the focus on normalcy. Many commentators simply believe that the ordinary life patterns described in the Noah illustration can coexist with the colossal distresses that run their course prior to Christ's second coming. But this seems

unreasonable'[22]. The great tribulation will not involve business as usual, or life carrying on as normal. It will completely disrupt normal life (being characterized by famine rather than eating and drinking, Rev. 6:5-6, and sexual immorality rather than people getting married, Rev. 9:21). Further, there will also be an awareness of divine judgment, even amongst the godless. They will acknowledge God's hand in judgment (Rev. 6:16-17), refuse to repent (Rev. 9:20-21) and instead blaspheme God's name (Rev. 16:9, 11). They will be defiant, not unsuspecting.

3. **No Signs**: There are no signs here that Christ is about to come. Hart asks, 'How can a "business-as-usual" attitude toward life exist at the precise time when the twenty-one tribulation judgments of Revelation are being poured out in all their intensity? ... [when] the calamities that precede the second coming of Christ will be so severe that the human race will be close to extinction apart from the Lord's intervention (Matt. 24:22)'[23]. If this is a post-tribulation rapture, we do not read of the armies of the world being gathered to fight at the battle of Armageddon, nor of the signs of the sun being darkened, the moon being turned to blood, and the stars falling from heaven. Christ's own words immediately after the 'two in the field/mill' verses emphasize the surprise and lack of signs: 'you do not know what hour your Lord is coming' (Matt. 24:42). This will not be true of believers during the great tribulation period – they will know that Christ is about to come. But there are no signs here in Matthew 24:40-42.

4. **Separation**: The rapture described here will separate the outwardly and seemingly similar – two men working in a field together, two women at a mill, two people in one bed (Luke 17:34). But it is unlikely that the saints will be living and working peacefully and quietly alongside the godless at the end of the great tribulation. Instead, because only those who have the Mark of the Beast are able to buy or sell, saints will find it all but impossible to survive in Antichrist's society alongside the godless. They will have to flee normal society (Matt. 24:16-20, Luke 17:31, Rev. 12:6, 14). The picture presented here of saints working alongside the godless does not match the conditions that characterize the end of the great tribulation period.

5. **Tribulation follows this Rapture**: If the scene describing the two in the field and the two at the mill is a post-tribulation rapture of the saved, then what are the ungodly 'left behind' for? 2 Thessalonians 1:8 speaks of the judgment of the godless at Christ's post-tribulation

---

[22] John F. Hart, *Evidence for the Rapture*, Moody, 2015, pp56-7
[23] Ibid, p57

return: 'in flaming fire taking vengeance on those who do not know God, and on those who do not obey the gospel of our Lord Jesus Christ'. But that is not the picture we have in Matthew 24:40-42 – we do not read of the godless being destroyed by fire from heaven. Instead, some people get raptured (the church, according to post-tribulationists), and some (the godless) get left behind, but for what purpose? In the parallel account in Luke 17:31-35, Christ says that when this 'rapture' happens people should head for the hills, because there is tribulation to come: 'in that day, he who is on the housetop, and his goods are in the house, let him not come down to take them away, and likewise the one who is in the field, let him not turn back ... I tell you, in that night there will be two in one bed, one will be taken and the other left. Two women will be grinding together: the one will be taken and the other left' (Luke 17:31, 34, 35). Christ thus follows up the description of the rapture with need for flight from coming persecution. Those who are 'left behind' are told to flee for their lives because of the coming tribulation period. How could this apply at the end of the tribulation? At the end of the great tribulation, believers will reign with Christ, and unbelievers will be overwhelmed by judgment at Christ's return – they will not be able to flee. In Luke, therefore, the rapture spoken of in the 'two in one bed verses' does not immediately end the lives of the ungodly 'left behind'. Luke's account makes it clear that there is still tribulation to come after this rapture.

It is thus very difficult to see Matthew 24:40-42 as a post-tribulation rapture. It is instead a rapture that occurs in non-tribulation conditions, a rapture which is followed by tribulation.

Many pre-tribulation advocates also believe that the description of the two in the field and the two at the mill depicts a rapture. However, some argue that it is not a rapture of believers before the tribulation, but a rapture of the ungodly after the tribulation at the return of Christ, who are taken away to stand in judgment before Christ. However, there are five problems with this idea:

1. **Two Raptures?** The idea of some pretribulation advocates that this is a rapture of the wicked at Christ's coming is strange because this means that there are actually two raptures, one for God's people before the tribulation and one for the ungodly after the tribulation. A rapture is an incredible and amazing event – millions of people instantly disappearing off the face of the earth – and while one rapture is

reasonable in view of the clear description in 1 Thessalonians 4:13-17, two raptures starts to strain credibility.

2. **Nowhere else Mentioned**. This rapture of the ungodly is nowhere else mentioned in God's Word, unless it be in this cryptic reference. We need good evidence from elsewhere in the Bible before accepting that there is a rapture of the unsaved as well as of the church.
3. **Christ's only Mention of the Rapture**. If this is a rapture (as it is), this is the only time that Christ Himself speaks of a rapture. The idea that the only rapture that Christ ever directly mentions in the gospels is a rapture of the ungodly seems strange. The rapture of the church is a major teaching of Paul's concerning the end-times. Surely, if Christ were going to mention any rapture, would it not be that of the church?
4. **Contradicts 'Sheep and Goats' Judgment**. If this rapture separates the righteous from the wicked at Christ's return to set up His Kingdom – with the ungodly taken away to be judged before Christ's throne – then it conflicts with the Parable of the Sheep and the Goats in Matt. 25:31-46. In that parable, the separation of the wicked and the righteous occurs before Christ's throne, not on the family farm. The separation of the wicked and the righteous occurs, not by a rapture but by Christ's word of judgment. If there were to be a second rapture, surely it would have to include all people (the sheep as well as the goats), for all people need transport to stand before Christ for judgment.
5. **No Purpose**. What is the purpose of a rapture of the ungodly? If they are being taken to stand before Christ in judgment, why can they not simply be gathered using normal earthly means of transport? Why should the ungodly be honoured and privileged to share in a similar rapture experience as the saved (or like Elijah, or the Lord's own ascension)? Such a rapture is both pointless, as well as unnecessary.

It therefore seems very unlikely that this is a rapture of the ungodly at the end of the tribulation.

Some suggest that this is a rapture of godly Israelites at the end of the tribulation, but Isaiah 11:10-16 shows that their regathering occurs on land, not via a rapture. Neither will there be any faithful Jews merrily working away in their fields at the end of the great tribulation that need to be raptured; they will be in hiding during the great tribulation (see Rev. 12:6, 14). Christ has already specifically told them to leave their fields (Matt. 24:18) – their normal places of work – when they see the 'abomination of desolation' and head for a place of hiding.

Instead, as we are about to see, it makes more sense to see it as a rapture of believers before the tribulation period. There are six good reasons for seeing these verses about the two in the field/mill as a description of a pre-tribulation rapture of believers.

1. **No Persecution or Tribulation.** As we detailed at length in previous pages, nowhere in the immediate context (Matt. 24:36–25:30) is there any hint of persecution or calamity or any other characteristic feature of the tribulation period. Instead, these verses picture perfect tranquility and normality: people working away at their farms and at the mill. The context of these verses is a non-tribulation coming of Christ – which means, of course, a pre-tribulation coming of Christ (for non-tribulation conditions only exist before the tribulation period and in the millennium afterwards, but no rapture happens in the millennium).

2. **A Sudden Surprise.** The immediate context also presents Christ's coming as a complete and sudden surprise, not a coming preceded by clear and unmistakable signs, like at the end of the great tribulation. This is seen in the verse which follows the two in the field, two at the mill: 'Watch therefore, for you do not know what hour your Lord is coming' (Matt. 24:42). The same idea of 'no one knows the day of Christ's coming' is stated five other times in Matt. 24:36, 39, 44, 50, and 25:13.

3. **Taken = Received.** Christ describes this rapture using the words, 'one will be taken and the other left' (24:40, 41). The word 'taken' here in Greek is *paralambano*. This word is used twice in verses 40 and 41, and it literally means to 'take along with', or 'take to oneself', or 'take to one's side'. It is translated as 'receive' fifteen times in the New Testament. Significantly, it is the very same word the Lord used in John 14:3 when He said, 'If I go and prepare a place for you I will come again and *receive* you to Myself, that where I am, there you may be also'. That is, it is the same word used by the Lord in John 14:3 to describe the rapture. It is a very different Greek word from the word 'took' (*airo*) used in v39 to describe the ungodly being taken away in judgement by Noah's flood. The common counter-argument is that *paralambano* is also used in John 19:16 where the soldiers took Jesus and led him away to be crucified. Thus, it is argued, *paralambano* is not always used of 'taking' someone in a friendly sense, or taking someone to some happy destination. But leaving aside whether *paralambano* is used in a pleasant sense in the NT or not (although it virtually always is), the important point is that *paralambano* means taking someone 'alongside' or 'along

with'. The central idea of the word is accompaniment, not whether the destination is good or bad. Whether the 'receiving' is for good or ill is a red herring. Seeing the word itself does not tell us whether the 'taking' is friendly or otherwise, it remains a strong possibility that Christ is using the same word here to connect Matt. 24:41-42 with the rapture in John 14:3, when Christ receives us to Himself (and also 1 Thess. 4:13-17 where we 'meet the Lord' and are 'always with the Lord').

4. **Left = Abandoned**. Furthermore, the Greek word used for 'left' here is *aphiemi*, and this word means to 'abandon' when its object is a person (see Matt. 4:22, 8:15, 19:29, 22:22, etc.). If this were a post-tribulation rapture of unbelievers, this means that believers are left behind – that is, abandoned. As Hart writes, '*aphiemi* could hardly be used of what the Father or the Son do with believers at the final return of Christ to the earth, i.e. to "leave" believers on earth to go into the millennium'[24]. Why would God abandon believers at Christ's visible return to reign? Christ promised never to 'abandon', 'forsake', or 'leave' believers (see John 14:18, Heb. 13:5).

5. **The Godly Escape Judgment**. Christ's allusion to Noah in verses 37-39 also suggests a pre-tribulation rapture. This is seen clearly in Luke's gospel where the lesson is expanded to include Lot's escape from Sodom. Luke's Gospel speaks about, 'the day Noah entered the ark, and the flood came and destroyed them all' and 'on the day that Lot went out of Sodom it rained fire and brimstone from heaven and destroyed them all' (Luke 17:27-29). Luke's Gospel shows that it is the godly who escape out of the way before judgment falls upon the world. The parallel with Noah and Lot is that believers will be taken out of this world so they will not come under God's wrath described in the Book of Revelation as it falls upon the ungodly.

6. **Addressed to Christ's Followers**. Notice Christ's words in Matthew 24:42, 'Watch therefore, for you do not know what hour your Lord is coming'. The words 'your Lord' indicate that Christ is here telling his followers to be ready at any moment for a rapture at His coming. This is a surprise, non-tribulation rapture for believers.

Thus, it would seem that there are good reasons for believing (a) that a rapture is being described, (b) that it is not a rapture of the ungodly, (c) that it is not a rapture of Jews, but rather (d) that it is a description of the rapture of believers in non-tribulation (i.e. pre-tribulation) days, in which,

---

[24] Hart, *Evidence for the Rapture*, p62

suddenly and without warning, 'in the twinkling of an eye' (1 Cor. 15:52), believers will be caught up in the air to meet Christ (1 Thessalonians 4:17). These verses do not refer to the ungodly being 'taken away' by judgments. They refer to the ungodly being left for the judgments of the tribulation whilst God's people are 'taken away' to be with Christ so that they do not go through that time of great tribulation.

Why does Matthew put the Rapture after the Tribulation?

This leaves one last question. If Matthew is describing a pre-tribulation rapture of Christians believers in Matthew 24:36 – 25:30, why does he describe the rapture *after* the great tribulation (Matthew 24:15-31)?

The post-tribulationist says that this is when the rapture happens – at the end of the great tribulation. Although we have seen that there are fatal flaws in this explanation, what does the pre-tribulationist say in response to this inverted order of events?

Firstly, although Moo argues that 'there is no basis for any transition from the posttribulational aspect of the Parousia in Matthew 24:31-35 (or -36) to its pretribulational aspect in verses 36ff'[25], we have already seen that there is a very good reason for a transition in the Olivet Discourse in Matthew 24:36 – the fact that this is where the Olivet Discourse originally ended, as seen in Mark and Luke. After this point, Matthew is giving us sayings by the Lord that were spoken on other occasions.

In Luke's account, after the Lord has spoken about the return of Christ (21:25-28), he goes on to speak about the response of His followers to this great event, firstly readiness in Luke 21:29-33, then moral preparedness in 34-35. Then, in Luke 21:36, the Lord says, 'Watch therefore, and pray always that you may be counted worthy to escape all these things that will come to pass, and to stand before the Son of Man'. This is a reference to the 'Rapture' – escaping from all the calamities of the tribulation, as well as standing before the Son of Man. Thus, in Christ's own teaching, the mention of the Rapture follows the talk of His Return.

Secondly, as John Hart says:

> This evidence [of a dramatic difference in the two parts of the Olivet Discourse] provides clear support for viewing the rapture in verses 36-44. The latter verses describe the imminent, unpredictable coming of the day of the Lord and the accompanying pretribulational rapture. Therefore, at verse 36, the Lord answers the first question of the

---

[25] Moo, "A Case for the Posttribulation Rapture", *Three Views*, p209

disciples (v. 3) about when the end-time events will begin. Here Jesus reveals that the inception of the day of the Lord itself and the accompanying pretribulational rapture cannot be known.[26]

The big question in Matthew 24 is this: when does Christ return? Christ says that 'of that day or hour no one knows, not even the angels of heaven, but My Father only' (24:36). But the reason why nobody knows this date is because no one knows when the sequence of end-time events starts. The first event in Matthew is the abomination of desolation (24:15). Even Christ does not say whether this occurs in winter (or some other season) or on what day of the week (a Sabbath or some other). The start date of the great tribulation period is unknown. But we have seen from Daniel 9:27 that there is another event that takes place even before this: the establishment of a seven year covenant (or treaty) between the Antichrist and the nation of Israel. If we knew when this happens, we would know when Christ will return. But is that treaty the very first event that takes place in the sequence of end-time events?

As we are going to see in the next chapter, the entire end-time sequence of events is called the Day of the Lord by Paul (in 1 Thess. 5:2 and 2 Thess. 2:2). The Day of the Lord includes far more than just the day Christ visibly returns at the Battle of Armageddon. It includes the entire reign of the Antichrist (see 2 Thess. 2:2-12). Paul tells us in 1 Thessalonians 4 and 5 that the rapture (1 Thess. 4:16) signals the start of the Day of the Lord (1 Thess. 5:2). It is the rapture which is the very first event in the entire end-times sequence, as we will show when we look at Paul's letters to the Thessalonians in the next two chapters.

Craig Blaising links Matthew 24:36 with Zechariah 14:7, and says:

> Most commentators are agreed that "that day or that hour" is not a reference to [the particular date of Christ's visible coming in the sky] in the earlier portion of the discourse.... Rather, "that day or that hour" looks at the day of the Lord itself – in a singular, comprehensive way... [Christ's words in Matthew 24:36 are] recalling Zechariah's comment that the day of the Lord is "a unique day, which is known to the LORD" (14:7 ESV) ... this part of the discourse [i.e. from 24:36 onwards] focuses on the coming of the day of the Lord as an entire event. ... The point is that the entire day of the Lord is a coming of the Lord in judgment. All of its destructive elements – ***for however long***

---

[26] John F. Hart, in *Evidence for the Rapture*, p52

their duration or however extensive their reach – are poured out by the God who has "come" enacting this judgment… The theophany at the end of the day of the Lord in Zechariah 14 climaxes ***an extended event*** in which he has come in judgment…. Following the imagery of a military campaign, the entire campaign, whether the devastation of the countryside or the siege and battle for the city – however long these last – is due to the coming of a general and his army who are perpetrating it. This coming is not merely his triumphal entry into the defeated city at the end of the campaign. His coming is the whole destructive event that completes itself when the city is defeated and he then makes his entry into it…. With this in mind, we can understand why in the Olivet Discourse Jesus speaks on the one hand of signs and on the other of no signs … All the signs are in the day of the Lord. They are signs leading up to his appearance at the end of this coming. The day of the Lord taken as a whole – the day of his coming in judgment and which culminates in his appearance – sets in to history without warning, without signs[27].

What Blaising is saying here might not be immediately clear to all readers, but his point is that the 'day of the Lord' is an extended event – it is another way of talking about the entire tribulation period when God intervenes in our world in judgment – that comes as a surprise upon the world, at a time only known to God. To understand more about the day of the Lord and its relationship to the Lord's coming, we need to look at Paul's letters to the Thessalonians and the book of Revelation. As we are about to see, Paul's letters to the Thessalonians clearly teach that the day of the Lord starts with the rapture.

---

[27] Craig Blaising, "A Case for the Pretribulation Rapture", in *Three Views on the Rapture*, Zondervan, 2010, pp48-50

22 THE LORD'S COMING: 1 THESSALONIANS

In Paul's first letter to the Thessalonians, he repeatedly discussed the subject of the Lord's coming. If we are going to understand what happens when Christ returns, we need to see what 1 Thessalonians says about it.

The Lord's Coming in 1 Thessalonians

Paul mentions the Lord's coming in each chapter of his first letter to the Thessalonians. It was obviously an important issue for early Christians. Paul says five things to the Thessalonians about the Lord's coming in 1 Thessalonians.

1. the Lord's coming is a comfort to grieving believers,
2. the Lord's coming has a warning message for non-Christians,
3. the Lord's coming is an encouragement to live a holy life,
4. the Lord's coming is a rescue from coming wrath, and
5. the Lord's coming is the Christian's hope and joy.

The Lord's Coming is a Comfort to Grieving Christians (4:13-18)

Paul wrote in 1 Thessalonians 4:16-17 about the rapture:

> 'the Lord Himself will descend from heaven with a shout, with the voice of the archangel and with the trumpet of God, and the dead in Christ will rise first. Then we who are alive and remain shall be caught up together with them in the clouds to meet the Lord in the air, and thus we shall always be with the Lord'.

Paul writes here to comfort believers in Thessalonica who were grieving over loved ones who had 'died in Christ'. Not only were they grieving, they were also worried and confused. Would their loved ones miss out on the Lord's coming? Paul's answer here is no – they are not going to miss out on this great event. He assures them there is going to be a resurrection of the dead saints along with the rapture of living saints, who are going to be caught up together in the clouds to meet the Lord in the air. We will be reunited with our loved ones in Christ. The Lord's coming thus brings comfort (v17).

THE END OF THE WORLD

The word 'Lord' is used five times in verses 15-17:

- In v15, Paul writes to them 'by the ***word of the Lord***'. What Paul says about the rapture is a word with the greatest possible authority. It is not Paul's own idea – it is God's Word.
- In v15, we have the '***coming of the Lord***'. Here is the greatest event the Christian is ever going to see. It would have been wonderful to see some of the Lord's miracles while He was on earth – raising Lazarus, healing blind people, walking on water. But we missed those miracles. However, this miracle is going to be better than any of them. Can you imagine millions of living Christians as well as resurrected saints caught up into the air. How amazing! We sometimes catch plane flights, and look out the windows when we are up above the clouds. But when the Lord comes we are going to be up in the air without a plane at all. We are also going to experience an incredible miracle in our own bodies. We are going to be changed. In an instant, we are going to have a spiritual, resurrection body, like the Lord had after His resurrection – He could walk through walls, or disappear. Not only is this amazing physical change going to take place, but we are instantly going to be like Christ, so that we will no longer sin. We will not be jealous of others as we are caught up into the clouds, or bitter, unforgiving. This will be the greatest miracle of all our lives, and we are not going to miss it, we will all be there. The coming of Christ, and the catching up of millions of saints into the air will be the greatest miracle we will ever experience.
- In v16, the ***Lord will descend***. He is not going to send another for us. He Himself is personally going to come for His church.
- In v16, we are going to be caught up to '***meet the Lord***'. We sometimes go to Christian conferences or meetings, and we look around to see who else is there. Can you imagine what this meeting will be like? Paul will be there, and all the other apostles. All the great preachers of the church, and the martyrs will be there. All those Christians who were a help to us in our spiritual lives – they'll be there. All our loved ones, they'll be there. We will all be reunited. This is going to be a meeting like no other. Best of all, we are going to meet the Lord. The hymn puts it like this, 'Face to face with Christ my Saviour, face to face what will it be, when with rapture I behold Him, Jesus Christ who died for me'. I don't think we'll be looking round too much at other people. I think our eyes will be gazing, transfixed on the face of the Lord Jesus – we'll just be staring at Him for the first half hour or so. But it doesn't

just say we will see Him – it says we will meet Him. We will hear Him speaking to us. We won't need to worry about mumbling something foolish when we meet him, either (like Peter on the Mount of transfiguration). We will have glorified sinless bodies. How wonderful!
- In v17, we are going to be *for ever with the Lord*, never more to be separated from Him or each other. There will be no more grieving then. Psalm 16, the resurrection psalm, says, 'In your presence is fullness of joy, at your right hand there are pleasures for evermore'. C. S. Lewis wrote, 'One million years from now, when the sun and stars no longer exist, you will still be alive'.

The Lord's coming should thrill us with joy and fill us with hope. We should be very excited about this great event.

Evidence that the Rapture is Pre-Tribulational (5:1-3)
Following straight on from the passage about the rapture, Paul writes about the Day of the Lord. He says the unsaved will not escape:

> But concerning the times and the seasons, brethren, you have no need that I should write to you ² for you yourselves know perfectly that the Day of the Lord so comes as a thief in the night, ³ for when they say "Peace and Safety", then sudden destruction comes upon them, as labour pains on a pregnant woman, and they shall not escape'.

Notice that instead of writing about *we* who are alive and remain, Paul switches pronouns here in 1 Thessalonians 5:1-3, and writes three times about '*they*' and 'them' – the unbelievers. Here Paul is writing about what will happen to unbelievers at the Lord's coming.

It seems clear that the 'times and seasons' Paul writes about here refer to the rapture and its timing. If Paul had been referring to the timing of something else, he would have specified what he was talking about. Paul is referring back to the last mentioned event in the previous verses: the rapture. But here, Paul uses the term the Day of the Lord in verse 2. It would appear that the rapture (1 Thess. 4:16-17) ushers in the Day of the Lord, which 'so comes as a thief in the night' (1 Thess. 5:1-3).

But what is the Day of the Lord? Is it a single 24-hour day? Post-tribulationists believe that the Day of the Lord is a 24-hour day, or a very short period of time. They believe the Day of the Lord is the Second Coming of Christ at the Battle of Armageddon at the end of the great tribulation[1].

However, there is a big problem with this idea: the Day of the Lord comes as a complete surprise upon the world (1 Thess. 5:1-3). How could the world be saying 'peace and safety' (1 Thess. 5:3) at the same time as the world's armies are gathering for the Battle of Armageddon (which is not a single day, but a prolonged war)? How could Christ's coming be a surprise when all the world must wear the Mark of the Beast to buy or sell, and must worship His image (Rev. 13)? How could Christ's coming be a surprise when we have the sign of the sun darkening, the moon being turned to blood and the stars falling (Matt. 24:29-31)? If the Day of the Lord occurs at the very end of the great tribulation, how can it be a surprise?

An even bigger problem with the post-tribulation position is found in 2 Thessalonians, where we read about the Day of the Lord again. It seems the Thessalonians thought that the Day of the Lord 'was present' (2:2), and that their persecution was part of the Day of the Lord – the tribulation period. But if the Day of the Lord was a single 24-hour day, or the return of Christ, they surely would have already seen Christ return. How can someone 'be present' in the Day of the Lord if it is merely Christ's visible return?

Paul writes Second Thessalonians to assure them that the Day of the Lord has not come. Paul says the Day of the Lord involves a number of things: the Man of Sin ruling the world, when he sets himself up as God in the temple of God, when he does Satanically-empowered miracles to deceive the world, and God sends a strong delusion on the unsaved and they believe the lie. The Day of the Lord is not just a 24 hour day, it is obviously an extended period of time – the tribulation period.

Here in 1 Thessalonians 5:2 we learn that the Day of the Lord comes suddenly and without warning. It will be like a thief in the night (verse 2). When they say, "peace and safety", then 'sudden destruction' comes upon them. It is like the labour pains of a pregnant woman – no one knows when they will start (v3). The rapture, ushering in the Day of the Lord, will be a surprise. There will be no signs or omens warning people that it is about to start. It will come like a gigantic shock to a sleeping world.

---

[1] See, for example, Douglas Moo in *Three Views on the Rapture* (2010), who writes: 'the "day of the Lord" in the New Testament refers to the climax of human history, a climax that follows the tribulation of this church age (including the final [i.e. great] tribulation')', p101. Moo argues that the Day of the Lord does not include the tribulation period; instead 'in the New Testament, the day [of the Lord] includes the destruction of the ungodly at the [post-tribulational] parousia of Christ, along with the rapture and the resurrection of the righteous dead', ibid, p203.

Nor is there any indication of either a pocket of 'peace and safety' or, contra Moo[2], a false sense of security during the great tribulation just before Christ returns. Those years leading up to Armageddon will be anything but 'peace and safety'. They will be three and a half of the most terrible years of human existence on earth, in which virtually everyone on earth dies by terrible calamities. Just before Christ returns, there will be an extended war which climaxes in the Battle of Armageddon, and before that, the whole world will be gathering its armies to war. How could people be lulled to sleep, blissfully unaware that anything is happening, in this period before the battle of Armageddon, with the signs in the sun, moon and stars (Matt. 24:29-31)? The thief in the night comes to surprise a slumbering, unsuspecting world, so how can Christ's words about the Thief in the Night refer to the end of the great tribulation period?

The Day of the Lord commences in non-tribulation (and that means pre-tribulation) conditions – with the rapture. Millions of people will disappear and then a succession of disasters will bring terrible judgment to the world.

The post-tribulation rapture view is thus very difficult to reconcile with the fact that the Day of the Lord is an extended period of time, including the entire 'great tribulation' period, that starts suddenly, in conjunction with the rapture, takes the world by complete surprise, and brings inescapable judgments (1 Thess. 5:1-3). While unbelievers are not going to escape the Day of the Lord, the church will escape the terrible judgments of the tribulation period because we are going to be raptured out of this world before it starts. Unbelievers had the chance to be saved, but when the Lord has come, there will be no more chance. It will be too late – Paul says, 'they will not escape'.

So while the Lord's coming is the most exciting event that a believer will ever experience, for the unbeliever, the Lord's coming is the most dreadful event to think about. If you are not saved, you need to be saved, and you need to be saved today. You don't have any guarantee of tomorrow. The Lord's coming will be a complete surprise, and it will usher in the terrible judgments of the Day of the Lord, the tribulation period.

Six Other Indications the Rapture Is Pre-Tribulational

I believe there are six other indications in Paul's words that this event – the rapture at the Lord's coming – could happen at any moment, and therefore that it could happen before the tribulation period.

---

[2] Moo, *Three Views*, p204

Firstly, it seems the Thessalonians were looking forward to seeing the Lord's return (cf. 1 Thess. 1:10). It is therefore probable that those who had died were also looking forward to the Lord's return. Further, it is clear from this passage that Paul himself hoped to see the Lord's coming during his lifetime. He says '*we* who are alive and remain to the coming of the Lord' (v15), and again, '*we* who are alive and remain shall be caught up together with them in the clouds to meet the Lord in the air' (v17). Why does Paul use the word 'we' twice in this passage, instead of 'those' or 'some people'? Simply because he himself was expecting to be alive at the coming of the Lord to experience the rapture. If Paul hoped to see the Lord's coming in His day, then we should look to see it in our day too.

In fact, we see Paul's personal hope to be alive at the Lord's coming in all the references to the rapture in the New Testament. I Corinthians 15:52 says, '*we* shall be changed'. Philippians 3:20-21 says, '*we* also eagerly wait for the Saviour, the Lord Jesus Christ, who will transform *our* lowly body that it may be conformed to His glorious body'. 1 Thess. 1:10 says [you] Thessalonians 'turned to God from idols to serve the living and true God and to wait for His Son from heaven, even Jesus the One delivering *us* from the wrath to come'[3], while 1 Thess. 5, says 'God did not appoint *us* to wrath but to obtain salvation through our Lord Jesus Christ'.

A second reason to think that the rapture could come before the tribulation period is this: if the rapture is not till the end of the great tribulation, which the church is going to go through, then we would have expected Paul to have told Christians about how they should prepare for the great tribulation. The great tribulation will be the most terrible event in the history of the world. If anyone takes the mark of the beast, they will be cast into the Lake of Fire and tormented forever (Rev. 14:9-11). Those wishing to escape the Lake of Fire will need to be prepared to lose their lives for the sake of Christ. Surely some advice or guidance or warning would be in order. But nowhere in any of his letters to any Christian churches does Paul ever tell Christians how to prepare for living during the great tribulation. E. W. Rogers writes,

> It is to be remarked that there is in New Testament epistles a total absence of any directions to the believer as to his preparing either for death or for the great tribulation. He is not told what to do in either eventuality. There is no such word as "Set thine house in order" or "When ye see ... then flee". Everywhere the eye is turned upward,

---

[3] Author's translation

and the hope of the Lord's return is presented as that which is constantly to be awaited[4].

This leads on to a third reason. If Paul was eagerly expecting the Lord to come in his lifetime, and if the church were to go through the great tribulation, we would expect that the Apostle Paul would have been one of the first people to boldly lay down his life as a fearless witness for Christ during this period. But Paul is not planning to die as a martyr during the great tribulation. Nor is he the sort of person to flee and hide, while others lose their lives for their testimony to Christ (Rev. 20:4). Paul is constantly looking forward to being alive at Christ's coming to be caught up in the air to meet the Lord. Why? The simplest and best explanation is because Paul expected Christ to come to take us to be with Himself before the tribulation period.

A fourth reason that suggests the rapture could happen at any moment is this: why doesn't Paul try to comfort the grieving Thessalonians by saying that their loved ones are in heaven with the Lord? Why doesn't he say they are 'absent from the body, present with the Lord' (2 Cor. 5:8), 'with Christ, which is far better' (Phil. 1:23)? Why does Paul instead point to the Lord's coming as the Christian's comfort?

The reason the Lord's coming is a comfort is that the reunion of living believers with those who have died in Christ – at the rapture – could happen at any moment. The Christian's hope is not to die and be reunited with our loved ones in heaven. There is something that could happen before that: the Lord's coming, which will reunite living believers with those who have died in Christ. We are not looking for the undertaker, we are looking for the up-taker. As the hymn says, 'The sky, not the grave, is our goal'.

A fifth reason which suggests the Lord's coming is pre-tribulational is that if the church is to go through the tribulation, Paul should have comforted the grieving Thessalonians by telling them that at least their loved ones had been spared the horrors of the great tribulation. As Kevin Zuber writes:

> If Paul believed the Thessalonians would "remain" through the tribulation, he should have comforted the Thessalonians regarding their departed loved ones by telling them that it was actually a blessing that, their loved ones, being dead, had missed that terrible time.

---

[4] E. W. Rogers, *Concerning the Future*, Pickering and Inglis, 1962, p60

Furthermore, he should have alerted them that they should take some thought and concern for themselves, for they themselves might soon be facing the hardships of the tribulation, should it come[5].

A sixth reason to believe that the rapture here is pre-tribulational is the fact that there is no mention of Christ's kingdom reign after His coming. If Christ's return here were post-tribulational, we might expect Paul to encourage the believers by looking off to the hope of reigning together with Christ. The fact that the apostle mentions neither the great tribulation before the Lord's coming or the Kingdom reign after suggests that the church is not envisaged as going through the great tribulation period. Instead, as Charles Wannamaker writes, Paul's imagery points to heaven:

> imagery (the clouds and being caught up to the Lord) are indicative of an assumption to heaven of the people who belong to Christ. That Paul adds his own definitive statement concerning the significance of this meeting in the clause 'and thus we will always be with the Lord' suggests that both dead and living Christians will return to heaven with the Lord, not only to enjoy continuous fellowship with him, but also, in terms of 1:10, to be saved from the coming wrath of God[6].

Admittedly, none of these six arguments are proof of a pre-tribulation rapture. They are suggestive rather than explicitly stated evidence. However, added to what Paul says about the extended Day of the Lord (i.e. the tribulation period) commencing with the rapture, they reinforce what is already strong evidence for a pre-tribulation rapture.

The Lord's Coming is an Encouragement to Godly Living (5:4-11)

Paul again turns his attention to believers in 1 Thessalonians 5:4-11 and says that we should be living in readiness for the Lord's coming. We shouldn't be living like the rest of the people around us, who are in darkness (v4). We should not be spiritually asleep (v6), but instead be watching and sober (v6).

I had a Greek Christian friend many years ago in London. He used to say that there will be two sorts of Christians at the Lord's coming: those

---

[5] Kevin Zuber, "Paul and the Rapture: 1 Thessalonians 4-5", in *Evidence for the Rapture*, ed. John F. Hart, Moody Press, 2015, p154
[6] Charles A. Wannamaker, *The Epistles to the Thessalonians*, NIGTC, Grand Rapids: Eerdmans, 1990, p175.

who are watching for the Lord's coming, and those who are watching TV. While he said it half-seriously, what he meant was that we should not be so absorbed in this world's affairs that we have forgotten the importance of being ready for the Lord's coming.

Verse 8 says we should be properly dressed, wearing the armour of God, the breastplate of faith and love and as a helmet the hope of salvation. We don't want to be embarrassed at the Lord's coming, found unprepared, or 'ashamed before Him at His coming', as John puts it in his first epistle. We need to be living the right way.

Let me ask my Christian readers: are you sitting at His feet hearing His Word every day, communing with Him in prayer? Are you being changed so that you become more like the Lord Jesus day by day, as you put off the works of darkness and do those things that please the Lord? Are you busy serving the Lord in some gospel outreach, are you using your gifts to encourage God's people? Or are you living a life that is not very different to the average non-Christian? Are your hopes and joys all earthly? Are you busy building a career, and your bank balance, and getting better at whatever hobby or sport you enjoy? Are you just getting on with life, or are you walking with the Lord and trying to please Him?

There is a story about a man who visited a villa in Italy. The grounds were kept in beautiful order, but he couldn't find anybody except the gardener. So he asked him, "When does the owner of this villa come here?" The gardener said, "I have been working here for twenty years, and he has only been here four times". "When was the last time that he was here?" "Twelve years ago". The man asked, "So who do you report to?" The gardener said, "I report to a steward in Milan". "That's amazing! You keep these gardens as if you were expecting the owner tomorrow". The gardener replied, "Today, sir. Today".

The last few verses of our passage also seem to teach a pre-tribulation rapture. Verse 9 says that 'God has not appointed us to wrath, but to obtain salvation through our Lord Jesus Christ'. That is, we are not appointed to go through that tribulation period, the time God pours out His wrath on the world. Why? Because the Lord Jesus Christ 'died for us' (v10) and we are saved, and when he comes again we are going to live together with Him.

Some would argue that 'not being appointed to wrath' refers to the wrath of God against sin generally, from which we have been saved by Christ's work at the cross. That is, we are not going to Hell. This is true, of course, however the context of this verse is about escaping the Day of the Lord (v3). Further evidence that the words 'not appointed to wrath' are speaking about escaping the Day of the Lord is seen in the fact that Paul adds, 'whether we wake or sleep, we should live together with Him' (v10). This takes us back to what was said in 4:13-17 about those who are 'alive and remain' as well as those 'dead in Christ' who 'sleep in Jesus' both being raptured to meet the Lord. Both the living and dead saints will escape the Day of the Lord because we will be raptured at the return of Christ.

The Lord's Coming is a Rescue from Coming Wrath (1:9-10)

Not being 'appointed to wrath' (5:9) also links up with what Paul said in 1 Thessalonians 1:9-10: the Thessalonians 'turned to God from idols to serve the living and true God, and to wait for His Son from heaven, even Jesus, the One delivering us from the coming wrath'. The Lord's return is going to be a rescue.

The KJV reads a little differently here: 'even Jesus which delivered us from the wrath to come'. This gives the impression that the deliverance is something that happened in the past, at the cross when Christ died for our sins. Of course, it is true that Christ saved us at the cross, but a more accurate translation reads 'Jesus the One ***delivering*** us from the coming wrath'. The participle 'delivering' is tenseless in Greek – that is, it could refer to the past, present or future – and it is only the context which determines what it is referring to. The context in 1 Thessalonians 1:9-10 is the Lord's coming from heaven, for which we are waiting, and the '***coming*** wrath'. These verses are looking to the future. The deliverance, or rescue, from the 'coming wrath' is therefore going to happen in the future. The Lord's coming is going to rescue or deliver us from the coming wrath of the tribulation period, from the Day of the Lord, the great time of trouble that is coming upon the earth.

We see this connection between the 'Day of the Lord' and God's wrath in the Old Testament, where the Day of the Lord is mentioned 70 times, and is a period characterized by God's wrath. For example, Isaiah 13:9 says, 'Behold, the day of the LORD comes, cruel, with both wrath and fierce anger, to lay the land (earth) desolate'. This is what Paul is speaking about here: the coming Day of the Lord, a period when God's wrath is going to be poured out on this world.

Whichever way we look at it, whether the wrath here refers to God's wrath in a future day, or God's general wrath against sin, we are not under any of God's wrath, because we are in Christ. God has not appointed us to wrath. We will not experience the wrath of God; instead, we will be rescued from it at Christ's coming.

Notice one final thing here: Paul taught the early Christians to wait for God's Son from heaven, not to wait for signs on earth. We are waiting for the Son, not signs, for Christ, not for Antichrist. We are not to look at the political scene, or the stock market, or stars in the sky – but for Christ.

I was once speaking with a Christian friend about the Lord's coming, and I told him that I believed in a pre-tribulation rapture. He replied: "I realize there are all sorts of debates over this subject, and I am not sure which viewpoint is right, but I was always taught a pre-tribulation rapture, and even if this is not correct, what it means is that I am living the right way, and expecting Christ's coming".

The Lord's Coming is the Believer's Hope and Joy (2:19)

'For what is our hope, or joy, or crown of rejoicing? Is it not even you in the presence of our Lord Jesus Christ at His coming?' (1 Thess. 2:19).

There was once an old preacher who said this: 'the Lord's coming is not a haunting nightmare, but a blessed hope'. What he meant was this: if we as Christians are supposed to go through the great tribulation, then that is a haunting nightmare. It takes a bit of the gloss off the hope and joy of Christ's coming. The great tribulation is the one part of the Bible that, more than any other, gives people nightmares.

But the New Testament does not present the Lord's coming as something we should dread or be troubled about. The Lord's coming is a blessed hope because Christ is going to rescue us from the wrath to come. We are not going to go through the tribulation period; we can look forward to Christ's coming with joy and hope.

23 THE COMING OF ANTICHRIST: 2 THESSALONIANS

The Lord's Coming in 2 Thessalonians

In 2 Thessalonians, Paul wrote to Christians who were losing their hope. There were three reasons their hope was being dimmed: firstly, they were being discouraged by persecution (chapter 1), secondly, they were being deceived by false teaching (chapter 2), and thirdly, they were being distracted from carrying out present responsibilities (chapter 3).

In particular, the Thessalonians were beginning to worry that the persecution they were enduring was evidence that they were in the Day of the Lord. They had become concerned that they were living through the end-time tribulation period.

In reply, Paul follows up his first letter by answering these concerns and addressing some additional questions that the Thessalonians had about the Lord's coming. This second letter presents us with four more reasons for believing that the rapture will occur before the tribulation

Were the Thessalonians Living through the Day of the Lord?

The main concern of the Thessalonians was that they were living through the 'Day of the Lord'[1]. Evidently, some Thessalonians had heard 'either by spirit or by word or by letter, as if from us' that the Day of the Lord was already present (or had begun)[2] (1 Thess. 2:2). The persecution the Thessalonians were enduring made them think that they were going through the tribulation period. In response, Paul assured these believers that they were not living through the Day of the Lord.

The simple fact that the Thessalonians thought they were living in the

---

[1] The KJV and NKJV have 'the Day of Christ' in 1 Thess. 2:2, but there is strong Greek manuscript evidence to read 'the Day of the Lord', as most modern Bibles have. In addition, Paul's second letter to the Thessalonians is a follow-up to the first, and Paul's mention of the Day of the Lord here alludes back to and enlarges upon what he said about the Day of the Lord in 1 Thessalonians 5:1-3.

[2] The KJV translates the Greek word *enesteken* 'is at hand' (2:2). But this is a mistranslation and misses the point. The Thessalonians' concern was not that the Day of the Lord was 'about to come' in the future, but that it 'had come' (NKJV) 'has come' (ESV, RSV, NASB), was 'present' (RV, Darby), and was 'already begun/arrived/here/come' (NLT/NJB/NET/NIV.)

Day of the Lord means that the Day of the Lord cannot be a single 24-hour period of time. Paul writes about the Day of the Lord in 2 Thessalonians 2 as an extended period of time with certain easily identifiable characteristics. These include the rule of the Man of Sin over the world, his enthronement in the temple of God demanding worldwide worship, his performance of Satanically-empowered miracles, and God sending a strong delusion upon the world so that all should believe the lie. Thus, the Day of the Lord is the entire tribulation period.

But this also leads to a very important conclusion: if we remember from 1 Thessalonians 5:1-3 that the rapture occurs at the same time as, and ushers in, the Day of the Lord (5:1), and, additionally, the rapture and the Day of the Lord come as a sudden surprise, the timing of which nobody knows (5:1-2), here we learn that the Day of the Lord is an extended period of time, roughly equivalent to the entire tribulation period. But if these three things are true, a post-tribulation rapture is impaled on the horns of a dilemma. Either:

1. The Day of the Lord is an **extended** period of time (the tribulation period, as we have seen from 2 Thessalonians 2) that comes as a surprise and is ushered in by the rapture (1 Thess. 5:1-3), or
2. The Day of the Lord is a **very short** period of time (the 24 hour day of Christ's return at Armageddon), but how is it possible for this day to come as a surprise?

Either (1) is true, which means that the rapture is pre-tribulational, or (2) is true (*contra* 2 Thessalonians 2 which shows that the Day of the Lord is extended period of time), but how do we then explain Christ's coming at the end of the tribulation period being a surprise?

In a post-tribulation rapture scenario, the rapture happens at the very end of the tribulation period just as Christ is about to come at the battle of Armageddon. The problem here is that Christ's coming would not be a sudden surprise at all, for all the world's armies are gathering for battle at Armageddon, and the Man of Sin has been ruling the world for a number of years, performing amazing miracles, demanding world-wide worship and insisting everyone wear the mark of the beast, let alone the signs in the sun, moon and stars. Anyone with any understanding of Bible prophecy (and post-tribulationists believe the church will still be on earth at this point) will know that Christ is about to come. How could there be any surprise about it?

Commentators who hold to a post-tribulation rapture argue that the

Day of the Lord is a brief period of judgment not much longer than an 24-hour day which occurs at Christ's coming at Armageddon at the very end of the tribulation period. Thus Robert Gundry writes, 'the day of the Lord will not begin until after the tribulation'[3]. But if the Day of the Lord is a 24-hour day or a very short period time, then how could the Thessalonians think that they are living through it or experiencing its ordeals? Surely, the Day of the Lord would be too short for any Thessalonians to be thinking that the persecution they were experiencing was the Day of the Lord.

Furthermore, if the Day of the Lord is simply the Second Coming of Christ at the Battle of Armageddon at the very end of the tribulation period, then the Thessalonians must have thought that all the events associated with the second coming had already happened: the Lord had returned, the rapture had already taken place, the dead had been raised, and the Battle of Armageddon already been fought. As Nathan Holsteen writes,

> This view [that the Day of the Lord occurs at the very end of the tribulation period] causes devastation to the text of 2 Thessalonians 2. Why? Because of the shape of the lie that the Thessalonian believers had been told. They had been told, "the Day of the Lord has come". But if the day of the Lord is identified as a post-tribulation rapture at the second coming (as Gundry suggests), the fact that the day of the Lord had already come could hardly be believed by the Thessalonians. They could certainly know they were not raptured and resurrected yet ... The view that the day of the Lord is a reference to the second coming of our Lord is completely incompatible with the context; such a view renders the whole message meaningless[4].

Holsteen uses an analogy to explain the situation:

> It is as if you and I were standing in the middle of downtown Dallas, and I were to say to you, "Please don't be upset by any reports to the effect that Dallas has been obliterated by a nuclear missile." Since a glance around you would immediately invalidate my concern, you would not be shaken in your composure – you would be concerned

---

[3] Robert H. Gundry, *The Church and the Tribulation*, Zondervan, 1973, p114
[4] Nathan D. Holsteen, "Paul and the Rapture: 2 Thessalonians", in *Evidence for the Rapture: a Biblical Case for Pretribulationism*, ed. John F. Hart, Moody, p181.

for my mental state![5]

Furthermore, if the church is meant to go through the tribulation period, this raises another problem: If Paul had taught the Thessalonians that the church was to go through the tribulation period, why would the Thessalonians have been alarmed or troubled by the idea that they were living through the tribulation? Surely they should have been encouraged by the thought that this meant that Christ's coming was near at hand?

Paul Feinberg writes:

> [Assuming that Paul had taught a post-tribulation rapture, then] If the Thessalonians thought they were in the Day of the Lord, even though erroneously, they should not have been unsettled and alarmed, for the coming of the Lord to rapture them was imminent; it was about to occur. Joy and expectancy should have been their attitudes. Those who were not working because they thought the Lord was about to return, were in fact vindicated. The rapture was about to occur[6].

As we have seen, Gundry, Moo and others who hold to a post-tribulation rapture argue that the Day of the Lord is a single brief event at the very end of the Tribulation period – the return of Christ at Armageddon. For proof, they point to 2 Thessalonians 2:3 which says that the Man of Sin must be revealed first, before the Day of the Lord: 'Let no one deceive you by any means, *for that Day will not come* unless the falling away comes first, and the man of sin is revealed, the son of perdition'[7]. Post-tribulationists argue that the Man of Sin must come before the Day of the Lord. Therefore, the Day of the Lord must refer to the second coming of Christ at the end of the tribulation period. However, this argument, instead of helping the post-tribulationist position, actually highlights yet another problem: 1 Thessalonians 5:1-3 has already told us that the Day of the Lord comes without any warning or sign. The Day of the Lord will come as a thief in the night, as a sudden surprise. How then can the Day of the Lord occur after such obvious signs as we are given in 2 Thessalonians 2, in particular, the Man of Sin sitting as God in the temple of God?

---

[5] Ibid, p188
[6] Paul D. Feinberg, "2 Thessalonians 2 and the Rapture", in *When the Trumpet Sounds*, eds. Thomas Ice and Timothy Demy, Harvest House, 1994, p306
[7] The words in italics are supplied in English, but virtually all commentators from all sides accept that they are required by the logic of the context, in this case the preceding verse with its talk about the Day of the Lord

The answer is that 2 Thessalonians 2:3 is not saying that the Man of Sin has to come before the Day of the Lord. What Paul is saying is the very reverse: that the revelation of the Man of Sin will be *evidence* that the Day of the Lord is already present – that it has already come. It is not a sign before the Day of the Lord, but a sign that the Day of the Lord is already begun. Robert Thomas uses an illustration to explain this verse:

> Suppose I say, "In the northern states, the fall season *will not come* unless the weather gets colder and the tree leaves change their colors." This sentence might imply that the weather gets colder and the tree leaves change their colors before the fall season comes. But this isn't true. These changes do not occur before the fall but are part of the fall season. But if I say, "The fall season *is not present* (is not here) unless first the weather gets colder and the tree leaves change their colors," this implies something different ... These two factors take place within the fall season and indicate its arrival. They don't occur before the fall season arrives. ... So, in 2 Thessalonians 2:3, the day of the Lord is not already underway unless two things happen: first, the apostasy must come, and then the man of lawlessness must be revealed. These are two major elements that take place within the day of the Lord, not before it arrives. If the falling leaves are signs within the fall season, they are not signs that precede the fall season[8].

Thus, Paul argues in 2 Thessalonians 2 that the signs that the Day of the Lord is present are the reign of the Man of Sin over the world, his worldwide worship and his Satanically-empowered miracles. The fact that these tell-tale signs show when the Day of the Lord has come means that the rapture cannot be post-tribulational, for how could a post-tribulation rapture then be a surprise, as Paul says in 1 Thessalonians 5:1-3? The rapture is a surprise that ushers in the Day of the Lord.

The Great Tribulation Period is Distinct from the Church Age

It becomes quite obvious when we read through 2 Thessalonians 2 that both Paul and the Thessalonians firstly thought of the Day of the Lord as an extended period of time equivalent to the tribulation period, and not a momentary event equivalent to Christ's coming at the Battle of Armageddon (as post-tribulationists hold). But secondly, it is also quite clear from 2 Thessalonians 2 that this extended period of time is a distinct

---

[8] Robert Thomas, "The Rapture and the Biblical Teaching of Imminency", in *Evidence for the Rapture*, Moody, 2015, pp38, 40, emphasis in original.

period of time from the church age, this day of grace.

Paul describes six features of the future Day of the Lord that the Thessalonians had not experienced, and thus assures the Thessalonians that they were not living through the Day of the Lord. Features that indicate that the Day of the Lord is underway include:

- **The Apostasy**: 'the falling away comes first' (2 Thess. 2:3)
- **The Revelation of the Antichrist**: 'the man of sin is revealed, the son of perdition, 4 who opposes and exalts himself above all that is called God or that is worshiped' (2 Thess. 2:3-4)
- **The Worship of the Antichrist**: 'so that he sits as God in the temple of God, showing himself that he is God' (2 Thess. 2:4)
- **The Restrainer is removed**: 'you know what is restraining, that he may be revealed in his own time. 7 For the mystery of lawlessness is already at work; only He who now restrains will do so until He is taken out of the way' (2 Thess. 2:6-7)
- **Satanic Signs and Wonders**: 'The coming of the lawless one is according to the working of Satan, with all power, signs, and lying wonders' (2 Thess. 2:9)
- **Divine Delusion**: 'for this reason God will send them strong delusion, that they should believe the lie, 12 that they all may be condemned who did not believe the truth but had pleasure in unrighteousness' (2 Thess. 2:11-12)

Notice how Paul contrasts two time-periods throughout 2 Thessalonians 2, the present church age and a future Day of the Lord. There are seven clear time-markers:

- 'you know what is restraining him [the Antichrist] *now*' (v6a, ESV)
- 'that he may be revealed *in his own time*' (v6b)
- 'the mystery of lawlessness is *already* at work' (v7)
- 'only He who *now* restrains will do so *until* He is taken out of the way' (v7)
- 'and *then* the lawless one will be revealed' (v8)
- 'for this reason God *will* (future tense) send them strong delusion that they should believe the lie' (v11)

All of these time-markers show that the Day of the Lord will be a *future*, extended period of time in which the Antichrist will be the focus of worldwide worship, proclaiming himself as God (v4), when multiple miracles will happen (v9), and when many people will believe this lie (v11).

Paul is thus teaching that there are two very distinct periods of time. The present-day church age is a different period from the future Day of the Lord when God's judgments fall upon the earth during the reign of Antichrist. We are certainly not living in a period when God is sending a strong delusion to make non-Christians believe Satan's lies. Nor are we seeing Satanically-empowered miracles happening on earth. We are not living in the Day of the Lord, because it is a yet-future period of time.

This was the crucial evidence that convinced J. N. Darby of the truth of dispensationalism. Darby saw from 2 Thessalonians 2 that there is going to be a period of time before the return of Christ which is distinctly different from the present church age. God will be dealing with the world in a very different way during the Day of the Lord to the way in which He is dealing with the world at the moment. Furthermore, Paul goes to great length to assure the Thessalonian Christians that they are not presently living through this different period of time. Why? The simplest explanation is that this different future period of time is not part of the church age at all, for it will only come when the church age has ended, and the church is no longer the focus of God's dealings with the world.

This is in line with a pretribulation rapture position, in which after God takes His church out of the world, a different period of time will begin in which God will deal with the world in a different way. By contrast, the post-tribulation rapture position holds that there is only one church age that runs right through the tribulation period until the second coming of Christ at the Battle of Armageddon – there are no dispensational distinctions or different eras in God's program for the future. Paul's words in 2 Thessalonians 2 disprove this.

The message of 2 Thessalonians 2 accords much better with the idea of a pretribulation rapture. The Thessalonians were worried that they were living through the Day of the Lord, the tribulation period. This alarmed and troubled them because they had been taught that the Day of the Lord commenced with the rapture of the church (1 Thess. 4:15 – 5:3). They thought they had missed the rapture and were now going through the tribulation period and would have to endure the terrible ordeal of Antichrist's reign. Paul reassures them that they are not in the Day of the Lord, for the tribulation period has not yet come, nor is it part of the church age.

The Restrainer

A third reason that 2 Thessalonians teaches a pretribulation rapture is found in verses 6 and 7:

> And now you know what is restraining that he might be revealed in his own time. ⁷ For the mystery of lawlessness is already at work, only He who restrains will do so until He is taken out of the way.

Paul writes about some force restraining or preventing the arrival of Satan's Man and the Day of the Lord. The restrainer is some*thing* (neuter, v6) as well as some*one* (masculine, v7). Who or What is this restrainer stopping the coming of Satan's Man?

There have been many suggestions including (a) human government (b) gospel preaching (c) Michael the archangel (d) the church (e) God's goodness (f) the Jewish state and (g) the Holy Spirit. However, when we consider what this Restrainer is holding back, we can make the following observations:

1. Seeing the Restrainer is holding back Satan's Man and plan, it must therefore be equal or greater in power to Satan himself, for 'the coming of the lawless one is according to the working of Satan' (v9). This suggests the Restrainer is Divine. Human government is not the answer, for Satan is far more powerful than any mere human government. Human government cannot hold Satan back; he is the very ruler of this age.
2. The lawless one is not only characterised by powerful miracles, but also by deception. The Restrainer must be the opposite, something that is presently restraining deception, and therefore a promoter of the truth. Again, the Restrainer is at least the equal of Satan, by whose deception the Man of sin works.
3. Since Satan's man is characterised by lawlessness, and the Restrainer is holding back 'the mystery of lawlessness' which is 'already at work' (v7), the Restrainer must be characterised by righteousness and holiness.
4. Seeing the Antichrist's character in 2 Thessalonians is a religious one, the Restrainer must be a force opposing false-religion, and promoting the gospel and the truth of God. Therefore again the Restrainer cannot simply be the secular power.
5. Seeing the rule of the Antichrist is going to be worldwide, the opposing power preventing his appearance must likewise be universal.
6. Seeing the Restrainer is a person (singular), he is not angels (plural).

7. Seeing the Restrainer is going to be taken out of the midst to allow the coming of the Man of Sin, He must currently be 'in the midst'.

The best candidate is the Holy Spirit, for the following reasons. He is powerful (point 1), He is the Spirit of Truth (point 2), He is holy (the Holy Spirit, point 3), He is the Spirit of God (point 4), He is omnipresent (point 5), He is a Person (singular, point 6), and He is the One who is in the church (point 7).

The interchange of neuter and masculine pronouns also strongly points to the Holy Spirit (point 5), who is elsewhere referred to both by the neuter (because the Greek word for 'Spirit' is neuter) and also as a Person, using the masculine (see the interchange of neuter and masculine pronouns with reference to the Holy Spirit in John 14:26, 15:26, 16:13-14).

Of the alternative suggestions, most are in fact included within the work of the Holy Spirit. This is because it is the Holy Spirit which (a) helps us pray for human government, (b) empowers our preaching of the gospel, (c) divinely directs the service of angels, (d) indwells the church, and (e) executes God's providential goodness. It is only through the working of the Holy Spirit in the church that we can act as salt and light in the world (i.e. live in a righteous way) and so restrain the working of Satan.

Someone might suggest that this Restrainer is simply a reference to God. However, the fact that the Restrainer is also described as 'what is restraining' suggests that it is not God, for the Bible never speaks of God in an impersonal way. Nevertheless, the Restrainer is also a person ('he') whose will and purpose align with God's in opposing and restraining Satan's working until the proper time comes for the revelation of the Man of sin. The Restrainer is not a force or an agent used by God unwittingly.

The main alternative suggested to the Holy Spirit by commentators is that human government is what Paul is speaking about. However, human government is not all-powerful, nor is it usually involved in promoting the truth of God. Indeed, it is often positively anti-Christian. While some of the alternatives are partially correct, none meet the full range of criteria, or match the full description, except the Holy Spirit.

That means, of course, that the Holy Spirit in the church is going to be taken out of this scene before the Day of the Lord. This in turn means that the church has to be raptured before the Day of the Lord.

E. W. Rogers writes:

> All kinds of suggestions have been made, such as ordered government,

the then existing Roman Empire. But it should be pointed out that whatever the restraint may be it is Something and Someone who wittingly, purposefully and designedly holds it in check with the view to ensuring that the Man of Lawlessness is revealed in his own proper time[9].

The 'Falling Away' or Apostasy

2 Thessalonians 2:3 reads 'Let no one deceive you in any way because that Day will not come unless the falling away comes first, and the Man of Sin is revealed'. Paul says the Day of the Lord cannot come unless the falling away has come first.

What is this 'falling away'? The Greek word 'apostasia' is only used once elsewhere in the NT (in Acts 21:21) and in Greek literature generally it usually refers to defection, a military revolt, a rebellion, or religious apostasy – i.e. departure from the truth.

However, some pre-tribulationists argue that this word should be translated the 'departure', by which they mean the rapture of the church. Thus, they translate 2 Thessalonians 2:3 as, 'that Day [i.e. of the Lord] will not come unless the Departure (the Rapture) comes first', which means that the Rapture must come first before the Tribulation. Evidence for translating the word as 'departure' is as follows:

- the verbal form of the word (*aphistemi*, found 15 times in the NT) means 'to depart', and is translated as such 13 times. For example, Anna did not depart from the temple (Luke 2:37), the Devil departed from Christ after the temptation (Luke 4:13), and the angel departed from Peter after his release from prison in Acts 12:10.
- 'Apostasia' is simply a later form of the classical Greek word 'apostasis', and one of the meanings of *apostasis* is 'departure, disappearance' (Liddell-Scott Greek lexicon). For example, Euripides, one of the three great tragic Greek playwrights (along with Sophocles and Aeschylus), in his play *Hippolytus*, wrote about death as a 'departure (*apostasis*) from life'. By the time of Paul, Euripides' plays were condensed into a 'school edition', used for school lessons. Thus, even school children in Thessalonica in Paul's day would have understood *apostasis* and its synonym *apostasia* to mean 'departure' in certain contexts.
- There are also examples of *apostasia* meaning 'departure' in patristic

---

[9] E. W. Rogers, *Concerning the Future*, pp64-65

Greek, that is, written by the post-apostolic church 'fathers'. For example, Lampe's *Patristic Greek Lexicon* gives an example of *apostasia* meaning 'departure'[10], which F. F. Bruce also refers to: 'the "departure" of the apostles with the Virgin Mary to Jerusalem from Bethlehem in the apocryphal writing *The Falling Asleep of the Holy Mother of God*[11].

- The idea that the 'apostasy' here means 'departure' is not a modern suggestion. The 4th century Latin Vulgate translated *apostasia* here in 2 Thessalonians 2:3 as *discessio*, which means 'departure'. All early English translations used the word 'departynge', including the Wycliffe Bible (1384), the Tyndale Bible (1526), the Coverdale Bible (1535) and the Cranmer Bible (1539). Other early English Bibles that translated it as 'departing' include the Breeches Bible (1576) the Beza Bible (1583) and the Geneva Bible (1608). This translation has a very long history.
- Another word related to 'apostasia' is 'apostasion', which is used in Matthew 5:32, 19:7, and Mark 10:4 for a bill of divorce (i.e. departure, separation). This again shows that the root idea of the word-family is departure, whether it is spatial departure, or spiritual departure, or political departure (i.e. revolt), or marital departure (i.e. divorce).

It is often stated today that *apostasia* cannot mean 'departure' in 2 Thessalonians 2:3 because it never means 'departure' in the New Testament, or in the Greek translation of the Old Testament (LXX). However, as there is only one other case of *apostasia* in the New Testament, and three in the Old, this argument is not very weighty. While the usual meaning of the word in Greek literature is either a military revolt or a religious defection, the word was occasionally used to mean 'departure' and this means that a 'rapture' interpretation is possible.

However, the fact that 'departure' is a possible translation does not mean that the rapture is being spoken of here. It is also possible that the meaning of the word here in 2 Thessalonians 2:3 is religious unfaithfulness (the same sense in which the word is used in Acts 21:21, and the three occurrences of this word in the Greek OT: Josh. 22:22, 2 Chron. 29:19 and Jer. 2:19). This option deserves consideration because the rest of 2 Thessalonians 2 tells us of the religious character of the Day of the Lord: we read of Antichrist setting himself up as god, people believing the lie, and God sending strong delusion, with those who rejected the gospel

---

[10] G. W. H. Lampe, *A Patristic Greek Lexicon*, Oxford University Press, 1969, p255
[11] F. F. Bruce, *1 & 2 Thessalonians*, Word Biblical Commentary, Nashville: Nelson, 1982, pp166-7

being condemned. So, we need to consider the possibility of a religious defection. But what sort of religious defection could this be? There are three options:

1. **The Abandonment of True Christianity**: William Hendriksen writes, 'by and large, the visible church will forsake the true faith'[12]. The problem with this idea is that this largely describes the situation in many parts of Christendom already – with denials of the virgin birth or the bodily resurrection – yet we are not in the Day of the Lord. There were even people who departed from the faith in the days of the apostles (2 Tim. 2:17-18, etc.). Despite all this religious apostasy, we are not yet in the Day of the Lord. How can apostasy from orthodox Christianity be a tell-tale feature of the tribulation period, when we have religious apostasy on every hand at present? There seems to be something special and different about the apostasy in the Day of the Lord.

2. **Antichrist's Religion**: secondly, a religious defection could refer to Antichrist's religion. The next verse (v4) speaks of Antichrist enthroning himself as God and being worshipped in the temple of God. However, it seems unlikely that Antichrist's religion is what is being spoken of here, because there is another end-time religion that fits the description of apostasy much better, and which occurs in the Day of the Lord before Antichrist's religion: Babylon the Great. Antichrist's religion is also problematic because it does not start out as orthodox Christianity and then deny the teachings of Scripture (which is what apostasy means) – it is a religion in total opposition to God. Antichrist also only sets up his religion at the mid-point of the tribulation period, while the Day of the Lord covers much more than the great tribulation period. Thus, while Antichrist's religion will be the ultimate form of false-religion at the end of the tribulation period, there is another form of apostate religion at the beginning of the Tribulation period.

3. **Babylon the Great**: the third option for the religious defection is the one-world religion we find at the beginning of the tribulation period. Babylon the Great is described as a harlot in Rev. 17: 1 and 5, and spiritual harlotry is a common metaphor in the Bible for false-religion

---

[12] William Hendriksen, *1 and 2 Thessalonians*, London: Banner of Truth, 1972, p170

(see Ex. 34:15, Jud. 2:17, Jer. 3, Ezek. 16, Hos. 1-3, etc.). Babylon stands in contrast to the Lamb's wife, the church (Rev. 19:7). It would seem that in the tribulation period the false-religions of the world will merge and unite into Babylon the Great. She is described as dominating the entire world in Rev. 17:1, 15. After the Antichrist's 'resurrection' he will destroy Babylon the Great and set up his own worship-system (Rev. 17:7-16). Thus Babylon the Great seems to best fit the description of 'the apostasy' in 2 Thessalonians 2:3; it will be a one-world religion denying the cardinal doctrines of Christianity.

But this raises a question. What is the difference between Babylon the Great and the general apostasy we see today? Today, despite all the apostasy, there are still many true believers who proclaim the truths of God's Word. Yet in a future day when 'the apostasy' (note the definite article) reaches its fullness, it will involve complete abandonment of the truths of the Christian faith. Even a post-tribulationist like George Müller wrote about the Apostasy as the complete and total abandonment of true Christianity:

> Not merely bad times in the Church, such as coldness, deadness, lukewarmness, lifelessness, but the Apostasy. Now what is the Apostasy? Entire rejection of everything that is divine; the fulfilment of the second Psalm—'Let us break their bands asunder, and cast away their cords from us;' let us have neither God, Christ, nor anything divine: the setting up themselves, the denying everything that is divine, the rejecting even the form of godliness, this is the Apostasy referred to … this has not been fulfilled in Popery. It is anti-Christian altogether[13].

But the complete denial of everything divine cannot occur until are no more believers to stand for the truth or protest its watering-down. We see this even with largely apostate Christian denominations today: a remnant within these denominations continue to stand up for the true gospel. Even where it seems that the true faith has been completely extinguished, light breaks out and shines forth again. As long as the Holy Spirit continues His work in this present church age, there cannot be 'the apostasy'. The apostasy therefore refers to something more than what we see today. It refers to a coming day in which there will be no true Christian witness

---

[13] "The Prophetical Signs of the Last Days of this Dispensation", a sermon by George Müller, delivered at the Clifton Conference, October 7th, 1884.

remaining on earth.

But for all true believers to be taken from the earth means virtually the same thing as the rapture. Either way, then, whether the word 'apostasia' means physical departure (i.e. the rapture) or total spiritual departure, the result is the same: the reason for the 'falling away' is that there is no one left standing up for the truth. Only the complete removal of all Christians from the world will permit the uniting of all the world's religions to form the end-time One World Religion, Babylon the Great. Whichever way we look at this passage, it appears to teach the departure of all believers from the earth before the Day of the Lord.

Conclusion

Paul commenced his argument in this chapter by mentioning the rapture: 'concerning the coming of our Lord Jesus Christ and our gathering together to Him' (verse 1). 'Our gathering together to Him' is a reference back to 1 Thessalonians 4:16-17. Therefore, as Robert Thomas writes,

> 'Our gathering together to Him' defines which aspect of Jesus' coming the writer has in mind. It reminds the readers of the great event described in 1 Thessalonians 4:14-17, the gathering of those in Christ to meet Him in the air *en route* to be with the Father in heaven. He wanted to emphasize that the day of the Lord cannot begin on earth until the saints are in heaven with the Father. Since Christ's reappearance to take the saints to heaven had not yet happened, the day of the Lord could not yet have begun. Therefore, the apostle asks them not to be shaken or troubled by the false message they had received. The gathering together had not yet occurred; hence the day of the Lord was not yet in progress[14].

---

[14] Robert Thomas, "The Rapture and the Biblical Teaching of Imminency", in *Evidence for a Pretribulation Rapture*, ed., John F. Hart, Moody, 2015, p37

24 THE CHURCH IN REVELATION

In this final chapter, we will look at the question of whether the church goes through the tribulation period by considering the book of Revelation. Here we will survey ten pieces of evidence (starting at the end of the book) that indicate that the Church will not go through the tribulation period. When we put them all together, we have good reason to be confident that the rapture of the Church will happen before the tribulation period.

1. Who are the Rebels in Revelation 20:7-10?
2. The Resurrection in Revelation 20:4 is not the Rapture
3. No Rapture Mentioned in Revelation 19
4. The Rewarded Church Comes out of heaven with Christ
5. The Church is not mentioned in Rev 4-19
6. What is the event in Rev 4-5 that starts the tribulation period?
7. Who are the twenty four elders?
8. Rev 3:10-11 – the promise to be kept.
9. Israel in the book of Revelation
10. Who are the 144,000?

1. Who are the Rebels of Revelation 20:7-10?
In Revelation 20:7-9 we read:

> Now when the thousand years have expired, Satan will be released from his prison [8] and will go out to deceive the nations which are in the four corners of the earth, Gog and Magog, to gather them together to battle, whose number is as the sand of the sea. [9] They went up on the breadth of the earth and surrounded the camp of the saints and the beloved city. And fire came down from God out of heaven and devoured them.

How is it possible for there to be rebel sinners at the end of the millennium? The only way this is possible is if some saved people enter the millennium in non-glorified bodies. These are mortal saints who live on into the millennium and go on to marry and have children during the millennium. At the end of the 1000 years, the descendants of these mortal saints will rise up in rebellion against Christ's rule. We see the same picture in Isaiah 65 where we read of people in paradise who are able to have children, sin, and even die.

This presents no problem for a pre-tribulation rapture position, which teaches that after the rapture, there will be people who are saved during the tribulation period, some of whom will enter the millennium in mortal bodies when Christ returns.

However, the problem for a post-tribulation rapture position is this: if all the saved are raptured and glorified at the end of the tribulation period, and no unsaved enter the millennium, then who are the mortal people of Isaiah 65, or the rebels of Revelation 20:7-9? The post-tribulation rapture position has no satisfactory answer to this question. Therefore, it is more probable that the pre-tribulation rapture scenario is correct, and that the rebels here are the descendants of people saved in the tribulation period after the rapture of the church.

2. The Resurrection in Revelation 20:4 is not the Rapture

Revelation 20:4 mentions a resurrection after Christ comes again, at the beginning of the millennial reign:

> And I saw thrones, and they sat on them, and judgment was committed to them. Then I saw the souls of those who had been beheaded for their witness to Jesus and for the word of God, who had not worshiped the beast or his image, and had not received his mark on their foreheads or on their hands. And they lived and reigned with Christ for a thousand years.

Post-tribulationists take the resurrection mentioned here to refer to the rapture and resurrection that occurs when Christ's returns, as in 1 Thessalonians 4:16-17. Thus, George Ladd (a post-tribulationist) argues that Revelation 20:4-6 is the only passage that indicates the time of the rapture – all other passages are inferences[1]. But there are three problems with identifying Revelation 20:4-6 as the rapture:

A. **Wrong Timing**: in the post-tribulationist view of Revelation 20:4, the resurrection occurs after Christ descends to earth (Rev. 19:11-18), defeats the Antichrist (Rev. 19:19-21), and then imprisons Satan for 1000 years (Rev. 20:1-3). But this is quite different to the

---

[1] George Ladd, *The Blessed Hope*, Eerdmans, 1965, p165

post-tribulation view of the rapture in 1 Thessalonians 4:16-17, where all Christians who have died are raised and caught up with living saints to meet Christ in the air during Christ's descent, immediately returning to earth with Him. 1 Thessalonians 4:16-17 teaches that the rapture occurs *before* the Lord comes to earth, but Revelation 20:4 puts the resurrection after He has returned to earth. Ladd's theory about Revelation 20:4 thus fails to match the time of the rapture.

B. **Wrong People**: the resurrection in Revelation 20:4 is different to the resurrection described in 1 Thessalonians 4. Here it is a resurrection of those who were martyred during the tribulation for not worshipping the beast. This passage makes no mention of the resurrection of Christians who died before the tribulation period. To be resurrected here, Revelation specifies that a person has to have been beheaded by the Beast. This is not the general resurrection of the saints.

C. **Wrong Reference**: there is no mention of a rapture at all in Revelation 20:4. There is no catching-up of living saints into the skies. There is only a resurrection. It is very hard to agree with Ladd's assessment that this passage explicitly gives the time of the rapture – because there is no rapture mentioned here at all. It is Ladd who is depending on inferences, for without a direct mention of any rapture, his argument is entirely speculative.

If the rapture occurs in Revelation 20:4, Christ is already on earth, so why would the saints be caught up into the air? A rapture here is 'not only posttribulational but postparousia, a virtual non-rapture' (Hultberg)[2]. In other words, if Revelation 20:4 is alluding to the rapture, it not only occurs after the tribulation period, but after the coming of the Lord altogether. That is a difficult timeline to harmonize with the rapture described in 1 Thessalonians 4:16-17.

3. No Rapture Mentioned in Revelation 19

Revelation 19:11-21 tells of the return of Christ to earth. Here is the most important passage in the book of Revelation, the climax of the entire book, and the most detailed description of the second coming of Christ in the New Testament. Yet there is no hint of any rapture associated with Christ's return in Revelation 19. If there is to be a rapture at the Lord's

---

[2] Alan Hultberg, "A Case for the Prewrath Rapture", in *Three Views on the Rapture*, Zondervan, 2010, p151

coming (as 1 Thess. 4 says), from a post-tribulation rapture viewpoint, we would expect the rapture to be described here, in Revelation 19. Yet, there is not a whisper of it. John Walvoord writes,

> Posttribulationists, if they follow 1 Thessalonians 4, must place the rapture of the church in the sequence of events as Christ is coming from heaven to the earth. . . . There is absolutely nothing in Revelation 19-20 to support the idea that there is a rapture of the church involved in the second-coming process. Posttribulationists attempt to turn the argument against the pretribulationists by saying that if there were a pretribulation Rapture, it ought to be stated in the book of Revelation. The opposite, rather, is the truth[3].

It is the post-tribulationist who has the problem, for Revelation is all about Christ's second coming. This is what the opening chapter looked forward to: 'Behold, He is coming with clouds, and every eye will see Him, even they who pierced Him, and all the tribes of the earth will mourn because of Him. Even so, amen' (Rev. 1:7). Revelation 19 describes Christ's return in vivid detail, but neither the resurrection nor rapture are part of the narrative.

Post-tribulationists believe that the resurrection of dead saints and the rapture of living saints happens while Christ is in the air, before He comes to the earth: the saints rise to meet Christ, and immediately return to earth with Him. Yet, there is no mention of any rapture or resurrection of the dead or a glorious U-turn of the saints, as they sweep up to glory and then swing in behind Christ as He descends to earth in Revelation 19. Thus, the rapture is not post-tribulational if Revelation 19 has any say in the matter.

4. The Rewarded Church comes out of Heaven with Christ

A fourth argument for a pretribulation rapture in Revelation comes from 19:11-14 where we read of Christ coming out of heaven to the battle of Armageddon, along with the armies of heaven:

> Now I saw heaven opened, and behold, a white horse. And He who sat on him was called Faithful and True, and in righteousness He judges and makes war. [12] His eyes were like a flame of fire, and on His head were many crowns. He had a name written that no one

---

[3] John Walvoord, *The Rapture Question*, Zondervan, 1979, p254

knew except Himself. [13] He was clothed with a robe dipped in blood, and His name is called The Word of God. [14] And the armies in heaven, clothed in fine linen, white and clean, followed Him on white horses.

Notice, particularly, the armies of heaven that accompany Christ out of heaven in verse 14. They are described as being 'clothed in fine linen, white and clean'. This is a description of the church, as can be seen from two facts. First, in Revelation 17:14 we have another description of those who accompany Christ as he returns to earth to the battle of Armageddon:

These [i.e. the Beast and the kings who rule under him] will make war with the Lamb, and the Lamb will overcome them, for He is Lord of lords and King of kings; and those who are with Him are called, chosen, and faithful.

Those who accompany Christ to war at the battle of Armageddon are 'called, chosen and faithful'. In other words, they are human believers. 'Believers' is a valid translation of the Greek *pistoi*, translated as 'faithful'. Angels are elsewhere described as elect (or, chosen), and the angels are also faithful. But angels are never described as 'called', for it is only human believers who respond to the gospel message of salvation. Here is a reference to the gospel call, and seeing angels never needed to be saved, it therefore indicates that those accompanying Christ are His saints.

Therefore, the church accompanies Christ out of heaven in Revelation 19:14. But this necessitates that the church was already in heaven before Christ began His descent. This in turn rules out a post-tribulation rapture where the church merely meets Christ mid-air and returns to earth with Him, without being taken to heaven, to the 'Father's house' (John 14:3).

Second, and even more significant, is the fact that the clothing of the armies of heaven is the same as the clothing of the Lamb's wife, the Bride, which has just been described: 'and to her it was granted to be arrayed in fine linen, clean and bright, for the fine linen is the righteous acts of the saints' (Rev. 19:8). White garments are also what was promised to the Christian believer in Revelation 3:4, 5, 18. Those returning with Christ (Rev. 19:14) are clothed in garments that identify them as the church.

These garments are highly significant. In Revelation 19:7-9 we read:

"Let us be glad and rejoice and give Him glory, for the marriage of the Lamb has come, and His wife has made herself ready". [8] And to her it was granted to be arrayed in fine linen, clean and bright, for the fine linen is the righteous acts of the saints. ⁹ Then he said to me, "Write: 'Blessed are those who are called to the marriage supper of the Lamb!'" And he said to me, "These are the true sayings of God".

Here we see a scene in heaven, just before Christ returns. The fact that this scene is in heaven can be seen from Revelation 19:1, which reads:

After these things I heard a loud voice of a great multitude in heaven, saying, "Alleluia! Salvation and glory and honor and power belong to the Lord our God!'"

Another three Alleluias ring out in verses 3, 4 and 6. Then in verse 7 we read about the Lamb's wife being made ready for the marriage of the Lamb. As we have noted earlier, the Lamb's bride is described as being 'granted to be arrayed in fine linen, clean and bright, for the fine linen is the righteous acts of the saints' (Rev. 19:8).

The fine linen, in which the church is dressed, is explained as the 'righteous acts of the saints'. This is not the imputed righteousness of Christ (2 Cor. 5:21), but rather the saints' own righteous acts – our good works of service for the Master. This suggests that the Church has already appeared before the judgment seat of Christ to be rewarded for how we have lived for Christ. The judgment seat of Christ would also need to have happened for the Lamb's Bride to have been made ready: there can surely be no marriage of the Lamb and 'reign with Christ' until we are 'made ready' by having our service assessed at the judgment seat of Christ.

If the church is seen here in heaven before the return of Christ, already wearing garments which speak of the reward for faithful service at the judgment seat of Christ, this again means that the Church must have been taken to heaven sometime before Christ's return, as the result of the rapture. The rapture therefore must either be pre-tribulational, or possibly mid-tribulational. But the rapture cannot be post-tribulational.

5. The Church in the Book of Revelation

Another evidence for a pre-tribulation rapture from Revelation is the fact that the word 'church' is not mentioned once during Revelation 4-19, the chapters describing the tribulation period on earth. This would not be particularly strange, except for the fact that chapters 1-3 of Revelation are full of references to the word 'church', and chapter 22 again mentions it. In chapters 1-3 and 22, before and after the tribulation, the word 'church' is mentioned 20 times. But the church is conspicuous by its absence in Revelation chapters 4-19.

The reason, it is suggested, why the church is not found in these chapters is that this is a period when God's wrath (Rev. 6:16-17, 15:1) and judgment (Rev. 14:7, 15:4, 17:1) are falling upon the world. Revelation chapters 4 to 19 describe the tribulation period, but the church is neither under God's judgment (John 5:24, Rom. 8:1), nor will we come under His wrath, for we 'wait for His Son from heaven . . . even Jesus, the One delivering us from the coming wrath' (1 Thess. 1:10), and 'God has not appointed us to wrath' (1 Thess. 5:9).

The book of Revelation, and particularly chapters 4-19, is full of the imagery of war (horsemen, trumpets), hell (torment), and mentions of God's wrath (6:16, 17, 11:18, 12:2, 14:8, 10, 19, 15:1, 7, 16:1, 19, 18:3, 19:15). The question needs to be answered: why would God declare war upon His own people in the church, or rain His wrath upon them via indiscriminate judgements affecting all people, such as are seen in chapters 4-19? What purpose would this serve? Surely it is only Christ-rejectors who deserve such tribulation.

While "absence of evidence is not evidence of absence", the fact that the church is not mentioned in these tribulation chapters is suggestive. It fits better with the idea that the rapture of the church takes place before the tribulation and that the church does not go through the tribulation period. Post-tribulationists argue that the church is mentioned in the tribulation chapters because of certain expressions like 'saints' (e.g. Rev. 13:7), those 'who follow the Lamb' (Rev. 14:4), those 'who keep the commandments of the Lord' (Rev. 12:17), and those 'who die in the Lord' (Rev. 14:13). However, this is not necessarily true, and indeed begs the very question, for it is possible that the saints of the tribulation period are a group of believers distinct from the New Testament church, just like the believers of the Old Testament period had many distinct differences from believers of the New Testament era.

6. What Event starts the End-times?
What event signals the start of the end-times? This question applies not only to the book of Revelation, but also to other events in the New Testament, like the reign of the Antichrist, a flood of lawlessness that will sweep the world when the restraining person/force is removed, and of the divine delusion that will be sent upon the world (2 Thess. 2). What event signals the start of these end-time scenarios? In the book of Revelation, this event is the opening of the seven seals, described in chapters 4 and 5.

This is what leads to all the terrible judgments that follow. But what event is this and when does it happen? Is the scene described in Revelation 4 and 5 the ascension of Christ (in the past), or is it what happens after a pre-tribulation rapture (in the future), or is it something else?

There are four main schools of thought about the book of Revelation:

a. **Preterist**: This view argues that the events described in the book of Revelation happened in the past, at the time of the Roman conquest over Judea in AD 67-70.
b. **Historicist**: this position sees Revelation as a description of Christian history from Christ's first coming until his return, but mostly in the past. For example, historicist interpreters explained the trumpet judgments (Rev. 8:7) to be prophecies of the invasions of the Goths, Vandals, Huns and Muslims.
c. **Idealist**: this position sees Revelation as a book with general lessons for Christians of all time-periods, based on a spiritualizing, allegorizing interpretative approach.
d. **Futurist**: the view takes Revelation to be a prophecy of future events that will occur just before the Lord returns.

Consider the event that starts the end-times. One option is that the scene described in Revelation chapters 4 and 5 depicts the ascension of our Lord Jesus Christ, in which He presents Himself before the throne of God following His death and resurrection and is given all authority in heaven and earth. Preterists, Historicists and Idealists might all take this view. But there are significant problems. Firstly, most scholars believe that John wrote Revelation in the AD 90s (thus making it difficult to accept the preterist view, which sees Revelation as describing the destruction of Jerusalem in AD 70). While there are flashbacks in Revelation (like chapter 12 where we read of Christ's birth), yet the general focus of the book is on events which are said to be still in the future. Thus, we read in the opening verse of the book that it concerns 'things which must shortly take place'. Again, in 1:19, the Lord tells John to 'write the things which you have seen, and the things which are, and the things which will take place after this'. These verses say that the book of Revelation deals largely with events in the future. The opening words of chapter 4 present us with a scene in which John is invited to come up into heaven 'and I will show you things which must take place after this'.

This would appear to indicate that the events of Revelation 4 and 5 take place in the future, at least from John's perspective. This means that

Revelation chapters 4 and 5 cannot refer to the ascension of Christ, which had already happened before John wrote Revelation. So what other event, comparable to the ascension, is described in Revelation 4 and 5, when Christ is given great authority and honour by God? What event is this which starts the whole end-times sequence?

The fact that the world has not yet experienced the events which immediately follow, the seal, trumpet, and bowl judgments, in particular the outpouring of the wrath of God (Rev. 6:16-17) with one half of the world's population dying as a result of the seal (Rev. 6:8) and trumpet judgments (Rev. 9:15), would appear to indicate that the scene in chapters 4 and 5 has not occurred yet either. Most significantly, seeing the narrative sweeps on to its climax at the return of Christ (an event which has obviously not happened yet), it seems likely that the scene in Revelation chapters 4 and 5 has not happened yet either.

Mounce writes, 'Since the vision moves on naturally to the breaking of the seals and ultimately to the unveiling of the close of history, it is best to understand it as referring essentially to a time yet future'[4]. This means, too, that the entire tribulation period is still in the future. But if the scene in Revelation 4 and 5 did not happen in the past, and is not happening in the present, but instead must yet happen in the future, what signals the start of this sequence of future, end-time events?

One clue is found in Revelation 6:17 at the end of the sixth seal. After a great earthquake, all the world's people, great and small, hide themselves in caves and rocks from God's wrath, saying, 'For the great day of His wrath has come, and who is able to stand?'. Notice what they say: the day of the Lord has come. In the Old Testament the 'day of the Lord' is a very prominent prophetic topic. It is the day of God's wrath (Isa. 13:9). The day of the Lord has been called the major theme of the minor prophets. But it is found right at the beginning of the prophetical books, too, in Isaiah 2:10-22. It is from this passage that Revelation 6:17 is directly quoting, and particularly Isaiah 2:21 in which men hide themselves in the clefts of the rocks 'from the terror of the Lord, and the glory of His majesty, when He rises to shake the earth mightily'. So, we conclude that the events involved in the seals judgements are part of the Day of the Lord, which is the time of God's wrath being poured out on earth, and that Christ opening the seals commences the Day of the Lord.

But it is clear from 1 Thessalonians 4 and 5 that it is the rapture that begins the Day of the Lord, the end-time period. Is there any rapture in

---

[4] Robert Mounce, *Revelation*, p132

the book of Revelation? In Revelation 4:1-2, John writes:

> After these things I looked, and behold, a door standing open in heaven. And the first voice which I heard was like a trumpet speaking with me, saying, "Come up here, and I will show you things which must take place after this". ² Immediately I was in the Spirit; and behold, a throne set in heaven, and One sat on the throne.

John is personally called by Christ, and transported from earth to heaven in the Spirit, to witness the scenes in chapters 4 to 22. John experiences his own personal rapture: a call, a trumpet sound, and an ascent to heaven. A similar thing happens to the Two Witnesses of Revelation 11 who, after their death and resurrection, 'heard a loud voice from heaven saying to them, "Come up here". And they ascended to heaven in a cloud, and their enemies saw them' (Rev. 11:12). This is a literal rapture, and the two witnesses are called to heaven using the exact same words "come up here" that John heard.

It is John's 'rapture' experience that starts the end-times sequence of events in Revelation chapters 4-19. John's personal 'rapture' in 4:1 is a miniature version of what the entire church will experience. While Revelation does not provide explicit proof that the church's rapture initiates the end-times sequence of events, perhaps we can say that John's personal 'rapture' provides a symbolic parallel with the church's rapture. Is it possible that here we have a hint that it is the church's rapture that commences the end-times sequence of events?

7. Who are the Twenty-Four Elders?

We get a further clue about what event starts the end-times when we look at who is present at the scene in heaven in Revelation chapters 4 and 5. I suggest there are good reasons for identifying the 24 elders of Revelation 4-5 with the church. This suggests that the church is in heaven during the tribulation period, and therefore absent from earth during Revelation chapters 4-19.

In Revelation 4, immediately after he is taken in the spirit to heaven (verse 1), John sees the throne-sitter, God (verses 2 and 3), and then he describes the 24 elders: 'Around the throne were twenty-four thrones, and on the thrones I saw twenty-four elders sitting, clothed in white robes; and they had crowns1 of gold on their heads. (Rev. 4:4). These 24 elders are described even before the 'seven lamps of fire burning before the throne, which are the seven Spirits of God' (verse 5), and the four living creatures (verse 6), the living cherubim chariot-throne (see 1 Chronicles 28:18) upon which God rides (verses 6-8). In other words, the 24 elders are very important; they are the 'inner circle' of heaven.

Notice the following descriptions of the 24 elders and the cross-references in Revelation which help to identify who these people are:

A. **They are wearing white robes** (Rev. 4:4). This is what was promised to the Christian believer (in Rev. 3:4, 5, 18). Thus, 3:5 says, 'He who overcomes shall be clothed in white garments, and I will not blot out his name from the Book of Life; but I will confess his name before My Father and before His angels'. Revelation 7:14 tells us that white robes are the clothing of those whose sins have been forgiven through Christ's blood; the great multitude who are converted during the great tribulation are described as follow as 'the ones who come out of the great tribulation, and washed their robes and made them white in the blood of the Lamb'.

B. **They are wearing gold crowns** (Rev. 4:4). This is the reward that was promised to the faithful Christian in 2:10: 'Do not fear any of those things which you are about to suffer . . . Be faithful until death, and I will give you the crown of life'. Similarly, 3:11 promises a crown to the faithful believer: 'Behold, I am coming quickly! Hold fast what you have, that no one may take your crown'. The Christian believer is also promised gold: 'I counsel you to buy from Me gold refined in the fire, that you may be rich; and white garments, that you may be clothed, that the shame of your nakedness may not be revealed; and anoint your eyes with eye salve, that you may see' (Rev. 3:18).

C. **They are overcomers**. Christ promised that the overcoming Christian would be 'seated on a throne' in Revelation 3:21: 'To him who overcomes I will grant to sit with Me on My throne, as I also overcame and sat down with My Father on His throne'. The word used for the crowns of the 24 elders wear is *stephanos* in Greek, the crown given to a victorious athlete, rather than *diadema*, a ruler's diadem. As already noticed, the white garments are also evidence that these are the overcomers of the church age (Rev. 3:5). There can, of course, be no crowned Christians in heaven until after Christ's return (see 2 Timothy 4:8 and Revelation 22:13 where rewards are only given after the Lord's return), which again suggests the events described in Revelation 4 are subsequent to Christ's return.. F. A. Tatford writes, 'The elders wore dazzling white garments and crowns of gold ... Their long pilgrimage and constant struggle were finished and they now sat resplendent in glory. The coronation of the saints occurs *after* Christ's return for His own people'[5].

D. **There are twenty-four elders**. The number twenty-four is not often found in the Bible. However, we find it in two chapters in the Old Testament, one after another. In 1 Chronicles 24, the priests in Solomon's temple were split into twenty-four divisions, or shifts, to serve God (these divisions were still in operation in the temple at the time of Christ's birth in Luke 1:5). Then, it is used again in the very next chapter, 25, in which the Levitical singers in the temple were split into twenty-four divisions, to give thanks and to praise God. Apart from these two chapters, there are no significant or relevant references to the number twenty-four elsewhere in the Bible (one of the giants of Gath had twenty-four fingers and toes, and there are a few references to twenty-four thousand, but that is it). The priests and the Levitical singers in the OT were engaged in the tasks of priesthood and praise, which is true of the elders in Revelation 4 also. These are also two things that apply to Christian believers. 1 Peter 2:9 says, 'But you are a chosen generation, a royal priesthood, a holy nation, His own special people, that you may proclaim the praises of Him who called you out of darkness into His marvelous light'. Also, in Revelation 5:8, we read that the twenty-four elders (along with the four living creatures) had harps to praise God. But significantly, while both men and angels can praise God, only men can be priests (see Hebrews 5:1).

E. **They are kings as well as priests**. Revelation 4:4 says 'Around the throne were twenty-four thrones, and on the thrones I saw twenty-four elders sitting'. The twenty-four elders have the character of kings, in that they sit on thrones. So, they appear to be kings as well as priests. Revelation 1:6 speaks about Christians being 'kings (or, a kingdom) and priests'. Revelation 5:10 says, 'And have made them kings (or a kingdom) and priests to our God; and they shall ***reign*** on the earth'.

F. **They are elders**. Another description that seems to point to these being people rather than angels is the fact that they are elders. Nowhere do we read of angels being called elders, however people in both testaments are described as such. Elders symbolize maturity, wisdom gained through experience, and those who have overcome adversity. The elders here seem to speak of those whose days of immaturity, learning and discipline are past. To borrow from the language of Hebrews, they appear to be 'the spirits of just men made

---

[5] F. A. Tatford, *Prophecy's Last Word*, London: Pickering and Inglis, 1969, p77

perfect' (although we have no indication of whether the elders in Revelation are merely spirits, or resurrected). The elders again seem to represent glorified saints in heaven.

G. **They cast their crowns before God.** In Revelation 4:10-11 we read, 'the twenty-four elders fall down before Him who sits on the throne and worship Him who lives forever and ever, and cast their crowns before the throne, saying 'You are worthy, O Lord, to receive glory and honour and power, for You created all things, and by Your will they exist and were created'. By casting their crowns before the throne they express their own unworthiness to be brought into such an exalted position. They are saying they do not deserve the crowns. The four living creatures do not make any similar protestations of unworthiness, for they have been created to stand before God. By casting their crowns before the throne, the elders acknowledge that God is the One to whom all the credit is due, and that it is by His grace that they occupy the position they find themselves in. Again, this is the language of the Christian, recognizing his unworthiness, and praising the grace of God that has brought them into such a position.

These seven descriptions of the elders in Revelation – which correspond with and fulfil the promises made to Christians overcomers in the churches in Revelation chapters 2 and 3 – suggest the elders are glorified Christian believers. Furthermore, the number 24 suggests that here we have the entire body of believers, all the different divisions of God's priestly people. They represent the church (and perhaps Old Testament saints as well?), and add their voice in worshipping God and in giving Christ all blessing and honour and glory and power. Representatives of the church get front row seats as all authority is given to Christ to open the seals and to initiate the tribulation period which will ultimately result in Christ returning to reign.

This suggests, too, that the church which has been described in its different degrees of success and failure in Revelation chapters 2 and 3 is now translated to heaven in Revelation 4, to appear before God's throne in glorified form.

8. Kept from the Hour

Revelation 3:10 seems to suggest that the church will be kept from the tribulation. The verse reads as follows: 'Because you have kept My command to persevere, I also will keep you from the hour of trial which shall come upon the whole world, to test those who dwell on the earth'.

This verse has been the subject of much debate. George Ladd argues that it 'need not be a promise of a removal from the very physical presence of tribulation. It is a promise of preservation and deliverance in and through it'[6]. Post-tribulationists argue that the words 'keep . . . from' mean 'guard from out of', indicating that God will preserve through and then bring the church out of it.

Another argument is that God will protect believers through the tribulation period because of a parallel passage in John 17:15 where Christ promised to keep believers from the evil one. This obviously did not mean taking us out of the world, so neither is the promise in Revelation 3:10 meant to be referring to God physically taking us out of the tribulation period. Post-tribulationists argue that it teaches the church will be protected through the time of tribulation, in a similar fashion to the way God protected the Israelites during the plagues on Egypt.

Pre-tribulationists point out in reply that the verse promises to keep God's people, not from the trial, but from the period of tribulation itself ('the *hour* of trial that is coming on the whole world'). Another problem with the post-tribulation argument that the church will be protected through the tribulation is that, in practical terms, it does not come true – for many saints living through the great tribulation will be martyred and beheaded.

Post-tribulationist Douglas Moo argues that the promise refers to spiritual protection rather than physical[7], but this not only admits the major problem with his position (saints will not be protected physically during the tribulation – which is what most post-tribulationists argue God will do). It also avoids the issue of people being kept from the time period itself – the hour of the trial. Coupled with the fact that the church appears to be absent from the tribulation period in Revelation 4-19, this verse seems to provide added encouragement for the view that the church will not be present during the time of the tribulation period, presumably via a pre-tribulation rapture.

9. Israel in the Tribulation

> Now a great sign appeared in heaven: a woman clothed with the sun, with the moon under her feet, and on her head a garland of twelve stars. Then being with child, she cried out in labour and in pain to give birth (Rev. 12:1-2).

---

[6] George E. Ladd, *The Blessed Hope*, Eerdmans, 1956, p85-6
[7] Douglas Moo, *Three Views on the Rapture*, 2010, p225

Who is this woman? The Bible is obviously not prophesying a literal pregnant woman travelling into space, because we are specifically told that this is a sign, that is, a symbol.

Roman Catholic commentators take this to be a reference to Mary because she gave birth to Christ, who 'was to rule all nations with a rod of iron, and her child was caught up to God and His throne' (Rev. 12:5). However, if this woman is Mary, when did Mary flee 'into the wilderness, where she has a place prepared by God, that they should feed her there one thousand two hundred and sixty days' (verse 6)? How did Mary grow two wings like an eagle to fly into the wilderness (verse 14)? Who, on a Roman Catholic reading, are 'the rest of her offspring' (verse 17), seeing they believe Mary was a perpetual virgin? Catholics cannot, with interpretational consistency, easily apply this language literally to Mary.

Some interpreters take this woman to picture the Church. However, the church is never spoken of in the Bible as Christ's mother, but instead as Christ's bride. If it is the church that has given birth to Christ, then the church is both Christ's mother and His bride, and the idea of Christ marrying His own mother presents a morally-jarring picture. If we remember from Ephesians 5:31-32 that Adam and Eve are an Old Testament type of Christ and His bride, it was Eve (the church in type) that came from Adam's (Christ's) side, not Eve that gave birth to Adam. The church is the fruit of Christ's suffering, but here in Revelation 12, Christ is the result of the woman's labour-pains. Further, if the woman here represents the Church, then who are 'the rest of her offspring' (verse 17)? If we say that these offspring are the members of the church, that makes the church three things: Christ's mother, Christ's bride, and her children. Sorry, but there are too many mixed metaphors! Why, if the church were in view here, did Revelation not simply call the woman Christ's bride, as elsewhere in Revelation, and leave it at that?

The third option is that this woman represents Israel. Although some commentators are reluctant to allow this possibility (they prefer lessons for the church), there are nevertheless four reasons why it seems that the woman here refers to Israel.

Firstly, because the sun, moon and twelve stars of Revelation 12:1 seem to be a reference to Joseph's dream in Genesis 37, where the sun, moon and twelve stars point to Jacob, Rachel and Jacob's twelve sons, and hence to the whole family of Israel as a unit. The woman of Revelation 12 is clothed with the insignia of Jacob's family. When we turn to the prophecy of the New Covenant in Jeremiah 31:35-36, God links His promise of Israel's national preservation with the sun and moon:

Thus says the LORD, who gives the sun for a light by day, the ordinances of the moon and the stars for a light by night, who disturbs the sea, and its waves roar (the LORD of hosts is His name): [36] "If those ordinances depart from before Me, says the LORD, then the seed of Israel shall also cease from being a nation before Me forever".

The number twelve is closely associated in the Bible with Israel, because of the twelve tribes that made up the nation. Even in the church, the reason there were twelve apostles was because the primary ministry of the twelve was to preach the gospel to ethnic Israel (see Galatians 2:7, and see also their connection to Israel in Matthew 19:28, Luke 22:30).

Secondly, in Rev. 12:7 we read about Michael and his angels fighting against the dragon who persecutes the woman, but Daniel 12:1 tells us that Michael is the special angelic guardian of the nation of Israel: 'at that time Michael shall stand up, the great prince who stands watch over the sons of your people (i.e. Daniel's people, Israel), and there shall be a time of trouble such as never was since there was a nation, even to that time, and at that time your people shall be delivered, every one who is found written in the book'.

Thirdly, Israel is often pictured in the Old Testament as a 'woman' who is married to Jehovah (Isaiah 50:1, 54:5-6, Jer. 3:14, 31:32, Hosea 2:2-8, 16-20), and also as a woman 'in labour' (Isaiah 66:7-8, Jeremiah 4:31, 6:24, 13:21, 22:23, 30:6, Micah 4:9-10, Hosea 13:13). This imagery goes back all the way to the curse upon Eve in Genesis 3:15-6, to whom God promised a seed (Christ) who would crush the serpent's head, but to whom God also said, 'I will greatly multiply your sorrow and your conception; in pain you shall bring forth children'. The suffering and hard labour of Jacob's wife Rachel's during childbirth (near Bethlehem of all places, Gen. 35:16-17, 19) is also perhaps a picture of the way in which the nation of Israel was to suffer because of their mission of bringing the Messiah into the world (Rachel is pictured as the 'mother' of the nation of Israel in Jeremiah 31:15 and Matthew 2:17-18). Israel's 'birth-pains' therefore symbolize the many sufferings of the chosen nation due to her special Messianic mission and the resultant Satanic opposition.

Fourthly, the immediate context of Revelation 12, coming directly after Revelation 11, would seem to indicate that Israel is the focus of attention. Revelation 11:1-3 shows us a picture of Jerusalem trodden down under Gentile domination and the two time markers used in those verses for the period of persecution ('forty-two months' and 'one thousand two hundred and sixty days') link up with the same time period of persecution mentioned in 12:6 ('one thousand two hundred and sixty days') and 12:14 ('time, times and half a time'). Thus, the persecution in Revelation 12 matches that of Revelation 11 and would suggest the same identity of the people persecuted: Israel.

Thus, while there are good reasons to see Revelation 12 telling us about Israel, and its persecution by Satan during the great tribulation, there seem no good reasons to think that the woman is the church, other than wish-fulfilment on the part of non-dispensational commentators.

We conclude that the tribulation period is a time when God will specially deal with the nation of Israel (see Hos. 2:14-15, Ezek. 20:33-38). This is why it is called the time of Jacob's trouble (not the church's) in Jeremiah 30:7. Israel will be brought back to God through the terrible discipline of the tribulation period. However, she will be delivered, and then come to faith in Christ: 'all Israel will be saved' (Rom. 11:26).

10. Who are the 144,000?

One of the more mysterious puzzles in the book of Revelation involves the 144,000 in Revelation 7, with 12,000 from each of the tribes of Israel.

Jehovah's Witnesses take these 144,000 to refer the highest caste of their cult, the first converts to their new religion in the early 20th century (as opposed to the later and more lowly 'hewers of wood and drawers of water' who will have a less exalted position in their future paradise).

Many interpreters take the 144,000 to refer to the Church. Some argue that we cannot take the references to Israel's tribes at face value because 'the twelve tribes no longer existed literally since hundreds of years before John wrote the ten northern tribes were taken into exile in 722 BC'[8]. This is not quite true, for we read of members of the ten 'lost' tribes in the Old and New Testaments (e.g. 2 Chron. 15:9, 30:11, Luke 2:36). Paul referred to the 'twelve tribes' as still being in existence in his day (Acts 26:7). God is able to identify them and knows where they are. Others take the 144,000 to refer to the church because the number is too precise to be other than symbolical. They see the 144,000 and the 'great multitude' in verses 9-17 to refer to the same group of people (the Church) in the same way as Christ is described as the lion and the lamb in Revelation 5. The other alternative is that the 144,000 people refer to 144,000 Jews who 'serve God' (Rev. 7:3) during the future tribulation period.

It is important to notice that in Revelation 7, we are not only introduced to the 144,000 in verses 1 to 8, but also to another group of

---

[8] Eckhard Schnabel, *40 Questions about the End Times*, Kregel Publications: Grand Rapids, MI, 2011, p86

people in verses 9-17 – the Great Crowd. These two groups are found in the same chapter, and there are both connections and contrasts between them.

Many commentators take this second group of people – the Great Crowd – to be the same as the 144,000. That is, both are symbols of the church. However, there are a number of obvious differences between them.

A. One group is **numbered** (144,000), while the second group is not simply unnumbered, but innumerable (Rev. 7:9).
B. One of the two groups is **identified by nationality** – Israel (the 144,000, of the 12 tribes of Israel, each tribe identified and numbered), whereas of the second group we read, 'a great multitude which no one could number, of all nations, tribes, peoples, and tongues' (Rev. 7:9).
C. The Great Crowd are an **unknown** group of people, for one of the elders comes to John and asks him, "Who are these arrayed in white robes, and where did they come from?" John replies, "Sir, you know". The elder said, "These are the ones who come out of the great tribulation, and washed their robes and made them white in the blood of the Lamb" (Revelation 7:13-14). If this group were the church, it would seem strange that John does not recognize them, or that he should have to ask. By contrast, the 144,000 are named as belonging to the twelves tribes of Israel.
D. The 144,000 are seen **on earth**, whereas the great multitude are seen in heaven. The word 'earth' is mentioned five times in the description of the 144,000 (see verses 1, 2 and 3). By contrast, the great multitude are said to be 'standing before the throne and before the Lamb' in verse 9, although they were previously upon the earth, for we read that 'these are the ones who come out of the great tribulation, and washed their robes and made them white in the blood of the Lamb' (v14).
E. The 144,000 are **protected** from the terrible sufferings of the tribulation period. The 144,000 are sealed in Revelation 7:2-4 before the harming of the earth and sea by the four angels. In a later chapter (Rev. 9:4) we are told that the 144,000 are not harmed by the torment of the locust-scorpions of the fifth trumpet: 'they were commanded not to harm the grass of the earth or any green thing, or any tree, but only those men who do not have the seal of God on their foreheads'. However, by contrast, the great crowd have suffered greatly during the great tribulation, even to death.

In addition to these differences in the descriptions of the two groups, we are given more details about the 144,000 in Revelation 14 that show they are in a class of their own.

Some commentators question whether the 144,000 in Revelation 7 are the same people as the 144,000 mentioned in Revelation 14. But there are three identifiers which point to them being the same. Firstly, their number is the same in both passages (144,000). Secondly, they are sealed on their foreheads (Rev. 7:3), while in 14:1, we read that they have the Lamb's 'Father's name written on their foreheads'. Someone's name written on the forehead signifies ownership; that is, sealing them as the possession of the person whose name is written on them. Then thirdly, they are described in Revelation 7:3 as 'the servants of our God', while in 14:4-5 we read about their exceptional adherence to the cause of the Lamb. We conclude that these are the same people in Revelation 7 and 14.

Who then are these 144,000? Revelation 14 gives us more details about who they are, and it very quickly becomes obvious that these are very special people. Notice five distinctive things about the 144,000 in Revelation 14 that set them apart from any others of the redeemed:

A. In heaven, before God's throne, they sing a special song that only they are entitled to learn and sing (v3). Their song is unique.

B. 'These were redeemed from among men, being firstfruits to God and to the Lamb' (v4). The expression 'firstfruits' in the Old Testament referred to the first ripe fruits of the harvest that were offered to God in thanksgiving. The first ripe fruits grow upon the best plants, the 'cream of the crop'. As 'firstfruits', these 144,000 appear to be the first installment of a harvest of redeemed people. They are a select group among the redeemed, the most exceptional members. Lastly, just as the firstfruits were offered back to God in thanksgiving in the OT, these are people who have unreservedly offered themselves to God.

C. Thirdly, they are unmarried virgins (v4). We read 'they are the ones who were not defiled with women, for they are virgins'. Some commentators have argued that these were people who had never committed adultery or some other sexual sin. But this is not what the Bible says: they are virgins who have not been defiled with women. Other commentators argue that we must take the entire picture allegorically as a picture of spiritual faithfulness[9]. However,

---

[9] Mounce argues that 'the 144,000 are here pictured as the promised bride of Christ who have kept themselves pure from all defiling relationships with the pagan world system.

The Church in Revelation

surely if this were a picture of the bride of Christ, they would have been described as females, rather than males. Or, if the verse were trying to say that the 144,000 had kept themselves pure from the seductive defilement of the great harlot Babylon, it might have simply said so. The discomfort of spiritualizing commentators arises from the fact that most ordinary Christians cannot be included in the 144,000 because they have either been married or are females, both of which exclude anyone from being among the 144,000. If, however, the 144,000 are a distinctive group who alone have a special song to sing before God's throne (v3), it makes sense to also accept that the 144,000 are not simply the same thing as the entire church of Christ. They are distinct, in that they are literally celibate people who have completely devoted themselves to God's service.

D. Fourthly, we read that 'in their mouth was found no lie' (v5). Again, some commentators struggle with these words; Mounce careers off into allegorical territory, arguing that they made no compromise with the heretical claims of Antichrist[10]. But, the verse says nothing about Antichrist or worldly compromise. It says that 144,000 are characterized by complete honesty.

E. Lastly, we read that they are without fault before the throne of God (v5). Some might argue that all Christians stand faultless before God's throne because of the work of Christ, and this is (of course) true. But verses 4 and 5 are talking about the moral characteristics of the 144,000 (celibacy, no lying), not the theological truth of imputed righteousness. It would seem best to take this last statement in the same vein as those preceding – literally.

We therefore conclude that the 144,000 are not the Church in its entirety. They are a distinctive, numbered group among the redeemed of the tribulation period, not ordinary, run-of-the-mill Christians.

We may also conclude that the Great Crowd are not the Church in its entirety from the simple fact that the Great Crowd lives during the great tribulation, which is not true of all Christians, or the Church generally. The fact that they have palm branches in their hands (7:9) suggests celebration of victory over the forces of darkness during the great tribulation.

They have resisted the seductions of the great harlot Rome with whom the kings of the earth have committed fornication. The apparent confusion of the sexes is of no moment since the entire figure is to be understood symbolically', Mounce, *Revelation*, p270

[10] Mounce, *Revelation*, p271

Just like the first group (the 144,000) are not the present-day church (they are distinctively special, extraordinary people: 'super-saints'), so too this second group, the Great Crowd, is also not the present day church – inasmuch as the Church is not presently living in the 'great tribulation'.

This would strongly suggest, also, that the 144,000 and the Great Crowd are two different groups who live during the great tribulation, who serve God during that future period.

What is their role in the book of Revelation, then? It would appear that during the great tribulation, there are going to be 144,000 servants of God who are totally dedicated to serving Christ (Rev. 14:3-5), who stand in contrast and distinction to a Great Crowd of other believers who also live through this period.

Try and imagine, for a moment, what sort of effect 144,000 'super-saints' will have upon the earth. Imagine 144,000 John the Baptists or Apostle Pauls unleashed upon the world, all at the same time, not only zealous for God but also protected against harm and danger during their service and witness. It would seem, by the fact that the two groups are described one after the other in Revelation 7, that the Great Crowd are the fruit and the result of the ministry of the 144,000 (the 'first-fruits'). No wonder there is an innumerably Great Crowd of millions of people saved during the great tribulation. It would seem to make all the more sense, then, that the 144,000 are literal ethnic Jews, a people-group who fit the psychological profile of religious zealotry that we find in Revelation 14:1-5. How much more so once they realize that Jesus truly is the Messiah, who their nation rejected in the days of His flesh, and down through the centuries since, who is returning soon to reign as King of Kings.

Their repentance and spiritual rebirth is indeed going to bring spiritual life to the entire world. As Romans 11:12 and 15 tells us, 'Now if their fall is riches for the world, and their failure riches for the Gentiles, how much more their fullness', and 'for if their being cast away is the reconciliation of the world, what will their acceptance be but life from the dead'. Revelation 7 is teaching that the greatest world-wide revival of all time is yet to come, during the first half of the tribulation period.

Please note that all we have done here is to show that an allegorical, method of interpreting Revelation 7 and 14 makes less sense and is more forced, while a literal approach is sensible and preferable. The attempt to read the church into these passages must repeatedly ignore or explain away the actual words of the text. The fact that a literal approach is preferable again lends support to a pre-tribulation view of the book of Revelation for the simple reason that a post-tribulation approach is continually forced to adopt allegorical interpretations, which are stretched and strained.

This, in turn, suggests that we should take references to Israel in the book of Revelation literally rather than as allegorical picture of the church:

- 'the temple of God' (11:1), in 'the holy city' (v2), 'where their Lord was crucified' (v8) is therefore best understood as a temple in Jerusalem.
- The two witnesses of Revelation 11:3 (flame-throwing, rain-stopping, turning waters to blood, cursing with plagues, devouring enemies) are not the church, but are two witnesses very much like Jewish Old Testament prophets (and their behaviour certainly does not represent the sorts of actions that the New Testament church preaching the gospel of grace is called to imitate).
- The 'woman clothed with the sun' with a 'garland of twelve stars' on her head (Rev. 12:1) who gave birth to the Messiah (12:5), is Israel.

This all means, too, that the more references we find to Israel in Revelation chapters 4 to 19, the less room we find in Revelation chapters 4 to 19 for the church.

Conclusion

One of my favourite preachers as a young Christian was Dr. Bill Peterson, who often preached on what the Bible taught about the future. Here, as we finish this book, are three of his sayings.

1. "We are on the winning side",
2. "The church will not enter into even the first day of the tribulation",
3. (about the Lord's coming): "Perhaps today".

GLOSSARY (and chapters where subjects are found)

666: number of the Beast required to buy or sell at end of world (9, 10)
Abomination of Desolation: idol set up in Jerusalem temple by Antiochus Epiphanes, similar idol to be set up at end of world (8, 12)
Amillennialism: belief there is no literal millennium (3, 4)
Antichrist: future Satanic world-ruler (10)
Antiochus Epiphanes: Syrian king who oppressed Jews 167 BC (11, 12)
Apocalypse: Greek name for last book of Bible, meaning 'revelation' (9)
Armageddon: great battle of all nations at the end of the world (11, 14)
Beast: name of the Antichrist in Revelation (10)
Covenants: promises God made to Abraham, David and Israel (3, 6, 19)
Daniel's Seventieth Week: last 7 year period before Christ returns (12)
Day of the Lord: when God intervenes at end of the world (22, 23)
Dispensationalism: belief that God operates in different ways during different periods; stresses difference between Israel and Church (19)
Eschatology: study of 'last things', from 'eschatos' ('last' in Greek).
False Prophet: Antichrist's lieutenant, his minister of propaganda (10)
Futurist: view of Revelation that sees its fulfilment to be still future (9)
Great Tribulation: last 3½ year period of intense persecution (8, 12, 21)
Historicist: view of Revelation that sees it fulfilled in church history (9)
Idealist: view of Revelation that says it teaches timeless lessons (9)
Imminence: belief that Christ could come at any time (20, 21)
Kingdom of God: God's reign over His people in His world (7)
Mark of the Beast: the number or name of the Beast (10)
Midtribulation: view that rapture happens in middle of last 7 years (20)
Millennium: 1000-year period when Christ reigns with saints (2-6)
Olivet Discourse: Jesus' teachings about future in Matthew 24-25 (21)
Parousia: Greek word meaning 'presence' or 'coming' used to refer to the coming of the Lord.
Postmillennialism: belief that Christ returns after the millennium (5)
Posttribulation: view that rapture happens at end of last 7 years (20)
Premillennialism: view that Christ returns before the millennium (6)
Pretribulation: view that rapture happens before last 7 years (20-24)
Preterism: view that future prophecies were all fulfilled in past (8, 9)
Prewrath: view that rapture happens before God's wrath falls (20)
Rapture: Christians being 'caught up' into air at Christ's coming (20, 22)
Replacement theology: view that the Church has replaced Israel (4, 19)
Supercessionism: belief that the Church has superseded Israel (4, 19)

Other Books by the same Author

Is the Bible Really the Word of God? The Doctrine of Scripture

Defends the Bible against modern critical attacks.

Reader Reviews:
- *intensely good reading – doing it slowly!*
- *has managed to pull together so many complex issues in this book! ... analysed each issue and then presents the reader with a well researched and balanced conclusion*

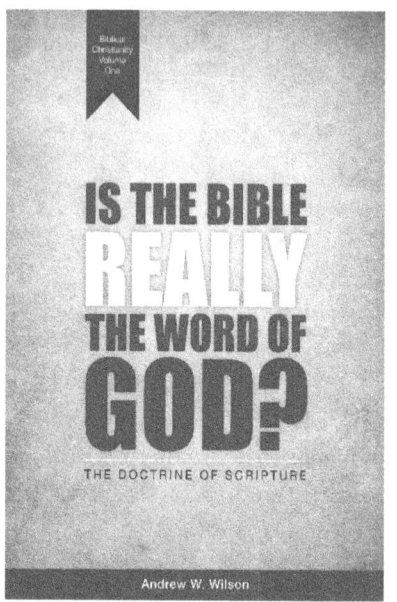

Do Not Quench the Spirit: a Biblical and Practical Guide to Participatory Church Gatherings

Explores the biblical picture of church gatherings, showing how the New Testament encourages the use of spiritual gifts by many.

'*A masterful defence of participatory church gatherings robustly supported from Scripture itself ... This is mandatory reading for anyone serious about church renewal and growth*'
Dr. Mel Heazlewood

Why there REALLY is a God and What You Need to Know about Him

Reader Reviews:
- *I really loved this book.*
- *I am not a reader, but I read all this book. Every Christian should read it.*
- *both scholarly and scientific, one of those compelling books that draws the reader into wanting to read the next chapter* (**Precious Seed magazine**).

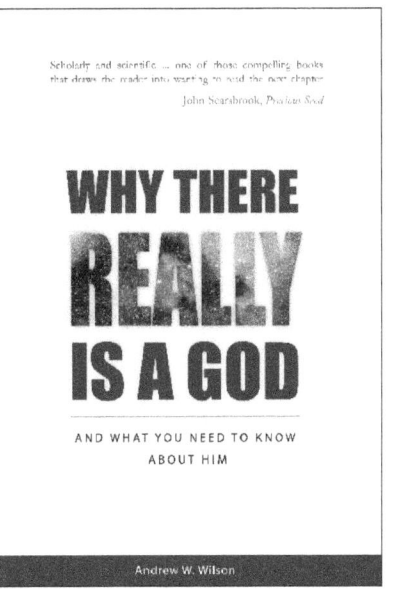

The Most Amazing Prophecy in the Bible: Daniel's Prophecy of the Seventy Sevens

What would be the chances of someone correctly predicting seven events, putting them in the right order, and even saying when they will occur? This is what we find in Daniel's prophecy of the Seventy Sevens. Daniel 9:24-27 is truly the most amazing prophecy in the Bible.

www.ingramcontent.com/pod-product-compliance
Lightning Source LLC
Chambersburg PA
CBHW070417010526
44118CB00014B/1791